Houghton Mifflin Company
Editorial Advisory Committee in Education

C. Gilbert Wrenn
Macalester College

Van Cleve Morris
University of Illinois at Chicago Circle

Samuel A. Kirk
University of Illinois

William Van Til
Indiana State University

Charles S. Benson
University of California, Berkeley

Robert H. Anderson
Harvard University

Education: A Beginning

William Van Til
Coffman Distinguished Professor
in Education
Indiana State University

Houghton Mifflin Company • **Boston**
New York • Atlanta • Geneva, Illinois • Dallas • Palo Alto

Copyright © 1971 by Houghton Mifflin Company.

All rights reserved. No part of this work may be reproduced or transmitted in any form or by any means, electronic or mechanical, including photocopying and recording, or by any information storage or retrieval system, without permission in writing from the publisher.

Printed in the U.S.A.

Library of Congress Catalogue Card Number: 74-142818

ISBN: 0-395-11255-9

For the Van Til family—
from Florence Alberta Van Til, born 1880,
to Linda Alison Nichols, born 1970,
and, somewhere in between,
Bee, Jon and Sally, Barbara and Bob, and Roy

Part opening photos courtesy of:
Part I (p. x): John G. O'Connor from Black Star
Part II (p. 128): Paul Conklin
Part III (p. 268): Katrina Thomas from Photo Researchers
Part IV (p. 456): Harvard Yearbook

Special thanks to Wayne State University Press for permission to use the boxed quotes in Chapters One and Sixteen. From August Kerber, *Quotable Quotes on Education,* copyright © 1968 by Wayne State University Press.
Material on pages 353-354 from *The Saber-Tooth Curriculum* by J. Abner Peddiwell, copyright © 1939 by McGraw-Hill, Inc. Used by permission of McGraw-Hill Book Company. Material on page 156 reprinted by permission from *The Story of the Eight-Year Study,* Volume I of *Adventure in American Education* by Wilford M. Aikin, copyright © 1942, by McGraw-Hill, Inc.
Material on pages 65-66 reprinted by permission of Dodd, Mead & Co., Inc., from *Good Morning, Miss Dove* by Frances Gray Patton, copyright © 1954 by Frances Gray Patton; copyright © 1947, 1952, 1954 by the Curtis Publishing Co.

PREFACE

Education: A Beginning is for you if you intend to teach or are thinking about the possibility of teaching. It is for you if you are a prospective teacher at any level of instruction from preschool through adult education. It is for you if you are a new teacher of any subject in any school or system.

Education: A Beginning is especially for you if you are a student in a first course in education. Such a course is often titled Introduction to Education or Social Foundations of Education, among many possible names.

I wrote *Education: A Beginning* during late 1969 and throughout 1970. It is a summing up of what I think is relevant to the new teacher for the 1970s. The book represents what I know from teaching in schools and in universities and from working in educational organizations. It represents too what I have learned from intensive study while writing the book. My hope is that *Education: A Beginning* may help you to make a difference through teaching.

I am grateful to many people to whom I owe much. Above all, I am grateful to thousands of my predecessors and contemporaries upon whom I have drawn in this book for insights on school and society. Only some of them are individually named in the footnotes and bibliographies.

Thanks also to leaders in American education who read, reacted to, and suggested improvements in this author's first draft of content related to their fields of specialization. They contributed markedly to whatever strengths this book may prove to have and their ideas were of the highest importance to this writer. Yet the author alone is responsible for this book and certainly for any inadequacies; until the book was published the readers named below neither saw any completed chapter or chapters which evolved from the first drafts nor the book as a whole.

Glen Robinson, Director, Research Division, National Education Association, Washington, D.C., and his associates (draft related to chapter 2)

Philip Rothman, Chairman, Education Department, Antioch College, Yellow Springs, Ohio (draft related to chapter 3)

Edgar L. Morphet, Project Director, Improving State Leadership in Education, Denver, Colorado (draft related to chapter 4)

Stanley Elam, Editor, Phi Delta Kappa Publications, Bloomington, Indiana (draft related to chapter 5)

W. Richard Stephens, Professor of Social Foundations of Education, Indiana University, Bloomington, Indiana (draft related to chapters 6, 7, 8)

C. Taylor Whittier, Commissioner of Education, Kansas State Department of Education, Topeka, Kansas (draft related to chapter 9)

Ronald C. Doll, Professor of Education, Richmond College, The City University of New York, New York City, New York (draft related to chapter 10)
William P. McLure, Director, Bureau of Educational Research, University of Illinois, Urbana, Illinois (draft related to chapter 11)
Helen Storen, Professor of Education, Queens College, City University of New York, Flushing, New York (draft related to chapters 12, 13)
Virgil A. Clift, Professor of Education, New York University, New York City, New York (draft related to chapters 12, 13)
Frank W. Jerse, Chairman, Department of Educational Psychology, Indiana State University, Terre Haute, Indiana (draft related to chapter 14)
Jack Allen, Chairman, Division of Social Science, George Peabody College for Teachers, Nashville, Tennessee (draft related to chapter 15)
Arthur G. Wirth, Professor of Education, Washington University, St. Louis, Missouri (draft related to chapter 16)
Fred T. Wilhelms, Executive Secretary, Association for Supervision and Curriculum Development, Washington, D.C. (draft related to chapter 17)
Gordon F. Vars, Professor of Education, Kent State University, Kent, Ohio (draft related to chapter 18)
Prudence Bostwick, formerly Supervisor, Denver Public Schools, Denver, Colorado (draft related to chapter 19)
Jean Marani Graetz, Supervisor of Interns, Sarasota Public Schools, Sarasota, Florida (draft related to chapter 20)
Merle M. Ohlsen, Holmstedt Distinguished Professor, Indiana State University, Terre Haute, Indiana (draft related to chapter 21)
David L. Jesser, Associate Director, Improving State Leadership in Education, Denver, Colorado (draft related to chapter 22)

Thanks to my editor at Indiana State University, Jane Angell.

Thanks to Russell McDougal, formerly Director of the Audio-Visual Center at Indiana State University, for his suggestions of specific aids; in annotations, the most likely source, whether producer or distributor, is suggested, and it is assumed that the reader will consult the major audio-visual indexes for full names and addresses of specified sources.

Thanks for research assistance from Marvin Kelly, now Assistant Professor of Education, University of South Florida; and Ronald M. Leathers, now Assistant Professor of Education, Eastern Illinois University.

Thanks to my secretaries and typists: Gail Rudd, who joined me as a freshman and will leave as a senior; Judy Braden; Ola Kelly, and Mitzi Williams.

Thanks to R. Joseph Dixon, who checked and verified the footnotes and the quotations, an unglamorous yet essential service.

Thanks to William MacDonald, my editor, and Mrs. Elaine Fritz and Miss Ellen Mattingly who copy-edited my manuscript at Houghton Mifflin.

Thanks to thousands of my former students and hundreds of my past and present colleagues.

Thanks especially to my wife Bee, my first mate and my publication factotum since our cruise down the Danube River.

William Van Til

CONTENTS

Preface vii

Part One. Decisions About Teaching

1. Do You Want to Teach in the 1970s? 3
2. Which Level Will You Choose? 23
3. Who Teaches in American Schools? 64
4. What Are Teachers Paid? 86
5. What Organizations Do Teachers Join? 102

Part Two. The Nature of American Schools

6. How Did the Public Schools Begin? 129
7. What Is the Work of the Public School Today? 152
8. What Are the Roles of Independent and Parochial Schools? 175
9. Who's In Charge Here? 195
10. What Is Expected of American Teachers? 218
11. Where Does the Money Come From? 240

Part Three. Foundations of Education

12. Who Attends School? 267
13. What Are the Community Backgrounds of Students? 294
14. How Do Learners Differ? 324
15. How Do Social Problems Affect Education? 352
16. What's a School For, Anyway? 378
17. What Should the Schools Teach? 413
18. How Do Curriculum Content and Organization Change? 435

Part Four. The New Teacher

19. What Does the New Teacher Worry About? 457
20. What Is the Work of the New Teacher? 479
21. What About Evaluation and Guidance? 504
22. What Will the Schools of the Year 2000 Be Like? 525
23. Is Teaching For You? 544

Index

PART ONE

DECISIONS ABOUT TEACHING

ONE

DO YOU WANT TO TEACH IN THE 1970s?

You have had considerable experience with schools and teachers that will help you decide whether you want to teach. After all, you've been going to school for a long time now, and have had contact with a rather large number of teachers of all sorts.

Some of your teachers you remember well; others you would just as soon forget. Your experience with teaching is based on a considerable number of persons who taught you well, badly, or indifferently during the fifteen years, more or less, that you have been a student.

But even though you are a veteran student, you have been on only one side of the desk; there is much to be learned from the other side—the teacher's side.

This book is intended to give you a look at the many aspects of education that must concern you as you make up your mind whether to teach and as you plan your future in the specialty and level you choose. In doing your own independent thinking you should take into account that the author's viewpoint will not be disguised. The author's view on "Why teach?" permeates this book.

WHY TEACH?

We must in all honesty admit that some of the tired old answers to the question "Why teach?" persist in the seventies. We are all familiar with them: "Because I don't know what else to do." "I'll teach until I get the degree I am really after—MRS." "After all, there are long vacations"—a dreary and unexciting list of mindless and expedient reasons for teaching.

But there are far better reasons than these for teaching in the 1970s. One of the best is the possibility of doing something socially useful with one's life in a decade that is dangerous, difficult, and explosive, yet simultaneously rewarding,

Teaching offers opportunities for personal satisfaction and for helping others. Courtesy of D. Worts from Harvard Graduate School of Education.

exciting, and meaningful. Many human lives will be needlessly destroyed in the 1970s, yet this same decade holds for more people than ever the promise of achieving their potential. The British novelist H. G. Wells was at his prophetic best when he wrote, "Human history becomes more and more a race between education and catastrophe."

Charles Dickens was describing a different revolutionary period than our own when he wrote *A Tale of Two Cities*. But he might have been writing of the

> **MORTIMER ADLER.** The best teachers are those who make the fewest pretensions.
>
> **BRONSON ALCOTT** The true teacher defends his pupils against his own personal influence. He inspires self-distrust. He guides their eyes from himself to the spirit that quickens him. He will have no disciple.
>
> **ANONYMOUS** Good teachers cost more, but poor teachers cost most.
>
> **ARISTOTLE** Those who educate children well, are more to be honoured than those who produce them; for these only gave them life, those the art of living well.
>
> **JACQUES BARZUN** Teaching is something that can be provided for, changed or stopped. It is good or bad, brilliant or stupid, plentiful or scarce.

American education must provide for and apply to varied life styles. Courtesy of United States Rubber Co. and Randal Partridge from EFL.

1970s in the opening sentences of his book when he wrote of the period before the French Revolution, "It was the best of times, it was the worst of times, it was the age of wisdom, it was the age of foolishness, it was the epoch of belief, it was the epoch of incredulity, it was the season of Light, it was the season of Darkness, it was the spring of hope, it was the winter of despair, we had everything before us, we had nothing before us, we were all going direct to Heaven, we were all going direct the other way." He was writing about the year 1775.

> **JAMES CASE** The original, the basic, the indispensable audio-visual device for every classroom is the teacher. No one has yet developed an aid to learning that is nearly as flexible, as dependable, as versatile—and probably no one ever will.
>
> **JOHN CIARDI** There are no dull teachers. There are only dull people in classrooms impersonating teachers.
>
> **ARTHUR COMBS** The good teacher is the one who has learned to use himself in an effective way. . . . Learning to teach is not learning to do but learning to be.
>
> **JOHN DEWEY** His (the teacher's) problem is to protect the spirit of inquiry, to keep it from becoming blasé from over excitement, wooden from routine, fossilized through dogmatic instruction, or dissipated by random exercise upon trivial things.

The first men on the moon. Courtesy of NASA.

Two centuries later it is also the best of times, the worst of times. Let us look at the state of the world, and more particularly the United States of America, as the 1970s were about to begin. What was the setting which humanity inherited?

July 20, 1969, was a significant date in the conquest of space. Less than a decade earlier on May 25, 1961, President John F. Kennedy had proclaimed: "I believe this nation should commit itself to achieving the goal, before this decade is out, of landing a man on the moon." After an expenditure of $24 billion for the Apollo program, Neil Armstrong and Edwin Aldrin emerged from a lunar module that looked like a rickety beach house on stilts and walked on the surface of the moon, gathering samples of the surface for scientific analysis. Hundreds of millions of earth-dwellers at their television sets heard the first words of the first man to set foot on the moon, "That's one small step for a man, one giant leap for mankind."

Courtesy of Equitable Life Assurance Society.

But some could not support the popular cry, "On to Mars!" In a still nationalistic, competitive, and antagonistic world, they pointed out that the giant leap was less for mankind than for American technology. They were skeptical of the priority given space programs on a planet beset by problems of overpopulation, pollution, hunger, war, and the threat of nuclear destruction. They were skeptical of priorities which gave enormous sums of money to space programs but insufficient funds to combat urban decay, poverty, and hunger. They likened the space spectacle to the bread and circuses with which the Roman emperors appeased the masses prior to the fall of the Roman Empire. They claimed that a contemporary Marie Antoinette in place of saying "Let them eat cake" on hearing that the people did not have bread, might now propose "Let them eat space."

Indeed, back on earth there was abundant evidence that "it was the best of times, it was the worst of times." The standards of living of the developed nations have steadily increased, yet the gap between the standards of living of

8 DECISIONS ABOUT TEACHING

the developed nations and the underdeveloped nations widens. New and effective techniques for population control have been developed, yet the population is increasing by leaps and bounds. An explosive element is inherent in any situation in which the rich get richer while the poor get children.

The United Nations continued to try to keep peace through mediation of small conflicts and through the activities of its worldwide agencies. The superpowers increased communication with each other and developed mutual compacts and agreements. But the superpowers also increased their offensive and

TABLE 1.1

These Are Typical Responses Given By Teachers-In-Training When Asked, "Why Do You Plan To Teach?"

"I want to help people."
"This world's in a hell of a mess. Education seems to be the only answer to our problems."
"Frankly, I think I've got a better chance of avoiding the draft by teaching."
"My father is a teacher, my mother is a teacher. I suppose I'm part of a tradition."
"I've always been a good student. I think I'll make a good teacher."
"The money gets better each year."
"It's simple, I like kids."
"As a black, I'm interested in black people. What we need is good education to compete with whitey."
"I had a great teacher in my sophomore year of high school who genuinely inspired me. I'd like to have that same effect on others."
"What I really want to do is go to law school. Teaching will give me some good experience and a few bucks."
"It's a good job for a married woman."
"The long vacations and the short hours are what I'm interested in."
"I like to work with people."
"It's a good life for a person who deals in ideas."
"I don't know what else to do."
"It's a good respectable profession. My parents want me to amount to more than they did."
"My fiance and I will be married following graduation. I'll teach to support us while he goes to graduate school."
"An education major is a snap course."
"I'm fed up with irrelevant education. I want to teach to tell it like it is."
"I don't plan to teach. A teaching certificate is a good insurance policy. If I can't find a better job, I can always fall back on teaching and support myself."
"Security. The fringe benefits are good."
"Teaching requires talents and personal attributes which I believe I have."
"I think I can make a difference through teaching."

defensive capacities with more and deadlier missiles, multiplied further the potential for overkill, and competed for the allegiance of minor powers and new nations. The military-industrial complex stockpiled devastating nuclear weapons and invented new horrors of chemical-biological warfare.

The citizens of the United States point proudly to a long period of continued economic growth accompanied by higher standards of living and interrupted only by occasional recessions. After the hungry depression-scarred decade of the 1930s, Americans have experienced the increasingly prosperous forties, fifties, and sixties. Yet it is obvious that this affluence has not been shared by large numbers of Americans, particularly many Negroes, Puerto Ricans, Mexican-Americans, and Indians, people in Appalachia and some Southern rural areas, the old, those of all ages who are untrained and unequipped vocationally, and residents of the slums and ghettos of American cities.

Americans point proudly to civil rights laws and economic gains by Negroes. But many white Americans, used to a society in which all real power is in white hands, and isolated from the realities of the black experience, are puzzled and frightened by the new sense of black pride, by the drive for power in black communities, and by the apathy and disillusionment of the still larger group whose sense of worth has been destroyed by the ugliness and frustration of ghetto life.

Americans are proud of the development of a universal education system available from elementary school through college and university for those who presumably have the ability, will, and funds to continue their education. But some of the citizenry are appalled by inadequate and outdated education.

JOHANN WOLFGANG VON GOETHE *A teacher who can arouse a feeling for one single good action, for one single good poem, accomplishes more than he who fills our memory with rows on rows of natural objects, classified with name and form.*

LAURENCE D. HASKEW *Teachers make teaching. And teachers are persons first of all, getting the results they get chiefly because they are personalities.*

THOMAS JEFFERSON *Enlighten the people generally and tyranny and oppressions of both mind and body will vanish like evil spirits at the dawn of day.*

SØREN KIERKEGAARD *To be a teacher in the right sense is to be a learner. Instruction begins when you, the teacher, learn from the learner, put yourself in his place so that you may understand what he understands and in the way he understands it.*

Moratorium Day, October 1969—Americans march for peace. Courtesy of Dan McCoy of Black Star.

Some are shocked by the violence and physical destruction directed against educational institutions by a revolutionary minority among the many students who seek changes.

Young men build and create, enjoy cultural resources and the expanding sports programs of the nation, live in comfortable homes, and take relatively well-paying jobs on graduation. But young American men have been drafted and killed in a despised war in Asia and are often blocked from the jobs they want by social and economic circumstances.

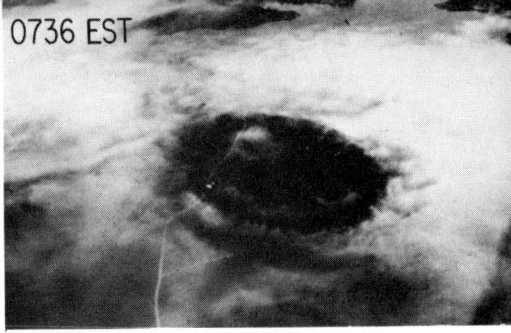

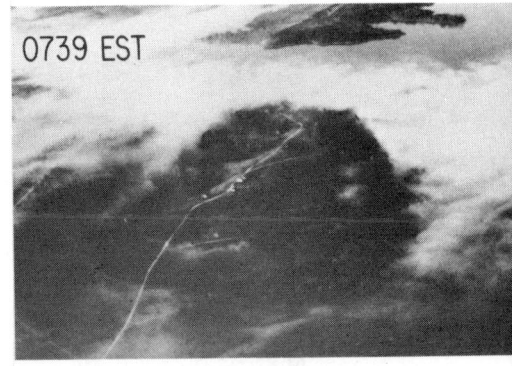

Among the marvels of modern technology are man's efforts to predict and control weather. The photos above were taken from a heliocopter as it cleared away fog. Courtesy of Air Force Cambridge Research Laboratories.

America builds marvels in the form of bridges, skyscrapers, highway systems, and planes. America also fouls its air, pollutes its waters, and ravages its landscape.

WILLIAM PENN   Good instruction is better than riches.

POPE PIUS XII   The teacher must make his teaching live, make his students think, and uncover for each of his students the talents he has at his disposal.

DAGOBERT D. RUNES   We have had teachers for the crown's sake, teachers for God's sake, teachers for Science's sake, teachers for business' sake, but none yet for man's sake.

BERTRAND RUSSELL   The thing, above all, that a teacher should endeavor to produce in his pupils, if democracy is to survive, is the kind of tolerance that springs from an endeavor to understand those who are different from ourselves.

TALMUD   Teach thy tongue to say, "I do not know."

Violence in the 1960s stunned and horrified America and the world. Courtesy of The New York Times Magazine.

America prizes its democratic dream of a nation in which each man is respected as an individual, where men work together for common concerns, and where the use of intelligence is the instrument of progress. Yet, Americans doubt themselves as gross and materialistic, careless and despoiling, and lacking in a worthy philosophy.

Into this setting comes a new generation of American teachers. Theirs is no easy task. Instead their job is tough and demanding. As to the outcome, the gods give no guarantees.

Unfortunately, every so often many Americans forget what education is supposed to do for human beings. Then cultural crises force a reassessment. This happened in America as the 1960s yielded to the 1970s.

Some of these crises were the Vietnam quagmire, rebellion of world youth against meaningless and obsolete educational practices, alienation and hostility

> **HORACE MANN** A teacher who is attempting to teach without inspiring the pupil with a desire to learn is hammering on cold iron.
>
> **ALEXANDER MEIKELJOHN** No one can be a genuine teacher unless he is himself actively sharing in the human attempt to understand men and their world.
>
> **H. L. MENCKEN** Next to the clerk in holy orders, the fellow with the foulest job in the world is the school master. Both are underpaid, both fall steadily in authority and dignity, and both wear out their hearts trying to perform the impossible. How much the world asks of them, and how little they can actually deliver!
>
> **THOMAS PAINE** One good school master is of more use than a hundred priests.
>
> **GEORGE HERBERT PALMER** Kindling of interest is the great function of the teacher. People sometimes say, "I should like to teach if only pupils cared to learn." But then, there would be little need of teaching. . . . Teaching may be defined as the awakening of another's mind, and, the training of its faculties to a normal self-activity.

of protesting students on scores of American campuses, decay of the central cities, the rioting and looting as Negro ghettos burned, persistence of poverty in the richest nation the world has ever known, fouling of the air we breathe and the waters that wash our shores, and assassination of such magnificent human resources as Martin Luther King and Robert F. Kennedy. Many Americans were forcibly reminded that education, which is supposed to improve human existence, faces tremendous tasks if it is to make a difference in people's lives.

Even so, some Americans are not aware of the major tasks before education. Some, even some teachers, blindly skirt the central challenges—the challenge to help young people cope with the social realities of our times; the challenge to relate learning to the motivation and concerns of the learner; the challenge to develop commitment to humane and decent values based on mankind's winnowed and reconstructed experiences. Such challenges as these are the proper foci for our best reflection, creativity, and action in education in the 1970s.

In the schools of the 1970s we must deal with the real and urgent problems of our times, including the most difficult problems of all, those of international understanding, pollution and population, and democratic human relations at home. We must see young people as individuals, each unique, with his own drives, tensions and concerns. We must recognize that the anger and intensity of the black and white activists and the indifference and apathy for current society by some of the hippies point to the crucial importance of educators helping young people develop valid values by which to live.

Fortunately, many educators are aware that education is inextricably related to people's lives. They recognize the challenges and seek ways to consider social realities, to relate to the individual's needs, and to encourage his search for values by which to live. They do not have all the answers, but they know what the crucial questions are. To ask the right questions is a step toward wisdom and intelligent action.

The new generation of teachers has an enormous potential to effect social changes. They may or may not be able to make education work for the goals and values they hold and are developing. But the potential is there.

Why teach? Because teaching offers a fighting chance to make a difference. There are other good reasons too, such as liking to work with people and liking the teacher's life styles. But the main reason for teaching, as the author sees it, is that teaching is where the action is—the action against ignorance and the stifling of human potential, the action of facing today's social realities, meeting the needs of learners, and developing humane values. Through teaching, one can make his life count.

HOW MANY OPENINGS ARE THERE FOR TEACHERS?

If you become an American teacher, you will join a sizable occupational group. According to the U.S. Office of Education, there were 2,775,000 Americans who listed their occupation as elementary, secondary, or higher education teachers in 1969.[1] At the opening of the 1969–70 school year, over two million of them were public elementary and secondary school teachers.

> **WILLIAM O. DOUGLAS** *The constitution guarantees freedom of thought and expression to everyone in our society. All are entitled to it; and none needs it more than the teacher.*
>
> **ALBERT EINSTEIN** *It is the supreme art of the teacher to awaken joy in creative expression and knowledge.*
>
> **ANATOLE FRANCE** *Let our teaching be full of ideas. Hitherto it has been stuffed only with facts. . . . The whole art of teaching is only the art of awakening the natural curiosity of young minds for the purpose of satisfying it afterwards.*

---

[1] U.S. Office of Education, *Digest of Educational Statistics,* 1969 ed. (Washington, D.C.: U.S. Government Printing Office, 1969), p. 5.

Not only is the occupation of teaching sizable—it is steadily growing. In the early years of the twentieth century, the number of teachers in American public elementary and secondary schools alone was approximately half a million. (For instance, in 1900 there were 423,062 teachers in American public schools.) By the time of the Great Depression, there were some 800,000 to 900,000 public school teachers. (In 1930 there were 854,263 teachers in American public

FIGURE 1.1

Classroom Teachers in Regular Elementary and Secondary Day Schools: U.S., Fall 1957–77 (includes effect of Elementary and Secondary Education Act of 1965)

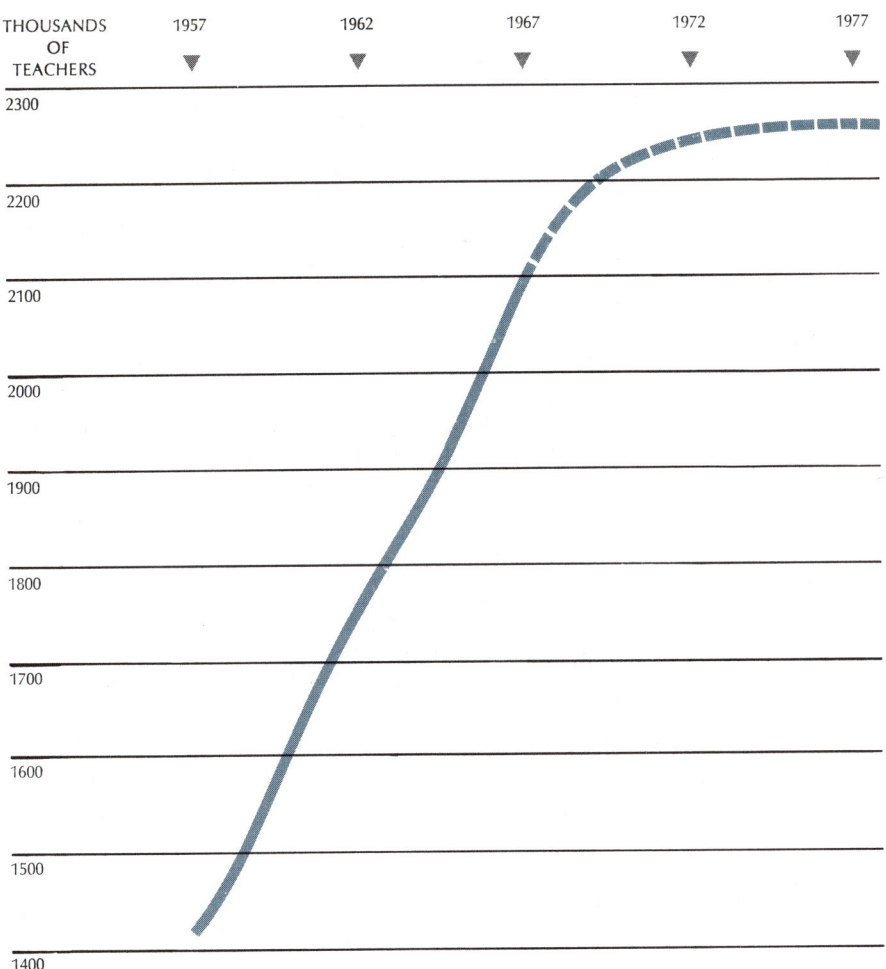

U.S. Office of Education, Projections of Educational Statistics to 1977–78 (Washington, D.C.: U.S. Government Printing Office, 1969), p. 45.

schools.) About the time today's college students were born, there were approximately a million American public school teachers. (In 1950 there were 913,671 teachers in American public schools.)[2]

Then the number of teachers really accelerated in public elementary and secondary schools. By 1967, the number of teachers in American public schools amounted to 1,855,000. When nonpublic school teachers were added, the total of American teachers reached 2,095,000.[3] The U.S. Office of Education projected 2,299,000 public and nonpublic elementary and secondary school teachers by 1977.[4] (See Figure 1.1)

What happened? One factor was a general population increase. If you were born in 1950, you were one of approximately 150 million Americans. Late in 1968 the American population passed the 200 million mark.

The increased number of teachers is explained not just by the general population increase in the twentieth century but more particularly by the expansion in school attendance which characterized the post–World War II period. This increase is dramatically demonstrated in school enrollment figures. In 1950, there were only 20,716,000 children between the ages of five and thirteen enrolled in schools. But by 1969 there were 35,999,000 such children. In 1950, there were only 8,143,000 young people fourteen to nineteen years old enrolled in schools. But by 1969 there were 17,803,000 school enrollees in this age group. Population has boomed and school attendance has grown in the age groups of greatest relevance to you if you are a prospective teacher of the five- to nineteen-year-old span, as the enrollment in this school-age group increased from 28,859,000 in 1950 to 53,802,000 in 1969.[5]

Because fewer children were born in the late 1960s than in earlier years, the rate of growth of the school-age population will decrease for several years. While the trend toward enrolling a larger proportion of the school-age populations will continue, it is not likely to offset the decreases resulting from fewer persons entering this age group. The students represented in the large increases in school enrollments which occurred in the early and mid-1950s have reached the age of college graduation and have enlarged the numbers of potential teachers available for entry into classrooms each year. These two factors—decreasing rates of enrollment growth in public schools accompanied by significant increases in the annual numbers of college graduates completing preparation to enter teaching, will make it likely that employment opportunities in the 1970s may not be as

---

[2] U.S. Bureau of the Census, *Historical Statistics of the United States, Colonial Times to 1957* (Washington, D.C.: U.S. Government Printing Office, 1960), p. 208.
[3] U.S. Office of Education, *Projections of Educational Statistics to 1977–78* (Washington, D.C.: U.S. Government Printing Office, 1969), p. 47.
[4] *Ibid.*
[5] U.S. Bureau of the Census, *Historical Statistics of the United States*, p. 214; and "School Enrollment in the United States: 1969," *Current Population Reports*, p. 2, Series P–20, No. 199 (Washington, D.C.: U.S. Government Printing Office, 1970).

FIGURE 1.2

Children Enrolled in American Schools 1950–69

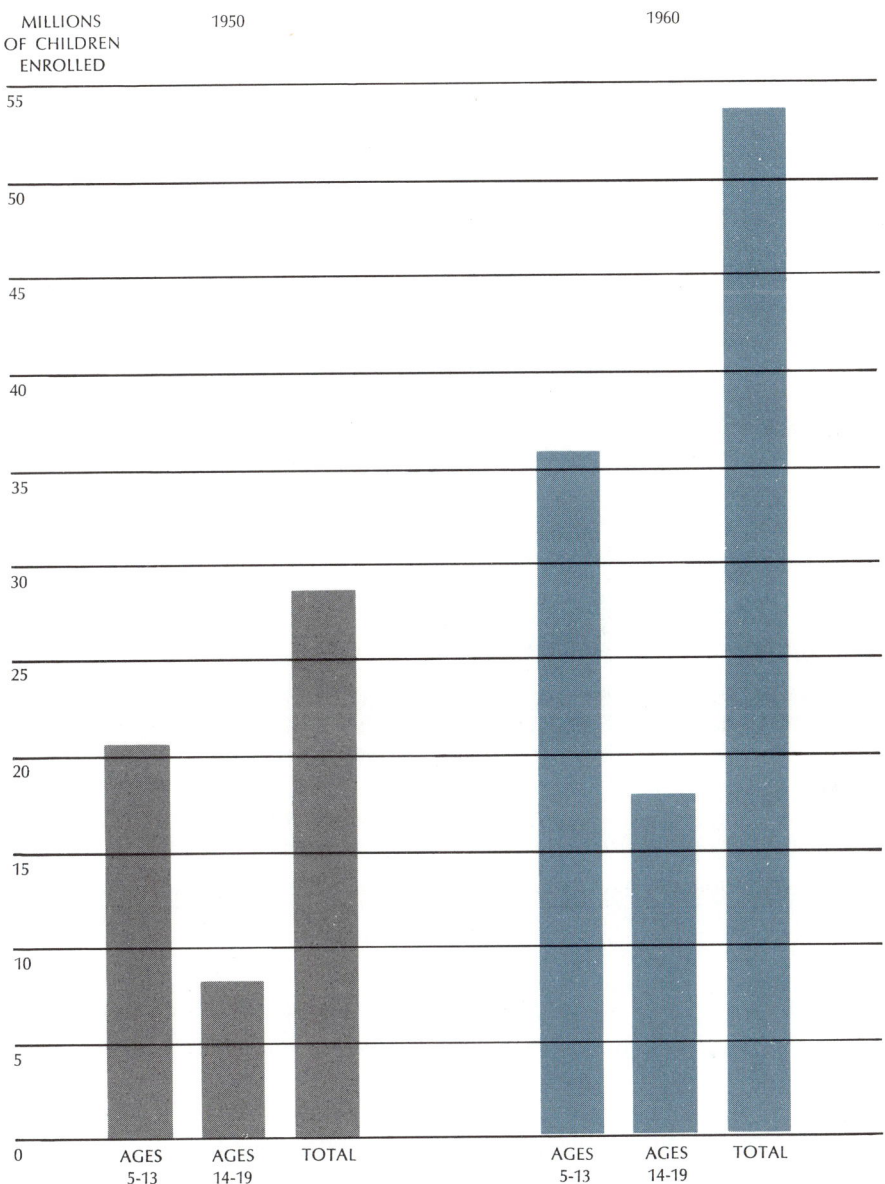

great as in recent decades. Opportunities may not even be available to all who choose to teach. However, if the American people require immediate attainment of minimum levels of quality staffing of schools, the demand for teachers will increase. (See Figure 1.3.)

FIGURE 1.3

Estimates of Supply of Teacher Education Graduates Expected to Enter Teaching and Demand for Beginning Teachers, 1969–70

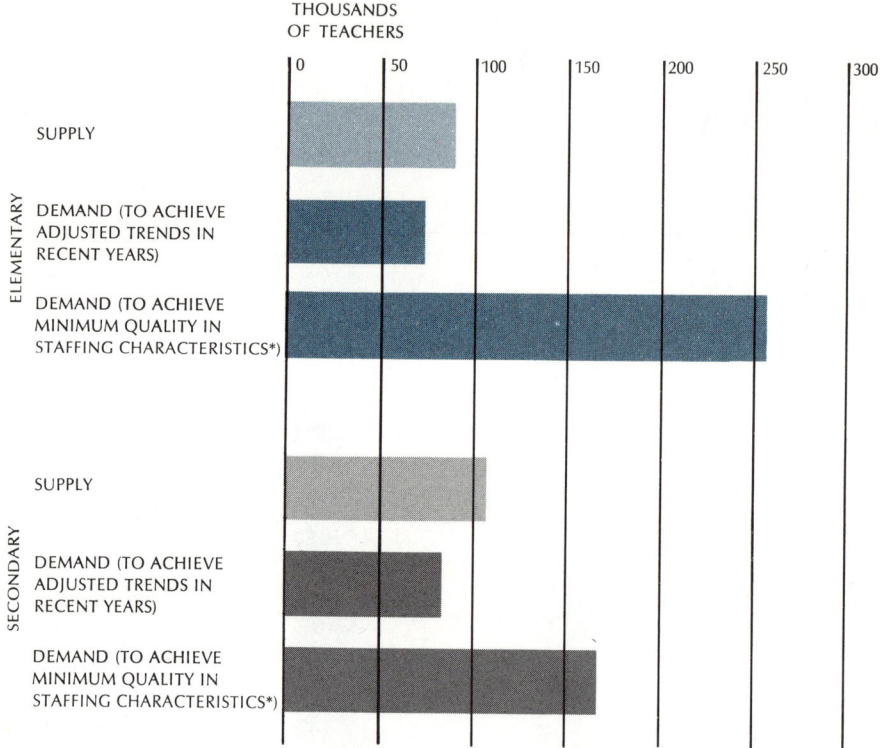

* The asterisks indicate the size of the educational staff needed to achieve quality education.

National Education Association, Research Division, *Teacher Supply and Demand in Public Schools, 1969,* Research Report 1969–R14 (Washington, D.C.: The Association, 1970), p. 49.

How about the influence on employment in education of such possible factors as social revolution or the new instructional technology? Would such developments sharply reduce the demand for teachers?

The world's experience with revolution is that immediately after an upheaval the revolutionaries find it essential to reestablish an educational system. The content of education may be changed and the attitudes sought may be different, but education continues and even expands after revolution.

As to the new instructional technology, any teacher who *can* be replaced by a machine *should* be! What cannot be replaced is the humanized, personalized, creative contribution to education of the vital, live teacher. Past precedent indicates that the new mechanisms will probably supplement the services of the teacher instead of replacing him. The experience of the Industrial Revolution indicates that new machines lead to a whole new series of related tasks and functions for people. Even if classroom teaching as now practiced should diminish in an era of highly accelerated instructional technology, the total occupation of education would probably flourish. After all, someone has to feed the machines a diet for educational purposes.

So you will be joining an already sizable occupation which is steadily increasing in numbers. Unlike the generation which came of age in the 1930s, those of the forties, fifties, and sixties had abundant employment opportunities. It appears that openings for teachers will not be as plentiful in the 1970s because of larger numbers of teacher education graduates and smaller rates of school enrollment growth. The U.S. Office of Education, projecting education statistics, foresees one million new teachers or returnees being employed in teaching during the six-year period from 1969 to 1974; during the preceding six-year period, it reported a demand for 1.2 million teachers.[6] Such predictions are based on the assumptions that: (1) education will continue to be one of the major priorities of the American people, (2) the usual number of teachers will continue to die or resign, (3) catastrophe such as nuclear war does not occur.

You will have to be a competent teacher in the 1970s. The days of employing incompetents to meet teacher shortages are over. A report from the American Association of Colleges for Teacher Education summarized the employment situation in the Fall of 1969:

There are now enough teachers to man most of the classrooms. The general teacher shortage, which has reached the critical point in recent years has ended, according to an NEA research report. Although the report is based on minimum standard of supply, a more balanced supply and demand condition will give a great boost to upgrading the quality of education. Of the states surveyed, only two Connecticut and Iowa, indicated a substantial shortage of teacher applicants. Alaska and California had an excess, while Michigan reported that it had enough applicants to fill all positions. Other states noted "some shortage" or had a shortage in some subject and regional areas and an excess in others. No state considered the situation more acute than it was in 1968. The most difficult positions to fill are in: mathematics, natural and physical sciences, industrial arts, special education, some vocational-technical subjects, women's physical education, and positions for elementary school librarians and guidance counselors.[7]

However, the October 1970 *Changing Times*, the Kiplinger magazine, commented on teacher supply and demand:

. . . according to some experts, there actually are not enough teachers on the job right now to meet the true needs of the schools. The problem, they say, is not an oversupply of teachers but an undersupply of money.

---

[6] U.S. Office of Education, *Projections of Educational Statistics to 1977–78*, p. 51.
[7] "General Teacher Shortage Is Over," *American Association of Colleges for Teacher Education Bulletin* (September 1969), p. 3.

School systems, faced by taxpayer resistance, are starved for the funds they need to lighten teacher loads, replace underqualified instructors and expand course offerings. When requirements like those are taken into account, says one report, there's a national shortage of close to 170,000 elementary school teachers, 60,000 secondary school teachers and 40,000 school librarians.

. . . Allan W. Ostar, executive director of the American Association of State Colleges and Universities, . . . makes this comment: "How can we talk of a teacher surplus when perhaps half of our communities are without kindergartens; . . . when according to a recent study at Harvard, almost half of the adult population 25 years old and over is functionally illiterate; when a new right-to-read program has been launched by the U.S. Office of Education as a top national priority; when in our high schools we have less than one counselor for every 500 students; when our rural and urban schools are woefully inadequate in meeting the special educational needs of our underprivileged children? There is no teacher surplus. There is an educational deficit which, for the first time since World War II, we now have an opportunity to correct."[8]

★ ★ ★

DISCUSSION

1. Consider your own teachers. Whom do you remember favorably and why? Whom do you reject and why? Can you generalize from these reactions on the qualities that you consider important in a "good" teacher?
2. In appraising yourself, do you find that you like to work with people, with things? In groups or alone?
3. What are some of the reasons some of your friends have gone into teaching? How would their responses compare with the answers quoted in the chapter in response to the question "Why do you plan to teach?"
4. Which of the reasons given by prospective teachers do you consider worthwhile? Which are selfishly motivated? Which reflect indifference? Which show some dedication to an idea or an ideal? Which are most similar to yours?
5. What is your own reaction to further space ventures by the United States? What do you consider top priorities?
6. What has happened to you and the world in your lifetime that indicates to you that you are living in the best of times? The worst of times?
7. What do you conceive to be the major tasks before American educators?
8. What is your answer to the question, "Why teach?" Why are you thinking seriously of entering the teaching field? What does teaching really mean to you?
9. Consider the growth in the number of teachers and the decline in teaching opportunities. What is the situation with respect to teacher supply and demand today in your state? Your community? What is the situation as it affects you?

[8] "Too Many Teachers?" *Changing Times* (October 1970), p. 44.

INVOLVEMENT

1. Make arrangements to visit a classroom (wherever convenient and of most interest to you) to see first hand a teacher and class situation. When you report back to your class, consider what you saw, how the teacher and class interacted, what your reactions were. (Caution: Always go first to the office of the principal of the school visited to request permission to visit.)
2. If the schools from which you graduated are nearby, go back to one of your schools and talk with a teacher whom you remember favorably about teaching.
3. In everyday conversations introduce the possibility that you will become a teacher and consider the ideas and reactions of your friends and relatives. Try out with them the idea that teaching can make a difference in people's lives.
4. Develop a simple questionnaire dealing with possible reasons why people wish to teach. Administer the questionnaire to some who are considering teaching, tabulate the results, and report to the group. (Best results are likely to occur when those answering remain anonymous.)
5. Try to bring to your class a first-year teacher to present his or her reasons for entering the field of education and to answer questions. Perhaps one speaker might be selected from the elementary and another from the secondary school level.

BIBLIOGRAPHY

Abraham, Willard. *A Time for Teaching.* New York: Harper and Row, 1964. A combination of a provocative choice of material with a witty style is characteristic of this introduction to the teaching profession.

Adams, Sam and John L. Garrett, Jr. *To Be a Teacher: An Introduction to Education.* Englewood Cliffs, N.J.: Prentice-Hall, 1969. Focus on "Shall I be a teacher?"

Beck, Carlton E., Normand R. Bernier, James B. Macdonald, Thomas W. Walton, and Jack C. Willers. *Education for Relevance.* Boston: Houghton Mifflin, 1968. A team approach to the social foundations of education, including historical, philosophical, sociological, comparative, and anthropological insights.

Foy, Rena. *The World of Education: An Introductory Text.* New York: Macmillan, 1968. Why education is important, who should be educated, who should be responsible for education, who should pay, and how education should be organized.

Haskew, Laurence D. and Jonathan C. McLendon. *This Is Teaching: An Introduction to Education in America,* 3rd ed. Chicago: Scott-Foresman, 1968. An overview of education in America, focusing on the individual who is to teach.

Hess, Robert D. and Roberta Meyer Bear, eds. *Early Education: Current Theory, Research and Action.* Chicago: Aldine, 1966. The published results of a conference on early childhood education sponsored by the Committee on Learning and the Educational Process of the Social Sciences Research Council.

Hughes, Monroe James. *Education in America.* New York: Harper and Row, 1970. A view of American education for college students who are considering entering the teaching profession and for citizens who are concerned about the course of education in this country.

James, William. *Talks to Teachers on Psychology: and to Students on Some of Life's Ideals.* New York: Henry Holt and Company, 1899. A classic. Collection of James's public lectures presented to teachers which emphasize concrete practical applications of his psychology to teaching.

Ohles, John F. *Introduction to Teaching.* New York: Random House, 1970. An overview of teaching, including help in finding answers to questions about teaching as a career.

Postman, Neil and Charles Weingartner. *Teaching as a Subversive Activity.* New York: Delacorte, 1969. A lively, refreshing book which calls for teaching to challenge and to generate excitement.

Richey, Robert. *Planning for Teaching: An Introduction to Education.* New York: McGraw-Hill, 1968. A widely used introduction to education which is comprehensive and and helpful.

Sharp, D. Louise, ed. *Why Teach?* New York: Henry Holt and Company, 1957. A collection of answers to the question "Why teach?" Short essays by people in all walks of life who pay homage to their own teachers or to teaching in general.

Van Til, William. *The Making of a Modern Educator.* Indianapolis: Bobbs-Merrill, 1961. A collection of essays and shorter writings which describe the author's experiences as a teacher in situations ranging from a reform school to a university.

AUDIO-VISUAL MATERIALS

Teach Me (TFC, 29 Min., Color) A selected segment from the film "Up the Down Staircase." It shows Sandy Dennis as a novice English teacher in a New York City school and the frustration and chaos which precede her successes.

Not by Chance (National Education Association, 28 Min., Color) Introduces many current practices in teacher education, such as admissions, classroom instruction, campus life, guidance activities, observation, and directed student teaching. The making of a good teacher is described.

Education—Challenge and Commitment (WSJTV, 55 Min.) The rapid change and social sophistication of modern society places new demands on methods of education. Individual growth and development is encouraged in the elementary grades so that a child retains self-confidence and self-motivation.

Career for You—Teaching (WUNC Television, 28 Min.) Illustrates the possibilities in a career in teaching.

I Want to be a Teacher (Educational Enrichment Materials, Inc., 30 frs., Color, Record) By questioning and observing children, this film reveals the workday world of a teacher.

The Teacher—A Community Helper (Sigma Educational Films, 10 Min., Color) Describes a typical day in the life of a primary school teacher. Shows her as she plans the lesson, teaches, confers with a parent, attends the university, and performs other duties as a mother, homemaker and responsible member of the community.

Your Future in Elementary Education (Guidance Associates, Harcourt, Brace and World, 79 frs., Color., Record) Discusses becoming a teacher and teaching in an elementary school. Explores student teaching, educational curriculum, requirements for certification and children's learning processes.

Education—Antidote to Poverty (University of Michigan TV Center, 30 Min.) Takes a look at movements in education designed to eradicate some of society's inequalities.

Teacher (National Film Board of Canada, 44 frs , Color) Describes educational and personal requirements for teachers, training in specialized fields, opportunities and advantages. Stresses the importance of the teacher in society.

TWO

WHICH LEVEL WILL YOU CHOOSE?

At what level of the American educational system do you propose to teach? This chapter will discuss the characteristics of each of the common divisions of the educational system.

INFANCY AND BABYHOOD YEARS

In America, no organized education now exists for the period from birth to the third birthday. Yet the importance of the first three years of life cannot be overestimated. Freudian psychology particularly emphasizes the importance of these early years, but one does not have to be a Freudian to recognize their significance in the shaping of the human being. The child is first molded by his family and the surrounding home environment during these three years. But in current American culture such education is informal and home-based rather than formalized and institution-located.

Education at home during infancy and babyhood is not a universal practice, however. Limited opportunities presently exist for educators to work with children during this phase of development; welfare agencies, children's hospitals, and orphanages often require the service of trained educators to help raise babies who have no families. Other societies of the world have developed alternative programs to the informal, home-based education of children during infancy and babyhood. For instance, Bruno Bettelheim in *The Children of the Dream* has written a fascinating account of the kibbutz method of rearing Israeli children, many of whom leave home shortly after birth for institutional upbringing. Bettelheim reports:

A meal on a kibbutz. Courtesy of the Israel Government Press Office.

The kibbutz experience clearly demonstrated to me that children raised by educators in group homes can and do fare considerably better than many children raised by their mothers in poverty-stricken homes, and better than quite a few raised at home by their middle-class parents.[1]

My conclusion must be that, despite published reports to the contrary, the kibbutz system seems quite successful in raising children in groups by other than their mothers, and this from infancy on. But up to now this success has only been demonstrated for relatively small societies, where an unusually high degree of consensus exists, where there is very little differentiation in style of life or in property rights, and where the entire society functions like an extended family.[2]

Knowing nothing of apartness, they are content with satisfactions not destroyed for them by having to fight for a sense of belonging. Neither must they strive for an individuation that might compensate, through a rich inner life, for what is absent from their group life. They feel no need to push ahead, but neither do they have the impulse to push anyone down. While such people do not create science or art, are neither leaders, nor great philosophers nor innovators, maybe it is they who are the salt of the earth without whom no society can endure.[3]

In the U.S., researchers are studying child development in the earliest years of life and particularly focusing on the differences between children of the poor and of the affluent. As Maya Pines reports, "If their research confirms that the

---

[1] Bruno Bettelheim, *The Children of the Dream* (New York: Macmillan, 1969), p. 43.
[2] *Ibid.*, p. 52.   [3] *Ibid.*, pp. 319–320.

A federally funded day-care center on a Cherokee reservation. Courtesy of Paul Conklin.

first three years of life largely determine a human being's future competence, these years can no longer be left to chance, they believe. Thus, armies of tutors could conceivably be sent into the homes of disadvantaged infants, and thousands of expectant parents enrolled in crash programs to teach them modern child rearing. We may be witnessing the end of society's traditional laissez-faire about the earliest years of a human being's life."[4] Though most students of human development now hope to produce improvements in the way parents, especially mothers, raise their children, some are considering as a possible strategy "starting kibbutz-like day-care centers in which trained teachers would give children an excellent education from earliest infancy."[5] As Pines points out, "As these ideas spread, the nation's educational efforts are likely to include ever younger children, and soon the years from birth to three may become a target of first priority."[6]

The federal government is becoming increasingly active in fostering the development of day-care centers for preschool children under five years old. On August 9, 1969, President Richard M. Nixon in an address to the nation outlining his proposals for welfare reform said, "I am also proposing . . . major expansion of day-care centers to make it possible for mothers to take jobs by which they can support themselves and their children." He added, "There is no single ideal to which this administration is more firmly committed than to the enriching of a child's first five years of life, and thus helping lift the poor out of misery at a time when a lift can help the most. Therefore, these day-care centers would

[4] Maya Pines, "Why Some 3-year-olds Get A's and Some Get C's," *New York Times Magazine* (July 6, 1969), p. 10.
[5] *Ibid.*, p 17.   [6] *Ibid.*

offer more than custodial care; they would also be devoted to the development of vigorous young minds and bodies. As a further dividend, the day-care centers would offer employment to many welfare mothers themselves." Such day-care centers would obviously include the children whom Pines describes who are in the first three years of their lives. So the day-care center for the first three years of the child's life may become the first rung on the evolving educational ladder in the United States.

NURSERY SCHOOL

Presently, the first level in American education is nursery school for children three, four, and five years old. These schools are relatively new to Americans; the value of such education has been underestimated in the past. Available records show that nursery school education in the United States dates back to 1920 when three nursery schools were in existence.[7] By October 1969, enrollment of public and private nursery schools had reached 860,000.[8] But even when one takes into account both public and private schools, including generously kindergartens with nursery schools, only one out of three children three to five years old was enrolled in nursery schools and kindergartens in the U.S. in October 1968.[9]

Nursery school education was encouraged by the federal government during the economic depression of the thirties and the manpower shortages of the forties as World War II raged. School services for young children were expanded through the Economic Opportunity Act and the Elementary and Secondary Education Act during the sixties as part of the war on poverty. The revision of the welfare system during the early seventies was accompanied by emphasis on opportunities for welfare mothers to be gainfully employed. Thus, social forces both in recent decades and today have resulted in federal government programs which supported the expansion of school services for young children. But nursery school education has a considerable distance to go before the widespread achievement of President Nixon's quoted goal, the enriching of a child's first five years of life.

In the United States today there are varied types of nursery schools for children under six years of age. Some of them are public, some private; some are sponsored by colleges and universities, others are organized by groups of parents, still others by church groups. A nursery school may be a laboratory nursery school associated with the university, a parent-cooperative nursery school supported by a group of parents, a church-sponsored nursery school. Some nursery

---

[7] Mary Dabney Davis, *Nursery Schools: Their Development and Current Practices in the United States* (Washington, D.C.: U.S. Government Printing Office, 1933), p. 2.
[8] U.S. Bureau of the Census, "School Enrollment in the United States," *Current Population Reports*, Series P–20, No. 199 (Washington, D.C.: U.S. Government Printing Office, 1970), p. 1.
[9] U.S. Office of Education, *Digest of Educational Statistics*, 1969 ed. (Washington, D.C.: U.S. Government Printing Office, 1969), p. 31.

A four-year-old works to improve his reading on a "talking typewriter," called SLATE (Stimulated Learning for Automated Typewriter Environment) used for remedial reading instruction and learning. Courtesy of Westinghouse.

schools are conducted as private enterprises or by community agencies and organizations. Some are designed for the exceptional child—blind, deaf, crippled, mentally handicapped, speech impaired. Some are designed for the educationally disadvantaged child and attempt to reduce possible retardation.

Some nursery schools are part of the regular public school system, serving as the "educational enterprise for the year or years preceding kindergarten, organized and maintained as part of the sequential program of the public elementary school under the direction of a qualified teacher."[10]

But nursery schools as part of the public school system are relatively rare. In a 1966–67 study, the Research Division of the National Education Association, after questioning all of the school systems in the United States with an enrollment of 300 students or more (a total of 11,970 systems), found among the responding systems only 148 which included nursery education as part of the established public school program. Almost all of these (141) responded to a questionnaire. The Far West and Mideast accounted for the largest proportion of the schools systems having nursery schools. School systems maintaining the fewest nursery schools were located in the Rocky Mountain region, the Southeast, and the Southwest.[11]

[10] NEA, Research Division, *Nursery School Education, 1966–67*, Research Report 1968–R6 (Washington, D.C.: The Association, 1968), p. 9.
[11] *Ibid.*, pp. 10–11.

TABLE 2.1

Primary Goals of Nursery School Education
in 141 School Systems, 1966–67

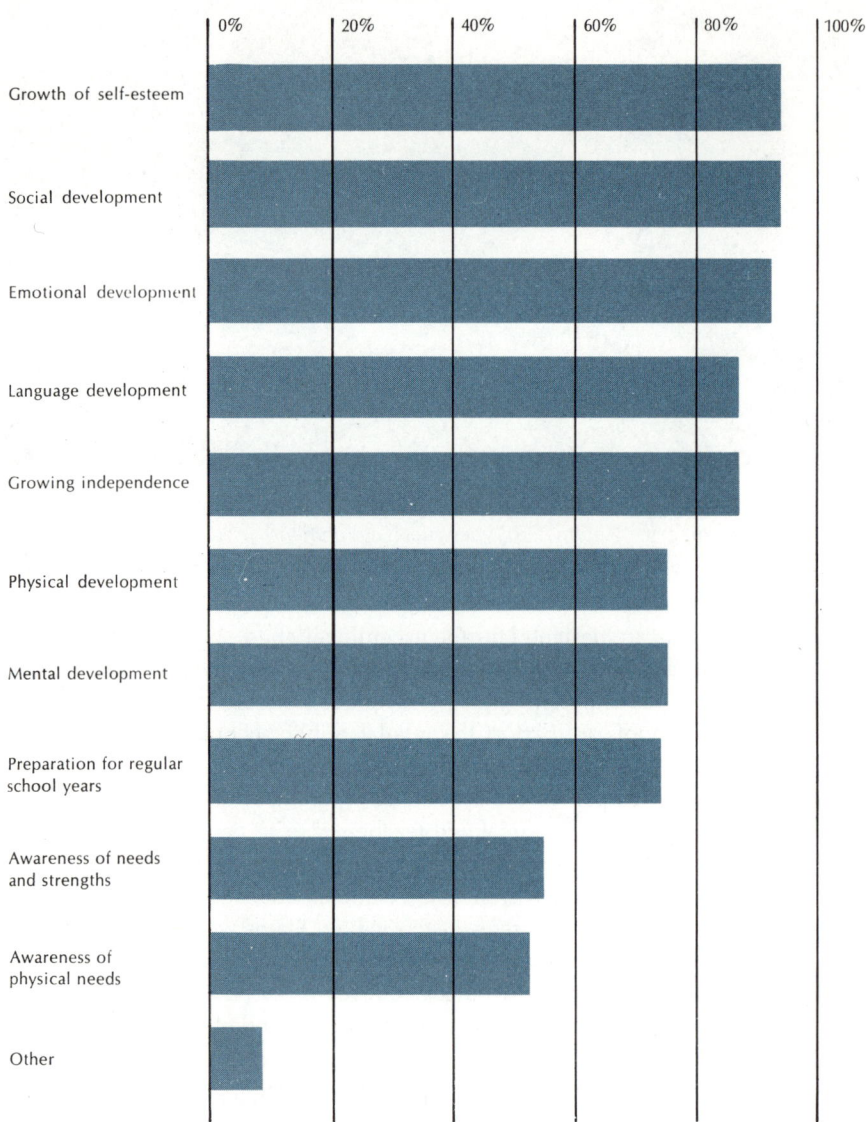

National Education Association, Research Division, *Nursery School Education, 1966–67*, Research Report 1968–R6 (Washington, D.C.: The Association, 1968), p. 18.

As to the programs of the public nursery schools, the report of the 141 school systems indicated that "about one-half, 51.1 percent, of the total systems had a daily program structure in which activities were provided in a regular sequence. Pupils moved from one activity to another with no regular sequence or definite time allotment in 24.8 percent of the systems. Of the total systems, 23.4 percent had a definite time allotment and sequence for each activity in the daily program. The daily program should be flexible and coincide with the pupil's needs and interests and the goals of the school; hence no one preferred structure exists."[12] The response of nursery school educators about their goals is reported in Table 2.1.

Katherine H. Read summarized the fundamental goal of nursery school education in *The Nursery School: A Human Relationships Laboratory:*

> The over-all goal of nursery school is to promote healthy growth. We are using the definition of health proposed by the World Health Organization as "a state of complete physical, mental, and social well-being, not merely the absence of disease or infirmity."[13]

KINDERGARTEN

The second established educational level is that of kindergarten. A kindergarten year usually takes place for a child (when it does occur) when he is five years old. The most frequently reported minimum age requirement for September enrollment was five by the following December 1 (34.4% of districts), and the second most frequently mentioned age was five by the following January 1 (18.0% of districts). More precisely, in a survey of 1968–69 school entrance age policies, only 5.2% of the school systems participating in the study would allow a child to enter kindergarten in September if his fifth birthday fell after the following January 1.[14]

The first private kindergarten in the United States was founded in 1856 and the first public kindergartens were established in St. Louis, Missouri, in 1873.[15] By 1888 the number of kindergartners enrolled in public schools almost equaled those enrolled in private schools—15,145 in public schools and 16,082 in private schools.[16] During the depression decade of the 1930s, enrollment in kindergarten declined, but aside from this decade, enrollment in public kinder-

---

[12] *Ibid.,* p. 18.

[13] Katherine H. Read, *The Nursery School: A Human Relationships Laboratory* (Philadelphia and London: W. B. Saunders, 1966), p. 86.

[14] NEA, American Association of School Administrators and Research Division, *Entrance Age Policies,* Educational Research Service Circular No. 5 (Washington, D.C.: The Association 1968), p. 2–3.

[15] Josephine Foster and Neith Headley, *Education in the Kindergarten* (New York: American Book Company, 1966), p. 26.

[16] *Early Childhood Education,* 46th Yearbook, Part II, National Society for the Study of Education (Chicago: University of Chicago Press, 1957), p. 46.

A New York City kindergarten in the late 1800s, based on Froebel's educational ideas. Courtesy of Culver Pictures.

gartens steadily swelled. By 1969, out of a total of 3,276,000 children in kindergarten, 2,682,000 or 82 percent were enrolled in public kindergartens, and 594,000 or 18 percent in private kindergartens.[17]

But provision of kindergarten as part of the public educational system varies greatly from state to state. In some states practically all local school districts provide public kindergartens. On the other hand, in a few states there are no public kindergartens. Equality of educational opportunity throughout the United States has not been established for kindergarten-age children.

The first kindergarten was designed by Friedrich Froebel in 1837 in Germany in order to provide an educational situation in which children's creative play might be organized constructively. Advocates of the kindergarten believe that through kindergarten experiences such as the use of songs, stories, games, group activities and simple materials, children can be helped to develop well and to mature.

One team of contemporary writers on the American kindergarten have generalized on the purposes of kindergarten as follows:

> The American kindergarten today attempts to give the child of five an education which is appropriate to his stage of development, which will be immediately satisfying to him, and which will help him build good foundations for the years ahead. In such an education, the child will develop all his powers—physical,

---

[17] U.S. Bureau of the Census, "School Enrollment in the United States: 1969," *Current Population Reports*, Series P–20, No. 199 (Washington, D.C.: U.S. Government Printing Office, 1970), p. 1.

Contemporary kindergarten, Early Learning Center, Stamford, Conn. Courtesy of Jonathan King of EFL.

emotional, mental, and social. Obviously, we do not seek to give him all the information he may need either now or in the future, but we do hope to help him develop the power to meet new situations by showing him how to use the information he possesses and how to gain other information he may need. We try through practice to help him develop skill in thinking. We are interested in discovering the traits and abilities of each child and in helping each child make the most of his potentialities.[18]

More specifically, Foster and Headley indicated that it is the aim of the kindergarten to provide each child with:

1. An opportunity to be in a social situation where his all-around readiness can be appraised before he must face the challenges of the first grade.
2. An opportunity to have a wide variety of experiences particularly adapted to his developmental needs.
3. An opportunity to mesh old and new learnings and, in so doing to build for himself a broad base of understanding.
4. An opportunity to be in many situations that will help him perceive relationships through problem solving.
5. An opportunity to be in social situations where he can feel needed.
6. An opportunity to be in situations where he can become increasingly aware of the relationships between freedom and responsibility.
7. An opportunity to have many experiences that will help him "grow into reading."[19]

[18] Foster and Headley, p. 44. [19] *Ibid.*, pp. 44–45.

Schoolroom around the time of the American Revolution. The schoolmaster was responsible for all age groups, usually in a crowded one-room schoolhouse. Courtesy of the Library of Congress.

ELEMENTARY SCHOOL

In the U.S. today, elementary education is part of required education. Unlike kindergartens and nursery schools (and, for that matter, colleges) all young Americans are required to attend elementary schools, which comprise the third educational level. In 1969–70, 27,428,000 young Americans attended public elementary schools, according to the United States Office of Education, and 4,300,000[20] attended nonpublic elementary schools, including private independent and church-related schools.

Elementary education, an idea inherited from Europe, began in the New World in the mid-seventeenth century. But elementary education in America progressed beyond the European conception of charity schools for paupers and moved toward common education available to all, and eventually free universal tax-supported elementary schools.

Colonial education was motivated by the needs for children to read so that they could understand and accept religious teachings, to know and comprehend laws, and to learn vocations.[21]

In the national period emphasis was placed on unity and citizenship as well

---

[20] U.S. Office of Education, *Digest of Educational Statistics,* 1969 Edition, pp. 22, 31.
[21] G. Wesley Sewards, "Elementary Education," *Encyclopedia of Educational Research,* 4th ed. American Educational Research Association (New York: Macmillan, 1969), p. 421.

Modern elementary school with movable walls, space for children to move around. Courtesy of EFL.

as on literacy and moral character. In the nineteenth century, history, geography, government, science and nature study gained stature in the program.[22]

In the first half of the twentieth century, strict subject matter teaching in the elementary schools was challenged by two reform movements. One called for more emphasis on the experience of learners and thus advocated more attention to the interests and concerns of pupils in a child-centered school. The other called for more emphasis on the concerns of society through the study of areas of living and of social processes. Some adaptations were made in the elementary school program but the schools remained largely subject matter centered rather than child-centered or society-centered. Subjects, however, were increasingly tied together and integrated; the major broad fields of the elementary school became language arts, arithmetic, social studies, science, art, music, health and physical education.[23]

In the 1960s, government-supported projects stressed ways to select subject matter and improve cognitive (knowledge-oriented) learning. Some students of elementary education foresaw for the 1970s more attention to affective (emotion-related) aspects and more concern for the program as a whole rather than

[22] *Ibid.*, p. 422.   [23] *Ibid.*, p. 424.

separate subjects or fields. Today new forms of organization are being used and new materials and media are becoming more generally available.

The elementary school in America has been changing. Even your own experience a decade or more ago is no longer a reliable guide to today's elementary schooling. A team of writers from Michigan State University make the following assessment of this change in the preface to their book on the modern elementary school.

> The evolution of the American elementary school during the past decade has been so rapid, so phenomenal, as to be termed a revolution. Disappearing is the "one teacher, one class, one room" concept of organization; scarce is the isolated teacher, who with few tools and little support is expected to educate youth in a vast complex of skills, concepts, and attitudes; rare is the school with drab "academic brown" cubic proportions. Dramatic changes are occurring not only in man's knowledge of how he learns but also in his use of instructional media, in school organizational patterns, and in multiple teaching strategies—all for more effective instruction. But as dramatic as these changes may seem to today's college students, they are but a prelude to even greater modifications in the elementary school of tomorrow.[24]

Looking to the future, Alfred Ellison of New York University describes an elementary school "for the day after tomorrow" which develops what he terms "tools for living."

1. Insight into the ideals, historical perspectives, and functioning of a democratic society to the extent of valuing it as a way of life, with consequent acceptance of full personal responsibility for participation in and defense of its instruments and institutions.
2. Respect for and understanding of one's self, leading to respect for others and skills in relating to them, maintaining the integrity of the individual personality as a primary value.
3. A rigorous intellectual development that provides an ability to evaluate facts, put them into proper perspective, and use them with purpose. Mere repetition and memory of a set of facts are inadequate; vitally important is the ability to think clearly and reason effectively.
4. Broad and deep insights into man's accomplishments and trials in his efforts to live together with others at personal, local, national, and international levels; and in his efforts to control, modify, and understand his physical and social worlds.
5. Aesthetic sensitivity—an ability to sense and participate in making the beautiful in a variety of art forms, with enough mastery of at least one art so as to provide a comfortable medium of personal expression.
6. An individual quirk of originality, inventiveness, creativeness, with corresponding strength to be nonconformist when important, so that the unique

[24] Calhoun C. Collier et al., *Teaching in the Modern Elementary School* (New York: Macmillan, 1967), p. v.

problems of an unknowable world ahead may find their necessarily unique solutions.
7. A high moral and ethical value structure as a basis for decision-making and personal living, one which serves to enhance the business of everyday living.
8. Knowledge of the many-faceted vocational propensities of a real world of work, including the new occupations now developing, together with techniques for realistic appraisal of one's personal abilities and aspirations.
9. Recognition of the excitement of discovery, the acceptance of intellectual challenge, the intensity of unfilled curiosity, with a fervor for the honest pursuit of ideas.
10. Skill in the communication of ideas, facts, and feelings in many forms and media.
11. Recognition of leisure time as an opportunity for the pursuit of private or public goals, with ability to use it wisely, creatively, and purposefully.
12. The achievement of optimum health through the interaction of the individual's physical well-being, his mental stability, and his personality fulfillment.[25]

JUNIOR HIGH SCHOOL

Junior high school, customarily grades 7, 8, and 9, constitutes the one educational level authentically invented in the United States. Americans inherited the organization and structures of the other educational levels, but the junior high school was first established in the United States in Columbus, Ohio in 1909. Some claim the birthplace to be Berkeley, California, which established its intermediate schools in January 1910, with a program specifically intended to meet the needs of young adolescents. However, Berkeley titled its schools "introductory high schools," a name which never caught on. The Ohio capital was the first city to use the name "junior high school."

Some students never attend an institution labeled "junior high school" because they go from elementary school into senior high in accordance with the popular nineteenth century organization, the so-called 8–4 system. Others spend their junior high school years in an institution which also encompasses the senior high school, the so-called 6–6 division. Yet about one-third of all public secondary schools are 2- or 3-year junior high schools.[26] Most schools are organized on the 6–3–3 or 6–6 basis (See Table 2.2).

---

[25] Alfred Ellison, "A School for the Day After Tomorrow," pp. 517–518 in Joe L. Frost and G. Thomas Rowland (eds.), *The Elementary School; Principles and Problems* (Boston: Houghton Mifflin, 1969).
[26] U.S. Office of Education, *Digest of Educational Statistics*, 1969 ed., p. 43.

TABLE 2.2

Number and Percentage of Public Secondary Schools by
Types of School: United States, 1919–20 through 1965–66

SCHOOL YEAR	TOTAL	TYPE OF SCHOOL			
		TRADI-[a] TIONAL	JUNIOR[b]	SENIOR[c]	JUNIOR[d] SENIOR
1919–20					
Number	14,326	13,421	55	22	828
Percent	100.0	93.7	0.4	0.1	5.8
1937–38					
Number	25,057	15,523	2,372	959	6,203
Percent	100.0	61.9	9.5	3.8	24.8
1951–52					
Number	23,746	10,168	3,227	1,760	8,591
Percent	100.0	42.8	13.6	7.4	36.2
1965–66					
Number	26,098	8,176	7,920	4,942	5,060
Percent	100.0	31.3	30.3	18.9	19.4

[a] Regular four-year high schools preceded by eight-year elementary schools.
[b] Two- and three-year junior high schools.
[c] Three- and four-year senior high schools preceded by junior high schools.
[d] Five- and six-year high schools.

U.S. Office of Education, *Digest of Educational Statistics,* 1969 ed. (Washington, D.C.: U.S. Government Printing Office, 1969), p. 43.

The newest competitor to the junior high school is titled the "middle school," a way of grouping grades which results in a three- or four-year middle school made up of the fourth through eighth or the fifth through eighth grades, followed by a four-year high school. Translated numerically, this form of organization involves 5-3-4 or 4-4-4 school groupings.

Regardless of how organized or where housed, the junior high school years are intended to: (1) continue the education needed by all citizens in a democracy (general education), and (2) provide experience especially suited to the diverse abilities, needs, and interests of widely varied adolescents (education for diversity). Fulfillment of these purposes imposes on the modern junior high school responsibility for the following functions:

1. Continuing and extending the general education program of the elementary school, including development of the basic skills.
2. Providing for a transition between the organization and approach of the elementary school and that of the senior high school.
3. Introducing new subject areas and additional specialization within basic areas.
4. Providing opportunities for students to discover and pursue their special interests and aptitudes.

Teachers discussing a comprehensive yet individual program for students. Courtesy of Ron Sherman of Nancy Palmer.

5. Providing appropriate experiences to assist and guide the rapid physical development that is characteristic of early adolescence.
6. Providing experiences that will develop the social competence needed as students enter young manhood and womanhood.
7. Providing experiences that will assist individuals in developing values and building a philosophy of life.
8. Providing ample opportunities for self-management and the development of leadership under supervision.[27]

As to the new middle schools which are emerging today, Theodore C. Moss recommends:

1. Clearly stated purposes must be developed for the middle school.
2. Careful attention to the growth characteristics of children and youth should precede curriculum construction.
3. An individualized skill building program should be developed for middle school students.
4. A core curriculum, including pupil interests and English–social studies teacher-planned units, is advocated for middle school youth.
5. A modern mathematics curriculum, adapted to at least four ability levels, is recommended for middle school students.
6. The middle school science curriculum should be based on a few carefully planned units, in depth, implemented through a tracking or nongraded program.

[27] William Van Til, Gordon F. Vars, and John H. Lounsbury, *Modern Education for the Junior High School Years* (Indianapolis: Bobbs-Merrill, 1967), p. 35.

Students take an active role in many of the decisions affecting their school lives. Courtesy of DeWys.

7. All middle school youngsters should receive instruction in at least one modern foreign language.
8. Artistically gifted and musically gifted students should receive separate instruction in programs designed to foster the development of their special talents.
9. Students with special dramatics ability should be assigned to a special dramatics class.
10. Middle school boys and girls should have an industrial arts program centered around tool use skills, correlated projects and technology.
11. A sound instructional program of health education is recommended as a separate subject for all middle school students.
12. Recreation, including individual and team sports and outdoor education, should be emphasized throughout the middle school years.
13. Physical fitness classes should be grouped by the physical maturation level of students.
14. The total middle school curriculum should foster general education for all students.
15. Middle school staff personnel responsible for administration, supervision, curriculum development and guidance should also teach students.
16. Guidance-oriented teachers, dedicated to the purpose of the middle school, must be recruited to teach 10- to 14-year olds.[28]

[28] Theodore C. Moss, *Middle School* (Boston: Houghton Mifflin, 1969), pp. 263–269.

One of the services and responsibilities of the school is providing counseling and guidance to all students. Courtesy of DeWys.

As to the future of the junior high school, an Association for Supervision and Curriculum Development publication, *The Junior High School We Need,* made the following recommendations a decade ago; they are still pertinent today.

1. *The junior high school of the future must continue to recognize the development of democratic values as its central commitment.* The junior high school of the future would, above all else, have a consistent commitment, in every instructional area and on the part of all personnel, to develop in young people a devotion to democratic values. . . .
2. *The junior high school of the future should rely upon a basic policy of experimental development of the instructional program.* So far as we now know or can predict, we never will have permanent answers regarding what constitutes the best education. . . .
3. *The junior high school of the future should seek continually to improve time arrangements for effective learning and teaching.* The quality of learning in almost all areas of the curriculum could be improved if the time allotments could be made more flexible. . . .
4. *The instructional process should be planned explicitly for the junior high school years.* If young people are to examine, study, and develop commitment to articulate democratic values in the junior high school, and if these are to be years of exploration and discovery in terms of self, vocational and life goals, then the kind of instructional process utilized must be geared to these purposes. The read-recite-quiz approach simply will not do. The

Modern technology has provided varied teaching and learning aids for the schools. Courtesy of Randal Partridge of EFL.

emphasis in junior high school classes increasingly must be upon discovery, upon finding out what constitutes a fact, what is an opinion, upon discrimination of sources of information and their relative reliability, and upon the process of problem solving. . . .

5. *The junior high school of the future should be an ungraded institution.* Today, the junior high school recognizes that many students cannot be easily classified by grade levels. In the future, students will be assigned to classes and courses on the basis of individual interests, achievement, and need. . . .

6. *The junior high school of the future should incorporate routines and patterns that encourage civility in living.* . . .

7. *Varying instructional procedures will be used to accomplish the purposes of junior high school education in the future.* It is widely agreed that during the years of early adolescence the student needs special attention and help for exploration and discovery. . . .

8. *The junior high school of the future should provide many means for the student to see himself as a significant individual in a larger world setting.* Many opportunities will be available to young people for experiences designed to help them develop personal values and commitments. One such opportunity can be provided by a school through establishing close ties with a school overseas. . . .

9. *The school year should be extended to provide a richer and more effective education program.* In many metropolitan and suburban areas, the junior high school youngster has few opportunities for constructive and satisfying activities after school. . . .
10. *Aesthetic and creative opportunities and experiences should be abundant in the junior high school of the future.* In today's world, individual maturity and serenity are hard to achieve. Yet, through aesthetic awareness and creative experiences, individuals can find ways in which life becomes more meaningful and manageable. . . .
11. *The junior high school of tomorrow should provide extended guidance for all students.* Adolescence is a crucial period in which many fateful decisions are made—to go to college, to leave school, to prepare for a vocation. Youngsters at this age need all the help that trained personnel can give them. . . .
12. *The staff in the junior high school of the future should be given differentiated assignments.* Just as we know that young people have different talents and strengths, so we must recognize that teachers vary in their skills. . . .
13. *New developments in technology and in materials of instruction should be utilized in the junior high school of tomorrow.* . . .
14. *Administrative responsibilities will be more clearly defined in the junior high school of the future.* . . .
15. *Gaining knowledge, skill and understanding are basic goals for junior high school pupils.* Knowledge must be meaningful; skills must relate to use; and understanding needs a foundation in reasoned and disciplined thought. . . .[29]

SENIOR HIGH SCHOOL

The high school today is either a three- or four-year institution, depending on whether the system uses the junior high school form of organization. The ancestry of the American high school includes the Latin grammar school, designed to teach academic knowledge, particularly the classics, to boys preparing for college; it also includes the academy, which was designed by Benjamin Franklin to foster useful knowledge rather than simply that knowledge which was ornamental.

From 1893 to 1918, five committees of distinguished educators reported to the nation on the functions of high school education. The first four of these committees stressed the responsibility of secondary school for preparing students for college; these committees were called the Committee of Ten on Secondary School Studies, the Committee on College Entrance Requirements, the Commit-

---

[29] Jean D. Grambs et al., *The Junior High School We Need* (Washington, D.C.: Association for Supervision and Curriculum Development, 1961), pp. 19–29.

Nineteenth century public high school in Boston, Mass. Courtesy of Culver Pictures.

tee on Economy of Time in Education, and the Committee of Nine on the Articulation of High School and College.[30]

But in 1918 came the historic report of the Commission on the Reorganization of Secondary Education. Unlike the earlier committees, this commission suggested that schools should base their instruction on the present and prospective lives of the students who attended. The report set forth as the principal objectives of all education and especially of secondary education these seven cardinal principles: health, command of the fundamental processes, worthy home membership, vocation, citizenship, worthy use of leisure, and an ethical character. Stress of the seven cardinal principles strengthened the curriculum claims of such high school subjects as industrial arts, home economics, music, fine arts, physical education and business education. Emphasis on the new objectives encouraged the development of a more unitary social studies program for citizenship rather than completely separate history, geography, economics, etc.

There have since been many campaigns in the struggle to make high school education less traditional. Nevertheless, most high schools continued to stress college preparatory programs, supplemented by vocational offerings for the non-college bound through vocational "tracks" within the comprehensive high school. Some large city systems separate academic and vocational education still further through developing a double system of academic high schools and vocational high schools.

With the Soviet Union's successful launching of Sputnik in 1957, American education placed new emphasis on the need for trained manpower to achieve national purposes. The high school curriculum was reconstructed subject by

---

[30] William Marshall French, *American Secondary Education* (New York: Odyssey, 1967), p. 147.

Modern schools usually try to give the impressions of space, light, and expansion—"room to learn." Courtesy of Freelance Photographers Guild.

subject, particularly with the aid of the original National Defense Education Act of 1958 which fostered the reconstruction of programs in science, mathematics, and world languages. With the development of concern for the culturally disadvantaged during the 1960s, the forces which urged a high school curriculum to meet the needs of all young people gained ground.

By 1969, public American secondary schools enrolled 18,196,000 students. Nonpublic high schools enrolled 1,400,000 students.[31] But the question of the high school's purpose was unresolved. Some believe the high school exists simply to prepare young people for college; others see it as an extension of general and specialized education intended to serve the needs of all young people whether college bound or not.

An important proposal for the future of the high school was made by Kimball Wiles of the University of Florida in 1963. Taking 1985 as a target date, Wiles envisioned a high school of the future in which "each pupil will develop a set of values to guide his behavior; acquire the skills necessary to participate effectively in the culture; gain an understanding of his social, economic, political, and scientific heritage; and become able to make a specialized contribution to society."[32] Wiles envisioned four educational phases: analysis of experience and values, acquisition of fundamental skills, exploration of the cultural heritage, and specialization and creativity.

In order to achieve analysis of experiences and values, Wiles proposed the pupil spend six hours a week in an "analysis group" with nine other pupils and

---

[31] U.S. Office of Education, *Digest of Educational Statistics*, 1969 Edition (Washington, D.C.: U.S. Government Printing Office, 1969), pp. 22, 31.

[32] Kimball Wiles, *The Changing Curriculum of the American High School* (Englewood Cliffs, N.J.: Prentice-Hall, 1963), p. 301.

Personal observation and involvement have become integral components of American education today. Courtesy of Franz Kraus from DPI.

a teacher-counselor discussing a variety of relevant problems. To acquire fundamental skills, he proposed dependence upon teaching machines, especially for learning mathematics, foreign languages and many scientific processes and formulas. To explore the cultural heritage, he proposed exposure to basic knowledge from such fields as the humanities, social sciences, and the physical and biological sciences through media which would be easily understood and dramatically and forcefully presented. He saw the analysis groups, the fundamental skills work, and cultural heritage courses as the program to be required of all. But in addition he called for each student to develop a specialization through work in shops, studios, work laboratories, work experience, seminars, etc. All students would also be encouraged to engage in creative activity through the varied arts and writing laboratories.

In 1969, nineteen writers contributed their reactions to Wiles' ideas in *The High School of the Future*. While the ideas of the authors naturally varied, there was fundamental agreement with Wiles' projection. For instance, this writer, after reviewing alternative futures of the high school, made the following predictions:

The most likely future high school, 1985–2000, will include as a component "analysis of experience and values," through small groups made up of students of varied social and racial backgrounds who will not only discuss but will also use various media in analyzing the value implications of their individual experiences and of society's social problems. . . .

The most likely future high school will include as a component "acquisition of individual skills" through core-like analysis groups, broad fields, and the specialized and creative approaches. Additionally, acquisition of individual skills will take place through individual study via computers, listening laboratories, and allied technology geared to individual levels and rates of learning.

The most likely future high school will include as its single heaviest component carefully selected "knowledge of the humanities, the social sciences and the physical and biological sciences." In addition, this component will include world languages because of the world power setting, and that important universal language used in the knowledge explosion—mathematics. Some of the work in these broad fields will be presented through large group instruction via multi-media. But much of it will take place through moderately sized groups characterized by questioning, discussion, and both individual and small group work. . . .

Specialization for the leadership group in a society of expanded higher education will be regarded as an indication of incipient potentiality which must be heavily supplemented on the collegiate and graduate level. Similarly, in a society with expanded on-the-job training for the ordinary worker, specialization in high school through work experience and vocational education will be regarded as little more than orientation. Specialization for those who are unemployable in a highly advanced society will be a problem possibly resolved by rotation in undemanding jobs or by new careers in the human-services field which may exist or be created. On the other hand, the creativity dimensions, through a variety of laboratory and field inductions into mental and physical leisure pursuits, will be heavily emphasized for the health of the social order and the fulfillment of the individual person in a society providing multiple options for the use of the abundant time on one's hands. Even the leadership group will be urged to develop creative pursuits, if for no other reason than enhanced productivity and more effective cogitation.[33]

COLLEGE AND UNIVERSITY

A college may be autonomous or it may be part of a university. The term *university* is far more comprehensive than the term *college;* they usually differ in size and scope of curriculum, and in the fact that a university grants graduate degrees.

The first college was established in the twelfth century in Paris. At Oxford and Cambridge the college became the principal center for learning within the university. The role of the university was to examine candidates for degrees and grant the degrees. From these seeds grew higher education. In the United States, higher education has reached substantial dimensions.

---

[33] William Van Til, "Alternative Futures of the High School," pp. 113–115 in W. Alexander (ed.), *The High School of the Future: A Memorial to Kimball Wiles* (Columbus, Ohio: Charles E. Merrill, 1969).

FIGURE 2.1

Estimated Retention Rates, Fifth Grade through College Graduation, U.S., 1959 to 1971

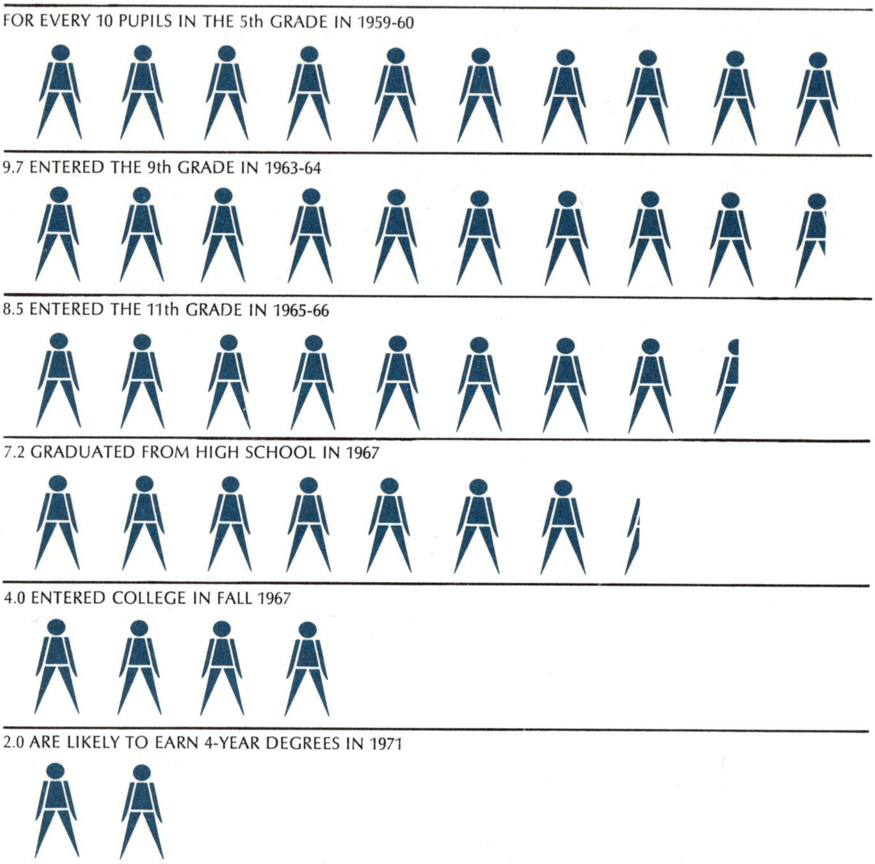

FOR EVERY 10 PUPILS IN THE 5th GRADE IN 1959-60

9.7 ENTERED THE 9th GRADE IN 1963-64

8.5 ENTERED THE 11th GRADE IN 1965-66

7.2 GRADUATED FROM HIGH SCHOOL IN 1967

4.0 ENTERED COLLEGE IN FALL 1967

2.0 ARE LIKELY TO EARN 4-YEAR DEGREES IN 1971

U.S. Office of Education, *Digest of Educational Statistics*, 1968 edition (Washington, D.C.: U.S. Government Printing Office, 1968), p. 8.

The U.S. Office of Education estimated that total expenditures on higher education during the school year 1969–70 was $22.7 billion, with $14.6 billion being spent on public institutions and $8.1 billion on private institutions. In the same year there were 5,100,000 students in public institutions of higher learning and 2,000,000 in private institutions. The total number of full-time and part-time instructional staff for degree-credit courses in Fall 1969 was estimated by the report at 532,000—344,000 in public institutions and 188,000 in private schools.[34]

Though the American colonies inherited the idea of colleges from the Old

---

[34] "Higher Education, 1969–70," *College and University Bulletin* (Washington, D.C.: American Association for Higher Education, October 1, 1969), p. 6.

World, Americans gave it a new twist. They developed the college as an institution separate from the university. A primary purpose was to educate young men for the ministry. The first American college was Harvard in 1636. There followed such colleges as William and Mary in 1693, Yale in 1701, Princeton in 1746, Columbia in 1754, Brown in 1765, and Rutgers in 1766. As the nation moved west, the settlers brought the college idea with them, and now the map of the nation is dotted with colleges, some of which have grown into universities.

In the latter half of the nineteenth century, tax-supported state colleges were formed. Through the Morrill Act of 1862, public lands were granted to the states for state agricultural and mechanical colleges. Out of such beginnings have grown such giants as the Big Ten[35] universities. Throughout the late nineteenth century and into the twentieth, the land grant colleges steadily moved to the status of universities by expanding to include professional schools and graduate instruction.

COLLEGES FOR WOMEN

Another American collegiate innovation was the establishment of colleges for women. The first women's colleges included Mount Holyoke, 1837; Elmira, 1853; Vassar, 1861; Wellesley, 1871; Smith, 1871; and Bryn Mawr, 1881. Women's colleges persist in the closing third of the twentieth century, but today the trend is to coeducation. Today many womens' colleges—the prestigious Seven Sisters,[36] for example—are developing further collaborative relationships with their male neighbors—for instance, Barnard and Columbia, Radcliffe and Harvard, Smith and Amherst, and Wellesley and M.I.T. Today the male sanctuaries, having earlier admitted women at the graduate level, are increasingly enrolling women undergraduates. Princeton and Yale were conspicuously in the news in the late 1960s as they cautiously opened their doors to women.

COLLEGES FOR BLACKS

The development of Negro colleges also reflects the American social setting. After the Civil War, colleges for black Americans came into existence partially through the philanthropy of such rich men as George Peabody and partially through the activities of Negro leaders like Booker T. Washington, who opened Tuskegee Normal and Industrial Institute in 1881.

In an era first of post–Civil War reconstruction and then of state-enforced segregation, Negro colleges struggled with the handicap that they were separate in status and unequal to white institutions in quality. Legally, the tide turned to desegregation in the late 1930s and the 1940s, when Supreme Court decisions

---

[35] Indiana University, Michigan State University, Northwestern University, Ohio State University, Purdue University, University of Illinois, University of Iowa, University of Michigan, University of Minnesota, University of Wisconsin.
[36] Barnard, Mount Holyoke, Smith, Radcliffe, Wellesley, Vassar, and Bryn Mawr.

Integration has come slowly in many areas. Courtesy of Black Star.

opened the door to the enrollment of Negroes in formerly all-white institutions. In a precedent-setting case, the Maryland Court of Appeals upheld a decision in which Donald Gaines Murray, a Negro graduate of Amherst, was ordered admitted to the University of Maryland School of Law in 1935.[37] In a similar case filed by Lloyd Lionel Gaines, the Supreme Court of the United States handed down a decision in 1938 which supported the earlier Murray decision and relied heavily on findings in that case.[38] Other suits followed in other states, so that by 1950 resort to legal action in school segregation questions was not an unusual practice.[39] Although twelve southern and border states and the District of Columbia had initiated desegregation in some of their institutions of higher learning to a limited degree prior to the 1954 Supreme Court ruling, court cases, such as the Brown case, provided the most influential prod to university desegregation.

Universities, sparked by the demands of black militants, initiated black studies programs in the late 1960s and into the 1970s; Negro colleges, largely in the South, were raided by northern colleges and universities suddenly eager to bring black men to their faculties for development of black studies programs. In addition, Negro colleges encountered economic problems brought about by the inflation of the fifties and sixties. They were also confronted by demands of black separatists and legal requirements that public education be desegregated. As a result of such social forces, Negro colleges are today struggling for survival.

[37] W. A. Low, "The Education of Negroes Viewed Historically," p. 54 in V. A. Clift, A. W. Anderson, and H. G. Hullfish (eds.), *Negro Education in America: Its Adequacy, Problems, and Needs* (New York: Harper, 1962).
[38] *Ibid.,* p. 55.   [39] *Ibid.,* pp. 55–56.

THE JUNIOR COLLEGE

The established four-year undergraduate college has been joined in the twentieth century by a college with a new time span, the junior college. Essentially, the junior college covers the first two years of the customary four-year span. Some junior colleges are private and independently supported, and some are affiliated with churches. But the most phenomenal growth is that of the public community college. In the late 1950s, approximately one out of five students in the nation began his undergraduate studies in a community college. But in the late 1960s, the number had grown to more than one out of three beginning college students. In the 1970s, it is reasonable to predict that the number will be one out of two. The growth of the community college is accounted for, in part, by the tremendous expansion of higher education in America in the twentieth century and by the demand for education on the part of the residents of the big cities.[40] Since community colleges are usually attended by commuters, dormitories are not needed—another factor which encourages growth of the community college concept.

Edmund J. Gleazer, Jr., executive director of the American Association of Junior Colleges, points out in a 1968 book, *This Is the Community College*, that "five hundred new community colleges have sprung up in the last ten years. . . . There was a community college within commuting distance of almost every person in New York State, Florida, and California. This will soon be the case in Illinois, Virginia, Michigan, and a score of other states."[41] "One out of three students enrolled in the community college will continue his work in a four-year college. The other two will not."[42]

GRADUATE SCHOOL

Increasingly, the master's degree is being taken for granted as a necessity for teachers—if not immediately after embarking on teaching, quite soon after. One form of master's degree is the MAT, designed especially for liberal arts graduates who decide to teach. Five years of education for teachers following high school graduation will almost certainly become one of the facts of teaching life which you should take into account.

Beyond the master's degree lies a one-year degree which still lacks a dignified title. It is sometimes referred to as the sixth-year degree or the advanced degree in education. This degree is for the practitioners who want to go beyond the master's degree but do not require specialization in research for their career development.

The ultimate degree in the American educational system is the doctorate. A doctor of philosophy (Ph.D.) or doctor of education (Ed.D.) degree has become

---

[40] Edmund J. Gleazer, Jr., *This Is the Community College* (Boston: Houghton Mifflin, 1968), p. v.
[41] *Ibid.*, p. 4.   [42] *Ibid.*, p. 66.

a must for the graduate staff member and a near must for four-year college teachers and school leadership posts.

Graduate education began in the United States in 1876 with the founding of the Johns Hopkins University. Many of the patterns now being disputed by some of the nation's youth were established at that time. The first president of the Johns Hopkins University, Daniel Coit Gilman, had in view:

> ... the appointment of professors who had shown their ability as investigators, whose duties as teachers would not be so burdensome as to interfere with the prosecution of their researchers, whose students should be so advanced as to stimulate them to their best work, and the fruit of whose labors in the advancement of science and learning should be continually manifested in the shape of published results.[43]

Sound familiar? This conception of the role of the graduate professor is now under attack from student dissenters who urge more activism and involvement by professors.

THE FUTURE OF COLLEGES AND UNIVERSITIES

As to the future of higher education, there is fierce debate and wide disagreement. The controversy goes far beyond the continuing and significant academic questions of how many courses should be required and how many should be elective, how much general or liberal education to include in the curriculum, or how much specialization in a single field. The questions now discussed with earnestness and passion involve the very role of these institutions. In the late 1960s and early 1970s demonstrations, strikes, arson, and closedowns swept through the colleges and universities because of student dissatisfaction on issues related in part to the role of the university in society.

Nineteenth century scholars such as John Henry Newman, a cardinal of the Roman Catholic Church, saw the university as an assembly of scholars who tested and shared ideas and created an atmosphere in which students could develop sound and creative habits of mind. As the twentieth century developed, classical ideals of liberal education such as Newman's were supplemented by demands that higher education prepare Americans for a variety of new professions and careers. Since World War II, the American university has increasingly served the government on a range of peacetime and war-related concerns.

In the 1970s, such established patterns were challenged by those who called for a much closer connection between the work of the university and pressing social problems of the times. Some called for more study of socially relevant problems in the curriculum; others called upon higher education to abandon its institutional neutrality and become a staging ground for political action within the democratic process; still others on the far left saw the colleges and universities as bases from which to launch a revolution. The question of whether social

---

[43] Fabian Franklin et al., *The Life of Daniel Coit Gilman* (New York: Dodd, Mead, 1910), p. 196.

Students protest, New York City. Courtesy of The New York Times.

activism in higher education can coexist with the earlier roles is central to the future of colleges and universities. Some think that student dissent and disruption have mortally wounded the American college and university. The historian and administrator Jacques Barzun, for instance:

By organizing hatred . . . by assaulting and imprisoning their teachers, dividing faculties into factions, turning weak heads into cowards and demagogues, ignoring the grave and legitimate causes for reform, advocating the bearing of arms on campus, and preferring "confrontation" to getting their own way, hostile students have ushered in the reactionary university of the future, medieval model.

For it is clear that once the traditions of deference and civility are broken they cannot be knit up again at will. No one can be sure of the future, but the past is not dumb. Medieval student power met its quietus when the aggressive traits of its leaders were, so to speak, taken over by the state. The students, losing their privilege, became subjects like any other and were put down. For the American university there is no telling whether the return to the Middle Ages will not be halted at the phase of royal repression. Already more than half the states have passed acts of control mild yet menacing by simply being there.

Nobody with a heart and a mind can look forward to the fulfillment of either reactionary hope—it took so long to develop the republic of learning in which *study* was the sole aim and test of the institution! Who can bear to think of reliving 1266 and All That?[44]

On the other hand, there are those who believe that increasing student participation in the life and governance of the university can lead to a far more significant collegiate education than that which has been characteristic of the past decade. For instance, Harold Taylor, formerly president of Sarah Lawrence College, is an outstanding proponent of this position:

> In this situation of the university, once more the students are its greatest allies, and if some of them have declared themselves to be its enemies, let them be met by those in the universities who know and can teach that the real enemy of the university is ignorance, force, and violence, and that the way to overcome these is by knowledge, a passion for justice, and a commitment to truth. . . .
>
> That is why education and the university must both be redefined so that they may become instruments through which the influence of persons on each other may act to secure the elevation of spirit and quality of life which it is the purpose of all education to induce. The university should be a place where students help their teachers to teach them, where teachers help their students to learn, where administrators help both to accomplish what they have come together to do. That is why the role of the students must also be redefined in order to make clear to them and to all others that students *are* the foundation of the university, that when everything else is taken away, as in fact it can be—the government contracts, the isolated research institutes, the alumni bodies, the services to industry, the travelling faculty, the organization men—what is left are persons working together to learn and to teach. . . .
>
> The education of students, therefore, means nothing less than their personal involvement in the conduct of the affairs of the mind. An equality of position in the polity of the community is a necessary condition of their involvement; otherwise they are playing a game the necessity for whose rules they never learn to understand—the commitment to play is never completely made.[45]

ADULT EDUCATION

No one claims that adult education has the rigor or scholarly apparatus of graduate education. Instead, adult education affords varied miscellaneous opportunities for adults to understand the problems of their world, to try to keep up with rapid social change, to prepare for new jobs, to remedy deficiencies in

---

[44] Jacques Barzun, "Tomorrow's University: Back to the Middle Ages?" *Saturday Review* (November 15, 1969), p. 61.
[45] Harold Taylor, *Students Without Teachers: The Crisis in the University* (New York: McGraw-Hill, 1969), pp. 320–321.

Education of America's adults has also received new emphasis in recent years. Courtesy of Paul Conklin.

their own backgrounds, and to engage in education simply for the love of learning something new.

Adult education is a kind of giant smorgasbord offering many dishes to please the tastes of varied individuals. It is almost impossible to define it closely. Perhaps the most useful definition is the simple one: "The term adult education is used to designate all those educational activities that are designed specifically for adults."[46]

Educational activities for adults may include the program of the Parent-Teachers Association or a luncheon club meeting, a correspondence course, in-service training program, a study discussion group, a public forum, or an evening class in a high school or university. These may be provided by public or private schools and colleges, public or volunteer health and welfare agencies, churches, businesses, industrial establishments, private clubs, proprietary schools, or the armed forces.[47]

Adult education includes academic education at the levels of elementary or secondary or university, fundamental education for literacy, education for older individuals to help them to a better life in their later years, creative arts education, liberal adult education such as study of the great books, public affairs education to develop knowledge and more effective citizenship, home and family life education, and community development education to aid in the improvement of community life.[48]

Though there are relatively few professional teachers in adult education, there are many volunteers. No one has reliably calculated the number of volunteer

[46] Coolie Verner, *Adult Education* (Washington, D.C.: The Center for Applied Research in Education, 1964), p. 1.
[47] *Ibid.*, p. 2.   [48] *Ibid.*, pp. 62–67.

Some adults have organized into groups to discuss common interests, such as community participation and child-rearing. Courtesy of Anna Kaufmann Moon.

adult education workers. For instance, think of the number of program chairmen in voluntary organizations in America. A second group of adult educators are the part-timers. These are the people who are regularly employed, often as teachers in universities and school systems; they take on additional work with classes of adults as moonlighting employment. They are seldom trained especially to work with adults and tend to find their way through the use of trial and error. Finally, there are the professionals in adult education, such as staff members of university extension programs, the agricultural extension experts, the adult education specialists in public schools, etc. Increasingly, such professionals work for graduate degrees.

CHOOSING AMONG LEVELS

If you are going to be a teacher, you will teach at one of the levels described. A small minority of new teachers may teach on two levels—for example, at both junior high and senior high school levels, or at both kindergarten and early elementary school levels. Or as his career intentions change, a teacher may move from junior high to a different level, perhaps to senior high school teaching. Sometimes an outstanding elementary or secondary school teacher, having achieved the doctoral degree, moves into college and university teaching. But most teachers stay at the level they originally chose.

How do you choose the teaching level that is right for you? Presumably you want to work with people to make a difference. But people at what stage of development? Perhaps the single most important factor to take into account is the age level of students with which you feel most comfortable and to which you are most attracted as a teacher. Do the unique experiences which you have had in your family, schooling, work or recreation lead you to prefer to work with one particular age group?

To decide the teaching level which you prefer, you might also take a realistic look at your own personality characteristics. If you are turned on by watching and helping individuals grow, you might seriously consider some of the lower levels of the educational systems; if teaching, to be rewarding to you, requires a lively interchange of ideas on a near peer basis, you might consider the highest levels of the educational system.

As part of your self-examination, you might also ask yourself what essentially you are trying to do through teaching.

If your primary interest is in the communication of a body of content which has awakened and aroused you, you might find yourself most at home on one of the higher educational levels—unless you have concluded that the earliest stages of learning your specialized content offer the most exciting challenge to you.

Or perhaps your motivation is to help human beings develop their values and approach to life. Such a commitment might lead you to work either with the very young, since presumably the young are still forming their values, or with older learners during those periods of their lives when they are reconsidering their life styles.

Perhaps your main interest is in research. Then you probably should plan to get your doctoral degree and teach at a four-year college or, preferably, a graduate school. For the teacher who wishes to teach on the college level but does not propose to become a research specialist, the American junior college movement, and especially the community college, offers great opportunities. About 9 percent of all junior and community college teachers hold the doctorate, reported Gleazer in his 1968 book, *This Is the Community College*;[49] however, the percentage will probably increase in the 1970s. In the mid-1960s a national study of teacher supply and demand reported that 30 percent of the new junior college teachers came directly from high school classrooms, 17 percent from college and university teaching, 24 percent from graduate schools, and 11.3 percent from business occupations.[50]

You cannot be sure that your early decision will be the best for you. But you must think it through carefully now. It is romantic folly to hope that you will become a professor of English in a university through preparing to become a teacher of English in a high school. The road to being a professor of English does

---

[49] Gleazer, p. 115.
[50] NEA Research Division, *Teacher Supply and Demand in Universities, Colleges, and Junior Colleges, 1963–64 and 1964–65*, Research Report 1965–R4, Higher Education Series (Washington, D.C.: The Association, April 1965), as reported by Gleazer in *This Is the Community College*, p. 114.

not lead through the high school or a college of education program, but requires graduate work in English at a major university.

Yet career changes can and do take place. For instance, it is quite possible that you may find yourself more interested in a career in adult education as you grow older, rather than immediately after college. In 1959 Brunner found that the median age of teachers in adult education was 46.4 years with two-thirds between the ages of 35 and 54. "Only four percent are under thirty which indicates that adult education is not a career line attractive to or holding much promise at present for young people seeking a lifetime professional affiliation."[51] However, since Brunner wrote, several institutions of higher education have instituted undergraduate programs to prepare young men and women for a lifetime career in adult education.

If your decision is both early and thoughtful, you will avoid such obvious errors as taking adolescent psychology instead of child psychology if you really intend to teach on the elementary school level; and also more sophisticated errors such as insufficient courses in the various social sciences when you intend to teach social studies in junior or senior high school. Each state has its own patterns of certification; your advisers are familiar with these. Should you find your advisor inadequate, most colleges or schools of education maintain an office of certification intended to help you meet certification requirements.

When you have established your goals, you can then concentrate on becoming the best possible teacher at the level you have chosen.

★ ★ ★

DISCUSSION

1. Which educational level presently most appeals to you? Why?
2. How much do you know about the kibbutz method of rearing children? What do you think about it?
3. What seem to be the advantages and disadvantages of the development of day-care centers for children from disadvantaged homes in America?
4. Why is there presently little or no formal education for the years from birth to age three?
5. Why did nursery school education come to the United States as late as it did? Why even now do so relatively few children attend nursery schools in the United States?
6. What do you know of nursery education in the community or communities in which you have lived? Who sponsors the nursery schools with which you are acquainted?
7. What do you think is the purpose of a nursery school?

---

[51] Edmund deS. Brunner, et al., *The Role of a National Organization in Adult Education* (unpublished report to the executive committee of the Adult Education Association, 1959), as reported by Verner in *Adult Education*, p. 47.

8. What do you think of the purposes of kindergartens that are proposed? Do you believe that kindergarten should stress reading? Why or why not?
9. What have been some trends in the development of elementary education in America? Can you cite any evidence to support the idea that elementary school education in America has been rapidly changing?
10. How would you revise Ellison's proposal for an elementary school "for the day after tomorrow"?
11. Can you see any reasons to prefer junior high schools, middle schools, or some other form of educational organization for the middle years?
12. Do the proposed purposes of the junior high school and those of the middle school seem fundamentally different to you in any ways? Do they seem alike?
13. What would be your own proposal for "the junior high school we need"?
14. What are some major developments in the history of the senior high school in America?
15. Why is the senior high school level particularly resistant to program changes? When the program does change, what forces particularly account for such changes?
16. As you see it, what is the relative importance of the four educational phases proposed by Wiles? In what ways do these phases correspond with the seven cardinal principles of education? In what ways do they go beyond them? Can you see any influence of Wiles' thinking in your own high school experience?
17. If you had your way, how would you change the current high school program? What is your picture of a desirable high school for the future?
18. Attendance at colleges and universities is steadily increasing. How is this desirable or undesirable? Is society forcing young people into college?
19. What is to be said for and against coeducation as contrasted to separate colleges for men and women? Do your reasons apply to all educational levels?
20. Speculate on the future of Negro colleges. Will they survive? If so, how will they be different from Negro colleges of earlier decades?
21. Why has the junior college movement boomed? What are the advantages and disadvantages of this form of educational organization?
22. What is the status of the junior college movement in your state? Are the junior colleges there a part of the state educational program? Does the junior college play a major or minor role in your state's higher education?
23. What are the current criticisms of Doctoral degree programs? Do you see any relationship between the Doctoral degree and the teaching ability of instructors and professors who have taught you?
24. What do you think of the emphasis on publications by professors which is characteristic of graduate school education? Is it valid to condemn higher education for so-called "publish or perish" policies? What is your conception of a desirable undergraduate or graduate school professor?
25. Fundamentally, what is a university or college for? Development of your mind? Vocational training? Social action?
26. Discuss the views of Barzun and Taylor. What is the role of students in your university? What should it be? Should students have voice and vote? Should they

have a degree of representation in policy-making groups? Should they have full equality with faculty in number of representatives?

27. Should students determine university and college matters related to tenure, promotion, salary increases of professors? Would academic freedom be threatened by student power?

28. What essentially is adult education? Why is adult education less systematically organized than higher education in America?

29. What is your own appraisal of your personality characteristics in relationship to teaching? How important to you is the exchange of ideas with students? How important is helping individuals grow?

30. In deciding to teach, how important is the subject matter in which you specialize? Do you propose to teach subjects or young people—or do you regard that as a false dualism?

31. Do your present ambitions tie into your long range aspirations? Can you make a case for going in one occupational direction after college and moving in a sharply different direction some years later?

INVOLVEMENT

1. Get in touch with and interview a member of one of the community agencies which deals with preschool children. Talk with this person about the differences between the behavior and problems of children of the poor and children of the affluent. Consider any differences which emerge and the implications they might have for education. Report to the class on your findings.

2. Visit a day-care center. Observe the teacher and the children and report things which seem significant to you. In what ways are these young children receiving good care? Speculate on whether or not some children are receiving better care than they might receive at home.

3. Visit a nursery school. After observing, ask the teacher why these particular children are in attendance. Do you find any relationship to social forces and developments?

4. Visit a kindergarten. Look for the purposes behind the various activities you observe. Try to find an opportunity to talk with the teacher about why the activities you observed are taking place. How would you handle (ideally) the program you observed?

5. Visit the oldest and the newest elementary schools in the community in which you live or study. Do you see any differences in the program related to the age of the buildings? Or are the differences due to other factors?

6. Draw up your own proposal for an elementary school geared to today's needs and tomorrow's demands. Consider the physical plant as well as the educational program.

7. Visit a school for the middle years. How is the program which you observe similar to or different from that recommended?

8. Interview a successful teacher who teaches at the level you presently prefer. Find out his or her reasons for teaching and why he or she chose that particular level.

9. Visit a senior high school. Make a point of going to other classes than simply those which represent your own field or fields. As you see it, what are the teachers

trying to do in their classes? In general, do the classes seem to be taught in modern or traditional manners?
10. Create an opportunity to talk with a high school teacher about Wiles' ideas concerning the high school of the future. How does this individual see the future of the high school?
11. Visit the campus of a junior college in your area. Go to the administration building and find the individual responsible for visitors. Talk with him about the role and future of the junior college and the nature of its staff.
12. Sum up the degree of engagement of your college or university in current campus dissent. What matters are in debate? What problems are latent, awaiting arousal?
13. Develop a few interview questions to raise with fellow students on the goals, program, problems, etc., of your college or university. Look for common denominators in answers.
14. Examine the process of student involvement in government and university life in general at your institution. Determine whether centers of power exist in the student body. Reexamine your own role and participation in student government and campus lite.

BIBLIOGRAPHY

Alexander, William M., ed. *The High School of the Future: A Memorial to Kimball Wiles.* Columbus, Ohio: Charles E. Merrill, 1969. Nineteen authors collaborate on examining a chapter on the high school of the future by Kimball Wiles. A lively and provocative collection.

Alexander, William M., Emmett L. Williams, Mary Compton, Vynce A. Hines, Dan Prescott. *The Emergent Middle School.* New York: Holt, Rinehart and Winston, 1968. For students initially preparing for middle school positions and personnel in-service retraining for continuing careers in new middle school programs.

Barzun, Jacques. *The American University: How it Runs, Where it is Going.* New York: Harper and Row, 1968. The American university as it looked to a scholar prior to the recent dissent and campaigns for increased student power in the university.

Blount, Nathan S. and Herbert J. Klausmeier. *Teaching in the Secondary School,* 3rd ed. New York: Harper and Row, 1968. Deals with foundations of creative learning, teaching-learning activities, and responsibilities and challenges.

Bettelheim, Bruno. *The Children of the Dream.* New York: Macmillan, 1969. A report by a leader in the behavioral sciences on young people reared in the Israeli kibbutz from birth through adolescence. Highly important to decision-making on the education of young children.

Brubacher, John S. and Willis Rudy. *Higher Education in Transition: An American History: 1636–1968.* New York: Harper and Row, 1968. A chronological study of the development of the college and university system from colonial times to the present.

Callahan, Sterling. *Successful Teaching in Secondary Schools.* Chicago: Scott, Foresman, 1966. To serve the needs of beginning teachers as well as in-service teachers.

Clark, Leonard H., ed. *Strategies and Tactics In Secondary School Teaching: A Book of Readings.* New York: Macmillan, 1968. A theoretical basis and some examples of the various techniques and methods incorporated in teaching strategies.

Collier, Calhoun C., et al. *Teaching in the Modern Elementary School.* New York: Macmillan, 1967. An overview of the work of the contemporary elementary school.

Conant, James B. *The Comprehensive High School: A Second Report to Interested Citizens.* New York: McGraw-Hill, 1967. A follow-up report a decade after the first Conant study of the American high school. Improvements are discussed and continuing inadequacies are detailed.

DeBoer, John J., Walter U. Kaulfers, and Lawrence E. Metcalf, eds. *Secondary Education: A Textbook of Readings.* Boston: Allyn and Bacon, 1966. On universal education, the high school population, goals and curriculum, subject fields developments, and trends.

Draper, Dale C. *Educating for Work.* Washington, D.C.: National Association of Secondary School Principals, NEA, 1967. An NASSP study on vocational education.

Fletcher, Margaret I. *The Adult and the Nursery School Child.* Toronto: University of Toronto Press, 1967. A summary of the importance of the nursery school to the child and a description of the role of the teacher in relationship to both children and parents.

Foster, Josephine and Neith Headley. *Education in the Kindergarten.* New York: Van Nostrand Reinhold, 1966. A useful introduction to the work of kindergarten teachers.

Frazier, Alexander, ed. *The New Elementary School.* Washington, D.C.: Association for Supervision and Curriculum Development, NEA, 1968. Concentrates on new ideas in elementary education in areas such as knowledge of how young children grow, patterns of content selection and organization, and new patterns of teacher education.

Frost, Joe L., ed. *Early Childhood Education Rediscovered: Readings.* New York: Holt, Rinehart and Winston, 1968. Presents the case for preschool education for all children, including the disadvantaged. Includes information on Montessori, Piaget, Head Start, etc.

Frost, Joe L. and G. Thomas Rowland, eds. *The Elementary School: Principles and Problems.* Boston: Houghton Mifflin, 1969. Elementary teachers and their interactions with the forces that directly or indirectly influence teaching and the elementary school curriculum.

Gleazer, Edmund J. Jr. *This Is the Community College.* Boston: Houghton Mifflin, 1968. Focuses on a type of junior college that has experienced change and growth during recent years and is now in the process of determining its future course—the public community college.

Grambs, Jean D., et al. *The Junior High School We Need.* Washington, D.C.: Association for Supervision and Curriculum Development, NEA, 1961. A lively and useful description of the directions in which the American junior high school should develop.

Hahn, Robert O. and David B. Bidna. *Secondary Education: Origins and Directions,* 2nd ed. New York: Macmillan, 1970. The origins of secondary education, along with the current state of secondary education.

Howard, Alvin W. *Teaching in Middle Schools.* Scranton, Pa.: International Textbook, 1968. Stresses fundamentals of teaching, classroom management, discipline, motivation, and individual differences in the middle grades.

Hymes, James L., Jr. *Teaching the Child Under Six.* Columbus, Ohio: Charles Merrill, 1968. Well written book on children ages three to six with implementing ideas for teaching them.

Keeton, Morris and Conrad Hilberry. *Struggle and Promise: A Future for Colleges.* New York: McGraw-Hill, 1968. The future of the liberal arts college, with in-depth studies of twelve such colleges together with reflections and recommendations.

Keith, Lowell, Paul Blake, and Sidney Tiedt. *Contemporary Curriculum in the Elementary School.* New York: Harper and Row, 1968. An introduction to modern curriculum based on foundations of education.

Kunen, James Simon. *The Strawberry Statement: Notes of a College Revolutionary.* New York: Random House, 1969. A diary by a student rebel with a sense of humor. Concerns experiences during the 1968 student dissent at Columbia University.

Margolis, John D. *The Campus in the Modern World.* New York: The Macmillan Co., 1969. Twenty-five essays which deal with goals, criticisms, and alternatives in higher education.

Morgan, Barton, Glenn E. Holmes, and Clarence E. Bundy. *Methods in Adult Education.* Danville, Ill.: The Interstate Printers and Publishers, 1963. Fundamental principles and techniques of teaching mature people through adult education programs.

Moss, Theodore C. *Middle School.* Boston: Houghton Mifflin, 1969. Presents practical methods and materials for teachers, guidance workers and administrators with respect to education for the middle years.

Nerbovig, Marcella H. and Herbert J. Klausmeier. *Teaching in the Elementary School,* 3rd ed. New York: Harper and Row, 1969. The revision encompasses the results of recent research and development aimed at improving teaching-learning practices.

Newman, John Henry, Cardinal. *The Ideal of a University.* New York: Longmans, Green, 1905. The classical case for the university as a place for the development of the mind.

Pines, Maya. *Revolution in Learning: From Birth to Six.* New York: Harper and Row, 1967. Developments of cognitive learning by preschool children which raise the question of whether America sufficiently emphasizes education at this level.

Ragan, William B. *Modern Elementary Curriculum,* 3rd ed. New York: Holt, 1966. Stress on learning experiences of children.

Read, Katherine H. *The Nursery School: A Human Relationships Laboratory.* Philadelphia and London: W. B. Saunders, 1966. A useful description of the place and purpose of the nursery school in America, with practical suggestions for teaching.

Salot, Lorraine and Jerome E. Leavitt. *The Beginning Kindergarten Teacher.* Minneapolis: Burgess Publishing, 1965. A resource book to assist the kindergarten teacher by providing practical suggestions which can be used in most kindergartens.

Sanford, Nevitt. *College and Character.* New York: John Wiley and Sons, 1964. The essence of a classic study, *The American College,* by the author and others, presented in shorter form.

Smith, Frederick R. and R. Bruce McQuigg. *Secondary Schools Today: Readings for Educators,* 2nd ed. Boston: Houghton Mifflin, 1969. Readable and lively compilation of controversies and conflicts in the field of secondary education. Deals with purposes, curriculum, students, new patterns of instruction, teachers, and centers of controversy.

Sewards, G. Wesley and Mary M. Scobey. *The Changing Curriculum and the Elementary Teacher,* 2nd ed. Belmont, Calif.: Wadsworth Publishing, 1968. A society and learner oriented book which is helpful to the elementary school teacher.

Taylor, Harold. *Students Without Teachers: The Crisis in the University.* New York: McGraw-Hill, 1969. An eloquent and provocative book by a former college president which supports the views of students who are critical of the contemporary university.

Thornton, R. James. *The Community Junior College.* New York: John Wiley and Sons, 1965. A book on the philosophy and place of junior colleges; the organization and administration of the junior college, its curriculum, and its student personnel problems.

Todd, Vivian Edmiston and Helen Heffernan. *The Years Before School: Guiding Preschool Children,* 2nd ed. New York: Macmillan, 1970. Affirmation of the importance of the early childhood years and practical assistance to early childhood teachers. Deals with day-care centers, nurseries, and kindergartens.

Van Til, William, Gordon F. Vars, and John H. Lounsbury. *Modern Education for the Junior High School Years*. Indianapolis: Bobbs-Merrill, 1967. A comprehensive textbook on the junior high school which treats of the present status of education for the junior high school years, the foundations of education, and developments in each of the subject areas.

Verner, Coolie. *Adult Education*. Washington, D.C.: The Center for Applied Research in Education, 1964. Broad coverage of adult education in America discussing the scope, needs, functions, and institutions that provide adult education.

Weaver, Gary R. and James H. Weaver. *The University and Revolution*. Englewood Cliffs, N.J.: Prentice-Hall, 1969. The impact of the university on the revolutionary movements sweeping the world today, as well as on the university.

Wiles, Kimball, *The Changing Curriculum of the American High School*. Englewood Cliffs, N.J.: Prentice-Hall, 1963. Well written advocacy of a curriculum stressing the needs of the individual learner. An especially provocative future-oriented final chapter.

Wills, Clarice Dechent and Lucile Lindberg. *Kindergarten for Today's Children*. Chicago: Follett Publishing, 1967. An overview of the modern kindergarten program stressing relevance, creativity, and involvement of the community.

Woodring, Paul. *The Higher Learning in America*. New York: McGraw-Hill, 1968. The diversity of educational institutions of higher learning in the nation—some of the problems faced by them and some possible solutions.

Zirbes, Laura. *Focus on Values in Elementary Education*. New York: G. P. Putnam's Sons, 1960. A powerful examination of values in relation to education. In this classic, elementary education is conceived as social change and as a means of projecting human values.

AUDIO-VISUAL MATERIALS

From Cradle to Classroom, Pts 1 and 2, (Twenty-first Century Series: CBS-McGraw-Hill, 50 Min.) Children from 3 months to 5 years in age are shown in many special types of teaching programs. Programs use professional teachers, nonprofessional instructors, teaching machines, educational toys, and association drills.

Teaching the 3's, 4's, and 5's, Part I: Guiding Behavior (Churchill, 21 Min.) Shows several nursery school children in situations where adult help is needed to guide group and individual behavior: a tantrum, a runaway, and other situations. Mistakes as well as examples of skillful handling of situations are shown.

Teaching the 3's, 4's, and 5's, Part II: Setting the Stage for Learning (Churchill, 22 Min.) Shows young children at play in a series of nursery school activities. Many simple "props" and play equipment are arranged to allow construction with wood, tests of physical powers, and use of imagination in family life play situations.

The Purple Turtle (ACI Productions, 13 Min., Color) Sights and sounds of kindergarten classes as children busy themselves with paints, crayons, and clay. Helps create an understanding of the value of art work.

Infant School (Educational Development Corp., 29 Min.) Explores a typical day in the Gordonbrook Infant School in London in an old building that has been adapted for new teaching methods. Examines the nongraded approach to instruction as practiced in England with children ranging in age from 5 to 7 years and grouped "family-fashion" for a wide variety of learning experiences.

Skippy and the 3 R's (National Education Association, 30 Min., Color) Shows how a first-grade child is taught reading and arithmetic by a teacher who utilizes the boy's interest to help him to realize his own need for learning.

A Long Time to Grow, Part III: Six, Seven, and Eight Year Olds—Society of Children (New York University, 28 Min.) Children ages six, seven, and eight at work and at play at the Poughkeepsie Day School. Their reactions and learning behavior through the day and in various activities.

Junior High—A Time of Change (McGraw-Hill, 11 Min., Color) Defines some of the problems which arise for the student upon entering junior high school. Suggests techniques to help in adjustment to the new type of school.

Your First Year in High School (Guidance Associates, Pt. 1–71 fr., Pt. 2–74 fr., Color, Record) Discussion of the problems, challenges and choices of the modern high school.

The High School (Frederick Wiseman) Filmed at Philadelphia's North East High. Depicts typical episodes in high school student life. Attempts to show that even a good high school may be out of touch with its students.

And No Bells Ring (National Association of Secondary Principals, 56 Min.) Dramatizes the new directions planned to improve the quality of education. Discusses how schools have adapted space and schedule changes.

The Junior College Story (California Junior College Association, 23 Min. color) Explains how a student can acquire professional and technical skills or prepare for advanced college work by attending a junior college. Outlines the types of vocational and academic subjects which are taught and discusses the counseling services which are available.

College (Pyramid Film Productions, 19 Min. Color) Explains the nature and function of an ideal college through the eyes of the scientist, poet and explorer. Ignores the exterior aspects of a college and concentrates on what occurs in students' minds. Filmed at San Fernando Valley State College, Northridge, California.

The College—(Vernon Zimmerman, 55 Min.) Paints an impressionistic picture of life at the University of Chicago by blending shots of classroom discussions, sports events and student political and musical activities, with students and faculty commenting on each.

The Columbia Revolt (San Francisco Newsreel, 50 Min.) Tells the story of the May 1968 revolt at Columbia University.

Learning for Life (NEA, 28 Min., Color) Reasons for adult education programs.

Hey, What About Us? (NET, 57 Min.) Depicts job situations after high school for the majority who don't go to college. Reviews the functions of counselors, industry training, employment agencies, and the military.

THREE

WHO TEACHES IN AMERICAN SCHOOLS?

What will your fellow teachers be like? First we must consider and dispose of stereotypes of the American school teacher. Stereotypes are distortions and caricatures which have highly limited validity, but they have a highly persistent quality. Through stereotypes, we describe all too glibly "the establishment," "the middle class," "student dissenters," "blacks," "professors," etc.

Unfortunately, the teacher stereotype we have inherited is not that of the wise and questioning Socrates, an intellectual gadfly. One old stereotype of the American teacher is that of the disciplinarian.

Take, for instance, Washington Irving's creation Ichabod Crane, who was pursued, as you may recall, by the Headless Horseman of Sleepy Hollow. Washington Irving vividly describes teacher Ichabod's pedagogy:

The schoolhouse stood in a rather lonely but pleasant situation, just at the foot of a woody hill, with a brook running close by, and a formidable birch tree growing at one end of it. From hence the low murmur of his pupils' voices, conning over their lessons, might be heard in a drowsy summer's day, like the hum of a bee-hive; interrupted now and then by the authoritative voice of the master, in the tone of menace or command; or, peradventure, by the appalling sound of the birch, as he urged some tardy loiterer along the flowery path of knowledge. Truth to say, he was a conscientious man, and ever bore in mind the golden maxim, "Spare the rod and spoil the child."—Ichabod Crane's scholars certainly were not spoiled.

I would not have it imagined, however, that he was one of those cruel potentates of the school, who joy in the smart of their subjects; on the contrary, he administered justice with discrimination rather than severity, taking the burthen off the backs of the weak, and laying it on those of the strong. Your mere puny stripling that winced at the least flourish of the rod, was passed by with

The Ichabod Crane and Miss Dove images of the schoolteacher persist in American education. Courtesy of Photoworld and Movie Star News.

indulgence; but the claims of justice were satisfied by inflicting a double portion on some little, tough, wrong-headed, broad-skirted Dutch urchin, who sulked and swelled and grew dogged and sullen beneath the birth. All this he called "doing his duty by their parents"; and he never inflicted a chastisement without following it by the assurance, so consolatory to the smarting urchin, that "he would remember it, and thank him for it the longest day he had to live."[1]

Washington Irving, a literary craftsman and humorist of the first half of the nineteenth century, portrayed the early Dutch schoolmaster of a Hudson River town as weird in appearance and devoted to the birch rod. As teaching became increasingly the work of females, Ichabod Crane, in effect, changed sexes. The resultant stereotype was equally odd-looking and equally devoted to her version of law and order in the classroom achieved through various coercive devices. Consider Miss Dove of Frances Gray Patton's *Good Morning, Miss Dove*.

How did any of Miss Dove's pupils, past or present see her? Off hand, that would seem an easy question. There was nothing elusive about Miss Dove's appearance and it had, moreover, remained much the same for more than thirty-five years. When she had begun to teach geography her figure had been spare and angular and it was still so. Her hair was more shadowy than it had once been but, twisted into a meagre little old-maid's knot, it had never had a chance to show much color. Her thin, unpainted mouth bore no sign of those

---

[1] Washington Irving, *Washington Irving, Selected Prose*, pp. 165–166 in Stanley T. Williams (ed.) (New York: Rinehart, 1958).

Movies such as "Up the Down Staircase" have portrayed the teacher's problems with student discipline and administrative bureaucracy. Courtesy of Movie Star News.

universal emotions—humor, for instance, and love, and uncertainty—that mark most mouths in the course of time. Her pale, bleached out complexion never flushed with emotion—a slight pinkness at the tip of her pointed nose was the only visible indication that ordinary human blood ran through her veins. . . . All in all, in bearing and clothing and bony structure, Miss Dove suggested that classic portrait of the eternal teacher that small fry, generation after generation, draw upon fences and sidewalks with nubbins of purloined chalk; a grown-up stranger, catching his first glimpse of her, might be inclined to laugh with a kind of relief, as if he'd seen some old, haunting ogress of his childhood turned into a harmless joke. . . . Even the elevated position of her desk—a position deplored by modern educators who seek to introduce equality into the teacher-student relation—was right and proper. The dais of aloof authority suited her as a little hill near Ratisbon suited Napoleon Bonaparte. . . .[2]

Miss Dove had no moods. Miss Dove was a certainty. She would be today what she had been yesterday and would be tomorrow. And so, within limits, would they. Single file they would enter her room. Each child would pause on the threshold as its mother and father had paused, more than likely, and would say—just as the policeman had said—in distinct, formal accents: "Good morning, Miss Dove." And Miss Dove would look directly at each of them, fixing her eyes directly upon theirs and reply: "Good morning, Jessamine", or "Margaret", or "Samuel." (Never "Sam", never "Peggy", never "Jess." She eschewed familiarity as she wished others to eschew it.) They would go to their appointed desks. Miss Dove would ascend to hers. The lesson would begin.[3]

Contemporary stereotypes have been created by books, films, and television

[2] Frances Gray Patton, *Good Morning, Miss Dove* (New York: Dodd, Mead, 1947), pp. 19–21.
[3] *Ibid.*, p. 8.

Lloyd Haines' television role illustrated a black male's experiences as a teacher. Courtesy of ABC.

programs of recent decades. For instance, James Hilton's Mr. Chips of the novel, film, and musical *Goodbye, Mr. Chips* was a warmhearted and generous dodderer who seemed to have been born an old man. Francis Prescott, "probably the greatest name in New England secondary education," was variously perceived as a tyrant, hypocrite, and hero by the characters of Louis Auchincloss's novel *The Rector of Justin*. Television's *Our Miss Brooks,* played by Eve Arden, was a loudmouthed, amiable, scatterbrained elementary school teacher, and *Mr. Peepers,* played by Wally Cox, was a shy, confused, and lovable high school science teacher. In recent television history, only James Franciosa, playing Mr. Novak, and Lloyd Haynes in *Room 222* supplied what psychologists term a desirable role model of the teacher. In movies based on novels, teachers were favorably portrayed by Sidney Poitier in *To Sir with Love* and Sandy Dennis in *Up the Down Staircase*.

Yet if a composite stereotype exists, it is of the teacher as a patient, tired spinster (though most female teachers are married), or as an ineffectual man. But look around you. Your future colleagues are individual human beings characterized by wide diversity in age, education, motivation, experience, and life style.

GENERALIZATIONS ABOUT THE AMERICAN SCHOOL TEACHER

It is, of course, possible to generalize about teachers. But these generalizations must be approached warily, for statistical figures often prove to be descriptions of the average or median person. Yet the many people on either side of those in the middle are just as real. With this warning, let us proceed to generalize on elementary and secondary school teachers.

SEX

As to which sexes teach on what levels, generalizations are easy. Teaching on the preschool or nursery level is a near monopoly of the female sex. So is kindergarten teaching. On the elementary school level, teachers are primarily women, a whopping 84.6 percent in 1969–70. There has been some increase in the number of male elementary teachers, but the increase has been small. For example, the number of men teachers increased only one percent in the decade 1959–60 (14.1%) to 1969–70 (15.4%). On the secondary school level, men teachers are now the majority. By 1969–70 the estimated percentage of male secondary school teachers was 53.5 percent.[4] In American public schools in 1969 approximately one out of every three teachers were male.

Men dominate as teachers on the college and graduate school levels. In the fall of 1966 men comprised 75.4 percent of college and university teachers and research personnel of all ranks.[5]

So the generalization is clear. The younger the learner, the greater the proportion of women teachers, although increasingly men are moving into the levels of elementary and secondary school historically dominated by women.

So your decision about the level at which you propose to teach should not be restricted by your sex. As a matter of fact, men are in high demand in elementary schools where their contribution as a male-role model for children is valued. Though discrimination against women persists in higher education (despite supposed enlightenment of professors) and though raising of eyebrows has occurred when male teachers choose the preschool or kindergarten levels (despite the cry for "father images"), sex barriers in teaching are steadily diminishing.

AGE

The age of the American teacher ranges from the late teens to the late sixties. Both entry into and exit from teaching are becoming increasingly delayed. In a society which prizes degrees and requires certification, few graduate directly from high school into teaching or leave college before graduation for a teaching post, though many did this in the nineteenth and early twentieth century. In a society of increasing longevity and increasing flexibility in retirement age, some universities and school systems defer teacher retirement or even make a point of employing retired people.

The average age of the American elementary and secondary school teacher is close to that age immortalized by the comedian Jack Benny—going on 39. To be precise, the average age was 38.7 in 1965–66, according to an NEA study pub-

---

[4] NEA Research Division, *Estimates of School Statistics, 1969–70*, Research Report 1969–R15 (Washington, D.C.: The Association, 1969), p. 14.
[5] Richard Beazley, *Numbers and Characteristics of Employees in Institutions of Higher Education* (Washington, D.C.: U.S. Government Printing Office, 1969), p. 11.

lished in 1967.[6] The best estimate of teachers' for 1969 was a median of 37.

The average female teacher is older than the average male teacher. In 1965–66, the average female teacher was 40½ years old, and the average male teacher was 35.[7] If you recall your elementary school teachers as older than your high school teachers, you are quite correct. The fact is that elementary school teachers —as you will recall, most are women—*are* older. A Spring 1969 random sample survey by the NEA Research Division showed that the median age of elementary school teachers was 39 and the median age of secondary school teachers was 34. Interestingly, the survey also reported that in 1969 the median age of *all* female teachers was 39 and the median age of *all* male teachers (in public schools) was 34.

So, should you ever meet our "average teacher," bear in mind that he or she, while younger than your parents, is nearer to their age than to your own. There may be some generation gap, since our "average teacher" was born some time after 1930, rather than after 1950, a date closer to your own birth.

EDUCATION

Do not underestimate the extent of schooling of your colleague-to-be, the average teacher. More than 95 percent of them have bachelor's or graduate degrees. Specifically, about two-thirds have a bachelor's degree (65.2 percent) and more than a quarter have a master's or higher degree (30.3 percent). Only 4.5 percent of all teachers now teaching have no degree whatsoever.[8]

MOTIVATION

The motivations which have led experienced teachers into the field are mixed, even as are the motivations of today's new teachers. They include wanting to work with children or youth; salary and community considerations; admiration or rejection of some of their own teachers; parental influence; a desire to make a difference in individual lives and American society; a drive to challenge students, motivate them to learn, and contribute to the solution of social problems. College juniors and seniors in a teacher education program at a mid-American university in 1970 were asked why they wanted to teach.[9]

Sydney stressed wanting to work with young people and improving democracy:

> I am going into teaching because one of the things I enjoy most is working with young people of all ages. I find it very rewarding to help set up situations in which people may discover, and learn to enjoy discovering, ideas and facts

[6] National Education Association, Research Division, *The American Public School Teacher, 1965–66*, Research Report 1967–R4 (Washington: The Association, 1967), p. 37.
[7] *Ibid.*
[8] NEA Research Division, *Teacher Supply and Demand in Public Schools, 1969*, Research Report 1969–R14 (Washington, D.C.: The Association, 1970), p. 53.
[9] Papers by students in education who plan to teach English gathered by Ronald Leathers (Charleston, Ill.: Eastern Illinois University, February 1970).

Students and teacher participating in civic affairs. Courtesy of Anna Kaufmann Moon.

about themselves and others. I find it challenging to help others to realize their own resources, to learn to think, to create, and to express themselves. I also have strong feelings about education in a democracy and its role in informing and motivating students to inform themselves as they come into a position of influencing the governing of the country.

Mary stressed belonging to a community:

I am from a small community in which the school is the main industry. The school is the center of activity and the hub of the community. As a student, I was a part of this hub, and I want to continue being an active, involved part. I enjoyed school from the first day through graduation, and I cannot picture myself any place except in a school. Wanting to be a part of a school organization is the first reason that I chose teaching for my career.

Other reasons reinforced my decision. I like working with young people. . . .

By teaching, I feel that I can satisfy a need in myself to help others. I can gain a sense of accomplishment by helping others achieve and by being a part of their learning and growing.

Marcia stressed steadiness of employment and assured salary:

My main reason for going into teaching is that it represents a steady job with a moderately good income. I have chosen to be an English teacher because I have had four years of training in this field. I also feel it is perhaps the best opportunity available for me to work with people, and in addition, it represents a serious challenge.

The child-teacher relationship can establish warm and free communication between two people. Courtesy of Lesley College.

Sharon stressed admiration of a former teacher:

I first thought about joining the teaching profession when I was in junior high school. My ambition, then, was to be a physical education teacher. I loved physical education and all types of sports. The most influential factor, however, was that my physical education teacher was my idol. I admired her and wanted to be just like her. It [teaching] would give me the opportunity to help people (I had always dreamed of being a social worker), it would give me the opportunity to prove and improve my knowledge, and it would be status-rewarding. Now, I look toward teaching as an opportunity to communicate my ideas and philosophies to others. I have chosen English. . . . I believe the themes and values of a great many authors can be of assistance to young people as they begin to develop their ideas and philosophies.

Norma wanted to teach better than she was taught:

When I was a high school student, I saw my teachers as three basic types. Those whom I personally disliked (but were, in a sense, effective at forcing learning) were in the majority. In the second category was the teacher who was

Teaching in an inner-city school. Courtesy of Anna Kaufmann Moon.

beloved by her students but who taught them little. The third group was composed of those who possessed both negative attributes. They were poor teachers and were thoroughly disliked by all their students. All but one of my high school English teachers fitted into the first classification. The remaining one was a wonderful person and friend to all her students. She was, however, completely unable to handle a class situation and teach effectively. I wished for just *one* who could do both. I wanted to change it all, to be different, to teach a course that would be enjoyable but beneficial. I still want this.

Tom stressed making a contribution through doing his thing:

Too many teachers hold that title only because they have earned an education degree and go to and from a school at 8 a.m. and 4 p.m. respectively each day. To those "educators" teaching is a guaranteed job, not easily lost and too easily obtained, or so it seems. But teaching involves more than just a laboring job; a good teacher makes a contribution to society by educating his pupils and invariably receives pleasure in "doing his thing" well. I hope to make this same contribution and receive this same pleasure whenever I enter the field of teaching and if I ever feel that I am not doing so, I shall no longer be a member of the teaching profession.

Joyce stressed dealing with social problems:

I have made my decision to become a teacher because it seems that it is a profession which could allow me to make a positive contribution to the development of my students' capabilities. . . . The teaching profession would give me the opportunity to contribute to the prevention of some of society's problems and to the cure of some social problems presently existing.

INTERESTS

Do the extent of the American teacher's educational background and the aspirations characterizing his motivation reveal themselves in his use of leisure hours? The Research Division of the National Education Association, after studying the reading and recreational interests of classroom teachers in 1965, reported these highlights of findings:

1. Practically all teachers read a daily newspaper fairly regularly: about one-half read one, and a little less than half read two or more.
2. Seven teachers in 10 read a weekly newspaper fairly regularly: four read one, and the remainder read two or more.
3. Nine teachers in 10 keep up with national, local and international news. About half or more read editorials, letters to the editors, columnists, and comics. About 9 teachers in 10 read feature stories on education.
4. The most popular columnists on national and international affairs are Drew Pearson and Walter Lippmann—read by about 4 teachers in 10. Ann Landers is the most popular specialized columnist—read by about half the teachers.
5. *Reader's Digest*, the magazine with the largest circulation (15 million) was the most popular with teachers: two-thirds read it fairly regularly. A close second was *Life*. In their reading of popular magazines, about 6 in 10 prefer nonfictional material.
6. About 8 teachers in 10 read at least one nonprofessional book in the three months preceding the questionnaire; about 1 teacher in 3 read four or more. In this type of reading matter, over 1 in 3 preferred fiction; 1 in 3 expressed no preference between fiction and nonfiction. Three teachers in 10 (or their spouses) belong to a book-purchasing club.
7. More than 8 teachers in 10 read at least one professional book in the three months preceding the questionnaire. About 3 in 10 read five or more.
8. Nearly 7 teachers in 10 read at least something in each issue of the *NEA Journal*; about 8 in 10, something in each issue of their state education association. The most popular items are teaching aids, articles on curriculum and instruction, and articles on controversial issues.
9. Preparing lessons and grading papers, and family and home responsibilities are the major limitations on the teacher's time for recreation.
10. Teachers attend football games more than any other spectator sport; the most popular active sport they engaged in is walking or hiking, followed closely by swimming.
11. In music, at least 7 teachers in 10 like semiclassical music, musical comedy, and folk music. They like rock and roll the least.
12. In movies, the greatest preference (8 teachers in 10) is for historicals, followed by drama, comedy, and musicals (at least 7 teachers in 10). Science fiction is liked the least. However, 4 teachers in 10 seldom or never attend a movie, and more than 1 in 3 attends only once in two or three months.
13. News reporting and commentary were most popular on both radio and TV.

More teachers (8 in 10) listened to or watched Chet Huntley and David Brinkley than listened to or watched any other commentator.[10]

TABLE 3.1
Membership and Participation in Organizations*

TYPE OF ORGANIZATION	VERY ACTIVE MEMBER	FAIRLY ACTIVE MEMBER	INACTIVE MEMBER	ANY TYPE OF MEMBERSHIP	NOT A MEMBER
Church or synagogue	24.4%	33.4%	27.7%	85.5%	14.5%
Youth-serving group	7.2	8.3	4.2	19.7	80.3
Women's group (women)	9.1	13.4	8.6	31.0	69.0
Men's service club (men)	4.4	7.9	3.6	15.9	84.1
Fraternal or auxiliary group	4.0	7.3	8.0	19.3	80.7
Civil liberties group	1.1	1.5	2.9	5.5	94.5
Veterans group (men)	1.9	2.6	6.7	11.2	88.8
Political party organization	1.4	5.9	14.7	22.0	78.0
Parent-teacher association	16.9	35.2	26.2	78.4	21.6
Hobby club	8.4	6.7	2.4	17.5	82.5
National Education Association	5.6	14.4	39.8	59.9	40.1
State education association	8.1	23.5	50.3	81.9	18.1
Local education association	15.3	33.7	34.1	83.1	16.9
Subject-matter or professional special interest association	7.7	14.7	15.1	37.5	62.5
American Federation of Teachers	1.3	2.9	3.8	7.9	92.1

* Reported by 2344 public school teachers in a 1965–66 nationwide survey conducted by NEA. NEA Research Division, *The American Public-School Teacher, 1965–66,* Research Report 1967–R4 (Washington, D.C.: The Association, 1967), p. 44.

Judging by the above, teachers are similar to many other Americans in their interests and choices. The major differences inferred from this table is that teachers tend to read more and to attend fewer movies than the typical American. Did you expect something more of the American teacher? What changes do you think there have been since this 1965 study?

[10] NEA Research Division, *Reading and Recreational Interests of Classroom Teachers,* Research Report 1967–R2 (Washington, D.C.: The Association, 1967), p. 5.

EXPERIENCE

In 1965–66 the average teacher had taught for almost a dozen years—11.8 to be exact. *She* had been teaching 13.1 years; *he* had been teaching 9 years. The average elementary school teacher had been teaching 13.4 years; the average high school teacher 10 years.[11] But the NEA Research Division random sample survey indicated that by 1969 the average teacher had only 9 years of total teaching experience.

MOBILITY

Every year about one out of twelve teachers leaves the teaching profession. As the NEA Research Division points out in a 1968 report, "Earlier studies in this series have used an estimate that the number of positions vacated by teachers who leave the profession each year equals about 8 percent of the total number of teachers."[12] Most who leave teaching resign from their posts; a minority are separated for the other reasons—13.6 percent of the teachers in large (25,000 or more enrollment) public school systems left teaching in the 1966–67 year, 11 percent of them through resignation and 2.6 for other reasons including retirement, deaths, dismissals, and promotions to nonteaching jobs.[13] Small systems have greater teacher holding power.

Meanwhile, one in every thirty-three teachers comes back annually (approximately 3 percent of the total teaching force), often because their children are grown, other jobs have been tried, or a second income in the family appears tempting. The difference between 8 percent leaving and 3 percent returning results in a 5 percent gap. These teaching posts are filled by beginning teachers.[14] In addition, beginning teachers are employed to fill new posts created by the population expansion and the increased holding power of the schools.

The majority of male teachers perceive themselves as willing to move out of the state to a better paying job, but not the majority of female teachers. More than 57 percent of the men teachers queried gave a migratory-minded "yes" to the question "Would you move to a school system in another state that is comparable to the one in which you are presently teaching if the superintendent of the school system offered you a sufficient salary increase and moving costs?" But 79.4 percent of women teachers answered "no" to the same question.[15] In general, the male teacher is mobile and the female teacher more bound to home and community ties.

Teachers who register for jobs are especially mobile. A study of some four

---

[11] NEA Research Division, *The American Public School Teacher, 1965–66*, Research Report 1967–R4 (Washington, D.C.: The Association, 1967), p. 12.
[12] NEA Research Division, *Teacher Supply and Demand in Public Schools, 1969*, Research Report 1969–R14 (Washington, D.C.: The Association, 1969), p. 29.
[13] NEA Research Division, *Selected Statistics of Local School Systems, 1966–67*, Research Report 1968–R11 (Washington, D.C.: The Association, 1968), p. 11.
[14] NEA Research Division, *Teacher Supply and Demand in Public Schools, 1969*, Research Report 1969–R14 (Washington, D.C.: The Association, 1969), p. 28.
[15] "Teacher Opinion Poll," *NEA Journal* (April 1968), p. 60.

thousand teachers who registered with the National Education Association's computerized job-locator service (SEARCH) in 1968 shows that 51 percent of these educators wished to move out of their present region of residence. Another 43 percent wanted to locate in another state in the same region.[16]

So teaching no longer means committing yourself to stay forever in your home community or even your state or region. Today's teacher is much more footloose than his predecessor.

IS THERE A NEW TEACHER IN THE SEVENTIES?

When considering what new teachers will be like in the seventies it is necessary to consider the possibility that patterns of the past, even the recent past, will not continue. One of the significant conditions of modern life is change—radical change affecting all aspects of life. In the forefront of today's change are many college students and recent graduates. The decade of the seventies began with the most unsettled year in the history of American higher education. A nationwide strike affected over one quarter of the nation's campuses in a direct fashion and most others at least indirectly.

To predict the outcome of a period of change is extremely difficult though it is possible to examine the prevalent experiences, values, attitudes, ideas, and actions and thus get some indication of likely outcomes. Yet in doing so there is some danger of developing a new stereotype, one which depicts the college student as an extremist. Let us eliminate this danger of substituting one stereotype for another by recognizing that no single description can encompass all college students or all new teachers. It is clear that present college students and new teachers represent a wide spectrum of types. However, this does not negate the presence of certain strong, formative influences which may make some new teachers very different from their predecessors.

Many new teachers will represent, in varying degrees, the results of a triple revolution—social, political and educational—which is making itself felt in our society. So far visible effects include increased pressure on schools to change, the development of short-lived private schools often called "free" or "alternative" schools, and conflicts in schools between teacher factions and between teachers and administrators.

THE SOCIAL REVOLUTION

Many young people have been evolving a new life style. They have made radical changes in such things as dress, language, music, sexual mores, ceremonies, and values. The problem of whether a school can control the length of its students' hair has been a major controversy in some schools, and has in many cases been brought to court. Schools have also been having trouble with dress

---

[16] "The Computer and the Peripatetic Teacher," *Today's Education* (February 1969), p. 13.

codes, while the use of drugs by students has become a national dilemma. Student newspapers, both underground and above, have challenged existing standards of obscenity and definitions of free speech. Increasingly, the traditional purposes of education have been challenged as irrelevant to contemporary human needs.

In colleges, all of these changes have been accepted, in varying degrees, by some students as appropriate—even necessary—behavior. The conflict may not remain a simple conflict of the school with its students, because some young teachers will bring with them their own experience with various forms of dissent. The act of graduation or achievement of certification will not bring about a rejection of a style of life which has been chosen as appropriate. There will be young teachers in the schools of the seventies who will find it increasingly difficult or distasteful to make compromises which the schools will seem to demand. Certain of these conflicts are already apparent, as in standards of dress and hair length for teachers. A considerable number of schools, sometimes reluctantly, are learning to live with young, bearded, long-haired, or Afro-styled teachers who wear dashikis or no tie, or even jeans as teacher apparel. Rock and soul music are heard in some classrooms. Some teachers have been in trouble with their administrators because they have not objected to taboo words in their students' writing, and have even used such words themselves in their own writing.

THE POLITICAL REVOLUTION

Through the sixties and into the seventies some young people have become increasingly involved in a wide variety of political activity. Many students have been involved with liberal reformist activity—for example, the campaign for Eugene McCarthy in the 1968 primary, the support of peace candidates in the congressional elections of 1970, or lobbying in Washington on behalf of their political stands. Others have been involved in radical politics including membership in such organizations as SDS (Students for a Democratic Society) or other new-left groups, or in conservative political action through organizations as YAF (Young Americans for Freedom). Other specific political movements attracting wide student interest and support have been women's liberation, the Black Panthers, antipoverty groups, environmental reform, and the various power groups—black, Mexican, and Indians, for example.

When these students become teachers, most will continue to involve themselves in the political activity of the community and nation. It is also likely that they will approve of and participate in political activities as part of their relationship to the schools. Political activity by teachers' groups, affiliates of both the National Education Association and the American Federation of Teachers, has been accelerating. Teachers' strikes and other vigorous organizational responses to the action of school boards and administrations have been increasing in recent years. Many young teachers will add to the militancy of such groups and will consider political activism by teachers as appropriate and necessary.

THE EDUCATIONAL REVOLUTION

Many young teachers believe that today's schools are not very good places for the young. Schools in the ghettos and other poverty areas are seen as failures in their mission of providing basic skills and information to those who need such basics in order to find a place in a technical society, and the schools in the suburbs are seen as failures in their role of providing meaning and understanding in the lives of children of an affluent society. New teachers often find the schools failing to deal with problems of institutional racism, pollution, and destruction of environmental resources, war and international tensions, and poverty in the midst of affluence.

Students in colleges often express dissatisfaction with their own schooling. Many have had no teacher whom they remember with appreciation and commendation. Some believe that schools are going to have to change radically. One of their major objections concerns the bureaucratic nature of school systems. They see the schools as one of the worst examples of depersonalization in modern society. They feel that students and teachers are treated as objects and recognized as numbers rather than as persons. They believe that school administrators are concerned with budgets, buses, and business rather than with students and learning. Such students wish to bring to the schools and to their jobs more direct personal relationships, more trust, more intimacy and more love. They have been influenced in these feelings by the nationwide movement expressed in colleges by such activities as T-groups or encounter sessions. They often support affective education. They have been impressed by views of education which have emphasized emotion and feeling, such as *Education and Ecstasy* by George Leonard,[17] *The Lives of Children* by George Dennison,[18] and *How Children Fail* by John Holt.[19]

Many young teachers question the purposes which our schools seem to serve. While recognizing the need for developing basic skills, they challenge the curriculum which seems to be more concerned with preparing students to fit into a society which to them is rapidly becoming obsolete, than with the development of individual self-realization and social improvement. They find confirmation for their misgivings in such books as *Summerhill* by A. S. Neill,[20] *Compulsory Miseducation* by Paul Goodman,[21] *Death at an Early Age* by Jonathan Kozol,[22] *Thirty-Six Children* by Herbert Kohl,[23] and *An Empty Spoon* by Sunny Decker.[24]

Some questioning young teachers enthusiastically accept the challenge of teaching the children of the poor in public schools in disadvantaged areas. They

---

[17] George B. Leonard, *Education and Ecstasy* (New York: Dell, 1968).
[18] George Dennison, *The Lives of Children: The Story of the First Street School* (New York. Random, 1969)
[19] John Holt, *How Children Fail* (New York: Pitman, 1964).
[20] A. S. Neill, *Summerhill: A Radical Approach to Child Rearing* (New York: Hart, 1960).
[21] Paul Goodman, *Compulsory Miseducation* (New York: Horizon Press, 1964).
[22] Jonathan Kozol, *Death at an Early Age* (Boston: Houghton Mifflin, 1967).
[23] Herbert Kohl, *Thirty-Six Children* (New York: New American Library, 1967).
[24] Sunny Decker, *An Empty Spoon* (New York: Harper and Row, 1969).

Education in the middle of a city—students in an outdoor art class. Courtesy of Philadelphia Parkways Program.

see an opportunity to make changes in the education of children and youth who have been neglected by society. But still others despair of the potential of public schools and turn elsewhere. Philip Rothman of Antioch College, for instance, reports as follows:

Despite working in innovative programs such as the Philadelphia Schools Parkway Project, and despite a usually comfortable and successful student teaching placement in Yellow Springs' mildly experimental public schools, the students are left with a feeling of frustration when faced with teaching in the public schools. By contrast, while not always in complete agreement with what goes

Students in an experimental school learn gemology from a local jeweler. Courtesy of Philadelphia Parkways Program.

on, the students feel a lot more comfortable with their experiences in the Antioch School, the Pinel School and other small, private, experimental or "free" schools. Many seniors speak of next year by saying, "IF I teach next year . . ." and, "I would like to find a small, private school . . ." It is true that this is not completely new, but the trend seems to have grown. The anti-institutional utopian bias seems to be challenging the public service ethos which had been predominant in the past.

. . . In recent years with the emergence of black identity as a major educational factor and with a growing emphasis on black control and leadership of black affairs, few white Antiochians continue to feel that they can serve useful purposes in predominantly inner-city black schools.[25]

---

[25] Philip Rothman, "Education Majors Found Turned Off By Public School Teaching Prospects," *Antiochian* (July 1970), p. 5.

A significant difference between new teachers and previous generations is their relationship to technology. Television has been an indigenous part of their culture since infancy, computers have increasingly been available and serving their needs, transportation and communication have provided direct access to ideas and places on a global basis, and they have accepted man's steps on the moon as a natural, if difficult, achievement. The writings of Marshall McLuhan on the uses of media have influenced their thinking. Consequently, they look to technology as a normal part of the school environment. They hope that computer-assisted instruction, film-making, video-taping and playback, rapid duplication facilities, and inexpensive paperbacks will be at hand so that they can individualize instruction, serve the interests of the students, meet different levels of ability and background, and provide students with a richness and diversity of materials and sources of information.

A TRANSITION PERIOD

The above description is not meant to be a portrayal of all young teachers as they are today or will be in the near future. A generalization does not describe a population, even if it is an up-to-date generalization. However, these characteristics do represent clear and strong trends which are shaping the young people who will be the new teachers of the seventies. Will the schools be able to accept these teachers, to accommodate their demands, and to help them use their abilities and energies? The most honest answer is that the evidence is mixed and conflicting. Schools are changing, but in many ways the change is reluctant and slow. Many school board members, school administrators, experienced teachers, taxpayers and parents recognize the changing characteristics of our times and, to different degrees, are in agreement with the younger teachers; others are strongly resistant. Their resistance may be strengthened by the recent shift in teacher supply and demand as reported in Newsweek, June 29, 1970:

In the coming academic year, according to the U.S. Office of Education, nearly 100,000 of 279,000 elementary and high school teachers now completing their training will have to find something else to fall back on—or else contribute to the highest academic unemployment rate since the supply of teachers first began to outdistance the demand.[26]

To put it bluntly, those resistant to these changes may be able to screen out some of the new teachers most inclined to dissidence.

So the seventies are likely to be a period of transition—a time of significant and sometimes disrupting change. The challenge to young teachers who recognize themselves in the description of the past few pages is to face the turmoil, tension, and trials of such a challenge with high competence.

---

[26] "Education—Supply and Demand," Newsweek (June 29, 1970), p. 58.

TABLE 3.2
Teacher Supply and Demand, 1965–1970

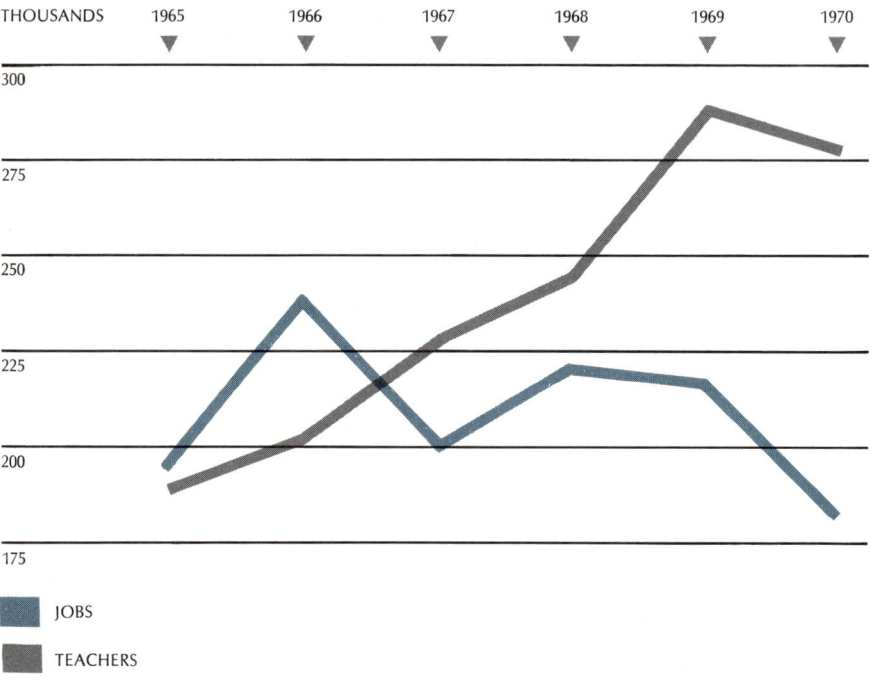

National Education Association (Washington, D.C.: The Association).

THE TEACHER IS AN INDIVIDUAL

Perhaps the most honest answer to our question "Who teaches in American schools?" is simply that more than two million individuals teach in America. They defy stereotyping. They are as varied as the American people.

Teachers have in common that, for multiple reasons, they have chosen to work with learners, whose lives they can influence. They have in common the possibility of making a difference through being teachers.

When you join American teachers in their work, you make an important choice. When you join them, you open up the potential of your own self-realization and of human betterment for others.

★ ★ ★

DISCUSSION

1. What has been your stereotype of a school teacher? Why?
2. Is there any validity in the common stereotype of the teacher?
3. What is the current situation as to men teachers in the early school years? How do you think more men can be attracted to the field?
4. Are women discriminated against in higher education teaching opportunities? To what extent has the women's liberation movement opened up further opportunities for women in higher education?
5. Why are increasing numbers of men entering teaching?
6. Teachers now customarily teach after receiving a bachelor's degree. Is this sufficient? Should a five-year higher education period of preparation be required?
7. What are the characteristic motivations of teachers, young and old? Which of the motivations described in this chapter seem to you most admirable?
8. What advantages and disadvantages do you see of teaching in one's home town? Home region?
9. Is mobility among teachers likely to grow? What factors might influence mobility in a particular direction?
10. What changes in your peers do you see that would support the statement, "The new young public school teacher will be a 'new breed of cat'?" What do you see to disprove such a statement? What forces might bring about a "new" teacher for the 1970s and help create a generation gap among teachers?
11. Essentially what do you find your friends and fellow students saying about education in general? Their own education? Administrators? Purposes of schools?
12. If your friends and fellow students in education had their way, in what types of schools would they teach? Public? Private? "Free"? Parochial?
13. What do you think of the likelihood of the dissenting new teacher finding a teaching post? If you think it would be difficult, do you think it should be?
14. Can you generalize on the American teacher in an intellectually reputable way?

INVOLVEMENT

1. Test the persistence of the traditional stereotype of the school teacher by asking a variety of people what they envision when you say "school teacher."
2. Develop a letter of support or criticism to a producer of a TV or radio program in connection with some portrayal of American teachers and share the response you receive with others.
3. Develop a simple questionnaire concerning motivations and try it out with a class of teacher education students and a class not planning to enter the field of teaching.
4. Develop a questionnaire parallel to the study cited of the reading and recreational interests of classroom teachers and administer it to your class. Compare the results with the NEA results.
5. Develop a series of character sketches of new teachers. Invite an administrator to class and ask him to react to the employment prospects of these new teachers sketched by you and other class members. When there is disagreement as to employability, explore the reasons for different perceptions.

6. Attempt to reach a consensus among class members as to the characteristics of the school in which they would like to teach. If consensus is not forthcoming, at least clarify different ways of looking at the ideal school.

BIBLIOGRAPHY

Ashton-Warner, Sylvia. *Teacher.* New York: Simon and Schuster, 1963. An unorthodox, readable account of a talented teacher's way of working with children of a culture foreign to her.

Benjamin, Harold R. W. *The Sage of Petaluma.* New York: McGraw-Hill, 1965. A purported biography of teacher J. Abner Pediwell which allows author Benjamin to be partially autobiographical yet also, as he himself said, "to lie a little."

Brenton, Myron. *What's Happened to Teacher?* New York: Coward-McCann, 1970. An examination of why teachers have changed, why they teach, why they strike, what they fear, and how they really view children.

Burrup, Percy E. *The Teacher and the Public School System.* New York: Harper and Row, 1967. The organization, operation, and offerings of educational institutions, the nature of teaching and teachers, and the shortcomings and deficiencies needing correction in teaching and teacher education.

Decker, Sunny. *An Empty Spoon.* New York: Harper and Row, 1969. An emotion-packed description of a young teacher's experience.

Foshett, John M. *The Normative World of the Elementary School Teacher.* Eugene, Ore.: University of Oregon, 1968. Presents the results of research on how teachers view their own position and how others view the position of teachers.

Highet, Gilbert. *The Art of Teaching.* New York: Alfred A. Knopf, 1950. A classic on teaching which considers characteristics and abilities of the good teacher, reviews powerful teachers of the past, examines the role of teaching in every day life, and stresses the responsibilities of the teaching profession.

James, Deborah. *The Taming: A Teacher Speaks.* New York: McGraw-Hill, 1969. Written humorously but seriously by a teacher frustrated by educational inadequacies.

Larson, Richard and James Olson, eds. *I Have a Kind of Fear: Some Reflections from the Notebooks of City Teachers.* Chicago: Quadrangle Books, 1969. Realistic contemporary picture of the difficulties faced by teachers in today's troubled cities.

Lieberman, Myron. *The Future of Public Education.* Chicago: University of Chicago Press, 1960. Lively and provocative volume stressing the importance of leadership by teachers if education is to improve.

Rousculp, Charles G. *Chalk Dust on My Shoulder.* Columbus, Ohio: Charles E. Merrill, 1969. Presenting by essay and anecdote in a plain-spoken document, the ordeals, the errors, and the triumphs that make a teacher's day and the contribution teachers make to American society.

Simpson, Ray H. *Teacher Self-Evaluation.* New York: Macmillan, 1966. Self-evaluation procedures and tools necessary for teacher self-diagnosis and self-improvement.

Stinnett, T. M., ed. *The Teacher Dropout.* Itasca, Ill.: F. E. Peacock, 1970. A symposium report by the Commission on Strengthening the Teaching Profession of Phi Delta Kappa. An exploration of the teacher dropout problem for insight into possibilities of strengthening the teaching profession.

Williams, George. *Some of My Best Friends Are Professors.* New York: Abelard-Schuman, 1958. The life of a college professor, written in a humorous vein.

Yamamoto, Kaoru, ed. *Teaching: Essays and Readings.* Boston: Houghton Mifflin, 1969. Varied views on teachers and teaching from a wide range of sources.

AUDIO-VISUAL MATERIALS

Portrait of the Classroom Teacher (National Education Association, 48 fr., Color, Taped Narration) Presents such data as age, marital status, experience, salary, preparation, and likes and dislikes of the typical teacher.

Every Teacher—An Active Political Citizen (National Education Association, 73 frs., Color) Discusses teachers' rights to participate in politics.

The Teacher (McGraw-Hill, 33 fr., Color) Illustrates how a good teacher can make the adjustment of a new pupil to a school a happy and successful one.

What is a Teacher? (University of Texas, 59 Min.) Twelve student teachers working with elementary school children in math, social studies, art and science. Indicates the role of the teacher in helping children to acquire knowledge and self-confidence.

FOUR

WHAT ARE TEACHERS PAID?

How important is the teacher's pay in your tentative decision to become a teacher? At one extreme are those new teachers who can honestly say that they are not concerned about salaries. They see their major goal as service to others. As dedicated agents of change, they are not especially interested in present or prospective financial compensation. At the other extreme are those who say with equal honesty, yet with a different social orientation, that the salary must be pretty good or they can be counted out. They are apt to point out that teachers and their families cannot live on dedication. Between these two groups are prospective teachers who realize that the financial compensation of educators is moderate and that one usually does not teach for the money in it; they know that the rewards are primarily in the teacher's recognition that he has made a difference in the lives of others. Most people want to be well informed as to the economic probabilities of their work. They recognize that they must take financial factors into account as they attempt to determine and establish their life styles. This chapter is intended for everyone who is at all concerned about financial compensation. It is intended neither to recruit you into nor to repel you from teaching; it is an objective account of some of the material aspects of teaching.

THE SALARY OF THE AMERICAN TEACHER

The estimated average 1969–70 salary of classroom teachers in public schools was $8,560 for the school year (nine months in most instances). Most secondary school teachers were paid more than elementary school teachers by over $500 a year, largely because their average length of preparation was greater than that of elementary teachers. The average salary of secondary school teachers in public schools in 1969–70 was $8,843. The average salary of elementary school teachers in public schools was $8,321.[1]

[1] NEA, Research Division, *Economic Status of the Teaching Profession, 1969–70*, Research Report 1970–R3 (Washington, D.C.: The Association, 1970), p. 10.

These averages do not reveal the differences between the beginner's salary and that of the experienced teacher who often holds graduate degrees. The average salary for the beginner holding a bachelor's degree in 1969–70 was $6,383; the average classroom teacher holding a doctor's degree and having sufficient years of experience to reach the maximum level in a school system was paid $12,452—more than $6,000 more. But these were also averages for the nation. The actual range in beginning salaries with the bachelor's degree was from a little less than $5,000 in some school systems to about $8,000 in others; maximum salaries with the doctor's degree ranged from about $9,000 in less wealthy areas to more than $16,000 in wealthier districts.

Between the extremes there are stages in compensation which depend upon both educational degrees and experience. In the average school system the beginner with a bachelor's degree who was paid $6,383 would eventually reach $9,000 or more. The beginner with a master's degree started at $7,058; with maximum experience, his salary would probably reach $10,000 or more. The beginner in the average system with a sixth-year degree, or the master's plus thirty additional hours of graduate work started at $7,673 and would presumably reach more than $12,000. The rare beginner who first taught after receiving a doctor's degree would begin at about $8,000 and might reach a maximum of twice that amount. Table 4.1 provides more detailed information regarding averages and trends, technically and more precisely described as "mean scheduled salaries."

TABLE 4.1

Mean Scheduled Salaries, 1962–63, 1965–66, 1969–70

PREPARATION LEVEL		SCHOOL YEAR		
		1962–63	1965–66	1969–70
Number of reporting systems		557	1,071	1,142
Mean Scheduled salary for:				
Bachelor's degree	—Min.	$4,331	$4,928	$6,383
	—Max.	6,426	7,278	9,278
Master's degree	—Min.	4,679	5,350	7,058
	—Max.	7,053	8,167	10,717
Six Years (M.A. + 30)	—Min.	5,310	5,900	7,673
	—Max.	8,236	9,416	12,002
Doctor's degree	—Min.	5,417	6,057	8,070
	—Max.	8,199	9,453	12,452

National Education Association, Research Division, *Salary Schedules for Teachers, 1969–70,* Research Report 1969–R13 (Washington, D.C.: The Association, 1969), p. 15.

In the U.S. public education system there are significant geographical differences in compensation. Take, for instance, regional differences in average annual salaries of the total instructional staff in public schools in 1969–70. If a beginning teacher made his decision of where to teach on the basis of salary alone (which doesn't happen to be the case), he would surely follow Horace Greeley's historic advice to his generation, "Go West, young man, go West!" In the Far West, the estimated average annual salary paid members of the total instructional staff was $10,412. The next most attractive regions, with respect to salaries, were the mid-Atlantic states, where the average was $9,664, the Middle states, where the average was $9,271, and the New England states where the average was $8,993. Markedly less attractive economically was the rest of the nation with an average annual salary in the Northwest of $7,700, in the Southwest of $7,645, and in the Southeast of $7,515.[2] Though contiguous, the states in the Far West paid instructional staff an average of over two and a half thousand dollars more than most states in the Southwest and Northwest. So, if salary were the sole consideration, many teachers might join a late twentieth century Gold Rush to California, or trek north to Alaska, which has the highest average salary of all the states—$10,560.

How do today's salaries compare with salaries of teachers during the past years? The general answer, of course, is that they have gone up, as have salaries in other fields of work. (See Table 4.2). Should we regard this increase "optimistically" or "pessimistically"? It depends.

If you look at the world through rose-colored glasses, you can truthfully point out that during the decade 1959–69 to 1969–70 the salary of the typical instructional staff member of the public schools increased by more than two-thirds (72.0%). But if you look at the world through dark glasses, you can equally point out that because of the inflation which changed the purchasing power of the dollar, the increase was only slightly more than one-third (36.8%).[3] To which the optimist might retort that an increase of more than a third in real income over a single decade is nothing to view darkly.

If you view the world through rose-tinted glasses, you might accurately point out that at the beginning of the decade, 70.7% of the teachers were below $5,500 in salary annually. You can apparently clinch your case by pointing out that only 2.9% of teachers received a salary of less than $5,500 in public schools at the close of the decade. Further, as one impressed by progress, you can correctly point out that, at the close of the decade, about two-thirds (65.4%) of teachers had salaries ranging from $7,500 to $10,500 or more; whereas, you might conclude, almost no teachers at the beginning of the decade had a salary of over $7,499.

But while you are polishing your rose-colored glasses, your colleague who sees the world pessimistically can justifiably remind you that the average salary of the beginning teacher with a bachelor's degree at the close of the decade was

---

[2] *Ibid.*, p. 9. Instructional staff includes principals and supervisors as well as classroom teachers and other instructional personnel.
[3] *Ibid.*, p. 6.

WHAT ARE TEACHERS PAID? 89

TABLE 4.2

Average Starting Salaries of Classroom Teachers Compared
With Those In Private Industry, 1964–65 and 1969–70

POSITION OR SUBJECT FIELD	AVERAGE STARTING SALARIES	
	1964–65	1969–70
Beginning teachers with bachelor's degree*	$4,707	$6,383
Male college graduates with bachelor's degree		
Engineering	7,356	9,960
Accounting	6,444	9,396
Sales-Marketing	6,072	8,088
Business Administration	5,880	8,100
Liberal Arts	5,712	7,980
Production Management	6,564	8,736
Chemistry	6,972	9,276
Physics	7,200	9,348
Mathematics-Statistics	6,636	8,952
Economics-Finance	6,276	8,304
Other Fields	6,360	8,796
Total—all fields (weighted average)	6,535	8,985
Women college graduates with bachelor's degree		
Mathematics-Statistics	6,108	8,484
General Business	4,848	7,104
Chemistry	6,468	8,532
Accounting	5,664	8,304
Home Economics	5,112	7,056
Engineering-Technical Research	7,224	9,672
Secretary	4,560	5,820

* in school systems enrolling 6000 or more pupils
National Education Association, Research Division, *Economic Status of the Teaching Profession, 1969–70*, Research Report 1970-R3 (Washington, D.C.: The Association, 1970), p. 55.

$6,383 (for approximately 9 months of service) and he will ask you to set this beside the beginning annual or 12-month salaries of male college graduates with a bachelor's degree in engineering, $9,960, or women college graduates in mathematics and statistics earning $8,484. To clinch his point of the comparatively low income of beginners in teaching as contrasted with beginners in other fields of work, he might point out that only women college graduates with bachelor's degrees who enter the field of secretarial work are paid less than teachers, and then only $563 less. (But secretaries who are employed for 12 months have less vacation time than teachers who are usually employed for about 9 months.) He, too, has statistics to which he can refer you. (See Table 4.3).

TABLE 4.3
Percent Distribution of Estimated Annual Salaries Paid
Classroom Teachers, 1959–60 through 1969–70

SCHOOL YEAR	PERCENT OF CLASSROOM TEACHERS PAID:								
	BELOW $3,500	$3,500-4,499	$4,500-5,499	$5,500-6,499	$6,500-7,499	$7,500-8,499	$8,500-9,499	$9,500-10,499	$10,500 OR MORE
	1	2	3	4	5	6	7	8	9
1959-60	12.8%	29.7%	28.2%	17.4%	11.9%	.....	.....	.....	.....
1960-61	9.2	26.0	27.2	19.3	10.9	7.4%	.....	.....	.....
1961-62	5.7	20.9	28.9	22.6	12.9	9.0	.....	.....	.....
1962-63	4.3	17.7	28.0	23.4	14.5	8.1	4.0%	.....	.....
1963-64	2.7	14.2	28.6	24.2	15.1	9.0	6.3	.....	.....
1964-65	1.6	11.9	27.0	24.7	16.6	10.1	5.5	2.6%	.....
1965-66	0.8	8.0	22.7	26.8	19.1	11.5	6.6	4.5	.....
1966-67	0.3	4.1	19.7	26.7	19.8	13.2	8.6	4.5	3.1%
1967-68	(......2.1.......)		11.5	25.5	22.0	15.3	10.5	6.6	6.5
1968-69	(......1.0.......)		7.0	19.9	22.5	18.5	13.6	9.2	8.3
1969-70	(............2.9............)			13.1	18.6	20.4	16.1	12.7	16.2

National Education Association, Research Division, *Economic Status of the Teaching Profession, 1969–70*, Research Report 1969–R3 (Washington, D.C.: The Association, 1970), p. 10.

HOW SALARIES AND INCREASES ARE DETERMINED

When the new teacher with the bachelor's degree is employed, he or she moves into the first niche on the salary scale of the employing public school system (or sometimes private or parochial school system). Since this first step is of the most immediate importance to you, you should be aware that beginners' salaries vary between public school systems. For the 1968–69 school year some beginners (1.9 percent of systems) earned salaries of $7,000 or more while a few others (0.6 percent of systems) earned less than $4,600. However, the more usual groupings were $5,800 to $6,199 for 27.4 percent of the systems and $6,200 to $6,599 for an almost equal number (27.3 percent). (See Table 4.4.)

TABLE 4.4

Range in Salaries for Beginning Teachers in 1968–69*

BACHELOR'S DEGREE, MINIMUM SALARY	
$4,599 or less	.6%
4,600–4,999	3.0
5,000–5,399	14.4
5,400–5,799	16.9
5,800–6,199	27.4
6,200–6,599	27.3
6,600–6,999	8.5
7,000 or more	1.9

* 1,172 reporting systems

NEA, Research Division, *Evaluation of Teacher Salary Schedules,* 1966–67, 1967–68, 1968–69, Research Report 1968–R14 (Washington, D.C.: The Association, 1968), p. 10.

With experience, continued study, and higher degrees, the teacher moves along the salary scale. Eventually, he reaches the maximum which he can earn in that particular system. Teachers within a school system have usually been paid on the basis of their experience and the extent of their higher education. There are currently several controversial questions about the way teachers are paid. Should there be a single salary scale, regardless of sex? Should elementary and high school teachers be paid on the same scale based on training and experience (which has been the policy during recent years) or should high school teachers receive higher salaries? The third question is the most heretical: Should teachers be paid on the basis of single salary schedule, or should they be paid at least partly on the basis of demonstrated merit? These questions have often been considered in discussions of American education. Though the direction in which decisions have gone during the past few decades in respect to each of these questions seem clear, the questions can still engender considerable warmth.

Elementary schools now offer children opportunities to partake of many classroom activities. Courtesy of EDC.

As to the question of the compensation of men versus women, the counter-arguments are clear. Those who favor higher compensation for men argue that men usually support families, while women usually do not, and that higher salary scales will attract needed males into teaching. The arguments for a single salary scale for both men and women stress sex equality and declare that many women are the single breadwinner for their families.

In the debate, sex equality has recently won out over sex discrimination in salaries. Legislation such as the Equal Pay Act of 1963, Title VII of the 1964 Civil Rights Act, and counterpart state legislation have finalized this issue in most school systems. Women teachers are now usually paid the same as men.

The question of whether high school teachers should be paid more than elementary school teachers also has a long history. The arguments for higher compensation for high school teachers have stressed the greater difficulty of teaching on the higher level, the need for more preparatory study and higher qualifications, and the greater importance of high school education as compared with elementary education. The opposite opinion denies these assumptions. Some elementary education protagonists even say that elementary school teaching, since it reaches young people at a stage when they are more malleable, is socially and educationally more important than high school teaching.

In practice, the single salary schedule without differentiation between levels has prevailed during recent years. The increased demand for teachers, professionalization of teaching, and increased understanding of the importance of early

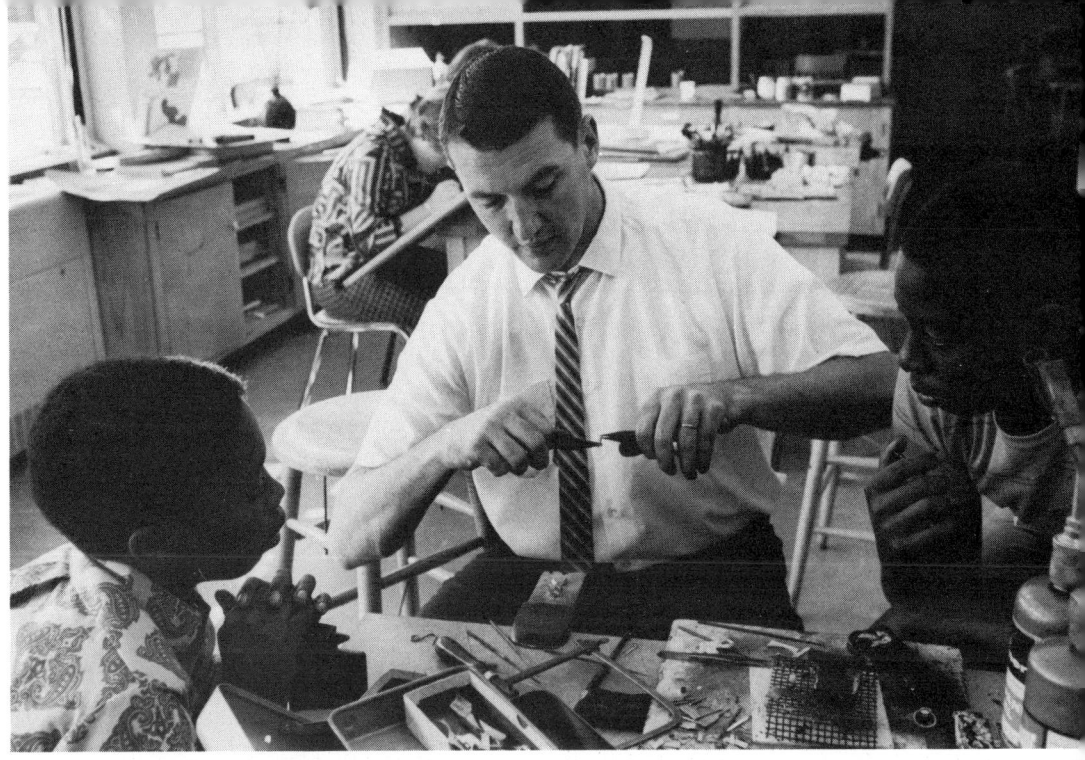

The schools concern themselves with courses other than those that are merely academic in order to expose the student to many experiences. Courtesy of Ivan Massar from Black Star.

education (among other things) are factors which have almost eliminated the dual salary schedule.

The most lively of the questions concerning compensation is the most fundamental—should teachers be compensated solely in terms of years of experience and advanced educational study undertaken or should they be compensated at least partly on the basis of merit as demonstrated by their teaching performances? This controversy has raged in many communities, often with substantial segments of community leadership advocating merit pay and substantial groups of teachers (with some community support) advocating compensation through fixed scales. The controversy centers around the desirability of using merit rating which if used must at least partially determine promotion, increases in pay, and advancement within a school system. Merit rating must determine the degree of effectiveness with which teachers perform their duties.

The argument for merit pay and attendant merit rating is clear. Essentially, the argument is that the superior teacher should be rewarded with higher pay. Proponents point out that in many fields, business for example, employees presumably are rated according to the effectiveness of their work and promoted and paid accordingly. But even in business and industry there are many deviations from this policy.

The viewpoint of those who reject merit rating and merit pay is that selecting superior teachers is very difficult, if not impossible. Generations of researchers have not been able to provide a workable and operational definition of superior teaching; as a result, no satisfactory system has yet been developed for selecting these supposedly superior teachers. It is argued that since teaching is a profession marked by cooperation and mutual support between colleagues, one should not be made to compete with other teachers for salary increases. Nor should administrators, supervisors and others spend their energies attempting to subjectively determine how an individual ranks in relation to a fellow teacher. Those who reject merit pay proposals insist that time and funds would be better invested in helping all teachers continue to improve.

Some state legislatures have initiated studies of merit rating plans. Sometimes such plans have been put into effect and then abandoned as they proved unacceptable or unworkable. Among the cities which in the past thirty years have had merit rating plans and discarded them are Washington, Philadelphia, Detroit, St. Louis, Pittsburgh, Atlanta, Buffalo, and Milwaukee. The number of systems having a quality-of-service provision in their plans of salary compensation has declined over the past twenty-five years.

According to a 1969–70 NEA study of salary schedules for teachers, of 1,142 school systems reporting (enrollment ranged from 6,000 through 100,000 or more) 90.3 percent had no merit pay provisions while 9.7 percent reported some form of payment for meritorious service. The smaller systems seemed more likely to have adopted or continued merit pay plans. None of the systems exceeding 100,000 enrollment reported merit pay provisions.[4]

Taking some of the edge off the merit pay controversy is a related idea which sometimes has been mistaken for merit rating. This is the approach of differentiated staffing and pay, making salary adjustments relate to increased responsibilities or differentiation of functions among staff members. Differentiated pay is increasingly used in American school systems. For instance, in school systems using team teaching, higher payment is sometimes provided for team leaders or head teachers. Staff members who take on semi-administrative or supervisory roles as staff assistants, heads of departments, etc., are usually compensated accordingly. Moreover, especially competent teachers in many school systems are sometimes selected and provided additional compensation for summer work on the curriculum and other related projects. Paraprofessionals (teacher helpers) with more limited preparation are also employed at somewhat lower pay scales in many school systems.

Yet the advocates of merit pay and merit rating still point out the existence of the system of evaluation and rating which you will probably encounter as a beginning teacher before you achieve tenure. Tenure assures an employee permanence in his position or employment as long as his work is satisfactory. With tenure, a teacher can theoretically only be dismissed after a hearing which determines that clearly defined unprofessional conduct has been demonstrated or that a teacher's service has been below acceptable standards. The beginning teacher who lacks tenure is appraised and evaluated by principals and others for

---

[4] NEA, *Salary Schedules for Teachers, 1969–70*, Research Report 1969–R13 (Washington, D.C.: The Association, 1969), p. 22.

Lunchtime provides an opportunity for the teacher to discuss programs and questions with colleagues. Courtesy of Patricia Hollander from HGSE.

approximately three years before he is accepted as a permanent member of the staff. During the non-tenure period, the novice teacher can be dismissed from the system provided he is notified of his dismissal within a reasonable or designated time. If the beginning teacher is rated and judged, argue the advocates of merit pay, why cannot the experienced teacher be so rated? Their opponents admit that the rating of beginning teachers is necessary, but deny its applicability or desirability for experienced professionals.

LENGTH OF THE SCHOOL YEAR AND VACATION PERIODS

Another economic characteristic of teaching is that traditionally teachers have worked far fewer days a year than people in most other occupations. For most teachers, the school year ends in May or more usually June and begins in September. Christmas vacation begins before Christmas and ends after New Year's Day. There is usually a week of vacation in the spring, often coinciding with an Easter week. Legal holidays are observed. All in all, teachers are employed for a school term of nine or at the most ten months.

But before you reach the conclusion that the teacher's life is a leisured one, consider some additional factors. During the approximately 185 (average) working days, the teacher's work is intensive. It often carries over into the evenings and weekends. Christmas and spring vacations are often used in part to catch up on work that simply cannot be handled during the regular teaching months. Bear in mind, too, the ongoing educational preparation of the teacher. The typical teacher begins as a bachelor's degree holder. For a number of reasons, which usually include both economic and professional improvement, the teacher works for higher degrees. When? Through late afternoon, evening, Saturday and summer term courses. No other profession makes such systematic provision for continuing education of its practitioners while they are employed.

For beginners in education, the fact of frequent and substantial vacations is an advantage and an inducement into the career of teaching. However, as the teacher grows more mature and the need for increased income becomes more important, many teachers (and most especially male teachers) come to view summer vacations in particular as an economic handicap. They would rather work and earn a better salary than be supposedly free. Such teachers welcome the growing trend in school systems to an extended term or a twelve-month contract that allows them Christmas and spring vacations and two to four weeks of summer vacation, but which occupies the rest of the summer season with teaching summer school classes, curriculum work, and committee activities aimed at improving education throughout the school system. In most school systems which use the extended term or twelve-month plan, a teacher has the option of working for the school system at additional compensation during summers or having the summer to devote to other activities.

Some teachers supplement their salaries by working at an additional job after hours. The term *moonlighting* has recently entered the American vocabulary; teachers helped make the invention of such a word necessary. By the middle of the 1960s regular school-year salaries of teachers accounted only for 91 percent of their total income. Of the remaining 9 percent, extra earnings amounted to almost 7 percent; the other 2 percent came from dividends, rents, interest, royalties, and other nonsalary sources.

Most of the extra income from extra work was earned during the summer months, sometimes from teaching or tutoring in the teacher's own school system but more often from outside jobs. The most usual outside summer jobs for teachers were in the areas of recreation, sales and retail, clerical-secretarial, teaching or tutoring outside of one's own school system, and the building trades.

During the regular school year some teachers also earned extra income. Some took on extra duties for extra pay in their own school system, largely by coaching athletic teams or directing recreational programs, occasionally through drama and music activities, and less often through administration and supervision, work with student teachers, special school duty, club sponsorship, or work with publications. Still others held outside jobs while teaching.

Men are especially inclined to moonlight because they are more often the family breadwinners. In the mid-1960s only 84 percent of the total income of the male teacher was earned through his salary for the regular school year. Sixteen percent came through extra earnings during the summer or the school year (more than 13 percent) or from nonsalary sources (less than 3 percent).[5]

To moonlight or not to moonlight? This is a decision which the teacher, particularly the male teacher, must often make. While it does increase income, moonlighting eliminates many opportunities for community action, further study, additional time devoted to instructional responsibilities, and opportunities for leisure and travel. One should become a moonlighter only after a careful assessment of priorities.

Presumably, as salaries increase for teachers, moonlighting will become less necessary. Yet as the general standard of living of Americans rises, so do the expectations of Americans for their own standards of living. Consequently, even with higher salaries for the traditional school year, moonlighting is likely to persist, especially for those not involved in extended term programs. Extra jobs, particularly in the summer, are attractive to many people psychologically as well as economically. For some, extra work is a solution to a twentieth century problem which our ancestors could not have anticipated: "What do I do with the time on my hands?"

FRINGE BENEFITS

The phrase *fringe benefits* is another twentieth century addition to the English language. Fringe benefits refer to various kinds of protection or benefits which make an occupation more attractive and more economically secure. Fringe benefits in teaching usually include group health insurance, income protection during disability, group life insurance, sick leave, retirement pay, and reasonable time off with compensation for self-improvement and for personal reasons other than illness.

But most young teachers in good health give little thought to the possibility of accident, illness, or aging. Like the Thomas Wolfe character in *Look Homeward, Angel* and *Of Time and the River*, Eugene Gant, they can't really believe that they will ever grow old, become ill, or die. They may recognize that time will prove them wrong, but it is natural that they do not choose to worry much about the distant future.

Consequently, the typical beginning teacher is seldom seriously concerned about fringe benefits when he accepts his first position; long-term planners are likely to appraise them more carefully. Fringe benefits become of greater concern to teachers as they grow older. They are taken into account in their decisions about whether to move to another post, and most particularly to another state with its different retirement system. If a teacher has accrued sufficient retirement benefits, it may not be in his interest to move. Thus, retirement systems, as well

---

[5] Statistics about extra income from NEA, Research Division, *The American Public School Teacher, 1965–66*, Research Report 1967–R4 (Washington, D.C.: The Association, 1967), p. 35.

as the supposed conservatism of age, inhibit mobility on the part of many teachers.

FROM YOUR VIEWPOINT

These then are some of the important facts that should be considered in your appraisal of economic prospects. They indicate that through teaching you will become neither a plutocrat nor a pauper. You may neither cruise the Mediterranean on your own yacht, nor starve romantically in a garret. You will be in a field of work in which salaries are rising—but you may ask whether they are rising fast enough. You will be in a field in which your salary increments are reasonably secure—but you may ask whether they are large enough. You will be in a field of work in which the rewards are not primarily financial—but you may wonder whether they are adequate. You can make a difference in lives of other people—but you may ask yourself whether your fellow citizens recognize the value of your contributions. As to your latter speculation, you may find useful some information about how your fellow Americans view your chosen field.

THE STATUS OF TEACHERS

Where does the American public place teaching in its ranking of the comparative status of occupations? Is the social status of teachers important to you? Should it be? The data which follow will answer the first question, but only you can answer the last two questions.

One early study of the prestige of occupations was conducted in 1947 by sociologists in cooperation with the National Opinion Research Center.[6] The study asked Americans to rank ninety occupations. When the scores were tabulated, the public school teacher was found to be thirty-sixth among the ninety occupations. Slightly above public school teachers were the artists who exhibit in galleries, factory owners who employ about a hundred people, sociologists, accountants for large businesses, biologists, musicians in symphony orchestras, authors of novels, captains in the regular army, building contractors, and economists. Clustered just below the public school teacher were the county agricultural agent, railroad engineer, farm owner and/or operator, official of an international labor union, radio announcer, newspaper columnist, and owner-operator of a printing shop.

The first ten places on the scale went to the U.S. Supreme Court Justices, physicians, state governors, cabinet members in the federal government, diplomats in the U.S. foreign service, mayors of large cities, college professors, scientists, United States representatives in Congress, bankers, and government

---

[6] National Opinion Research Center, *National Opinion on Occupations: Final Report of a Special Opinion Survey Among Americans 14 and Over* (Denver: University of Denver, 1947).

scientists. Two-thirds of the way down the list were ranked mail carriers, carpenters, automobile repairmen, plumbers, garage mechanics, local officials of labor unions, owner-operators of lunch stands, corporals in the regular army, and machine operators in factories. Lowest on the list, in descending order, were dock workers, night watchmen, laundry clothes-pressers, soda fountain clerks, bartenders, janitors, sharecroppers (who own no livestock or equipment and do not manage a farm), garbage collectors, streetsweepers, and finally shoeshiners.

So the public school teacher was not at the top of the reported ranking of occupations and social status as reported by the NORC study in 1947. But he was also a long distance from the bottom. His closest occupational kin, the college professor, shared seventh place with scientists and congressmen. Incidentally, Albert J. Reiss, Jr., in a book which reported, analyzed, and criticized the NORC study, commented that younger people tended to rank teachers lower than did older people.[7] You might wish to speculate on why this was the case.

Some scholars who were interested in occupational prestige in America used a sample of 651 persons in June 1963 to replicate the 1947 NORC scales. They found that the public school teacher shared twenty-ninth place. The sociologist was still slightly ahead of him, but the public school teacher had passed the factory owner, contractor, artist, musician, novelist and economist. Moreover, the public school teacher had not been passed by anyone below him in the prestige order.[8] So the teacher in the public school is gaining respect in the eyes of Americans. Changes in the social status of teaching appear to be continuing. The *New York Times* on August 17, 1969, reported a February 1969 poll on education as follows:

> Spokesmen for Gallup International said the survey, "based upon a representative sampling of all adults" in the country, was the "most extensive" it had conducted on the subject.
>
> The Gallup organization said it had found that the teaching profession "has probably never been held in higher esteem."
>
> The survey concluded: "Probably no better measure of the public's high esteem for teaching could be found than parents' views toward teaching as a profession. When asked if they would like to have a child take up teaching in the public schools as a career, three out of every four said they would. And in the case of parents with children now in the public schools, the ratio is even higher—four out of five."[9]

As the 1970s opened, the social status of teaching as an occupation was rising. Again, as with salaries, some potential teachers are not seriously concerned about status considerations. Other potential teachers may regard the social

---

[7] Albert J. Reiss, Jr., *Occupations and Social Status* (New York: Free Press, 1961), p. 187.
[8] Robert W. Hodge, Paul M. Siegel, and Peter H. Rossi, "Occupational Prestige in the United States: 1925–1963," p. 324 in S. M. Lipset and R. Bendix, *Class, Status and Power*, 2nd ed. (New York: Free Press, 1966).
[9] *New York Times* (August 17, 1969), pp. 1, 66.

status of an occupation as of major importance. But most potential teachers will probably be pleased to know that regard for teaching appears to be rising, yet may conclude that there are more important considerations in career decisions. Among the most important considerations for any teacher are his self-respect and the way he views his work. Of greatest importance is whether the individual can achieve his own personal and social goals and whether through teaching he can make a difference in others' lives.

★   ★   ★

DISCUSSION
1. What position do you take on the importance of teacher salary in deciding to enter teaching? What are the arguments about the importance of the teacher's salary? What assumptions lie beneath different positions?
2. How different is the salary paid in the communities you know best from the 1969–70 salaries reported in this chapter? What are the factors which determine the salaries of teachers?
3. In broad terms, how should salaries in differing fields of work be determined? How are they determined now? Ideally, how would you advocate they be determined?
4. What is your viewpoint on equality of pay for men and women? For those who are teachers and professors?
5. What is the case for and against merit pay? What is your own conclusion? How about teacher tenure? What factors must be taken into account in reaching a decision on tenure and its desirability or undesirability?
6. Is the long summer vacation of teachers an actual advantage or disadvantage to teachers? To society? To children and youth?
7. What do you think of "moonlighting"? Is it good? bad? necessary? detrimental?
8. What specific areas of education are often compensated for with extra pay when additional assignments are undertaken or responsibilities accepted? Should such differential compensation be paid? What criteria determines decisions in this respect? Are these valid?
9. How important are fringe benefits to you? What fringe benefits do you regard as important? Are there additional fringe benefits you would suggest?
10. How important is the status of teachers to you? To the class? To teachers as a whole? Does the ranking seem too high or too low?
11. How important are these economic and status factors in your tentative decision to enter the teaching field?

INVOLVEMENT
1. Get in touch with the office of your local teacher's association or the office of a school district and obtain a copy of the current salary schedule of teachers in your community. Note the increments for each year of teaching experience and for each additional step in preparation.

2. Attempt to determine the salary you would receive if you were employed in the school or school system in which you currently think you might like to be employed.
3. Obtain salary schedules for several school systems in which you would like to teach. Compile your collection with those of other class members and create a master file for reference.
4. Get in touch with the office of your state teacher's association for the average salary figures for the current year. From the schedule, find the salary for the beginning teacher in your state, for the teacher with the master's degree and ten years of teaching experience, and for the teacher with a advanced degree in education and twenty years of teaching experience. Contrast these figures with the figures presented in the chapter in order to see the direction of the trend.
5. Obtain information on differentiated pay (in contrast to merit pay) in school systems to which you are contemplating applying for positions. Inquire about the extent of moonlighting and summer jobs in local school systems from local educational association or teachers' union officials.
6. Determine the fringe benefits in school systems to which you contemplate applying for a position.
7. Develop an adaptation of the status questionnaire and administer it to your class, to a sample of "people in the street," and to students on campus. Note any differing views expressed by the varying groups.

BIBLIOGRAPHY

Caplow, Theodore and Reece J. M. McGee. *The Academic Marketplace.* New York: Doubleday, 1965. A realistic and provocative discussion of professors in the "marketplace"—how they find new posts, what is valued by employers, surrounding working conditions.

Keyserling, Leon H. *Goals for Teachers' Salaries in Our Public Schools: A Vital Test of the Sincerity of our Great National Purposes.* Washington, D.C.: Conference on Economic Progress, 1967. The case for better teachers' salaries, utilizing charts, graphs, and tables to show trends, goals, and present salaries.

NEA, Research Division. *State Minimum-Salary Laws for Teachers, 1968–69.* Washington, D.C.: The Association, 1969. Helpful for comparisons of states.

———. *Index Salary Schedules for Teachers, 1968–69.* Washington, D.C.: The Association, 1969. Information on salary schedules.

———. *Some of the Highest Salary Schedules for Teachers, 1968–69.* Washington, D.C.: The Association, 1969. Presentation of salary levels achieved by some in education.

———. *Economic Status of the Teaching Profession, 1968–69.* Washington, D.C.: The Association, 1969. Broad presentation of a variety of economic and welfare information.

———. *Beginning Salaries for College Graduates, June 1969.* Washington, D.C.: The Association, 1969. Useful data for all college graduates.

Reiss, Albert J., Jr., *Occupations and Social Status.* New York: Free Press, 1961. A useful commentary on studies of the social status of various occupations.

FIVE

WHAT ORGANIZATIONS DO TEACHERS JOIN—AND WHY?

WHY JOIN ORGANIZATIONS?

When a teacher joins an organization of fellow educators, what kinds of services are provided the teacher in exchange for the dues paid? A general benefit is joining with other like-minded persons to advance shared interests and common ideas.

Your selected organization (or your several organizations) is your spokesman in the field of education. Presumably the organization wants to communicate many of the same ideas about your interests that you want to communicate individually. The organization can usually communicate these ideas and advance your interests, often including economic interests, more effectively than you can alone, unless you are unusually influential or eloquent.

Support for organizations can contribute to the advancement of education. Vigorous organizations can be heard at the local, state, and national levels; they can play a role in the decision-making that goes on in boards of education, in community governing bodies, in state legislatures, and in the Congress. Vigorous organizations can extend academic freedom, the freedom to teach that every teacher requires for self-respect and for effective performance in the profession. They can fight against the kinds of loyalty oaths which single out teachers for special statements of their allegiances not required of other citizens. They can help in the development of such statements as the Code of Ethics developed by the National Education Association (NEA) and adopted by a number of other organizations and of the Bill of Rights of the American Federation of Teachers (AFT), documents which are at the close of this chapter.

For instance, the National Education Association supplies a wide variety of special services for its members, in addition to helping them toward higher salaries. The organizational divisions that perform these services are at the heart of NEA's activities; the substance of what NEA does for the educational profession is typically conceived, implemented, and coordinated by a wide variety of professional interest organizations, commissions, councils, and committees of educators working with full-time staffs maintained at the Washington, D.C. headquarters. (See Figure 5.1).

FIGURE 5.1
Organization Chart

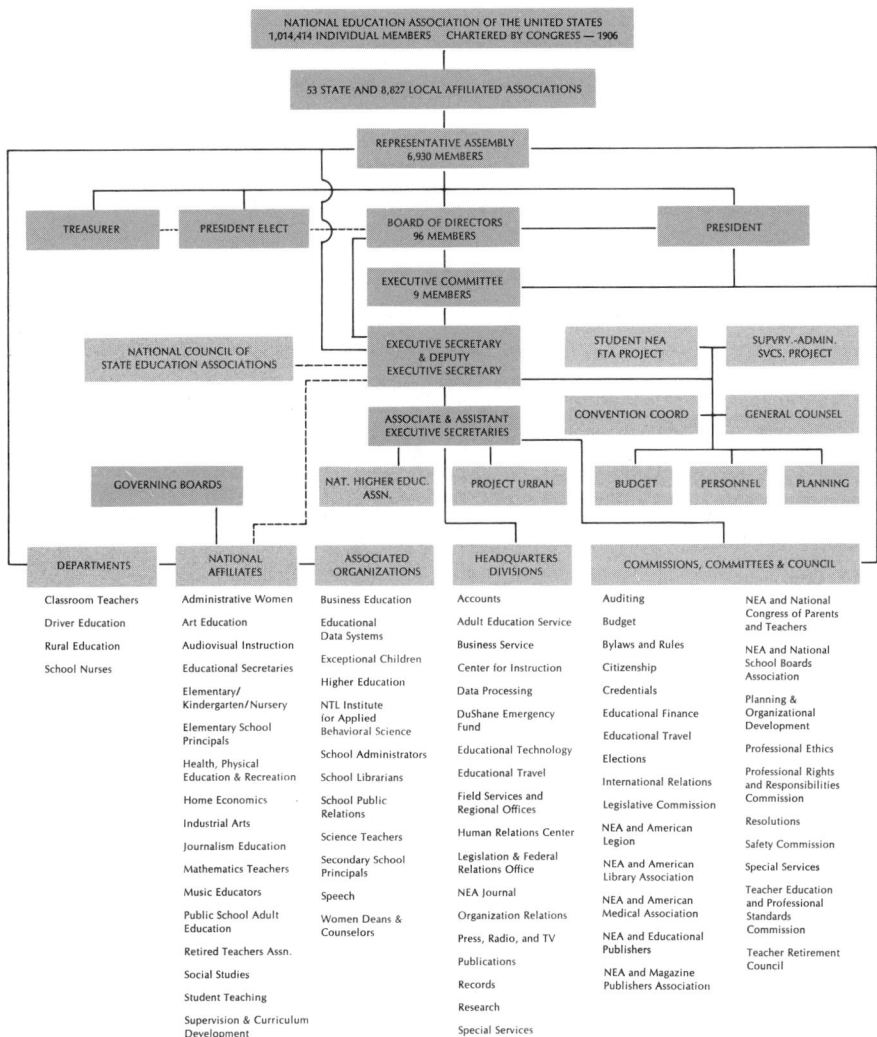

National Education Association, *NEA Handbook* (Washington, D.C.: The Association), p. 17.

George Fischer of the NEA with Congressmen. Courtesy of Joe DiDio from NEA.

For example, the Legislative Commission represents the teaching profession before Congress and generally promotes legislation favorable to the interests of public education and teachers. The Commission on Professional Rights and Responsibilities works to protect the professional, civil and human rights of educators and to investigate alleged violations of these rights. The Dushane Emergency Fund Division supples funds to ensure fair treatment of educators when their rights are threatened. The Research Division produces a constant flow of research reports on salaries, court decisions, teacher supply and demand, school statistics, etc., as well as publishes the quarterly *NEA Research Bulletin*. NEA services include such benefits as a computer-based job locator service (SEARCH); a program of educational travel for educators; insurance, annuity, and mutual fund programs; and an auto leasing program.[1]

The American Federation of Teachers also performs a variety of special functions for its members, as well as helping them in collective bargaining and in improving working conditions. Such organizational divisions as the Legal Counsel and Teacher Defense Commission, the Council on Professional Standards, the Legislative Department, and the Department of Research are similar in function to parallel NEA groupings. In addition to such generalized services, the AFT provides members with insurance coverage of the professional liability, accident and life varieties, and protection against unfair disciplinary or dismissal action through the activities of the federation and the resources of the AFT Defense Fund. (See Figure 5.2).

Early in the new teacher's career he will make a decision, either conscious or by default, whether or not to play an active part in whatever organizations he joins. The democratic tradition of active citizenship supports a decision to be

[1] For a more complete explanation of NEA services, see the *NEA Handbook*, published annually.

FIGURE 5.2

Organization Chart

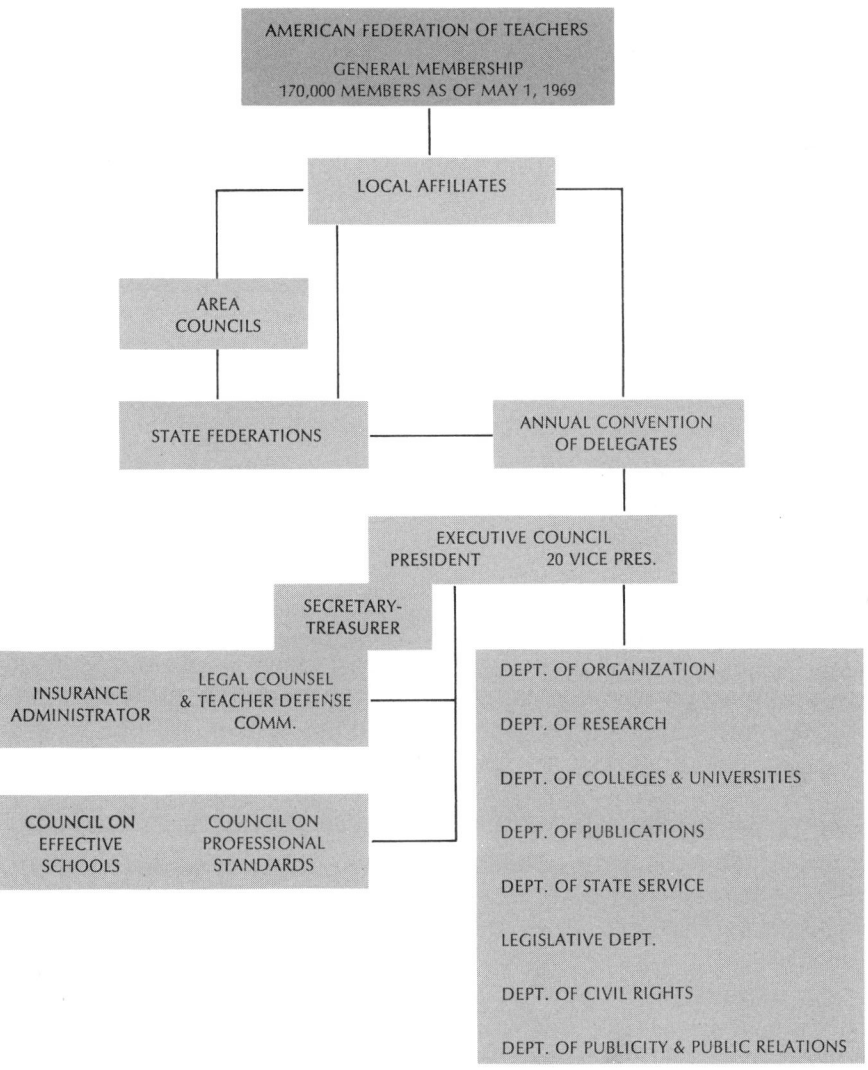

Constitution of the American Federation of Teachers (Washington, D.C.: The Federation, 1969).

an active participant. Both self-interest and advancement of one's social concerns also support active participation by the individual in organizations in which he holds membership. If one refrains from participation, he can scarcely complain in good conscience about the operation of the organization.

Another membership benefit is that you are entitled to participate in the national, regional, state, or local meetings your organization may have. You are entitled to play a role in the development of the organization's program through your elected representatives and sometimes through your own role as a representative.

If you are active in the organization, you can experience personal and professional relations with people who have many of your interests and concerns. If you choose to be a relatively passive participant, you can still receive the publications which almost all such organizations issue.

Many organizations include among their publications a journal or magazine which may either be distributed every school month, quarterly, or sometimes on a six-issue schedule. Such a magazine usually contains articles, columns, and news information related to the teacher's specialty. Many organizations have, in addition, a more informal "house organ" type of publication containing news about the work of the organization and mention of the activities of members. All such publications help the teacher stay up-to-date. For instance, the National Education Association publishes a journal, *Today's Education*, and the American Federation of Teachers publishes a tabloid, *American Teacher*, and a journal, *Changing Education*.

For some specialized organizations which deal with particular subject matter fields or other interests, publications include a yearbook which, as the name implies, is an annual publication on some topic of special concern to the group. The yearbook is usually made up of chapters contributed by intellectual leaders or prominent practioners in a specialized field, and it often deals with a topic of current controversy or of concern in the field. In addition, many organizations distibute pamphlets, usually prepared by selected members, on topics of interest to the membership.

THE STRUGGLE BETWEEN THE NEA AND AFT

In legend and in literature, there have been historic feuds. A famous example is the nineteenth century feud of the Hatfields and McCoys in the mountains of North Carolina and Kentucky. A feud between the Montague and the Capulet families in Verona resulted in the death of a pair of "star-cross'd lovers," Romeo and Juliet.

As a teacher in the 1970s, you may be a participant in the final act of another famous feud, the struggle between the American Federation of Teachers and the National Education Association. The 1970s may see the termination of the battle between these major organizations; the struggle for power may be resolved through some degree of reconciliation or accommodation or through a merger.

THE BACKGROUNDS OF NEA AND AFT AND THEIR DIFFERENCES

The National Education Association was created in 1857 when forty-three people met in Philadelphia to organize the "National Teachers' Association."

After World War I, the organization began to grow toward its present impressive size. As the 1970s opened, membership in the National Education Association totaled approximately 1,100,000 (1,085,589 in 1970).

The American Federation of Teachers was organized and granted affiliation with the American Federation of Labor in 1916. By the beginning of the 1970s membership in the AFT totaled about 175,000.

The National Education Association and the American Federation of Teachers are rival organizations. Historically, they have had differing perceptions of their educational roles, and of each other.

The National Education Association historically has seen itself as the major professional association for American educators. Though teachers have always constituted a majority of the membership (the Department of Classroom Teachers enrolls some 700,000 members), departments of the NEA have enrolled such groups as administrators, supervisors and curriculum directors, high school principals, elementary school principals, and others in administrative and supervisory posts. The NEA has long been devoted to enhancing the professional stature of teachers as well as promoting their economic welfare. Consequently, the organization has stressed a broad spectrum of publications, conventions to improve the competence of teachers and add to their sense of belonging to a profession, and representation of the cause of education in Congress.

The American Federation of Teachers has seen itself as an integral part of the American labor union movement and is affiliated with the AFL-CIO. The organization is made up almost exclusively of teachers; administrators are generally barred from membership. The AFT stresses its devotion to the improvement of the economic welfare of teachers; it suspects that too much talk about "professional" status serves as a smokescreen obscuring the real economic issues. Nevertheless, in recent years the AFT has expanded its interest into such professional matters as the support of research, promotion of international education in the curriculum, and the encouragement of such educational reforms as New York City's "More Effective Schools." The AFT provides a rallying place for teachers who resist both the inadequate compensation offered by many communities and the authoritarianism of some educational administrators.

The fundamental differences between the two organizations are that the National Education Association serves an umbrella function for varied educational groups, including administrative groups, while the AFT is affiliated with the labor union movement. Myron Lieberman, a frequent spokesman for the AFT and a onetime candidate for its presidency, pointed out these differences more than a decade ago.

> Essentially, there are two basic issues which divide the two organizations. One is the fact that the NEA has no restrictions upon administrator membership. The other is AFT's affiliation with the AFL-CIO.[2]

[2] Myron Lieberman, *The Future of Public Education* (Chicago: The University of Chicago Press, 1960), pp. 231.

Supporters of the two organizations have often been openly hostile to each other. The NEA has been criticized by supporters of the AFT as a company union, a monolithic giant, a spokesman for the educational establishment, a clumsy and loose bureaucratic federation, an administrator-dominated organization which coerces teachers into membership, and a racially conservative force which once tolerated segregation within its state affiliates and local organizations. Meanwhile, NEA supporters have criticized the AFT as a tool of Big Labor, a pygmy pretending to stature, a haven for malcontents, an open violator of state laws, a user of such unprofessional tactics as strikes, a left-leaning force which appeals primarily to metropolitan dissidents and administration-haters, and an organization of clock-watchers who simply put in their time. Such name-calling by some has hampered the relationships of members of both groups.

Relationships between the NEA and the AFT were not always bad, however. In fact, some of the earlier leaders of the AFT were also leaders in the NEA. When the AFT was founded in 1916, some thought that it would represent teachers on welfare issues such as wages and tenure while the NEA would work mostly with research and curriculum and methodology.[3] But as the American Federation of Teachers began to grow following World War I, competition developed. In the period from 1918 to 1921, efforts were made by teachers who had sought affiliation with the labor movement to take over the NEA or to bring its policies in line with the AFT view. At the 1918–1921 conventions of the National Education Association, for instance, the Chicago Federation of Teachers urged emphasis upon welfare matters such as salaries, tenure, and pensions. The NEA responded with its usual insistence on professional development and the inclusion of all educators in a concerted effort at educational improvement.[4]

In 1918 the memberships of the NEA and the AFT were approximately equal— each had fewer than 10,000 members. By 1960 the NEA had 713,000 and the AFT 60,000. By the beginning of the 1960s some of the leaders of organized labor had become deeply interested in enrolling teachers in teacher unions. They reasoned that if teachers could be persuaded to join unions, other white-collar workers and professional people would follow, which seemed appealing since union rolls were suffering from the decrease in the percentage of blue-collar workers in the nation's work force.

The focus of AFT activity in the early sixties was New York City. After a successful breakthrough in New York City in December 1960—the United Federation of Teachers, an AFT local, won exclusive right to bargain for teachers— the AFT began to grow. The growth occurred primarily in large cities like New York, Chicago, Detroit, Los Angeles, St. Louis, Boston, and New Orleans. By 1966 the AFT had doubled its membership while the NEA had moved close to one million members.

The battlegrounds of the two organizations were the big cities. The campaigns took the form of competition between the two organizations to serve as the

---

[3] Edward B. Shils and C. Taylor Whittier, *Teachers, Administrators and Collective Bargaining* (New York: Thomas Y. Crowell, 1968), pp. 539–540.

[4] T. M. Stinnett, *Turmoil in Teaching* (New York: Macmillan, 1968), p. 19.

representative of teachers in bargaining and negotiations. Each side had its victories and defeats, but in general the National Education Association maintained a firm hold in rural, small town and small city America while the AFT gained in the larger cities, particularly in the northeast quarter of the U.S.

With respect to size, the NEA remained Goliath and the AFT remained David. But the AFT gains were disturbing to NEA supporters. Since the 1890s the U.S. had been steadily developing as an urban and industrial nation and had grown away from its earlier rural and agricultural orientation. So although the NEA still heavily outnumbered the AFT in memberships throughout the 1960s, the speed of growth of the teachers' unions in big cities and in some suburbs threatened the NEA's controlling position. A nationwide sample survey of public school classroom teachers conducted in the spring of 1969 by NEA's Research Division revealed that of teachers responding just over half (54.1 percent) belonged to the NEA; much larger proportions, 80.3 percent and 81.9 percent, belonged to NEA-related state and local education associations respectively. Almost 7 percent (6.7 percent) of the sample group belonged to the AFT.[5] Only 22.2 percent claimed membership in some specialized subject-matter organization.

COLLECTIVE BARGAINING VS. PROFESSIONAL NEGOTIATION

For a while, a clear distinction could be made between the major groups of educators as to the instruments of power they used in gaining concessions from boards of education. The AFT used the historical labor union tactics of collective bargaining and strikes; the NEA used the processes of professional negotiations and sanctions.

T. M. Stinnett, a student of the dispute, points out that "collective bargaining" was defined by the Taft-Hartley Act as "the performance of the mutual obligation of the employer and the representatives of the employees to meet at reasonable times and confer in good faith with respect to wages, hours, and other terms and conditions of employment for the negotiation of any agreement or any question arising thereunder, and the execution of a written contract incorporating any agreement reached if requested by either party, but such obligation does not compel either party to agree to a proposal or require the making of a concession." "Professional negotiation" was defined by the National Education Association as "a set of procedures to provide an orderly method for teacher associations and school boards, through professional channels, to negotiate on matters of common concern, to reach mutually satisfactory agreement on these matters, and to establish educational channels for mediation and appeal in the event of impasse."[6]

Certainly there is a similarity. Is there a difference? Stinnett, a longtime worker in the National Education Association and an admitted advocate of the NEA point of view, believes there is and states his position as follows:

---

[5] NEA, Research Division, *Teacher Opinion Poll, 1968–69* (July 1969) (mimeo).
[6] Cited by Stinnett, p. 90.

The differences are that collective bargaining:
1. Is designed for private employees, and its use is mandatory under law.
2. Uses procedures that are subject to Federal and state laws and interpretations of the courts. Administration of collective bargaining is under jurisdiction of Federal and state labor departments or agencies.
3. Employs, in cases of impasse, the strike, which is recognized under the laws as the weapon of the employee.

In contrast, professional negotiation:
1. Is designed for public employees (teachers).
2. Requires that all processes are to be through professional channels; that is through education personnel and agencies.
3. Must use educational channels for appeals or mediation of impasse.
4. Does not advocate or consider legal the use of the strike as a weapon.

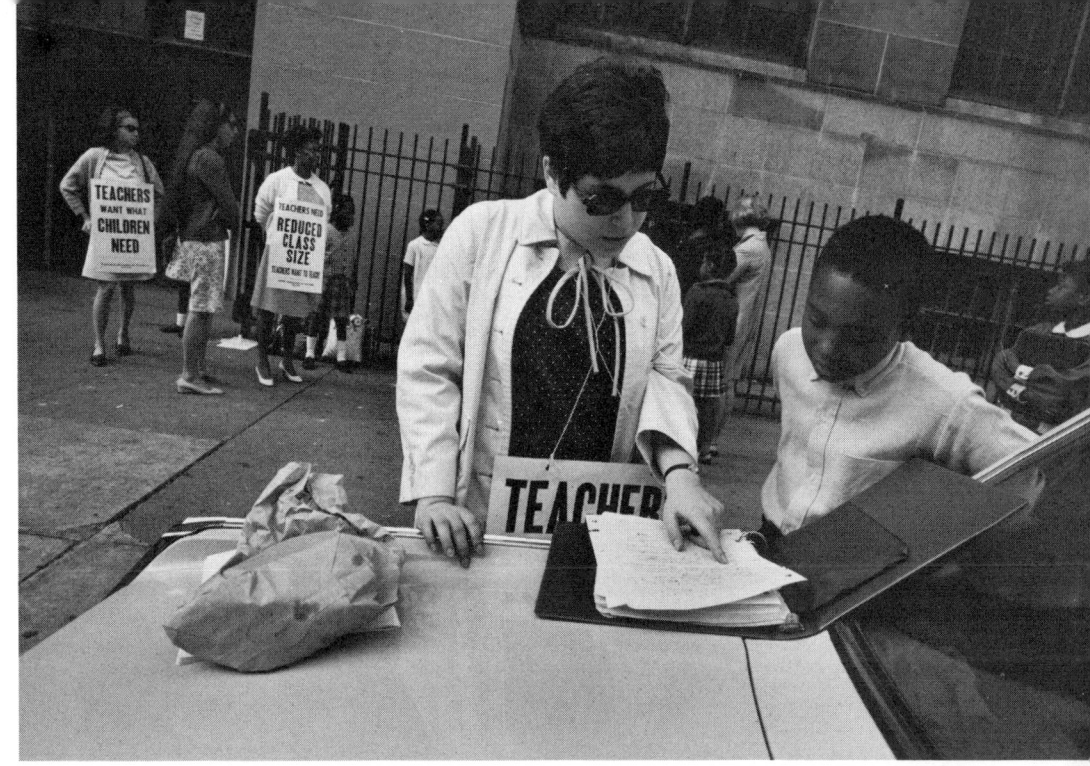

Many object to teacher strikes because of their effects on students, but others argue that striking is sometimes the only way to achieve better educational situations. Courtesy of Henry Monroe from DPI. Photo on preceding page courtesy of Clayton J. Price of Black Star.

In short, professional negotiation seeks to keep public employees (teachers) out of labor techniques as defined in labor laws. The rationale is that schools and factories are not analogous; schools are not profit-making enterprises, and management and employees are not natural enemies fighting over divisions of profits.[7]

STRIKES AND SANCTIONS

To others, the distinctions between collective bargaining and professional negotiation appear less obvious. To them, the difference diminished further as the NEA advocated not strikes but sanctions. A sanction involves curtailment or withdrawal of services of teachers to a given district or state school system. A first step involved is publicizing the dispute; the association involved then requests its members who are employed elsewhere not to seek or accept positions in the unsatisfactory school district. All instruction personnel are then requested to boycott the school district. Finally, the Association declares it professionally unethical for either newcomers or present staff to accept employment in the school district.

[7] Stinnett, p. 90.

Again is there a difference between the strike and the sanction? Stinnett thinks there is:

There are several differences. Sanctions do not violate a contract. Services to children are not interrupted. Teachers serve out their contracts for the current school year. Under sanctions, there are no picket lines. Under sanctions, school districts are given several months' notice and told that existing conditions make possible only inferior programs for children, that professional people cannot, under the existing conditions, provide first-rate services. As a general rule, sanctions are made effective in the succeeding school year except in the case of withdrawing extracurricular services.[8]

AFT proponents are quick to counter, however, that sanctions do, in fact, negatively affect services to children, particularly in the later stages of a sanction effort. They also argue that strikes do less long-term damage to a district and are usually briefer and "cleaner." In other words, a strike may end and the entire original staff resume teaching, whereas sanctions may result in the departure of teachers over a long period of time.

THE DECLINE OF DIFFERENCES BETWEEN NEA AND AFT

Increasingly, NEA local associations used work stoppages which resembled strikes. However titled, work stoppages, strikes, mass resignations, withdrawals, and sanctions were used by both the NEA and the AFT to withhold teacher services. In his final chapter, Stinnett comments sadly,

Like the teachers' unions up to 1962 with respect to collective bargaining, the NEA and its affiliated associations began advocating professional negotiation in muted tones and with promises of responsible and reasonable action by teachers. Gaining a foothold in some places now, teachers' associations and unions are exhibiting increasing truculency and growing demands. Turmoil and strife have grown alarmingly in frequency.[9]

Edward B. Shils and C. Taylor Whittier summed up the disappearance of differences between the NEA and the AFT in *Teachers, Administrators and Collective Bargaining* as follows:

The earlier differentiation between the NEA as a professional organization and the AFT as a labor union is gradually disappearing in the cold light of local organizing actions and tactical planning at national headquarters. Both organizations train organizers, employ strikes and threats of strikes, aim at contracts that are highly complex, and whittle away at traditional staff and board prerogatives, and advocate firm grievance procedures ending with final and binding arbitration. Little by little, the NEA at the local level, like the AFT, is driving principals, supervisors, and administrators out of the bargaining unit. Both organizations

---

[8] *Ibid.*, p. 127.   [9] *Ibid.*, pp. 356–357.

press hard for exclusive representation and the NEA is getting as tough in the fighting as the AFT. The two organizations are busy lobbying the legislatures for laws to their own liking that will mandate elections and recognition in each district. While each organization specializes in a particular approach—the educational channels versus the labor channels—their respective lobbyists, in due time, will press for amendments not far apart.[10]

Symptomatic of the point of view of the above authors as to the gradual disappearance of operational differences between the AFT and the NEA is the increasing frequency of the use of the phrase "collective negotiations," a hybrid of collective bargaining and professional negotiations. Shils and Whittier say, "In view of the militancy engaged in by both the NEA and the AFT the difference between NEA's professional negotiations and AFT's collective bargaining is a matter of nomenclature."[11]

THE POSSIBILITY OF MERGER

As the 1970s opened, the feud between the AFT union and the NEA professional association went on, though the two organizations increasingly resembled each other in their daily operations at the community level as to teacher welfare. Indeed discussion of merger was proposed by the AFT in 1968, but was rejected by the NEA. Yet talk of possible merger in the 1970s was rife in publications dealing with education. As the 1970s opened, an educators' newsletter reported:

A merger of the National Education Association (NEA) and the American Federation of Teachers (AFT) may be closer than many educators think it is. The key may be talks now under way in Los Angeles that could result in the merger of the Association of Classroom Teachers of Los Angeles, an NEA affiliate, and the Los Angeles Teachers Union, an AFT local. Teacher groups in cities across the country are watching Los Angeles very carefully. If merger occurs there, and many believe that it will, other cities are expected to follow this lead.[12] One merger, in Flint, Michigan, is already a fact. Other cities, especially on the West Coast, and even statewide organizations are reportedly talking merger. Although officials at the national level deny that they have begun to discuss uniting, both George D. Fisher, NEA president, and David Selden, AFT president, have gone on record as favoring a merger.[13]

At the present writing, the NEA and AFT exist as separate organizations. Membership in such educational organizations is voluntary and thus a matter of individual teacher choice. Thus, one can choose to be a member of the National Education Association or of the American Federation of Teachers or neither.

---

[10] Shils and Whittier, p. 540.   [11] Ibid., p. 549.
[12] The two Los Angeles teacher groups did merge. A strike followed in the Spring of 1970.
[13] *Education U.S.A., The Weekly Newsletter on Education Affairs* (December 15, 1969) (Washington, D.C.: The National School Public Relations Association), p. 92.

Conventions offer teachers opportunities to learn about new innovations, publications, and methods as well as to exchange ideas with others of their profession. Courtesy of Joe DiDio from NEA.

(A few teachers hold membership in both.) One can choose to belong to a local union of the AFT or the state or local affiliates of the NEA, or belong to none. (However, one cannot join a local of AFT without paying national dues, a percentage of which goes to the AFL-CIO.)

However, as teachers in local communities increasingly decide that, for purposes of "collective negotiations," they will be represented either by the union or the professional association, a surrounding climate of opinion develops among fellow teachers which strongly encourages the new teacher to join the dominant group. It is quite possible that the 1970s will see such labor techniques as the closed shop with compulsory checkoff of dues mandated by agreements and supported by law. Many contracts negotiated by AFT locals call for dues deductions to be made from salary checks; the money withheld is paid directly to the union by the board.

SPECIALIZED ORGANIZATIONS

One can choose whether or not to belong to a specialized organization within the broad field of education. Here we refer not to the variety of locals of the American Federation of Teachers from the large United Federation of Teachers of New York City down to a handful of union-oriented teachers working toward recognition in a small community, nor to the influential state associations of the

National Education Association and the local associations at the community level. Instead, we refer to the many specialized organizations which bring together teachers with common interests in a particular subject matter or some other basis. Some of these are affiliated with the National Education Association in an increasingly loose relationship; others are independent. (See Table 5.1.)

TABLE 5.1

Special Organizations for Teachers

Some Organizations Affiliated with the National Education Association

The address for all these organizations is: 1201 Sixteenth Street, N.W., Washington, D.C.

American Association for Health, Physical Education and Recreation
American Driver and Traffic Safety Education Association
American Industrial Arts Association
Association for Supervision and Curriculum Development
Council for Exceptional Children
Department of Elementary-Kindergarten-Nursery Education
Department of Foreign Languages
Department of Home Economics
Journalism Education Association
Music Teachers National Conference
National Art Education Association
National Association for Public School Adult Education
National Business Education Association
National Council for the Social Studies
National Council of Teachers of Mathematics
National Science Teachers Association
Speech Association of America

Some Independent Organizations

American Association of Teachers of Physics
1201 16th Street, N.W.
Washington, D.C.

American Educational Research Association
1126 16th Street, N.W.
Washington, D.C.

Association for Childhood Education International
3615 Wisconsin Avenue, N.W.
Washington, D.C.   20016

Delta Kappa Gamma
416 West Twelfth Street
Austin, Texas

The John Dewey Society for the Study of Education and Culture
John Dewey Project
Southern Illinois University
Carbondale, Illinois

Kappa Delta Pi
Box A
West Lafayette, Indiana

National Association of Biology Teachers
1420 N Street, N.W.
Washington, D.C.

National Congress of Parents and Teachers
700 North Rush Street
Chicago, Illinois

National Council of Teachers of English
508 South Sixth Street
Champaign, Illinois

Phi Delta Kappa
Eighth Street and Union Avenue
Bloomington, Indiana

You are a social studies teacher? For you there is the National Council for the Social Studies. You are research-oriented? For you there is the American Educational Research Association. You are a teacher of the language arts? For you there is the National Council of Teachers of English. You are concerned about the curriculum? For you there is the Association for Supervision and Curriculum Development. Those educators who believe that education should increasingly become a profession rather than an occupation often become members of such specialized groups to share ideas and interests with fellow professionals.

IS EDUCATION A PROFESSION?

A persisting problem for educators has been whether education is a profession in the fullest sense of that honorable word.

Myron Lieberman supplies eight characteristics of a profession:

1. A unique, definite and essential social service.
2. An emphasis upon intellectual techniques in performing its service.
3. A long period of specialized training.
4. A broad range of autonomy for both the individual practitioners and for the occupational group as a whole.
5. An acceptance by the practitioners of broad personal responsibility for judgments made and acts performed within the scope of professional autonomy.

6. An emphasis upon the service to be rendered, rather than the economic gain to the practitioners, as the basis for the organization and performance of the social service delegated to the occupational group.
7. A comprehensive self-governing organization of practitioners.
8. A code of ethics which has been clarified and interpreted at ambiguous and doubtful points by concrete cases.[14]

Should education be a profession marked by this complex of characteristics? *Is* education currently a profession marked by these characteristics? If one is to answer these questions, some specific elements in the definition must be taken into account.

1. A unique, definite and essential social service. Is education unique, to be carried on only by educators? Or can an untrained person teach well? Is there agreement on the function of education? Or is there substantial disagreement and uncertainty over what education is intended to do? Is education essential to the welfare of children in our society? Or is education a social luxury which should be available only to those who can pay for it?
2. An emphasis upon intellectual techniques in performing its service. Does education require of the teacher complex intellectual operations which are characteristic of professions? Or is education simply a matter of using physical techniques in carrying on the work?
3. A long period of specialized training. Are the four years of college work toward the baccalaureate, including some education courses, equivalent to a "long period of specialized training"? Would the requirement of a master's degree for teaching constitute a sufficiently "long period of specialized training" necessary for a profession? Is the professional training received by teachers-to-be primarily intellectual? Or is it primarily nonintellectual?
4. A broad range of autonomy for both the individual practitioners and for the occupational group as a whole. Does teaching involve freedom to exercise independent skill and judgment? Or must teaching be closely supervised by authorities who make the basic decisions and solve the major problems? Do teachers have a great deal of say in regulation of their profession? Or do teachers lack freedom to decide such things as admission to the profession, suspension from work, and the characteristics of ethical conduct?
5. An acceptance by the practitioners of broad personal responsibility for judgments made and acts performed within the scope of professional autonomy. Do teachers accept responsibility for their work and its outcomes? Or do they regard responsibility for outcomes as residing with others outside of their field of work?
6. An emphasis upon the service to be rendered, rather than the economic gain to the practitioners, as the basis for the organization and performance of the social service delegated to the occupational group. Do teachers take pride in the service they render? Or do teachers work simply because of the pay involved?

[14] Myron Lieberman, *Education as a Profession* (Englewood Cliffs, N.J.: Prentice-Hall, 1956), pp. 2–6.

7. A comprehensive self-governing organization of practitioners. For instance, do teachers have an organization or organizations to foster the profession by setting standards of certification, disseminating new ideas, raising the general and social economic status of the professional group? Or do teachers not have an organization or organizations concerned for the standards and advancement of the profession?
8. A code of ethics which has been clarified and interpreted at ambiguous and doubtful points by concrete cases. Is there a code of ethics for the teaching profession which has been interpreted in practice? Or is there no such code?

As you check over the questions raised in connection with each of the ingredients of the definition of a profession, it is quite possible that you will answer affirmatively to some questions which describe professional status, affirmatively to some questions which describe education simply as an occupation but not a profession, and ambiguously to others. If so, your conclusion will probably be that education is partially but not totally a true profession at the present time.

We will refer hereafter to education as a "profession" throughout this book. But we hope you will keep in mind that we too recognize that the professional status of education has not been fully achieved. Codes and bills of rights such as those which follow contribute to the achievement of professional standing for teaching.

National Education Association
Code of Ethics of the Education Profession

Preamble

The educator believes in the worth and dignity of man. He recognizes the supreme importance of the pursuit of truth, devotion to excellence, and the nurture of democratic citizenship. He regards as essential to these goals the protection of freedom to learn and to teach and the guarantee of equal educational opportunity for all. The educator accepts his responsibility to practice his profession according to the highest ethical standards.

The educator recognizes the magnitude of the responsibility he has accepted in choosing a career in education, and engages himself, individually and collectively with other educators, to judge his colleagues, and to be judged by them, in accordance with the provisions of this code.

Principle I
Commitment to the Student

The educator measures his success by the progress of each student toward realization of his potential as a worthy and effective citizen. The educator therefore works to stimulate the spirit of inquiry, the acquisition of knowledge and understanding, and the thoughtful formulation of worthy goals.

In fulfilling his obligation to the student the educator—
1. Shall not without just cause restrain the student from independent action in his pursuit of learning, and shall not without just cause deny the student access to varying points of view.

2. Shall not deliberately suppress or distort subject matter for which he bears responsibility.
3. Shall make reasonable effort to protect the student from conditions harmful to learning or to health and safety.
4. Shall conduct professional business in such a way that he does not expose the student to unnecessary embarrassment or disparagement.
5. Shall not on the ground of race, color, creed, or national origin exclude any student from participation in or deny him benefits under any program, nor grant any discriminatory consideration or advantage.
6. Shall not use professional relationships with students for private advantage.
7. Shall keep in confidence information that has been obtained in the course of professional service, unless disclosure serves professional purposes or is required by law.
8. Shall not tutor for remuneration students assigned to his classes, unless no other qualified teacher is reasonably available.

Principle II
Commitment to the Public

The educator believes that patriotism in its highest form requires dedication to the principles of our democratic heritage. He shares with all other citizens the responsibility for the development of sound public policy and assumes full political and citizenship responsibilities.

The educator bears particular responsibility for the development of policy relating to the extension of educational opportunities for all and for interpreting educational programs and policies to the public.

In fulfilling his obligation to the public the educator—

1. Shall not misrepresent an institution or organization with which he is affiliated, and shall take adequate precautions to distinguish between his personal and institutional or organizational views.
2. Shall not knowingly distort or misrepresent the facts concerning educational matters in direct and indirect public expressions.
3. Shall not interfere with a colleague's exercise of political and citizenship rights and responsibilities.
4. Shall not use institutional privileges for private gain or promote political candidates or partisan political activities.
5. Shall accept no gratuities, gifts, or favors that might impair or appear to impair professional judgment, nor offer any favor, service, or thing of value to obtain special advantage.

Principle III
Commitment to the Profession

The educator believes that the quality of the services of the education profession directly influences the nation and its citizens. He therefore exerts every effort to raise professional standards, to improve his service, to promote a climate in which the exercise of professional judgment is encouraged, and to achieve conditions which attract persons, worthy of the trust to careers in education. Aware of the value of united effort, he contributes actively to the support, planning and programs of professional organizations.

In fulfilling his obligation to the profession, the educator—

1. Shall not discriminate on grounds of race, color, creed, or national origin for membership in professional organizations, nor interfere with the free participation of colleagues in the affairs of their association.
2. Shall accord just and equitable treatment to all members of the profession in the exercise of their professional rights and responsibilities.
3. Shall not use coercive means or promise special treatment in order to influence professional decisions of colleagues.
4. Shall withhold and safeguard information acquired about colleagues in the course of employment, unless disclosure serves professional purposes.
5. Shall not refuse to participate in a professional inquiry when requested by an appropriate professional association.
6. Shall provide upon the request of the aggrieved party a written statement of specific reason for recommendations that lead to the denial of increments, significant changes in employment, or termination of employment.
7. Shall not misrepresent his professional qualifications.
8. Shall not knowingly distort evaluations of colleagues.

Principle IV
Commitment to Professional
Employment Practices

The educator regards the employment agreement as a pledge to be executed both in spirit and in fact in a manner consistent with the highest ideals of professional service. He believes that sound professional personnel relationships with governing boards are built upon personal integrity, dignity, and mutual respect. The educator discourages the practice of his profession by unqualified persons.

In fulfilling his obligation to professional employment practices, the educator—

1. Shall apply for, accept, offer, or assign a position or responsibility on the basis of professional preparation and legal qualifications.
2. Shall apply for a specific position only when it is known to be vacant, and shall refrain from underbidding or commenting adversely about other candidates.
3. Shall not knowingly withhold information regarding a position from an applicant, or misrepresent an assignment or conditions of employment.
4. Shall give prompt notice to the employing agency of any change in availability of service, and the employing agent shall give prompt notice of change in availability or nature of a position.
5. Shall not accept a position when so requested by the appropriate professional organization.
6. Shall adhere to the terms of a contract or appointment, unless these terms have been legally terminated, falsely represented, or substantially altered by unilateral action of the employing agency.
7. Shall conduct professional business through channels, when available, that

have been jointly approved by the professional organization and the employing agency.
8. Shall not delegate assigned tasks to unqualified personnel.
9. Shall permit no commercial exploitation of his professional position.
10. Shall use time granted for the purpose for which it is intended.[1]

American Federation of Teachers
Bill of Rights

The teacher is entitled to a life of dignity equal to the high standard of service that is justly demanded of that profession. Therefore, we hold these truths to be self-evident:

I

Teachers have the right to think freely and to express themselves openly and without fear. This includes the right to hold views contrary to the majority.

II

They shall be entitled to the free exercise of their religion. No restraint shall be put upon them in the manner, time or place of their worship.

III

They shall have the right to take part in social, civil, and political affairs. They shall have the right, outside the classroom, to participate in political campaigns and to hold office. They may assemble peaceably and may petition any government agency, including their employers, for a redress of grievances. They shall have the same freedom in all things as other citizens.

IV

The right of teachers to live in places of their own choosing, to be free of restraints in their mode of living and the use of their leisure time shall not be abridged.

V

Teaching is a profession, the right to practice which is not subject to the surrender of other human rights. No one shall be deprived of professional status, or the right to practice it, or the practice thereof in any particular position, without due process of law.

VI

The right of teachers to be secure in their jobs, free from political influence or public clamor, shall be established by law. The right to teach after qualification in the manner prescribed by law, is a property right, based upon the inalienable rights to life, liberty, and the pursuit of happiness.

VII

In all cases affecting the teacher's employment or professional status a full hearing by an impartial tribunal shall be afforded with the right of full judicial

---

[1] *National Education Association Handbook, 1969–70* (Washington, D.C.: The Association), pp. 87–89.

review. No teacher shall be deprived of employment or professional status but for specific causes established by law having a clear relation to the competence or qualification to teach, proved by the weight of the evidence. In all such cases the teacher shall enjoy the right to a speedy and public trial, to be informed of the nature and cause of the accusation; to be confronted with the accusing witnesses, to subpeona witnesses and papers, and the assistance of counsel. No teacher shall be called upon to answer any charge affecting his employment or professional status but upon probable cause, supported by oath or affirmation.

VIII

It shall be the duty of the employer to provide culturally adequate salaries, security in illness and adequate retirement income. The teacher has the right to such a salary as will: a) Afford a family standard of living comparable to that enjoyed by other professional people in the community; b) Make possible freely chosen professional study; c) Afford the opportunity for leisure and recreation common to our heritage.

IX

No teacher shall be required under penalty of reduction of salary to pursue studies beyond those required to obtain professional status. After serving a reasonable probationary period a teacher shall be entitled to permanent tenure terminable only for just cause. They shall be free as in other professions in the use of their own time. They shall not be required to perform extracurricular work against their will or without added compensation.

X

To equip people for modern life requires the most advanced educational methods. Therefore, the teacher is entitled to good classrooms, adequate teaching materials, teachable class size and administrative protection and assistance in maintaining discipline.

XI

These rights are based upon the proposition that the culture of a people can rise only as its teachers improve. A teaching force accorded the highest possible professional dignity is the surest guarantee that blessings of liberty will be preserved. Therefore, the possession of these rights imposes the challenge to be worthy of their enjoyment.

XII

Since teachers must be free in order to teach freedom, the right to be members of organizations of their own choosing must be guaranteed. In all matters pertaining to their salaries and working conditions they shall be entitled to bargain collectively through representatives of their own choosing. They are entitled to have the schools administered by superintendents, boards or committees which function in a democratic manner.

★ ★ ★

DISCUSSION

1. For what reasons should a teacher join an educational organization? Should he or she take an active part? Why? Do you think membership should be compulsory?
2. Essentially what is the difference between the two major organizations of teachers and the specialized organizations of teachers?
3. What are the fundamental and historical differences between the National Education Association and the American Federation of Teachers?
4. What current perceptions do the members of the two major organizations have of each other? Is the past hostility decreasing?
5. What are the past differences and present similarities between the two major organizations as to "strikes"; "negotiations"?
6. If you were forced to choose between the two major organizations, which would you choose to join? Why?
7. What forces tend toward merger of the National Education Association and the American Federation of Teachers? Which forces discourage merger?
8. Discuss the advantages and disadvantages of a possible merger of the National Education Association and the American Federation of Teachers.
9. Toward which specialized organizations do members of your class incline?
10. What is the meaning of the word profession? To what extent is education today a profession?
11. What would you add to Lieberman's list of eight characteristics of a profession?
12. Is it possible for a profession to consist of some professional teachers who meet all of the standards set forth in Lieberman's eight characteristics of a profession while simultaneously others in the profession do not meet these standards?
13. What is your reaction to the code of ethics of the NEA and the bill of rights of the AFT? Can you accept both? Do you think one is preferable? Why?

INVOLVEMENT

1. If you have a strong commitment to either the National Education Association or the American Federation of Teachers, volunteer your services to the local unit of the organization for a specified number of hours per week. Learn the ways and the work of the group.
2. Begin reading regularly the publications of either or both of the two major national organizations.
3. Attend a school board meeting at which representation of a group position is made either by the local unit of the National Education Association or the American Federation of Teachers.
4. Organize and conduct a debate on the topic: "Resolved: Professional teachers should belong to a professional organization" or on the topic: "Resolved: Working teachers should belong to a labor-affiliated organization."
5. Interview an officer of the local teacher's association and the local American Federation of Teachers, if these groups exist in your community. Ask them why they are active in their organizations and why they believe their organization is "the" one for teachers.

6. If there is an opportunity to study a strike in actual operation, take advantage of it.
7. Obtain and examine a journal of the professional organization most closely aligned with your particular area of interest (level of teaching or subject matter area). In what ways could this material be of value to a teacher in a particular interest area?
8. Attend a meeting of a specialized organization in education. Information as to time and place can readily be obtained from one of your professors who specializes in the work of that organization.
9. Interview teachers about their viewpoints on the major organizations and the specialized organizations in education. Obtain their advice on affiliation.
10. Compare the teachers whom you know best against the characteristics of a professional suggested in this chapter and discussed by your class.
11. Debate on whether or not education is a profession.

BIBLIOGRAPHY

American Federation of Teachers. *In Search of Excellence*. Washington, D.C.: American Federation of Teachers AFL-CIO, no date. Questions and answers about the AFT.

Brinkmeier, Oria A., Gerald C. Ulben and Richard C. Williams. *Inside the Organization Teacher: The Relationship Between Selected Characteristics of Teachers and Their Membership in Teacher Organizations*. Danville, Ill.: Interstate Printers and Publishers, 1967. An attempt at measurement and analysis of differences between members and nonmembers of a professional organization. A report of the findings of three research studies and their implications.

Corwin, Ronald G. *Militant Professionalism*. New York: Appleton-Century-Crofts, 1970. Professionalism in a bureaucratic setting involves a degree of conflict as competing principles of organizations clash.

Dreeben, Robert. *The Profession of Teaching*. Glenview, Ill.: Scott, Foresman and Company, 1969. Nature of the work of teachers, settings, careers, and educational associations.

Dorros, Sidney. *Teaching as a Profession*. Columbus, Ohio: Charles E. Merrill, 1968. The profession of teaching: goals, ethics, accreditation, certification, economic welfare, organizations, etc.

Elam, Stanley, Myron Lieberman, and Michael Moskow, eds. *Readings on Collective Negotiations in Public Education*. Chicago: Rand McNally, 1967. A comprehensive and varied collection relating to the new relationships of teachers, administrators, school boards, and the public in respect to teacher salaries and working conditions.

Lieberman, Myron. *Education as a Profession*. Englewood Cliffs, N.J.: Prentice-Hall, 1956. Analysis of the aspects of a profession and the degree to which education can be so categorized.

Lieberman, Myron and Michael Moskow. *Collective Negotiations for Teachers: An Approach to School Administration*. Chicago: Rand McNally, 1966. Knowledgeable specialists in negotiations procedures sum up their views and recommendations.

Mayer, Martin. *The Teachers' Strike: New York, 1968*. New York: Harper and Row, 1969. An account of a "great disaster"—the teachers' strike in New York City in 1968. The author places blame for it on the great foundations, the universities, and the mayor's office rather than on the participants in the strike.

National Education Association. *Implementing the Code of Ethics of the Education Profession and Strengthening Professional Rights.* Washington, D.C.: The Association, 1964. Procedures to protect rights and to enforce obligations of educators. Actions of local, state, and national organizations.

NEA Handbook. Published Annually. Washington, D.C.: The Association, 1969. "The purpose of this handbook is to elevate the character and advance the profession of teaching and to promote the cause of education in the United States." Basic data about NEA.

Nolte, M. Chester, ed. *Background Materials on Collective Bargaining for Teachers.* Denver, Colo.: University of Denver, 1968. A collection of available pertinent materials on collective bargaining for teachers. Contains varying points of view, current status of legislation, and issues facing legislators in dealing with demands for legislation.

Schmidt, Charles T., Jr., Hyman Parker, and Bob Repas. *A Guide to Collective Negotiations in Education.* East Lansing, Michigan: Social Science Research Bureau, 1967. An overview of all aspects of the negotiating process for use by those involved in negotiations in the state of Michigan, where laws concerning negotiations became effective earlier than in other states.

Shils, Edward B. and C. Taylor Whittier. *Teachers, Administrators and Collective Bargaining.* New York: Thomas Y. Crowell, 1968. The total area of collective negotiations by two competent authorities.

Stinnett, T. M. *Professional Problems of Teachers,* 3rd ed. New York: Macmillan, 1968. Provides college students preparing for teaching and experienced teachers with information regarding problems they must face as practitioners and as members of the profession.

Stinnett, T. M. *Turmoil in Teaching.* New York: Macmillan, 1968. An account by an experienced NEA worker of conflicts and difficulties as the NEA and the AFT vied power.

AUDIO-VISUAL MATERIALS

Those Who Care (NEA, 20 Min., Color) Policy statements of NEA leaders. Discusses teachers today and describes an individual case study in which NEA legal assistance was required.

The Cutting Edge (NEA, 15 Min., 76 frs.) To stimulate group discussion in leadership training workshops—for orientation of members in understanding local positions of associations.

Quiet Too Long (Guggenheim Productions, Inc., 29 Min.) John Uram and Bill Adams reflect the new militancy among teachers—those who are rising in protest against poor school facilities, teaching conditions and benefits.

Teachers Tenure (National Tape Recording Project, 15 Min.) The question of tenure for teachers and its implications.

Professional Commitment—A Confrontation with Integrity (Educational Filmstrips, 70 frs., Color, Record) Discusses the professional commitment of teachers and educators.

Teaching Today (University of South California, 14 Min. color) Promotes teaching as a top quality professional calling. Analyzes the marks of a profession and shows how school teaching fulfills these qualifications.

# PART TWO

THE NATURE OF AMERICAN SCHOOLS

SIX

HOW DID THE PUBLIC SCHOOLS BEGIN?

One function of this book is to provide you with information so that you can responsibly make some important decisions. In the next two chapters we will consider the public education system, its origin, development, and present challenges. A third chapter will deal with private independent schools, and schools sponsored by religious groups, especially the largest such school system, that of the Roman Catholic Church. In what kind of system will you teach—with the large majority of educators in public schools or with those who teach in either private independent or religiously sponsored schools?

AMERICAN PUBLIC SCHOOLS

There are many things we take for granted. We press a switch and assume the electric lights will come on; we open a book and know there will be print before our eyes; we desire an education and expect the American public school system to provide it. We take so much for granted that we almost forget that there had to be an Edison to discover the uses of electricity, a Gutenberg to invent movable type, a Horace Mann to "invent" the public school system.

Even American historians take American public education so much for granted that they sometimes pay it the dubious compliment of *not* sufficiently including it in their histories. One is apt to find mention of many minor military and industrial figures yet find little recognition of one of the most creative of all American social developments—universal public education.

The idea of universal public education—the opportunity for every child to have a good education sponsored and financed by everyone—is a central idea in American education. The phrase is so familiar you probably consider it an ancient concept; in reality it is uniquely American, and therefore relatively new in the history of educational thought. Education for the elite has far more worldwide historical precedent.

American education has not always been guided by this ideal of universal public education. In fact, the public support part of the idea was not applied to all the major educational levels until the final quarter of the nineteenth century, and educational opportunity for all did not become a reality until into the twentieth century. The history of this unique, complex, and something less than perfect institution is important for you as a potential American teacher. To know what teaching is requires knowing something about the people, processes, and forces which have created it. David Tyack in his *Turning Points in American Educational History* argues in favor of the study of educational history:

As general education for teachers, educational history can rarely be useful or functional in a narrow sense. Instead it should be a kind of knowledge which is interesting and valuable in its own right, though it also can give educators lasting insights and habits of analysis which will benefit them professionally. Inquiry into educational history can assist teachers to interpret and generalize their experience and to free themselves from unexamined routine.[1]

Hopefully, as you prepare for and later practice your chosen specialty, you will continue inquiry into the history of education in more depth than is provided here.

BEFORE UNIVERSAL PUBLIC EDUCATION

Our ancestors from Europe, Asia, and Africa did not bring universal public education with them when they came to the New World. They couldn't, as it had not yet been invented. The most advanced of the continents as to education—Europe—regarded education as a privilege of the wealthy and assumed lack of education inevitable for the masses. So England established tutorial systems and preparatory schools and universities for the children of the prosperous classes. Originally, education was for the children of the landed aristocrats; but increasingly the children of the rising new industrialists were included. Education was still not conceived of as education for all, however; instead it was for the sons (and less frequently for the daughters) of the upper class that they might become the elite leaders of society. It was not until the twentieth century that Europe achieved a school system for children and youth of all social classes.

Some European nations did initiate laws requiring local communities to feed, clothe, and shelter paupers; tied to such legislation were provisions for the schooling of charity cases. In 1601, for example, the English Poor Law was passed, and as a result England developed "charity schools," providing a degree of literacy to some impoverished children.[2] But these charity schools were a far cry from the free public elementary schools that were to develop first in the United States and then in Europe.

---

[1] David B. Tyack, *Turning Points in American Educational History* (Waltham, Mass.: Blaisdell, 1967), p. xii.
[2] Robert Holmes Beck, *A Social History of Education*, Foundations of Education Series (Englewood Cliffs, N.J.: Prentice-Hall, 1965), p. 75.

Page from The New England Primer. *Puritan education was closely associated with Puritan religious beliefs. The hornbook on the following page is now in the Bulkeley Collection of the Connecticut Historical Society.*

EDUCATION IN COLONIAL AMERICA (1600–1776)

To a large extent, colonial life in America was an extension of European, and particularly English, social, political, and commercial systems. As a result, the educational patterns which emerged in the seventeenth century followed European, especially English, models. The Old World dual system of education which provided formal instruction for the upper classes and charity schools and some apprentice training for the lower classes was widely practiced throughout the colonial and early national periods. But there were religious, political, and social forces operative in the American colonies which caused the American educational system to differ significantly from the European tradition.

Most influential of these forces was the religious motive of the Quaker, Catholic, Anglican, and Puritan colonists who early established church sponsored and controlled schools. As the educational historians Butts and Cremin point out, this religious-educational diversity inhibited the development of a strong colonial educational system under English civil control and thereby provided the climate for distinctively American ideas to develop.[3]

[3] R. Freeman Butts and Lawrence A. Cremin, *A History of Education in American Culture* (New York: Henry Holt, 1953), p. 98.

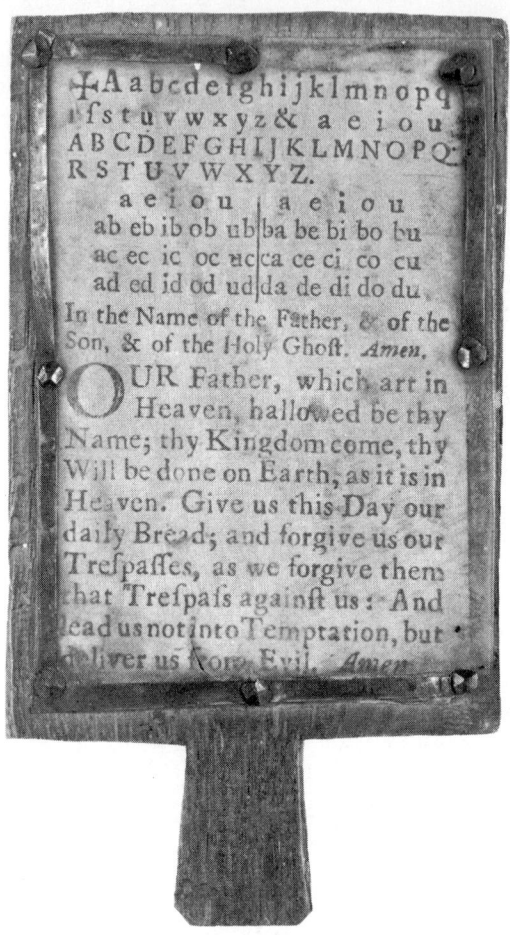

PURITAN INFLUENCE IN NEW ENGLAND

Among no religious group was education more integral to the social and theological order than among the Puritans of New England. In 1629 these English businessmen and craftsmen founded Massachusetts Bay Colony under royal charter to establish a "New Jerusalem" where their rigid Calvinism could be both the religious and civil code. Puritan theology defined both child and adult as sinners, totally depraved and worthy of nothing except God's punishment. Since salvation was always uncertain, it was only natural that the "perfecting of the saints" should be the primary and oftentimes harsh business of the schools.

As early as 1635 the citizens of Boston started the first "public" Latin grammar school for the education of boys between the ages of eight and fifteen. The following year Harvard College was funded from public and private sources and by 1638 was operating in Cambridge, Massachusetts, with one professor and one building. These early schools—models for New England education—placed great emphasis upon the practical Puritan ideal of education for the perpetuation of a "hellfire and damnation" morality, using, paradoxically, the pagan Greek and

Roman classics prominently in the curriculum. The Puritans respected education as instrumental in developing reason, in making man a more willing instrument in the hands of God, in counteracting the wiles of Satan, in providing a learned clergy and literate congregation, and in allowing the Bible to be read from the older Latin translations. Consider, for instance, this excerpt from *The New England Primer* which illustrates the Puritan viewpoint on the proper purpose of reading.

Praise to God for Learning to Read

The praise of my Tongue
   I offer to the Lord
That I was taught and learnt so young
   To read his Holy Word.

That I was brought to know
   The Danger I was in,
By Nature and by Practice too
   A wretched slave to Sin.

That I was led to see
   I can do nothing well;
And whither shall a Sinner flee
   To save himself from Hell.

Dear Lord this Book of thine,
   Informs me where to go
For Grace to pardon all my sin,
   And make me holy too.

Here I can read and learn
   How Christ the Son of GOD
Has undertook our great concern,
   Our Ransom cost his Blood.

And now he reigns above,
   He sends his Spirit down
To show the wonders of his Love,
   And make his Gospel known.

O may that Spirit teach,
   And make my heart receive
Those Truths which all thy Servants preach,
   And all thy Saints believe!

> Then shall I praise the Lord
> in a more cheerful Strain,
> That I was taught to read his Word,
> And have not learnt in vain.[4]

In addition to the Latin grammar schools, so-called "dame schools" operated on a tuition basis. These schools provided reading, ciphering, and religious instruction for a town's young children. For the older child, tax and tuition supported grammar schools appeared as a response to the growing need for education.

As the Bay Colony grew and prospered, the Massachusetts General Court sought to exercise some regulatory influence over education in the various towns with the passage of a 1642 law requiring parents to see to the education of their children or be fined for noncompliance. This act was followed in 1647 by a more important piece of legislation, commonly called "The Old Deluder Satan Act," which required that every village of fifty families provide a school for instruction in reading and writing. Towns of one hundred or more families were required to employ schoolmasters to prepare young boys for college. Considering that by 1647 Massachusetts "had nearly 20,000 people, some 30 towns, 30 to 40 churches, 7 grammar schools, and a college,"[5] the impact of this law is quite impressive.

In the early years of the New England colonies the church and the state were so closely united that they were essentially one. The church, however, was dominant when any differences arose. So colonial Massachusetts was able to impose the Puritan creed on all citizens by state legislation. The phraseology used in the 1647 law stressed the struggle against the Devil, "it being one chief object of the old deluder Satan to keep men from the knowledge of the scriptures as in former times by keeping them in an unknown tongue. . . ." Though the religious motive was dominant, there were other concerns in the 1642 and 1647 Acts. The 1642 Act specified that parents and masters were required to teach children not only "the principles of religion" but also "the capital laws of the country." The 1647 Act was intended to protect the colonist from "the old Deluder," but it also emphasized "that learning may not be buried in the graves of our fathers in Church and Commonwealth." The responsibility for enforcement of such acts was placed with the community's "chosen men appointed to manage the prudential affairs" rather than with any state organization.

Although the New England schools were predecessors of the modern public school insofar as they were under community control, were in theory open to all a town's children, and were partially supported by public funds, they were not free schools in the contemporary sense. Parents were usually obligated to provide additional support in the form of fees and tuition. Also, of course, these schools

---

[4] From the *New England Primer* (Boston: Ginn, Twentieth Century reprint; Boston: Draper, 1785–90).

[5] Edward A. Krug, *Salient Dates in American Education* (New York: Harper and Row, 1966), p. 9.

were not dedicated to free inquiry but to the maintenance of Puritan moral and religious beliefs.

Butts and Cremin have summarized the control of New England schools in the following way:

1. The state could require children to be educated.
2. The state could require towns to establish schools.
3. The civil government could supervise and control schools by direct management in the hands of public officials.
4. Public funds could be used for the support of public schools.[6]

Some change in this pattern developed in the eighteenth century, however, as the colonial legislatures of New England increasingly transferred the control of schools to local districts. This decentralization rapidly took hold and became the dominant system throughout most of America as school districts multiplied with westward expansion.

EDUCATION IN THE MIDDLE AND SOUTHERN COLONIES

Not all of the colonies were as homogeneous in religious allegiance as Massachusetts under the domination of the Puritans. In the Middle colonies, though religion was still a motivating concern in the establishment of schools, diversity of religious beliefs prevailed. Consequently, the state could hardly force one religion upon a diverse people through education. Instead, the responsibility for education was left to a variety of individuals and institutions, including families, churches, religious and philanthropic organizations.

While Puritan education was spreading through the New England colonies, the Dutch Reformed Church in New York and the Quakers in Pennsylvania were among those establishing educational systems in the Middle colonies. Prior to the English takeover of New Amsterdam (New York) in 1664, the Dutch had instituted a civil-controlled educational system under the agency of the Dutch Reformed Church. Following the collapse of Dutch control, these town schools became solely church operated, and other religious sects moved to establish their own schools. William Penn, founding Pennsylvania in 1681, likewise sought to develop state responsibility for education. But state influence later faltered, leaving education under the control of church and private interests during most of Pennsylvania's colonial history.

The Dutch schools were similar in curriculum and method to the Puritan schools, but the Quaker approach to education was much more humane. William Penn, in his *Some Fruits of Solitude in Reflections and Maxims,* said children should "be making of Tools and Instruments of Play; Shaping Drawing, Framing, and Building, &c. than getting some rules of propriety of Speech by Heart. And those also would follow with more Judgment, and less trouble and Time."[7]

[6] Butts and Cremin, p. 103.
[7] Cited in Rena L. Vassar, *Social History of American Education,* vol. 1 (Chicago: Rand McNally, 1965), p. 34.

The Southern colonies were slowest to mandate a system of public-supported education. The system of slavery required an elitist education for the sons of the white gentry who would themselves soon become slave masters; a tutorial system of classical education became the dominant practice. The education of the slave was antithetical to Southern society, and was prohibited by law in many states, as indicated by the following excerpt from a 1740 South Carolina Act prohibiting teaching slaves to write:

XLIV. And whereas, the having of slaves taught to write, or suffering them to be employed in writing, may be attended with great inconveniences: BE IT ENACTED BY ETC. that all and every person and persons whatsoever, who shall hereafter teach, or cause any slave or slaves to be taught to write, or shall use or employ any slave to be taught to write, or shall use or employ any slave as a scribe in any matter of writing whatsoever, hereafter taught to write; every such person and persons, shall, for every such offence, forfeit the sum of $100 current money.[8]

Meanwhile, among the poorer white settlers, there existed a rudimentary or nonexistent education in the home. Consequently, education in the South lagged behind that of the Middle and New England colonies.

THE ENLIGHTENMENT

The eighteenth century saw ideas imported from Europe which challenged the older religious orthodoxies. The resulting shift in thinking has been described by Butts and Cremin:

. . . proposals for change in the older ways of thinking and acting carried appeals to *human* reason rather than divine law, to *natural* rights rather than supernatural rights, to *scientific* method rather than to established truths, to *social* agreements and *individual* freedom rather than authoritarian control, and to *humanitarian* and *democratic* faith rather than aristocratic privilege. The results of this shift in emphasis in intellectual sanctions were felt in theology and religion, in philosophy, and in political, economic, and social theory. They were likewise seen in the emergence of new forms of educational theory and proposals for educational change that eventually led to changes in educational practice.[9]

Prominent among Americans who exemplified the new emphasis on human reason was Benjamin Franklin. Though he lent his insights and talents to a variety of endeavors, his educational proposals are of particular importance as indicative of directions American education would take.

---

[8] *An act for the Better Ordering and Governing of Negroes and Other Slaves in this Province*, in South Carolina, Statutes, *The Public Laws of the State of South Carolina from its Establishment as a British Province down to the Year 1790, inclusive* (Philadelphia: R. Aitkin & Son, 1790), p. 174.

[9] Butts and Cremin, pp. 43–44.

The University of Pennsylvania had its beginnings in Franklin's idea of an academy to teach the young ". . . every Thing that is useful . . ." Courtesy of HPS.

In 1749 he wrote his *Proposals Relating to the Education of Youth in Pennsylvania*, followed in 1751 by the *Idea of the English School, Sketch'd Out for the Consideration of the Trustees of the Philadelphia Academy*. He proposed that an academy for the education of youth be chartered in Philadelphia, suggesting that: "It would be well if they could be taught *every Thing* that is useful, and *every Thing* that is ornamental; But Art is long and their Time is short. It is, therefore, propos'd that they learn those Things that are likely to be *most useful* and *most ornamental,* Regard being had to the several Professions for which they are intended."[10]

The academy was opened in Philadelphia in 1751 with a curriculum patterned after the one outlined by Franklin. Although the school did not long maintain the practical directions Franklin had mapped for it, it presaged the secondary school. The emphasis on English grammar in private schools of this type also led the way for the study of English at all levels and thereby worked to insure that America would be a one-language nation.

EDUCATION IN THE EARLY NATIONAL PERIOD (1776–1865)

Two of the most significant educational events which immediately followed the Revolutionary War were the passage of the Land Ordinance Act of 1785 and the Northwest Ordinance of 1787. First stated in the 1785 law and reinforced by the 1787 legislation was a provision to reserve section 16 of each township of

[10] Cited by Tyack, p. 74.

public land for educational purposes. The Northwest Ordinance, which provided specifically for the territorial organization of that area roughly bounded by the Ohio and Mississippi Rivers and the Great Lakes, contained an often quoted indication of the new government's concern for education. "Religion, morality, and knowledge being necessary to good government and the happiness of mankind, schools and the means of education shall forever be encouraged." Thus, the colonial emphasis upon education was an early tradition of the new nation.

The government instituted by the Articles of Confederation in 1781 was superseded in 1789 by a more centralized government under the present United States Constitution. The new Constitution had nothing specific to say about education; but its silence on this issue is highly significant, for it left education completely under the control of the states rather than laying the foundation for a national system of education. This question of state versus national control has been an important one throughout American educational history; today such debates are evident in conflicts over busing, private segregated schools, and religion in the schools.

There was a relentless trend in the development of American society toward education for all the people. Thomas Jefferson, an advocate of a nation composed of sovereign individual states, probably best expressed the necessity of education in a republic. In a proposal to the Virginia Assembly in 1779, a Bill for the More General Diffusion of Knowledge, Jefferson said:

... it becomes expedient for promoting the publick happiness that those persons, whom nature hath endowed with genius and virtue, should be rendered by liberal education worthy to receive, and able to guard the sacred deposit of the rights and liberties of their fellow citizens, and that they should be called to that charge without regard to wealth, birth or accidental condition or circumstance; ... it is better that such should be sought for and educated at the common expense of all. . . .[11]

He went on to call for a common school system organized and governed on a county basis. All free children were to be provided the first three years tuition free; the superior students were then to be selected and sent to regional grammar schools; yearly, the best students in each grammar school were to be selected and sent to the College of William and Mary for a full college education, all of which would be paid by the public. This plan, calling for only three years of common education, was highly selective in nature. Nevertheless, it was a milestone in the slow move toward universal public education. Regrettably, the Virginia Assembly, imbued with the popular notion that education was a private matter, rejected Jefferson's bill. But the basic ideas were incorporated in legislation passed in 1796 for a comprehensive system of elementary schools and in 1810 for a system of aid from the State of Virginia to counties in order to support public education.

[11] Cited by Vassar, pp. 109–110.

Essentially what Jefferson wanted was the three R's for all, plus the opportunity for bright boys to obtain schooling at the expense of the state. That opportunity, thought Jefferson, must be extended to include university education. So persuaded was Jefferson of the importance of the university that he instructed that his tombstone carry the fact that he was not only the drafter of the Declaration of Independence but also a founder of the University of Virginia.[12]

Jefferson knew that education of the people was essential to freedom. In a letter to Du Pont de Nemours, April 24, 1816, he said, "Enlighten the people generally, and tyranny and depression of body and mind will vanish like evil spirits at the dawn of day."[13] And in a letter to William Charles Jarvis, September 28, 1820, he said, "I know of no safe depository of the ultimate powers of the society but the people themselves; and if we think them not enlightened enough to exercise their control with a wholesome discretion, the remedy is not to take it from them, but to inform their discretion."[14]

Nor was Jefferson alone. As Thayer and Levit point out, "In 1786 Benjamin Rush in Philadelphia produced a plan for the education on a national scale of all American youth, including both sexes, a plan specifically designed to emphasize the principles of democracy and to insure an understanding of the machinery of government with which to maintain the institutions of democracy."[15] Rush also outlined a plan for public schools in Pennsylvania that was comparable to Jefferson's. He called for a four-level system with a free school in each township, an academy in each county, four state colleges, and one state university. He, too, failed to get his plan adopted.

THE COMMON SCHOOL MOVEMENT

Despite these early failures, the first three decades of the nineteenth century were marked by a rising clamor for public schools. This was the "era of the common man," personified by Andrew Jackson who was elected president in 1828 largely as a result of support from the "common people." It was these people, the small farmers, the immigrants, the urban laborers, who most vigorously voiced their demand for schools for their children. Encouraged by the democratic promise, they feared that existing selective educational systems would promote the development of an aristocratic society which would lock their children in the bonds of ignorance and poverty.

It was not that there were no schools. Tyack points out that except in the South and a few rural areas there were schools, but they were a hodgepodge of public, semi-private, private, and religious institutions with little common direction. They certainly did not adequately meet the demands of the new social

---

[12] John Dewey, ed., *The Living Thoughts of Thomas Jefferson* (New York: Fawcett World Library, 1963), p. 9.
[13] John Bartlett, *Familiar Quotations*, Fourteenth Edition (Boston: Little, Brown, 1968), p. 473.
[14] *Ibid.*
[15] V. T. Thayer and Martin Levit, *The Role of the School in American Society* (New York: Dodd, Mead, 1966), p. 59.

conditions—"urbanization, industrialism, immigration, and the democratization of politics."[16]

The movement did not proceed unresisted, however. Religious and private interests which controlled the largely private system of education actively opposed the creation of schools which would lessen their control (in the case of the churches) and profits (in the case of school owners). But public education was gaining more support. Labor spokesmen demanded schools for the children of workers which were not charity schools for paupers or schools dependent upon the whims of rich industrialists. Simultaneously, some of the more perceptive of the middle-class leaders and the imaginative business leaders supported public education for its potential contribution to a prosperous society. As a result, the states increasingly began to set up funds to help communities fulfill their educational responsibilities. Massachusetts became the first state to establish a free, public, tax-supported, common school system.

The first American high school, enrolling 176 boys, opened in Boston in May 1821. By 1823 a school committee was alarmed that seventy-six pupils had dropped out and that some of the teachers had already deviated from the plan in the disposition of the studies. Said the committee, some teachers had even introduced some studies not originally included. The committee urged that the high school maintain its original purpose and that the most useful and practical studies be taught the first year. Confirming its displeasure with the swing toward a strictly academic curriculum, the committee recommended that the high school's name be changed from "The English Classical School" to "The English High School."

HORACE MANN AND PUBLIC EDUCATION

Historians regard Horace Mann as the outstanding nineteenth century proponent of public schools. He was educated in law at Brown University, entered the legal profession in 1823, and was elected to the Massachusetts legislature in 1827. While a member of that body, he led the fight against the state's increasing abdication of responsibility for education and aided in the successful drive for the creation of a State Board of Education. In 1837 he accepted the position of secretary of the board, thus becoming the chief, though somewhat powerless, administrative officer of Massachusetts' public schools.

The energy and vision which he brought to the office soon, however, made it an influential forum for his views. In his reports to the state on the condition of education, Mann combined several arguments to persuade the citizens to support public schools. He played heavily on the self-interests of businessmen and industrialists in pointing out the economic value of education. Simultaneously, he stressed the potential of education for the elimination of both social problems and individual defects. Mann could combine practical economic arguments with appeals to utopian beliefs:

... education has a market value; that it is so far an article of merchandise, that it may be turned to pecuniary account; it may be minted, and will yield a

[16] Tyack, pp. 120–121.

Horace Mann, 1796–1859. Courtesy of the Library of Congress.

larger amount of statuable coin than common bullion. . . . The aim of industry is served, and the wealth of the country is augmented, in proportion to the diffusion of knowledge.[17]

Mann could also make the following sweeping idealistic claim:

. . . there is by nature little or perhaps no distinction among men with respect to their original power of intellect. The seeds of knowledge, of refinement, and of literary excellence are implanted with a liberality, nearly or completely equal, in the mind of the ignorant peasant, and in the mind of the most profound philosopher.[18]

Cremin has summarized the common school idea which Mann so vigorously promoted:

The commanding figure of the early public-school movement, he had poured into his vision of universal education a boundless faith in the perfectibility of human life and institutions. Once public schools were established, no evil could resist their salutary influence. Universal education could be the "great equalizer" of human conditions, the "balance wheel of the social machinery,"

[17] Cited by Thayer and Levit, p. 6.   [18] *Ibid.*, p. 5.

and the "creator of wealth undreamed of." Poverty would most assuredly disappear, and with it the rancorous discord between the "haves" and the "have-nots" that had marked all of human history. Crime would diminish; sickness would abate; and life for the common man would be longer, better, and happier. Here was a total faith in the power of education to shape the destiny of the young Republic. . . . Little wonder that it fired the optimism of the American public.[19]

COMMON SCHOOLS REALIZED

Of course Horace Mann was not the only influential supporter of public schools. He was joined by men such as Henry Barnard, John Pierce, and Samuel Lewis.

The reformers emulated each others' articles in the journals, regarding work in other states as social laboratories for reform ideas. Though ranging from Massachusetts to California, the crusaders came to similar conclusions about the purpose and institutional character of the common school. Out of the diversity of American education in the early nineteenth century had come, by mid-century, a remarkable degree of consensus.[20]

The struggle for educational reform spanned twenty-five years, but by the beginning of the Civil War public supported education at the elementary level was fairly widespread. Cremin sums up the advances made by the common school movement as follows:

A majority of the states had established public school systems, and a good half of the nation's children were already getting some formal education. Elementary schools were becoming widely available; in some states, like Massachusetts, New York, and Pennsylvania, the notion of free public education was slowly expanding to include secondary schools; and in a few like Michigan and Wisconsin, the public school system was already capped by a state university. There were, of course, significant variations from state to state and from region to region. New England, long a pioneer in public education, also had an established tradition of private education, and private schools continued to flourish there. The Midwest, on the other hand, sent a far greater proportion of its school children to public institutions. The southern states, with the exception of North Carolina, tended to lag behind, and did not generally establish popular schooling until after the Civil War.[21]

Public education came about when democratic ideals, labor support, increasing acceptance by the middle classes, and the needs of an increasingly industrial age resulted in a demand for education for more than the few.

---

[19] Lawrence A. Cremin, *The Transformation of the School* (New York: Knopf, Vintage, 1961), pp. 8–9.
[20] Tyack, p. 125.
[21] Cremin, p. 13.

EDUCATION IN EXPANDING AMERICA (1865–1920)

The half century following the Civil War was a period of intense educational activity. The common school gains of the first half of the nineteenth century were consolidated and extended in a variety of important ways. Specifically, the federal government created a Department of Education; Negro education increased; the common school idea was extended to secondary education; public education included the education of the immigrant; and vocational education became an accepted function of the schools.

In 1867 a Department of Education was created by Congress for the purpose of "collecting such statistics and facts as shall show the condition and progress of education in the several States and Territories, and of diffusing such information, respecting the organization and management of schools and school systems, and methods of teaching, as shall aid the people of the United States in the establishment and maintenance of efficient school systems, and otherwise promote the cause of education throughout the country." The name was later changed to the Office of Education in 1868, then to the Bureau of Education in 1870 for 59 years, and finally back to the United States Office of Education in 1929.

The first Commissioner of Education was Henry Barnard, an educator of Horace Mann's era who had made considerable contributions to education as the chief educational officer in Connecticut and Rhode Island. As Cremin notes, however, it was William Torrey Harris, the "commanding figure of his pedagogical era" who towered above post–Civil War commissioners.[22] Prior to his appointment as commissioner, he had distinguished himself as the superintendent of schools in St. Louis from 1868 to 1880. During his superintendency and his tenure as commissioner (1889–1906), he worked to entrench the common school in American tradition.

NEGRO EDUCATION

For the education of the Negro, the post–Civil War period was not a time for consolidation but for beginning. There had been some scattered interest in educating the Negro during the colonial and early national periods, but for the most part the slave of the "cotton" South had been systematically deprived and denied the benefits of education, often by law, since a slave was seen as mere property to be used as necessary for personal gain. To educate the Negro was to threaten the entire social and economic system of the South—a system which through enslavement violated the personal rights and dignity of human beings.

Although the door to education did open somewhat for the Negro before the Emancipation Proclamation, various forces worked to discourage mass education of the black population. The reorganization of education forced by reconstruc-

---

[22] Cremin, p. 8–9.

Tuskegee Institute, Tuskegee, Alabama. Courtesy of Tuskegee Institute.

tion policies was for most Southern states the beginning of free public schools for whites and blacks.

The early progress that was made can be credited primarily to the educational programs of the Freedmen's Bureau and various church groups, the support of northern philanthropists, and the concern of civic leaders in the North. These forces combined to start the slow development of Negro education.

Ultimately, true progress had to await the emergence of Negro leaders. Among this group—which included W. E. B. DuBois, Lucy C. Laney, Mary McLeod Bethune, and Charlotte Hawkins-Brown—Booker T. Washington, founder of Tuskegee Institute (1881), was preeminent. He regarded equality as a commendable goal but one that was probably distant. Consequently, in a speech before the Atlanta Cotton States and International Exposition in 1895, he advanced what has come to be known as the "Atlanta Compromise." He said, "In all things that are purely social we can be as separate as the five fingers, yet one as the hand in all things essential to mutual progress." The fateful idea of "separate but equal" was born. The following year the Supreme Court made it the law of the land in their *Plessy v. Ferguson* decision. Separate school systems were established for the two races, and they were far from equal. Education for Negroes usually was decidedly third rate—separate but not equal.

Although this decision was invalidated by the Supreme Court in 1954 (*Brown v. the Board of Education of Topeka*), de facto segregation has continued throughout many parts of the country. One of the many challenges to education in the 1970s is to provide high quality education without discrimination.

EDUCATION FOR THE IMMIGRANTS

Immigration to the U.S. began in substantial volume in the 1830s and 1840s. Many emigrated from Ireland with the failure of potato crops in 1845–46. After the Civil War large numbers of Englishmen, Germans, Irishmen, and Scandinavians came looking for a better life than Europe had offered them. In the 1880s and 1890s nineteenth century immigration reached its peak with southern and eastern European contributing an increasing share of the almost 9,000,000 newcomers. In the next two decades (1901–1920) more than 14,500,000 people arrived.

From the early part of the nineteenth century, the schools had played an important part in Americanizing the newcomers. As the incoming numbers increased in the 1880s and 1890s, however, education was forced by public opinion to respond in a more systematic and deliberate way. The immigrants who came at this time tended to congregate in urban centers and to retain their languages and cultures. Poverty, anti-immigrant attitudes of the white middle class, and political corruption combined to handicap the immigrants. Many Americans who considered themselves the "true" Americans because their families had been here earlier wanted the schools to absorb these newcomers and to eliminate their "foreign" language and cultural patterns. Education for conformity became for some an ideal. In the late nineteenth century a movement to reform the public schools developed. Though humanitarian motivations were held by some school reformers, such as journalists and social workers, many Americans were largely concerned to assimilate the "new immigrant" into the capitalist economic system and endow him with the "virtues" of the Protestant ethic.

To men such as Professor Ellwood P. Cubberley of Stanford University the new immigration represented a threat to American society. They called for the schools to adopt an explicit policy of Americanization in which Anglo-Saxon values would supplant what they considered the inferior ethnic patterns of immigrants from countries like Italy, Austria-Hungary, and Russia. As a result, more attention was paid to English instruction, civics, American history, and the inculcation of values that white, Anglo-Saxon, Protestant America prized.

Cubberley wrote:

> These Southern and Eastern Europeans were of a very different type from the North and West European who preceded them. Largely illiterate, docile, often lacking in initiative, and almost wholly without the Anglo-Saxon conceptions of righteousness, liberty, law, order, public decency, and government, their coming has served to dilute tremendously our national stock and to weaken and corrupt our political life. . . . Our national life, for the past quarter of a century, has been afflicted with a serious case of racial indigestion.[23]

---

[23] Ellwood P. Cubberley, *Public Education in the United States* (Boston: Houghton Mifflin, 1934), pp. 485–486; also see Ellwood P. Cubberley, *Changing Conceptions of Education* (Boston: Houghton Mifflin, 1909), p. 15.

To assimilate these people into our national life and citizenship is our problem. We must do this and we must, if possible, give them the impress of our peculiar institutions and ideals. National safety and welfare alike demand that we not only teach these peoples to use the English language as our common tongue, but that they be educated also in principles and ideals of our form of government. Even under the best of conditions this will require time, and it calls for a constructive national program if effective work is to be done. Social and political institutions of value are the product of long evolution, and they are safe only so long as they are in the keeping of those who have created them or have come to appreciate them. Our religious, political, and social ideals must be preserved from replacement by less noble ideals if our national character is not to be weakened.[24]

Needless to say, the school did not go unchanged. While the motives many times were based on prejudice, the result was that children of many backgrounds were educated together. And eventually what was learned by educators contributed to the educational move away from a subject matter orientation, characteristic of American education from colonial times, toward a greater concern for the individual and the society in which he lived.

PUBLIC SECONDARY EDUCATION DEVELOPS

It would be a mistake to assume that public elementary and secondary education developed concurrently. The public elementary school was consolidated after the Civil War, but it remained for the educators of the second half of the nineteenth century to extend the common concept up through the secondary level.

The early Latin grammar schools were not strictly secondary schools in the contemporary sense, for their students were not adolescents until the last two or three years. It was the academy, however, which was the prototype of the secondary school to come. Benjamin Franklin's idea had caught on as the nation moved into the nineteenth century, and by 1850 it is estimated that there were 6,000 academies in existence. These schools varied in curriculum from the Latin grammar school classicalism to the more comprehensive English-influenced school of Franklin's type, to the patently vocational school. They were generally not under public control and were not free. They were the best available, but their selectivity was not in the spirit of the democratic ideal which education was increasingly called on to serve.

Consequently, laymen and professional educators alike began to think in terms of a publicly supported educational system spanning the elementary and secondary years. But as the movement started in this direction in the third quarter of the nineteenth century, it met heavy resistance, as had the elementary common school fifty years earlier. Butts and Cremin point out, however, that

---

[24] Ellwood P. Cubberly, *An Introduction to Education* (Boston: Houghton Mifflin, 1925), pp. 26–67.

the earlier fight had been to get education laws on the books while the secondary education issue was centered on whether or not these laws furnished the legal basis for upward extension.[25]

This question was first answered conclusively in the Kalamazoo case of 1874. The Michigan State Supreme Court upheld the Kalamazoo school district's right to collect taxes for the support of a high school. The decision, written by Justice Thomas M. Cooley, pointed out that Michigan had already provided for a tax-supported elementary system and a state university and that it was inconsistent to exclude secondary education. This decision clarified the legal status of public secondary education in Michigan and set the stage for the national expansion of public high schools.

Development to 1890 was slow, however. Raubinger et al. in *The Development of Secondary Education* point out that by 1890 only 203,000 students were enrolled in public high schools as compared to 12,500,000 in public elementary schools. For the approximately 6,000 public high schools in existence by this date, the average enrollment was less than forty.[26] Clearly, much had to be accomplished if universal public secondary education was to become a reality.

VOCATIONAL EDUCATION

As the American economy became increasingly commercial and industrial in makeup, there was a parallel increase in vocational education interest and activity. In the early 1900s industry and organized labor collaborated with the National Society for the Promotion of Industrial Education in supporting the passage of federal legislation to underwrite substantial financial assistance for vocational education. The result was the Smith-Hughes Act of 1917.

Specifically, this legislation allowed the federal government to cooperate "in paying the salaries of teachers, supervisors, and directors of agricultural subjects, and of teachers of industrial subjects, and in the preparation of teachers of agricultural trade and industrial and home economics subjects." The continuing interest in vocational education in the nation's high schools is largely due to this piece of legislation and other laws which followed it.

By 1920 the public schools were somewhat more socially relevant. The decline of classical courses was accompanied by the introduction of vocational agriculture, home economics, business and secretarial training, vocational guidance, and industrial arts.

★ ★ ★

---

[25] Butts and Cremin, p. 418.
[26] Frederick M. Raubinger, et al. (eds.), *The Development of Secondary Education* (London: Collier-Macmillan, 1969), pp. 2–5.

DISCUSSION

1. What does "universal public education" mean to you? Do you support literally education for everybody? Do you believe that public support should apply to all rungs of the educational ladder? What is the case for the alternatives to "universal public education?"
2. React to the statement "The opportunity for a good education for every child and young person paid for by everybody is a central idea in American education." Is this the way it is? Is this the way it ought to be?
3. What accounts for differences between New England education and Middle States education in the American colonies? What accounts for differences between colonial New England education and Southern education?
4. What are the shifts in thinking brought about by ideas from the Enlightenment?
5. Why does Franklin hold a significant place in American education?
6. What was Jefferson's point of view on education? What was the political basis of his educational convictions?
7. How did Jacksonian democracy encourage the development of public schools?
8. What were the views of Horace Mann? How did he use his position to foster public education?
9. What combination of factors fostered public education in nineteenth century America? What stages did education for blacks go through?
10. What were the circumstances which explain why Booker T. Washington took the position on separation of the races that he did? Do you think his position was necessary or a cop-out?
11. What problems did immigration pose for American schools? What support from society did historian Cubberley have for his position on "Americanization" of the immigrant? What criticisms can be directed against his position?
12. How did academies differ from public schools? How did they differ from today's independent schools?
13. What is the significance of the oft-cited Kalamazoo case?
14. What influence did the need for vocational training have on the American public schools program?

INVOLVEMENT

1. To learn more of the tenor of Puritan education, turn to histories of education or collections of early documents to read more about the first learning materials used in American schools.
2. Expand your knowledge of Franklin's ideas through his autobiography and collections of his writings.
3. Expand your knowledge of Jefferson's views through biographies and excerpts from his writings. Study the interrelationship of his educational ideas and his political philosophy.
4. Find out when your college or university was founded. Was it originally a land grant college, a denominational college, state school or other? Report to the class on its background and the place it takes in the history of education.

5. Become more familiar with Horace Mann's contribution through biographies of Mann and books on his educational contributions. Try your hand at using historical sources by finding and reading one of his famous reports to the state on the condition of education.
6. Grow familiar with the lives and accomplishments of nineteenth century Negro leaders. Attempt to understand the total social situation which influenced their convictions and approaches.
7. Trace the development into the twentieth century of ideas as Cubberley's which attribute inferiority to certain "stocks." What are some of the social consequences in our own times of the continuance of such views?
8. Interview your grandparents concerning their educational backgrounds. What changes or innovations in education do they remember as significant in their lives? How do they view education differently from you and your contemporaries?
9. Without indicating the source, try out with friends and family members some of the educational theories characteristic of an historical figure described in this chapter. After obtaining reactions, tell the individual with whom you have been talking the name of the historical figure. Does learning the name affect his agreement or disagreement with the ideas?

BIBLIOGRAPHY

Bailyn, Bernard. *Education in the Forming of American Society.* New York: Random House, 1960. An historical exposition of early American education accompanied by enlightened criticism. The book evaluates Puritanism, philanthropy, race relations, and the growth of sectarianism, among educational forces.

Beck, Robert Holmes. *A Social History of Education.* Foundations of Education Series. Englewood Cliffs, N.J.: Prentice-Hall, 1965. A book for prospective teachers to give them perspective on the social history of education from prehistory to the present.

Bennett, Lerone, Jr. *Confrontation: Black and White.* Baltimore: Pelican Books, 1965. A history of America by a black historian. Stress on past and present conflicts.

Best, John Hardin, ed. *Benjamin Franklin on Education.* New York: Bureau on Publications, Teachers College, Columbia University, 1962. A report of the many contributions made to education by Benjamin Franklin, including the academy and the University of Pennsylvania.

Butts, R. Freeman and Lawrence A. Cremin. *A History of Education in American Culture.* New York: Holt, Rinehart and Winston, 1953. A sound historical foundation upon which to base judgments about American education; this chapter draws on insights from this book.

Cremin, Lawrence A., ed. *The Republic and the School: Horace Mann On the Education of Free Men.* New York: Teachers College, Columbia University, 1957. Horace Mann's legacy—his annual reports.

Cubberley, Ellwood P. *An Introduction to Education.* Boston: Houghton Mifflin, 1925. An introduction to education on which an older generation grew up. Currently criticized for its conservative social orientation by a new generation of educational historians.

———. *Public Education in the United States.* Boston: Houghton Mifflin, 1934. History of education in the United States marked by a nativist interpretation of immigrants and their place in American society.

DuBois. W. E. B. *The Souls of Black Folk.* New York: New American Library, 1969 (original date, 1903).

Good, H. G. *A History of American Education,* 2nd ed. New York: Macmillan, 1962. A comprehensive chronological survey of the philosophical background and developing institutions of American education.

Greene, Maxine. *The Public School and the Private Vision: A Search for America in Education and Literature.* New York: Random, 1965. A contrast of American educational optimism and the darker outlook of such writers as Melville and Hawthorne.

Hillway, Tyrus, ed. *American Education: An Introduction Through Readings.* Boston: Houghton Mifflin, 1964. A collection of basic readings that provides access to the documents and literature of American education.

Holmes, Dwight Oliver Wendell. *The Evolution of the Negro College.* New York: Arno Press, 1969. The circumstances surrounding the establishment and development of the Negro college. The present place and function of this group of schools in the scheme of higher education for America.

Krug, Edward A. *The Shaping of the American High School.* New York: Harper and Row, 1964. The American high school as it developed and matured, as reported by a competent educational historian.

———. *Salient Dates in American Education.* New York: Harper and Row, 1966. Useful chronology of American education.

Mayer, Frederick. *A History of Educational Thought,* 2nd ed. Columbus, Ohio: Charles E. Merrill, 1966. An analysis of the evolution of educational thought from ancient Oriental to modern American concepts, stressing the impact of religious and philosophical ideas and the contributions of leading personalities.

Meyer, Adolph E. *An Educational History of the American People.* 2nd ed. New York: McGraw-Hill, 1967. The vista of American educational history.

Potter, Robert E. *The Stream of American Education.* New York: American Book Company, 1967. Examination of current educational problems in their historical context to enable teachers to evaluate new concerns as they arise.

Thayer, V. T. and Martin Levit. *The Role of the School in American Society.* New York: Dodd, Mead, 1966. History of education marked by abundant discussion of controversial issues. Especially helpful on church–state relations.

Tocqueville, Alexis de. *Democracy in America,* Richard D. Heffner, ed. New York: New American Library, 1960. A classic account of impressions of the new American democracy by a French visitor in 1831–1832. The freshness and wisdom of de Tocqueville's comments and their relevance to today's America.

Tyack, David B. *Turning Points in American Educational History.* Waltham, Mass.: Blaisdell, 1967. Vigorous interpretations by a leading educational historian of the contemporary generation.

Vassar, Rena L., ed. *Social History of American Education.* 2 vols. Chicago: Rand McNally, 1965. The development of education from colonial times to the present. Comprehensive history of American education.

AUDIO-VISUAL MATERIALS

Education in America: The Seventeenth and Eighteenth Centuries (Coronet, 16 Min., Color) The beginnings of American education are re-enacted from the early New England school laws to the Northwest Ordinance. Includes scenes of dame schools, Latin grammar schools, church schools, and pauper schools.

Education in America: The Nineteenth Century (Coronet, 16 Min., Color) Discusses development of schools from the Northwest Ordinance to 1900, including westward movement, change to secular education, rise and decline of district schools, struggle for tax support, and contributions of educational pioneers.

Education in America: Twentieth-Century Developments (Coronet, 16 Min., Color) Effects of industrial revolution, the influence of Binet, Dewey, Thorndike, and others, junior high school movement, growth of graduate school, consolidated schools and effects of new court decisions.

Then and Now (NCAT, Indiana University) A series of 53 programs on the results of what people have said and done in the past. Sample: Americans Plan for Education—Beginning of Public Education—15 Min.

Horace Mann (McGraw-Hill, 43 fr., Color, Record) Shows how Horace Mann was motivated to work for improvement in the schools throughout the United States during a critical early period.

SEVEN

WHAT IS THE WORK OF THE PUBLIC SCHOOLS TODAY?

The past half century has been a period of quest for more significant and appropriate education. The public schools had been created and their powers extended in earlier periods. The question now became what should be the work of public schools in a rapidly changing twentieth century? Concern shifted to the nature of programs of the public schools.

PROGRESSIVE EDUCATION

A PROGRESSIVE MOVEMENT IN EDUCATION

Lawrence A. Cremin in *The Transformation of the School,* by choosing 1876 as the beginning date for his history of progressivism in American education, reminds us that progressive education did not suddenly appear on the American scene in the 1920s. Social forces—including increased interest in vocational education, the development of settlement houses, the campaign to improve country living, the development of science, the emergence of Darwinism, and nineteenth century reformist ideals—contributed to the movement for progressive education before the twentieth century. As early as 1875, Francis W. Parker, a school superintendent whom John Dewey once called the father of progressive education, introduced concepts of progressive education in the schools of Quincy, Massachusetts. At the Centennial Exposition in Philadelphia in 1876, Americans learned about manual training and vocational education developments in Europe. By 1896 John Dewey had established a laboratory school at the University of Chicago to test his emerging theories. Progressive education, according to Cremin, grew out of the Progressive Movement in the emerging urban and industrial civilization of the last half of the nineteenth century.[1] Cremin writes:

Actually, progressive education began as part of a vast humanitarian effort to apply the promise of American life—the ideal of government by, of, and for the people—to the puzzling new urban-industrial civilization that came into being during the latter half of the nineteenth century. The word *progressive* provides the clue to what it really was; the educational phase of American Progressivism writ large. In effect, progressive education began as Progressivism in education; a many-sided effort to use the schools to improve the lives of individuals. In the minds of Progressives this meant several things.

First, it meant broadening the program and function of the school to include direct concern for health, vocation, and the quality of family and community life.

Second, it meant applying in the classroom the pedagogical principles derived from new scientific research in psychology and the social sciences.

Third, it meant tailoring instruction more and more to the different kinds and classes of children who were being brought within the purview of the school . . . .

Finally, Progressivism implied the radical faith that culture could be democratized without being vulgarized, the faith that everyone could share not only in the benefits of the new sciences, but in the pursuit of the arts as well.[2]

In the 1920s, the momentum of the progressive movement in education accelerated. Private schools such as the Ethical Culture Schools and the Walden School in New York City, the Beaver Country Day School in Massachusetts, and the John Burroughs School in St. Louis challenged traditional approaches to education. Schools associated with universities, including the Lincoln School of Teachers College, Columbia University, experimented with progressive programs. Even more significant was the spread of progressive education into suburban public school systems such as Winnetka, Illinois; Bronxville, New York; Shaker Heights, Ohio; and Pasadena, California. City school systems such as Denver, Colorado, also began to initiate programs marked by progressive ideas.

Because of the various personalities and forces behind progressive education, experimentation proceeded in numerous ways and directions. However, progressive education in the 1920s inclined to a child-centered school in which the program reflected the felt needs of the learners. The characteristic progressive school of the 1920s stressed the importance of the drives and interests of individuals, and emphasis was placed on teacher-pupil planning through which young people participated in determining content, methods, and program. Teachers were proud of student activity in self-initiated projects; the focus of instruction moved increasingly from formal subject matter to the self-initiated and self-directed

---

[1] Lawrence A. Cremin, *The Transformation of the School: Progressivism in American Education, 1876–1957* (New York: Alfred A. Knopf, 1961).
[2] Cremin, pp. viii–ix.

Children in a progressive-oriented classroom have opportunities to vary their activities. Courtesy of Education Development Center.

activities of children. Critics, of course, claimed that children were allowed to "run wild."

With worldwide economic depression and the rise of fascism in the 1930s, progressive education became increasingly oriented to social needs and interests. Rather than stressing the importance of child needs alone, progressive schools attempted to include content to help Americans meet urgent and pressing social problems. Consequently, progressive schools of the 1930s included in their programs studies of international relations and alternatives for the American economy.

The issues of secondary education which seemed important to educators in the middle thirties were stated by the Department of Secondary School Principals of the National Education Association as follows:

1. Shall secondary education be provided at public expense for all normal individuals or for only a limited number?
2. Shall secondary education seek to retain all pupils in school as long as they wish to remain, or shall it transfer them to other agencies under educational supervision when, in the judgment of the school authorities, these agencies promise to serve better the pupils' immediate and probably future needs?
3. Shall secondary education be concerned only with the welfare and progress of the individual, or with these only as they promise to contribute to the welfare and progress of society?

4. Shall secondary education provide a common curriculum for all, or differentiated offerings?
5. Shall secondary education include vocational training or shall it be restricted to general education?
6. Shall secondary education be primarily directed toward preparation for advanced studies or shall it be primarily concerned with the value of its own courses, regardless of a student's future academic career?
7. Shall secondary education accept conventional school subjects as fundamental categories under which school experiences shall be classified and presented to students, or shall it arrange and present experiences in fundamental categories directly related to the performance of such functions of secondary schools in a democracy as increasing the ability and the desire better to meet socio-civic, economic, health, leisure-time, vocational, and pre-professional problems and situations?
8. Shall secondary education present merely organized knowledge, or shall it also assume responsibility for attitudes and ideals?
9. Shall secondary education seek merely the adjustment of students to prevailing social ideals, or shall it seek the reconstruction of society?
10. Granting that education is a "gradual, continuous, unitary process," shall secondary education be presented merely as a phrase of such a process, or shall it be organized as a distinct but closely articulating part of the entire educational program, with peculiarly emphasized functions of its own?[3]

The impact of the progressive movement on education was obvious.

EVALUATION OF PROGRESSIVE EDUCATION

As progressive education developed, interest in evaluating its outcomes grew. Consequently, the Progressive Education Association, formed in 1919, appointed a Commission on the Relation of School and College. In the 1930s 300 colleges and universities agreed to cooperate in an eight-year experiment and to release a selected group of secondary schools from the usual pattern of requirements for college admission. Students from the progressive high schools would be admitted to college and a careful evaluation would be made of the success of these students in college. The resulting study, sometimes called the Eight-Year Study or the Thirty Schools Study involved 1,475 matched pairs of students. Each graduate from the thirty schools was matched with another student in the same college who had taken the prescribed courses, who had graduated from some school not participating in the study, who had met the usual entrance requirements, who was of the same age, sex, race, scholastic aptitude scores, home and community background, interests, and even probable future. The college follow-up found that the graduates of the thirty schools:

---

[3] Department of Secondary Principals of the National Education Association, "The *Issues* of Secondary Education," Bulletin No. 59 (Washington, D.C.: The Association, January, 1936).

1. Earned a slightly higher total grade average.
2. Earned higher grade averages in all subject fields except foreign language.
3. Specialized in the same academic fields as did the comparison students.
4. Did not differ from the comparison group in the number of times they were placed on probation.
5. Received slightly more academic honors in each year.
6. Were more often judged to possess a high degree of intellectual curiosity and drive.
7. Were more often judged to be precise, systematic, and objective in their thinking.
8. Were more often judged to have developed clear or well-formulated ideas concerning the meaning of education—especially in the first two years in college.
9. More often demonstrated a high degree of resourcefulness in meeting new situations.
10. Did not differ from the comparison group in ability to plan their time effectively.
11. Had about the same problems of adjustment as the comparison group, but approached their solutions with greater effectiveness.
12. Participated somewhat more frequently, and more often enjoyed, appreciative experiences in the arts.
13. Participated more in all organized student groups except religious and "service" activities.
14. Earned in each college year a higher percentage of nonacademic honors (officership in organizations, election to managerial societies, athletic insignia, leading roles in dramatic and musical presentations).
15. Did not differ from the comparison group in the quality of adjustment to their contemporaries.
16. Differed only slightly from the comparison group in the kinds of judgments about their schooling.
17. Had a somewhat better orientation toward the choice of a vocation.
18. Demonstrated a more active concern for what was going on in the world.[4]

The College Follow-Up Staff said:

Some of the differences were not large, but wherever reported, they were consistent for each class. It is apparent that when one finds even small margins of difference for a number of large groups, the probability greatly increases that the differences cannot be due to chance alone.

It is quite obvious from these data that the Thirty Schools graduates, as a group, have done a somewhat better job than the comparison group whether

---

[4] Wilford M. Aiken, *The Story of the Eight-Year Study*, vol. 1 in Commission on the Relation of School and College of the Progressive Education Association (ed.), Adventure in American Education Series (New York: Harper and Bros., 1942); also, pp. 199–200 in Frederick M. Raubinger et al., *The Development of Secondary Education* (London: Collier-Macmillan, 1969).

success is judged by college standards, by the students' contemporaries, or by the individual students.[5]

If the proof of the pudding lies in these groups and a good part of it does, then it follows that the colleges got from these most experimental schools a higher proportion of sound, effective college material than they did from the more conventional schools in similar environments. If colleges want students of sound scholarship with vital interests, students who have developed effective and objective habits of thinking, and who yet maintain a healthy orientation toward their fellows, then they will encourage the already obvious trend away from restrictions which tend to inhibit departures or deviations from the conventional curriculum patterns.[6]

In the 1940s, the Educational Policies Commission of the National Education Association and the American Association of School Administrators proposed better programs for two illustrative communities, which the commission called Farmville and American City. They called for a common learnings course, interdisciplinary in nature, as an important component of secondary education to deal with the major personal and social problems of young people of high school age. The Commission set forth ten imperative needs of youth:

1. All youth need to develop salable skills and those undertakings and attitudes that make the worker an intelligent and productive participant in economic life. To this end, most youth need supervised work experience as well as education in the skills and knowledge of their occupations.
2. All youth need to develop and maintain good health and physical fitness.
3. All youth need to understand the rights and duties of the citizen of a democratic society, and to be diligent and competent in the performance of their obligations as members of the community and citizens of the state and nation.
4. All youth need to understand the significance of the family for the individual and society, and the conditions conducive to successful family life.
5. All youth need to know how to purchase and use goods and services intelligently, understanding both the values received by the consumer and the economic consequences of their acts.
6. All youth need to understand the methods of science, the influence of science on human life, and the main scientific facts concerning the nature of the world and of man.
7. All youth need opportunities to develop their capacities to appreciate beauty in literature, art, music, and nature.
8. All youth need to be able to use their leisure time well and to budget it wisely, balancing activities that yield satisfactions to the individual with those that are socially useful.

---

[5] Dean Chamberlin et al., *Did They Succeed in College?* vol. 4, Commission on the Relation of School and College of the Progressive Education Association (ed.), Adventure in American Education Series (New York: Harper and Bros., 1942); in Raubinger et al., p. 200.
[6] *Ibid.*, Raubinger et al., p. 201.

9. All youth need to develop respect for other persons, to grow in their insight into ethical values and principles, and to be able to live and work cooperatively with others.
10. All youth need to grow in their ability to think rationally, to express their thoughts clearly, and to read and listen with understanding.[7]

But many high schools disregarded the needs-oriented recommendations of *Education for All American Youth* or the proposals of the Progressive Education Association. When the typical high school experimented with the "ten imperative needs," such as the need to be an intelligent consumer, it more often offered an elective course or placed an emphasis on the problem in an established course, such as consumer education, rather than creating the interdisciplinary "common learnings" course. Most high schools continued to stress college preparatory programs, supplemented by vocational offerings for the non–college bound.

During World War II, the energies of the nation and school men turned increasingly to the international struggle. Reconstruction of the program of the schools assumed a subordinate position and when it did occur it was often in the interest of meeting wartime demands for manpower and homefront support. The report of the Eight-Year-Study was given less attention than it would have been given had it not been published during World War II.

REACTIONS AGAINST PROGRESSIVE EDUCATION

RIGHT WING CRITICISM

Reactionary rightist criticism of the public schools flourished in the early 1950s. Public school education was condemned by some as communistic and socialistic, as godless and atheistic, and as disloyal and unpatriotic. This wave of criticism, coinciding with the late Senator Joseph McCarthy era, represented an educational counterpart to the McCarthyism which accused government employees of being disloyal, liberals of having communist sympathies, and the United States Army of harboring traitors. The National Education Association was portrayed by some rightists as a part of a communist conspiracy to take over the country.

A cause célèbre of the period was that of Willard Goslin, an outstanding American educator. Goslin, as superintendent of schools in Pasadena, California, was assailed because of his support for UNESCO, his inclusion of sex education in the curriculum, his concern for Negroes, his advocacy of racial integration, and his support of progressive education. A vigorous reactionary minority forced his resignation.[8]

---

[7] Educational Policies Commission, *Education for All American Youth* (Washington, D.C.: NEA, 1944), pp. 225–226.
[8] David Hulburd, *This Happened in Pasadena* (New York: Macmillan, 1951).

In attempted responses to criticisms of the public schools, educators faced a familiar dilemma. On the one hand, the public schools belong to the people and should never be exempt from critical examination and appraisal by the people; nor should schoolmen be unduly defensive or smug about claimed achievement for schools. On the other hand, the attacks on the schools were incited and supported by a minority and were manifestly unfair and distorted. Schoolmen had to resist or good school systems would be picked off one by one.

ACADEMIC CRITICISM

A second major wave of criticism of education came from a quite different source, the academic critics of progressive education. Because this criticism immediately succeeded that of the reactionary right wing, and because the academic critics also singled out progressive education as a foe, some educators mistakenly lumped the two criticisms. Actually, the academic criticism was an expression of an educational counter-philosophy to the progressive education philosophy which had contributed to what historian Cremin called "the transformation of the school."

The academic critics were led by Arthur Bestor, a liberal arts professor at the University of Illinois, and by Hyman Rickover, an admiral in the United States Navy and the developer of the nuclear-powered submarine. They urged an alternative conception of education. Steadily maintaining that they were supporters and not enemies of public education, the academic critics called for an end to "life adjustment education" and "life problems in schools." Instead they called for increased emphasis upon the separate disciplines of knowledge. Bestor, an historian, described the social studies as "social stew." He urged the teaching of history, geography, and political science as separate disciplines rather than as taught in interrelationship with each other:

> The "social studies" purported to throw light on contemporary problems, but the course signally failed, for it offered no perspective on the issues it raised, no basis for careful analysis, no encouragement to ordered thinking. There was plenty of discussion, but it was hardly responsible discussion. Quick and superficial opinions, not balanced and critical judgments, were at a premium. Freedom to think was elbowed aside by freedom not to think, and undisguised indoctrination loomed ahead. I am surprised at how accurately we as students appraised the course. I cannot now improve on the nickname we gave it at the time: "social stew."[9]

Bestor generalized his arguments in another statement and referred to all the disciplines:

> What is falsely called "integration" in most secondary schools and many colleges is actually a fallacious but disguised attempt to bypass the stage of

---

[9] Arthur Bestor, *The Restoration of Learning* (New York: Alfred A. Knopf, 1955), pp. 142–143.

analysis entirely . . . the programs themselves, when examined with care, turn out to be schemes for finding a shortcut to intellectual discipline. They propose, contrary to all reason and experience, to train men to perform the culminating acts of thought while skipping all the antecedent steps . . . we must remember . . . that the various disciplines can only be coordinated; they cannot be fused. If a real synthesis of knowledge is to take place, it must take place in the mind of the student. Our responsibility as teachers is to aid him in acquiring a range of intellectual powers—each clear-cut, precise, and controlled—which he can employ in various combinations to solve problems that may never arise in our lifetimes.[10]

Rickover, alarmed at what he saw as the Soviet threat to American military strength, charged that neglect of science and mathematics by the schools had weakened the American capacity to survive in a physically dangerous world:

. . . the Russians are increasing their engineering and scientific talent faster than we are. Mr. Allen Dulles, director of our Central Intelligence Agency, estimated that between 1950 and 1960 Soviet Russia will have graduated 1,200,000 scientists and engineers, compared with 900,000 in the United States. And by 1960 it is estimated she will have more scientists and engineers than we. Thereafter, the situation will steadily worsen unless we take steps to upgrade mathematics and science teaching in the high schools and increase enrollment in our engineering colleges.[11]

The greatest mistake a nation can make is to underestimate a potential enemy. Russian engineering and scientific development constitute a threat to our military power. We cannot allow this challenge to stand and I, for one, do not believe that a democracy must of necessity be less efficient than a total state . . . it has been evident some years now that our scientific training is deteriorating. Yet we have done little about it. The first step we must take is to improve the technical and scientific training of our young people. We are faced with a national problem of the first order and nothing less than an overriding effort by all of us will meet it. There is no lack of knowledge of *what* must be done.[12]

Bestor's and Rickover's criticisms were supported by others, such as Mortimer Smith, president of the educationally conservative Council for Basic Education, Albert Lynd who wrote *Quackery in the Public Schools* and *And Madly Teach,* and John Keats, a journalist, who wrote *Schools Without Scholars.*

RECONSTRUCTION OF DISCIPLINES

The academic critics' school of thought received its greatest support from an external development—the launching of the first space vehicle, a Sputnik, by the Russians in 1957. In the United States anxiety intensified as people feared for the survival of the nation as Russia moved ahead in the space race.

[10] *Ibid.,* pp. 61–65.
[11] Hyman G. Rickover, *Education and Freedom* (New York: E. P. Dutton, 1959), p. 45.
[12] *Ibid.,* pp. 50–51.

Sputnik and the accompanying ferment gave impetus to a movement to reexamine subject matter. Americans were appalled at the notion that our great technology was not as effective in space probing as that of the Soviet Union. National pride was offended; national goals were threatened; physical survival seemed at stake.

Consequently, national legislation to support certain aspects of education was sponsored. Selected subjects were fostered and favored for their potential usefulness in defense of the nation. One highly influential piece of national legislation that singled out certain fields for financial support made no secret of the intention of the congressional sponsors—the National Defense Education Act. This 1958 legislation supported training, equipment, and programs in fields judged vital to defense. Science, mathematics, modern languages, and guidance were selected for favor. Preferential treatment was often accompanied by stern warnings that upon these fields depended survival of a free people. Americans were warned that they were living in a world in which communism moved relentlessly forward.

Both national interest and available funds coincided. Scholars had a genuine opportunity to reconstruct the content of their separate subjects, first on the high school level, later at the elementary school level. To many leaders of reconstruction of the separate subjects the way to proceed seemed to be to call together university scholars who most intimately knew a particular subject. Some skilled high school or elementary school teachers of the subject who could be of special help at the methodological level were also often included. Funds were readily available from either the federal government or from foundations. As a result there were meetings and conferences at which specialists attempted to discard the obsolescent and to include necessary new knowledge. Staffs of specialists then worked out new content and approaches.

The scholars who reconstructed the subject matter which they knew best were capable people. Many of them recognized that many pupils were simply amassing isolated bits of knowledge. Scholars stressed, instead, the understanding of concepts and principles, the development of processes of inquiry, and the understanding of relationships. The better among the scholars developed genuinely new insights into education; others contributed little more than reaffirmation of insights which leaders in professional education had long taken for granted. The ideas of John Dewey and the other leaders of progressive education were often rediscovered and restated. Less perceptive scholars occasionally proclaimed already established insights as their personal new discoveries. One result of the work in the separate subject matters was that new and improved course content developed. Obsolescent materials were discarded; new content was developed.

Unfortunately some educators adopted new programs for the disciplines without sufficient scrutiny of the claims of the proponents; some hastened to jettison any general education which was interdisciplinary, and some proclaimed progressive education obsolete. Any passing bandwagon attracted many so-called educators.

Ironically, such flights from convictions took place despite sober second

A school in Appalachia. Courtesy of Bill Strode.

thoughts by many scholars. In developing the study of the disciplines, the scholars found that a fundamental progressive education doctrine—the importance of inquiry—was essential. Increasingly, they subscribed to the importance of motivation, another staple in the progressive creed. Increasingly, the scholars recognized the importance of interdisciplinary studies in a scholarly world in which disciplines stubbornly rejected the isolation of each from the other.

So the academic criticism of modern education, which began with glorification of academic learning and rejection of interdisciplinary studies of significant problems, increasingly settled for a hybridization of academic and progressive insights.

THE CAMPAIGN FOR THE DISADVANTAGED

CRITICISMS OF RELEVANCE OF EDUCATION TO DISADVANTAGED

Meanwhile, a counterforce to overemphasis on academic education was developing. It took the form of criticism of academic education as irrelevant to the needs of disadvantaged children and youth. To the emerging social critics, the forgotten Americans of the 1960s were the poor, including many blacks and other minority group members.

Suburban school; compare with photo on previous page. Courtesy of Morton Tadder.

The campaign for the disadvantaged was supported governmentally. Aided by the efforts of the National Education Association, the 88th U.S. Congress in 1964 broadened the National Defense Education Act to include improvement of the qualifications of individuals "who are engaged in or preparing to engage in the teaching or supervising, or training of teachers of history, geography, modern foreign languages, reading, or English in elementary or secondary schools"[13] and those "who are engaged in or preparing to engage in the teaching of disadvantaged youth and are, by virtue of their service or future service in elementary or secondary schools, enrolling substantial numbers of culturally, economically, socially, and educationally handicapped youth in need of specialized training."[14]

The Civil Rights Law of 1964 contained provisions to "render technical assistance to such applicant (school boards, etc.) in the preparation, adoption, and implementation of plans for the desegregation of public schools," "for special training designed to improve the ability of teachers, supervisors, counselors, and other elementary or secondary school personnel to deal effectively with special educational problems occasioned by desegregation," for "in-service training in dealing with problems incident to desegregation," and for employment of "specialists to advise in problems incident to desegregation."[15]

[13] Public Law 88–665, National Defense Education Act Amendments, 1964, Title XI.
[14] *Ibid.*
[15] Public Law 88–352, Civil Rights Act of 1964, Title IV.

Head Start programs have attempted to expose the disadvantaged to more varied experiences. Courtesy of Michael Sullivan from Black Star.

In 1964, the Congress also enacted an Economic Opportunity Act (the so-called Anti-Poverty Bill) which was intended to help the culturally disadvantaged avoid cultural obsolescence.[16] The Manpower Development and Training Act Amendment developed programs to train unemployed youth and functional illiterates.[17] President Lyndon B. Johnson hoped that he would be remembered as the president who fostered education; it is a sad irony that he may be remembered instead for the Vietnam War.

With funds available and national interest aroused—the same combination that prevailed when reconstruction of the disciplines flourished—a variety of programs to aid the disadvantaged were developed. Best known is Head Start, a program for preschool children from culturally disadvantaged backgrounds. The theory supporting Head Start was that poor children, including many blacks and minority group members, were socially disadvantaged as compared to middle-class children because of the lack of opportunities for good audio-lingual development, limited neighborhood and community trips with family members, and few stimulating experiences or materials, such as books and educational toys. A preschool experience, it was urged, would provide disadvantaged children the head start needed so that they might enter the first grade at the same level as middle-class children.

The same concept of compensation for social deprivation characterized such junior and senior high school programs as New York City's Higher Horizons. The idea was to open up greater opportunities for slum youth through increased guidance, remedial programs, parental education, and—the most highly pub-

---

[16] Public Law 88–452, Economic Opportunity Act, 1964.
[17] Public Law 88–214, Manpower Development and Training Act Amendment, December 19, 1963.

licized aspect of the programs—trips to historical locations and cultural institutions. For instance, New York City's Higher Horizons students visited Franklin D. Roosevelt's home in Hyde Park, college campuses, Philharmonic concerts, and the Modern Art and Metropolitan museums.

Similarly, at the precollege level, Upward Bound programs were developed for disadvantaged students who required some degree of additional help beyond their high school programs in order to qualify for college entrance. During the summers, such young people attended special high school or college classes, received help from tutors and remedial education specialists, and had such group experiences as trips, living in college dormitories, etc.

In addition to many such programs as the above, schools adapted content to the special needs of the culturally deprived students. New textbooks were developed especially at the primary levels to recognize the variety of skin colors of Americans. Some early efforts were rightly dismissed as "color me brown" books—the same textbooks except for darker faces. Increasingly, books adapted to the realities of urban life and the actualities of the black experience were published. Historians rewrote textbooks to include the black experience and to weed out prejudicial statements. Progressive education techniques such as planning with students, recognition of learner needs, attempts to identify and use relevant content came back into vogue as their necessity became apparent, though the term progressive education stayed out of style.

Yet, by the 1970s, compensatory education, as such programs came to be called, was not a success when measured by realistic evaluators using objective measures. Societal handicaps, disadvantaged family backgrounds, and educational inadequacies were harder to overcome than optimists had thought. Researcher James Coleman, for instance, described the problems facing attempts to develop such programs:

> Several points are obvious: It is not a solution simply to pour money into improvement of the physical plants, books, teaching aids, of schools attended by educationally disadvantaged children. For other reasons, it will not suffice merely to bus children to otherwise achieve pro forma integration.
>
> The only kinds of policies that appear in any way viable are those which do not seek to improve the education of Negroes and other educationally disadvantaged at the expense of those who are educationally advantaged. This implies new kinds of educational institutions, with a vast increase in expenditures for education—not merely for the disadvantaged, but for all children. The solutions might be in the form of educational parks, or in the form of private schools paid by tuition grants (with federal regulations to insure racial homogeneity), public (or publicly subsidized) boarding schools (like the North Carolina Advancement School), or still other innovations. This approach also implies reorganization of the curriculum within schools.
>
> Such curricular innovations are possible—but again, only through the investment of vastly greater sums in education than currently occurs.[18]

[18] James S. Coleman, "The Imbalance in Educational Opportunity," p. 66 in William P. Lineberry (ed.), New Trends in the Schools (New York: W. W. Wilson, 1967).

SOME PROBLEMS OF AMERICAN PUBLIC EDUCATION

A fair analysis requires the recognition that in recent years some Americans have concluded that universal public education has failed in several areas.[19] It has not yet provided a relevant education for blacks who experienced centuries of slavery followed by decades of enforced segregation. It has failed the children of many poor Americans, whatever their skin color. It has not produced the social understandings which Jefferson said were requisite for an educated citizenry. It has not solved the social and personal problems which Horace Mann confidently anticipated that it would soon conquer. In the 1970s public education, because of such failures, is under attack by many who judge it inadequate.

Criticisms of big city schools are particularly vigorous. Some blacks, despairing of help from the entrenched bureaucracies of large public school systems, call for decentralized education in large cities. They favor greater community control of schools in black ghettos. They believe that black schools manned by black teachers would be superior to the present centralized city systems largely controlled and staffed by whites. Those, both black and white, who disagree see this course as the road back to segregation.

The viewpoint of militant blacks is still within the tradition of support for public education. Indeed, it may be argued that the contemporary black demands for black community control are simply an extension of Jefferson's decentralization concept. But whether decentralization is the best way to achieve good education in a nation characterized by increasing centralization in government is difficult to determine.

Some critics of public education even express the belief that rather than universal tax-supported education, individuals should be given a sum for education to spend as they see fit, in public, private, or parochial schools. Competition among such schools, accompanied by accountability through rigorous appraisal of results, would be an improvement for education, it is argued. To those who oppose this, the danger of throwing out the baby with the bath seems imminent.

But experimentation with "tickets to schools" began, and on June 4, 1970, the *New York Times* reported:

The Federal Government is planning in the fall of 1971 to establish in one or two localities an "education voucher" system under which parents who are dissatisfied with their neighborhood schools could "buy" alternative forms of education for their children.

All parents in the locality would receive a voucher, or ticket into the classroom, for each child of elementary school age. The voucher would be equal in value to the local public schools' current per-pupil expenditure on education.

A parent would then enroll his child in any public school in the experimental district—including the neighborhood school—or in any private school that chose

---

[19] See Rush Welter, *Popular Education and Democratic Thought in America* (New York: Columbia University Press, 1962), and Henry J. Perkinson, *The Imperfect Panacea: American Faith in Education, 1865–1965* (New York: Random, 1968).

Dispute over community control of school, Brooklyn, N.Y. Courtesy of Ted Cowell from Black Star.

to take part in the program. Upon his child's enrollment, the parent would give the voucher to the school, which in turn would present it to the local government for reimbursement.

The voucher plan, which has been discussed in some quarters for years, appears to be coming to fruition at a time when public schools in urban areas are under increasing attack by dissatisfied parents and students who believe that administrators and boards of education are unresponsive to their complaints.

"There is sort of a general agreement that the traditional, politically controlled system for keeping educators accountable has broken down in the big cities," Christopher S. Jencks of Harvard University, chief author of the plan, said in an interview today.

The plan also comes at a time when some parents and students in a number of cities are leaving the traditional schools and setting up their own classrooms.

School integration has been one of the U.S.'s foremost dilemmas in the past few decades. Courtesy of Paul Conklin.

A major objective of the voucher experiment would be to stimulate the establishment of such alternatives to publicly managed education, thereby spurring competition for the public schools.[20]

The voucher plan was immediately criticized by those who instead called for greater investment in public school education in the slums and the ghettos of the inner cities. The president of the American Federation of Teachers warned that the voucher plan would bring more problems than it would solve, including "hucksterism" as competing schools attempted to sell parents on their peculiar merits. The chairman of a commission on law and social action of the American Jewish Congress saw the plan as a disaster for the country because of the possible proliferation of hundreds of school systems segregated on the basis of religion.[21]

[20] *New York Times* (June 4, 1970), pp. 1, 36.
[21] *Education U.S.A.*, National School Public Relations Association (July 1, 1970), p. 225.

Private school in Canton, Miss. established to avoid desegregation. Courtesy of UPI.

WHETHER OR NOT TO TEACH IN PUBLIC SCHOOLS

In American education, the dominant position is certainly occupied by the public school system. So dominant is it, as the figures cited earlier in Chapter One indicate, that for many young teachers the question of whether to teach in public schools is academic. Clearly, public education is where the overwhelming majority of the nation's youth and teachers are.

When a conscious decision to teach in the public school system is made by new teachers, some material factors are also taken into account. Public school teaching usually offers better pay, more security, and firmer tenure than teaching in either independent private schools or religiously sponsored schools. Too, in many public schools the available equipment and resources are more numerous and superior to that of nonpublic schools. For some new teachers, these material considerations are a determining factor.

Yet there are also some factors which have to do with the mission of public education. Some teachers will regard these factors as self-evident; others will consider them as idealistic, a word they use as synonymous with sentimental. How you view these factors depends on your social point of view. For, as even a cursory survey of the development of public education indicates, American public education is a great American experiment based on a faith that the common man is educable and that education for all is essential to democracy. Thus, to many prospective educators, American public education with all of its difficulties and complexities is the place where the action truly is. It is the opportunity to realize the American dream through the education of all, regardless of race, creed, or class; it is the opportunity to make a better world.

Doubters point out that, given our social structures, education in public schools is often racially segregated, and sometimes exclusive and socially classified. As evidence they point to both ghetto and homogenized suburban schools. Others are appalled by the extent of the challenge of educating the disadvantaged and underprivileged. To them, the American dream of a viable public school system for all is an unattainable dream.

So the question of whether or not to teach in the public school system eventually comes down to the matter of one's basic philosophy and aspirations.

★ ★ ★

DISCUSSION

1. How did the progressive movement in education come about? Did John Dewey "invent" progressive education?
2. What is the essential meaning of a "child-centered school"? What weaknesses or strengths do you see in such a school program?
3. Why did an increasing social orientation come into the progressive education movement? Do you see any possible strengths or weaknesses in a socially oriented school program?
4. What were the fundamental findings of the Thirty Schools Study? What are the implications of such findings for college entrance? For school programs? For controversies on education? Why was so little attention paid to the Thirty Schools Study after it was completed?
5. How did the report of the Educational Policies Commission on ten imperative needs of youth reflect the emphases of the progressive education movement?
6. Why do most high schools continue to stress separate subject college preparatory programs rather than create the interdisciplinary "common learnings" course?
7. What was the nature of right wing criticism of public schools in the 1950s? What dilemmas did educators face in attempting to respond to such criticism?
8. How did the academic criticism of education in the 1950s differ from right wing criticism? What did the two have in common?
9. What was Arthur Bestor's fundamental criticism of progressive education? How is this similar to or different from Admiral Hyman Rickover's?
10. What social events in America and the world contributed to the reconstruction of certain disciplines in American schools during the 1950s?
11. How did the scholars perceive their task of reconstructing the disciplines? How did they proceed? What were some of their triumphs and perplexities?
12. What accounts for the development of educational concern for the culturally disadvantaged? What legislative enactments supported programs for the disadvantaged?
13. So far, how successful has the campaign against culturally disadvantaged backgrounds been? Which programs are currently receiving support? Which programs seem to be minimized today?

14. What social problems hinder the programs of compensatory education of yesterday and today?
15. Some critics say that American education is failing. In what respect? Do you agree?
16. What proposals are currently being made for the improvement of education in large cities?
17. What are the pros and cons of the voucher plan? How would it affect American public education and financial support for public education? How would it affect parochial schools? Segregated schools? Independent schools?
18. What have been the latest Supreme Court rulings involving education? What has been the latest legislation enacted that affects education?
19. What advantages and disadvantages can you see in teaching in the American public school system? How might a decision to teach or not to teach in the public schools be related to one's philosophy of life? Philosophy of education?

INVOLVEMENT

1. Learn which school available to you for a visit is popularly regarded as the "best" school in the community or region. Visit the school to observe whether it has characteristics of what has been termed progressive education. In what ways does it differ from what you understand progressive education to be? Do you see evidence of child-centering? Do you see evidence of social orientation?
2. Seek out the reports of the Thirty Schools Study. Through the indexes to the volumes, locate the names of schools nearest to your own geographical situation. Read about these schools and compare or contrast their present programs with their programs of that era.
3. Interview three persons who were young adults during the depression years (1929–1935). Do they see the depression as related to educational failures? As a force for change in the pattern of public education?
4. From news weeklies, and reports by educational journals, determine what are the current criticisms of schools by right wing forces in America; left wing forces. To what extent are the criticisms similar to those of the 1950s?
5. Review your own educational experience to determine whether the projects which followed the launching of Sputnik influenced your own high school experiences and education. In retrospect how do you see the importance and significance of these projects? Do you have any criticisms of them?
6. Visit some outstanding contemporary compensatory programs for the disadvantaged. After asking questions of teachers and sponsors, reach some tentative conclusions on their influence and success. (Caution: quick conclusions may be inaccurate.)
7. Visit an Upward Bound program for high school students and a Head Start program for young children. What do they have in common and how do they differ?
8. Obtain recent figures for unemployment and for persons on welfare rolls in the United States. Look carefully at percentages, at trends. Do these comparisons lead you to form any theories about the needs of people today?
9. Interview the director of the local unemployment services to obtain his view on the success or failure of the Manpower Development and Training Act and its programs to train unemployed youth and functional illiterates.

10. Draw up your own bill of particulars in support of American public education and in criticism of American public education. Venture possible improvements.
11. Foster a debate on whether or not to teach in American public schools.

BIBLIOGRAPHY

Bernstein, Abraham. *The Education of Urban Populations.* New York: Random House, 1967. An introduction to education for urban teachers stressing problems of urban education and solutions. Deals with sociology in Part I and educational practices in Part II.

Bestor, Arthur E. *Educational Wastelands: The Retreat from Learning in Our Public Schools.* Urbana, Ill.: University of Illinois Press, 1953. A criticism of public education deploring its lack of purpose, over-emphasis on "practical" education and "life-adjustment" training, together with suggestions of how to bring about reform, reorganization, and restoration of "liberal" education.

———. *The Restoration of Learning.* New York: Alfred A. Knopf, 1955. A sequel to *Educational Wastelands* in which Bestor reiterates his criticisms but also offers specific proposals for action to implement the changes he deems necessary in American education.

Cremin, Lawrence A. *The Genius of American Education.* New York: Random House, 1965. Three essays stressing the commitment to popularization of American education and how this commitment historically has affected the structure, nature, and politics of present-day education.

———. *The Transformation of the School.* New York: Alfred A. Knopf, 1961. Definitive history of the development of the progressive education movement from 1876–1957 and its influence in transforming the schools. Stresses the social origins of educational developments.

Dix, Lester. *A Charter for Progressive Education.* New York: Bureau of Publications, Teachers College, Columbia University, 1939. The basic principles, curriculum designs, and strategies of progressive education.

Dropkin, Stan, Harold Full, and Ernest Schwarcz, eds. *Contemporary American Education: An Anthology of Issues, Problems, Challenges.* 2nd ed. New York: Macmillan, 1970. An anthology on the current concerns and problems of schools in transition, presenting a variety of viewpoints.

Educational Policies Commission. *Education for All American Youth.* Washington, D.C.: NEA, 1944. Now a classic in the field, this book still provides a vision of good education toward which the contemporary high school might well aspire.

Educational Policies Commission. *Education for All American Youth: A Further Look.* Washington, D.C.: NEA, 1960. Outlines the Commission's recommendations for a problem-centered curriculum which emphasizes the development of reflective thinking.

Ehlers, Henry and Gordon C. Lee, eds. *Crucial Issues in Education,* 4th ed. New York: Holt, Rinehart and Winston, 1969. Anthology of articles concerning controversial issues in contemporary educational thought. Presents conflicting views and encourages dialogue about differing sets of values.

Graham, Patricia Albjerg. *Progressive Education: From Arcady to Academe.* New York: Teachers College Press, Teachers College, Columbia University, 1967. Focuses upon the history and development of the Progressive Education Association and the progressive education movement.

Havighurst, Robert J. *Education in Metropolitan Areas.* Boston: Allyn and Bacon, 1966. An experienced scholar of the disadvantaged sets forth the achievements and problems of education in American cities.

Havighurst, Robert J. and Bernice L. Neugarten. *Society and Education,* 3rd ed. Boston: Allyn and Bacon, 1966. The relationship of education to the social structure. Emphasizes problems of urban areas and the disadvantaged pupil.

Hulburd, David. *This Happened in Pasadena.* New York: Macmillan, 1951. Lively account by a journalist of the dismissal of an outstanding American superintendent of schools under pressure from the radical right.

Keats, John. *Schools Without Scholars.* Boston: Houghton Mifflin, 1958. A journalist's critique of public education with emphasis on what he feels should be taught in our public schools.

Kerber, August, and Barbara Bommarito, eds. *The Schools and the Urban Crisis.* New York: Holt, Rinehart and Winston, 1966. Readings on the urban community, its schools and influences, youth problems, teachers, improving urban schools, controversial issues, and new directions.

Lerner, Max. *America as a Civilization.* New York: Simon and Schuster, 1957. An ambitious and classic overview of American life by one of America's most versatile social scientists.

Lynd, Albert. *Quackery in the Public Schools.* Boston: Little, Brown, 1953. A criticism of trends in education and in educational leadership engaged in what Lynd terms "quackery."

Miller, Harry L. and Roger R. Woock. *Social Foundations of Urban Education.* New York: Dryden Press, 1970. A comprehensive examination of sources of massive educational retardation of lower-class minority groups in the cities.

O'Neill, William F., ed. *Selected Educational Heresies.* Glenview, Ill.: Scott, Foresman, 1969. Readings presenting controversial criticisms of educational practices and proposing alternative ideas and systems.

Orlich, Donald C. and S. Samuel Shermis, eds. *The Pursuit of Excellence: Introductory Readings in Education.* Cincinnati, Ohio: Van Nostrand Reinhold, 1965. Readings on history, goals, organization, and administration, financing, forces, and education as a profession.

Perkinson, Henry J. *The Imperfect Panacea: American Faith in Education, 1865–1965.* New York: Random House, 1968. A history of education in America from 1865–1965. A discussion of the unwarranted, unrealistic, and harmful demands often made on education and an account of some of the achievements and failures of the American dream in education.

Raubinger, Frederick M., Harold G. Rowe, Donald L. Piper, and Charles K. West. *The Development of Secondary Education.* New York: Macmillan, 1969. A source book of the developments and documents which have been significant in American secondary education over the past seventy-five years.

Resnik, Henry S. *Turning on the System.* New York: Pantheon Books, 1970. An account of the effort of the Philadelphia schools to relate to children and youth in the urban situation. The authors view is that the effort was a noble one but that it did not succeed.

Rickover, Hyman G. *Education and Freedom.* New York: E. P. Dutton and Co., 1959. A criticism of American education contained in a series of speeches which point out the need for upgrading the scholastic standards of our schools. The book concentrates on the supposed inadequacies of the American educational system in the 1950s.

Scanlon, John and Paul Woodring, eds. *American Education Today*. New York: McGraw-Hill, 1963. A variety of essays selected from *Saturday Review* under the editorship of Woodring and Scanlon. The emphasis is upon conflict and variety of viewpoints on today's educational problems.

AUDIO-VISUAL MATERIALS

Our Schools Have Kept Us Free (National Education Association, 30 Min. color) Based on an article of the same title by Henry Steele Commager. Discusses the role of education in helping to shape and preserve democracy in the United States.

Freedom to Learn (National Education Association, 28 Min. color) When, due to the well-meaning fears of parents, a high school social studies teacher is charged with teaching communism, she explains why she teaches about communism and why she believes it important that students know the facts about subjects they discuss.

The Sound of a Stone (Centron Corporation, 28 Min.) A high school teacher becomes suspect because a book he recommends is considered subversive. The waves of gossip and hate touch shores for which they were never intended. Community leaders and the parent who made the accusation try to undo the damage, but the reverberations continue in sinister and startling ways.

The High School Curriculum for Life Adjustment (Bureau of Auditory Education, 12: dia., 33 speed) The case for "life adjustment" education presented by Harl R. Douglas.

Education as Intellectual Discipline (NET., 29 Min.) Arthur Bestor comments on the importance of a disciplined mind and outlines the methods of obtaining intellectual discipline in a democratic society.

Education—For What and For Whom (Center for Study of Democratic Institutions, 30 Min.) Robert M. Hutchens, Admiral Rickover, and Rosemary Park in an analysis of educational problems.

Conant on Public Education (University of Michigan UMITV, 30 Min.) An interview with James B. Conant on the future of public education in the United States.

Education for a Free Society (NET 29 Min.) R. Freeman Butts discusses freedom from constraint, freedom of thought, religion, speech and press, and freedom to make choices and to act on those choices.

Education for National Survival (NET, 29 Min.) Emphasizes that our national strength depends much upon a high level of educational achievement and that we must discover and develop our best talent.

EIGHT

WHAT ARE THE ROLES OF INDEPENDENT AND PAROCHIAL SCHOOLS?

Though the large majority of American teachers teach in public schools, alternative forms of organization are the private schools (or to use the phrase which private school educators think more appropriate, "independent schools"), and church systems of education, such as maintained by the Roman Catholic church, commonly called parochial schools. Both of these are nonpublic.

Both independent and parochial schools which meet the legal requirements of a state, when such requirements exist, have been adjudged legal alternatives to public schools. In other words, approved independent and parochial schools are deemed able to achieve the same goals that public schools achieve while accomplishing their own characteristic objectives. This principle was confirmed by the United States Supreme Court in the 1925 Oregon Decision. The Oregon legislature had passed a law in 1922 which required all normal children who were between eight and sixteen years of age and who had not completed the eighth grade to attend the public schools. Both a church school and a nonsectarian military academy challenged the law. The court ruled:

We think it entirely plain that the Act of 1922 unreasonably interferes with the liberty of parents and guardians to direct the upbringing and education of children under their control.... The fundamental theory of liberty upon which all governments in this Union repose excludes any general power of the State to standardize its children by forcing them to accept instruction from public teachers only. The child is not the mere creature of the State; those who nurture him and direct his destiny have the right, coupled with the high duty, to recognize and prepare him for additional obligations.[1]

---

[1] Pierce, Governor of Oregon et al. v. Society of Sisters; and Pierce, Governor of Oregon et al. v. Hill Military Academy, Appeals from the District Court of the United States for the District of Oregon, Nos. 583, 584. Argued March 16, 17, 1925; decided June 1, 1925.

AMERICAN INDEPENDENT SCHOOLS

The private or independent school is a school which is open to selected students, rather than a school committed to a public responsibility for educating children in a particular neighborhood or community. Independent schools are supported primarily by tuition and by philanthropic funds. Yet such private schools are not completely independent of government control or supervision; they are subject to whatever state supervision or controls exist. They are also subject to whatever community controls are established; for instance, a headmaster and a board of trustees cannot conduct a school in a firetrap. A useful definition is supplied by an official of the National Association of Independent Schools:

What is an independent school? In contrast to the public school, it is supported chiefly by nonpublic funds, and it is controlled by a nonpublic body, usually a board of trustees. It is relatively independent of state control; conditions and regulations vary from state to state, but as a general rule it has considerable freedom to set its own standards and curriculum, admit and dismiss students, and hire and dismiss teachers, without state supervision or control. It is free, legally, to incorporate religious teaching in its curriculum, and free, practically, to encourage discussion of controversial topics. Of course, it must meet health, fire, and safety standards, and the state has ultimate control in the equivalency laws.[2]

The independent school is usually nonsectarian, but a degree of church affiliation occasionally exists. Whenever the independent school's board is essentially the controlling force and control by the church is actually or relatively nonexistent, as in the case of many Friends and Episcopal schools, the school is usually regarded as an independent school. When a school is essentially under the control of a central church authority, as are Roman Catholic parochial schools, it is not usually regarded in the independent category.

The variety of state patterns of regulation of independent schools is dramatized in a report by Donald Erickson which indicates that twenty states make no real provision for regulation, another twenty states have regulations ranging from moderate to demanding, and the remaining ten states regulate some phase of the operation of independent schools, such as curriculum, teaching methods, and ratio of pupils to teachers.[3] Wide variation also exists in accreditation; some independent schools comply with all provisions for accreditation and others refuse to do so in the interest of freedom in the employment of teachers regardless of their professional training.

---

[2] Francis Parkman, "Independent Schools," p. 633 in American Educational Research Association, *Encyclopedia of Educational Research*, 4th ed., 1969.
[3] Donald Erickson, "On the Role of Nonpublic Schools," *School Review*, 69 (Autumn 1961), pp. 338–353.

THE ORIGINAL PRIVATE INDEPENDENT SCHOOLS

Private independent schools have a long lineage. Private education antedates public education; the first schools established in centers of civilizations such as ancient Egypt or classical Greece were private schools. The Egyptians had schools for royal children in early times, and later such schools trained young men to conduct government. The Greeks did not have free schools. But the son of an Athenian citizen began attending a private school at the age of seven. He was taught reading, writing, literature, and arithmetic; then he went to another school for physical training. At sixteen, he entered the "gymnasium," a state school, and learned the duties of citizenship. The famed philosophers had no classrooms; they gathered students around them on tree-shaded athletic grounds. Plato met his pupils in the field called the Academy, and Aristotle held sessions with his students in the Lyceum. Later, the Romans founded schools on the Greek pattern.[4]

When European universities arose in the twelfth and thirteenth centuries, Latin was the language of the scholars. So Latin schools were established to prepare young scholars for the universities. By the fourteenth century, some cities established schools for the teaching of arithmetic, reading, and writing of the common speech rather than of Latin, and to teach other subjects of practical value to merchants and traders.

As Europe moved from medievalism, when education was a church function, into the modern world, private education became a part of the home; aristocratic families employed tutors or teachers to instruct young family members. In time education moved from a room within a family home to a building or cluster of buildings termed a school. Great Britain developed its famous private schools in which generations of British leaders were educated. Eton College, largest and most famous of the English private schools, was founded by King Henry VI in 1440; Harrow was established in 1571. Such schools were called by the British "public schools," a phrase baffling to the American ear and requiring reverse translation, since in our terms these schools are private.

PRIVATE INDEPENDENT SCHOOLS IN AMERICA

The American colonies followed the pattern of private education. "Dame schools" were first taught by housewives in their own homes in exchange for payment by their students' families. Later, early American schoolmasters conducted private schools in school buildings.

Some independent schools, still existent, date from the seventeenth century. They include the Roxbury Latin School in Massachusetts (1645), the Collegiate School in New York City (1638), the Hopkins Grammar School in New Haven, Connecticut (1660), and the William Penn Charter School in Philadelphia (1689).[5]

---

[4] For a broader, more detailed discussion, see Frederick A. G. Beck, *Greek Education: 450–350 B.C.* (New York: Barnes and Noble, 1964).
[5] Parkman, "Independent Schools," *Encyclopedia of Educational Research,* p. 634.

Phillips Exeter Academy, First Academy Building, restored. Courtesy of Phillips Exeter Academy.

So America, too, developed outstanding private schools, which specialized in preparing young men for entry into such colleges as Harvard, Yale, and Princeton as part of the education of a young elite who were to become American leaders. Phillips Academy in Andover, Massachusetts, for example, was opened in 1778 and chartered in 1780 by Samuel Phillips, a state senator from Massachusetts. The school, often called Andover or Phillips Andover, is the oldest incorporated academy in America. Phillips Exeter Academy was chartered in 1781 and opened in 1783 by John Phillips, an uncle of Samuel Phillips and a provider of financial backing to both schools.

Academies flourished in the mid-nineteenth century when more than 250,000 pupils were enrolled in 6,000 academies.[6] However, today private independent education is a minority segment of the total American educational enterprise. After pointing out that the large majority of nonpublic schools in the mid-sixties were Roman Catholic parochial schools, Parkman says, "The remainder comprises some 1,000 non-church-related and 2,900 church-related elementary schools with about 400,000 students and in the secondary area about 1,500 schools (800 nonsectarian, 700 church-related) with nearly 200,000 students. According to our definition, not all of these schools can be counted as truly independent schools but certainly a large part of them can be. Over 90 percent are nonprofit schools."[7] By contrast, enrollment in Catholic education was over

[6] *Ibid.*   [7] *Ibid.*

5,000,000 and enrollment in public schools was about 43,000,000 in the mid-1960s.

A new development in the private sector of American education is the "alternative" or "free" or "innovative" schools, developed to provide alternatives to the restrictiveness of some public schools. In March 1970, Donald W. Robinson reported that over 700 alternative schools have been founded during the past three years, about half of them in the inner cities.[8] Many alternative schools are child-centered and youth-centered. Harvey Haber, founder of the New Schools Exchange which publishes a directory of such schools, estimates the average life of a new school at eighteen months, after which it may die completely, merge with another school, or alter its course so severely as to cease to be a radically innovative institution.[9]

WHETHER OR NOT TO TEACH IN PRIVATE INDEPENDENT SCHOOLS

A new teacher contemplating whether or not to teach in the private independent schools should take into account some of the advantages and disadvantages.

A strong argument for teaching in a private independent school is the freedom to experiment and from some of the claimed restrictions characteristic of public school education. Classes are frequently small; there is a low pupil-teacher ratio. Independent schools, it is sometimes said, are free from the petty hobbles placed on teachers by the public school bureaucracy, from the restrictions of conformity-centered public educators, from the system-wide homogeneity of public schools. Under creative leadership, the private school teacher is free to innovate and as Ralph Waldo Emerson put it, "to do his thing." In such circumstances, the only test is whether the teacher achieves educational results. For instance, approximately half of the schools in the Progressive Education Association's Eight Year Study were independent. Independent schools fostered the advanced placement programs of the 1950s and 1960s.

But the skeptic with a counter argument quickly points out that the independent school teacher may have merely traded one master for another. Upper- and upper-middle-class parents are notoriously concerned about their children's entrance into the best colleges. They are apt to throw their weight in conservative rather than experimental directions. Most independent schools are educationally conservative and oriented to close conformity to college entrance requirements, rather than progressive or experimental in approaches. Headmasters and principals, it is said, have been known to sacrifice their principles to the practical goal of parental support manifested by the continuing payment of tuition. So the supposed freedom from restrictions and for experimentation may be illusory.

---

[8] Donald W. Robinson, " 'Alternative Schools': Challenge to Traditional Education," *Phi Delta Kappan*, 51 (March 1970), p. 374.

[9] *Ibid.*, p. 375. The address of New Schools Exchange is 2840 Hidden Valley Lane, Santa Barbara, California.

The skeptic adds that independent school teachers are seldom tightly organized in a teachers' union or educational association and must pay for their supposed individualism by acceptance of lower salaries and even more administrative controls than public school teachers. "Alternative" schools often die quickly despite (or perhaps because of) their Utopianism, say the doubters.

Controversy also exists as to the social class biases of independent schools. Parkman of the National Association of Independent Schools, after citing the volume of scholarships granted by private schools, defends independent schools against "misconceptions held by the public":

> Many people cherish one or another (and some people all) of the following illusions; that independent schools are run for somebody's private gain, that they are all richly endowed, that they are "exclusive," that they are only for the rich and/or for disciplinary cases, that children from poor families cannot gain admission, that attendance at an independent school guarantees admission to highly selective colleges, that the New England boarding school is typical of all independent schools.[10]

An opposing view frequently advanced against teaching in independent schools is that independent schools, except for "alternative" schools, are essentially "class" institutions in which education has been and remains, despite scholarships, essentially for the upper- and upper-middle classes. In the independent school, the new teacher essentially works with an American elite, which is sometimes conscious of being an elite and in which social snobbery occasionally exists. Critics say that the independent private schools evade the social challenge of public education to educate the children of the common people that they may improve the quality of their lives.

Some new teachers teach in private schools precisely because they want to teach upper-income children who accept upper- or middle-class values, who do not present as many discipline problems, and who are culturally advantaged. Such a teaching situation is precisely what some new teachers prefer, even though their more socially motivated colleagues may regard them as copping out on the tougher responsibilities.

An interesting footnote to the matter is provided by the junior and senior high school dissent of the late 1960s which was led by upper-middle-class youth. In the 1970s will the new teacher who prefers the private independent school, or his public school counterpart who prefers the upper-class suburbs, be able to escape student anger and hostility through his choice of a privileged setting?

PAROCHIAL EDUCATION

Several religious groups have developed their own schools in America, among them the Lutherans and the Jews. But by far the largest of the private religion-related school systems is that of the Roman Catholic Church. Consequently,

---

[10] Parkman, p. 637.

only the Catholic educational system is treated here. Roman Catholic schools represent the second major type of school system in the United States, surpassed only by the public school system in size.

Catholic schools were established to provide for the religious formation of the young. As early as 1606, Franciscan missionaries established a short-lived school in St. Augustine, Florida. In the nineteenth century, Catholic schools were created in response to both the secular theory of the public schools and the religious practices of Protestant Christianity—such as reading the King James Bible and holding prayers—which were a daily part of nineteenth century public schools. Catholics initially sought to free the public schools of such religious practices but without success. After several court decisions favoring Protestant religious practices in public schools and after several "religious riots" in cities such as Philadelphia, Catholics began their own school system in order to ward off the Protestantizing of their children.[11]

As early as 1840 there were 200 Catholic schools in the United States.[12] They were created largely because Catholic citizens of the New World wanted to keep alive their religion in the minds and hearts of their children. The development of Catholic schools was encouraged by nineteenth century immigration, including the major migration of the Irish in the decade of the 1840s.[13] In 1820 there were only 195,000 Catholics in the United States but by 1850 there were 1,606,000.[14] Catholic schools often reduced the immigrants' shock of transition.

Support for the establishment of a parochial school system came from American Catholic bishops gathered at the Third Plenary Council of Baltimore in 1884. The Council decreed:

That near every church a parish school, where one does not yet exist, is to be built and maintained in perpetuum, within two years of the promulgation of this council, unless the Bishop should decide that because of serious difficulties a delay may be granted.

That all Catholic parents are bound to send their children to the parish school, unless it is evident that a sufficient training in religion is given either in their own homes, or in other Catholic schools; or when, because of a sufficient reason, approved by the Bishop, with all due precautions and safeguards, it is licit to send them to other schools. What constitutes a Catholic school is left to the decision of the Bishop.[15]

---

[11] For references see John F. Wilson, *Church and State in American History* (Boston: D. C. Heath, 1965); Merle Curti, *The Social Ideas of American Educators* (Paterson, N.J.: Littlefield, Adams, 1959), Chapter X; and Lloyd P. Jorgenson, "Historical Origins of Non-Sectarian Public Schools: The Birth of a Tradition," *Phi Delta Kappan* (June, 1963).

[12] George N. Shuster, *Catholic Education in a Changing World* (New York: Holt, Rinehart & Winston, 1967) p. 26.

[13] Shuster, p. 27.

[14] Neil G. McCluskey, S.J. *Catholic Viewpoint in Education* (New York: Doubleday, 1962), p. 189.

[15] Reginald A. Neuwien (ed.), *Catholic Schools in Action: A Report, the Notre Dame Study of Catholic Elementary Schools and Secondary Schools in the United States* (Notre Dame, Ind.: University of Notre Dame Press, 1966), p. 9.

A progressive Catholic classroom. Courtesy of Boston Globe.

In practice, prior to the twentieth century, the usual pattern of Catholic education in the United States placed great emphasis on the elementary and college levels. "The first provided most of the schooling the average youngster received, and the second was relied upon to provide, among other benefits, the supply of teachers needed. In the Catholic system, the elementary school was a place in which children were taught discipline—at an earlier stage, rigorously, and later on, persuasively—as well as the rudiments of their religion, while learning secular subjects appropriate to their time of life. The sexually segregated college, which was often an adaptation of the European Gymnasium or lycée to the American environment, was normally conducted by a religious community."[16] In recent years, and especially in the twentieth century, Catholic secondary education has grown markedly.

WHO ATTENDS CATHOLIC SCHOOLS TODAY?

Catholic education is now a sizable form of schooling in the United States of America. By the school year 1966–67, enrollment in Catholic elementary schools totaled 4,245,786. Enrollment in secondary schools totaled 1,107,767. In the more than ten thousand Catholic elementary schools and more than two thousand Catholic secondary schools, 112,786 teachers were employed in elementary education and 55,783 were employed in secondary schools.[17] In the school year 1968–69, enrollment in Catholic elementary schools totaled 3,895,751

[16] Shuster, p. 7.   [17] Shuster, pp. 237–238.

and enrollment in secondary schools totaled 1,086,528 according to *Catholic Education Today, An Overview*, published by the National Catholic Education Association.

For years, Catholic leaders supported the idea of the bishops of 1884 of educating every Catholic child in a Catholic school. However, in the present age of ferment in the world and in Catholicism and especially following the Second Vatican Council, Catholics have reopened the discussion of the desirability and practicality of this. A Notre Dame study reports that as of 1962–63 only 52.21 percent of Catholic children in the United States were enrolled in Catholic elementary schools—in other words, somewhat more than four million of a potential enrollment of more than eight million.[18] Only 32.22 percent of eligible Catholic children were enrolled in Catholic secondary schools—slightly more than a million of a potential enrollment of more than three million.[19]

With the dwindling of immigration, the characteristic enrollment in the Catholic school has changed. George N. Shuster says, "The comment is often made that Catholic education serves 'nice' middle class boys and girls. To a certain extent, due allowance having been made for the pejorative quality of the adjective, this is true. The average Catholic-school youngster, apart from a few exceptional diocesan elementary and high schools, has a better family background, a higher I.Q., and more learning motivation than does the average public school child . . . the situation arises because not all who would like to attend Catholic schools can do so."[20] Shuster concludes, "By reason of the structure of its schools, particularly from the admissions point of view, the Church in the United States may be in some peril of becoming an intellectualized Church and of losing what for a lack of a better term we may call the working-class."[21]

A great debate now rages in Catholic educational circles as to which aspects of the total educational structure are most vital for Catholic education. The problem is complicated by financial considerations because Catholic schools depend heavily upon instruction by the members of religious orders and by the relatively low-paid lay teachers. Some Catholic educators believe the best course would be reduction of elementary education and particularly the early years of elementary school programs. Shuster points out, "Notable is a trend, first seriously inaugurated by the Archdiocese of Cincinnati, to lop off the earlier grades of the elementary school. Also, we read reports that schools are being closed in a number of smaller towns and cities, presumably because keeping them going is too difficult. Do these things portend a serious effort to curtail, if not indeed to abandon, the elementary school?"[22] ". . . We have now come to the point where not only laymen but priests, religious, and even bishops are asking whether it may not be wise and necessary to think of a drastic curtailment of the parochial school effort."[23] "Whether it is desirable to concentrate on the high school, in order to provide a measure of Catholic education for all children whose parents wish them to have it, is a query which must be submitted to those

---

[18] *Ibid.*, pp. 55–56.
[19] *Ibid.*, p. 56.
[20] *Ibid.*, pp. 78–79.
[21] Shuster, p. 80.
[22] *Ibid.*, pp. 171–172.
[23] *Ibid.*, p. 172.

in charge of Catholic education as a whole. As has been said, its adoption would not automatically mean the demise of the parochial school, but that school would henceforth be in some measure peripheral."[24]

ISSUES IN CATHOLIC EDUCATION

Like the public schools and the private independent schools, Catholic schools face fundamental problems today. Two sociologists, Andrew M. Greeley, who is a Catholic priest, and Peter H. Rossi, who is a non-Catholic, have explored these issues in *The Education of Catholic Americans*, a study conducted by the National Opinion Research Center. In the preface to the book, several issues are set forth:

> The first of these concerns is the major manifest reason for the establishment and maintenance of the Catholic school system—the preservation of religious faith. Since the *raison d'être* of religious schools is that they assist in the teaching of religion, it is crucial that any research project on Catholic schools address itself to the question: "Are the people who attend Catholic Schools better Catholics?" . . .
>
> A second issue of major concern in discussions of Catholic education has been the question of the potentially divisive nature of a separate, value-oriented educational system. Does the Catholic school system set its students apart from other Americans and create barriers to their cooperation with Protestants and Jews? . . .
>
> A third issue which underlies the research project is the evaluation of the part which Catholic education plays in preparing individuals for economic success. The significant question here concerns the competency of Catholic schooling to prepare one for life in a secular world, where occupation success not only contributes to his general level of economic well-being but also has a significant impact on his general social status.[25]

The authors conclude that:

> The first theoretical question was whether the values of a religious group can be effectively taught in a religiously oriented educational system. Our answer to this question is that, to some extent, they can. The students who attend such schools can be expected in adult life to do even better those things which most members of their religious group do reasonably well. Value-oriented education can affect behavior in adult life in precisely those areas in which adults can be expected to adhere to the norms of their religious group even without education. Those who have the education will simply be even more likely to exhibit the desired behavior.
>
> The second theoretical question was whether such separate systems of educa-

---

[24] *Ibid.*, pp. 176–177.
[25] Andrew M. Greeley and Peter H. Rossi, *The Education of Catholic Americans* (Chicago: Aldine, 1966), pp. vi–viii.

Teacher's union picketing at St. Johns University, Queens, N.Y., over academic freedom and dismissal of faculty members. Courtesy of UPI.

tion were "divisive." We could find no evidence that the products of such a system were less involved in community activities, less likely to have friends from other religious groups, more intolerant in their attitudes, or less likely to achieve occupationally or academically. On the contrary, we found that they were slightly more successful in the world of study and work and—after the breaking point of college—much more tolerant. The achievement, and perhaps even the tolerance, seems to be related to the degree to which a young person was integrated into his religious subculture during adolescence.[26]

WHO TEACHES IN CATHOLIC SCHOOLS?

A Notre Dame study shows that, though members of religious orders substantially outnumbered lay teachers in Catholic schools, the lay staff was growing rapidly during the 1950s. Between 1950 and 1961 "the number of lay teachers had grown approximately four times as fast as the number of religious at the secondary school level, and nearly twenty-three times as fast at the elementary school level.[27] From 2,768 lay teachers in 1946, the number grew to 44,000 in Catholic elementary schools in 1965–66.[28]

[26] Greeley and Rossi, pp. 228–229.
[27] Shuster, pp. 56–57.
[28] C. Albert Koob, "Parochial Schools—Roman Catholic," p. 927 in American Educational Research Association, *Encyclopedia of Educational Research*, 4th ed., 1969.

By the close of the 1960s, a newsletter on educational affairs could report:

Lay teachers are rapidly outnumbering religious teachers in Catholic elementary and secondary schools. The New York Archdiocese and the Brooklyn Diocese report that the number of lay teachers has passed 50% this fall. The National Catholic Education Association (NCEA) says more than 25 other major school systems have a majority of lay faculty. In all Catholic school systems in Florida and Louisiana, religious teachers are in the minority. NCEA reports that national-wide totals do not reflect the strength of the trend because New England parochial schools still retain a higher proportion of religious teachers than do other areas. The pressure of paying higher salaries to lay teachers is increasing the already tight financial squeeze on Catholic education. In turn, Catholic educators are having to plead harder for public funds to keep their schools running.[29]

Among the problems encountered by lay teachers in Catholic schools is the lack of career opportunities to become administrators. These posts are usually reserved for the Sisters and Brothers who are in religious orders. In addition, salaries of lay teachers in Catholic schools are lower than the salaries in public schools.[30] The high enrollment in elementary schools results in larger classes; the situation in regard to median class size was somewhat better in secondary schools than in elementary schools.

WHETHER OR NOT TO TEACH IN CATHOLIC SCHOOLS

As teachers contemplate service in Catholic schools, many factors will have to be taken into account. How deep is the individual's commitment to a distinctive Catholic education? If the commitment is deep, to what extent does it reflect traditional approaches to Catholicism or to what extent does it reflect the new self-examination that followed Pope John and the Second Vatican Council? Will the individual be content with a presumably lower salary than is paid in the public schools and will he or she accept presumably fewer opportunities to move ahead to administrative posts? Can the teacher adapt to larger class size than is characteristic of public schools? Will parochial elementary schools be curtailed?

As to continuance of the Roman Catholic educational system, Greeley and Rossi say:

Our opinion, for what it is worth, is that discussion by Catholics and non-Catholics alike concerning whether there will be Catholic schools is quite irrelevant. A system which involves one out of every seven (sic) school children in our republic does not go out of business, either all at once or gradually. It seems to us, rather, that the relevant question is how the distinctive system of Catholic schools can make the strongest possible contribution to the health of

---

[29] *Education, U.S.A.*, National School Public Relations Association (Washington, D. C.: The Association, Fall 1969).
[30] Shuster, p. 61.

American society. In the fierce exchanges between those who are "pro" and those who are "con" this question is often overlooked. Yet, being for or against a school system with over five million students is like being for or against the Rocky Mountains; it is great fun but it does not notably alter the reality.[31]

An official of the National Catholic Education Association concludes his contribution to the *Encyclopedia of Educational Research* with several questions concerning Catholic parochial education:

Should an all-out effort be made to expand the system in order to meet the rising demands of the immediate future, or should the system be held at its present level of size or even cut back, while efforts are concentrated instead on new educational and religious formation programs? If the decision is for expansion, where will the money to build the schools and pay the teachers come from? Will the American public, legislatures, and courts accept the arguments of parochial school proponents that their institutions and/or students are constitutionally entitled to aid from tax funds, or will decisions of public policy or constitutional interpretation instead go against the interests of parochial education? Can parochial schools continue to meet the mounting demands for educational excellence?[32]

You take all of these questions into consideration as you decide about teaching in Catholic schools.

CONTROVERSIES OVER RELIGION AND SCHOOLS

Since 90 percent of America's nonpublic schools are Catholic and a substantial proportion of the independent schools are church-related to some degree, religion is an important factor in nonpublic education. The right of a nonpublic school to instruct in the tenets of the sponsoring religious group is not in dispute in the United States today. But does the government have any responsibility for the financial support of religiously controlled nonpublic schools? And does the public school, an institution maintained by public funds for the benefit of a highly diverse population as to religion, have any responsibility for religious instruction in the public schools?

The principle of separation of church and state is embodied in the first amendment to the United States Constitution, "Congress shall make no law respecting an establishment of religion, or prohibiting the free exercise thereof." The new nation chose freedom of religion rather than the earlier colonial concept of an established church supported with public funds.

To the Founding Fathers, the religion clause of the first amendment meant that a "wall of separation" was erected between church and state. For instance, Thomas Jefferson wrote in 1802, "I contemplate with sovereign reverence that

---

[31] Greeley and Rossi, p. 231.
[32] Koob, p. 929.

act of the whole American people which declared that their legislature should 'make no law respecting an establishment of religion or prohibiting the free exercise thereof,' thus building a wall of separation between church and state." James Madison who wrote the first amendment said, "We maintain, therefore, that in matters of religion no man's right is abridged by the institution of civil society; and that religion is wholly exempt from its cognizance."

Supporters of the "wall of separation" interpretation of the first amendment believe that it has saved America from the religious conflicts which troubled the Old World, has permitted a great religious diversity in which approximately 300 sects and denominations exist peaceably, has guaranteed religious freedom for all, and has given religions the opportunity to be free, independent, and strong.

But some interpret the first amendment as simply intended to keep the Congress from establishing a national church. Some Catholic spokesmen, for instance, have argued for a limited and literal interpretation of the amendment. James M. O'Neill, in *Religion and Education Under the Constitution,* says that "the question of 'an establishment of religion' for the whole United States . . . was a subject which Congress should not touch. It neither approved nor disapproved of the established religions existing in the States. It made explicit the fact that Congress was powerless to act in favor of an establishment of religion for the nation."[33]

Another interpretation of the first amendment calls for friendly cooperation between church and state and increasing flexibility. For instance, an official of a council of the United Church of Christ says:

Between the poles of "nonestablishment" and "free exercise" lies a vast realm of functional interaction which cannot—and should not—be proscribed by legal and judicial acts. Instead of a "wall" we ought to have a "wavy line" between church and state. They are in dynamic relation to each other and the boundaries of their respective spheres cannot be determined once and for all.[34]

The Supreme Court of the United States has frequently been called on to rule on cases involving separation of church and state. In the *Everson* decision in 1947, the Court said:

Neither a state nor the Federal Government can set up a church. Neither can pass laws which aid one religion, aid all religions or prefer one religion over another. Neither can force nor influence a person to go to or remain away from church against his will or force him to profess a belief or disbelief in any religion. No person can be punished for entertaining or professing religious beliefs or disbeliefs, for church attendance or nonattendance. No tax in any amount large or small can be levied to support any religious activities or institutions, whatever they may be called, or whatever form they may adopt to teach or practice religion. Neither a state nor the Federal Government can, openly or secretly,

---

[33] James M. O'Neill, *Religion and Education Under the Constitution* (New York: Harper and Bros., 1949), pp. 9–10.
[34] Ray Gibbons, "Protestantism and Public Action," *Social Action* (February 15, 1949).

participate in the affairs of any religious organization or groups and vice versa. In the words of Jefferson, the clause against establishment of religion by law was intended to erect a "wall of separation between church and state."[35]

But in the *Everson* decision, the Court held that the state could provide free bus transportation to children attending private schools, including church-related schools. In 1968, in the *Allen* case, the United States Supreme Court upheld the constitutionality of a New York State statute requiring local boards of education to lend secular textbooks which were approved by public school authorities to children in nonpublic schools, including parochial schools, without charge. Operating on a "child benefit" theory which conceived the loan of textbooks as aid to children rather than aid to religious schools, the Court said:

. . . Private education has played and is playing a significant and valuable role in raising national levels of knowledge, competence and experience. Americans care about the quality of the secular education available to their children. They have considered high quality education to be an indispensable ingredient for achieving the kind of nation and the kind of citizenry that they have desired to create. Considering this attitude, the continued willingness to rely on private school systems, including parochial systems, strongly suggests that a wide segment of informed opinion, legislative and otherwise, has found that those schools do an acceptable job of providing secular education to their students. This judgment is further evidence that parochial schools are performing, in addition to their sectarian function, the task of secular education.[36]

Several other Supreme Court rulings have affirmed that the public school must be a secular institution—the Court's rulings in the *Everson* case, the *McCollum* decision against "released-time programs" for religious instruction on public school premises, the *Engel v. Vitale* case declaring unconstitutional the recitation in the public schools of a prayer composed by the New York Board of Regents, and the *Schempp* case holding that devotional reading of the Bible and school-sponsored prayers are violations of the First Amendment. But with the Allen case, it became obvious that the question of how far the state may go in aiding parochial schools or their students has not yet been fully determined.

Under the "child benefit" theory, public aid is frequently shared by public and nonpublic schools. The Elementary and Secondary Education Act (ESEA) of 1965 was a compromise providing funds for educationally deprived students in both public and nonpublic schools. Grants to public school children were shared by nonpublic school students through educational radio and television programs, mobile educational services, library resources, textbooks and other instructional materials, and "dual enrollment" programs through which the school time of children was shared between state-supported schools providing general educa-

---

[35] U.S. Supreme Court, *United States Reports,* October Term, 1947, *Everson v. Board of Education,* 330 U.S., pp. 59–60.
[36] U.S. Supreme Court, *United States Reports,* October Term, 1967, *Board of Education v. Allen,* 392 U.S., pp. 247–248.

tion and church-supported schools providing the religious emphasis of a denomination. Individual states, led by Pennsylvania in 1968, today are providing aid to those aspects of instruction in parochial schools which are deemed secular. Meanwhile, antagonists in the controversy debate whether or not any education in a religious-related school can be deemed secular rather than sectarian, and whether or not all instruction in a parochial school is permeated by religion. In 1970 a Supreme Court decision on Pennsylvania case was in the offing.

The argument over public aid to parochial schools grows increasingly tense as predictions are made that the Catholic system of education will collapse without further support and, therefore, will load the already overburdened public schools with the one student in approximately nine who now attends Catholic schools.

But opponents of public aid doubt that Catholic schools will collapse without government support and advise instead investment of federal funds in inner-city public schools which are sadly in need of money. They point out that many parochial schools are attended by middle- and upper-class children and that public support for such schools would divert the church from increased social work in the slums. They quote Matthew Ahmann, Executive Director of the National Catholic Conference for Interracial Justice, who has said, "The Church school serves the middle class community. The sisters are tied to slavery in service to the middle class rather than being free to serve the slums of the inner-city."[37] Such spokesmen believe that the better ecumenism is not cooperation in Catholic appeals for public funds but instead encouragement of redirection of church activities toward social service on behalf of underprivileged groups.

Meanwhile, what is termed "parochaid" had been voted by legislatures in Pennsylvania, Connecticut, Rhode Island, and Ohio by the spring of 1970. *The New York Times* for March 8, 1970 reported as follows concerning Michigan where the legislature neared completion of a bill:

Under the parochaid plan, nearly 900 schools with more than 10,000 teachers and about 280,000 pupils would qualify for aid from the state treasury.

The parochial schools would receive up to 50 percent of the estimated average salary of $8,800 paid 5,800 certified lay teachers of secular subjects like English, mathematics, and science. Salary reimbursement would rise after the first year to 75 percent, subject to an over-all ceiling of two percent of total state, local and federal spending of school operations.[38]

A new dimension of disputes concerning federal support for nonpublic schools is the appearance in some southern states of white private schools created by segregationists in order to avoid desegregation of the schools. Such white-only schools have been tax-exempt, as are other nonpublic schools. Whether they should receive a tax exemption, in light of the Supreme Court decision of 1954 against segregation in public schools, is being vigorously discussed. In 1970 the

---

[37] John M. Swomley, Jr., "Ecumenism and the School Aid Issue," *The Christian Century* (June 4, 1969), p. 780.
[38] *The New York Times* (March 8, 1970), p. 55.

Nixon administration initiated action against tax exemption for the new white-only schools. To avoid using the educational vouchers (discussed in Chapter 7) for purposes of racial discrimination, Christopher Jencks specifies in his plan that half the places in a school accepting vouchers be filled by a lottery among participants. As to parochial schools, however, the New York Times reports, "Mr. Jencks said financially strapped parochial schools would probably find the vouchers a boon."[39]

★ ★ ★

DISCUSSION

1. On what basis has the United States Supreme Court ruled that independent and parochial schools are legal alternatives to public schools?
2. What are the characteristics of an independent private school?
3. To what extent is an independent school subject to state regulation? How might the existence of state regulations relate to you and your career and training if you chose to work in an independent school?
4. What are the major developments in the evolution of the private independent schools in America?
5. How do the so called "alternative" or "free" or "innovative" schools differ from the established private independent schools?
6. What are the advantages of teaching in an independent school, according to its proponents? What are the disadvantages, according to its critics? What is your own point of view on advantages and disadvantages?
7. What accounts for the development of parochial schools in America in the nineteenth century?
8. What reactions do you have to the 1884 decree that "all Catholic parents are bound to send their children to the parish school"? Have there been changes in the interpretation or implementation of this decree in recent years?
9. Why did parochial education place great emphasis on the elementary and college levels? Does this seem to you to have been a wise decision from the point of view of its sponsors or the public at large?
10. Who enrolls in Catholic schools? Are social class factors involved?
11. What have been some recent trends in Catholic education as to levels of instruction to be stressed and maintained? What do you think of the advisability of these tendencies?
12. According to *The Education of Catholic Americans,* what are the fundamental issues being faced by Catholic schools today? What conclusions do the authors of the cited study reach? Do you agree with their conclusions?
13. Who teaches in Catholic schools? What are the trends as to employment of lay and religious teachers? What seem to be likely future developments as to Catholic teachers?

[39] *New York Times* (June 4, 1970), p. 36.

192 THE NATURE OF AMERICAN SCHOOLS

14. What are the factors to take into account in deciding whether or not to teach in Catholic schools? What seem to you to be the advantages and disadvantages advanced by proponents and critics and perceived by yourself? What would be your own tentative decision as to whether you, if a Catholic, or a friend of yours, if a Catholic, should teach in parochial schools?
15. What are the central religious issues in the schools? What are some subordinate issues?
16. What interpretations have been advanced of the meaning of the first amendment pertaining to schools? What position do you take on the matter? Why?
17. What position has the United States Supreme Court historically taken on separation of church and state? What position is the Court currently taking on the public schools as secular institutions?
18. Do you see any possible shift in the United States Supreme Court position through the "child benefit" theory? In what ways do parochial schools now share with public schools resources provided by public funds?
19. What are the arguments about public funds for the support of religiously sponsored education?
20. If the Catholic schools were to close, could the public schools meet the resulting increased cost of education?
21. What are the newest developments in what has been termed "parochaid"? What are the latest decisions of the Supreme Court in connection with such support?
22. Is there any relationship between aid to integrated parochial schools and aid to segregated white academies? Can aid by the national government be given to one while excluding the other?

INVOLVEMENT

1. Have a panel of students describe the program and problems of independent private schools, if your class includes students who have attended such schools.
2. Make arrangements to visit a class in an independent school. From personal observation, what do you see as differences between this class and those you have observed in public schools?
3. Through panels, debates, extended discussions, etc., explore the pros and cons of teaching in private independent schools, including the new "alternative" schools. Include fundamental issues such as student characteristics and the values of teachers.
4. If a "free" or "alternative" school exists in your region, visit it to learn of its program and problems. How stable or impermanent is this school?
5. Determine the dates of the founding of private independent schools in the region in which you live or attend school.
6. Invite an administrator or teacher or sponsor of an independent school to class to describe the program and problems of his school.
7. Sponsor an exchange visit or a shared class session with a teacher education class in a Catholic college if you attend a non-Catholic college, or plan to visit a public college if you are attending a Catholic institution. Explore similarities and differences in programs. Look for agreement and clarify different ways of seeing education.

8. Talk to selected Catholic leaders, both members of the clergy and laymen, concerning probable directions of Catholic education. Invite nuns to class to talk with you on the matter.
9. Write your own summary of the major issues in Catholic education.
10. Make arrangements to visit a class in a parochial school. From personal observation, what do you see as differences between this class and those you have observed in public schools?
11. During a visit to a parochial school attempt to talk to both lay and religious teachers. Are there apparent differences in their points of view? Similarities?
12. Draw up a check list of factors to be taken into account in deciding about teaching in Catholic schools. Include in your list the possible advantages and disadvantages.
13. Research the various positions people take with respect to religion and the schools. Organize panel presentations of the varying viewpoints with documentary support.
14. Visit programs in your community in which parochial schools share a degree of public support. Do the programs you observe seem to be "secular" or "sectarian"?

BIBLIOGRAPHY

American Association of School Administrators. Commission on Religion in the Public Schools. *Religion in the Public Schools.* Washington, D.C.: NEA; 1964. A report from an AASA Commission on the effect of Supreme Court decisions. Suggestions for guiding the development of local policies and practices in response to the Court's decisions.

Blanshard, Paul. *Religion and the Schools: The Great Controversy.* Boston: Beacon Press, 1963. Vigorous criticism of the Catholic position on church and state.

Butts, Freeman. *The American Tradition in Religion and Education.* Boston: Beacon Press, 1950. The history of separation of church and state by an able educational historian.

Clayton, S. Stafford. *Religion and Schooling.* Waltham, Mass.: Blaisdell, 1969. The place of religion in the American public school system, including examination of patterns of European countries.

Dierenfield, Richard B. *Religion in American Public Schools.* Washington, D.C.: Public Affairs Press, 1962. Examines religious observances, activities, and instruction to provide a base for forming opinions and decisions in this controversial area.

Erickson, Donald A., ed. *Public Controls for Nonpublic Schools.* Chicago: University of Chicago Press, 1969. A collection of essays reflecting ideas which grew out of a 1967 national conference on government regulations and private schools.

Fraser, W. R. *Residential Education.* New York: Pergamon Publishing, 1968. Explores the nature of the residential school conceptual frameworks for its existence and its struggle to function successfully.

Greeley, Andrew M. and Peter H. Rossi. *The Education of Catholic Americans.* Chicago: Aldine Publishing, 1966. Research study on how Catholic education is similar to and different from public education in achieving its goals.

Jacobson, Philip. *Religion in Public Education.* New York: American Jewish Committee, 1969. A compact and objective guide to discussion of the major issues, upon which a section of this chapter draws.

Koob, C. Albert, ed. *What Is Happening to Catholic Education?* Washington, D.C.:

National Catholic Educational Association, 1966. Recent developments and critical issues in Catholic school curriculum development.

McCluskey, Neil G., S.J. *Catholic Viewpoint in Education*. New York: Doubleday, 1962. A capable and considered case supporting the Catholic viewpoint on education.

——. *Catholic Education in America: A Documentary History*. New York: Bureau of Publications, Teachers College, Columbia University, 1964. A review of the intellectual, societal, and historical foundations of Catholic schools.

Morgan, Richard E. *The Politics of Religious Conflict: Church and State in America*. New York: Pegasus, 1968. Political dimensions of the problem of church-state relations.

Neuwien, Reginald A. *Catholic Schools in Action: A Report, the Notre Dame Study of Catholic Elementary Schools and Secondary Schools in the United States*. Notre Dame, Ind.: University of Notre Dame Press., 1966. Research study of the strengths and weaknesses of parochial education in the United States in our time.

O'Neill, James M. *Religion and Education Under the Constitution*. New York: Harper, 1949. Historical facts, with opinions and interpretations, on the background of church and state controversies by a Catholic writer.

Pfeffer, Leo. *Church, State and Freedom*. Boston: Beacon Press, 1966. A defense of separation of church and state.

Shuster, George N. *Catholic Education in a Changing World*. New York: Holt, Rinehart and Winston, 1967. A distinguished Roman Catholic college president looks at the development of Catholic education in a world of educational and religious ferment. A presentation of what has been learned and what changes should be expected in the future.

Thayer, V. T. *The Attack Upon the American Secular School*. Boston: Beacon Press, 1951. The case for separation of church and state and a response to criticisms of secular schools.

Wilson, John F. *Church and State in American History*. Boston: D. C. Heath, 1965. Source for ideas on the historic relations between church and state.

AUDIO-VISUAL MATERIALS

Children as People (Polymorph Films, Inc., 35 Min.) A school in which children are free to move about, to talk, and to plan and direct their own work. How they look and talk and how they relate to the adults in the school and how they manage their lives and learning. An "alternative" school.

Bible Reading in the Public Schools, A Report on the Supreme Court Decision, NCAT, University of Minnesota, 56 Min. One aspect of the problem of religion and the schools.

Roman Catholic View of Education, A (NET 29 Min.) Professor Father Robert J. Henle discusses a Roman Catholic view of education.

NINE

WHO'S IN CHARGE HERE?

The teacher works in a particular school, usually in a particular public school system in a particular community. What are the surrounding conditions and forces influencing the teacher in such a public school? In other words, who's in charge here?

INFLUENCES ON THE PUBLIC SCHOOL IN THE COMMUNITY

THE POWER STRUCTURE

Within the specific community in which the new teacher will work, it is probable that a power structure exists. The term *power structure* was popularized by the Southern sociologist Floyd Hunter in a study of the early 1950s.[1] He recognized that one could not simply explain decision-making in communities through reference to the legal channels alone. Social class also influences the decision-making process. So Hunter studied a city of over 500,000 population and found that decision-making was largely the province of a few men who dominated the economic system of the city. The influential men in this informal power structure usually did not hold public offices; instead they were the key industrialists, financiers, and commercial leaders of Regional City, as Hunter called his actual community. The public officials followed the decisions of the men in the informal power structure; few citizens actually participated in community decisions.

Not all of the studies which followed Hunter's found the degree of monopolization of power that Hunter did in Regional City. Yet most studies agreed that only a small percentage of the people were involved in basic community decisions. For instance, Robert Presthus concluded from his studies, "In sum,

[1] Floyd Hunter, *Community Power Structure* (Chapel Hill, N.C.: University of North Carolina Press, 1953).

our findings in Edgewood generally support earlier research of sociologists who found a tendency toward elitism in community power structures which were usually dominated by economic elites. In Riverview, the decision structure remains highly concentrated, but political leaders play the major role. Regarding the restriction of active participation to the few, the more recent findings of political scientists are quite similar."[2]

Recognizing the importance of the question of who makes the basic decisions in communities concerning public education, students of power such as Ralph D. Kimbrough have explored the process of educational decision-making.[3] Stephen K. Bailey and others examined particularly the relationship of school decisions and politics.[4] While the students of decision-making in school systems recognized that the community power structures differed from one school district to the other, they were able to generalize on some common characteristics. Based on their conclusions, the new public school teacher might well assume that, despite the equalitarian ideals of democracy, power in a school district is not equally distributed among all the people. At the top of the structure are usually the influentials, for instance a powerful industrialist. Below them are the leaders who perform a variety of roles in the school system, such as a superintendent or an important politician.

In power systems there are ground rules, or procedural norms, which vary in accordance with the type of power structure, the people involved, their interests and goals. People who do not observe these rules usually lose their power to influence the system. Latent centers of power composed of people who potentially have strength but who do not usually choose to exercise their power must also be considered. Given a community crisis, those who are silent yet powerful may be heard from.

THE TYPES OF POWER STRUCTURE

Students of community power structures in relationship to schools have identified four main types of community power structures. Kimbrough, for instance, recognizes the *monopolistic power structure* in which the influentials, through consulting together, dominate the decisions, though often with some opposition. *Multi-group noncompetitive structures* are often found in rural areas where each village has its own power structure and where political change comes about through temporary unions of the influentials from the different villages. *Competitive elite structures* exist when power struggles occur between coalitions of influentials. *Pluralistic power structures* occur in which power groups specialize on particular fields; for instance, those providing leadership

---

[2] Robert Presthus, *Men at the Top* (New York: Oxford University Press, 1964), p. 430 (quote found in Kimbrough, *Administering Elementary Schools*, pp. 70–71).
[3] Ralph B. Kimbrough, *Political Power and Educational Decision Making* (Chicago, Ill.: Rand McNally, 1964).
[4] Stephen K. Bailey, Richard L. Frost, Paul E. Marsh, and Robert C. Wood, *Schoolmen and Politics* (Syracuse, N.Y.: Syracuse University Press, 1962).

in the field of education may not be heavily involved in other areas of community activity.[5]

Kimbrough also points out that the resultant power systems may be open or closed. He cites his research in Florida in two counties he refers to as Beach County, a closed social system, and River County, an open social system. In Beach County, the few dominant influentials, largely from the business groups, were hostile to outside influences, opposed to economic and social changes which might threaten the status quo, and were, in general, conservative. In such a closed system, educational innovation would be difficult to carry on, particularly if it required funds from outside sources such as the federal government. However, in River County, with a more varied group of influentials including some active educational administrators, there was much more openness to and interest in change. River County was closer to the democratic ideal than Beach County; yet even within River County, characterized as it was by an open competitive elite, there was far from maximum effective democracy. However, the climate for innovation was favorable in open River County, partly due to the fact that many new residents had recently come into the county because of a new economic development in the area.

INFLUENCES ON THE TEACHER IN THE SCHOOL SYSTEM

THE BOARD OF EDUCATION

High in the legal framework in public schools is the local school board, which holds the general policy-making authority in communities. Though most frequently called the school board or the board of education, the local governing body for public education is sometimes called a committee; the members of the board are sometimes described as the school directors, trustees, commissioners, or inspectors.

Though the board is the local controlling agency and though there can be no school district without a school board, it is important to bear in mind that this local agency's powers and operation are influenced by the state legislature as the controlling state authority. The school board is a civil subdivision of the state; it looks to state statutes for its administrative powers. Yet school board members have substantial autonomy to make decisions.

In 1968 there were approximately 21,000 school boards in the United States and, assuming that a typical board had five members, approximately 105,000 school board members.[6]

The American school board grew out of the early New England town government. Committees of selectmen carried through the decisions of the New Eng-

---

[5] Ralph B. Kimbrough, *Administering Elementary Schools: Concepts and Practices* (New York: Macmillan, 1968), pp. 73–74.
[6] Stephen J. Knezevich, *Administration of Public Education* (New York: Harper and Row, 1969), p. 213.

land town meeting. In 1721 the heavily burdened selectmen of Boston appointed a committee on school visitation. At first such school committees were the agents of the selectmen, but an 1826 Massachusetts law established school committees as a separate entity. So school boards governed separately from other community governing bodies date from the early nineteenth century in America.

School boards are usually elected directly by the people: a commonly accepted estimate is 85 percent; the remaining 15 percent are appointed by public officials such as mayors or occasionally by the governor. The usual number of members is from five to seven though the size of local school boards sometimes ranges from one to fifteen members; a school board member usually serves from three to six years, though again the length of a term may range from one to seven years. The large majority of school board members receive no pay but perform their office as a public service. The large majority are men who, relatively speaking, represent the higher social levels in their community. They are generally better educated than the population of the community which elects them; most of them are college graduates. Historically, school board members come from backgrounds more representative of the haves than the have-nots. Among school board members, there are a disproportionate number of lawyers, businessmen, and doctors.[7]

Today, despite increasing minority group representation, a general disproportionate distribution of power still exists. Consequently, many school board members are consciously or unconsciously predisposed to the interests of the more prosperous and propertied members of the community. They often interact with such associates in their daily work and they often encounter them in school affairs, since the propertied and prosperous carry the largest burden of taxation and are sensitive to getting their money's worth.

The responsibilities of a local school board were summarized by Knezevich as follows:

1. To satisfy the spirit as well as the word of state laws dealing with education and of the regulations of the state education authority.
2. To ascertain goals or objectives of public education and to prepare general policies in tune with them.
3. To select a superintendent of schools, designate him as the chief executive officer, and work harmoniously with him.
4. To strive continuously to develop further and improve the scope and quality of educational opportunities for all children and youth in the district.
5. To create policies which will attract and retain professional and other personnel needed to realize educational objectives.
6. To provide educationally efficient and safe school-plant facilities.

---

[7] This was noted as early as 1927 by George Counts in his study, *The Social Composition of Boards of Education: A Study in the Social Control of Public Education.*

7. To plan for and obtain financial resources necessary to achieve educational goals.
8. To keep the people of the district informed and aware of status, progress, and problems of their schools.
9. To appraise activities of the school district in the light of its objectives.
10. To discharge its responsibilities as a state agency by participating in statewide efforts to promote and improve public education.[8]

The single most important responsibility of a school board is to determine policy for the school system. A policy statement is a guideline which describes an objective to be achieved. Increasingly school board policies are written; written policies save time, money, and effort, reduce inconsistencies in school board action, and prove especially useful when community controversies develop. They are particularly helpful to the staff; all should be familiar with them. However, too often the teacher is unaware of these statements.

School board policies usually deal with such matters as the work of the board and the superintendent, personnel relations, the instructional program, school food services, business matters, student transportation, selection and retention of personnel, policies about pupils, and public relations.

School boards are constantly exhorted by experts on school organizations to make a clear distinction between policy-making and administration; nevertheless, a gray area persists. A major function of a school superintendent and his team is to supply leadership and thus constantly advise and consult with the board on the development of policy. On the other hand, a board member wants to see his policies embodied in rules and regulations and thus is likely to take a substantial interest in the precise courses of actions which are developed to carry out the broad framework of policy.

Meetings of school boards are usually open to the public. But sometimes a school board finds it desirable to hold an executive session in such cases as disciplinary action directed against particular pupils, accusations brought against teachers, and decisions on the purchase of school sites. But when boards use executive sessions too frequently and use open sessions primarily for voting with a minimum of discussion, they are naturally subject to suspicion by the public and the mass media.

The school board member has a difficult job. He not only has the responsibility for formulating policy but also for evaluating results. He is expected to play down his own self-interests and play up board unity. He is expected to support the superintendent who, after all, was selected by the board. He should be a leader and be effective in personal human relations; he must also be able to relate to teachers and to the administrative staff. Above all, he should have the courage of his convictions in situations beset by pressures.

School boards operate in increasingly difficult circumstances. Today there is a demand for high quality education; teachers are increasingly militant, and

---

[8] Stephen J. Knezevich, *Administration of Public Education* (New York: Harper and Row, 1968), pp. 216–217.

decisions about salaries and working conditions are difficult. The federal government enters the picture through court decisions and through special programs of aid and support. The school is increasingly regarded as an institution to deal with problems traditionally viewed as noninstructional and to correct social injustice. Pressure groups increase and grow more vigorous. Innovation is expected from schools. Criticisms proliferate. Many community forces and varied expectations must be taken into account. Yet few citizens are enthusiastic about helping board members obtain the kind of financial support the schools need to meet such demands.

One problem today is how the residents of a local district will exercise influence over their schools. In some cases minority groups claim they must have authority to hire and fire neighborhood principals and teachers, thus carrying decentralization of decision-making to a point where it is difficult to see the relationship of these functions to the total school district. This is defended as a way of involving minorities in the vital process of education. But it raises the question of whether local residents not organized as a board of education have the competence, authority, and final accountability to carry out their wishes. Consequently, proposals for community control within large cities should be accompanied by plans for community boards of education with defined legal powers and a carefully spelled-out relationship to any centralizing board and administration.

Citizens of a community often know very little about how a board operates; teachers are frequently suspicious of boards. Meanwhile the power structure continues to operate, regardless of whether board members are high in the power structure or not. So the typical board of education in America presides over a situation marked by considerable conflict. The board member often relies heavily upon his executive officer, particularly the superintendent.

THE SCHOOL SUPERINTENDENT

The general executive agent for a school system is the superintendent, sometimes known as the general superintendent, the supervising principal, or the district school superintendent. The superintendent is the implementer and the executive for the board.

In the early years of American education the executive and implementing body was the school committee itself, operating through a standing committee of the board of education. But the demands on such standing committees grew heavier as school systems grew more complex. By 1837, Buffalo and Louisville established the post of school superintendent. Some of the early city school superintendents were elected by popular vote, and though this approach was soon terminated, election of county and state superintendents still exists in many states.

The early superintendent was the "the board's man" and was responsible for a variety of chores rather than for leadership. His work was primarily superintending instruction; it was not until the twentieth century that he took over financial and building functions.

Even today some superintendents are bogged down with "administrivia." However, more superintendents are assuming leadership responsibilities.

In 1967–68 there were about 13,265 local superintendents of public schools and 1,750 intermediate school superintendents.[9] The job of the superintendent today is a complex one. Knezevich describes it as follows:

1. The superintendent is the chief executive officer of the board.
2. He is responsible for carrying out all policies, rules, and regulations established by the board. In matters not specifically covered by board policy, he is to take appropriate action and report the same to the board not later than the next regular meeting.
3. All individuals employed by the board are responsible directly or indirectly to the superintendent of schools.
4. The superintendent has the authority to prepare regulations and to give such instruction to school employees as may be necessary to make the policies of the board effective. He may delegate responsibilities and assign duties. Such delegation and assignment do not relieve the superintendent of responsibility for actions of subordinates.
5. Except when matters pertaining to his reemployment are being considered, the superintendent is to be present at all meetings of the board and its special committees.
6. He is responsible for preparing and submitting the budget to cover school operations.
7. The superintendent has the authority, within limits of major appropriations approved by the board, to authorize and direct all purchases and expenditures.
8. He recommends all candidates for employment. The board has the authority to reject specific candidates recommended, but personnel finally accepted should be employed only upon the recommendation of the superintendent.
9. The superintendent formulates and recommends personnel policies necessary to the functioning of the school.
10. The superintendent provides professional leadership for the educational program of the schools and is responsible for developing a system of regular reporting to the board on all aspects of that program.
11. The superintendent is responsible for keeping the school board informed on all vital matters pertaining to the school system.
12. He is responsible for the development of a program of maintenance and improvement or expansion of the buildings and the site. This includes recommendation for employment and supervision of all building custodians.
13. He is responsible for formulating and administering a program for supervision for all schools.
14. The superintendent is responsible for submitting an annual report on the operation of the school system.[10]

---

[9] Knezevich, p. 238.   [10] *Ibid.*, p. 239.

Yet, in a sense, the superintendent is still the "board's man" for the board still retains the right to dismiss him. But a school board should not too lightly dismiss a superintendent. If a superintendent is to be more than a puppet, he may well be involved in disagreements with board members or indeed the board as a whole. The relationship of the school board members and the superintendent should be one of mutual responsibility in which each supplies his ideas, listens to the others and all work for the best interests of the school.

Today's superintendents have usually had a broad background of experience and interests, and have been especially concerned with the social aspects of education. "The fields of major study most frequently listed by superintendents were the behavioral sciences (sociology, economics, psychology, anthropology, and human relations), 17.6 percent; education, 16.8 percent; physical and biological sciences, 14.8 percent; history and political science, 14.7 percent; mathematics, 11.4 percent; and English, 8.6 percent."[11] Almost all superintendents have a master's degree. By 1968 more than a fourth of the school superintendents of the country had a doctorate and others were working toward this.

Yet today as the post of superintendent involves increasing competence in politics and human relations, some school systems are turning from the educator-superintendent to the nationally prominent civic figure in the search for capable superintendents. Recently, New York City, seeking a superintendent, sounded out such national figures as Ralph Bunche, Arthur Goldberg, and other well-known Americans. Because of rising costs and the need for managerial skills in conducting large enterprises, some boards have considered selecting a superintendent from the top ranks of industrial leadership. But the professional educator is still the usual choice for the superintendency.

THE CENTRAL OFFICE ADMINISTRATIVE AND SUPERVISORY STAFF

If the superintendent is to serve as the executive for the policy-making school board, he needs help from a team or staff. This is particularly true as the school system grows larger and as school programs grow more complicated. The early American superintendents sometimes found themselves responsible not only for administering the schools but for some of the teaching. Boards of education soon found it necessary to relieve superintendents of such assignments and to supply them with secretaries and similar clerical assistance in order to get the job done. But even secretaries and clerks were not enough; professional assistance in staff positions had to be provided. This was the beginning of the professional team, usually headquartered and working with the superintendent in the central office of the school system.

The size and organization of the supporting staff depends on the size and nature of the school system. For instance, it is still possible in small systems for the superintendent to have no more help than a school secretary. But the larger the school operation, the more special functions emerge—such as the general

---

[11] *Ibid.*, pp. 243–244.

supervisor whose task is to help teachers, system-wide, to improve the quality of their teaching, or the curriculum director whose function it is to update and improve the curriculum through teacher participation in curriculum-building. In the larger school systems, the general supervisor who attempts to better instruction in all fields and at all school levels yields to specialized supervisors, who know intimately particular specialized fields, such as music or science, or are especially informed about a particular level, such as elementary or junior high school or senior high school.

A logical first addition to the superintendent's staff was the assistant superintendent, first appointed in the large cities in America in the middle of the nineteenth century. In small systems, the general superintendent and his assistant superintendent still handle matters of personnel, instruction, business management, and public relations.

Assistant superintendents are often placed in charge of major responsibilities within the school system. For instance, an assistant superintendent may be in charge of elementary education, or secondary education, or business affairs, or curriculum, or professional personnel, or services to pupils. In other words, an assistant superintendent may work with an instructional area or a service function of the school.

As cities grew and the number of assistant superintendents in big city systems increased, the post of deputy superintendent was created to coordinate the work of various assistant superintendents. The geographical sprawl of big cities also necessitated the appointment of area or district superintendents who are in charge of geographic areas within a large city though ultimately responsible to the superintendent. As the current drive for greater decentralization of the school bureaucracies of big cities grows, the district or area superintendent will probably increase his responsibilities and influence.

If a system contains a considerable number of supervisors, they may be responsible to a director of supervision who in turn reports to an assistant superintendent. In addition to supervisors, school systems often develop directors or coordinators of special functions. The audio-visual function is an illustration. The audio-visual director or coordinator may be responsible to the assistant superintendent who is in charge of curriculum or instruction.

Supervisors were first conceived to be inspectors, and it was first thought that laymen could do this job. After the Civil War, however, professional inspectors or evaluators became necessary.

In time, American educators learned that there were more effective ways of helping teachers than to place inspectors or evaluators over them. In the twentieth century supervision became increasingly concerned with helping teachers improve their instruction through classroom observation by supervisors, rather than inspection or rating. With the growth of emphasis upon human relations techniques both in industry and in education, supervision became an earnest attempt to help teachers develop as professionals and to encourage curriculum changes through teachers. But, the old image of the supervisor as an inspector or evaluator who reports to "the boss" persists.

In an attempt to eliminate, or at least reduce, the inspector-evaluator image, school systems have developed a distinction between "line" and "staff" officers. The line officer is the individual who is directly subordinate to the superintendent, yet has the authority to act as a chief almost as if he were himself the superintendent. People in line positions can and do exert their authority with respect to those who are subordinate to them in the educational structure. On the other hand, a person in a staff position, though still subordinate to the superintendent, sees himself primarily as a person acting as a service agent. Such a person can exert no direct authority; he or she attempts to be perceived as a helper or consultant. Supervisors today usually prefer the role of staff worker rather than line authority.

In professional baseball, when the manager of a ball club is fired, the coaches he has brought to the club are usually dismissed too. When a new manager takes over a ball club it is usually assumed that he will bring his own coaches with him. To a lesser degree this is the same situation when a superintendent is employed or dismissed; his top level staff may go with him. Lower level line officers and almost all staff officers still stay on, for they are regarded as "career" people within the school system, even as, despite changes in a national administration, the "career diplomats" of the State Department stay on. One result is that the key men around the superintendent are sometimes more personally loyal to him than those somewhat removed from the superintendent's "cabinet."

In today's complicated operation the superintendent needs staff members who have specialized skills he lacks. In the effective large system, the operation becomes a team effort in which the superintendent coordinates the efforts of several specialists. Yet because a common training pattern for all members of the superintendent's staff often persists, the superintendent may find himself working with staff members with skills like his own rather than with the specialists who are really needed.

In the day-to-day decisions that carry out the board policies and the superintendent's rules and procedures many different interpretations may develop. The problem of communication, both written and oral, can result in countermanding an "order" from the superintendent. Getting through to principals and teachers is difficult and almost impossible if those in the line want to block or modify the message. The reverse is also true. The teacher who wishes to communicate with the superintendent has a long and difficult road, especially in a large system.

Though the headquarters of the varied members of the superintendent's team is frequently the central office (or, with decentralization, the office of the district or area superintendent) members of the superintendent's team are frequently found at work in individual schools. This is particularly true of the staff officers. Thus, members of the superintendent's staff form an important ingredient in the answer to the question "Who's in charge here?" Sometimes their relationships with the man who is supposedly in charge in the individual school—the principal —grow complex indeed.

The principal's responsibilities include conferring with teachers. Courtesy of Black Star.

THE SCHOOL PRINCIPAL

The school principal is the chief executive officer or administrator of the basic unit of the school system—the individual school. Today there are substantially more than 100,000 principals or assistant principals in American public elementary and secondary schools. The smaller the school the more likely it is to have only a principal; the bigger the school the more likely it is to have one or more assistant principals.

The evolution of the principalship resembles the evolution of the superintendency and the superintendent's team. The early American schools were staffed only by teachers. Then certain teachers were charged with some responsibilities for the school's administration. A later step was the hybrid of principal-teacher with administration responsibilities primary and teaching secondary. Latest was the creation of the full-time principal. Yet even today one finds, particularly in rural or in small communities, situations where the principal also teaches.

In the evolution of the principalship, the principal started out as a glorified clerk. In the twentieth century, the principal's major responsibility is seen as leadership for his students, teachers, and building or buildings. A good principal today skillfully uses the special services and supporting staff from the central office and encourages the development of improved instruction through resource people within the school itself, such as "helping teachers." But even the good principal is sometimes perplexed as to what services he should supply and which come from central staff people or delegated individuals within the school.

Concerning the work of the principal, Knezevich says,

> The principal in a public school, whether at the elementary or secondary-school level, is a counselor of students, the school disciplinarian, the organizer

of the schedule, the supervisor of the instructional program, the pupil-relations representative for the attendance area, the liaison between teachers and the superintendent, the director and evaluator of teaching efforts, the manager of the school facilities, the supervisor of custodial and food-service employees within the building, and a professional leader. Little wonder that this is a demanding position as well as one of considerable significance determining the direction of public education.[12]

The high school principal occupies a higher status position than other principals, partly because there are fewer high school principals than elementary or junior high school principals. Since the high school is usually the largest of the community's schools, the high school principalship is viewed as a senior position. But the reasons are also largely historical. One of the most prestigious posts of the nineteenth century was headmaster of an academy, the predecessor of the American high school. The high school principalship preceded the development of either the superintendency or the elementary principalship. Thus in the nineteenth century there was sometimes conflict as to authority between the high school principal and the superintendent.

THE TEACHER

Teachers within a school constitute still another force affecting decision-making in the individual school. The "good old days" in which the American teacher was a humble and subservient follower of orders seems to be gone—and few forward-looking people mourn this passing. With the new teacher militancy, teacher concerns have gone beyond salary and immediate welfare conditions and have included participation in shaping the curriculum. No precise design for teacher participation in the conduct of the school has yet emerged, but greater participation by teachers is a reality.

Two tendencies appear to support this development. Enlightened supervisors and other central office staff members have long been saying that teachers should be a genuine force in the shaping of the school's program. So supervisors have long secured participation by teachers in shaping and forming the curriculum, rather than simply implementing what others have mandated. A second tendency is for many teachers to recognize that, if they are to be maximally effective, their concerns must go beyond salaries and working conditions and into the realm of curriculum. True, some demands by teachers' unions or associations may have been misguided; they may have been too concerned about the time which teachers devote to committee work and too anxious to avoid the authority of principals and central staff members. But there is great promise and potentiality in teacher union and teacher association participation in creating a more relevant curriculum.

---

[12] Knezevich, p. 283.

Teachers in an in-service training session. Courtesy of Education Development Center.

THE STUDENT

Nor can the teacher of the 1970s afford to overlook the student as a participant in decision-making. Again, granted that student participation has often been clumsy, conflict-oriented, and even violent, the potential of student participation is clear. Recently New York City accepted a forward looking code concerning students' rights:

1. In each high school there should be established an elective and representative student government with offices open to all students. The student government will establish reasonable standards for candidates for office. All students should be allowed to vote in annual elections designed to promote careful consideration of the issues and candidates.

a. The student government shall have the power to allocate student activity funds, subject to established audit controls and the by-laws of the Board of Education. Extracurricular activities shall be conducted under guidelines established by the student government. The student government shall be involved in the process of developing curriculum and of establishing disciplinary policies.
b. Representatives selected by the student government shall meet at least monthly with the principal to exchange views, to share in the formulation of school student policies and to discuss school-student relations and any other matters of student concern.
2. A parent-student-faculty consultative council, as established by previous Board of Education resolutions, shall meet at least monthly to discuss any matter relating to the high school. The Consultative Council shall organize a subcommittee to consider matters of school-wide concern submitted by individual students. The subcommittee shall place such problems on the agenda of the consultative council when appropriate.

The consultative council shall establish a continuing relationship with the principal to secure information regarding the administration of the school, to make recommendations for the improvement of all school services and to promote implementation of agreed upon innovations. Its structure and operating procedures shall be placed on file with the chancellor.
3. Official school publications shall reflect the policy and judgment of the student editors. This entails the obligation to be governed by the standards of responsible journalism, such as avoidance of libel, obscenity and defamation. Student publications shall provide as much opportunity as possible for the sincere expression of all shades of student opinion.
4. Students may exercise their constitutionally protected rights of free speech and assembly so long as they do not interfere with the operations of the regular school program.
   a. Students have a right to wear political buttons, armbands and other badges of symbolic expression, as long as these do not violate the limits set in 4c, below.
   b. Students may distribute political leaflets, newspapers and other literature at locations adjacent to the school.
   c. Students shall be allowed to distribute literature on school property at specified locations and times designated. The principal and the student government shall establish guidelines governing the time and place of distribution at a site that will not interfere with normal school activities. They will also provide for sanctions against those who do not adhere to prescribed procedures.

   No commercial or obscene material, nothing of a libelous nature or involving the defamation of character nor anything advocating racial or religious prejudice will be permitted to be distributed within the school. In noting these exceptions it is clearly the intention of the Board of Education to promote the dissemination of diverse viewpoints and to foster discussion of all political and social issues.

The high schools have also become involved with civil and human rights movements. Courtesy of Howard Petrick from Nancy Palmer.

    d. Students may form political and social organizations, including those that champion unpopular causes. These organizations, however, must be open to all students and must abide by Board of Education policies as developed in guidelines established by the student government acting in concert with the principal. These organizations shall have reasonable access to school facilities.
5. Faculty advisers shall be appointed by the principal after consultation with the student group.
6. Students have the right to determine their own dress, except where such dress is clearly dangerous, or is so distractive as to clearly interfere with the learning and teaching process. This right may not be restricted even by a dress code arrived at by a majority vote of students, as Dr. Ewald Nyquist, Acting State Commissioner of Education held this year in Decisions No. 8022 and 8023.
7. Students shall receive annually upon the opening of school a publication setting forth rules and regulations to which students are subject. This publication shall also include a statement of the rights and responsibilities of students. It shall be distributed to parents as well.
8. A hearing must be held within five school days of any suspension as prescribed by law and the circulars of the Chancellor (Superintendent of Schools).
9. The extent and definition of student rights and responsibilities are subject to discussion by the consultative councils. Appeals from the decisions of the head of the school, relating to rights and responsibilities herein enume-

rated, must first be lodged with the assistant superintendent in charge of the high schools, then the Chancellor and finally the central Board of Education. All such appeals shall be decided as quickly as possible.

10. Rights also entail responsibilities. One of the major goals of this document is to establish a new trust, one based on the humane values of self-respect and respect for others. No student has the right to interfere with the education of his fellow students. If dialogue is interrupted or destroyed, then the bonds that hold us together are broken. It is thus the responsibility of each student to respect the rights of all who are involved in the educational process.

Explanation. This resolution is an attempt to state systematically some of the rights and responsibilities of senior high school students. In no way does it diminish the legal authority of the school officials and of the Board of Education to deal with disruptive students. The resolution recognizes the student's responsibility for his conduct and at the same time extends the range of his responsibility. It is meant to foster greater understanding so that students, parents, teachers and administrators can more effectively participate in an active educational partnership.[13]

Let us grant that students cannot possibly know completely what is best for them. Yet the fact remains that they are the ultimate consumers of the curriculum. They too deserve a voice in the making of decisions. The quality of their education is involved. After a period of struggle which may be particularly sharp in schools that previously have been indifferent to viewpoints of students, we may move into a period in which the student relationship to decision-making proves productive. This is a frontier on which the new teacher, who is nearest to the contemporary student generation, might be active.

THE CURRICULUM

The curriculum is also a force in decision-making in the individual school. Some educators believe it to be a more important force than the individuals who supposedly make the decisions as they set policies, administer, and teach.

The curriculum is made up of all of the learning experiences under the control of the school. Therefore, such subjects as arithmetic in the third grade or French in high school, are part of the school curriculum. Whatever learning experiences a school affords are part of the curriculum. (The curriculum will be defined further in Chapters 17 and 18.)

The curriculum of the specific school in which you will teach is influenced by historic backgrounds and social forces. The curriculum is influenced by whether the school is public, parochial, or independent. It is influenced by individuals, by the broad educational policies, and by the various forces which exist in the system and school in which you work.

---

[13] Board of Education's amended resolution on "Rights and Responsibilities of Senior High School Students," *New York Times* (July 8, 1970), p. 16.

If we look for the central defining agency of the curriculum of your school, we must again turn to the individual state. For the broad framework of subjects and requirements are set forth by the state legislature and are more specifically defined by the state department of public instruction or education. The law of a state often defines in a general way the minimum curriculum offerings. Sometimes laws go further to specify particular areas or emphases, such as American history or driver's education, which must be taught in all the schools.

Despite this apparent restriction, local school systems have substantial latitude in arriving at curriculum decisions. After all, it is the local board of education that is responsible for broad curriculum policies and it is the superintendent and supporting staff who must execute these policies and realize the goals set by the board. So curriculum making is an activity which utilizes the energies of many educators at the local level. In the United States there is considerable variation in the degree to which local school systems depend on standardized resources supplied by the state and by textbook publishers and the degree to which they depend on local initiative and teacher-influenced curricular approaches.

For instance, some school systems depend heavily upon whatever courses of study or curriculum guides are provided by the state. Such courses of study are often prepared by a single individual or a few "experts." In some schools, the "curriculum" is almost synonymous with textbooks adopted for use throughout the state. What some teachers teach is exactly what a textbook prescribes.

Fortunately, educators are becoming increasingly independent of restrictive emphases. Today, when curiculum guides are used they are often the products of high level curriculum projects carried on jointly by scholars in the disciplines and by educators, including teachers. Projects such as PSSC (physics) or BSCS (biology) or SMSG (mathematics) are the products of scholars organized in a physical science study committee, a biological science curriculum study, and a school mathematics study group respectively.

Today even more enterprising educators stress curriculum development to meet the needs of students in the individual school situation. Such curriculum development even refuses to be bound by the names of established subject matter. Out of such experimentation has grown concern for interdisciplinary problems, such as race relations and international relations. Out of such experimentation has grown the combination or fusion of subjects, such as the combining of English and social studies into a unified studies or core program.

WHO IS IN CHARGE HERE?

This chapter has emphasized forces contributing to decisions in a particular school within a particular school system. The question is, "Who *is* in charge here anyway?" Nominally within the individual school it is the principal, who, it is important to remember, works within a larger setting. He is in constant and sometimes complex interaction with members of the superintendent's team. Because he represents only one school, he sometimes conflicts with adminis-

212 THE NATURE OF AMERICAN SCHOOLS

trators who must make decisions that affect all schools in the district. He is very much subject to decisions made at the level of the superintendent of schools and to the policy-making responsibility of the board of education. The surrounding power structure, whether completely understood by him or not, plays its part in the complex process of decision-making. The individual principal also has to take into account the students and teachers in his school and those who live in the immediate area of the school and the views of all these individuals.

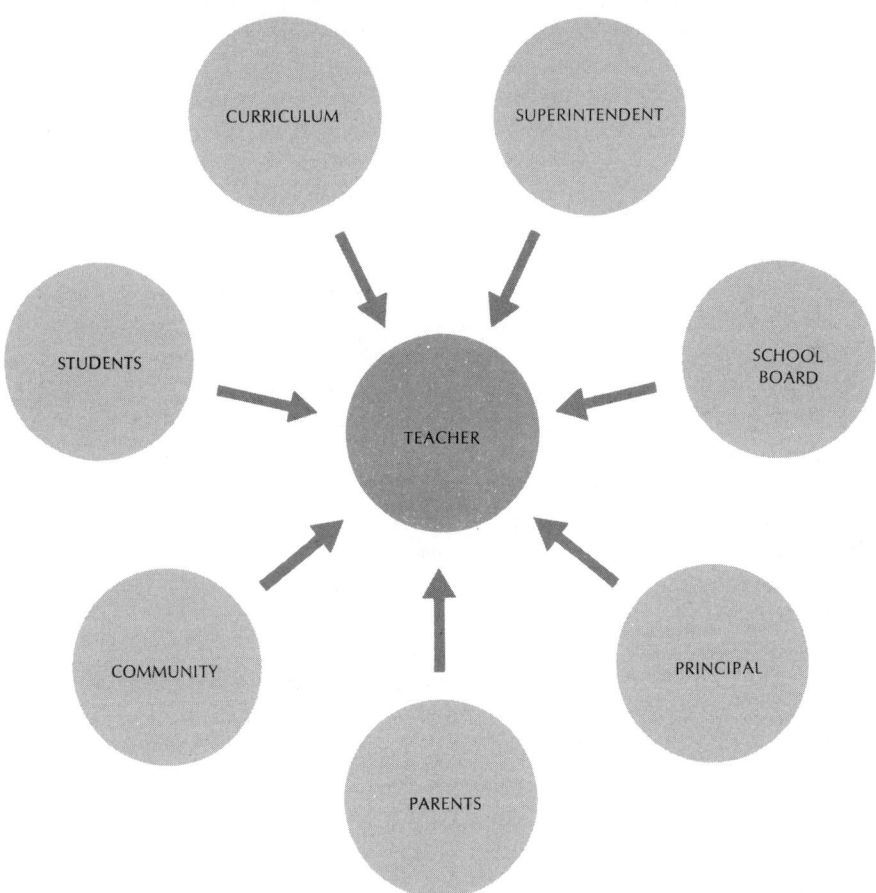

FIGURE 9.1
Influences on the American Teacher

Perhaps the best answer to our question is to recognize that no single person is "in charge here," as there would be within an authoritarian system. Instead, the affairs of the individual school are subject to the interaction of a variety of forces, some far beyond the community at the national level. These forces interrelate and shape and reshape each other and out of the interplay come the decisions reached within the individual school.

The wide variety of individuals responsible for decision-making makes it all the more important to identify the goals and objectives which are to be achieved, and the degree to which each person contributes. A mechanism must be applied to hold each accountable for his contribution.

The new teacher may look with some degree of anxiety at a situation marked by dynamic forces and constant flux. He may prefer the security of clear-cut decisions made by clearly identifiable persons. As Erich Fromm pointed out, many people fear freedom; perhaps such individuals will be unhappy in a situation marked by a balance of forces rather than by a dominating decision-maker (whether it takes the form of a human being such as a principal or a medium of instruction such as the textbook for the course).

On the other hand, the new teacher may have the type of personality that welcomes the challenge of flexibility and flux. The very existence of a variety of influences gives him the opportunity to make decisions for himself, particularly with respect to his classrooms and students. Rather than imposing a high degree of restriction on his teaching, the variety of forces influencing the program of individual schools often results in less restrictiveness than the new teacher expects.

Yet this great variation often causes parents to ask questions about common standards and the determination of ways of measuring achievement. Teachers must be willing to develop and respect evidence which will show whether or not they are successfully carrying out their assignments. Educators must be accountable for their work and they must be aware of the varied expectations held for them by many individuals and groups having different perceptions of their role.

DISCUSSION

1. What is the meaning of power structure as applied to American communities? To American education? What are the variations in power structures in America, according to students of power?
2. What seems to you to be the power structure in the community in which you live or in which you study? Find out how valid your reported impressions are.
3. In the schools you attended did you see any evidence of pressure groups at work in establishing or changing school policy or emphases in the curriculum?
4. In what ways might a large number of new people moving into a community create a change in the community's educational system?
5. What is the usual role of board of education members in the power structure? What are possible roles in the power structure which board of education members could play?
6. Why did boards of education come into being in the United States?
7. What is the usual social composition of boards of education? What is the situation in your own community? Is any change in the social composition becoming

obvious? Discuss and revise the list of responsibilities of a local school board summarized by Knezevich.
8. What is the function of written policy statements for a school system? Do they exist in your community?
9. What are some illustrations of distinctions between policy-making and administration in education? Have there been any controversies in this connection in your community?
10. How has the work of the school board member grown increasingly complicated in recent years?
11. How did the superintendent's responsibility change over the years?
12. What are the academic backgrounds of the superintendents in school systems which have been attended by members of your class?
13. Revise the cited list of responsibilities of the superintendent in accordance with your perception of his proper responsibilities.
14. To what extent is the American superintendent "the board's man"?
15. How did the central office staff evolve? What were some first additions to the staff? What is the nature of the staff in the community you know best?
16. What are some issues in the question of centralization or decentralization of the administration of school systems?
17. How does a supervisor perceive his responsibility?
18. What are the usual channels of communication between members of the public or teachers and the superintendent of schools and the board of education? How can these channels of communication be improved? What is the situation in your own community?
19. Basically, what is the role of the school principal? How did this post evolve?
20. To what extent are teachers participants in decision-making in schools? Should they be? What gains or losses come from greater teacher participation?
21. Should students play a role in the determination of educational matters? In determining the curriculum? In presenting and handling grievances? In teacher rating? In promotion and tenure and salaries?
22. How is the curriculum a force in decision-making in an individual school?
23. Who has been in charge in the schools you have attended? Do you agree that this individual or combination of individuals should have been in charge? Who do you think should be in charge in an individual school?

INVOLVEMENT
1. With the help of a sociologist, work out approaches to determine the power structure in a community. Interviews and questionnaires might be employed. Conclusions should be drawn with care, and throughout the investigation the possible negative repercussions should be recognized.
2. Attempt to generalize on the nature of the power structure in the community you know best.
3. Find the names, educational backgrounds, and areas of work of the members of your local board of education. Does your board membership represent the more affluent

and socially prominent elements of your community? Does it represent pressure groups? Are minority groups represented? In what ways does it reflect the model outlined in the chapter? In what ways does it differ?
4. Attend some meetings of the board of education of your home community or the community in which you are a student. Inquire how people attain their posts on school boards, their positions on issues before the board, etc. If an opportunity occurs, speak up for any viewpoint which you think the board should take into account.
5. Locate a copy of the Policy Handbook of your local school corporation. What areas does it cover generally? What are some of the exact rules and regulations it spells out? What kinds of implications do you see in these?
6. Draw up some distinctions between policy-making and administration for consideration by the class.
7. Invite the superintendent or one of his representatives to describe the program and problems of a local school system to your class. Ask the superintendent or his representative about recent changes in his work, including negotiations regarding salary, etc.
8. Invite a school supervisor to class to describe his relationship to the new teacher and the help he attempts to provide.
9. Invite a school principal to class to discover the kind of teacher he would like to employ. Discuss the desirable characteristics of such a teacher.
10. Visit the central office of your local school district. Obtain or make a chart of the organization of the administrative staff including both line and staff officers.
11. Invite several teachers to class to discuss their role in decision-making in schools. Attempt to clarify differences and similarities among them.
12. Interview a teacher you admire and ask him or her to frankly report to you his or her views of the functions and responsibilities of the school principal and the supervisor.
13. Invite the president of the school government organization and a student critic of his school to your class to comment on the proper role of the students in decision-making.
14. Ask teachers about the role of the curriculum in decision-making within a particular school. If specific materials are cited as influential in decision-making, attempt to obtain copies of them.
15. Sum up what you have learned about who is in charge in a particular school system. Advance your own theory on who should be in charge. In so doing, take into account the variety of influencing forces.

BIBLIOGRAPHY

Anderson, James G. *Bureaucracy in Education*. Baltimore: Johns Hopkins Press, 1968. A discussion of the causes of bureaucracy in education highlighting the critical dilemma of how to reconcile autonomy and individual responsibility with the bureaucratic hierarchy's demand for centralized control.

Bailey, Stephen K., Richard L. Frost, Paul E. Marsh, and Robert C. Wood. *Schoolmen and Politics*. Syracuse, N.Y.: Syracuse University Press, 1962. Realistic analysis of the political roles and relationships of educators in community settings.

Bowers, C. A. ed. *Education and Social Policy: Local Control of Education*. New York: Random House, 1970. Original readings dealing with the complex relationship between politics and public education with essays by Seymour M. Lipset, James S. Coleman, Jules Henry, and Edgar Z. Friedenberg.

Burbank, Natt B. *The Superintendent of Schools: His Headaches and Rewards.* Danville, Ill.: Interstate Printers and Publishers, 1968. Picture of the high pressure area in which a superintendent works.

Campbell, Roald F., John E. Corbally, and John A. Ramseyer. *Introduction to Educational Administration,* 3rd ed. Boston: Allyn and Bacon, 1966. A major book in administration reflecting the views of a group of administrative theorists who draw heavily on the behavioral sciences.

Dykes, Archie R. *School Board and Superintendent: Their Effective Working Relationships.* Danville, Ill.: Interstate Printers and Publishers, 1965. A study of the local unit of school administration, the school district, and its governing body, the board of education. An analysis of the interaction of school boards and superintendents.

Franklin, Marian Pope, ed. *School Organization: Theory and Practice.* Chicago: Rand McNally, 1967. Readings giving a comprehensive, concise view of school organization as it is and describing possibilities of new directions.

Frey, Sherman H. and Keith R. Getschman, eds. *School Administration: Selected Readings.* New York: Thomas Y. Crowell, 1968. The school administrator and his role in influencing the direction of growth and change in American society.

Heald, James E., Louis G. Romano, and Nicholas P. Georgiady, eds. *Selected Readings on General Supervision.* New York: Macmillan, 1970. A variety of articles on current trends and practices in effective supervision.

Hunter, Floyd. *Community Power Structure.* Chapel Hill, N.C.: University of North Carolina Press, 1953. Classic analysis of the concept of the power structure. The resultant pressures and tensions in American communities.

Kimbrough, Ralph B. *Administering Elementary Schools.* New York: Macmillan, 1968. The application of systems theory to behavioral problems in administering elementary schools. Emphasis on the importance of fusing knowledge of human behavior and management.

———. *Political Power and Educational Decision Making.* Chicago, Ill.: Rand McNally, 1964. Descriptions of the role of the power structure in actual American communities based on substantial research. The political role of educators in decision-making and policy development.

Knezevich, Stephen J. *Administration of Public Education,* 2nd ed. New York: Harper and Row, 1969. Useful, comprehensive volume on administration upon which this chapter draws.

Leeper, Robert R., ed. *Supervision: Emerging Profession.* Washington, D.C.: Association for Supervision and Curriculum Development, NEA, 1969. An anthology on supervision made up of selections from *Educational Leadership,* the magazine of ASCD.

Lucio, William H. and John D. McNeil. *Supervision: A Synthesis of Thought and Action.* New York: McGraw-Hill, 1969. Theories of supervision in education, including the scientific management theory, the human relations theory and the authors' revisionist view.

Masters, Nicholas A. *State Politics and the Public Schools: An Exploratory Analysis.* New York: Alfred A. Knopf, 1964. Examination of power and pressures at the state level.

Ovard, Glen F. *Administration of the Changing Secondary School.* New York: Macmillan, 1966. Administrative theory as well as practice.

Presthus, Robert. *Men at the Top.* New York: Oxford University Press, 1964. Scholarly examination of the procedures and practices of dominant individuals in contemporary society.

Rogers, David. *110 Livingston Street: Politics and Bureaucracy in the New York City School System.* New York: Random House, 1969. Detailed critical study of the workings of the largest school system in the United States.

Tuttle, Edward Mowbray. *School Board Leadership in America.* Danville, Ill.: Interstate Printers and Publishers, 1958. The services of local school boards and the purposes and functions of school boards associations in America.

AUDIO-VISUAL MATERIALS

School Buildings, 1967 (American Association of School Administrators, 154 fr., Color) Examines school building programs—views of interiors, exteriors, sites and plans of schools ranging from elementary through junior college level.

School Board in Action (National School Boards Assn., 26 Min., Color) Depicts, in a series of school board meetings with citizens, the manner in which the community and board deal with issues such as censorship of textbooks, salary increases, school board elections, and the floating of a bond issue to build a new school.

The Principal (McGraw-Hill Textfilms, 40 frs., School Helpers series) Designed to make students aware of the contributions made in their behalf by the school.

TEN

WHAT IS EXPECTED OF AMERICAN TEACHERS?

The word *role* once meant simply a part or a character to be played by an actor or actress. In more recent years, however, it has been borrowed from the theatre for sociological and educational purposes, and an adaptation has been made of its secondary definition, "the proper or customary function of a person or thing." Grace Graham, for instance, writes,

> Adolescents, like adults, have many statuses and roles. Status refers to one's position in a group, and *role* to the behavior associated with a particular status. A teen-ager may be a son, a brother, a steady boy friend, a buddy, a part-time employee, a student, a football player, a class president, and a leading character in a school play. In each of these statuses, he plays a different role. How he plays the role is determined to a considerable extent by the manner in which others expect him to play it.[1]

Harold L. Hodgkinson specifically compares the theatrical role with the individual's role in society: "Just as an actor learns a given role which he will perform, so each indivdual acquires a role for each reference group to which he refers. This role represents the desired norms and performances of the reference group."[2] Educators apply this concept to the varied people related to the educational process.

---

[1] Grace Graham, *The Public School in the New Society* (New York: Harper & Row, 1969), p. 336.
[2] Harold L. Hodgkinson, *Education in Social and Cultural Perspectives* (Englewood Cliffs, N.J.: Prentice-Hall, 1962), p. 3.

THE ROLES OF THE TEACHER

Today the individual teacher is expected to assume a variety of activities and behaviors. If you are to be an effective teacher, you must be familiar with your self-expectations and with the expectations others hold for you. With an understanding of these differing expectations, you can better recognize and react to praise and criticism you will necessarily encounter. If you become skillful in managing your responses to criticism, you may be better equipped to anticipate potential conflicts and either minimize them or provide support for your own viewpoints.

If your knowledge of roles is supplemented by an understanding of social realities, of your students' personal-social needs, and of an educational philosophy in which you are confident, you will be well-equipped for the conflicts and criticisms that arise.

But not all citizens are critics of teachers. In general, American community members regard teachers with a degree of respect; the status studies described in Chapter Four indicate that Americans consider teachers well within the upper third of occupational groups. The perceptions of community members vary according to community locales, parental and social class backgrounds, and inevitably, according to individual idiosyncracies.

COMMUNITY EXPECTATIONS IN DIFFERING LOCALES

Rural community members are often well acquainted with the community's teacher. The rural teacher customarily lives in or near the village or town in which he teaches. He is one of the neighbors and is known not only as a teacher but as a resident, householder, a citizen, and a participant in community life. As a result, he is frequently appraised in these roles rather than just as a teacher. If the morality of the community tends toward provincialism, he is usually expected to conform to what the community regards as reasonable limits on ideas and behavior. This does not mean that he is denied some degree of individuality, or indeed, eccentricity; it does mean that he is usually denied conspicuous violations of the community's accepted codes.

In the city, the situation is somewhat different. In the first place, the teacher often lives outside the neighborhood in which he teaches. Though he is far from wealthy, he is by background or has become by occupation a middle-class person. As such, he may be somewhat removed in ideas as well as in income from the poorer or wealthier section of the city in which he may teach.

Since the middle classes steadily leave the city, the middle-class teacher usually either joins the flight to the suburbs or lives in one of the remaining middle-class neighborhoods. He is therefore less often encountered by the community as a householder or community participant than his rural counterpart. In the urban community the teacher is often viewed somewhat impersonally and is met only on those occasions that community organizations or individual necessities bring the community member to the school. The result is twofold: more freedom or opportunity for variation in the teacher's personal life style, and more parent and student interest in his teaching role and performance than in his total personality. This does not mean that the teacher's personal life can outrage the urban community's sensibility; it does mean that his personal life is less visible to community members in the city setting.

Almost the same relationship of the teacher to the community is present in the suburb as in the city, though to a different degree. Few teachers can afford to live in conspicuously upper-income suburban communities. Indeed, some prefer not to live in such communities because perceptions of them as community service persons might interfere with their social patterns of living. Similarly, teachers are usually paid at a higher level than most residents of working-class suburbs and often prefer to live elsewhere. Many middle-class suburbs do exist in which teachers both live and work, and where teachers become known as householders and participants. A suburban teacher may also live in a middle-class community near the community in which he teaches. Since suburban newspapers often cover a county-wide area, or at least a larger area than one community, teachers may become known to citizens in the community in which they teach through accounts of community and social activities, community participation, etc.

PARENTAL EXPECTATIONS

A teacher encounters expectations and perceptions by community members which are closely related to the social class backgrounds of the particular neighborhood. For instance, an upper-class parent's expectations of the teacher may be to impart to the child the technical skill and knowledge he or she will need to enter the college of his choice. Support for educational innovation also exists in such communities, particularly on the part of parents alert to psychological insights and convinced of the importance of motivation; these parents, as a rule, take pride in having their schools do the "in" thing. But even supporters of innovation seldom support change at the expense of student admission into the best colleges.

Socioeconomic factors account for some contrasting parental conceptions concerning the community's teachers which may be surprising, or even alarming to the young teacher. Some rich persons equate teachers directly with the servant class. The comment of a matron in a wealthy suburb of Westchester County, New York, represents the view of a few very wealthy persons: "I don't see why that nice young school teacher hasn't married one of our chauffeurs." On the other hand, some first generation Americans from middle- or working-class neighborhoods highly respect teachers and want their children to teach.

Until recently, the characteristic experience of a teacher in a working-class district was to encounter few parents. The typical working-class community member seemed to assume that the school as an institution knew what it was doing and that teachers knew far more than community members about educa-

Counselor visits home of a juvenile delinquent to discuss problems and school program with family. Courtesy Ford Foundation.

tion. Only when school authorities required their presence because of their children's misbehavior did parents appear at the school. The prevalent attitude was not so much indifference as a feeling that education was not the parent's business.

In the last half of the 1960s this attitude has been replaced in some communities by militant concern by the poor, especially blacks and other minority groups, regarding the quality of education their children were receiving. Rather than passive acceptance, a tone of disappointment, anger, and hostility often characterizes the new relationships of some local community residents to the schools. Militant community members have not only picketed and demonstrated; they have sometimes entered the schools in sit-ins or have withdrawn their children from schools in boycotts or strikes. In some major cities there have been confrontations between striking teachers and militant community members bent on keeping the schools open. Charges of racism by blacks against predominantly white teaching staff members and by teachers against black militants have become commonplace.

The spokesmen for militant community groups charge that the schools have failed to teach many children to read, write, spell, and handle arithmetic adequately. Repeatedly, some minority group children have failed tests devised by educators to appraise the success of outcomes of teaching. Curriculum content relevant to blacks and other minority groups in America has been ignored or dealt with lightly, say the critics. Demands have mounted for school studies which take into account the black experience, including black history. The qualifications of whites to teach blacks have been sharply questioned by vigorous proponents of relevant education. Some communities have demanded the replacement of white teachers and administrators by members of their own group. In many communities, the former passivity of parents has been replaced by involvement and often turmoil.

Parents register their views on sex education at the New Jersey State Assembly. Courtesy of UPI.

Simultaneously, some residents of white working- or middle-class districts have grown suspicious of schools and teachers because of what some white residents regard as favoritism and partiality to minority group members. Parents in such communities have sometimes resisted programs of intercultural or intergroup education and have demonstrated against minority group students being bused into "their neighborhood," or majority group students being bused out into minority group neighborhoods. Though such white groups are currently less well organized, their anger and hostility are growing and their potential influence on school programs is evident.

In community conflict situations, the parents of students play an important part. They see themselves as being most intimately concerned, for it is their children's welfare and lives which are at stake.

INDIVIDUAL EXPECTATIONS

Teachers at any level of a public school system can testify to the completely individualized set of perceptions and problems brought to school by the parents of individual children. Even some of the most helpfully motivated Parent Teachers Association members often have difficulty in dealing with the real issues concerning the needs of a school in general because they are so concerned for the welfare of their children. Differing individual expectations concerning the purposes of education are characteristic of parents in communities which appear homogeneous but which actually are not.

Let us illustrate impressionistically the variety of individual expectations by describing the views of some citizens of a supposedly homogeneous suburb, as this author pointed out in an article about his neighbors:

A neighbor who works for Bell Telephone Laboratories says, "There has been a tremendous explosion of knowledge in the past few years. Do you realize that 87 percent of all the scientists who ever lived are alive at this very moment? Knowledge is multiplying fantastically. I want my son to master concepts and relationships and to have the skills to acquire and use the new knowledge, especially in the sciences and modern mathematics."

Another neighbor, who is a member of the local League of Women Voters, says, "I listen to my daughter's friends when they're sitting around our house. They want to make a difference in this world but they have no idea of how to go about it. High schools ought to teach them how to participate in community life as young citizens and how to deal with social forces and problems."

Another of my neighbors has a deserved reputation as a good mother. She says, "I want my children to be good human beings. For instance, I hope they will hear and play music, read widely and love knowledge, be creative in the arts, take part eagerly in sports, and enjoy their leisure. The need is for well-balanced people who hold to humane values. I hope the high schools help the young to solve their problems and to live with themselves."

Another neighbor owns a garage. He says, "Not everybody goes to college for further education and for preparation for a professional career. High schools ought to teach practical skills too so that a youngster can move into a job after he gets his high school diploma. Girls ought to know more than they do about making a good home; they get married young these days and homemaking and child raising soon become their jobs. Now the courses my son and daughter are taking. . ."

My neighbors and your neighbors have a variety of ideas on what their children should be taught in high schools. And no wonder. A variety of young people from a wide diversity of family and economic backgrounds go to high schools today.[3]

ADMINISTRATIVE EXPECTATIONS

The administrators with whom the teacher usually has the closest working relationship, whether good or bad, are the school principal and/or assistant principal. The principal is usually a former teacher who has been recognized for his ability in organization and his skill in human relations. The assistant principal, who carries on those functions delegated to him by the principal, has usually had even more recent experience in teaching than the principal. Since both types of leaders usually have come to their posts via teaching responsibilities,

---

[3] William Van Til, "What Makes a Good High School Curriculum?" *Woman's Day* (October 1964), pp. 42, 104.

they may be expected to view education in somewhat the same way as the teacher.

In addition to practical classroom experience, today's building administrator holds a master's degree and has taken a number of graduate courses in administration; the more ambitious are working towards a doctoral degree in education. Thus they are acquainted with current ideas on organization, curriculum innovation, supervision, human relations, and administrative procedures in general. This background inclines them to look with approval on teachers who are experimental and innovative. But, at the same time, the responsibility which they feel for the efficient administration of their schools inclines them to lack sympathy with those who unduly cause problems. Administrators do not often enjoy conflict or particularly appreciate teachers who are controversial; teachers who able to manage their own affairs within the classroom without excessive calls upon the principal's office are valued. Administrators are inclined to view with distinct reservations those teachers who bring them long lists of grievances or a variety of complaints.

Thus, the principal is pulled in two directions. In general, his graduate work and his own perceptions of himself as a former teacher and present administrative leader conflict with his desire to "run a tight ship" and to minimize conflicts. Consequently, principals have been known to talk one way about desirable innovations and experimentation and to behave in another way by rewarding conformity.

But it is extremely difficult to generalize on the expectations of principals since principals are as varied as teachers. Whenever possible, the new teacher might attempt to include an interview with the principal prior to accepting a post. The quality of the principal and his administrative staff can make a great difference in the experience of the new teacher.

The superintendent, though a vital factor in the development of the school system, is often a somewhat remote figure to the classroom teacher. In some school systems, the superintendent is seen as he presides over the opening of school in-service education sessions before or after each Labor Day; then he becomes invisible to the teacher for the balance of the year as he presides over mysterious operations developed through the central office. Obviously, this is not the case with the better superintendents who participate ex-officio in many committees and who are familiar figures in individual schools. Yet even the most active superintendent must depend heavily on his supporting staff for supervision and the improvement of curriculum and instruction.

Consequently, in the usual school system the teacher encounters the superintendent's supporting staff more often than the superintendent himself. The superintendent's supporting staff members may include assistant superintendents, curriculum directors, personnel directors, and business managers with whom the new teacher often comes into contact during interviews, contract negotiations, certification procedures, curriculum planning, and supply requisition.

The role of the supporting staff is to improve the quality of the school system in the particular area of specialization represented by the supporting staff member. He gains his professional recognition and salary increments through success in his specialization. Consequently, many supporting staff members are genuinely eager to help teachers perform better—especially in the area of the staff member's specialization! If the teacher's perception of his work coincides with that of the specialist, a harmonious relationship is predictable. If the teacher's perception varies to a noticeable degree, it is likely that the supporting staff member will attempt, preferably (but not invariably) through democratic procedures and human relations techniques, to modify the teacher's approach. Whether the supporting staff member will be regarded by the teacher as a helpful person or as a menacing "snoopervisor" depends heavily upon the personalities and the professional skills of the interacting individuals. Fortunately, during the past decade supervision has moved steadily away from a scientific-management approach toward a human relations-oriented approach and from authoritarian procedures toward democratic processes.

BOARD OF EDUCATION EXPECTATIONS

Members of boards of education occupy a strategic place in the total pattern of perceptions and expectations in a school system. The board member sees himself as responsible to his community. Yet at the same time, he is not bound to simply reflect the community majority; in many cases he is a vigorous spokesman for education in community debates concerning financing schools or in criticisms directed against the school. Ideally, he is a spokesman for good education and a mediating force between the school and the community.

The typical school board member is more often called upon to deal with financial factors, such as the ever-pressing questions of budget and financial support for the schools, rather than with matters of content and instruction. Unless curriculum matters become controversial in the community, the board member tends to leave content and instruction to the professionals. The school board member thus often finds that his role is political in nature rather than a role of educational leadership.

As teachers increasingly bargain collectively, the board of education member may find himself cast in the role of antagonist to the teacher. Increasingly, teachers discriminate between those board members who are "for" them and those who are "against" them. Thus, the school board member has an ungrateful task. Though he supplies unsalaried service to the community, he is sometimes unpopular with large or small segments of the community and the professional staff. Seldom is this more evident than in matters which are financially controversial such as determining salaries, or in situations which are programatically controversial such as sex education, teaching about communism, etc. If one wishes to be universally loved, one does not become a school board member.

The school board member's expectation of the teacher is that the teacher "do a good job." But definitions of what is a good job vary from board member to board member, even as performance of a good job varies from teacher to teacher.

STUDENT PERCEPTIONS AND EXPECTATIONS

Relatively innocent of such community and administrative expectations are the students. While other forces may react to teachers as a collective group, the student is usually much more concerned with the specific teachers who teach him than with intangible abstractions concerning the "teacher." Studies have been made as to what students value in teachers. A common thread running through such studies is the preference of students for teachers who are fair though firm, who have a sense of humor, who see and help students as individuals, who know their subjects, and who try to make their teaching relevant to students' experiences and lives.

In a 1969 study, for example, Hulda Grobman asked members of her New York University undergraduate education class who had no previous teaching experience to list "things they hoped as teachers they would never do in the classroom." The top seven items on their list were the following: "be ill-mannered; lose temper, scream; lack love of all individual students; pick a favorite or scapegoat; use sarcasm; be unfair (closeminded); do the same routine each year."[4] In a study also published in 1969, Alton Harrison, Jr. and E. G. Scriven asked students at Northern Illinois University to "describe the best teacher you ever had and state why you selected that particular teacher." These students indicated that the most important teacher characteristics are "respects students, empathetic, understanding, provides student participation, encourages self-direction, excellent presentations, knowledgeable."[5]

The consistency of such preferences is evident from a 1964 study in which Ann Healy Kirtland asked 371 adolescents "what they remembered best about the fifth grade." The results revealed that student memories, whether positive or negative, were "predominantly concerned with teacher personality." The statements of a few of Healy's subjects were recorded as follows:

"Our fifth grade teacher really understood our troubles and helped us solve them."
"She always gave everybody a chance."
"She was patient, but firm."
"She helped us to make friends and even to understand our enemies."
"I felt free to express myself as I wanted to."
"It was fun never knowing what might come next."
"My teacher explained math so that even I could understand it."
"She made hard things simple, and dull things exciting."
"The teacher got mad a lot. She was hard on everybody."
"She let two boys pick on other children."
"He was always talking about the Golden Rule, but he never practiced it."
"We wrote all day long. I was bored mean."

---

[4] Hulda Grobman, "To See Ourselves as Others See Us," *Childhood Education*, 45 (March 1969), p. 396.
[5] Alton Harrison, Jr. and E. G. Scriven, "Is There a Relevancy Gap in Education?" *Peabody Journal of Education*, 46 (March 1969), pp. 303–307.

"It was her first year. She didn't know school subjects and she didn't care for kids."

"The teacher told us everything. We never found out anything for ourselves."[6]

FELLOW TEACHER PERCEPTIONS AND EXPECTATIONS

Colleagues also have their perceptions and expectations of the new teacher. Since teaching is essentially not a competitive business, as is, for example, advertising, the new teacher is usually welcomed by his colleagues. The typical teacher who, you will recall, averages nearly thirty-nine years in age in contrast to the new teacher who is about twenty-two, often adopts a semiparental as well as professional attitude toward the newcomer. So the experienced colleague is likely to adopt the role of an insider advising an outsider as to the practical facts of life in respect to students, program, administration, and even other teachers. Some experienced teachers make a point of putting an arm around the shoulder of the new teacher, figuratively if not always literally, and advising him or her to forget the nonsense learned in teacher education programs and to proceed in accordance with the experienced colleague's advice—which will then immediately be tendered the newcomer. Such advice should be carefully listened to, appraised, and evaluated by the new teacher. The natural insecurity of the newcomer should not lead him to abandon in panic all that he has learned and planned. Above all, advice from the veterans should not lead him to reject his own teaching style arrived at through his own experience in living and his thoughtful consideration of education. Sensible modifications, yes; total rejection, no. Respectful listening without express commitment accompanied by attempts to develop good human relationships with the colleague seem to be the best approach for the new teacher.

As the months go by, the new teacher will probably build intellectual identifications and sometimes friendships with particular teachers who are closest to his life style and goals, accompanied by increasing respect for the perceptions and expectations of such selected colleagues. Simultaneously, the teacher may experience a degree of widening gap between himself and other colleagues who do not see things his way. But life will be better for all involved if the new teacher not dramatize the gap through publicly or privately expressed contempt for the ideas, techniques, or performance of colleagues. Professional ethics supports mutual toleration, as does enlightened self-interest, since experienced colleagues may have developed their own ways of manifesting disapproval of their untenured young colleagues.

As America learned in the 1960s, wars should be chosen with great caution and care. Choosing one's "wars" applies not only to countries but also to the individual. A new teacher should be quite sure of the harmfulness of a colleague to whatever the new teacher holds vital before he engages in any warlike activities. The new teacher should carry his torch as a person of conviction, but should avoid burning people with it.

---

[6] Ann Kirtland Healy, "I'll Remember You Always," *NEA Journal*, 53 (December 1964), p. 66.

THE TEACHER'S SELF EXPECTATIONS

The most crucial and complex of the variety of expectations and perceptions of the teacher's role are those held by the teacher himself. To suggest a fixed pattern of desirable expectations which you should hold would be presumptuous and unrealistic. Instead, we suggest some factors to take into account in arriving at your own expectations. Above all, you might ask yourself why you have chosen teaching as your career. What do you hope to achieve through teaching? What is your guiding philosophy? What contribution to society do you hope to make through teaching? What kind of teacher do you want to be?

The young teacher's self-expectations are often unrealistically high; conversely, his self-image is often unrealistically low. He tends to over-estimate the influence that he is expected to have on his students and he is often alarmed at the exhaustion which he experiences as he encounters the myriad of responsibilities and long hours of work related to teaching. He is often fearful during his first weeks of teaching that the expectations of his supervisors, students, community, and fellow teachers are too high for his background and ability.

There is no substitute for thinking through your self-expectations, for recognizing the existence of expectations by others, and for using your own intelligence in reconciling conflicting expectations. Recognize that being a teacher will be a learning experience for you, yet that you have much to contribute. Rely on yourself yet be able to respect the varying outlooks of others and to evaluate their suggestions.

WHO OWNS THE SCHOOLS?

Even though you understand the differing self-expectations of the teacher and the varying perceptions of teachers by individuals and groups, you still face a perplexity. In such a context, who should set the broad policies to guide the schools? What forces should determine the general direction in which education should go? Whose schools are these anyway?

Part of the answer is found in the modifiers of the word "school." If a school is private, it essentially belongs to the private board in which responsibility for policy-making is vested. If a school is parochial, it belongs to the church which administers it. If it is a public school, it belongs to the people.

THE PEOPLE OWN THE PUBLIC SCHOOLS

But, you may ask, how about the teachers? Do the public school teachers own the public schools? They own the public schools no more than Lyndon B. Johnson or Richard M. Nixon owns the American presidency. In the American political system, whoever happens to be President occupies the Presidency but does not own the Presidency. Presidents can be removed and have been removed by the electoral process or even, at the people's discretion, by the impeachment process. Similarly, teachers occupy their positions by virtue of the people and at the discretion of the people.

Certainly the people should give substantial autonomy to those they have empowered to teach. But when the chips are down, public school teachers are the representatives of the people and not the owners of the schools. The ultimate power and ownership of the schools is vested in the American people. You may have possibly met teachers and administrators of whom it was said, "They act as if they own the school." But they don't own the school—the people do.

But "the people" is a large and amorphous abstraction. How have the people exercised their responsibility for setting the broad policies concerning the public schools?

THE DEMOCRATIC CONSENSUS

As we have seen, colonial governments such as Massachusetts required communities to establish schools. With the formation of the nation and through the mechanism of the U.S. Constitution, education was delegated to the states as one of their "implied powers." Article X of the additions and amendments to the United States Constitution states, "The powers not delegated to the United States by the Constitution, nor prohibited by it to the States, are reserved to the States respectively, or to the people." Education was not specified as a power of the Congress; indeed, education is not mentioned in the U.S. Constitution. Through the states, the people established free public education in the nineteenth century and wrote provisions for free schools into the constitutions of nearly all of the states.

Obviously, with education the province of a number of expanding states, no mandate by a centralized federal government as to the proper work of the schools was ever handed down from Washington, D.C. Yet nations have a way of developing a general consensus without specific mandates. To the extent that a consensus as to the responsibilities of education exists in the United States, it is a reflection of the democratic values of Americans.

Americans vary in their ways of phrasing their constellation of values. Yet important in American value patterns, however variously phrased, is respect for the worth and dignity of the individual. Important too is concern for the general welfare to be achieved by working together for common purposes. Important is freedom to use one's own intelligence rather than accept authoritarian dictates. The history of ideas in America testifies to the American dedication to such central ideas in the democratic creed even though the pages of our history are blotted with violation of democratic values.

SOCIETAL SPOKESMEN FOR THE DEMOCRATIC CONSENSUS

Abraham Lincoln, for instance, was an outstanding spokesman for the American consensus on the importance of the democratic way of life. He once said, "As I would not be a slave, so I would not be a *master*. This expresses my idea

"Our reliance is in the love of liberty . . ."

of democracy. Whatever differs from this, to the extent of the difference, is no democracy."[7]

In the Lincoln-Douglas debate, Lincoln spoke of,

> . . . the eternal struggle between these two principles—right and wrong—throughout the world. They are the two principles that have stood face to face from the beginning of time; and will ever continue to struggle. The one is the common right of humanity, and the other the divine right of kings. It is the same principle in whatever shape it develops itself. It is the same spirit that says, 'You toil, work and earn bread, and I'll eat it.' No matter in what shape it comes, whether from the mouth of a king who seeks to bestride the people of his own nation and live by the fruit of their labor, or from one race of men as an apology for enslaving another race, it is the same tyrannical principle.[8]

He also said,

> When . . . you have succeeded in dehumanizing the Negro; when you have put him down and made it impossible for him to be but as the beasts of the field; when you have extinguished his soul in this world and placed him where the ray of hope is blown out as in the darkness of the damned, are you quite sure that the demon you have roused will not turn and rend you? What constitutes the bulwark of our own liberty and independence? It is not our frowning battlements, our bristling sea coasts, our army and our navy. These are not our reliance against tyranny. All of those may be turned against us without making

---

[7] Fragment (August 1, 1858?). From Roy P. Basler, *The Collected Works of Abraham Lincoln,* Vol. 2 (Rutgers University Press, New Brunswick, N.J.: 1953), p. 532.

[8] *Ibid.*, vol. 3, p. 315. Reply, seventh and last joint debate, Alton, Illinois (October 15, 1858).

us weaker for the struggle. Our reliance is in the love of liberty which God has planted in us. Our defense is in the spirit which prized liberty as the heritage of all men, in all lands everywhere. Destroy this spirit and you have planted the seeds of despotism at your own doors. Familiarize yourselves with the chains of bondage and you prepare your own limbs to wear them. Accustomed to trample on the rights of others, you have lost the genius of your own independence and become fit the subjects of the first cunning tyrant who rises among you.[9]

Theodore Roosevelt expressed his ideas of democracy during one of his political campaigns, that of 1921 (after his presidency) when he was defeated as the candidate of a third party. He said,

... I believe in pure democracy. With Lincoln, I hold that 'this country, with its institutions, belongs to the people who inhabit it. Whenever they shall grow weary of the existing government, they can exercise their constitutional right of amending it.

We progressives believe that the people have the right, the power, and the duty to protect themselves and their own welfare; that human rights are supreme over all other rights; that wealth should be the servant, not the master, of the people.

We believe that unless representative government does absolutely represent the people it is not representative government at all.

We test the worth of all men and all measures by asking how they contribute to the welfare of the men, women, and children of whom this nation is composed.

We are engaged in one of the great battles of the age-long contest waged against privilege on behalf of the common welfare.

We hold it a prime duty of the people to free our government from the control of money in politics.

For this purpose we advocate, not as ends in themselves, but as weapons in the hands of the people, all governmental devices which will make the representatives of the people more easily and certainly responsible to the people's will.[10]

In the twentieth century, Franklin D. Roosevelt phrased the American aspiration in terms of four freedoms. In a message to Congress some months before the United States entered World War II he said,

In the future day, which we seek to make secure, we look forward to a world founded upon four essential human freedoms. The first is freedom of speech and expression—everywhere in the world. The second is freedom of every person to worship God in his own way—everywhere in the world. The third is freedom from want . . . everywhere in the world. The fourth is freedom from fear . . . anywhere in the world.[11]

[9] Speech, Edwardsville, Illinois (September 13, 1858).
[10] Theodore Roosevelt, Address, Columbus, Ohio, February 21, 1912.
[11] The State of the Union Message (January 6, 1941).

"And if we cannot end now our differences, at least we can help make the world safe for diversity." Courtesy of Southern Pacific Historical Collection.

In the last year of his life, John F. Kennedy said,

So let us not be blind to our differences—but let us also direct attention to our common interests and the means by which those differences can be resolved. And if we cannot end now our differences, at least we can help make the world safe for diversity.[12]

In his inaugural address in 1969 Richard M. Nixon said,

Our greatest need now is to reach beyond government, to enlist the legions of the concerned and the committed. What has to be done has to be done by government and people together or it will not be done at all. The lesson of past agony is that without the people we can do nothing; with the people we can do everything.[13]

Martin Luther King, Jr. spoke for the American dream. He said,

I have a dream that one day this nation will rise up and live out the true

---

[12] Allan Nevins, ed., *The Burden and the Glory* (New York: Harper and Row, 1964), p. 57.
[13] Inaugural Address (January 20, 1969).

"I have a dream that one day this nation will rise up and live out the true meaning of its creed . . ." Courtesy of Jerry Frank from DPI.

meaning of its creed: "We hold these truths to be self-evident; that all men are created equal."

I have a dream that one day on the red hills of Georgia the sons of former slaves and the sons of former slaveowners will be able to sit down together at the table of brotherhood. . . .

I have a dream that my four little children will one day live in a nation where they will not be judged by the color of their skin but by the content of their character.

I have a dream today.[14]

BROAD INFLUENCES ON EXPECTATIONS

Despite the consensus on a constellation of values defining the democratic way of life, expectations of public school teachers are influenced by many factors. Even though there may be agreement at a verbal level on respect for the individual, fostering the common welfare through working together for

[14] Speech delivered to March on Washington participants, Washington, D.C. (August 28, 1963).

common purposes, and the use of intelligence in human affairs, there exist variant perceptions of what these mean in practice.

SPECIAL INTEREST GROUP INFLUENCES

For instance, special interest groups have varying expectations of teachers. But special interest groups do not own the school—though they too sometimes act as though they do, particularly when their members are high in the community power structure. The schools do not belong to any special group, however praiseworthy or deplorable. For instance, the schools do not belong to the League of Women Voters, or to the American Legion, or to the Parent-Teachers Association, or to the Chamber of Commerce, or to the Ku Klux Klan, or to the Black Panthers, or to the Episcopal Church, or to the John Birch Society, or to the Southern Christian Leadership Conference, or to the Young Americans for Freedom, or to the Students for a Democratic Society—and so on ad infinitum. The schools neither belong to those who are permanent in the community power structure nor to those who challenge the existing power structure. All such groups are heard and should be heard in the continuing debate on the work of the schools. Many individual members of such groups will also be heard. But the schools belong to the people as a whole, not to any special group or its spokesmen, not to any power structure or its challengers.

Though the schools do not belong to the special interest groups, such groups bring their influence to bear on the shaping of education. Often they see themselves as representatives of American values; infrequently they are frankly antidemocratic. But their interpretations of the values they support are often influenced by their special interests. Often they do not see eye-to-eye with other protagonists. They bring their influence to bear on behalf of their interpretations of their values and often, in the process, attempt to influence the work of schools. So the programs of the schools are influenced through the policies of voluntary organizations, whether they be labor or management groups, peace or war groups, religious or agnostic groups, minority or majority groups, etc.

HIGHER EDUCATION INFLUENCES

Simultaneously, influences on educational policies and on expectations of teachers are also being exerted by groups within the field of education, even though they too do not own the public schools. The colleges, as a component of American higher education, influence the policies pursued by the schools through college entrance requirements. Since college is the next educational level beyond high school and since college education is highly valued both as a means of making a better person and as a means of upward mobility occupationally, colleges can exert substantial influence on schools and on expectations of teachers through their prescriptions as to what content and even what personality characteristics are necessary for college entrance.

Meanwhile, in the 1970s, formidable social pressures are being applied to colleges to revise their college entrance requirements to admit a larger proportion of relatively disadvantaged youth, especially disadvantaged blacks. Consequently, such a university system as that of the City of New York has markedly relaxed college entrance requirements to achieve open admissions. But some scholars and political leaders foresee the decline and decay of higher education if student and community pressures result in wider admissions. Thus, conventional college entrance requirements, as one operating force in higher education, encounter counterforces in the form of pressures for open admissions.

Another influence on the policies of schools comes from the various faculties of the institutions of higher learning. Differing perceptions as to desirable educational programs have long existed between liberal arts faculties and teacher education faculties within colleges and universities; individual proponents often sound as though they owned the public schools. This cold war between faculty members centers on such questions as the most appropriate content, materials, and methodologies for use in schools. Liberal arts faculty members incline to established academic approaches to education; teacher education faculties incline to learner-adapted approaches. Consequently the college student is apt to hear from the liberal arts faculty member the claim that if one knows his subject, he can teach it without taking education courses, and from teacher education faculty members the contention that much knowledge concerning the learner and society exists and much adaptation of subject matter to the learner and to society is necessary for effective education. While the debate is less heated than it used to be and while reconciliation of the conflict has been achieved on some campuses, the debate on many campuses between the variant perceptions among professors still goes on.

FINANCIAL SUPPORT INFLUENCES

Still another influence on school policies and expectations of teachers derives from sources which can supply financial aid to school systems which must chronically cope with a shortage of financial support. One such source of support is the philanthropic foundation, typified by the largest of all such foundations, the Ford Foundation. Such foundations frequently make supplementary funds available to schools for the development of new media such as television, or for use with special groups of learners such as the disadvantaged, or to support certain content areas such as citizenship education or science. No school system is forced to accept foundation funds. But school systems, notoriously needy, often do. The acceptance of funds often leads to an acceptance of the emphasis supported by the philanthropic foundation.

Today the federal government, and to a lesser extent state governments, play similar roles with respect to the provision of funds. Federal aid to schools is for special purposes presumably related to the national interest. The federal government supplies help for special concerns, such as vocational education early in the twentieth century, or support for programs for the culturally disadvantaged in our own times. Again, school systems are under no compulsion to accept such

Courtesy of Robert Perron.

aid. Yet their needs are great and, consequently, certain aspects of the school programs are strengthened through selected "categorical" programs of federal aid to education.

Broad policies which supply American education its mandate are also influenced by the action of state legislators. Though there is common agreement among educators that state legislatures should not prescribe the content of specific courses, but should rather depend upon their state education department to establish standards for instruction and to provide leadership, some legislatures do prescribe specific content. Perhaps the most famous illustration of prescription by a legislature is the evolution law passed by the Tennessee Legislature which mandated a Biblical interpretation of the origin of man rather than the evolutionary thesis.

RELATIONSHIPS OF TEACHERS AND GROUPS

The realistic new teacher knows that such influences exist and that they affect the expectations of individuals and groups as to his role. He must acknowledge their influence yet attempt to maintain his own integrity and his responsibility to the American people. For despite the pressure of a variety of interests, in a democracy the schools must belong to the people.

★   ★   ★

DISCUSSION
1. What is the meaning of "role" as used in sociology and education? How does it differ from "status"?
2. What are the various roles you as an individual play as you go about your daily life? As you assume the role of teacher what changes in your life style do you see yourself making?
3. How do community expectations generally differ in rural, urban, and suburban areas? What about expectations of the teacher in the community you know best?
4. How do parental expectations differ? To what extent does social class appear to be a factor? To what extent do individual differences within the groups appear?

5. How have the expectations of teachers by lower income Americans—especially members of minority or disadvantaged groups—changed in recent years?
6. What are characteristic administrative expectations of the teacher? The school board members? The superintendents? The central staffs? The principals?
7. What are characteristic student perceptions and expectations of the teacher? What were your own expectations of the teacher at varying stages in your school life?
8. How important are the perceptions and expectations of fellow teachers? On what basis is the new teacher likely to be judged by his colleagues?
9. What are some of the self expectations which members of your class hold? Which do you hold?
10. What can be done to help the young teacher identify realistic self-expectations?
11. What are the possible viewpoints on who "owns" the public schools? What is the relationship of teachers to the people, in broad terms and in specific instances with which you are acquainted?
12. Does a democratic consensus on the work of the schools exist? If so, how might it be phrased? Who has contributed to it? What other public figures have expressed themselves on the goals of American society and the proper goals of American schools?
13. What special interest groups affect education nationally? What special interest groups have influenced the schools with which you are most familiar?
14. How does higher education influence school programs? In the college or university you know best, is there some degree of disagreement among liberal arts professors and education professors?
15. How might financial factors influence the program of schools? How do philanthropic foundations relate to school systems? Federal government?

INVOLVEMENT
1. Talk with friends or family members about their expectations of schools. Attempt to relate their expectations to class backgrounds, community backgrounds, individual preferences, etc.
2. Visit a meeting of a PTA reputed to have more than routine meetings. Attempt to determine the characteristic expectations of teachers held by parents and, conversely, the expectations of parents held by teachers.

3. Try a "man in the street" interview as to the expectations of schools by varying individuals. Look for similarities and differences.
4. Attempt to become acquainted with a board of education member by personal relationship or interview. Try to understand his perceptions and how they are similar to or different from your own and those of your friends. Consider the reasons behind these similarities or differences.
5. Visit an administrator or invite a representative of administration to class in order to learn of his expectations of a teacher. Clarify similarities and differences of his point of view with those of students engaged in the interview or as an audience.
6. Invite several teachers to class to discuss their expectations of their colleagues, both new and experienced.
7. Recall your own expectations of teachers at various points in your experience as a student. Talk with contemporary elementary and high school students to see what differences in perception might exist.
8. Extend further your study of the democratic consensus. Read the ideas of others who have contributed to viewpoints on the proper role and responsibility of schools.
9. Talk informally with both liberal arts and education professors to determine their ideas about what constitutes a good teacher and what they expect of American education.

BIBLIOGRAPHY

Brubaker, Dale L. *The Teacher as a Decision-Maker.* Dubuque, Iowa: Wm. C. Brown, 1970. A variety of cases are set forth, each requiring decisions by teachers.

Coles, Robert. *Children of Crisis: A Study of Courage and Fear.* Boston: Little, Brown, 1967. An account of Southern children attending schools in the era of pressures related to segregation and integration.

Conant, James Bryant. *Shaping Educational Policy.* New York: McGraw-Hill, 1964. Discusses policy-making for the public school system in light of contemporary problems. Includes special emphasis on racial strife.

Grambs, Jean. *Schools, Scholars, and Society.* Englewood Cliffs, N.J., Prentice-Hall, 1965. Insights into the educational process in society through the application of sociology to education.

Hass, Glen, Kimball Wiles, and Arthur Roberts, eds. *Readings in Secondary Education.* Rockleigh, N.J.: Allyn and Bacon, 1970. A collection of articles which combine discussion of educational theory and attention to practical problems of teaching. One section devotes particular attention to the high school teacher's role in school and community.

Heald, James E. and Samuel A. Moore, II. *The Teachers and Administrative Relationships in School Systems.* New York: Macmillan, 1968. Answering for beginning teachers such questions as: "How are school systems run?"; "Where do I as a teacher fit into the total operation?"; "What kind of interactions should I expect?"; and "How can I participate in changing the system"?

Herriott, Robert E. and Nancy Hoyt St. John. *Social Class and the Urban School: The Impact of Pupil Background on Teachers and Principals.* New York: John Wiley and Sons, 1966. How teachers and principals of schools of different social class composition view pupils and parents. The racial composition of schools and social class differences.

Hodgkinson, Harold L. *Education in Social Perspectives.* Englewood Cliffs, N.J.: Prentice-Hall, 1962. Ways of looking at the schoolhouse, teacher, administrator, and children.

Kaufman, Bel. *Up the Down Staircase.* Englewood Cliffs, N.J.: Prentice-Hall, 1964. A poignant and humorous description of an aspiring teacher's experiences in a New York City school. Supervision comes off badly in this book; the author portrays the bumbling of various administrative officials.

Lane, Willard R., Ronald G. Corwin, and William O. Monahan. *Foundations of Educational Administration: A Behavioral Analysis.* New York: Macmillan, 1967. An analysis of some of the functions of a school leader.

Ostrander, Raymond H. and Ray C. Dethy. *A Values Approach to Educational Administration.* Cincinnati, Ohio: Van Nostrand Reinhold, 1968. Emphasizes that the educational administrator must constantly develop and redesign his personal values as a guide in setting goals and making decisions.

Pullias, Earl V. and James D. Young. *A Teacher Is Many Things.* Bloomington, Ind.: Indiana University Press, 1968. Observations and experiences of the authors concerning the significance and the substance of teaching. The many roles of the teacher are described.

Troy, Rena. *The World of Education.* New York: Macmillan, 1968. A general education text with an excellent section on who should be responsible for education.

Usdan, Michael D., David W. Minar, and Emanuel Hurwitz, Jr. *Education and State Politics.* New York: Teachers College Press, Columbia University, 1969. The relationship of elementary and secondary education to higher education in the context of state politics, including problems of financing the schools.

Weaver, Warren. *U.S. Philanthropic Foundations: Their History, Structure, Management and Record.* New York: Harper and Row, 1967. A useful appraisal of the power and social influence of philanthropic organizations.

Wiles, Kimball, *Supervision for Better Schools.* 3rd ed. Englewood Cliffs, N.J.: Prentice-Hall, 1967. A case for a supervision marked by democratic human relations and group processes rather than the former traditional authoritarian conception.

AUDIO-VISUAL MATERIALS

How Good Is Your Child's School? (NEA, 80 fr., Color, Record) Appraisal of elementary and secondary schools by lay individuals and groups and criteria for evaluation.

Pressure Groups In Action (Republic Steel Corporation, 20 Min.) The need for pressure groups in our contemporary political system.

Approach to School Site Development (International Film Bureau, 22 Min., Color) A case study in Ann Arbor, Michigan, shows the planning committee, various classes and teachers, local citizens and youth groups helping develop the environment and utilizing the natural features of the land for an enriched educational program.

Is Anybody Home? (NCAT, University of Texas) A series of 37 tapes on home and family life education. For instance: What a Teacher Expects of Her Student—15 Min. What a Teacher Expects of Parents—15 Min. Are Teachers Necessary?—15 Min.

Teachers Contributing to Educational Advance (Ohio State University, 51 frs., Color) Presents a review of curriculum activities. Describes the role of the teacher as a creative personality responsible for developing creativity in his pupils and contributing to their educational advancement. Discusses the special responsibility of the laboratory school.

ELEVEN

WHERE DOES THE MONEY COME FROM?

Public education is a major enterprise in the United States. As Herold C. Hunt has pointed out in his introduction to Charles S. Benson's *The Economics of Public Education,* "Nearly thirty percent of our population is enrolled in schools and colleges; if we include participants in various types of informal education, teachers, and administrators, education involves more than a third of the population of the United States. This trend is certain to continue."[1] Obviously, so large and crucial a service must be financed in some way.

SOURCES OF FINANCIAL SUPPORT

SUPPORT FROM LOCAL, STATE AND FEDERAL GOVERNMENTS

The American educational enterprise is a decentralized public activity. School districts are the primary units of local government charged with responsibility for education, a responsibility delegated by the state legislatures. Other local governments such as township, municipal, and county units provide some services including tax collection, fire and police protection, water and sanitation, etc. In addition, about half of the states have regional agencies such as county school offices to provide services to the local districts. State governments affect education through the legislature, the state department of education, and agencies such as the revenue department and the state judiciary. The federal government exercises its educational activities through all major departments as well as the United States Office of Education.

---

[1] Charles S. Benson, *The Economics of Public Education* (Boston: Houghton Mifflin, 1968), p. v.

Local control is still a key concept in financing public education and local authorities still receive most of the funds for schools through local tax revenues. But, since an individual school district is limited in its ability to raise funds, local funds are supplemented by grants from federal and state governments. Though the federal government plays a greater role in the funding of education than it formerly did, state and local governments are still the major participants in the financing of education.

About one-half of the direct outlay for elementary and secondary public schools comes from funds of local governments. State governments supply approximately two-fifths of school revenue. The third partner is the federal government which supplies the remainder, constituting 7 to 8 percent most years during the 1965–66 through the 1969–70 period. Federal participation has almost doubled since the period 1959–60 through 1964–65 when the percentage of school revenues derived from federal sources averaged about 4 percent annually. Table 11.1 shows the percentages of revenues from these sources from 1959–60 through 1969–70. Meanwhile in the eleven school years from 1959–60 through

TABLE 11.1

Distribution of Total Revenue Receipts for Public Elementary and Secondary Schools 1960 through 1970

SCHOOL YEAR	PERCENT OF SCHOOL REVENUE DERIVED FROM:		
	FEDERAL SOURCES	STATE SOURCES	LOCAL AND OTHER SOURCES
1959–60	4.4	39.1	56.5
1960–61	3.8	39.8	56.4
1961–62	4.3	38.7	56.9
1962–63	3.6	39.3	57.1
1963–64	4.4	39.3	56.4
1964–65	3.8	39.7	56.5
1965–66	7.9	39.1	53.0
1966–67	7.9	39.1	53.0
1967–68	8.0	39.3	52.7
1968–69	7.4	40.0	52.6
1969–70	6.6	40.7	52.7

National Education Association, Research Division, *Estimates of School Statistics 1969–70*, Research Report 1969–R15 (Washington, D.C.: The Association, 1969), p. 18.

1969–70, the percentage of school revenue derived from local sources dropped from 56.5 percent to 52.7 percent. Over the same time the percentage of all school revenue derived from state sources increased from 39.1 percent to 40.7 percent. The absolute amount increased from each source during this decade.

SPENDING FOR SCHOOLING

What is the revenue, whether from local, state, or federal funds, spent for? Primarily for salaries. The salaries of the teaching staff of public elementary and secondary schools account for approximately 50 percent of the combined local, state, and federal expenditures for education. The salaries of the nonteaching academic staff such as administrators, librarians, and counselors account for about 15 percent. When auxiliary staff such as bus drivers, custodians, and other noninstructional personnel are included, when the cost of retirement programs are included, and if the school system is not spending large amounts for school building, "it is common to find that salaries and fringe benefits account for roughly 80 percent of the annual budget."[2]

School revenues, then, are derived from local, state, and federal sources. Salaries are the largest category in the spending of those revenues. Salaries of the instructional staff (teaching and other academic personnel) constitute about two-thirds of the operating expenditures for public schools. Quite soon the instructional staff may include you, and your salary may depend on revenues which are derived from taxation. Yet, can you think of anything more unpopular with people than taxes?

Nevertheless, all signs point to an increase in the cost of education. America's large governmental activity—public elementary and secondary education—grows larger and costlier annually. The U.S. Office of Education predicts that total expenditures (in 1967–68 dollars) for public elementary and secondary schools, will move from the 17.1 billion spent in 1957–58 to an estimated 40.9 billion in 1977–78, an increase of 139.2 percent.[3]

WHY TAX-SUPPORTED EDUCATION?

If you become a public school teacher, you may often be called on to defend the support of education through taxation. You should therefore be familiar with the arguments for tax-supported education.

You may propose as a possible defense for public education that individuals will be benefited. Any comparison of what a person earns after various stages of graduation—from elementary school, from high school, from college, from graduate school—demonstrates the economic benefits of education to the individual. But this is essentially a *private* argument; it may not persuade many citizens that they have any financial responsibility for education. A more persuasive argument with the tax-paying citizen is that education provides a substantial amount of social benefit as well as private benefit.[4]

A first defense for public support of education is the contention that education of the common man is necessary in a democracy. In a nation which proposes to

---

[2] Benson, p. 14.
[3] U.S. Office of Education, *Projections of Educational Statistics to 1977–78* (Washington, D.C.: U.S. Government Printing Office, 1969), pp. 78–79.
[4] Benson, p. 30.

be a free society, the people must participate in the democratic process. They can do so only if they are an educated citizenry.

There are strong economic arguments for public education as a social benefit. There is a relationship between expenditures for education and the extent of the national economic growth. Theodore W. Schultz, formerly president of the American Economic Association and a professor of the University of Chicago, once said that there are long-standing puzzles about economic growth, changes in the structure of wages and salary, and changes in the personal distribution of income that can be substantially resolved by taking account of investment in human capital.[5]

Increasingly, economists point out that the most productive investment in human capital that can be made is education. As Professor William G. Bowen has put it, "The results obtained for the U.S. economy do offer rather consistent (some might say surprisingly consistent) support for the notion that education on the average, has paid significant financial as well as nonfinancial rewards."[6]

Yet some contend that these economic benefits could come from a private education system just as well if not better. Therefore, some propose that school services be provided more by private sources than they are now. But the arguments against this point of view stress that, along with economic benefits, public education provides desirable noneconomic outcomes. Public schools help develop the common values of the democratic way of life; public education contains the potential to reduce class distinction and to provide equal educational opportunities to every individual for fullest development. Thus, public education is needed to achieve the democratic way of life, to reduce class distinctions, and to combat segregation.

SOURCES OF TAXATION

Taxes are collected at the three major levels of government: federal, state, and local. "At the time of the 1967 Census of Governments, the United States had one federal government, 50 state governments, 3,049 county governments, 18,051 municipalities, 17,107 townships and New England towns, and 43,046 special districts, including 21,782 school districts."[7] Each unit of government mentioned has a relationship to the levying of taxes.

There are three large sources of tax money for state and local governments. Property taxes are the largest single revenue producer, though their proportion in the local and state tax structure is steadily declining. Following property taxes in importance are sales and gross receipt taxes, including general and selective (earmarked) taxes which are levies on retail sales of particular articles and

---

[5] Theodore W. Schultz, *Economic Value of Education* (New York: Columbia University Press, 1963), p. 65.
[6] William G. Bowen, *Economic Aspects of Education: Three Essays* (Princeton, N.J.: Princeton Industrial Relations Section, Princeton University, 1964), p. 32.
[7] Cited by Benson, p. 88.

services, such as gasoline, cigarettes, or liquor. The third large source, increasing in importance during recent years, includes individual and corporate income taxes. (See Table 11.2.) But all of the tax money collected by state and local government still totals less the the amount collected by the federal government.

TABLE 11.2

State and Local Government Revenues
and Expenditures 1967–68

GENERAL REVENUE BY SOURCE	AMOUNT (IN MILLIONS)	PERCENTAGE
Property taxes	$ 27,747	23.59
Sales and gross receipts taxes	22,911	19.49
Individual income taxes	7,308	6.22
Corporation income taxes	2,518	2.14
From Federal Government	17,181	14.61
All other	39,916	33.95
Total	117,581	100.00

GENERAL EXPENDITURES BY FUNCTION	AMOUNT (IN MILLIONS)	PERCENTAGE
Education (all)	$ 41,158	35.41
Highways	14,481	12.46
Public welfare	9,857	8.48
All other	50,738	43.65
Total	116,234	100.00

U.S. Department of Commerce, *Governmental Finance in 1967–68*, Government Finances /GF68 No. 5, Bureau of Census, p. 18.

Where does the federal government turn for revenue? Over 80 percent of tax revenues for the federal government come from individual income taxes, corporate income taxes, and employment taxes. The rest come to the federal government through excise taxes, insurance trust funds, estate and gift taxes, customs, duties, and miscellaneous receipts. (See Table 11.3.) No wage earner in the United States can be unfamiliar with the income tax which withholds income for tax purposes from one's weekly or monthly pay. Individual income taxes alone accounted for approximately 45 percent of federal administrative budget receipts in 1968.

As a concerned citizen and as a new school teacher you should consider which types of taxes should be depended on for future revenue. A commonly accepted tax standard is equal treatment of equals. In other words, people who have equal amounts of economic goods should contribute equally; none of the equals should be arbitrarily favored by the tax structure. But obviously not all people are equal in their ability to pay; some have a much higher income than others. Therefore, another proposed tax standard is that the tax burden should be shared according to the amount of income of the individual or corporation. Such a tax is called a "progressive" tax, one under which the high income household pays a higher ratio of tax than a low income tax family.

TABLE 11.3

Federal Budget Receipts by Source, 1968 and 1969

SOURCE	1968 ACTUAL		1970 ESTIMATED	
	AMOUNT (IN MILLIONS)	PERCENTAGE	AMOUNT (IN MILLIONS)	PERCENTAGE
Individual income taxes	$ 68,726	44.72	$ 90,400	45.49
Corporate income taxes	28,665	18.65	37,900	19.07
Employment taxes	29,223	19.01	39,863	20.06
Unemployment taxes	3,346	2.17	3,575	1.79
Contribution for insurance and retirement	2,050	1.33	2,431	1.22
Excise taxes	14,079	9.16	15,700	7.90
Estate and gift taxes	3,051	1.98	3,400	1.71
Customs duties	2,038	1.32	2,300	1.15
Miscellaneous receipts	2,498	1.62	3,117	1.56
Total	$153,676		$198,686	

Council of Economic Advisers, *Annual Report of the Council of Economic Advisers* (Washington, D.C.: U.S. Government Printing Office, 1969), p. 299.

PROGRESSIVE AND REGRESSIVE TAXES

It is frequently said that the only things which are certain are death and taxes. We might add that, as to how to distribute taxes, it is equally certain that people will quarrel about what is fairest or best. If there is a consensus among economists on this controversial issue, it is quite possibly the one expressed by Benson:

In general, economists express a preference for a progressive rate structure and on two grounds: (1) Taxation should not take dollars that are necessary for a minimum standard of living. As long as demand for government services are high and as long as there are several million very poor households in the country, it follows that taxation will have to be levied at proportionately higher rates on the rich than on the poor; (2) Taxation should do something to reduce extreme inequality in disposable income.[8]

[8] Benson, p. 94.

Standards as to fairness might be kept in mind as we examine the four major types of taxes used for support of education in the opening of the 1970s. The four types are property taxes, sales taxes, state income taxes, and federal income taxes.

The property tax, it will be recalled, is the primary source of revenue for local governments. A property tax is collected from owners of property and is presumably based on the value of the taxable property of the owner. The property tax taxes real property, a phrase for land and the improvements upon the land including houses, garages, etc. In addition, in most states certain kinds of tangible personal property are taxed. Tangible personal property includes automobiles, furniture, clothes, jewelry, business and farm equipment, farm animals, etc. Of these two, the more important source of revenue is locally assessed real estate. Though the assessment is supposed to represent the market value of the real estate, the county or district assessor usually assesses property at less than its actual present buying and selling assessing value.

Property taxes are usually regressive rather than progressive taxes. "A 'regressive tax' is one under which the ratio of tax paid to income is greater in poor families than in rich."[9] A regressive tax results in poor families paying a greater ratio of tax with respect to their incomes than do the rich.

Since property taxes are regressive, they are unpopular with many people, particularly those who are not rich. If a tax is unpopular, the person advocating taxes for a social service, such as education, is often ineffective in making his case, despite his possible eloquence as to the social benefits of the service.

Yet the property tax persists because of its long tradition and a certain convenience. It is a stable tax producing a stable yield. Property tax rates can be raised or lowered without much difficulty. A bill is received in a household once or twice a year and a check or money order made out—not a very complex process. The property owner knows how much he is paying and thus the tax is visible; the payer of a visible tax may be more inclined to keep his eye on how the government spends his money.

A second type of tax is the sales tax, usually levied by the state. The tax on sales (or gross receipts) may be, for instance, as low as 2 percent, regarded as fairly low, or as high as 6 percent, regarded as fairly high. Sales taxes are also regressive taxes. The poor spend more of their income in sales taxes than the rich, while the poor are able to save a lower proportion of their income than rich families. Rich families usually spend more of their money than poor families on travel, education, and personal services, on which there is usually no sales tax.

The state has another recourse in collecting taxes to be used in large part for education. This is the state income tax, now used in many states. The state income tax is similar to the federal income tax except that exemptions are usually higher and rates usually much lower. The income tax, whether state or

---

[9] *Ibid.*, p. 94.

federal, is a progressive tax because the ratio of tax paid to income is larger for the high income family than for the low income family.

The tax of which one most often hears is the federal individual income tax. This tax is not simply the major source of revenue for an increasingly large federal government; it has genuine consequences in the economy, and has become an instrument of social policy. For instance, sometimes the government raises income taxes to fight inflation by reducing the amount of money individuals and corporations have for the purchase of goods and services.

The federal individual income tax asks the taxpayer to total his taxable sources of income; it then allows him certain deductions and exemptions for himself and the members of his family, and it specifies a tax rate to be paid on the difference between his income and his deductions and exemptions.

The income tax has proven a highly productive source of funds for government. It is, of course, a progressive tax and the result is that rich people pay far more than poor families. All taxes are unpopular. But the federal income tax tends to be particularly unpopular with the wealthier segment of the community.

In summary, then, four types of major taxes supply revenue for the support of education. Two of them are primarily regressive taxes—the property tax levied by local government and the sales tax levied by states. Two of them are primarily progressive taxes—the state income tax and the federal income tax. Overwhelmingly, local government uses the property tax as its instrument and the federal government uses the income tax.

State governments, however, have a choice of whether to use the income tax or sales tax. Those states which use both have the choice as to which one to use more heavily. Those legislators who favor regressive taxes tend to favor the sales tax; those who favor progressive taxes tend to favor the income tax. In broad terms, labor usually supports the income tax while business supports the sales tax. The educator is frequently recruited on either side of the battleground. Clearly, there is no tax on which all harmoniously agree.

Each tax base—property, sales, and income—can be evaluated individually. We have mentioned the most fundamental considerations such as equity, administrative feasibility, cost of collection, and regressivity. Complete evaluation of any one tax base cannot be made solely by examining the base without reference to the combined effect of all taxes. For example, some authorities on taxation believe that after making special allowances for extremely low income families, retired persons, and other adjustments, the regressivity of property and sales taxes may not be unfair, particularly when viewed in relation to the progressivity of income taxes. The end result of all taxes is the best basis on which to make final judgment on the reasonableness of any one tax base.

An illustration of variations in percentage of income spent in each of these tax forms by home-owning families with three family members is shown in Table 11.4. These percentages do not provide all the information necessary to judge either a particular tax base or the total of all three. However, they do represent the context for making a fair and rational evaluation.

TABLE 11.4

Percentages of Income Spent on Taxes by Home Owners, 1968*

INCOME (FAMILY OF THREE)	$3,000	$5,000	$7,000	$9,000	$13,000	$20,000
Property tax	7.2	4.0	3.1	2.9	2.8	2.2
Sales tax	2.9	2.4	2.1	1.9	1.6	1.4
Federal income tax	3.2	8.0	10.7	12.1	14.0	18.4
Total	13.3	14.4	15.9	16.9	18.4	21.6

* Data from a survey of homeowners in Illinois in 1968.
William P. McLure, "Major Issues in School Finance," *Educational Administration Quarterly* (Fall 1969), p. 6.

Sweeping reforms of school financing have been proposed by a few individuals and groups from time to time during the past quarter of a century. In 1969 an education newsletter reported a fundamental proposal for change in Michigan:

Michigan's governor has rocked the education world with a plan calling for the state to take over the entire cost of education—a controversial step which other states may be forced to follow. The proposal, a "total reform of education," would also eliminate the state board of education, replace the state superintendent of public instruction with a state director of education appointed by the governor, and change the complexion of negotiations. The reform suggested by Gov. William G. Milliken, which requires legislative approval and state constitutional changes, substitutes a uniform statewide property tax for local school taxes. And it would probably cause a sharp increase in the state income tax. Milliken says the primary purpose of his proposal is to equalize educational opportunity throughout the state and end the inequalities caused by differences in local wealth. He also stresses making school systems accountable for the money they spend.[10]

The concept of shifting the full cost of local schools to the state is not a new one; this idea has been around for a long time, though it has not received wide acclaim in this country. In recent years this approach has been proposed as an alternative to the traditional one of using state and locally shared revenues. Examples of state central financing of public schools are found in Australia, France, some provinces of Canada, and even in Hawaii. This concept was advocated in a recent report by the Advisory Commission on Intergovernmental Relations, a commission of twenty-six members established by an act of Con-

---

[10] "Michigan Governor Seeks State Take-over of all School Costs," *Education U.S.A., The Weekly Newsletter on Education Affairs* (October 6, 1969). Published by the National Public Relations Commission, Washington, D.C.

gress in 1959 for continuing relationships among, local, state, and federal levels of government.[11]

EQUALIZING SUPPORT FOR PUBLIC SCHOOLS

INEQUALITIES IN STATE AND LOCAL SUPPORT

The question of support for education is more than a question of what are the most appropriate taxes to levy and administer. Anyone who thinks seriously of the importance of the educational enterprise must take into account the entire program needed by a nation in order to avoid shortages or surpluses in the national life. As the economists remind us, economic goods are by definition scarce and must be used wisely and in relationship to the basic purposes and goals of the people of a nation.

The fact of life is that in the United States there is inequality in income distribution. Consequently, school districts that are among the less wealthy have some of the greatest social needs and yet the least available economic support and educational opportunities. Not only are some districts prosperous and others poor in this land which contains both rich suburbs and miserable slums; this is also a nation of prosperous states such as California and New York and poorer states such as Mississippi and Arkansas.

The decisions concerning the extent of financial support for schools are not made by educators. Basically such decisions are made by the people or their representatives. Thus, the matter of financing of schools is essentially a political decision. At all levels of government, some political administrators are most concerned for what they term the interests of the taxpayer; others are more concerned about fostering the broad welfare of the nation by spending for education. Consequently the tug-of-war for funds goes on between taxpayer-oriented and education-oriented members of state legislatures on the state level, and members of school boards on the local level. On the state level, various pressure groups vie for their share of the state budget. On the local level, the board of education is one group among many competing for a share in the local tax dollar. However, only a very few boards operate under special laws requiring them to argue their case before county trustees, council members, mayors, etc; with few exceptions, school boards make decisions on amount of local tax levies for schools within limitations set by state laws. Federal funding decisions channel through the Congress of the United States, which, in turn, is subject to a variety of pressures from the people and their representatives as to priorities.

That there are inequalities in educational opportunity is apparent. A 1965 study by Harrison and McLoone showed that about two out of every hundred of America's young people were attending schools which had four times the financial support of schools in which two out of a hundred young people at the

---

[11] Advisory Commission on Intergovernmental Relations, *State Aid to Local Government*, ACIR Report A–34.(Washington, D.C.: The Commission, April, 1969.)

other extreme of the economic scale were enrolled.[12] To use a current illustration of inequality of opportunity among residents of different states, in 1969–70 Alabama was spending an estimated $438 and New York was spending an estimated $1,251 per pupil in average daily attendance.[13]

Inequality among states is not a matter of malice or penury on the part of a particular state. There are great variations among the states in financial ability to provide support. For example, in 1967 New York had more than twice the personal income for each school-age child (five to seventeen) than did Mississippi.[14] At the same time there are major differences as to spending within each state. In some states, some districts support education at twice the level of other districts.

So the social question which arises is whether or not a nation has an obligation to provide equal educational opportunities for its citizens. Does a nation at least have an obligation to move toward greater equalization of opportunity? All states apply the principle of equalization in their state finance plans, but there is a wide variation in the extent to which the actual distribution of state aid accomplishes this purpose.

Most states use a "foundation" plan to equalize a minimum level of support. Each school district is expected to make a local contribution at some prescribed level, applied uniformly to estimated property tax valuations. The state provides the difference between the funds raised locally and the cost of the foundation. In other words, a basic foundation as to scope and cost of education is guaranteed for all districts.

There are reasons, however, why this plan falls short of equalization of educational opportunity among school districts, even in the states judged by the most competent analysts to have the best finance plans. School districts have leeway to raise local taxes beyond the amount required to participate in the foundation; those with high taxing ability can raise more beyond the foundation than those with low taxing ability. There are numerous special aids, state and federal, that are distributed without reference to funds otherwise available. Equal amounts of funds per pupil alone cannot accomplish equal educational opportunity; some pupils require twice, perhaps three or four times, as much to be spent to meet their needs. Since some districts have a higher proportion of pupils with special needs than do other districts, an average amount per pupil will not provide comparable fiscal capacity among districts. While some states use procedures for "weighting" pupils with high cost needs, these methods do not fully compensate for the basic differences. Finally, most states distribute flat grants to those districts that do not qualify for equalization aid, thus creating a degree of disequalization.

---

[12] Forrest W. Harrison and Eugene P. McLoone, *Profiles in School Support: A Decennial Overview*, U.S. Office of Education, Miscellany No. 47 (Washington, D.C.: U.S. Government Printing Office, 1965), pp. 1–7.

[13] NEA Research Division, *Estimates of School Statistics 1969–70*, Research Report 1969–R15 (Washington, D.C.: The Association, 1969), p. 37.

[14] NEA Research Division, *Rankings of the States*, Research Report 1969–R1 (Washington, D.C.: The Association, 1969), p. 33.

FEDERAL AID TO EDUCATION

The federal government also enters into greater equalization of educational opportunity through *categorical aid*. Categorical aid is support for special aspects of the educational program considered important to the development of the nation. Typically, categorical aid relates to such national concerns as defense or full employment or elimination of educational deficiencies associated with poverty. Table 11.5 shows the extent of the federal program for education and manpower.

TABLE 11.5

The Budget for Fiscal Year 1971
Education and Manpower
[In millions of dollars]

PROGRAM OR AGENCY	1969 ACTUAL	OUTLAYS 1970 ESTIMATE	1971 ESTIMATE	RECOMMENDED BUDGET AUTHORITY FOR 1971
Elementary and secondary education:				
Early childhood development	350	324	327	339
Children from low-income families	1,092	1,200	1,324	1,394
Education of handicapped children	56	75	84	97
Indian Education (Department of the Interior)	176	229	257	233
Formula grants to States	322	209	173	116
Assistance to schools in federally impacted areas	398	397	128	
Proposed legislation			212	425
Other	86	234	205	199
Higher education:				
Student grants, direct loans, and guaranteed loans	418	582	632	651
Construction of facilities	596	643	580	100
Other	216	170	237	197
Vocational Education	262	266	329	379
Science education and basic research:				
National Science Foundation	490	490	490	513
Other education aids:				
Educational research and development	85	94	100	118
Library of Congress and Smithsonian Institute	97	109	112	102
National Foundation on the Arts and the Humanities	12	23	40	40
Corporation for Public Broadcasting	5	15	22	22
Other	174	193	137	95
Subtotal, education	4,835	5,253	5,389	5,020

TABLE 11.5 (cont.)

The Budget for Fiscal Year 1971
Education and Manpower
[In millions of dollars]

PROGRAM OR AGENCY	OUTLAYS			RECOMMENDED BUDGET AUTHORITY FOR 1971
	1969 ACTUAL	1970 ESTIMATE	1971 ESTIMATE	
Manpower training:				
Proposed legislation (additional first-year cost)			25	45
On-the-job training	121	216	397	455
Institutional training	456	384	404	406
Work experience	356	357	377	376
Special targeting	173	327	411	369
Program direction and research	87	84	106	121
Other manpower aids:				
Federal-state employment security program	630	711	769	776
Other manpower programs	181	217	264	277
Subtotal, manpower	2,003	2,297	2,754	2,824
Deductions for offsetting receipts:				
Proprietary receipts from the public	−13	−13	−14	−14
Total	6,825	7,538	8,129	7,830

The Budget of the United States Government, 1971 (Washington, D.C.: U.S. Government Printing Office, 1970), p. 138.

Many educators urge that categorical aid should be eliminated or restricted to support only a few selected aspects of school programs and that most federal support be *general aid* that provides revenue from national taxation for the use of schools throughout the nation. In effect, what they urge is a type of foundation program not simply at the state level but at the federal level. Yet the counter argument made is that with increasing federal (or state) support comes increasing control by the fund suppliers. Still others argue that laws can be developed which could safeguard against encroachments and unreasonable federal or state controls.

The present probability seems to be that categorical aid will be continued while general federal aid to education increasingly gains favor. Some believe that the supposed threat of federal control can be reduced by allocating federal monies to the state for control and administration. Yet this raises the question of whether the states, through their agencies, have made the best and most effective utilization of funds in the past, or whether adequate procedures exist to utilize the best intelligence for judging effectiveness. Some observers fear that racial discrimination or political chicanery might sometimes affect distribution of funds in some states.

Supporters of federal aid to education point to a long history of federal support which is sometimes overlooked by critics. Federal legislation supporting schooling in America began far earlier than is sometimes assumed. (Table 11.6 gives a list of major federal acts on education.) A considerable body of legislation existed previous to the mid-century federal legislation which provided schooling for veterans of World War II through the G.I. Bill of Rights and prior to the National Defense Education Act which grew out of American fears that the schools were not sufficiently geared to a Space Age.

TABLE 11.6

The Federal Government and Education, 1780–1969

MAJOR PRE-SPUTNIK CONGRESSIONAL ACTIVITY IN EDUCATION

Land Ordinance	1785	Provided an orderly format for distribution and settlement of public lands and encouraged use of public monies to establish and maintain public schools in the newly created townships.
Northwest Ordinance	1787	
Ohio Statehood Enabling Act	1802	First of the Enabling Acts which provided land grants (a total of 98 million acres) for public schools in newly created states.
Morrill Act	1862	Provided 30,000 acres of land per congressman for establishment of agricultural, scientific, and industrial colleges; assisted 68 institutions currently enrolling 40 percent of the nation's college population.
Hatch Act	1887	Provided land grants for agricultural experimental stations at land grant colleges.
Second Morrill Act	1890	Provided permanent annual endowment for developing instructional programs in agricultural and technical colleges and universities; original $15,000/year/state appropriation eventually increased to $50,000/year/state.
Smith-Lever Act	1914	Created Agricultural Extension Service to "aid in diffusing . . . useful and practical information on subjects pertaining to agriculture and home economics"; original $5 million/year appropriation eventually increased to $50 million/year.

Smith-Hughes Act	1917	Provided matching funds to help states develop high school vocational programs; original $1.7 million program expanded four times and incorporated in 1958 NDEA.
"New Deal" Activity	1930s	Encouraged education as part of the Public Works Administration, Civilian Conservation Corps, National Youth Administration, Works Progress Administration, etc.
Lanham Act	1941	Provided funds to construct and operate schools where war-incurred federal activity created burdens upon local governments; expanded in 1950 by Impact Laws 815 and 874 which provided money for school construction and district operating costs respectively.
Serviceman's Readjustment Act (GI Bill)	1944	Provided education and training for returning World War II veterans; expanded subsequently to include veterans of wars in Korea and Vietnam.
National School Lunch Program	1946	Provided funds for school lunch programs in public and nonpublic school; expanded in 1954 to include a school milk program.
National Science Foundation	1950	Established a federally supported foundation to provide scholarships and fellowships for study and research in scientific fields.
School Construction Act	1957	Provided $325 million/year for four years for financing school construction.

MAJOR POST-SPUTNIK CONGRESSIONAL ACTIVITY IN EDUCATION

National Defense Education Act	1958*	Provided graduate fellowships in education—particularly in the sciences, mathematics, and foreign languages; extended in 1964.
Area Redevelopment Act	1961	Provided funds to train persons in redevelopment areas throughout the nation.
Peace Corps Act	1961	Established a program to supply teachers and technicians for underdeveloped nations for two-year periods of time.
Manpower Development and Training Act	1962	Established up-to-date training programs for youth whose lack of education prevents them from obtaining employment; expanded in 1963.
Higher Education Facilities Act	1963*	Provided grants to all colleges, public and private, for improvement of facilities.

* Legislation providing the core of federal activity in education since Sputnik.

Vocational Education Act		Extended 1950 Impact Laws and NDEA and provided funds for construction of vocational schools and development of expanded vocational education offerings.
Economic Opportunity Act	1964	Provided the legislative weapon for the war on poverty; intended to improve the lot of the disadvantaged through educational and community projects. Head Start, Job Corps, Neighborhood Youth Corps, VISTA, and other work-experience and community programs; expanded, but with restrictions a year later.
Civil Rights Act	1964	Intended to discourage racial discrimination throughout society, with particular emphasis upon hastening desegregation in the nation's schools.
Juvenile Delinquency and Youth Offenses Control Act Amendment	1964	Intended to research fully the effects of compulsory school attendance and child labor laws upon juvenile delinquency.
Elementary and Secondary Education Act	1965*	Provided large sums of money for a broad range of educational concerns.
National Foundation for the Arts and Humanities	1965	Established a federally supported foundation to complement NSF and provide scholarships and fellowships for study and research in the arts and humanities.
Higher Education Act	1965*	Provided large sums of money for institutions, students, and teachers involved in higher education.
International Education Act	1966	Provided grants in institutions of higher education for establishment, strengthening, and operation of research centers for study of international education.
Education Professions Development Act	1967	Amended the 1965 Higher Education Act to improve the preservice and inservice training of educational personnel.

---

* Legislation providing the core of federal activity in education since Sputnik.

John M. Nagle, "The Tenth Amendment and Uncle Sam," *The Educational Forum* (November 1969), pp. 23, 28.

Despite the long history of federal aid to education and the substantial sums now being spent for federal support of education in the nation, the debate over federal aid to education is still heated. Here are the more frequent arguments used on both sides of this issue, as adapted from Howard R. Jones' more expanded treatment in *Financing Public Elementary Education and Secondary Education*.[15]

The proponents of federal aid to education say:
1. Every American child, regardless of whether he happens to grow up in a rich state or a poor state, should have at least a minimum level of opportunity to receive an education and, at most, the quality of educational opportunity provided to most American children and youth.
2. The United States needs all of its citizenry to be well educated, in the interest of both national welfare and national security. Even more broadly, educational opportunity for all is necessary if we are to consider ourselves a democracy.
3. Some states and regions of the nation have been particularly handicapped economically in their efforts to supply sufficient classrooms and employ adequate teachers. Even though great improvements have taken place, some areas of the country still face substantial problems.
4. Since most of our taxes are collected at the federal level, primarily through an income tax which reflects the individual's ability to pay better than do state and local taxes, a substantial amount of federal aid derived from the income of the entire nation and used on behalf of the entire nation is eminently fair.
5. Federal aid is the greatest reservoir of resources for taxation; local and state taxes for education have grown tremendously and the capacity for further use of these resources is more limited than at the federal level.
6. The federal government collects taxes relatively efficiently as compared to state and local sources.
7. People in the United States frequently move and this mobility supports national programs for greater equalization.
8. We are spending millions abroad through foreign aid in behalf of the educational programs of newly developing countries. The educational welfare of our own children is at least equally important.
9. If the federal government is able to build highways, protect the public health and provide housing, it should be able to make a substantial investment in the welfare of children.

The opponents of federal aid to education urge:
1. The responsibility for education in the American system rests with the states. Education is not even mentioned in the United States Constitution.
2. Federal control is a reality; schools adapt their purposes and programs in order to receive federal funds. The agency which controls the purse strings will control the educational product.
3. This is no time to add responsibility for education to the national priorities. The present staggering costs of federal government should be decreased, not increased.
4. The emergency is over with respect to the public schools. The boom in elementary enrollment is past, so why support federal spending now?

[15] Howard R. Jones, *Financing Public Elementary and Secondary Education* (New York: The Center for Applied Research in Education, 1966), pp. 103–106.

5. Wealthy states should not be taxed more heavily than poor states to achieve within their own borders the equalization desired.
6. When tax money must be funneled into Washington before being distributed to the states, substantial overhead and administrative costs will be incurred.
7. Since private and parochial schools may not constitutionally be granted federal support, many citizens with children in private and parochial school programs may be expected to resist expanded federal taxation for education.
8. Perhaps the federal government should support other state activities such as welfare, road building, etc., through grants to the states and thus leave the states more funds for state support of education so there will be less necessity to call upon the federal government.

As the controversy has continued, federal aid has steadily grown, though it has taken the form of federal support for certain aspects of the educational program. It has been a response to emergencies in the name of national interest and in the form of categorical aid. For instance, when during World War I vocational education seemed to be sadly lagging, the Smith-Hughes Act was inaugurated. During the depression of the 1930s, schools were built through federal funds, in large part to provide employment. When the veterans returned from World War II, more educational opportunities were made available through federal funds. School lunch programs came about in large part because of the desire to use America's agricultural surplus. As we have already seen, the National Defense Education Act came about because of fears that the United States was lagging behind the Soviet Union in a space age and most particularly as to subjects judged necessary for national survival—mathematics, science, and modern languages. The federal stress on programs for the disadvantaged was a recognition of a national problem in the inner cities, involving the poor and the culturally disadvantaged in general.

So, until the present time, financial help provided by the federal government has taken the form of assistance to parts of the school program which seemed to be falling behind, thus potentially or actually handicapping the national interest. Other support to schools came about as a by-product of attempts to aid aspects of the economy.

The result was not general aid to education but what might better be described as a broken-front approach on the part of the federal government. A crucial problem for the seventies is whether or not the federal government has a responsibility to provide aid so that at least a minimum program for all children and possibly a program of genuine educational equalization might be established throughout the nation.

THE EXPANSION OF EDUCATIONAL EXPENDITURES

THE GROWTH OF EDUCATIONAL EXPENDITURES

The total expenditures for the public schools have risen sharply during the last decade. When one includes both current expenditures of elementary and secondary schools, the outlay for capital and the payment of interest, one finds that in the period from the 1959–60 school year through the period of the 1969–70 school year the total amount spent has increased 152.9 percent. Table 11.7 shows the total expenditures for public schools each year from

TABLE 11.7

Expenditures for Public Elementary
and Secondary Schools 1960 through 1970

SCHOOL YEAR	TOTAL EXPENDITURES*		
	AMOUNT (IN THOUSANDS)	PERCENT INCREASE OVER 1959–60	PERCENT INCREASE OVER PREVIOUS YEAR
1959–60	$15,613,255		
1960–61	16,807,934	7.7	7.7
1961–62	18,373,339	17.7	9.3
1962–63	19,735,070	26.4	7.4
1963–64	21,324,993	36.6	8.1
1964–65	23,029,742	47.5	8.0
1965–66	26,248,026	68.1	14.0
1966–67	28,352,330	81.6	8.0
1967–68	31,917,850	104.4	12.6
1968–69	35,777,575	129.2	12.1
1969–70	39,489,137	152.9	10.4

* Current expenditures plus capital expenditures plus interest on debt service.

SCHOOL YEAR	CURRENT EXPENDITURES ONLY		
	AMOUNT (IN THOUSANDS)	PERCENT INCREASE OVER 1959–60	PERCENT INCREASE OVER PREVIOUS YEAR
1959–60	$12,329,389		
1960–61	13,147,075	6.6	6.6
1961–62	14,729,270	19.5	12.0
1962–63	15,606,328	26.6	6.0
1963–64	17,218,446	39.7	10.3
1964–65	18,548,925	50.4	7.7
1965–66	21,053,280	70.8	13.5
1966–67	22,854,760	85.4	8.6
1967–68	25,769,474	109.0	12.8
1968–69	29,039,741	135.5	12.7
1969–70	32,280,569	161.8	11.2

NEA Research Division, *Estimates of School Statistics, 1969–70*, Research Report 1969–R15 (Washington, D.C.: The Association, 1969), pp. 19–20.

1959–60 through 1969–70. Despite inflation during the period, this is an increase which has far out-distanced inflationary forces. The increase over this same

TABLE 11.8

Current Expenditure Per Pupil in
Average Daily Attendance 1960 through 1970*

SCHOOL YEAR	CURRENT EXPENDITURE PER PUPIL IN ADA FOR ELEMENTARY AND SECONDARY DAY SCHOOLS		
	AMOUNT	PERCENT INCREASE OVER 1959–60	PERCENT INCREASE OVER PREVIOUS YEAR
1959–60	$375		
1960–61	393	4.8	4.8
1961–62	419	11.7	6.6
1962–63	433	15.5	3.3
1963–64	460	22.7	6.2
1964–65	484	29.1	5.2
1965–66	537	43.2	11.0
1966–67	573	52.8	6.7
1967–68	634	69.1	10.6
1968–69	702	87.2	11.1
1969–70	766	104.3	9.1

* Current expenditure per pupil in ADA increased from $375 in 1959–60 to an estimated $766 in 1969–70, a rise of 104.3 percent. Variations among the states in expenditures per pupil are great. Estimated expenditure per pupil in ADA for 1969–70 varies from a low of $438 to a high of $1,251.

CURRENT (1969–1970) EXPENDITURE PER PUPIL IN ADA FOR ELEMENTARY AND SECONDARY DAY SCHOOLS	NUMBER OF STATES
$400–449	1
450–499	1
500–549	5
550–599	1
600–649	9
650–699	7
700–749	5
750–799	6
800–849	5
850–899	6
900 and over	4

NEA Research Division, *Estimates of School Statistics, 1969–70* (Washington, D.C.: The Association, 1969), p. 20.

period for current operating expenses only, excluding capital outlay and interest on debt, was 161.8 percent.

The changes in total expenditures do not reflect the effects of increased numbers of pupils, the relative economic status of employee salaries, and the qualities of capital facilities and other inputs. Some idea of the relative change in current operating expenditures over this past decade may be seen in Table 11.8 by comparing average expenditures per pupil. The percentage increase in average expenditure per pupil from 1960 to 1970 was 104.3 percent. The difference between this figure and 161.8 percent shown for gross current expenditures on Table 11.7 indicates that much of the increase was spend on additional pupils.

Table 11.8 also shows a distribution of average current expenditure per pupil by states in 1969–70. The ratio of the highest state average to the lowest state average is nearly three to one; the variations of school district averages within some states are even greater.

THE FUTURE OF EDUCATIONAL EXPENDITURES

The probability is that expenditures for schools will continue to rise. Take, for example, the recommendation of a fifty-member Urban Education Task Force, appointed in March 1969 by Robert H. Finch who was then the Secretary of Health, Education and Welfare, to help him shape long-range proposals for legislation and financing. The Task Force concluded that the problems of big-city education were crucial and thus proposed an Urban Education Act to support a comprehensive master plan for inner cities. In order to improve the education of fourteen and one-half million inner-city youngsters, they proposed boosting educational resources including equipment, teachers, and counselors, by at least one-third. The Task Force informed President Nixon that their recommendations would call for somewhere between five and seven billion dollars in federal aid.

So there is no doubt that the problem raised in this chapter as to "where's the money coming from?" is a real and continuing one. As a new teacher, you have the social responsibility of knowing not only the dimensions of the problem but thinking through your viewpoint on the social issues involved. You need to consider whether public education should be supported by tax funds, and, if so, why. You need to consider the types of taxes which should be depended on for revenue in the future. You need to consider the social implications of progressive and regressive taxation. You must determine your position on inequalities in support for the schooling of Americans, and you need to think about the desirability or undesirability of federal aid and whether the present program of grants-in-aid for special national needs is preferable to a broader program of general aid from federal sources. If your decisions are to be well based, you will have to continually expand your knowledge of finances to become a reasonably literate person in this field.

Your decisions are important in your role as a citizen and they are crucial in your role as a teacher.

★ ★ ★

DISCUSSION

1. In what way is American education a decentralized public activity? How important is local control?
2. Where does the money for public education come from? What are the relative proportions of contributions from the various sources?
3. Should public education be supported by tax funds? If so, why? If not, how?
4. What is to be said for achieving economic and social benefits through a private rather than a public system of education?
5. What are the sources of taxation in America? What proportion of taxes go to education?
6. How would you defend the support of education through taxation?
7. Show the relationship between expenditures for education and the extent of the national economic growth. Examine the claimed relationship critically.
8. Discuss the difference between a progressive and regressive tax.
9. Why does a regressive tax measure aid the wealthier segment of our population? How does a progressive tax aid the poorer segment? What are the taxes in your state that are characterized as being regressive? Progressive?
10. What seem to you to be appropriate standards for tax equity? What is the case for, respectively, property taxes, sales taxes, and income taxes? What are some trends and tendencies with implications for the future?
11. Can you document the existence of inequality in income distribution and consequent inequality of educational opportunity in the United States? How do these inequalities manifest themselves in particular states? In local communities?
12. What essentially is the meaning of a "foundation" plan? Could the idea of a "foundation" be equally used at the federal level?
13. How has the federal government contributed to education?
14. What is the case for "general" versus "categorical" aid from the federal government?
15. Were aspects of your own elementary or secondary education at least partially supported with federal aid funds or programs? If so, what? Why were these particular aspects singled out?
16. What are the pros and cons on federal aid to education? Which of the arguments seem particularly impressive to you? What social forces encourage and discourage federal aid to education?
17. To what extent have educational expenditures grown in past years and to what extent do they simply reflect inflationary forces? What seems to be the probable future for expenditures for education?
18. What arguments support large additional sums of money being spent on public education? Which oppose? Give specific examples.
19. Should additional funds be allocated by governing bodies to determine and implement a more effective—preventive and developmental—compensatory education program?
20. Discuss this comment: "Adequate financial support alone does not solve the problems facing the school: it facilitates their solution."

INVOLVEMENT

1. Attempt to determine community and state support of education through local and state sources in your community.
2. Obtain from local school sources the budget for the local school system. How do the proportions spent compare with the national figures contained in this chapter?
3. Interview a school administrator. Which funds are earmarked for special activities from the federal government? Which from the state? If additional funds were available to him, what would be his priorities for spending them?
4. Determine where your state stands nationally with respect to educational expenditures. (Relevant data might be obtained from your State Department of Education.)
5. Appoint a member of your class to visit the legislature when educational appropriations are under consideration. Better still, plan a group visit by your class to the legislature which might include visits with your own representatives.
6. Report on the federal budget. Attempt to determine the current proportion of funds invested in support of education and in support of the military establishment of the nation. Consider the views of various class members on desirable national priorities.
7. Write to your senators or congressmen concerning your opinions on educational support and solicit their positions on educational appropriation. Share with them your own point of view on federal aid to education and ask for their viewpoint.
8. Interview the student personnel services administrator in your school district. What groups of children need the largest educational expenditures?
9. Develop panel presentations concerning the arguments concerning increased expenditure for public education. Include value factors.

BIBLIOGRAPHY

Benson, Charles S. *The Cheerful Prospect: A Statement on the Future of American Education.* Boston: Houghton Mifflin, 1965. The economic setting, sources of revenue, and the allocation of educational resources.

———. *The Economics of Public Education.* Boston: Houghton Mifflin Company, 1968. Fundamental and perceptive treatment of problems related to financing of schools upon which this chapter heavily draws.

———. *School and the Economic System.* Foundations of Education Series. Chicago: Science Research Associates, 1966. 117 pp. Interrelationships of education and economics by an authority.

Bowen, William G. *Economic Aspects of Education: Three Essays.* Princeton, N.J.: Princeton Industrial Relations Section, Princeton University, 1964. The case for the importance of education in the economy. Summary of insights on financing the schools. Part of a larger series of similar concise reports on education.

Bowles, Samuel. *Planning Educational Systems for Economic Growth.* Cambridge, Mass.: Harvard University Press, 1969. Considers the economic characteristics of the production of educated labor in the schools and conceptual foundations for determining an efficient allocation of resources in the education sector.

Brighton, Stayner. *Financing Public Schools: A Study Guide.* Washington, D.C.: Committee on Educational Finance, NEA, 1965. Principles concerning why we spend money on schools, how schools obtain their revenues, and how they spend for services and materials.

Chamber of Commerce of the United States. *An Investment in People.* Washington, D.C.: Chamber of Commerce, 1964. 57 pp. The case for education as good business as viewed by the Chamber of Commerce.

Corbally, John E. *School Finance.* Boston: Allyn and Bacon, 1962. 288 pp. Basic textbook in the field of financing schools.

Garvue, Robert J. *Modern Public School Finance.* New York: Macmillan, 1969. A review of educational finance which makes the case for more financial commitment based on the premise that education is actually an investment in human capital.

Gauerke, Warren E. and Jack R. Childress, eds. *Theory and Practice of School Finance.* Chicago: Rand McNally, 1967. Basic book for study of school finance problems.

Gerwin, Donald. *Budgeting Public Funds: The Decision Process in an Urban School District.* Madison, Wisc.: University of Wisconsin Press, 1969. A research study exploring how public budgeting decisions are actually made in a school district. Utilizes newly developed techniques in administrative theory.

Johns, Roe L. and Edgar L. Morphet. *The Economics and Financing of Education,* 2nd ed. Englewood Cliffs, N.J.: Prentice-Hall, 1969. Educational finance and many of the major problems and issues. The implications of educational finance policies for the total social system.

Jones, Howard R. *Financing Public Elementary and Secondary Education.* New York: The Center for Applied Research in Education, 1966. A compact summary of issues in financing public schools, with an especially good analysis of the pros and cons of federal aid to education.

Kneller, George. *Education and Economic Thought.* New York: John Wiley and Sons, 1968. Relates economics to educational concerns, particularly the support of public education.

McCloskey, Gordon. *Education and Public Understanding,* 2nd ed. New York: Harper and Row, 1967. Implications of research and the use of modern communications media which provide opportunities to obtain financial and moral public support for schools.

National Education Association. *Interdependence in School Finance: The City, the State, the Nation.* Washington, D.C.: Educational Finance Committee, The Association, 1968. Recognition of the necessary interrelationships of all sources of funds in a sound system of financing public education.

National Education Association, Committee on Educational Finance. *Financial Status of the Public Schools.* Washington, D.C.: The Association, 1970. Useful statistics on the financial background of public schools as the 1970s began.

———. *What Everyone Should Know About Financing Our Schools.* Revised ed. Washington, D.C.: The Association, 1967. The case for adequate school support. Why costs of education are increasing and why educational expenditures are an investment. Local, state, and federal sources of public school support.

AUDIO-VISUAL MATERIALS

Breakthrough to Better Schools (NEA, 70 fr., Color) Discusses the need for federal aid to schools to equalize the tax burden.

Criteria of a Good Tax System (New York City Board of Education, 30 Min.) A demonstration lesson for teacher training which discusses criteria of a good tax system.

Can America Afford Better Schools? (National Education Association, 14 Min. color) Shows a newspaper reporter interviewing a superintendent, principal and classroom teacher for an explanation of the rise in school costs. Gives reasons for quality education which depends on quality teachers.

PART THREE

FOUNDATIONS OF EDUCATION

TWELVE

WHO ATTENDS SCHOOL?

To this point in the book we have talked largely of teachers. We have mainly dealt with decisions you as a new teacher must make. Knowledge of the social and historical setting in which education takes place and of the forces to be taken into account is essential in your decision-making. But important though your decisions and surrounding forces are, there is another element in education which is of high importance to you and your work. After all, education is for students, young or old. This chapter will deal with the social class and ethnic backgrounds of these students.

The sheer number of human beings who attend schools is impressive. The simplest statistic to describe the volume is three-tenths of the nation. We live in a learning society. It's no wonder that education is occasionally referred to as America's major enterprise. The population of the U.S. is now well beyond the 200,000,000 figure—about 60,000,000 of which were enrolled in schools in 1970. Some 46,000,000 pupils were enrolled in public schools; 5,000,000 in Catholic schools; 700,000 attended independent or private schools; while for higher educational institutions, the figure was around 8,300,000. And that does not include the hard-to-estimate number involved in adult education.

But the people who attend schools in America are not statistics—they are individual human beings. Even within categories, students still remain individuals. An impressionistic description of the high school population, which the writer once wrote for the readers of a popular magazine, may illustrate the point of individuality:

What a range of young people attend our public high schools in America! Here's Susan: brilliant, already accepted by one of the "Seven Sisters" colleges, studying PSSC physics devised by the best brains of M.I.T. and elsewhere, speaking French fluently, reading William Faulkner and Jean Paul Sartre, wrestling with calculus, learning international economics, planning to travel on the Continent with her family next summer.

Here's Mike: indifferent, ready to quit high school, attending remedial reading class, seeing some sense in the industrial arts program he calls "shop" but repelled by geometry and world history, counting the days till he's sixteen and free to make the wrong decision.

Here's Jane: of average ability, reading *Silas Marner* at school and movie fan magazines at home, doing well in the health unit in biology but poorly in civics, finding mathematics only tolerable, coming fully alive only in home economics and band, confiding in her counselor that there's only one degree she wants—the MRS.

Here's Joe: alienated from both school and society, hating every moment spent in every subject, proud of being chosen War Lord by his gang, itching for the next rumble or, better still, for some student or teacher to knock off the invisible chip he wears to school, when he comes to school at all.

Here's Maria: physically deprived of good nutrition, adequate housing and clothing; culturally deprived of books, magazines, newspapers except for gutter journalism, games, travel, dinner table conversation, privacy, and desperately trying to master ways of living and learning she has never known which are taught to her in a strange foreign tongue.

Here's Harry: creative and individualistic, understanding what the poetess, Edna St. Vincent Millay, meant by saying "Euclid alone has looked on beauty bare" now that he has fallen madly in love with mathematical analysis. He pays no attention whatsoever to his other subjects.

Add to Susan, Mike, Jane, Joe, Maria and Harry . . . other young people who attend all types of secondary schools today. Include those wondrously individual youngsters whom you know best from your own family and immediate neighborhood.[1]

SOCIAL CLASS IN AMERICA

Groupings do exist to help us categorize, however loosely, highly varied people. One such grouping is social class. A society characterized by divisions of people into relative strata or ranks is a society characterized by social classes. To some, the mention of social class is anathema, for they associate social class only with the theories of Karl Marx who conceived capitalist societies as divided into two hostile, antagonistic classes: the proletariat versus the bourgeoisie. But, increasingly, students of society are looking at social class more dispassionately; they recognize that social class has been a characteristic of past societies and is characteristic of American society today. Twentieth century sociologists such as W. Lloyd Warner, August B. Hollingshead, and Herbert Gans; educators such as Robert J. Havighurst and Allison Davis; novelists such as John O'Hara and John P.

---

[1] William Van Til, "What Makes a Good High School Curriculum?" *Woman's Day* (October 1964), pp. 42, 104.

Marquand; and even cartoonists such as Al Capp, creator of Li'l Abner and the society of Dogpatch, testify to the existence of a social class structure in America.

To describe American social classes, some sociologists have adopted the conventional divisions of a society into upper, middle, and lower classes. They have then subdivided each of the major divisions. As a result, W. Lloyd Warner and his followers, by dividing each category into upper and lower, describe the lives of upper-uppers, lower-uppers, upper-middles, lower-middles, upper-lowers, and lower-lowers. The subdivisions are based on how people perceive other people as to their relative status and rank in the total society.[2]

Some fellow sociologists have criticized Warner's six-fold structure (reduced for some communities to five) as more applicable to an America of the past, characterized essentially by towns and small cities than by modern, complex metropolitan giants. It is true that Warner carried on his studies primarily in the 1940s, but his categories still provide a useful introduction to major class categorizations, despite the date of his field research and the difficulty of making sharp demarcations between classes in contemporary America.

UPPER-UPPER AND LOWER-UPPER

Warner found that the upper-upper group is distinguishable from other social classes in that it is made up of families long established in the community and exercising considerable influence in the making of important community decisions. Upper-uppers are prominent in what we earlier described as the power structure. Since this group is prosperous, such families often live in old and well-kept residences in what the community considers the most desirable section. The clubs to which family members belong are the most exclusive in the community; they include clubs based on the length of one's ancestry in America and exclusive organizations that raise money for charities. Such families derive their income from inherited wealth, investments, and property ownership.

Children and youth from upper-upper families are carefully trained for their roles in life. They have no worries about food, clothing, and shelter. They too belong to the exclusive groups of the community; for them these groups often provide instruction in social dancing and etiquette. Upper-upper youngsters often learn their sports skills, such as tennis, through special tutors and camps; national and international travel is taken for granted. In some communities, public school teachers never encounter such students because they often attend exclusive independent schools. Babies may be enrolled at birth for future attendance at a particular prep school. Sometimes these children are sent to public schools in a conscious attempt at democratization of their experiences.

---

[2] W. Lloyd Warner, *Social Class in America: A Manual of Procedure for the Measurement of Social Status* (Chicago: Science Research Associates, 1949). See also W. Lloyd Warner and Leo Srole, *The Social Systems of American Ethnic Groups* (New Haven, Conn.: Yale University Press, 1945) and W. Lloyd Warner and Paul S. Lunt, *The Status Systems of a Modern Community* (New Haven, Conn.: Yale University Press, 1942).

Below the upper-uppers in the social scale, yet sometimes equivalent to upper-uppers in wealth, are the lower-uppers who are also influential in the power structure. Yet, according to Warner and his school of thought, the lower-uppers are not perceived by the community as equivalent in social status to the upper-uppers because lower-uppers represent families that have more recently acquired their substantial share of the world's goods. Though their dollars may be just as green as upper-upper dollars, lower-uppers are regarded by communities as *nouveau riches* who are not top level in status because they are not the long-time possessors of wealth.

The homes of such lower-upper families are among the best in town; sometimes parents have been known to purchase the mansion (though not the status) of an old family. Their clubs are outstanding but not as exclusive as those of the upper-uppers. Membership is usually held in the country club. Entertaining is frequent and may be more lively than gracious. The men of the families work for a living as top-level business leaders, doctors, lawyers, etc. Cars are new and numerous. Alliances with the upper-uppers as a way of social climbing, particularly through marriages, are frequent.

The child or youth from such a family background is somewhat more likely to attend public schools than the upper-upper young person. But since his school is located in the most exclusive section of town, he usually does not have much relationship with social classes other than his own and the upper-middle class, along with the upper-uppers who happen to be in attendance at public rather than private school. Like the upper-upper young person, the young lower-upper family member is often trained for the social struggle through social dancing lessons, ballet, tennis instruction, and sometimes fencing. He or she often is destined by his family for entrance into either the best college of the region or an exclusive college on the East or West coast. Families are deeply concerned for academic success which will ensure college admittance into the selected college. Today, the usual lower-upper youth follows the patterns established by parents. But in our turbulent times, some totally repudiate their training and adopt the ways of hippies or other dissenters.

In some communities, particularly old communities in New England or in the South, the distinction between upper-upper and lower-upper classes is clear. In some Middle Western communities and often in young communities, this distinction blurs. Sociologists consequently report, in such communities, a single upper class. Such was the case in Jonesville, a small city of 6,108 in Abraham County, state of North Prairie, a fictional title for an actual community near Chicago described by W. Lloyd Warner in *Democracy in Jonesville*.[3]

In Jonesville the upper group was represented by the Will Taylor family which lived in a fine old mansion built by Will's grandfather. The Taylor home was located in Top Circle, the best section of town. The Taylor family were social leaders, prosperous and secure, people in the society pages. Earlier generations

---

[3] W. Lloyd Warner, *Democracy in Jonesville: A Study in Quality and Inequality* (New York: Harper and Row, 1949).

of the family often thought of moving to Chicago and taking part in social life there, but the men of the family wanted to be near their farm lands in order to confer with the farm managers on the crops and to see how the tenants were producing. People like the Taylors in Jonesville belonged to the country club and a social club; other similar upper-class people belonged to organizations open only to those whose ancestors lived in America during settlement and colonization. According to Warner, the upper class—approximately three percent of Jonesville—included both the few old and respected families who had lived a long time in the community and a few new families of wealth who were accepted by the old families. As to prestige and influence, the lines between upper-uppers and lower-uppers in Jonesville blurred.

UPPER-MIDDLE AND LOWER-MIDDLE

The upper-middle group in an American community consists of families in which the men are prominent in managerial and professional work and active in the community through luncheon clubs, community-support organizations, and community affairs. The women of the upper-middle group are frequently active in such organizations as the League of Women Voters, the Parent-Teacher Association, and the American Association of University Women. The homes of upper-middle-class citizens are comfortable and pleasant, often located in the better suburbs or in urban apartments regarded as desirable though not top level. Adults of such families are usually regarded as solid and substantial citizens.

Children and youth from upper-middle families are often taught (by example, if not directly) the desirability of being well-liked by contemporaries and of making good impressions; teamwork is stressed. In a sense, such families often emphasize the salability of personalities in American life. Perhaps because of this conformity emphasis, it is from this group and the lower-upper class that much of the contemporary youth rebellion stems. From the point of view of many young people the lives that their parents have led are not worthwhile. Some see their parents as too materialistic, insufficiently concerned with the larger issues in society, too conventional and conforming. Studies of youth dissent show that the leadership in protest comes particularly from upper-middle group young people in revolt against what they regard as a trivial and superficial heritage.

Warner and his associates dramatized the upper-middle group through the George Hill family of Jonesville. The father was a successful businessman who had never questioned the desirability of working hard and "getting somewhere" in life. He was active in the Rotary Club, and his wife was a community leader in town. He lived in one of the better residential districts in town, sometimes called the Country Club district. But the George Hill family was not as well off or as accepted in high society as the Taylors. Instead, Jonesville citizens described people like the George Hills as community leaders, respected citizens, prominent business and professional people. The adults of the Hill family worked with community-oriented luncheon clubs and service organizations rather than with exclusive society-oriented organizations. Approximately 11 percent of Jonesville residents were upper-middle-class, according to Warner.

In the American class structure, there is a difference in prestige between the upper-middle-class and the lower-middle-class members. Families in the lower-middle class often earn their living from white-collar jobs such as sales positions, clerical pursuits, and employment in small businesses. Their houses, while perhaps neat and tidy, seldom resemble the advertising displays found in the homes and gardens magazines. The clubs to which they belong are certainly not exclusive; often they are lodges which also sponsor women's auxiliaries. Characteristic lower-middle-class life is marked by a good deal of work by the family about the house and the yard. Domestics are not employed; the lower-middle class does its own work in the house and on the lot. Since Warner conducted his studies, many highly skilled and well-paid workers have joined the lower-middle-class group. Many of the building construction workers (termed "hard-hats" by the journalists) who demonstrated in New York City in 1970 against student dissent and to support the Cambodian invasion and who carried signs supporting the "Establishment" were probably lower-middle-class Americans.

The children and youth of lower-middle American families are sometimes regarded as typical young people. They are in school primarily, as they see it, to ready themselves for a place in the world of work. Yet they are not usually great social or financial strivers. Today they are usually somewhat more conventional than the youth above them in the social scale, and often, like their parents, they actively or passively oppose rebels and dissenters.

Warner in *Democracy in Jonesville* personified the lower-middle class in the Henry Johnson family. As a clothing store clerk, Henry Johnson drew a regular weekly salary. His family lived in an ordinary bungalow which was in a part of town not regarded by Jonesville as the worst part of town or the best part. Henry was a simple man who enjoyed his vegetable gardening and his lodge meetings; his wife was proud of her ability to keep the house without any paid help. People of Henry Johnson's class often worked as small shopkeepers, skilled workers, or clerks; they received salary checks for their office work or obtained weekly wages in pay envelopes for semi-skilled jobs in mills or factories. Warner indicated that approximately 31 percent of Jonesville people might be grouped as lower-middle.

UPPER-LOWER AND LOWER-LOWER

The upper-lower class is roughly synonymous to the working class. Upper-lowers pour steel in Pittsburgh, assemble cars in Detroit, mill flour in Minneapolis, and sew garments in New York City. They are usually labor union members; they strike when necessary but usually without revolutionary enthusiasm and they may or may not follow their union leaders on political endorsements. They work primarily with things rather than people, and they are relatively unskilled and not as well paid as skilled building trades workers. Their homes are usually relatively simple but clean, but they do not live in the best section of town.

Children of this class are often disadvantaged by their parents' somewhat limited outlooks. Often, from the parental point of view, education is simply a way of entering a vocation; consequently, parents tend to deprecate the academic aspects of education. Family travel takes the form of short vacations or day-long trips to the beach or to the park. Books are scarce though newspapers are read and reread. Conversation seldom deals with social or political issues; when it is judged appropriate at the dinner table it usually deals with family affairs, sports or local activities. While higher education is often aspired to, there is little knowledge of the ways of obtaining scholarships or other financial support.

For the young, the temptation to drop out of school is strong. They often envy their friends who have dropped out and are working and making money; the fact that many of them are in dead-end jobs is harder to see.

If one judges by middle-class standards, the upper-lower young people are often culturally disadvantaged. Yet there often is a closeness and affection in a working class family which compensates for certain disadvantages. This closeness is not always evident in the upper-middle-class suburban family where commuting distances are long and father's work often takes him out of town.

Warner portrayed the upper-lower class through Joe Bird. Joe, who had a steady job at the mill, was perceived by other residents as a man who had little money and not much of a house. But the town saw him as personally honest and as raising a respectable family. When Jonesville described families like the Bird family they talked of "good substantial working-class people," "ordinary folks," "poor but honest," "decent and hard working," "respectable." Joe's work was steady. When economic recession or depression occurred, Joe moved onto relief but moved off as fast as he possibly could. He joined the lower-middles in clubs and lodges while his wife attended women's auxiliaries. He liked small informal groups to play poker or gossip with. In Jonesville, upper-lower residents amounted to a substantial 41 percent of the citizens.

Essentially, the upper-lowers are different from the lower-lowers in the way they are regarded by the community: lower-lowers are regarded as no-account. The difference between upper-lowers and lower-lower on the social scale is not strictly financial: much of it relates to the way society perceives and ranks people as to their status. On one thing all upper classes seem agreed—the lower-lowers are not "good people." The community often thinks they don't particularly care or try; and they are often regarded as "trash."

Not only are they often unemployed, but they make little effort to get off relief, according to their neighbors. Their homes are not particularly well-kept. Fathers occasionally disappear (rather than go through the formalities of divorce, a custom more popular in upper and upper-middle classes). The lower-lower seldom belongs to a club or organization. He and his family are often isolated and alone.

As a result, children and youth from lower-lower families find themselves extremely handicapped in a materially-oriented upward-aspiring society. The scholars searching for identifying group features regard them as culturally disadvantaged. Their neighbors above them on the social scale regard them as young people from undesirable backgrounds. By this, people mean that their families, judged by conventional American standards, are disreputable. Young people themselves scarcely have any way to avoid assuming undesirable family characteristics.

Dropping out of school is particularly attractive to young people of this social group, for everything in the school experience and life experience seems to conspire against them. Without a middle-class background, they often find school highly unrealistic and irrelevant. Often these young people experience repeated failure unredeemed by any particular success in the school framework. When their best friends drop out at 16, and find jobs that temporarily sound attractive or do not get jobs but insist they are enjoying life just hanging around, it is very difficult for these young people to stay in school. Since their parents have no great respect for education, they do not provide much encouragement to staying in school either. As a result, most lower-lower young people leave school at relatively low educational levels and thus cut themselves off from opportunities to rise in American life. To put it bluntly, the dice are loaded against the lower-lower class children and youth. To many observers they represent a self-perpetuating American tragedy.

Yet other observers warn us not to sell some of the values of lower-lower life short. They point out that there is a kind of tough realism in many lower-lower young people, that there exists a quality of loyalty to those who belong to their immediate groups, that struggles for survival have taught lower-lower youth a kind of ingenuity, that buried beneath expression in the form of profanity and obscenity lie genuine creative responses. Others regard such claims as sentimentalism and arrant nonsense for they see little that is redeeming in lower-lower-class culture.

Again Warner dramatized the lower-lowers through the Tom Dow family. As seen by Jonesville people, Tom was shiftless and lazy. He didn't try because he didn't care. He was definitely poor and certainly not respectable. He had no regular work and made no great effort to stay off the relief rolls. He did as little as he could about the house and the yard and he escaped through drinking when he could. He was not active in clubs and organizations, though he complained loudly about life. He certainly did not bring up his children according to Spock. People like the Dow family constituted approximately 14 percent of Jonesville.

INTERACTION AND SEPARATION AMONG JONESVILLE YOUNG PEOPLE

In *Democracy in Jonesville,* Warner and his associates did not particularly report on the interaction and the separateness among the young people. But from the Jonesville data provided and from August B. Hollingshead's *Elmtown's Youth*[4] (Elmtown and Jonesville are the same community) we can readily visualize

[4] August B. Hollingshead, *Elmtown's Youth: The Impact of Social Classes on Adolescents* (New York: John Wiley and Sons, 1949).

the relationships. It is quite apparent that belonging to one group or another affected the young person. It made a difference in whom a teenager had as friends, where he went for recreation and what he did, whom he dated, whether he graduated from high school, and whether he got a job after graduation and the kind of job it was.

Who were the friends of these high school students? Who made up these small informal groups of about five friends who stood around talking before school, who tried to sit together at lunch and at the drug store, who went to classes together, who went somewhere together after school? Ask a Jonesville High student and he would say, "I never particularly thought of *who* they are. I guess they are people like me."

He was right. They were like him. About four out of five members of his group were in the same grade. Also the members of his group resembled each other in that about three out of five of them were from family backgrounds similar to his. The chances in Jonesville High were strongly against belonging to a crowd two levels away from the social group of any one's family. When a Jonesville High School student did happen to belong to such a group, people frequently commented about it.

Whom did Jonesville High students date? Six out of ten of their dates were with people from similar family backgrounds. Almost four out of ten of their dates were with young people in the next family background group.

Did Jonesville youth intend to go around with and date people with family backgrounds like their own? Or did it just happen? A little of both. For instance, two fashionable out-of-school clubs of high school students, the G.W.G., a girls club, and the Cadet Club, a boys club, consisted of members largely from upper and upper-middle class families who belonged to the Country Club. The other students called the two groups "the combine" because it was understood that the majority of the Cadets dated G.W.G.'s and the majority of G.W.G.'s dated Cadets.

All of Jonesville's youth of high school age were not found in Jonesville High. Young people in Jonesville could choose one of two alternatives. One— usually taken by the upper, upper-middle and the lower-middle youth—was that of attending classes, enjoying himself with school friends, taking part in extra-curricular activities, holding part-time jobs, doing homework, and taking examinations. The other path was taken by the upper-lower and especially the lower-lower youth who often dropped out of school. He looked for a job, and —if he found one—got used to long, regular hours, divided his earnings between himself and his parents, made job friends, and frequently came to realize that without more education it was hard to get ahead.

Two major explanations by students for dropping out of school are: the need for money and the feeling of not belonging and of being left out or far behind. But do these explanations go far enough? Why do some children from families with little money drop out of school while others, equally poor, stay in? Why do some children and not others feel that they don't belong and that they are left out of things?

The underlying explanation is closely related to family social-class background and the attitude of the family toward education. Some parents with little money are eager for their children to have an education; many believe that education will help their children "do better than their parents." They sacrifice to keep a child in school and they encourage him in his schoolwork. It is quite a blow to them when one of their children drops out.

Frequently, lower-lower class families are opposed or indifferent to much education. Sometimes they tell their children: "Your father never had a high school education," or "It's up to you; I don't care." When the family is uninterested or hostile or they do not provide an appropriate atmosphere in which to study, there is a greater chance that children will drop out.

So the way Jonesville-Elmtown families were regarded or rated or thought about by many people in the community made a great difference in the young person's life. It influenced whom he had as friends, who belonged to his group and whom he dated. The family background was important in whether he stayed in school and had a better chance for a better job or whether he dropped out early and eventually settled in a poorer job.

OTHER STUDIES OF SOCIAL CLASS

During the past two decades, sociologists have studied the class patterns of other American communities and have investigated the ways of living of many American sub-groups within social classes. For instance, Arthur Vidich and Joseph Bensman in a study of a small town they called "Springdale" reported five classes: the middle class, a marginal middle class, the old aristocracy (which was a fallen upper-upper group), the traditional farmers, and the "shack people."[5] C. Wright Mills explored the traditions and values of the American middle classes symbolized by the white collar,[6] and in another study reported on three powerful groups in what he termed the power elite: the corporation executives of big business; the political influentials in Washington; and the military leaders of the Pentagon.[7] Herbert Gans has studied the residents of a massive housing development, Levittown, and reported on the patterns and interactions of the several classes represented in the community.[8] Gans has also reported on ethnic groups in the city in *The Urban Villagers*.[9] A useful appraisal of contemporary social class relationships is Gerhart Lenski's *Power and Privilege*.[10]

---

[5] Arthur Vidich and Joseph Bensman, *Small Town in Mass Society* (Princeton, N.J.: Princeton University Press, 1958).
[6] Charles Wright Mills, *White Collar: The American Middle Classes* (New York: Oxford University Press, 1951).
[7] Charles Wright Mills, *The Power Elite* (New York: Oxford University Press, 1956).
[8] Herbert Gans, *Levittowners: Ways of and Politics in a New Suburban Community* (New York: Pantheon Books, 1967).
[9] Herbert Gans, *The Urban Villagers* (New York: Free Press, 1962).
[10] Gerhart Lenski, *Power and Privilege: A Theory of Social Stratification* (McGraw-Hill, 1966).

ETHNIC BACKGROUNDS OF STUDENTS

Young people in the United States are not only affected by their social class backgrounds. Despite the melting pot ideal in American life, leading to the disappearance of ancestral backgrounds and the emergence of a standard "American type," ethnic differences do exist and are often sharpened in our own times.

No tidy and neat classifications exist for the ancestral backgrounds of Americans. So we will use three broad and admittedly clumsy classifications for want of better groupings. These are the Americans who came early from the British Isles and Western Europe; the Americans who came from Southern and Eastern Europe; and the Americans collectively called minorities and typified by the original Americans (the Indians), the Negroes or blacks who came early but in chains, and such groups as the Spanish-speaking people from Mexico and from Puerto Rico.

IMMIGRATION, SETTLEMENT AND MORE IMMIGRATION

In broad terms, settlement in America from the Colonies to the middle of the nineteenth century was largely a story of people from the British Isles and Western Europe who colonized, settled and conquered the wilderness, and built towns and cities. American history books chronicle the traditions they brought with them and developed, including political democracy, concern for civil liberties, the free enterprise system, the belief in hard work, the creation of a legal system, and an ethic which was primarily Protestant in orientation. Subconsciously, and often consciously and blatantly, the descendants of such people think of themselves as being the "real Americans." They often appoint themselves to the roles of the protectors and guardians and extenders of what they see as an early American heritage.

Aside from the Indians who were here when the English landed at Plymouth Rock and in Virginia, and aside from the Negroes who were imported early as slaves and chattels, the first major wave of what came to be called the "new" immigration to the United States consisted of middle and southern Europeans with a sprinkling of people from border lands in the Near East and North Africa. Such immigrants often brought with them faiths different from the prevailing Protestant faith—notably Catholic and Jewish. These new immigrants, especially in the late nineteenth and early twentieth centuries, saw America as the land of opportunity; they had magnificent and misguided stereotypes of gold in the streets and easy acceptance in American life. Actually, they encountered resistance from those who had come earlier. Because they landed at the large city ports and knew little of the country, they tended to concentrate in these areas of the Eastern seaboard and to a lesser extent on the West coast. With time, they fanned out across the country and created new centers, somewhat oriented to their own ethnic backgrounds, in rural areas as well as cities.

America's ethnic groups have often retained much of their cultures while adding aspects of these cultures to the American scene. Courtesy of John T. Urban.

Their ethnic identities still exist, typified by the Polish in Chicago, the Italians in New York or the Irish in Boston. They acculturated and they intermarried. Yet they retained some of their distinctiveness with respect to such customs as cookery, child rearing, and religion. Their stories are well-chronicled by scholars such as Nathan Glazer and Daniel P. Moynihan in the *Beyond the Melting Pot*[11] and Milton M. Gordon in *Assimilation in American Life*.[12] They struggled for acceptance and their share of the American dream in an America which was essentially becoming more industrial and capitalistic.

[11] Nathan Glazer and Daniel P. Moynihan, *Beyond the Melting Pot* (Cambridge, Mass.: MIT Press, 1963).
[12] Milton M. Gordon, *Assimilation in American Life* (New York: Oxford University Press, 1964).

Family of Japanese origin in Honolulu. Courtesy of Vivienne.

Many members of ethnic groups from Southern and Eastern Europe achieved what Americans have traditionally termed "success." Many others stayed at relatively low levels in the American status system. They were not alone in this; we have only to recognize the persisting economic problems of low-income whites from the British Isles and Western Europe to recognize that all do not automatically rise to "the top" in American life. Some of those left behind in the American success race were particularly alarmed by what they conceived as an infringement on their lives by those from the minorities who also wanted to stake their claims to a share in American life. So as the United States entered the 1970s, an increasing uneasiness and even hostility was apparent particularly toward new immigrants from Mexico, the Orient, and Puerto Rico and toward longer established but unassimilated groups such as blacks and Indians.

THE AMERICANS OF MINORITY GROUP BACKGROUNDS

Since the American history courses you have taken and the history textbooks you have read have been permeated by accounts of the backgrounds of Americans from the British Isles and Western Europe and the later Americans from Southern and Eastern Europe, we will not elaborate on the backgrounds of these groups and the consequent influences on their descendants. Until recently, the Indian, Negro, and Spanish-speaking American experience has been relatively unreported in American history and in American history textbooks. To help right the balance we are including here a summary, all too brief, of the experience of these minorities.

THE AMERICAN INDIANS

To some observers of the American scene, the minority with the greatest concentration of human and social problems are the Indians, who were, paradoxically, the first Americans. Despite originally friendly relations, wars between whites and Indians soon occurred. Whites made their conquests not only with guns and treaties but also through some of the harmful accompaniments of so-called civilization—disease and alcohol. Eventually, the Indians were forced back into reservations.

On the reservations there was always ambivalence as to whether education should absorb the Indian into American majority patterns or respect his civilization and identity. The vacillation between opposing poles of thought was accompanied by the growth of a large governmental bureaucracy, notably the Bureau of Indian Affairs. Report after report was prepared and filed by governmental and philanthropic groups, with very little change in the low economic level of the remaining members of the Indian tribes. Today the desperate situation of many Indians is documented in their high suicide and alcoholism rates, and their alienation from white society. Indians have recently re-assumed a forceful and militant attitude and have become more determined to receive the benefits of American society. In 1969 some Indians dramatically took over Alcatraz Island in San Francisco Bay and proposed it as a future center for Indian cultural development.

There are approximately one million Indians in the United States. Four hundred thousand of these live on reservations. About 500,000 are urban Indians and the remaining 100,000 are in scattered bands.[13] Indian reservations amount to 52 billion acres distributed across 26 states and they represent home for the people of 315 different Indian tribal groups.[14] Today there is a major conflict as to whether reservations should be "terminated" or maintained. The conflict is reflected in education as some Indian groups demand control of education on reservations through the creation of Indian school boards. The conflict is partly

---

[13] Vine Deloria, Jr., "The War Between the Redskins and the Feds," *The New York Times Magazine* (December 7, 1969), p. 47.
[14] *Ibid.*, p. 82.

American Indian boys on reservation in Concho, Oklahoma. Courtesy of Bureau of Indian Affairs.

related to the broader social conflict as to minority policies between integrationist and separationist tendencies. The new cry in the continuing conflict is "Indian power"; the automobile bumper stickers which increasingly report American viewpoints now include such slogans as "Indians discovered America" and "Custer had it coming."

BLACK AMERICANS

In Jamestown, Virginia, in August 1619, twenty black people were brought ashore to be farmed out as servants. The American tragedy of slavery was about to begin. Sociologist Nathan Glazer has called American Negro slavery "the most awful thing the world has ever known."[15] The brutal facts are that the Negro slave in America had no protection from organized society; his children could be sold; his wife could be both violated and sold. He could be subject to any barbaric action his master deemed appropriate. He was sharply cut off from a past that he could learn little about. Laws specified that he could not be

[15] Nathan Glazer, "Introduction," p. 9 in Stanley M. Elkins, *Slavery* (New York: Grosset and Dunlap, 1963).

taught to read or write without the specific permission of his master. He could not even practice any religion through meeting with his fellow slaves unless a white were present.

Lerone Bennett, Jr. describes the situation:

No slave could stand up to life as a human being. To live, for a slave, especially a male slave, was to renounce, to renounce anger and love and indignation, to renounce hate and human hurt, to renounce the claims and the rewards of love, the responsibilities of parenthood and the pride of ownership—to renounce these things not voluntarily in the service of a higher ideal, but at the command of another human will arbitrarily imposed by society. . . . Slavery destroyed the Negro's family, emptied his mind, and impoverished his soul. More than that, it made him doubt himself.[16]

The institution of slavery troubled the consciences of some of the makers of the United States Constitution. But it did not trouble them sufficiently to result in the abolition of slavery and, as the American nation began, the quality of life was being destroyed for 600,000 human beings, the slaves who existed in America in 1790.

It is little wonder that earnest men deplored slavery. Possibly the first recorded protest came from a group of German Mennonites in Pennsylvania in 1688. They asked, "Pray, what thing in the world can be done worse towards us, than if men should rob or steal us away and sell us for slaves to strange countries; separating husbands from their wives and children?"[17] It is no wonder that physical struggles for human rights took the form of slave mutinies and insurrections. These occurred during the eighteenth century and reached their culmination shortly before the Civil War. Notable uprisings included the revolt by Cato in 1739 near Stono, South Carolina. Probably best known are the Virginia rebellion of Nat Turner in 1831 and John Brown's famous raid on Harpers Ferry in 1857 immortalized in the song *John Brown's Body*. There were hundreds of less celebrated struggles. Yet by 1860 there were almost four million slaves in America.

The white abolitionists, such as William Lloyd Garrison and Wendell Phillips, crusaded, as did the black abolitionists such as Frederick Douglass. But the final confrontation of the Civil War had to take place before the Emancipation Proclamation by Abraham Lincoln freed the slaves of the South. The war was followed by the thirteenth, fourteenth, and fifteenth amendments to the Constitution that forbade slavery, fostered equal protection laws, and specified that rights of citizens to vote should not be denied.

But as the reconstruction period ebbed, racial segregation was established throughout the South by both law and custom. The North acquiesced and practiced its own version of segregation. The Negro response was first a policy of accommodation, typified by the educational efforts of Booker T. Washington.

---

[16] Lerone Bennett, Jr., *Confrontation: Black and White* (Baltimore: Penguin Books, 1965), p. 27.

[17] John W. Caughey, John Hope Franklin, and Ernest R. May, *Land of the Free* (New York: Benziger Brothers, 1966), p. 113.

Courtesy of Fred deVan of Nancy Palmer.

But more militant leadership emerged, as evidenced in 1905 at Niagara Falls in Canada and a year later at Harpers Ferry. The Negro leaders who convened wrote, "We will not be satisfied to take one jot or tittle less than our full manhood rights." Organization of the National Association for the Advancement of Colored People followed in 1910.

In the middle twentieth century, after numerous sit-ins, marches, and protests, the struggle took place in the courts and the legislatures. The civil rights drive got support from the Supreme Court school desegregation decision of 1954 and the Civil Rights Law of 1964. Many racial strategies combined to achieve these triumphs. They included the vigorous legal pressure under the leadership of the NAACP and such men as Thurgood Marshall and Roy Wilkins. They reflected the direct action strategy of A. Phillip Randolph who sponsored influential marches. They were inspired by Martin Luther King who developed a combination of passive resistance and social action through the activities of the Southern Christian Leadership Conference. They were stimulated by the militancy of the rebels of the Student Non-Violent Coordinating Committee (SNCC), the Congress of Racial Equality (CORE), and the anger of the Black Muslims and Malcolm X.

Today the confrontation continues. Clearly, civil rights laws are not enough. There are too many people whose lives remain the same despite such laws. They see themselves as still powerless, subordinated, and lacking full rights. Too many people are not treated as free and equal. So militancy grows, particularly among young blacks. It spilled over into rioting during the summer of 1964 in Harlem, in 1965 in Watts, in 1966 in Hough in Cleveland, in 1967 in the burning of sections of Detroit, in 1968 in the violence which accompanied the assassination of Martin Luther King, in 1969 and 1970 in scores of smaller cities.

This is part of the heritage of black children who will be attending many of the schools in which you will teach. It is part of the background which accounts for much of the anger, hostility and militant rebellion which the new teachers of the 1970s, black or white, will encounter.

Some wonder why there is rebellion and militancy on the part of the blacks when conditions are seemingly growing better for them. In some areas of employment and in some areas of human endeavor conditions are better for some blacks. Yet there still remains a wide gap between whites and blacks in America. In some aspects of life, the gap even widens.

The nonwhite infant mortality in 1940 was 70 percent higher than the white rate. In 1960 it was 90 percent higher.

Maternal mortality among nonwhite mothers in 1940 was 2.4 times the white rate. In 1960 it was 3.8 times higher than the white rate.

A Negro boy born in 1962 has as much chance of surviving to 20 as a white boy has of reaching 37. A Negro girl could look forward to reaching 20 as confidently as a white girl to reaching 42.

In employment, the best years for Negroes only come up to the recession levels for whites. In 1964, a prosperous year, when white unemployment dropped to less than 3.5 percent, the Negro rate was still almost 10 percent. That was half again as high as the worst white rate since the depression. These figures are for adults 20 or older. For 16- and 17-year-old Negroes, unemployment has not dropped below 20 percent in 10 years.[18]

President Kennedy stated the situation thus:

The Negro baby born in America today, regardless of the section or state in which he is born, has about one-half as much chance of completing high school as a white baby born in the same place on the same day; one-third as much

---

[18] National Advisory Council on the Education of Disadvantaged Children, "Schools for an Open Society," *Integrated Education* (March–April 1968), pp. 11–12.

chance of completing college; one-third as much chance of becoming a professional man; twice as much chance of becoming unemployed; about one-seventh as much chance of earning $10,000 per year; a life expectancy which is 7 years less; and the prospects of earning only half as much.[19]

SPANISH-SPEAKING AMERICANS

Two Spanish-speaking groups are among the contemporary minority groups in the United States. Though their cultures are substantially different, Americans from Puerto Rico, and the Hispano-American immigrants from Mexico trace part of their heritage back to Spain. The common problems of the recent migrants from Puerto Rico and Mexico include mastery of English and adaptation to an industrial and technological civilization.

The close relationship of Puerto Rico with the United States dates back to the Spanish-American War of 1898. Puerto Rico is now a Commonwealth of the United States. Ever present on the island is the necessity to understand two cultures through mastery of bilinguality. In Puerto Rico social problems are pressing. Young Puerto Ricans must learn to earn their livings on an island steadily shifting from rural to urban ways, in an economy engaged in Operation Bootstrap, in a world that permits easy migration to the mainland U.S. Young Puerto Ricans are improving their lives through still further conquest of island problems of health, sanitation, housing, nutrition, safety, resource use, production, and consumption. As citizens of their localities and of the Commonwealth, as potential migrants to the mainland of the United States, they are learning to participate in democratic government, despite a social heritage marked by the authoritarianism of colonialism and imperialism. Young Puerto Ricans are also learning to improve human relationships in the kaleidoscope of colors, classes, and cultures which characterize Puerto Rico. As young people in a space age, young Puerto Ricans must become more versed in the mathematical and scientific underpinnings of scholarship which have led them into island industrialization.

Puerto Rican youngsters are facing life problems on their island which bewilder them. They are trying to relate to parents who are struggling with the urban-rural transition and the breakdown of older village traditions of family control. They are trying to find their way in peer groups colored both by island ways and by American ideas imported via mainland television, magazines and publications, sometimes influenced for better or worse by youth who have returned from the streets of New York City. They must learn the new ways of recreation which are now superimposed on the older patterns. They must come to terms with their roles as men and women in society, with early maturation

---

[19] President John F. Kennedy, "Special Message to the Nation on Civil Rights," February 28, 1963 (Reprinted in The Keystone in the Arch, Compilation of Major Remarks on the Subject of Education by the Late John F. Kennedy, President of the United States; Committee on Education and Labor, House of Representatives, Eighty-eighth Congress, 2nd Session, April, 1964, p. 62.)

and early marriage. They are threading their way through the maze of vocational decisions and preparation on an island where unskilled work persists, yet new opportunities for the skilled proliferate as Operation Bootstrap attracts investments and industries.

Complex choices are presented individuals through the continuing restless migration from village and *barrio* ways to the urbanization of San Juan, Ponce, Mayaguez, and a dozen other major centers, and from the rural stretches of sugar cane and coffee and tobacco lands and from the cities of large plazas and colorful houses and ever open windows to the canyons of cold New York lined by tenements, marked by strange folkways, and, sadly enough, by less than a warm welcome for "the foreigner." Many young Puerto Rican immigrants have to decide whether to band together in street gangs, whether to use militant techniques of confrontation.

For teachers of very low-income Puerto Ricans, Oscar Lewis' *La Vida*[20] is essential reading. This frank and haunting book describes the experiences of a Puerto Rican family first in San Juan and then in New York, always living in the culture of poverty.

Helping Puerto Rican young people to think for themselves should be an important goal in mainland and island education. Respect for each individual personality must prevail over vestigial class consciousness and invidious racial distinctions inherited from earlier aristocratic traditions. Fortunately, the democratic value of working together for common purposes commonly arrived at had strong roots in the *barrio* and is emphasized today through a determined campaign by the Commonwealth government, using many agencies of social work, education, and information, to help Puerto Ricans work together toward a rising living standard and a good life.

Puerto Rico moves ahead rapidly; migration to the mainland ebbs and flows according to job opportunities on the island and mainland. While New York City is usually the first home of the Puerto Rican newcomer, many have now moved into New York's suburbs, into adjoining states, and to metropolises throughout the nation.

A lively political struggle is taking place in Puerto Rico over the desirability of Commonwealth status involving immunity from United States income tax (but also no voting representation in the U.S. Congress) versus complete independence from the U.S. versus complete immersion in the U.S. by way of statehood. A teacher in the 1970s who works with Puerto Ricans should at least be aware of the varying stances on this issue.

Puerto Rico is part of the United States whereas Mexico is an independent nation, our neighbor to the south with which we share a long common boundary. Throughout history, people from Mexico have crossed that border to live permanently or temporarily in the United States.

Indeed, some Spanish-speaking Americans lived in what is now the United

---

[20] Oscar Lewis, *La Vida: A Puerto Rican Family in the Culture of Poverty* (New York: Random, 1966).

Courtesy of OEO.

States long before the present border with Mexico existed. States that are now the Southwestern and Western U.S., including Arizona, New Mexico, Texas, and California, were first settled by Spanish-speaking Americans, many of whom came north from Mexico during Spain's colonization of the New World. So some families of Spanish-speaking ancestry have lived on United States soil for centuries; if their children visit Mexico it is as tourists since their birth place is the United States. To term such families "Mexican" or "Mexican-American" is a questionable use of language. How many generations does one have to live in the United States to be regarded as a native?

The terms Mexican-American or Hispano-American or Spanish-American apply more properly to twentieth century immigrants, including those who cross the border for temporary or permanent residence in the United States. Workers from such families have long labored in the fields and ranches and mines of the Southwest and today often work in the industries of such growing cities as Los Angeles, San Francisco, Oakland, and Denver, as they fan out through California and the Rocky Mountain states and into urban centers of the midwest and east. Since Mexico, despite gains for the common people growing out of its early twentieth century revolution and despite the growth of a middle class, is a land in which the living standard is still below that of the U.S., the migrants to the U.S. are usually poor people searching for a better life and a higher standard of living. Some plan to settle permanently in the United States; others plan to return to Mexico. Some intend to find permanent work; others have come as *braceros,* entering as authorized temporary agricultural laborers; a few have crossed the Rio Grande as "wetbacks" in illegal immigration.

The families participating in the contemporary immigration from Mexico face many problems. For many, theirs is the culture of poverty. Economically, they are often exploited. Their homes are frequently rural or urban slum shacks or migrant work camps. Only recently, through such charismatic leaders as Cesar Chavez who led the grape-pickers strike, are they beginning to organize effective agricultural unions.

The educational problems of their children in U.S. schools are formidable. Their native language is Spanish and in Mexico bilingual instruction has not been as essential as in Puerto Rico. Schooling is interrupted by frequent moves to follow the crops from region to region within the states or to return home to Mexico. Low standards of living, sometimes including hunger, handicap effective education. When their parents reside in cities, the entire family faces the problems of adjustment that rural people worldwide are forced to make to the strange ways of cities. To cap the problem of education, their culture is essentially Mexican and the schools, even when sensitive adaptations such as bilingualism are made, are essentially oriented to U.S. culture.

The median number of school years attained by Mexican-Americans fourteen years old and over is as follows: Arizona 8.3; California 9.2; Colorado 8.7; New Mexico 8.8; and Texas 6.7.[21]

An educational attainment of eight years or less is automatically bracketed with the occupational capability and income level of a manual worker. As automation invades clerical and related occupations, educational preparation for those who are to hold the new jobs must advance at least through high school and, sooner or later, beyond. As an ethnic group, therefore, the Mexican-Americans have a present handicap of from four to seven years vis-à-vis the rest of the population. The rapid general increase in high school and college enrollment of the recent past serves but to emphasize the gap.[22]

Among the very young, different, though equally pressing, cultural gaps appear. On one side stand the impoverished households, the alien family style, the ancestral language, the insecure community. On the other there is the school with its inadequate budgets, its administrative molds, its distance from the families of its pupils. Between them is the preschooler who speaks only Spanish, who falters in his first and crucial encounter with Anglo-American because his native speech is still regarded as a barrier and not a road and because in addition he brings with him all the handicaps of poverty.[23]

A self-identification as "chicanos" has arisen among Mexican-American youth. The chicano is frequently impatient with those who term themselves Spanish-Americans and who seem to the chicano to be aristocratically inclined upper-class people proud of their Spanish past and disdainful of Mexican origins. The chicano prefers to be loyal to *La Raza* and to the Mexican and Mexican-American people. He sees his people as an exploited group who must assert

---

[21] Ernesto Galarza, Herman Gallegos and Julian Samora, *Mexican-Americans in the Southwest* (Santa Barbara, Calif.: McNally & Loftin, 1969), p. 38.
[22] *Ibid.*, p. 39.   [23] *Ibid.*, pp. 46–47.

themselves more aggressively. As he expresses his anger and demands, the chicano often finds himself at odds with the Anglo majority in community and school environments.

For teachers of Hispanic-American students from Mexico, books by Oscar Lewis of the University of Illinois are must reading. They include *The Children of Sanchez*,[24] the autobiography of a Mexican family, and *Five Families*,[25] case studies in the Mexican culture of poverty. *Mexican-Americans in the Southwest*, quoted above, is a helpful source of factual data.

RELATIONSHIPS OF CLASS AND ETHNIC BACKGROUNDS TO EDUCATION

The outcomes of education are related to the social class of students; this relationship holds for majorities and minorities. The educational attainment of an individual student is related both to his social class and to social class level of his classmates. The *Equality of Educational Opportunity* survey—one of the most extensive studies of student attitudes and performance ever made—found that the greatest proportion of the achievement differences among students are accounted for by the differences in their social class.[26] In a study of Richmond, California, performed for the U.S. Civil Rights Commission by Professor Alan Wilson of the University of California at Berkeley, the relationship between a student's social class and his school achievement was assessed; social class was found to be an important factor closely related to the academic achievement of children in the early grades.[27] Attitudes and aspirations of students seem directly related to their social class.

In addition to suffering educational damage which stems from poverty, many minority group children develop negative self-images and low self-esteem because of segregation and discrimination. These differences do not suggest, however, that to be of low social class or of minority status in America necessarily implies failure in school. They do suggest that, on the average, the social class and ethnic status of a student have a strong relationship to his academic success and aspirations.

There has been no general agreement among educators as to the best way to remedy the academic disadvantage of the lower social classes and minorities. The search for remedies has been made more difficult by controversy that often accompanies such efforts. Disputes and controversy rage over neighborhood schools, racial imbalance, and the selection of school sites for construction.

---

[24] Oscar Lewis, *The Children of Sanchez: Autobiography of a New Mexican Family* (New York: Random, 1961).
[25] Oscar Lewis, *Five Families: Mexican Case Studies in the Culture of Poverty* (New York: Basic Books, 1959).
[26] James S. Coleman, *Equality of Educational Opportunity*, U.S. Department of Health, Education and Welfare, Office of Education, 1966, pp. 298–300.
[27] Alan Wilson, *Educational Consequences of Segregation in a California Community*, A Report of the U.S. Commission on Civil Rights, 1967, I, 165–206.

Many sections of the nation are faced with a critical yet imperfectly understood educational problem: how to improve the educational achievement of the poor and minorities. School systems generally have taken one of two basic approaches and have sometimes used both—compensatory education or school desegregation. At present there is disagreement over the relative efficacy of these approaches.

One of the most challenging and compelling educational problems of this decade will be that of providing equal and adequate education for all groups in America.

★ ★ ★

DISCUSSION
1. To what extent do the classifications of social classes proposed by Warner and his followers seem valid to you? To what extent invalid? Do contemporary sociologists conceive social class in large cities as being somewhat different from the Warner conception based on towns and small cities?
2. Elaborate upon the life experiences and educational backgrounds of upper class families based both on your own reading and your own experiences in living. Do the same thing for each of the other major social class groups.
3. In what ways have the behaviors and life experiences of the various classes described by Warner changed in the past two decades?
4. Of what social class do you consider yourself a member? What are the distinguishing characteristics of this class? Do you belong to the same social class as your parents? Your grandparents? If not, what has made the difference?
5. What is the meaning of culturally disadvantaged? Who judges? To what extent can both upper-lowers and lower-lowers be described as culturally disadvantaged in America today?
6. Relate your own experiences in growing up to social class theory. Any influences on friends, dates, college entrance, etc.? Does the Elmtown story reflect your own experiences?
7. Are the immigrant ethnic groups from Europe currently "forgotten"? Do you think another group is the "forgotten" one?
8. What are the most recent government proposals for improving the life of the American Indians? What is your own view on the maintenance of Indian reservations or their phasing out through absorption of Indians into the mainstream of current American life?
9. What are some possible influences of slavery and a long period of segregation on the personalities of blacks? Do you think it likely that such characteristics might be passed on to later generations?
10. Define the present gap between opportunities of blacks and whites in America.
11. How is life for the Puerto Rican young person different on the island than on the mainland?
12. What are the major educational problems of Mexican children and youth?

13. How does an individual's class or ethnic background relate to his probable educational experience? What are the alternative methods to improve the educational achievement of the poor?

INVOLVEMENT

1. Study Warner's system of arriving at social class rankings in *Social Class in America*. Apply his approach to your own background and that of friends and acquaintances.
2. Develop a categorization of social classes for the community with which you are best acquainted.
3. Trace your ancestry to the time your family came to America. To which ethnic groups do your ancestors belong? How has this background affected your life?
4. If your school is not located in an inner-city area, develop as a class project a trip to a major metropolis which will include opportunities to become acquainted with the patterns of living of a variety of ethnic and racial groups.
5. Look for opportunities to develop relationships to people of groups other than your own, whether they represent majorities or minorities. Find, if you can, opportunities through recreational leadership, settlement house work, community action programs, etc.
6. Invite to class representatives of a variety of minority groups. Do not overlook ethnic groups from Europe, if substantial clusters of Americans from such backgrounds exist in your community. Groups which might supply speakers include the National Association for the Advancement of Colored People, the Urban League, Mexican-American groups, etc.
7. Discover and take advantage of opportunities to tutor children and youth of minority group backgrounds or those from disadvantaged homes. Church and community groups are often sources of information.

BIBLIOGRAPHY

Brameld, Theodore. *The Remaking of a Culture*. New York: Harper and Row, 1959. A book on the interrelationships of Puerto Rican culture and life by an outstanding social reconstructionist philosopher. Of high importance to anyone teaching Puerto Rican students, whether on the island or the mainland.

Caughey, John W., John Hope Franklin, and Ernest R. May. *Land of the Free*. New York: Benziger Brothers, 1966. A high school history textbook which includes the black contribution to American life.

Clift, Virgil A., Archibald W. Anderson, and H. Gordon Hullfish, eds. *Negro Education in America: Its Adequacy, Problems, and Needs*. New York: Harper, 1962. A comprehensive and scholarly examination of Negro education in America by black and white authors. A yearbook of the John Dewey Society.

Coles, Robert and Al Clayton. *Still Hungry in America*. Cleveland, Ohio: World, 1969. An angry and poignant account of how hunger in affluent America still plagues the black and white poor.

Conant, James B. *Slums and Suburbs*. New York: McGraw-Hill, 1961. This book contrasts suburbs and slums. It concludes that what a school can do is determined by the status and ambitions of the families being served.

Cordasco, Francesco and Eugene Bucchioni, eds. *Puerto Rican Children in Mainland Schools*. Metuchen, N.J.: Scarecrow Press, 1968. Readings bringing together material on Puerto Rican culture, family, experience on the mainland, and experience of children in North American schools.

Elkins, Stanley M., ed. *Slavery.* New York: Grosset and Dunlap, Inc. 1963. Direct and unsparing account of an American evil.

Galarza, Ernesto, Herman Gallegos, and Julian Samora. *Mexican-Americans in the Southwest.* Santa Barbara: McNally and Loftin, 1969. Fact-filled account of handicaps experienced by Mexican-Americans.

Gans, Herbert. *The Urban Villagers.* New York: Free Press, 1962. Account of ethnic groups in the urban situation.

Glazer, Nathan, and Daniel P. Moynihan. *Beyond the Melting Pot.* Cambridge, Mass.: MIT Press, 1963. Sociologists' view of developments in the experiences of Americans from immigrant backgrounds.

Gordon, Milton M. *Assimilation in American Life.* New York: Oxford University Press, 1964. Useful treatment of questions related to absorption of new Americans and to cultural pluralism.

Gregory, Susan. *Hey, White Girl!* New York: Norton, 1970. The experiences of the only white student in an all-black Chicago high school.

Hollingshead, August B. *Elmtown's Youth: The Impact of Social Classes on Adolescents.* New York: John Wiley and Sons, 1949. A classic study of an American high school demonstrating the power of social class in shaping the lives of young people.

Lenski, Gerhart. *Power and Privilege: A Theory of Social Stratification.* McGraw-Hill, 1966. Contemporary scholarly book on recent thinking on social class and related issues.

Lewis, Oscar. *The Children of Sanchez: Autobiography of a Mexican Family.* New York: Random House, 1961. An intimate account of a Mexican family by a distinguished anthropologist who has lived closely with the family and reported their words through tape recordings.

———. *Five Families: Mexican Case Studies in the Culture of Poverty.* New York: Basic Books, 1959. Detailed account of the lives of Mexican families. Stresses the concept of the culture of poverty.

———. *La Vida: A Puerto Rican Family in the Culture of Poverty.* New York: Random House, 1966. A harsh and shocking but frank and realistic account of a Puerto Rican family living first in San Juan and then in New York City, yet always existing in what Lewis describes as "the culture of poverty." The book is told in the words of family members and does not evade the brutal aspects of their existence.

Lipset, S. M. and R. Bendix. *Class, Status and Power,* 2nd Edition. New York: Free Press, 1966. Consideration of class relationships by outstanding sociologists.

Miller, S. M. and Frank Riessman. *Social Class and Social Policy.* New York: Basic Books, 1968. By a social economist and a social psychologist in response to the issues of the day, relevant to the underlying issues of social class in America.

Morsbach, Mabel. *The Negro in American Life.* New York: Harcourt, Brace and World, 1967. A broad picture of Negro participation in the progress of the nation.

Sexton, Patricia. *Education and Income: Inequalities of Opportunity in Our Public Schools.* New York: Viking, 1961. A hard-hitting explanation of how the quality of one's education is related to the relative affluence of his background. A plea for much greater equality in American schools.

Tumin, Melvin M. *Social Stratification: The Forms and Functions of Inequality.* Englewood Cliffs, N.J.: Prentice-Hall, 1967. An analysis of the conditions under which various forms and amounts of social inequality arise and are sustained and what their consequences are for the societies in which they operate.

Vidich, Arthur and Joseph Bensman. *Small Town in Mass Society*. Princeton, N.J.: Princeton University Press, 1958. A study of a small rural community in upstate New York which tries to maintain its own identity in a world in which the larger society constantly impinges.

Warner, W. Lloyd. *Democracy in Jonesville: A Study in Quality and Inequality*. New York: Harper and Row, 1949. Classic study of social class in an American community upon which this chapter heavily draws.

———. *Social Class in America: A Manual of Procedure for the Measurement of Social Status*. Chicago: Science Research Associates, 1949. Procedures to follow in determining the social status of students.

Warner, W. Lloyd and Paul S. Lunt. *The Status System of a Modern Community*. New Haven, Conn.: Yale University Press, 1942. Concerning Yankee City: studies by Warner and associates on social class, status relationships, etc.

AUDIO-VISUAL MATERIALS

Social Class in America (McGraw-Hill Textfilms, 16 Min.) Shows the difference social class makes in the lives of three high school boys. Also explains how one boy is able to raise his social status.

The Summer We Moved to Elm Street (McGraw-Hill, 28 Min., Color) Produced by National Film Board of Canada. Portrays the effect of constant movement from one home to another on a young child. The neighborhood becomes familiar to her, friendships are established, and social activities begin, only to all end when her parents move again.

Prior and Present Experience (NET, 30 Min.) Explains the need for the teacher to consider the differences between her background and that of her students as shown by language used and assumptions made.

The Negro American (Bailey, 14 Min.) Discusses the contributions of the Negro to American civilization and advocates education on the part of both Negroes and whites as a basis for better understanding.

No Hiding Place (NET, 59 Min.) A study of the tensions which divide the Negro and white communities. Ghetto youth, housewives, the local NAACP president, an alderman, and others are interviewed on racial problems of the town.

Operation Head Start (Paul Burnford, 16 Min.) Tells the story about the home and classroom experiences of an underprivileged American child who is participating in the Head Start program.

Operation Head Start (U.S. Office of Economic Opportunity, 29 Min.) Shows the need for the Head Start project, various facets of the program, and its policies as observed in a variety of localities. Includes scenes of the poverty existing in urban and rural ghettos.

The Way It Is (NET, 60 Min.) Presents the chaos of the ghetto school and reports on a New York University special learning project in Junior High School 57, Brooklyn. Shows visits with parents, teachers' meetings and project workers in classrooms.

Portrait of a Disadvantaged Child: Tommy Knight (McGraw-Hill, 16 Min.) Brings the viewer face to face with the reality of a day in the life of a slum child. Many of the factors that affect Tommy's ability to learn are shown.

Mexican-American: A Historic Profile (Anti-Defamation League, 30 Min.) Traces the history of the Mexican-American from the time of the Spanish period to the present. Particular emphasis on the various prejudices against migrants during the last one hundred years.

THIRTEEN

WHAT ARE THE COMMUNITY BACKGROUNDS OF STUDENTS?

American communities are classified by the Census Bureau as either urban or rural. The term rural is limited to farm families, to hamlets which contain less than 500 people, and to villages or towns in which 500 to 2500 persons live.[1] Any place with 2500 or more inhabitants or any area with 1500 or more people per square mile is defined as urban. As a result, "urban" becomes an omnibus category which includes not only large and small cities but also many suburban communities.

However helpful this distinction between rural and urban may be for purposes of the census takers, a somewhat sharper contrast is needed to understand the ways of living that will be encountered by new teachers. A more helpful categorization for purposes of sketching American community backgrounds is threefold: (1) rural communities including farms, hamlets, villages and towns, (2) small and large cities, and (3) suburbs.

RURAL BACKGROUNDS

If you choose to teach in a rural area, you will be working among a dwindling group. America is steadily moving from rural areas to urban centers. The farm population dropped from 15 million in 1960 to 10 million in 1970. In 1960, farmers and their families comprised about 8 percent of the U.S. population. In 1970, the ratio had fallen to about 5 percent.

---

[1] United States Bureau of the Census, *The U.S. Book of Facts, Statistics, and Information for 1969* (Washington, D.C.: U.S. Government Printing Office, 1968), p. 16.

Rural life has been eulogized by many Americans as the quiet, unharried life, but in recent years rural areas have lost large percentages of their population; now less than 30% of America's population lives in rural areas. Courtesy of Grant Heilman.

RURAL COMMUNITIES

What happened? In 1890, America crossed a "watershed of American history," as the historian Henry Steele Commager phrased it. On the nineteenth century side of the watershed lay a country that was essentially rural and agricultural. On the twentieth century side emerged a primarily urban and industrial nation. In 1900 approximately 40 percent of the American people lived in the locations classified by the census as urban; but by 1967 approximately 70 percent of the American people lived in such areas. In the twentieth century, Americans steadily moved from the farms, hamlets, villages, and towns, and took up residence in large and small cities and in the suburbs.

In addition, the life style of those who remained in the rural communities became more urban-oriented as rural people increasingly assumed the characteristics of those who live in cities. Mechanization, the mass media, and mobility steadily influenced the traditional rural ways of living celebrated in nineteenth century American literature. True, some isolated pockets of homespun and sturdily independent farmers persisted, particularly in the hill country of Appalachia and the Ozarks. But such American yeomen were becoming rare.

Mechanization changed the farm. Electricity became commonplace and with it came electric ovens, freezers, and household appliances. Farming itself became mechanized with increasing use of tractors, combines, potato harvesters, cotton pickers, corn pickers, hay stackers, citrus sprayers, etc. Many farms have become, in Carey McWilliams' classic phrase, "factories in the fields" conducted by businessmen of the soil.

The outside world entered the farm home through mail delivery, the telephone and the mass media. Newspapers and magazines are read; radios play; television is watched. Mobility characterizes the farmer and his family.

The automobile ended the isolation of the American farm early in the twentieth century. Outside communities are now within an easy cruising range of farm families. Even the village and town cannot hold the mobile rural residents, for the automobile has brought the big city into the farmer's range for buying and selling. Along with the world-changing force which Henry Ford fostered, came superhighways, supermarkets, and super-governments. Shopping by mail order developed; national advertising campaigns were launched. With the rural resident no longer dependent upon a single trade area, the historic justification for the village or town disappeared. Some villages and towns were able to make the adjustments and continue to attract some rural customers. Some turned to tourism as an income-producing resource. But, in general, the rural community is declining and the young are leaving for the cities.

Though, historically, farming has been the reason for living in rural areas, today only about one-fourth of rural residents are farmers. Many are local business and professional men; others are daily commuters to jobs in the cities. Some residents of rural areas are among the most prosperous of Americans; they are successful in their city occupations but prefer to live in the country.

But no one should leap to the conclusion that farmers and village and town residents who remain in rural areas are universally prosperous. Many farm laborers and tenant farmers who stayed with the rural areas have a miserable standard of living. Some live on subsistence farms; some shuttle between city and farm; some become migrant workers. Rural poverty is a reality in America today, as a trip off the turnpike on the backroads will readily demonstrate to the city resident. As Michael Harrington pointed out in *The Other America,* poverty has a way of hiding up back roads. In his book, which encouraged a federal governmental war on poverty, Harrington wrote of Appalachia:

> Though the steep slopes and the narrow valleys are a charming sight, they are also the basis of a highly unproductive agriculture. The very geography is an anachronism in a technological society. Even if the farmers had the money, machines would not make much difference. As it is, the people literally scratch their half-livings from the difficult soil. . . .
>
> This, for example, is how one reporter saw the independent yeomanry, the family farmers, and the laid off industrial workers in the Appalachians: "Whole counties are precariously held together by a flour-and-dried-milk paste of surplus foods. The school lunch program provides many children with their only decent

Poverty in rural America—Appalachia. Courtesy of Paul Conklin for OEO.

meals. Relief has become a way of life for a once proud and aggressively independent mountain people. The men who are no longer needed in the mines and the farmers who cannot compete with the mechanized agriculture of the Midwest have themselves become surplus commodities in the mountains."

One study, for instance, estimated that the Appalachians would need slightly more than one million new jobs if the area were to begin catching up with the rest of America. As of now, the vicious circle is at work making such a development unlikely; the mountains are beautiful and quaint and economically backward; the youth are leaving; and because of this poverty modern industry hesitates to come in and agriculture becomes even more marginal.[2]

As Robert Coles points out, there are many rural people "still hungry in America" years after the war on poverty began.[3] Researchers are increasingly pointing out causal relationships between poverty and mental retardation. For instance, Rodger L. Hurley in *Poverty and Mental Retardation* says:

The thesis of this book is that the supposed mental retardation of many of the poor is not mental retardation at all but environmental deprivation. . . . It appears that on many occasions we are not measuring mental retardation but our society's callousness toward the poor.[4]

With the loss of population and economic power in the rural areas may come some possible losses to American life. Historically, the small town has been cele-

[2] Michael Harrington, *The Other America* (New York: Macmillan, 1962), pp. 41–42.
[3] Robert Coles, *Still Hungry in America* (New York: World Publishing, 1969).
[4] Rodger L. Hurley, *Poverty and Mental Retardation: A Causal Relationship* (New York: Random, 1969), p. 44.

The town meeting in colonial and early national periods was the primary form of government. Courtesy of The Bettmann Archive.

brated for the sense of belongingness it cultivated, for neighborliness at grass-roots level, for day-by-day personal relations and for a simple homespun philosophy. Its civic contribution is symbolized by the New England town meeting in which the neighbors get together for full participation in the civic decisions affecting their lives.

However, some observers do not see the decline of the small town and of rural life as catastrophic. Contributors to American literature such as Hamlin Garland and Sherwood Anderson have long decried the small town as dull and lifeless and provincial. They feel that there is no loss in the disappearance of patterns of small town conformity which have been based on narrow and provincial morality. So some commentators on American life welcome the movement to urban areas where the educational level of the residents is higher, the people are more cosmopolitan, and more women are included in the labor force.

RURAL CHILDREN AND YOUTH

If new teachers in rural areas are to be realistic in their education of rural children and youth, the steady movement toward erasing distinctions between rural and urban personalities in contemporary America must be taken into account. In the nineteenth century and well into the twentieth century, it could be taken for granted that rural young people, because of their backgrounds, experienced life differently from urban young people, and consequently viewed the world and behaved differently. Living close to the soil, and working closely with their parents, rural children and youth tended to be more conservative and more accepting of traditional American values; they were characterized by close-knit family loyalty and a degree of reserve rather than ready acceptance of strangers. Some personality tests in past decades have indicated that rural young

Present-day New England town meeting. Courtesy of DPI.

people were more likely than urban young people to be shy, self-deprecating, withdrawn, and submissive. Such tests showed that farm children tended to be less poised, less confident, and less articulate. Rural children depended more upon parents and their authority than did urban children, were less likely to rebel against authority, and were not particularly optimistic about the power of human beings to improve and better the surrounding environment.[5] Such self-perceptions, along with few horizon-widening experiences, particularly in poor farm homes, contributed to rural young people making lower scores than urban young people on tests of school achievement and of mental ability.

To some extent, these differentiations continue to exist in rural areas. But as the outside world increasingly enters the rural home and as modern transportation brings increasingly easy access to larger towns and urban centers, the differences between rural and urban youth steadily diminish. Today there is much less difference or, some even say, no significant difference between rural and urban youth as to their attitudes and ideas. Youth opinions increasingly tend to be alike, regardless of whether the individual lives in the city or the country. So the new rural teacher cannot count upon rural young people supporting individualism, hard work, or fixed moral standards to the degree that rural parents support these values.

In addition, rural youth, when grown up, continue to leave the farm for the city. The continuing movement in America from an agrarian to an industrial society sweeps them up. The good rural school and teacher therefore have the extremely difficult job of helping those rural young people, now a minority, who plan to stay with the farm and small town while simultaneously helping those

---

[5] Grace Graham, The Public School in the New Society (New York: Harper and Row, 1969), p. 220.

Courtesy of Grant Heilman.

others who (whether they currently plan to or not) will migrate toward the larger community.

Because they have been accustomed to educating youth for rural life, country schools do better with the first task than the second. Yet vocational agriculture, a frequent offering in the rural schools, does little to prepare rural youth for the forthcoming city experience. In the city, more emphasis is placed on verbal abilities and skills; reading, writing and speaking are more in demand. Specialized occupational skills are required if one is not to remain at the lowest vocational levels or find himself technologically obsolete. Other people constantly impinge upon one's life even though, paradoxically, the city can be a lonesome place for the newcomer. The more isolated and culturally disadvantaged the background of the young rural migrant, the greater these problems loom. Yet it is the schools from such areas that have the least relevant curriculum.

Consequently, rural schools must adapt to urban demands rather than rest content with agricultural programs alone. Realistic teachers must stress the acquisition of social skills along with enhanced knowledge of industry through studies of occupations accompanied by trips, student exchanges, and outside visitors.

The establishment of vocational and technical schools in rural areas is helpful to adjustment to a broader occupational scene. Yet many rural parents, who provide the financial support for rural schools, resist. As they see it, the establishment of area technical institutes or urban-oriented community colleges is a way of financing and supporting competition to their rural way of life and thus encouragement to rural youth to leave their homes.

Not the least of rural education difficulties is that teachers too tend to move cityward. Teachers, like young people, tend to reject what they sometimes regard as the more restrictive and limited environment of the village. Yet for those who do choose to stay with rural education, the challenges are many and the opportunities to make a contribution are great. Not all of the ghettos and the poverty are found in the cities. One can find many mountain and other relatively isolated areas where a teacher's contribution could make a significant difference in the life of rural children. Writers like Jesse Stuart, a mountain poet and teacher, testify to the rewards of teaching in the hills.

> Seldom if ever did one of my Lonesome Valley pupils stay out of school because he wanted to. He stayed out of school usually for one of three reasons: he was sick; he had to help harvest the crops; he didn't have sufficient clothes, shoes, or books. . . .
>
> My attendance was down considerably in September. There wasn't an attendance officer to see why they didn't come to school. If the pupil went, it was all right. If he didn't, it was all right too. It was a land of freedom and work. But we had made our school so attractive in appearance that the pupils loved the place. They had had a hand in helping to make it beautiful—to make their school their home during school days, their workshop, their beehive. This was their place and my place. It was the liveliest spot in our community. It was the only place they could go, and many would never go beyond this school. Their education ended when they finished at Lonesome Valley. . . .
>
> I thought of these things when I taught my pupils all the practical things I could teach them. How to write letters, measure land, be clean with drinking water, about personal sanitation, screens for their windows, and so many things aside from the dry-as-powder, uninteresting textbooks I was forced to teach because they were *standard,* selected by someone in the state department who didn't teach, perhaps never had, and if he had taught once upon a time was far removed from it now.[6]

CITY BACKGROUNDS

Despite the warnings of the devoted agrarian Thomas Jefferson, cities have grown. In 1790 there were only two U.S. cities of more than 25,000 population. By 1970, the nation contained 25 metropolitan areas ranging in size from 11,410,000 (New York City) to 1,259,000 (Miami).

The word "cities" was no longer comprehensive enough to describe the size of the biggest cities; even the word "metropolis" would not suffice. A new description—"megalopolis"—was borrowed from the Greeks to describe emerging intermeshed cities such as Boswash, a complex of interlocking metropolises stretching from Boston through Philadelphia and New York to Washington; Chipitts, a middlewestern complex stretching from Chicago through the Great Lakes to Pittsburgh; and Sansan, stretching initially from San Diego to Santa Barbara and eventually to San Francisco. Kahn and Wiener predicted in *The Year*

---

[6] Jesse Stuart, *The Thread That Runs So True* (New York: Charles Scribner's Sons, 1949), pp. 57–58.

2000 that these three developing megalopolitan complexes would hold almost half of the American people by the end of the twentieth century.[7]

A complex of circumstances led the American people into the cities. Changes in science and technology, which influenced developments in production, power, transportation, and communication, resulted in vastly increased urbanization, particularly throughout the twentieth century. Technical developments in industry combined with social developments—stable central government, expanded markets throughout the world, and the specialization of labor—to foster the growth of cities. Steadily Americans migrated to the cities. Once, at the time of the American Revolution, approximately 90 percent of the American people were employed in agriculture. Today the reverse is true; only 10 percent are so employed. The remaining 90 percent now are engaged in work other than the production of food; much of this work necessitates cities.

URBAN COMMUNITIES

Sociologists have looked for patterns of living or characteristic life styles within cities. One popular sociological theory in the first half of the twentieth century stressed the loss of relationships to the community which came with the movement from rural to urban areas. The theory emphasized the impersonality of urban life. City people, it was pointed out, meet many people, so many people that they pass them by indifferently with little or no recognition. Searching for more intimate relationships, city people join special groups which reflect their own special interests, whether occupational or avocational. So the city dweller was perceived as a sophisticated cosmopolitan and individualistic person who found his common interests in groups made up of people from across the city.

In recent years, this conception of the urban style has been modified by scholars who believe that insufficient emphasis has been placed on urban neighborhoods, where people resemble each other in life styles. Frequently their social class and ethnic backgrounds are similar. Such neighborhoods are by no means as closely knit as rural neighborhoods, yet the city neighborhood has not disappeared, as assumed in the earlier theory. Nor have family relationships disappeared in cities. Urban dwellers do visit relatives and friends and neighbors, as traffic tie-ups on weekends testify.

But the urban dweller is often isolated in respect to relationships with people who are not of his familial group or neighborhood. Particularly, he is separated from people across class, racial, and ethnic lines. Yet as equal employment opportunities increase, he meets a greater variety of people through his job. Sometimes romance defies family lines, as in the love affair of Maria and Tony in *West Side Story;* marriages across ethnic, racial, and class lines do occur and are increasing. But in general the city remains a mosaic of social worlds; the ways of

---

[7] Herman Kahn and Anthony J. Wiener, *The Year 2000* (New York: Macmillan, 1967), p. 61.

Los Angeles traffic pattern "The Stack" (at least four levels of roadways). Courtesy of Georg Gerster from Rapho Guillumette.

living of the jet-setter and the solid middle-class citizen and the slum-dweller differ markedly from each other.

All city-dwellers are vulnerable to breakdowns in their environment, whether they be newspaper or garbage collection strikes, power blackouts or brownouts, smog or pollution, riots or crime in the streets. Some residents are more vulnerable than others; usually the poorer the individual the more vulnerable he is to the events which result in social disorganization.

Crucial to any prospective teacher's appraisal of city life is a frank recognition of the wide diversity of life patterns in the city. The patterns vary with areas and with degrees of wealth. The variation grows more noticeable as the middle classes flee to the suburbs.

With the migration of the middle classes toward the suburbs, a city increasingly becomes a place of extremes. Left behind are the wealthy and the poor. The wealthy live on their social islands, often huge, self-contained apartments, hotels, and town houses with preempted views of the lake, river, park, or other city scenic attraction. Sometimes the park overlooked by plush housing is not safe for walking after dark. The transportation to work or play or school is by cab or private bus, car or limousine or, when very hurried, by subway. The poor people, conspicuously including the most recently arrived groups such as the Puerto Ricans and Negroes in New York, Negroes in Chicago, Mexicans and Negroes in Los Angeles, live in run-down areas, including once-respectable brownstone houses now crowded with families. They sit on the front steps and occupy the roofs in hot weather. They jam the subways and elevateds and public buses returning from their work at a variety of unskilled and semiskilled jobs. The middle-class group, a potential mediator between extremes, steadily dwindles through flight to the suburbs. Only high income and inheritance taxes, which reduce the wealth of the rich, and the steady job availability, which employs the poor, keep the extremes from being still more obvious.[8]

Playwrights have long dramatized city contrasts of rich and poor living side by side, but increasingly in the cities, the neighborhoods grow more residentially distinct. Both income and life styles contribute to the succession of social islands which make up a modern city. For example, clerical workers who frequently earn less than blue collar workers live in more prestigious neighborhoods primarily as an expression of life style and desired social differentiation from working class people.

CITY CHILDREN AND YOUTH

In so diverse a city pattern, the life and the educational experience of children and youth depends heavily upon the neighborhood in which the individual lives. In turn, the neighborhood situation is heavily influenced by social class and ethnic backgrounds.

There still exist in American cities enclaves (distinctly bounded areas enclosed within the larger area) in which upper class city-dwellers and their children live. Sometimes the enclave is a city neighborhood in which large and imposing houses persist; Riverdale in New York City is such a section. More often in contemporary times the enclave takes the form of luxury apartment buildings grouped together, each with its own doorman and security system. Babies and small children from such families are often taken to nearby parks or playgrounds by maids and household employees playing the role formerly occupied in Britain by nannies. School-age children are frequently transported by car to private schools which combine both academic and recreational facilities. The cultural resources of the city are often used by both old and young upper-class family members. Vacations are frequently taken at a considerable distance from the city. In general, the patterns of living of children and youth of such families are the urban counterpart of the upper-upper and lower-upper social class experiences described in the last chapter.

Similarly, upper-middle- and lower-middle-class youth frequently live in city neighborhoods much in the manner described in the section on social class. However, middle-class families in cities increasingly move to the suburbs when opportunities occur. Moving to the suburbs is a way of bettering oneself and of living the good life in America, as many middle-class Americans see it. Unfortunately, it is also a way of separating middle-class citizens from the problems

---

[8] William Van Til, Gordon F. Vars, and John H. Lounsbury, *Modern Education for the Junior High School Years* (Indianapolis: Bobbs-Merrill, 1967), p. 95.

The city offers few play areas for its young people. Courtesy of Laurence Fink for Nancy Palmer.

experienced by the lower-class who remain of necessity in the city. Many white middle-class Americans see themselves as beleaguered by pressures from lower income city dwellers and, more particularly, from blacks and other minority groups. As new migrants who are largely of upper-lower and lower-lower class background press in upon the borders of former middle-class neighborhoods, the residents grow increasingly uneasy. They perceive any lower-class groups as bringing with them the virus of crime and neighborhood blight. Reaching the conclusion that "the old neighborhood is not what it used to be," they move. They rationalize the move as "being good for the children."

Many middle-class young who remain in the city stem from the ethnic group backgrounds related to the earlier immigration waves. Some middle-class young people in urban areas, however, stem from the contemporary minorities; their ethnic backgrounds are largely Negro, Puerto Rican, Mexican-American, etc. Their way of looking at the world is heavily influenced by middle-class backgrounds.

Some middle-class children and youth from minority group backgrounds accept the conventional American system of economic rewards and work within it toward good jobs and material satisfactions. Within the system they hope to achieve better housing, better opportunities for the use of leisure time, and better total social surroundings. Often they are just as eager as minority group members to move out of the city to the conventional grass-surrounded house in the suburbs. Thus, a new teacher would make a grave error by stereotyping young people from upwardly mobile families as having the same attitudes and reactions as socially disadvantaged children.

The errors schools sometimes commit because of insensitivity to changing social class circumstances in neighborhoods verge on the ludicrous. For instance, Estelle Fuchs in *Pickets at the Gates* tells of one minority group rising toward middle-class status, which was misinterpreted by the schools. In a dilapidated area which had long been populated by working class Negro people, new housing developments arose, including Skyview Terrace Apartments. Skyview Terrace attracted as tenants 60 percent Negro, 20 percent Puerto Ricans, and 20 percent others. The heads of families were semi-skilled and skilled workmen and many were at the factory-foreman level. Still others were civil service employees including postal workers, policemen, and teachers. To the Slater School came children from Skyview Terrace (45 percent) and children from the old neighborhood outside the project (55 percent). The more articulate new residents of Skyview Terrace became active in the P.T.A.

The community exploded in anger when the principal of Slater School wrote a well-intentioned but misguided letter to his faculty which over-generalized on the disadvantaged backgrounds of the children. Resentful parents petitioned for his removal from the principalship, on the basis that he had made the following comments about the community, parents and children:

Compared with middle class homes, they are poorer financially, academically, socially.
Many of our children are on welfare . . . the school lunch is the best meal they get.
The mother is so busy with her brood that the individual child is lonely.
Many of our children have no fathers at home.
Our children are living in a noisy atmosphere.
There is a lack of encouragement at home to achieve.
Families on welfare for the third generation lack academic drive.
Coming from a poor environment, socially, culturally, economically, physically, it is no wonder that our children are not ready for school.
The people of the Appalachian Mountains, the Ozark hill-billies, the Mexican-American migrant workers, have these attributes as well as poor Negroes and poor Puerto Ricans.[9]

Larry Cuban in a book on teaching in the inner city, *To Make a Difference*, comments on the same situation. He says of the principal:

Where had he erred? First, he misread totally the diversity of social economic

---

[9] Cited by Estelle Fuchs, *Pickets at the Gates* (New York: Free Press, 1966), pp. 10–11.

class that exists in segregated neighborhoods. Second, his middle-class prejudices (the ones he warned new teachers about) slipped into the discussion and colored his views of youngsters and parents. Third, he combined sense and nonsense in his descriptions of children and parents by borrowing generalizations from sociology and psychology and applying them uncritically to the children and the community his school serves. . . . He discovered that he did not know the range of income and style of living of his students and their parents.[10]

Historian E. Franklin Frazier in *Black Bourgeoisie* described with a degree of irony the renunciation of their heritage by some upwardly mobile Negroes.[11] Members of the black bourgeoisie are sometimes called "strivers" and a section of Harlem is even referred to as Strivers Hill. Contemporary invective directed against them includes "Oreo," a reference to the product of a biscuit company which is a cookie black on the outside and white on the inside.

But a contemporary, E. Franklin Frazier, would find that much of today's leadership in minority group struggles to attain status is being taken by adult and youthful ethnic group members from families who have become middle class. Today the middle-class status of some minority group youths does not necessarily mean they will accept conventional economic and social American patterns. For instance, leadership in black militancy and Puerto Rican and chicano dissent often stems from young people who are not themselves poverty-stricken. Their deep loyalty to the cause of underprivileged blacks, Puerto Ricans, and Mexican-Americans leads them into social activism on behalf of the group with which they identify.

Crucial to the urban problem of America in the 1970s are the children and youth of the lower classes, especially the lower-lowers. Frequently, they live within what the sociologists have termed the inner city—that section of the city which includes slums and ghettos and which houses those who have the least materially. Many inner-city residents today are from black, Puerto Rican, and Mexican-American ethnic backgrounds.

The past decades have been periods of substantial migration of the poor, of all racial and ethnic backgrounds, to the cities of both the North and the South. Though the parents of many children and youth have come to the city in search of a better life, they have often encountered deprived living conditions. They have moved into the neighborhoods in which they could find the least expensive housing, which is usually also the oldest and most deteriorated. They have often been exploited by absentee landlords who refused to maintain the buildings and who have charged exorbitant rents. The jobs they found (when they could find them) were low paying and primarily for the untrained and unskilled. The new migrants have swelled the relief rolls.

A sixth grade child in Harlem describes a block in such a neighborhood:

My block is the most terrible block I've ever seen. There are at lease 25 or 30

[10] Larry Cuban, *To Make a Difference: Teaching in the Inner City* (New York: Free Press, 1970), pp. 18–19.
[11] E. Franklin Frazier, *Black Bourgeoisie* (New York: Free Press, 1957).

narcartic people in my block. The cops come around there and tries to act bad but I bet inside of them they are as scared as can be. They even had in the papers that this block is the worst block, not in Manhattan but in New York City. In the summer they don't do nothing except shooting, stabbing, and fighting. They hang all over the stoops and when you say excuse me to them they hear you but they just don't feel like moving. Some times they make me so mad that I feel like slapping them and stuffing a bag of garbage down their throats. There's only one policeman who can handle these people and we call him "Sunny." When he come around in his cop car the people run around the corners, and he won't let anyone sit on the stoops. If you don't believe this story come around some time and you'll find out.[12]

Increasingly America is having to face up to the fact that the education being received by upper-lower- and lower-lower-class children and youth in the inner city as yet cannot compensate for the environmental conditions which these young people experience. Indeed, some of the irrelevant education which lower-class children receive even adds to their handicaps. The handicaps brought to school with the child from the slums already include deteriorating housing, the weak family structures in some (but by no means all) families, the prevalence of crime in the neighborhood, the spread of drug addiction, the lack of recreational facilities, the incidence of disease, etc. Take any index of social ills in America and you will find that the lower-class bears the brunt of the burden.

The schools of the cities, historically conceived as institutions in which young people of all backgrounds could come together, have become increasingly one-social-class and one-ethnic-group institutions. This is particularly true of elementary schools which are usually located so as to be within walking distance of the young child; it is less true of the high schools which draw young people from a wider area. Schools, like the neighborhoods, are part of the urban mosaic. But *each* elementary school and *each* neighborhood is not likely to have the characteristics of a mosaic because contemporary urban living results in limited interaction among people who live in differing social worlds. The walls between lower- and middle-class neighborhoods may be invisible, yet they do exist in psychological terms. So lower-class groups feel estranged from other groups.

The children of lower-class groups in large cities often share societal alienation. Forces encouraging alienation include the isolation and insecurity of children in the environment of the cities. It is no accident that two outstanding black novelists have titled their books *The Invisible Man* (Ralph Ellison) and *Nobody Knows My Name* (James Baldwin). In such a setting, low self-esteem combines with low motivation. One of the hardest things for whites to understand is that riots, such as the summer disturbances of the late 1960s, and social anger such as that of the Black Panthers are ways troubled people use to establish self-identity and self-esteem. One of the problems facing American society is whether alienation can be replaced by identity only through violence or whether, on the

---

[12] Herbert Kohl, *36 Children* (New York: The New American Library, 1967), p. 36.

other hand, the schools can play a role in establishing identity and reducing alienation through education.

Teachers in inner-city schools often encounter formidable difficulties. The buildings in which they work are often old; needed equipment is frequently lacking. And, above all, the children who are to be educated are beset by problems. Sometimes they are emotionally disturbed. Sometimes they reject the discipline which the school attempts to maintain. Sometimes they bring into the schools the obscenities of the streets and the anger communicated to them by role models in homes and neighborhoods. As a result, many such children respond with anger and hostility.

On the other hand, some say that school systems and the teachers themselves help create their difficulties. Critics say that educators do so through insistence on irrelevant curriculum, by taking for granted that if one is poor and from a minority group background he will be unable to learn, by expecting little or nothing from disadvantaged students, and by blaming all school failures upon the community and the environment which surround the student. Consequently, scholars like Kenneth B. Clark believe that "the schools are presently damaging the children they exist to help."[13]

But in an effort to help, a torrent of books replete with suggestions has poured from the presses during the 1960s. They include *The Disadvantaged Early Adolescent* by Helen F. Storen;[14] *Education in the Metropolis* edited by Harry L. Miller and Marjorie B. Smiley;[15] *The Leftouts* by Sandra A. Warden;[16] *The Schools and the Urban Crisis* edited by August Kerber and Barbara Bommarito;[17] *Education in Metropolitan Areas* by Robert J. Havighurst;[18] *The Education of Urban Populations* by Abraham Bernstein;[19] *Education for the Disadvantaged* edited by Harry L. Miller;[20] *How to Teach Disadvantaged Youth* by Allan C. Ornstein and Philip D. Vairo;[21] *Education of the Disadvantaged* edited by A. Harry Passow, Miriam Goldberg, and Abraham J. Tannenbaum;[22] *The Disadvantaged* by Mario D.

---

[13] Kenneth B. Clark, *Dark Ghetto* (New York: Harper and Row, 1965), p. 124.
[14] Helen F. Storen, *The Disadvantaged Early Adolescent: More Effective Teaching* (New York: McGraw-Hill, 1968).
[15] Harry L. Miller and Marjorie B. Smiley (eds.), *Education in the Metropolis* (New York: Free Press, 1967).
[16] Sandra A. Warden, *The Leftouts: Disadvantaged Children in Heterogeneous Schools* (New York: Holt, Rinehart and Winston, 1968).
[17] August Kerber and Barbara Bommarito (eds.), *The Schools and the Urban Crisis* (New York: Holt, Rinehart and Winston, 1966).
[18] Robert J. Havighurst, *Education in Metropolitan Areas* (Boston: Allyn and Bacon, 1966).
[19] Abraham Bernstein, *The Education of Urban Populations* (New York: Random, 1967).
[20] Harry L. Miller (ed.), *Education for the Disadvantaged: Challenge to Education* (New York: Free Press, 1967).
[21] Allan C. Ornstein and Philip D. Vairo, *How to Teach Disadvantaged Youth* (New York: David McKay, 1969).
[22] A. Harry Passow, Miriam Goldberg, and Abraham J. Tannenbaum (ed.), *Education of the Disadvantaged* (New York: Holt, Rinehart and Winston, 1967).

Fantini and Gerald Weinstein;[23] *School Children in the Urban Slum* edited by Joan I. Roberts;[24] *Deprivation and Compensatory Education* by Helen E. Rees;[25] and *Developing Programs for the Educationally Disadvantaged* by A. Harry Passow.[26]

Since the new teacher is likely to be assigned to schools containing substantial proportions of poor children, he has an obligation to read current literature concerning the disadvantaged and to be willing to train in deprived areas. For much still needs to be done to change both school and community situations which perpetuate the problems of the disadvantaged. Jules Feiffer, the cartoonist, developed a series of drawings to illustrate the following ironic comments, attributed to a sad-looking tired man:

> I used to think I was poor. Then they told me I wasn't poor, I was needy. Then they told me it was self defeating to think of myself as needy, that I was culturally deprived. Then they told me deprived was a bad image, that I was underprivileged. Then they told me underprivileged was overused, that I was disadvantaged. I still don't have a dime, but I do have a *great* vocabulary.[27]

SUBURBAN BACKGROUNDS

Though cities have grown markedly during the twentieth century, the fastest growing community grouping in the United States today is the suburb. The *New York Times* reported on June 21, 1970, that according to census experts, the suburbs in 1970 became "the largest sector of the population, exceeding for the first time both central cities (59 million) and all the rest of the country outside metropolitan areas (about 71 million)."[28]

SUBURBAN COMMUNITIES

When Americans think of the suburbs, they often visualize an upper- or upper-middle-class setting. But with the growth of the suburbs, other types of suburbs must be included—lower-middle-class suburbs and working-class suburbs in which some upper-lower Americans live. One cannot make the assumption that all suburban teachers work in affluent communities.

The suburbs resemble the frontier in American history. Like the frontier, the suburbs refuse to be confined; they move steadily outward. What used to be an

---

[23] Mario D. Fantini and Gerald Weinstein, *The Disadvantaged* (New York: Harper and Row, 1968).
[24] Joan I. Roberts (ed.), *School Children in the Urban Slum* (New York: Free Press, 1967).
[25] Helen E. Rees, *Deprivation and Compensatory Education: A Consideration* (Boston: Houghton Mifflin, 1968).
[26] A. Harry Passow, *Developing Programs for the Educationally Disadvantaged* (New York: Teachers College Press, 1968).
[27] Jules Feiffer, *Reader's Digest* (March, 1967), p. 145.
[28] *The New York Times* (June 21, 1970), p. 54.

One of the complaints against suburbia is that its very physical arrangement encourages and is a reflection of its conformity. Courtesy of J. R. Eyerman.

inner suburb has often been embraced by the city as city limits expand. Houses that once were surrounded by vacant space are then often surrounded by looming apartments. The outer suburbs grow more populated and new outer suburbs develop far beyond what formerly was thought reasonable commuting distance. Eventually the suburbs give way to the exurbs, that strange new blend of suburban and rural.

A common characteristic of suburbanites, whether inner, outer or exurban, is to be acutely aware of travel time. The typical suburbanite works in a city, returns home to his bedroom community, and spends a substantial fraction of his life in commuter trains, buses or automobiles.

The more well-to-do of the upper-class or upper-middle-class communities usually lie a considerable distance from the central city. Homes are along quiet tree-shaded streets, lawns are well-kept. The men commute regularly; the women play a considerable role in social life and community affairs. In the comfortable homes of the prosperous suburban community there is considerable emphasis upon entertaining, gardening, and college entrance. Critics often blast such communities for conformity, striving to outrank others, and a general complacency. For instance, Fred M. Hechinger says:

> Too many of the suburbs have become compounds which, even though they are not protected by the barbed wire of their military counterparts in occupied territories, nevertheless set their inhabitants apart from the "outside" world. They are pervaded by a sameness—in income levels, in taste, in mutual entertainment and admiration, in outward indicators of material status and attainments, and in aspirations, especially for the children's collegiate careers.[29]

[29] Fred M. Hechinger, Foreword, p. 5 in Alice Miel with Edwin Kiester, Jr., in *The Shortchanged Children of Suburbia* (New York: Institute of Human Relations Press, 1967).

If you ask the typical prosperous suburbanite why he has come to the suburbs, he usually responds that this is the best place to raise his children. By this, he (or she) means that near home there is space for the young to play and opportunities for them to attend good schools. Critics of suburbia claim that one of the actual reasons for moving to suburbia, yet one not often mentioned, is to avoid lower-class contacts for the family as a whole, especially contacts with blacks, Puerto Ricans, and other minorities.

Lower-middle-class suburbs are increasing. Frequently they are made up of nearly identical houses in a development which has been bulldozed from farm lands and denuded of trees. The occupational status of the residents is not as high as in the upper- or upper-middle-class suburbs. In both types of suburbs, family relationships continue to be important. Neighboring with the people in nearby houses is frequent.

The working-class suburb is also different from the various upper-or middle-class suburbs. Sometimes such suburbs are actually small cities on the edge of larger ones; sometimes they are genuine residential suburbs from which people travel to the central city. These suburbs differ from the middle-class suburbs in that the residents are largely skilled or semi-skilled workers often classifiable as upper-lower-class. More minority group members live in working-class suburbs than in upper- or upper-middle-class suburbs. Customarily people in working-class suburbs have less formal education than those who live in the upper-middle-class suburbs. Their homes are not used for the massive entertaining, such as cocktail parties, characteristic of the upper-middle-class suburb. Instead, entertaining in the working-class suburb often takes the form of having relatives in for dinner. Organization membership is not so high in the working-class suburbs as in the upper-middle-class suburbs.

The exurbs are a kind of community smorgasbord. Since they are located at the meeting place of urban and rural, one hardly knows whether to categorize them as suburban or rural. Residents vary from necessarily gregarious residents of trailers to isolates living on extensive estates. Since the area is not restricted by building regulations and is characterized by little community organization, anything goes with respect to residences. Residences may be expensive homes or shacks. They may house people who work in the city or who work on the farm. The life styles of people are mixed and varied; the exurbs are marked by great heterogeneity.

SUBURBAN CHILDREN AND YOUTH

The social class of the area in which the suburban child lives makes a difference in his life.

In the relatively upper-class suburb, the schools are frequently oriented to college entrance. The programs, while academic, frequently reflect the best that a coalition of scholars can develop for instruction in the varied disciplines. Many students in such situations are acceptant of their schools and willing to play by the implicit rules of the game. So they struggle for grades and attempt

Standardized tests often encourage learning merely to do well on these exams. Courtesy of College Entrance Examination Board.

to qualify themselves for the college of their choice. Yet such programs have also spawned contemporary rebels. Drug addiction worries suburban residents today. Confrontation with the administration of schools by dissidents grows.

James A. Meyer says of suburbia,

> At first glance most of our suburban youth share a common background of comfortable homes, loving parents, "good schools," high intelligence, excellent health, and almost unlimited opportunities for self-development. They have almost all the advantages that many of their mothers and fathers growing up during the Great Depression and World War II were denied. Yet many of today's middle-class suburban youngsters exhibit disturbing character qualities—sexual libertarianism, vehement rejection of adult authority, and a widespread disposition to experiment with drugs.[30]

Dan Dodson, director of the Center for Human Relations and Community Studies at New York University, has long pointed out that a problem for upper- and upper-middle-class young people in suburbs is "their essential uselessness." Young people are supported by their parents and often can make little contribution to the family except to strive for good grades, says Dodson. Consequently, the "college rat race" becomes surpassingly important to many such young people, as Francis R. Link points out in an article on pressures on youth.

---

[30] James A. Meyer, "Suburbia: A Wasteland of Disadvantaged Youth and Negligent Schools?", *Phi Delta Kappan*, 50 (June 1969), p. 575.

The youth of suburbia is a young person under pressure, and the pressure for him is "awesome." It "preys" on his mind; it is a continual sense of foreboding and dismay. One suburban teenager said, "It is the feeling, as each academic day breaks, that there is always something, or rather some million things, to be done, and all count terribly much and hold enormous importance for the future."

When he says future, the suburban youth means college. He must get into a "good" college. It requires getting good grades, taking part in extracurricular activities, and "taking tests until your eyes fall from their sockets." This necessity bombards the suburban high school student from all possible angles, from parents, teachers, and counselors, whose bywords are: "Don't forget that every test counts," and "A college will look at your total record." The pressure sometimes seems impossible, sometimes murderous, but it must be lived with, for in our society there is no other way, no alternate route—to 'success.'

... The child of suburbia is the organization child, and his social and psychological pressures, as well as his solutions to them, are very significantly rooted in the family, in the nature and quality of family interaction.[31]

Upper- and upper-middle-class suburban schools are often made more pleasant for those who attend them by an emphasis on student participation and the use of modern teaching methods, such as committee work, independent study, and problem solving. In addition, suburban schools are noted for the variety and extent of the extracurricular or cocurricular programs. So even when students are not stirred by classroom experiences, they do have opportunities for educational challenges in athletics, school publications, dramatic clubs, and a host of other activities.

Yet the forgotten person in such schools is often the individual who is not oriented toward college and who needs vocational preparation during his secondary school years. Since suburban schools are frequently weak in vocational education because of community emphasis on the academic program, such children and youth are overlooked or pressured to conform to the majority pattern. The upper- and upper-middle-class suburban school, despite a peaceful outer appearance, is often a frustrating place for those who are not academically inclined.

Some feel that upper-upper-, lower-upper-, and upper-middle-class youth in suburbs are cheated of an opportunity to live and work together with young people of varied backgrounds. Alice Miel and Edward Kiester, in *The Shortchanged Children of Suburbia* point out that in relatively upper income suburbs, the housing situation itself deprives the young of the opportunity to know lower-class students, though their future success may often depend heavily on their human relations skills with people of a variety of economic groups. Young people in "lily-white" suburbs are cheated of the opportunity to know young people of minority backgrounds, particularly black, Puerto Rican, and Mexican-American, though the rapidly changing occupational patterns makes it almost

---

[31] Francis R. Link, "Pressures on Youth: Suburbia," *Theory Into Practice*, vol. 7 (February, 1968), p. 23–24.

inevitable that as adults they will work with these people. Though the world has become a global village populated largely by colored races in lands less industrialized than the U.S., suburban children and youth experience only their own homogeneous villages. It is difficult to bring about meetings of such young people with other young people different from themselves.

Miel and Kiester say:

. . . the child of suburbia is likely to be a materialist and somewhat of a hypocrite. In addition, he tends to be a striver in school, a conformist, and above all a believer in being "nice," polite, clean and tidy. Besides dividing humanity into the black and the white, the Jew and the Christian, the rich and the poor, he also is apt to classify people as "smart" or "dumb," "clean" or "dirty," and "nice" or "not nice." What is more, he is often conspicuously self-centered.

In all these respects the suburban child patterns his attitudes and goals chiefly after those of his parents. But he can never be sure that he won't fall short of their hopes for him—that he is measuring up to the standards (especially of academic achievement, behavior and tidiness) that they have set for him. He is therefore likely to be an anxious child. Our study as well as other inquiries indicate clearly that to grow up in an American suburb today is not a wholly enviable lot.[32]

Such an analysis enrages some suburban parents who regard it as a distorted version of their lives and their children's lives. But some proportion of suburban parents admit a degree of validity in the authors' portrait of "New Village" and support their recommendations that upper- and upper-middle-class suburban schools should (1) develop higher thought processes, (2) foster understanding of the students' own community, its structure and operation, (3) help children attain some insight into their own values and those of others, and (4) develop an empathic understanding of others.[33] Such parents are sometimes active in programs of suburban-urban pupil exchange aimed at breaking down the barriers between cities and suburbs. They work actively through P.T.A.'s and school boards so that their children experience the social learning necessary to the achievement of the American dream and so that no social shortchanging takes place.

Because substantial financial support and well-equipped modern school plants are available, and genuine concern for their children is manifested by parents, education in upper- and upper-middle-class suburban communities has high potential. Needed are more adventuresomeness in the teaching of controversial issues; more and better use of resources outside the classroom in the suburban community and in the neighboring city; more opportunities for the young to clarify and achieve democratic values; and above all, the creation of opportunities for suburban children to become acquainted with and to work beside others of a variety of racial, religious, national, and socioeconomic backgrounds.

[32] Alice Miel and Edwin Kiester, Jr., *The Shortchanged Children of Suburbia* (New York: Institute of Human Relations Press, 1967), p. 43.
[33] *Ibid.*, pp. 57–59.

Children taking part in an urban-suburban exchange program. Courtesy of Anna Kaufman Moon.

Through use of a wide variety of books, magazines, visitors, social travel, shared experiences, open discussions, etc., suburban schools can more fully realize their potential for a relevant late twentieth century education. Rather than handicap suburban students in the college education which lies ahead for most of them, such a program can lead to greater motivation for acquiring a college education and a broader and more realistic college experience.

Somewhat different are the experiences of children and youth living in lower-middle-class suburbs. Herbert J. Gans reported of Levittown, New Jersey, a community he described as three-fourths lower-middle-class, that while children are allowed to be themselves and to act as children they are at the same time raised strictly. Parents are fearful of spoiling children. Parents do not give up control over their children quickly in lower-middle-class homes; they hope that schools will support the home and its values and keep the children in line. Young people from such families are often encouraged to go to college primarily because college is necessary for a respectable and good paying job and for a good marriage. Social adjustment of young people is frequently regarded as at least as important as academic success.

All suburbs are not middle-class, despite the popularity of the stereotype of suburbia. Dobriner has pointed out in *Class in Suburbia,*

In fact, many suburbs are not essentially middle-class and accordingly do not exhibit those middle-class patterns too often mistaken as suburban patterns. Indeed, Berger's study of a working-class suburb in California failed to sustain the findings of the Park Forest and Drexelbrook studies of William Whyte, the

Crestwood Heights researches of Seeley and his associates, and those of the Gordons in *The Split-Level Trap.* Berger found that his working-class suburbanites still voted Democratic, they did not become Republicans as the Myth has it. They did not rediscover religion—more than half of the respondents said they went to church rarely or not at all. They had no great mobility aspirations; the great majority did not regard their suburban homes as a transient watering place, but rather as "paradise permanently gained." Furthermore, recent studies by Lazerwitz point out that the suburbs are losing whatever middle-class monopoly they might once have enjoyed, that streams of semiskilled and skilled workers are steadily moving to the suburbs.[34]

Gans describes a working-class subculture in Levittown of blue-collar workers, and white-collar workers, who, in general, did not graduate from high school. He says,

. . . Husbands and wives exchange love and affection, but they have separate family roles and engage in little of the companionship found in middle classes. The husband is the breadwinner and the enforcer of child discipline; the wife is the housekeeper and rears the children. Whenever possible, husbands spend their free time with other male companions, woman with other women. Entertaining is rarer than in the middle class, and most social life takes place among relatives and childhood friends. When they are not available, there is occasional visiting with neighbors and also a tendency for husband and wife to draw closer to each other.[35]

Gans reports parent-child relationships in working-class cultures to be adult-centered rather than child-centered. Children are expected to behave and are often strictly disciplined. There are many rules by which the child must live; working-class parents expect the schools to cooperate in enforcing discipline. Children often react by leaving the house for peer groups as soon as possible and, paradoxically, achieving freedom earlier than the typical middle-class child. Gans says that working-class parents of Levittown "often expect the child to get into trouble by the time he reaches adolescence and accepts its occurrence fatalistically. By then the child, especially the boy, is expected to be a near adult and responsible for himself."[36]

The working-class parent knows that education is important if his children are to attain good jobs. However, he is quite doubtful of educational "frills" and usually unhappy about the rise in tax rate. If the boy is academically successful, the parents will make an effort to send him to college for vocational purposes. College education for girls is sometimes approached with more reserve. Fathers hope sons will do better than they have, but upward social or economic mobility

---

[34] William M. Dobriner, *Class in Suburbia* (Englewood Cliffs, N.J.: Prentice-Hall, 1963), pp. 13–14.
[35] Herbert J. Gans, *The Levittowners* (New York: Random, 1967), pp. 25–26.
[36] *Ibid.,* p. 26.

318 FOUNDATIONS OF EDUCATION

is not as marked an aim as in middle-class groups. A team of sociologists writing about working-class youth say,

> Asked what he is or would like to be, he would most likely say: A good guy. This translates to some degree into someone who is both tough and sentimental, someone who can be pushed just so far, but no one—including himself—appears to know just how far that is.[37]

The authors also say,

> With his father he essentially shares an outlook characterized by resignation, but resignation without a basis in experience. He is, in relative terms, active rather than introspective. He is not a moralist. He is prepared to take life as it comes, expecting frighteningly little as long as it comes in predictable ways. It is when it does not come this way, when it becomes unpredictable, and he is required to respond, that he does so as a moralist and a very rigid moralist indeed.[38]

Schools in working-class suburbs can make a contribution by helping young people examine themselves, their values and goals, and recognize that education is more than simply vocational training. The development of understanding of people at other economic levels and of those who dissent from established values (which the working-class youth often takes for granted) is particularly desirable in the interest of broader American unity.

THE INFLUENCE OF COMMUNITY BACKGROUNDS

So, community factors such as rural, city, or suburban backgrounds continue to make a difference in the lives of American young people. As we try to illustrate in the next chapter, individuality remains, despite all attempts at grouping. Despite all of the conditioning influences in our backgrounds, the human being is unique and develops in ways which are often unpredictable.

DISCUSSION
1. How do the census definitions of categories differ from the groupings employed for explanation of community backgrounds in this chapter?
2. Why is the rural American "the disappearing American"?

---

[37] William Simon, John H. Gagnon, and Donald Carns, "Working Class Youth: Alienation Without an Image," *The National Association of Secondary School Principals Bulletin*, vol. 53 (September 1969), p. 64.
[38] *Ibid.*, p. 68.

3. What were formerly the characteristics of rural youth, according to studies? Do these characteristics differ from those of rural youth today? How and why?
4. What is the dual task of many rural schools?
5. What accounts for the steady growth of urbanism in America?
6. What are the varying theories of life styles within American cities? Specifically how do urban theories of the 1930s differ from contemporary theories concerning neighborhoods, etc.?
7. What are the characteristics of life in the city as experienced by children and youth of different social classes?
8. Why do some young people aspire to and others reject upward economic mobility? Why do some young Americans accept while others reject middle-class patterns?
9. What were the major misinterpretations by the principal in the account of Skyview Terrace and Slater School?
10. Why are the problems of the poor so pressing in American life today? Why is the problem more exaggerated than it was in earlier years?
11. What are the handicaps which the slum child brings to school with him? What are the actions of schools which sometimes increase those handicaps? What are the actions of schools which decrease such handicaps? What are the difficulties against which the city teacher struggles in teaching children and youth from slum and ghetto areas?
12. How do teachers in the inner city sometimes help create their difficulties?
13. What do you consider the role of a teacher of culturally disadvantaged students? Should he or she adapt his or her approach to meet individual differences or maintain a careful uniformity in relationships with all students?
14. What are some major cues from books on the disadvantaged to help new teachers who will work in the inner cities?
15. Distinguish among various types of suburbs. Discuss the emphasis of Dobriner and others on the existence of suburbs other than upper-class communities.
16. Why do people move to the suburbs? Is there any difference between what people say in explanation of moving to the suburbs and their true reasons?
17. Can you generalize on children and youth from the upper-income suburbs? From the lower-income suburbs? How do their school experiences differ? How important is social class in accounting for differences in patterns of behavior?

INVOLVEMENT
1. Use students in your class who have rural or urban or suburban backgrounds as resources for a panel presentation on the characteristics of such community backgrounds and the influences they believe these backgrounds have had upon them.
2. Make arrangements and visit a classroom in an inner-city school, a suburban school, and a rural school. Note any significant differences you discover—differences in pupils, teachers, settings, facilities, methods, etc.
3. Make a conscious attempt to see the different neighborhoods of the city nearest you. A group may visit a particular neighborhood and generalize on it to the class.
4. Interview a teacher or an administrator who has been in an inner-city school for

at least ten years. Get his reactions to the changes in the pupils and their family backgrounds.

5. Volunteer your services to the administration of a school in the inner city. Learn of the challenges to education in such a school by immersing yourself in the environment of that school. Then write an objective account of your experiences.
6. Develop your own reading program of books by authors who have grown up in the inner city, typified by James Baldwin's *Nobody Knows My Name* and Claude Brown's *Manchild in the Promised Land*.
7. Compile a list of suggestions for working with disadvantaged children and youth from class members' reading on the culturally disadvantaged.
8. Develop and carefully plan at least two major trips for the class as a whole. One trip would explore living patterns and experiences in a community background familiar to the students whether rural, urban, or suburban. The other would explore a community background quite unfamiliar to the students. In each case, emphasize not only the physical experience of being in a neighborhood but also exchange ideas with residents through meetings, discussions, etc.

BIBLIOGRAPHY

Anderson, Margaret. *Children of the South*. New York: Farrar, 1966. A warm account of the children who found themselves caught in the crossfires related to the desegregation of schools in the South in the 1960s. By a high school teacher and counselor.

Brown, Claude, *Manchild in the Promised Land*. New York: Macmillan, 1965. A bitter and colorful account of what it was like to grow up in Harlem in recent years. Extremely helpful in understanding some of the attitudes of contemporary blacks.

Clark, Kenneth B. *Dark Ghetto*. New York: Harper and Row, 1965. An account of life in Harlem which stresses the pathologies which grow out of ghetto life.

Cuban, Larry. *To Make a Difference: Teaching in the Inner City*. New York: Free Press, 1970. Outspoken and practical guide to the work of the teacher in the ghetto and slums of America. Stresses what educators can do, rather than shifting the blame to families.

Dobriner, William M. *Class in Suburbia*. Englewood Cliffs, N.J.: Prentice-Hall, 1963. Points out that the conception of suburbia as exclusively upper class is a myth. Describes emerging working-class suburbs.

Fantini, Mario D. and Gerald Weinstein. *The Disadvantaged*. New York: Harper and Row, 1968. Collaboration by students of the inner city who draw upon community projects and philanthropically supported programs with which they have worked.

Frazier, E. Franklin. *Black Bourgeoisie*. New York: Free Press, 1957. Classic history of the upwardly mobile Negro in American society.

Fuchs, Estelle. *Pickets At the Gates*. New York: Free Press, 1966. Lively accounts of school situations focusing on problems of civil rights, including the Skyview Terrace incident reported in this chapter.

Gans, Herbert. *Levittowners: Ways of and Politics in a New Suburban Community*. New York: Pantheon Books, 1967. Comprehensive description of a massive new American community in which many lower-middle-class Americans live.

Ginzberg, Eli, et al. *The Middle-Class Negro in the White Man's World*. New York: Columbia University Press, 1967. Case studies of the career plans of middle-class Negro males in college or college-bound.

Graham, Grace. *The Public School in the New Society.* New York: Harper and Row, 1969. A basic text for students of social foundations of education focusing on the most significant of the many social influences causing problems in contemporary education.

Greene, Mary Frances and Orletta Ryan. *The Schoolchildren: Growing Up in the Slums.* New York: Pantheon, 1965. Teaching experiences and children's problems in two New York City public schools.

Harrington, Michael. *The Other America: Poverty in the United States.* New York: Macmillan, 1962. A rare book that has had a distinct social influence through calling the attention of Americans of the early 1960s to the reality of poverty in the United States. A book which heavily influenced the development of programs during the Johnson administration.

Hurley, Rodger L. *Poverty and Mental Retardation: A Causal Relationship.* New York: Random House, 1969. Recognition of the interrelationships between poverty and mental retardation formerly attributed to causes other than societal deprivation.

McGeoch, Dorothy M. *Learning to Teach in Urban Schools.* New York: Teachers College Press, Columbia University, 1965. Realistic practical procedures for the teacher scheduled to teach in urban schools and usually with disadvantaged children. Includes accounts of experiences by four new teachers.

Miel, Alice, and Edwin Kiester, Jr. *The Shortchanged Children of Suburbia.* New York: Institute of Human Relations Press, 1967. Lively and controversial pamphlet on suburban influences on upper- and upper-middle-class young people, particularly as to their inadequate education for human relations.

Miller, Harry L., ed. *Education for the Disadvantaged.* New York: Free Press, 1967. A compilation of articles helpful to the new teacher contemplating work with the disadvantaged. Emphasis on schooling, testing, curriculum issues, teachers, and desegregation.

Noar, Gertrude. *Teaching the Disadvantaged.* Washington, D.C.: Association of Classroom Teachers, NEA, 1967. The characteristics of the disadvantaged and their problems, one of the "What Research Says to the Teacher" series, which summarizes the research findings on various aspects of instruction.

Ornstein, Allan C. and Philip D. Vairo. *How to Teach Disadvantaged Youth.* New York: David McKay, 1969. A how-to-do-it book on working with disadvantaged learners. Emphasis on practicality.

Passow, A. Harry, ed. *Developing Programs for the Educationally Disadvantaged.* New York: Teachers College Press, Columbia University, 1968. Seventeen papers on setting, compensatory programs, research, reading, segregation and racial imbalance.

Rees, Helen E. *Deprivation and Compensatory Education.* Boston: Houghton Mifflin, 1968. Substantial information on programs and projects for disadvantaged children and adults.

Riessman, Frank. *The Culturally Deprived Child.* New York: Harper and Row, 1962. One of the earliest books which called the attention of Americans to the existence of cultural deprivation among young people by raising questions as to characteristics and possible emphases.

Storen, Helen F. *The Disadvantaged Early Adolescent: More Effective Teaching.* New York: McGraw-Hill, 1968. Help for the teacher of the middle school and junior high school years by an experienced teacher and professor.

Stuart, Jesse. *The Thread That Runs So True.* New York: Charles Scribner's Sons, 1949. Nostalgic account of teaching in the American hill country.

Terkel, Studs. *Division Street: America.* New York: Pantheon Books, 1967. A series of interviews with people in Chicago in the late 1960s demonstrating the mosaic of views on society and life which exists in America.

Warden, Sandra A. *The Leftouts: Disadvantaged Children in Heterogeneous Schools.* New York: Holt, Rinehart and Winston, 1968. Educationally disadvantaged children scattered throughout homogeneous schools and "left out" of opportunities because age mates are better prepared for schooling academically and socially.

Webster, Staten W., ed. *The Disadvantaged Learner: Knowing, Understanding, Educating.* San Francisco: Chandler, 1966. A realistic helpful introduction to the disadvantaged learner through 73 articles edited by a black scholar well qualified to report research developments.

AUDIO-VISUAL MATERIALS

A Desk for Billie (National Education Association, 57 Min.) The true story of a child of migrant parents and her struggle to get an education in the public schools.

The Search for Excellence (N. C. Film Board, 29 Min.) Discusses the role of the consolidated school with reference to changing communities, boundary shifts and teaching resources. Photographed in Winston-Salem, Greenville, Charlotte and Waynesville areas.

Teaching Deprived Kindergarten Children (Teachers College Press Columbia University, 91 frs., Color, Record) Describes an experimental program for teaching kindergarten children from a disadvantaged neighborhood in New York City. Outlines the major teaching strategies, discusses the formulation of academic needs and concept development and shows how these needs can be met.

Critical Moments in Teaching: Tense Imperfect (Holt, Rinehart, and Winston, Inc., 11 Min., Color) Problems of teaching adolescents of a low economic area secondary school. A stimulus for discussion and analysis of the situation.

Critical Moments in Teaching: First and Fundamental R (Holt, Rinehart and Winston, 12 Min., Color) An elementary class of culturally deprived children is making very little progress in learning to read. The children are inattentive and generally uninterested. The problem of what to do is explored.

Portrait of the Inner-City School—A Place to Learn (Vision Associates, 19 Min.) Discusses some of the creative ways in which school teachers and administrators can approach the problem of teaching pupils from the disadvantaged inner city. Points out how these pupils view school. Underscores the importance of the classroom climate.

Portrait of the Inner City (Vision Assciates, 15 Min.) Pictures life in the inner-city slum area. Shows both the positive and negative aspects of growing up in poverty-stricken areas.

Teaching the Disadvantaged (National Education Association, 52 frs. Color, Record) Describes the characteristics of disadvantaged children and discusses their learning handicaps. Contrasts the teaching methods by which they may be reached with those which are ineffective, and points out some of the problems of each age group.

Children Without (Guggenheim Productions, 29 Min.) This picture was filmed in the Franklin School in Detroit, Michigan, where special programs have been established to work with underprivileged children.

John Kenneth Galbraith: The Idea of the City: History, Economics, Future (University-at-Large, 29 Min. color) Galbraith traces the historical transition from the preindustrial to the industrial city and explores the nature and consequences of commitment to "economic efficiency." The inadequacies of our present cities are analyzed. The forces already reshaping our cities are diagnosed and Galbraith develops a new organic concept of the modern city.

Four Families, Part 1 (National Film Board of Canada, McGraw-Hill, 28 Min.) Discusses family life and child care in India and France. Intra-family relations, duties and responsibilities, and relationships to child care are discussed by Margaret Mead.

Four Families, Part 2 (National Film Board of Canada, McGraw-Hill, 29 Min.) Family customs in Japan and on the Canadian prairies are explored. Margaret Mead discusses infant dress, roles of family members, eating patterns, bathing the baby and the child's place in the home.

FOURTEEN

HOW DO LEARNERS DIFFER?

No matter how we try to group people, we eventually have to acknowledge individuality. To get some clues to human behavior we may use such sociological groupings as those described in the last two chapters: social classes, ethnic backgrounds, and community backgrounds. Yet experience repeatedly tells us that the resulting classifications are imperfect. Each person remains an individual. Regardless of measurements—whether they be anatomical, biological, physiological, mental, or social—human beings differ each from the other.

The inevitability of individuality is certainly apparent in education and the schools. No matter how we try to group children and youth we find that each young person is unique; each differs in interests, motives, talents, aptitudes, ideas. Each has different habits and different life styles; each differs in his needs and in his sensitivities. In education as in life the norm is a myth.

Yet societies develop schools with supposedly natural groupings. American society provides rough groupings in the form of rural, city, and suburban schools, since students come to the schools from these community backgrounds. American society often provides still more supposedly homogeneous groupings—neighborhood schools attended by students of some particular ethnic background whose families live in that particular neighborhood.

When students appear at the doors of these schools, educators attempt to group them further, presumably on the assumption that greater homogeneity leads to better instruction. One such grouping, until recently taken for granted as desirable, is grouping on the basis of age. The popular educational assumption is still that all first graders must be six years old and all high school graduates (to whom we allow a slightly higher degree of variability) should be approximately seventeen or eighteen.

Only recently, through the device of the nongraded school which groups young people from several grades (such as a primary years grouping or a middle years grouping), have we challenged the long accepted age separation of grades. By definition, nongrading breaks away from conventional grade-level instruction

In this nongraded Early Learning Center in Stamford, Conn., children of ages 2–8 learn together. Courtesy of George S. Zimbel from EFL.

(see chapter 18), and it enables students to advance according to their individual capabilities. Many school systems with nongraded programs use multi-age groupings which bring together in a nongraded class students who are at similar levels of accomplishment in one or more subjects.

Certainly, all children or youth of the same age are far from alike. Sorting children into age groups is far from a satisfactory way of dealing with human diversity.

DIFFERENCES IN INTELLIGENCE

In the quest for "natural" groupings, educators group students on the basis of intelligence. Yet psychologists are far from able to define what intelligence is. Nonetheless, they have developed a variety of intelligence tests which purport to measure intelligence, and in present day American society such tests have a powerful influence on decisions important to all of us. They are frequently an important determinant in who goes to which college, who joins the armed forces or gets drafted, and who gets which job. Intelligence tests may well be the single most important and influential invention of the profession of psychology; they have increasingly become centers of controversy not only in American education but also in American life.

DEVELOPMENT OF INTELLIGENCE TESTS

The practice of intelligence testing began in the latter part of the nineteenth century. James McKeen Cattell first used the phrase "mental test" in 1890.[1] In

---

[1] Read D. Tuddenham, "Intelligence," *Encyclopedia of Educational Research*, 4th. ed., p. 654.

1905, a Frenchman, Alfred Binet, developed the first widely used intelligence test.[2] He asked his subjects to engage in a variety of tasks such as defining words, repeating sentences and numbers, counting, and copying simple figures. Binet's scale enabled examiners to determine if a child had the ability to perform the same tasks as the "average" child of his age.[3] In a revision of his scale, Binet proceeded to allocate items according to age in months. So he developed a mental age score which was the same as the age of a supposedly average child who passed the same number of items on the test.

The term and the concept "intelligence quotient" was suggested in 1912 by the German psychologist, William Stern. An American, Lewis M. Terman, pushed the testing movement further in 1916 when he published a standardized revision of Binet's scale and called it the Stanford-Binet Scale. Through his test, Terman became the "father" of intelligence testing in the United States because, although there were others who preceded his attempts, none were as successful.

The Stanford-Binet became the test against which most subsequent tests were measured and mental testing spread rapidly and widely in American schools. The IQ was calculated by dividing a young person's mental age as measured on the test by his chronological age and multiplying the result by 100. The Stanford-Binet Scale was revised and restandardized on new norms in 1937 and again in 1960.[4] As statistical sophistication increased, the 1960 version used a newer approach to determine the IQ. Today the Stanford-Binet test is one of the most frequently used intelligence tests.

Despite the widespread use of intelligence tests by the nation's social institutions, especially the schools in recent decades, the basic question of what *is* intelligence has remained incompletely answered. Both the cynical and the serious have sometimes said that intelligence is what the tests measure! But surely this is not a sufficient definition.

An early interpretation of intelligence was that the test measured not only specific factors but also a general factor, called "g"; it was thought that there existed a measurable unitary trait of general intelligence. Charles E. Spearman stressed this concept, and he proposed that a single test be substituted for the heterogeneous collection of items found in most intelligence tests.

But later researchers concluded that there were multiple factors in intelligence. J. P. Guilford recognized three broad classes which he termed operations, products, and content. Content factors are essentially figural, symbolic, semantic, or behavioral. Product factors involved units, classes, relations, systems, transformations, or implications. Operations factors have to do with memory, cognition, divergent thinking, convergent thinking, and evaluation.[5] Today many psychologists increasingly think that intelligence is not a simple unitary trait, but a complex combination of many components.

---

[2] Henry Clay Lindgren, *Educational Psychology in the Classroom* (New York: John Wiley and Sons, 1962), p. 434.
[3] *Ibid.*   [4] *Ibid.*, p. 436.
[5] Tuddenham, p. 657.

NEW DIMENSIONS CONCERNING THE IQ

Yet as the psychologists have struggled with their definitions of intelligence, the schools have continued using the relatively simple instrument called the IQ test. However, the familiar assumptions concerning IQ tests are being increasingly challenged today.

The earlier mental testers thought that the IQ remained constant throughout one's life (assuming that the original basic test and follow-up tests were well conducted). Yet, while it is true in general that the bright remain bright and the dull remain dull, it is not true that an individual IQ always remain constant. Shifts as high as fifty IQ points have occurred; the more usual changes, however, do not go beyond fifteen points in the school years of the child.

How can such large changes as fifty points be accounted for, asssuming the tests were competently handled? According to the strict advocates of the importance of heredity, such marked changes should never take place. According to the exponents of the power of the environment, such changes can be accounted for through changes in the setting and situation in which the young person grew up. The English scholar-philosopher, John Locke, recognized the two schools of thought on this question. As early as 1693 Locke wrote, "God has stamped certain characters upon men's minds, which, like their shapes, may perhaps be a little mended but can hardly be totally altered and transformed into the contrary."[6] Yet in his discussions on the choice of a tutor and on the relative influence of the home and school on the child's upbringing, he was well aware of environmental influences on the individual's behavior.[7]

The conflict between proponents of the power of heredity and supporters of the strength of environment has persisted through the centuries and each side has had its say. In the struggle about "nature" (heredity) and "nurture" (environment), contemporary scholars increasingly take a middle position. They hold that both the genes and the social situation are important. This middle position supports the possibility that an IQ can be influenced by the intellectual or educational level of the family or, indeed, by migration to a more stimulating geographical environment. For instance, a study by Everett S. Lee showed that Negro children who moved from Southern situations which were largely rural and segregated to the more "stimulating" environment of a Northern city and its desegregated school system, raised their IQ scores. The younger the child, the more likely was the rise in IQ.[8]

Research has documented that, *in general*, the higher the individual's social class the higher he will score on the usual IQ tests. Similarly, in the past Negroes have *in general* recorded lower scores on the usual intelligence tests than whites. Some have attributed such differences to racial characteristics but psychologists

---

[6] F. W. Garforth (ed.), *John Locke: Some Thoughts Concerning Education* (Woodbury, N.Y.: Barron's Educational Series, 1964), p. 92.
[7] *Ibid.*, pp. 24, 98 ff.
[8] Everett S. Lee, "Negro Intelligence and Selective Migration: A Philadelphia Test of the Klineberg Hypothesis," *American Sociological Review*, 16 (April 1951), pp. 227–233.

overwhelmingly reject this theory. The question was reopened by Arthur Jensen in the *Harvard Educational Review,* Winter 1969.[9] Vigorous criticism of Jensen's position by fellow psychologists followed in the Spring issue of the *Review,*[10] and the debate continues.

Studies of intelligence of blacks and whites show wide overlap between distributions of scores, rather than support the assumption that "all" whites are superior in intelligence through hereditary factors to "all" Negroes. Differences within the white race are equally as large as differences within the black race. Studies of intelligence of Negroes also show that regional differences within those Americans who were classified as blacks, particularly Northern-Southern differences, can be as large as the differences between the races. Similarly, studies of American Indians and Mexican-Americans do not support those who believe that innate differences exist and that such minorities are "inferior people as to brains."

The question of whether or not environment is a powerful factor which makes a significant difference in the IQ scores engages many scholars. That it does is indicated by such studies as that of Benjamin Bloom which testify that impoverishment of the environment may depress the IQ by as much as twenty points.[11] Many scholars have pointed out that IQ tests are not completely culture free or culture fair. Recent reconsiderations of intelligence testing lend support to those who refuse to accept the result of intelligence tests as a necessary predestination for the individual.

Too long have children and youth suffered from teachers learning of an individual's IQ score and then promptly assuming that nothing can be done for the relatively low scoring individual. Scholars now think that there is a range within which the individual can operate. Whether he operates toward the bottom or the top of his range depends on factors susceptible to change—such as family influences, the quality of the environment, and—most important of all to teachers—the quality of the educational experience he encounters.

So the assumption is invalid that an intelligence quotient provides us with so remorseless a natural grouping that we can ignore the law of diversity. What is learned by each individual differs from what is learned by the rest of a group, despite similarities in IQ.

CATEGORIES AS TO INTELLIGENCE

It can be argued that generations of work with intelligence quotients have been useful in helping educators divide young people into broad descriptive categories—mentally retarded, normal, gifted, etc. The terms used for such

---

[9] Arthur R. Jensen, "How Much Can We Boost IQ and Scholastic Achievement?" *Harvard Educational Review,* 39 (Winter 1969), pp. 1–123.
[10] Jerome S. Kagan, J. McV. Hunt, James F. Crow, Carl Bereiter, David Elkind, Lee J. Cronbach, and William F. Brazziel, "Discussion: How Much Can We Boost IQ and Scholastic Achievement?" *Harvard Educational Review,* 39 (Spring 1969), pp. 273–356.
[11] Tuddenham, p. 663.

categories are not completely standardized, so do not be surprised if your professor of psychology or of psychology of education uses somewhat different cut-off points concerning categories than those described below.

Lowest of the IQ categories is the grouping of the mentally deficient, feeble-minded or mentally defective who range from zero to 50 on IQ scales. They include the nontrainable level, technically defined as between zero and about 20 or 25 on intelligence tests, who are noneducable and nontrainable; these people can learn no more than a two year old. The trainable level ranges from about 25 to 50 on IQ scales. People at this level are trainable to carry out simple routines or to care for their bodily needs; they are not educable in the usual sense of the word.

People with a tested IQ between approximately 50 and 70 are sometimes called the mentally handicapped or mentally retarded. Today the usual term is educable. Such people are educable in the sense that they can learn to read, write, and do simple arithmetic. They can develop limited occupational proficiency and can manage in society. Unlike the nontrainable and trainable, they attend regular schools and are often enrolled in classes titled "special education" or "education for the mentally retarded." Increasingly, the educable mentally retarded are placed in special classes rather than educated with other children and youth. Working with the mentally retarded is a field which calls for specialized training.

The higher up the IQ scale analysis goes, the more difficult it is to describe precisely the categories. This is the case with the borderline or slow learner category made up of people with IQs ranging roughly from 70 to 90. Even the category of "slow learner" is controversial, for some researchers—including Leona E. Tyler, a specialist on individual differences—warn us that slow learning or dull children are often slow developers. Such children may move to higher levels of understanding in time, but achieving understanding will take them longer. It is worth recalling that the British statesman Winston Churchill was thought by some of his teachers to be a slow learner!

Some authorities have estimated that about 20 to 24 percent of the child population falls into the category variously described as borderline or dull, slow learner or slow developer. Whatever the title given such a child, the fact remains that he is usually found in a regular class where he faces real difficulty in dealing with skills or information that normal or gifted children can readily acquire. School is a constant and frequently losing struggle for him.

Which grouping for the slow learner is best? Some educators attempt to resolve the problems by regarding the separation of the mentally retarded (IQ range of 50 to 70) as desirable, particularly when skillful and trained teachers of special education use appropriate methods and materials with such students. They argue that the gap separating the retarded individual from members of the regular class is too large and that the mentally retarded child is likely to be overwhelmed in the setting of the regular class and to be rejected by classmates. On the other hand, educators sometimes say that the slow learner (IQ range of 70 to 90) is sufficiently like the rest of the regular class in personality and background that he will be socially accepted, may make friends who may challenge him, and may not perceive himself as a failure.

The middle category is, of course, the average or normal range made up of children with IQs from approximately 90 to 110. Since about 45 to 50 percent of the population of pupils falls into this middle category, teachers who have difficulty dealing with individual differences often aim their lessons and teaching at this middle group.[12] Whether they hit their target is another matter.

Above average or superior students as to IQ are those whose intelligence quotients fall somewhere in the range between 110 and 130. Pleasant names are applied to them—rapid learners, superior students, able people, apt students, etc. They too are usually found in the regular classes. Consequently, they are often the class leaders academically and socially; teachers point to them with pride.

In the category of an IQ ranging roughly from 130 to 170 are the students who are classified as gifted or very superior. Such students often regard school work as a "breeze." If the teacher focuses his instruction only on the average student and ignores individual differences, a gifted youngster may soon become bored and may even develop antisocial behavior in the classroom. It is sometimes surprising to a new teacher to learn of the sizable number of gifted people attending his school.

There is a good deal of controversy as to what IQ constitutes the lower level of giftedness. When a school begins a program of grouping certain students as gifted, the controversy is particularly sharp. In some situations, the gifted group is open to only those above 140; in other situations, a student with a measured IQ of 115 may be admitted. Contrary to the prevalent stereotype, gifted children are not usually sickly, weak, and nonathletic; studies show them to be above average in general in health, strength, and physical agility.[13]

At the top of the groupings by intellect is, of course, the category made up of persons who are exceptionally superior. Arbitrarily, the lower level for this category has sometimes been set at 170. There is no known upper cut-off point. Such people at the very top of the intellectual scale are often well rounded as to various aspects of intelligence, at least well rounded enough to score above 170 on intelligence tests. The need for recognizing individual differences in the case of the exceptionally superior thinker, sometimes called "the genius," is obvious. The word genius, incidentally, might best be reserved for those who have produced works of genius through significant contributions of enduring value, as in the case of the musical genius or the artistic genius or the scientific genius, a person of magnificent virtuosity regardless of his IQ score.

HOMOGENEOUS VERSUS HETEROGENEOUS GROUPING

With respect to intellectual differences among children and youth, educators face a familiar dilemma. On one hand, they cannot help but be aware of the existence of individual differences. On the other hand, the school is not organ-

---

[12] R. Murray Thomas and Shirley M. Thomas, *Individual Differences in the Classroom* (New York: David McKay, 1965), p. 90.
[13] *Ibid.*, p. 91.

ized today as an individual tutorial system but operates through groups, some of them quite large. How can there be provisions for individual differences in an institution geared not to individuals but to groups? Possibly the new technology being developed for schools, such as computer-aided instruction, will contribute in the future to the achievement of greater individualization. In the past and the present, educators have attempted to resolve the dilemma by making groups more consistent or homogeneous; but in the process many problems have emerged because educators also have to deal with individuality.

Possibly the most popular way of attempting to meet individual differences that relate to learners' intellectual abilities involves the organization of groups. One organizational way of dealing with divergent intellectual abilities which has been used in American education is "homogeneous" grouping on the basis of intelligence. Homogeneous grouping brings together students who are presumably similar in intellectual ability. It is the opposite of "heterogeneous" grouping which involves grouping together students who represent a wide range of intellectual ability.

In homogeneous grouping pupils are usually first sorted according to grade levels, which primarily represent divisions according to age. Then the students are divided according to their ability, frequently on the threefold basis of slow, normal, and fast learner.

Proponents of homogeneous ability grouping advance several arguments. They claim that when the materials and methods and specific objectives are adjusted to the particular learning group, students make better academic progress in a class with others with the same ability range than if they were in a heterogeneous class. In this case the teacher does not have the problem of dealing with as wide an ability range. Nor is it fair to the learner to expect him to compete with a person of superior ability or to be held back by slow learners. In general, parents support ability grouping (though they sometimes have inaccurate but firm ideas to to which group their own child should be in!), and in general teachers prefer teaching intellectually similar children to teaching diverse children in heterogeneous groups.

The case for homogeneous ability grouping sounds persuasive; why then does ability grouping not universally prevail? Why does the introduction of ability grouping ebb and flow in American education, rising in one period and falling during a subsequent decade?

Opponents of ability grouping contend that in large part the difficulty is traceable to the undeniable fact of human individuality. While the bright tend in general to be bright in all ways and the dull tend in general to be dull in all ways, significant individual variations persist. As a result, an elementary school student may rate placement in the bright group in verbal abilities but only in the normal group in quantitative abilities. The supposedly dull student may prove to be quite competent in some particular subject. And even in the group which appears homogeneous intellectually, there is actually a considerable range of variation. If the teacher of this group does not individualize through a variety of techniques—just as he presumably individualizes in teaching in a heterogenous group—learning will not go forward very briskly.

Another argument used against homogeneous grouping is of a social nature. The American democratic ideal envisions the classless and integrated school which teaches children and youth of all backgrounds to live and work together with mutual respect and acceptance. What happens to the dream in schools which use homogeneously grouped classes in a society in which the supposedly intellectual differences actually reflect differing social and cultural backgrounds? Is the result a degree of snobbery on the part of the "superior" group often made up of socially advantaged young people? Is the result submission or rebellion on the part of the "inferior" group, often composed of the socially disadvantaged?

Another claimed disadvantage of homogeneous grouping has a psychological base; it can best be comprehended by considering the "slow learners." Their perceptions of themselves must be taken into account, too, and their self-identities must not be derogated. Each person has a picture of himself which he learns in large part from the way others see him. He tends to accept this picture of himself as true and behave accordingly. If this be so, say the psychologists, the lesson may be driven home every day to the slow learners that they are the dull and stupid, the dummies who will never amount to much. Would they not build more constructive and positive self-identities if placed in heterogeneous classes?

One compromise offered as an alternative to homogeneous grouping is assigning students to special classes or to tutoring for part of the school experience, perhaps through an hour or two during the school day or after school. A slow learner might have remedial reading experiences or a gifted child might work in a science laboratory or an honors class. Special interests and needs are thus maximized.

ACCELERATION AND RETENTION

Another approach in the eternal quest by the school to place supposedly similar children and youth together and thereby outwit the law of human variability, takes the form of acceleration and retention, sometimes called "skipping" or "being left back."

Accelerating the child a grade or a half grade on one or more occasions gives him the opportunity to take on advanced work. Since presumably his ability level is closer to the intellectual level of students a grade level beyond him than to the intellectual level of his present classmates and age mates, the child or youth is advanced to the higher grade. Yet the haunting question as to acceleration is whether possible resulting social, physical, and emotional handicaps are worth the possible intellectual gain. Consequently, when acceleration takes place, forward-looking educators find it advisable to take into account not only intellectual factors but also the social maturity, emotional stability, the physical prowess, and even quite literally the size of the individual. One well known study which has reassured some educators concerning the effects of acceleration was conducted by the same Lewis E. Terman who developed IQ tests. Terman and his associates in *Mental and Physical Traits of a Thousand Gifted Children*[14] and *The Gifted Child Grows Up*[15] reached the conclusion that acceleration was not usually harmful, in general, to the gifted child's social, physical, or emotional development. Terman pointed out that in most cases feelings of inferiority were soon overcome. Yet some educators are not persuaded of the desirability of acceleration and the haunting question persists.

As to retention, the idea that a student will benefit from nonpromotion has not been supported by research. Retention or nonpromotion is often defended on the assumption that the student would master on a second try the material he did not understand before and that he would work harder because of a fear of failing. As early as 1954, Henry J. Otto in a book on elementary education made the following statements:

> It is now evident that practically all of the notions previously held about the value of nonpromotion or the motivating value of the threat of failure have been exploded. Out of a group of repeaters, about 20 percent will do better than they did the preceding term, about 40 percent will show no change, and about 40 percent will actually do worse. If doubtful cases are divided into two groups appropriately matched on essential items, and one group is promoted and the other group is held back to repeat the grade, several studies have shown that the achievement of the promoted group, as measured by standardized tests, is equal to or greater than the achievement of the group held back. . . . As far as personality adjustment is concerned, group studies show that the adjustment of pupils of low achievement is not more satisfactory when they are retained in grade groups more nearly representative of their levels of achievement. Numerous cases are on record which show the contribution which nonpromotion, especially repeated nonpromotion, has made to the personality maladjustment of individual cases.[16]

Those educators favoring retention cannot defend their case through the argument that the child benefits; consequently, they fall back on arguments that school standards must be maintained and that the work of the teacher will be simplified by retention. Opponents retort that standards must be flexible and individual-related and that schools are for learners, not for the convenience of teachers.

DIFFERENCES IN CREATIVITY

Just as children and youth differ in intellectual competencies, they also differ

---

[14] Lewis M. Terman, *Mental and Physical Traits of a Thousand Gifted Children* (Stanford, Calif.: Stanford University Press, 1925).
[15] Lewis M. Terman and Melita H. Oden, *The Gifted Child Grows Up* (Stanford, Calif.: Stanford University Press, 1947).
[16] Henry J. Otto, *Elementary School Organization and Administration* (New York: Appleton-Century-Crofts, 1954), pp. 268–269.

The preschool offers very young children varied experiences to help their total development. Courtesy of William Simmons from Ford Foundation.

with respect to special abilities. Some are especially creative in the arts or music or science, etc. Throughout history man has been aware of the existence of especially creative people. Indeed, man's recorded history is largely the account of the activities of such people. But only since approximately 1955 has substantial research begun on a variety of unknown matters relating to creativity.[17] Among the present findings of the scholars of creativity is the conviction that all people are to some degree creative or potentially creative, regardless of their age, their cultural background, or the field in which they specialize. Yet students of creativity also recognize the law of individual variability, for they assure us that individuals differ in their creative potential in various fields and in their varied ways of expression.

One of the lively arguments concerning creativity deals with the extent to which the creative person is or is not identical with the intellectual person. Few deny some degree of relationship; students of creativity have also pointed out differences. Calvin Taylor, a researcher and writer in the field of creativity, says:

> Certain intellectual characteristics, for instance, appear to have some relationship with creative performance; these fall within the categories of memory, cognition, evaluation, convergent production, and divergent production. The divergent-production factors, including fluencies and flexibilities, seem to be most important. The fact that these intellectual aspects of creativity are relatively

---

[17] Calvin W. Taylor, (ed.), *Creativity: Progress and Potential* (New York: McGraw-Hill, 1964), p. 2.

Education involves much more than only academics. Both photos courtesy of DeWys.

distinct components indicates the probability of multiple types of creative talent. The generally low correlation of these factors with intelligence test scores suggests that creative talent is not only various, but relatively different from intelligence.[18]

No one claims that all frontiers of creativity, including its relationship to intelligence, are yet explored. Among the scarcely known areas of high interest to students of creativity are explanations for the decrease in creativity which seems to occur in the early school years. Too, we know relatively little about the development of creativity during the later school years. Still further specific suggestions, tested materials, and procedures are needed if we are going to develop, rather than block, creative learning at the various school levels.

But some suggestions of ways to develop creativity are ventured, as those summarized by E. Paul Torrance who considers nurturing creativity in elementary schools:

1. Value creative thinking.
2. Help children become more sensitive to environmental stimuli.
3. Encourage manipulation of objects and ideas.
4. Teach how to test each idea systematically.
5. Develop tolerance of new ideas.
6. Beware of forcing a set pattern.
7. Develop a creative classroom atmosphere.
8. Teach the child to value his creative thinking.

[18] *Ibid.*, p. 179.

9. Teach children skills of avoiding or coping with peer sanctions without sacrificing their creativity.
10. Give information about the creative process.
11. Dispel the sense of awe of masterpieces.
12. Encourage and evaluate self-initiated learning.
13. Create "thorns in the flesh," making children aware of problems and deficiencies.
14. Create necessities for creative thinking.
15. Provide for active and quiet periods.
16. Make available resources for working out ideas.
17. Encourage the habit of working out the full implications of ideas.
18. Develop skills of constructive criticism.
19. Encourage acquisition of knowledge in a variety of fields.
20. Be adventurous-spirited yourself.[19]

In general, it makes good sense for the creativity-fostering teacher to introduce all youth to various media and opportunities in such fields as art and music. It is helpful to open up many possibilities to the student. The teacher should also individualize potential creative experiences by using such techniques as working in small groups, giving individual assignments, sponsoring projects, and generally individualizing classroom procedures so that as many students as possible can realize their creative potentials.

DIFFERENCES IN HANDICAPS

Just as there are intellectual and creative abilities which differ widely, handicaps also unfortunately exist and greatly differ. Physical obstacles of students most often encountered by teachers include those of sight, hearing, speech, crippling, disfiguring, and cerebral palsy.

With respect to such handicaps, the first necessity is to recognize them. The teacher certainly recognizes total blindness, deafness, inability to communicate, etc. But the teacher may not be equally aware that he can expect approximately 20 percent of children to suffer from visual defects, 5 percent or possibly more from hearing problems, and about 5 to 10 percent from speech problems serious enough to require special attention. Many children and young people with such handicaps will be found in the regular classroom.

Too, the teacher sometimes fails to diagnose the problems he encounters with a sufficient degree of accuracy. Many hard-of-hearing students who are not deaf but who are below the normal hearing level are wrongly diagnosed by teachers as slow learners. Some stutterers are thought to suffer from an unremediable physical handicap, though actually it may be some degree of emotional disturbance. However, many teachers are increasingly aware of the non-physiological origins of speech handicaps and of the availability of speech therapy resources. The referral of handicapped children to such specialized sources,

[19] Ibid., pp. 92–93.

whether within the school or the community, is desirable. But special help, when available, will only be used if the teacher is sensitive to the existence of a problem.

After recognition of handicaps and seeking help from available school and community sources, the teacher might well stress two approaches. For one, the teacher should do all of the common sense things by way of adaptation of the school environment to reduce the degree of the individual's handicap. These include attention to lighting problems, moving hard-of-hearing young people within close range of the center of the classroom action, and special attention to children and youth with speech handicaps. The most useful adaptation of all is individualizing instruction.

There is an additional adaptation which cannot be overlooked—working with the class as a whole for greater understanding and acceptance of the individual with the handicap. How easy it is for a child with a handicap to become the butt of the cruelty, however innocent or unintentional, directed against him by classmates! The scorn or jeering of classmates can contribute further to the difficulties the handicapped child may be experiencing, not only in attempting to cope with his handicap but also in his relationships with his parents and with others outside the school. With an understanding teacher and accepting classmates, the handicapped child may have a fighting chance of being able to live with or even conquer his handicap. Without these supports, he is in deep trouble.

DIFFERENCES IN INDIVIDUAL BEHAVIOR PROBLEMS

Individual differences occur not only with respect to the intelligence, creativity, and physical handicaps of children and youth. Individual differences in the form of behavior variations also occur, and are myriad. From the teacher's point of view, behavior differences are particularly obvious when they take such negative forms as delinquency or dropping out of school. These two deviant behaviors are, of course, only a small sample of possible behavioral manifestations growing out of the pressures of the surrounding society. Would that teachers were always especially sensitive to positive behavior, such as the behavior of children and youth who exercise constructive leadership in the school and community! But behavior problems are more obvious and appear more urgent to new teachers.

JUVENILE DELINQUENCY

In a period in which Americans are deeply troubled by the prevalence of crime, juvenile delinquency poses a major problem for schools. Who is the juvenile delinquent? Juvenile delinquents are people who are in trouble. He or she can be of any race or social class. The delinquent reacts to his problem with outward aggressive behavior. He does so in a society which finds his conduct bothersome and contrary to how it believes life should be. Again, we must recognize that he is an individual and must be treated as such.

Social forces largely account for delinquency. Today few hold to the obsolete theories of the nineteenth century Italian criminologist Cesare Lombroso, who compared anthropological measurements of human beings and reached the conclusion that the criminal was a type marked by distinct physical traits. The related idea that criminality is somehow inherited through the genes has also been abandoned. This is not to deny that criminals may not breed criminals through family environmental influences. But the locus of the making of the criminal and the delinquent, it is commonly agreed, is to be found in his surroundings rather than in the bumps on his head or in his genetic history.

According to research studies of delinquency, summarized by William C. Kvaraceus among others, the delinquent is more likely than the nondelinquent to be characterized by the following environment and experience:

Living in slum areas
Overcrowded, poorly furnished and badly kept homes
Poverty and deprivation
Bad home conditions
No family recreation
Parents less interested in his future
Home characterized by quarreling, rejection, and indifference
Discipline, if not completely lacking, depending heavily on physical punishment
Less mental ability
Ten points lower than nondelinquent on IQ scales
Instability
Resentment of authority
Emotional conflicts
Inclination to look for adventure away from home
Disliking school
Lacking career plans
Doing poorly in school
Receiving low grades
Failing to be promoted
Behaving badly
Escaping through truancy.

A word of caution is in order. As you read such characteristics as "living in slum areas," "poverty and deprivation," "bad home conditions," the thought may occur to you that you know of—or you may even know personally—some delinquents who live in relative affluence surrounded by good home conditions in privileged communities. Yes, juvenile delinquency does exist in America's Scarsdales and Evanstons and in exclusive "Main Line" and "North Shore" communities, as well as in the bitter city slums. But the generalization nevertheless holds—the life of the delinquent is *more likely* to be marked by the characteristics cited above than the life of the nondelinquent. Yet your recognition of the reality of delinquency among upper-middle- and lower-upper-class young people supplies further evidence that the juvenile delinquent, like other human beings, must ultimately be seen as an individual.

Members of two gangs take part in a work project combatting delinquency. Courtesy of Arthur Leipzig from Ford Foundation.

Schooling is no panacea for juvenile delinquency. The roots of delinquency are social, emotional, and deep. Juvenile delinquency is complex; it is multiple-caused.

A good illustration of what is meant by "multiple-caused" and the significance of this conception is furnished by the history of investigations into the causes of delinquency. During the 1920's and 1930's, investigators such as Shaw and McKay (1931, 1942) provided data indicating that there is a relationship between urban delinquency rates and distance from the center of the city. The highest rates were found near the center of the city, with rates decreasing gradually as one moved away from the center. Although there was a significant correlation, it was not high. There were many exceptions. This led Healey and Bronner (1936) to pose the question, why, of two children living in the *same* home and under the *same* environmental conditions, one becomes delinquent and the other does not. Their inquiry involving 105 delinquents paired with 105 sibling controls, indicated that a variety of blocked emotional forces such as feeling rejected, deprived, or thwarted, internal mental conflicts, or a sense of guilt, characterized 96 of the 105 cases. The remaining nine without marked emotional stress revealed such factors as various social pressures, lack of supervision, and poor family standards. . . .

Recent studies of the role in delinquency of the self concept (Lively and others, 1962; S. Smith, 1965; Scarpitti, 1965; Fannin, 1965), attitudes engendered by social status (Robins and others, 1962), opportunities to achieve (Cloward and Ohlin, 1960; Landis and Scarpitti, 1965), and difficulty in developing an ego

One of the counselor's services is discussing job possibilities with students. Courtesy of Rondal Partridge for EFL.

identity (Erik Erikson, 1959) further extend the list of factors suspected of having causative roles in deviant behavior.[20]

Delinquency similarly requires multiples cures, some of which are hard to apply. For instance, we know delinquents often need love; yet of all the persons whom it is hard to love, it is the angry, hostile, suspicious juvenile delinquent! Nevertheless, the need for love is inescapable.

If a school—or even one teacher—can create for the potential or actual juvenile delinquent an atmosphere of acceptance, belongingness, affection, and being wanted, the delinquent may be helped. Delinquents need such a surrounding atmosphere for they are short on acceptance and understanding. In many cases, they have not found it in their homes. Too often they can find acceptance and understanding only in the antisocial behavior of their gang. They will not find acceptance and understanding in the type of school in which coldness and suspicion and tension are dominant and where rigidity and unnecessary regulations are paramount.

It may be that what the juvenile delinquent needs most of all from his school is some humane person to listen to him. This may be the guidance counselor; it might also be his classroom teacher.

You have probably heard the charge that education contributes to juvenile delinquency. Usually this is accompanied by the advice to teachers that they "get tough," an admonition sometimes accompanied by references to going back to the nineteenth century use of the razor strap and the woodshed for physically punishing young people. Yet beatings may only harden the delinquent in his belief that he is alone in the world and must regard all men as his enemies.

---

[20] Ralph H. Ojemann, "Behavior Problems," *Encyclopedia of Educational Research*, 4th. ed., p. 101.

The school can also be a recreational area for its students. Courtesy of Gerald Davis from Pictoral Parade.

The irony of the situation is that education may be a causative factor in delinquency—but because of restrictiveness rather than over-permissiveness. To the degree that education may be guilty of contributing to delinquency, the true contributor may be the teacher who manages his classroom arbitrarily and autocratically and who ignores the needs of the class members. In such classes the behavior problem may the teacher rather than the student!

But love alone, however important, is not enough. A vital curriculum is also needed. A good school can also help by giving young people a chance to take part in their education through working in groups, speaking out frankly in discussions and participating in extracurricular activities. The juvenile delinquent is usually active and adventurous; he needs outlets for his activities and for expression and he needs to come in contact with an increasingly wider world. If his school is one in which students sit passively while teachers tell them exactly what to do and exactly how to do it, there is likely to be classroom warfare between the teacher and the increasingly rebellious delinquent.

The potential juvenile delinquent especially needs a curriculum which includes vocational education and work experience. College entrance is seldom a motivating goal for a delinquent. A school which forces youngsters to work toward unattainable and/or irrelevant goals only contributes to delinquency. We should not forget that the typical delinquent is more likely to be a slower learner than others and often needs remedial help.

Certainly one major contribution to the prevention and control of delinquency which can be made by the schools is early identification of the problem. Once identified, the young person should be referred to diagnostic facilities so that the variety of factors operating in his case may be studied and remedial programs developed. Increasingly, remedial programs provide for consultation by mental health workers with teachers and other school personnel working closely with the youth involved. Though still woefully lacking, such diagnostic facilities are fortunately on the increase. They take the form of community child-guidance clinics, which have resulted in part from the work of the National Institute of Mental Health, and of residential receiving centers for juvenile delinquents. Diagnostic approaches are also provided by an increasing number of school psychological and guidance services. The best diagnosis of the difficulty and an appropriate plan of action is more likely to come from a multi-dimensional approach involving a variety of agencies, such as community clinics, schools, churches, employment facilities, recreational facilities, and health agencies rather than from any single source. Teachers should learn to work with a variety of community agencies if they are serious about combating delinquency.

Important though diagnosis may be, the importance of primary prevention should not be minimized. A delinquent child may benefit from the understanding help of a teacher or a counselor and a delinquent youth may be helped by placement in a job. But if other social circumstances remain the same and the delinquent returns nightly to a slum area or an inadequate family, there may be little real progress. The multiple causation of delinquency includes persisting social problems.

THE DROPOUT

The dropout is also an individual. A combination of circumstances account for his leaving school before graduation; each combination is different. Yet generalizations on the dropout can be stated, though not every dropout will represent each generalization.

Who is the typical dropout? The dropout is more likely to be a boy than a girl. He is usually just beyond his sixteenth birthday. His intelligence is average or slightly below average, as measured by intelligence tests. But he is usually not reading at his appropriate grade level. It is a good bet that academically he will rank in the lowest quarter of his class. He is probably slightly older than others in his grade for he has usually had the experience of having been held back once during the elementary and junior high school grades. The typical dropout leaves after the junior high school years and does not enter the doors of the senior high school.

The average dropout has encountered discipline problems in his career. But, contrary to an erroneous stereotype, the usual dropout is not a juvenile delinquent; most dropouts have no police record. Yet as compared with the non-dropout, the dropout has been in trouble more frequently with the law and more often has a police record.

The dropout feels that the school is not for him. He seldom takes part in extracurricular activities; he feels that the school and its representatives reject him and he in turn rejects the school. For instance, students at Modesto (California) High School who graduated and students who dropped out answered questions about their self concepts. Sixty-two percent of the dropouts answered affirmatively to the question "Do you feel spiteful toward other pupils?" whereas only 11 percent of the graduates answered affirmatively. Thirty-nine percent of the dropouts answered yes to question "Has a teacher ever rewarded or praised you?" whereas 88 percent of the graduates testified that this was the case. Sixty-two percent of the dropouts responded yes to the question "Do you feel you are a slow learner?" whereas 18 percent of the graduates saw themselves in this role. Forty-one percent of the dropouts answered affirmatively to the question "Do you have any skills that will help you get a job?" whereas 90 percent of the graduates thought they had such skills.[21] Feeling rejected by the school, the dropout in turn rejects the school.

The parents of the dropout often were themselves dropouts; it is more than likely that the dropout's older brothers and sisters also dropped out of school early. His friendships are usually made with people outside of the school and these include older dropouts.

His explanations as to why he dropped out of school are profuse and often anti-school. He frequently says that school is uninteresting, that he wants to earn money for himself, that he wants to contribute to his parents' support, etc. It is understandable that he cannot describe, at this stage of his life, the combination of factors which made his dropping out predictable. The dropout often explains that he intends to work for a high school diploma at night or through correspondence. But he usually does not achieve that diploma.

After dropping out, he has a hard time finding and keeping a job. Some studies have shown that at least half of the dropouts are unemployed for a substantial period immediately after leaving school. The jobs dropouts do get are frequently menial, such as washing cars, mowing lawns, cleaning up, household help, etc. Unemployment is usually markedly higher in the age groups from sixteen to nineteen than in other age groups. If the dropout also happens to be a member of a minority group, his chances of unemployment are usually still higher. The lifetime income of the dropout is substantially lower than that of the individual who graduates from high school. A 1964 calculation by the United States Department of Labor reported that the average lifetime earnings of males was $149,687 for elementary-school graduates, and $215,487 for high school graduates.[22]

Whether we seem to be doing well or badly in the 1970s on the problem of dropping out depends on how we state the situation. We can, for instance, say that in 1900, of every 100 pupils who made up the fifth grade only seven graduated from high school. By 1950 of every 100 pupils in the fifth grade, more than half graduated from high school. By the end of the 1960s, of every 100 pupils in the fifth grade about two-thirds graduated from high school. Thus, the percentage of students who dropped out before high school graduation has declined steadily throughout the twentieth century and nears one-fourth of all students in the early 1970s, with one-sixth anticipated as the probable dropout proportion in the mid-1970s.

[21] Daniel Schreiber, "Dropout Causes and Consequences," *Encyclopedia of Educational Research*, 4th. ed., p. 314.
[22] *Ibid.*, p. 309.

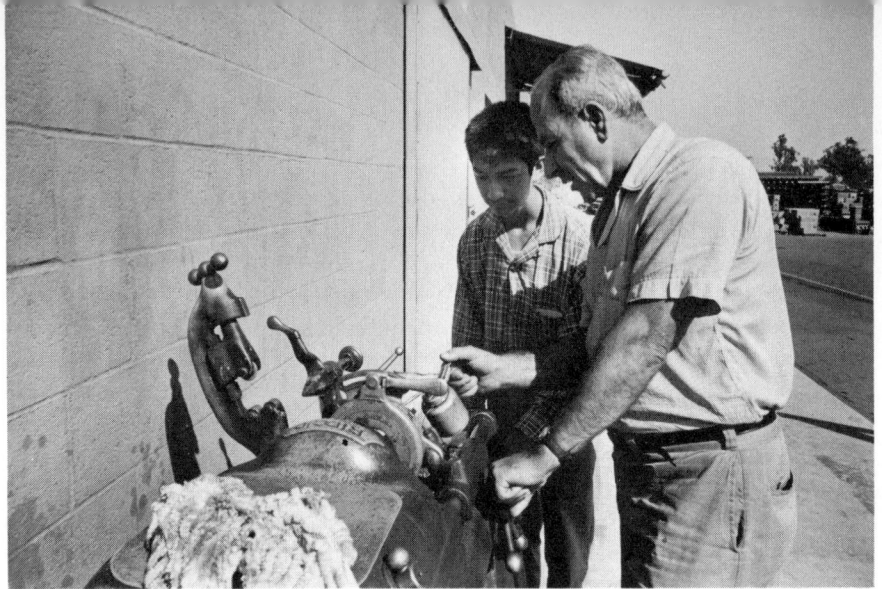

Students learning through a work-study program developed to keep young people in school. Courtesy of Arthur Leipzig from Ford Foundation.

Ours is a land in which college education is increasingly regarded as important to successful and happy living. Take six young people today; only one of them graduates from college. Of these six people, two left school without even graduating from high school, two graduated from high school but did not go on to college or related forms of advanced education, and one of them went to college but dropped out along the way.

To conquer the dropout problem, educators must develop programs adapted to the reality of individuality. Carl L. Byerly, after long experience as an administrator in public schools, recommends:

1. Building flexibility of various kinds into the program so that individual or group needs may be met when they occur. This may include length of periods, sequence of learning experiences, size of classes, combinations of content subjects, access to special services and so on.
2. Adaptation of both materials and procedures of instruction to the understanding, the cognitive level of the children concerned. This is recognition that intelligence, rather than being already fixed by genetic factors at birth, emerges as it is nurtured. Each stage of development carries with it possibilities for the acquisition of new abilities, new ways of processing information.
3. Strengthening the ego, building a positive self-image, as a primary objective of the school and its program. This means that each student has some successful learning experiences each day and that recognition is given when tasks are performed successfully. Teachers demonstrate confidence in and respect for the individuals in their classes.
4. Mustering the resources of social service agencies and professionals from other disciplines that are recognized as a necessary adjunct to bolster and

undergird the work of the school. This is recognition that (a) the competencies of the social worker, the psychologist, the psychiatrist, and the guidance counselor are needed to supplement the skill and abilities of teachers, and (b) that the home and the community provide a learning environment which may conspire to defeat the necessarily limited effort of the school unless a conscious effort is made to counteract their influences.[23]

HOW THE NEEDS OF LEARNERS ARE ALIKE

Throughout this chapter emphasis has been placed on how learners differ because of the inescapable fact of individuality. But individuality does not mean that no likenesses among people exist, including among learners in schools. There do exist basic human needs or urges or drives. Some of these are clearly physical, some are related to ego satisfaction, some arise through the social nature of man, and some occur because of man's insistent desire to know. For instance, John E. Horrocks lists twelve categories of psychological needs:

1. Acceptance. The need to feel that others' attitudes toward one are favorable or positive. To feel that others respect, sanction, or approve of one. To be secure in the feeling that one is a worthy person in another's eyes. To feel that others regard one as equal. To feel that one is not rejected.
2. Achievement. The need to acquire, gain, receive, win, or strive to accomplish goals, tokens of status and respect, or knowledge. To attain, secure, prove, surmount through praiseworthy exertion.
3. Affection. The need to be loved, cherished, emotionally wanted for one's own sake; to receive unconditional love and affection. To receive emotional love from parents, relatives, friends or lovers.
4. Approval. The need to have others' behavior toward one indicate that one is a satisfactory person, or that one's deeds are satisfactory. To seek overt rewards or other signs of approval. To be given overt demonstration by others of one's worthiness. To avoid blame, criticism, punishment.
5. Belonging. The need to feel a part of a group or institution. To identify oneself with a person, group institution, or idea. To be a member of a congenial group.
6. Conformity. The need to be like others, to avoid marked departure from the mode. To yield or conform to custom. To avoid being different in dress, behavior, attitudes, ideals.
7. Dependence. The need to have to ask for or depend on others for emotional support, protection, care, encouragement, forgiveness, help.
8. Independence. The need to be free of external control by friends, family, associates, and others. To do things in a self-determining manner, to make one's decisions, to be self-sufficient, to rely on oneself.

---

[23] Carl L. Byerly, "A School Curriculum for Prevention and Remediation of Deviancy," p. 280 in Daniel Schreiber (ed.), *Profile of the School Dropout* (New York: Vintage, 1967).

9. Mastery-dominance. The need to control, to be in power, to lead, to manage, govern, overcome people, problems, obstacles. To influence the behavior, feelings or ideas of others.
10. Recognition. The need to be noticed, to become known. To avoid effacement of one's individuality. To be identified by others as a unique individual, to be distinguished from others. To find one's place, to be regarded as an important human being.
11. Self-realization. The need to function at one's ability level. To learn, understand, perform to the best of one's ability, to avoid performing at a mediocre level. To strive for increasingly better accomplishment within the limits of one's capacity.
12. To be understood. The need to feel in sympathetic rapport with parents, relatives, friends, associates. To feel at one with others. To feel free to express one's innermost thoughts and problems to one or more persons without loss of affection or personal status. To feel that another identifies with oneself.[24]

Yet even with respect to such recognized human needs, one must recognize variation in intensity of a need among different individuals. The strength of the drives differ from learner to learner. Some categories of needs may be so weak as to approach the point of disappearance.

One of the verified laws in the behavioral sciences upon which educators can rely is that of individuality.

★ ★ ★

DISCUSSION
1. Why do schools group on the basis of age? What is the case for and against the use of age grouping?
2. In what ways have intelligence tests made an important difference in American life? What have been some of the social results of using intelligence quotients?
3. What are some possible meanings of intelligence? What seems a reasonable definition?
4. What is the point of view of the advocates of "nature"? Of "nurture"?
5. What seems to be the relationship of social class and ethnic backgrounds to scores on intelligence tests? What are the theories that attempt to account for the results? Which theories seem to have the greatest scientific support?
6. What are the dangers of abuse of IQ scores by teachers and parents?
7. What are the major categories of human intelligence? How reliable do they appear to be?

[24] John E. Horrocks, *The Psychology of Adolescence* (Boston: Houghton Mifflin, 1962), pp. 507–508.

8. What is the case for teaching the educable mentally retarded child in a special education class rather than absorbing him in a "regular" class? What is the case for teaching the "slow learner" of an IQ range of 70 to 90 in a special class rather than a "regular" class? Should the highly gifted be taught in separate classes or in relatively homogeneous classes with their fellow students?
9. Do you know of any recent legislation in the area of special education? What have been the results of earlier legislative decisions for education?
10. What special services are available to your school district's classroom teachers in serving the needs of children with special problems?
11. What constitutes giftedness? At what measurable level with respect to IQ does giftedness begin? Do you consider this accurate or arbitrary?
12. What are the arguments for and against homogeneous versus heterogeneous grouping in school? Is there a middle position? What types of groupings are most defensible?
13. What are the arguments for and against the use of acceleration by schools? The use of retention? Does supporting evidence for any of the positions in controversy exist?
14. To what extent are intelligence and creativity synonymous? To what extent do they differ?
15. What are some ways of developing creativity in elementary school? In high school? In higher education?
16. What are some common sense things a teacher can do to reduce an individual's physical handicap through adaptation of the school environment?
17. What are some characteristics of "positive" or "healthy" behavior? Why are these sometimes of less concern to the new teacher than negative or unhealthy manifestations of behavior?
18. Essentially, who is the juvenile delinquent? What characterizes him?
19. What do we know of possible ways of working against juvenile delinquency? What can the community contribute? What can education contribute?
20. Essentially, what are the characteristics of the dropout? How does he differ from the young person who stays in school?
21. What are some approaches to meeting the dropout problem?
22. To what extent are the needs of learners alike? Different? Do the common needs of learners invalidate the claim that one of the verified laws in the behavioral sciences is the law of individuality?

INVOLVEMENT
1. The next time you visit a school look particularly for whether or not the school provides "natural" groupings by way of the dimensions of social class, ethnic background, community background, age, homogeneous ability grouping, etc. According to your observations, do the resultant groupings markedly reduce the degree of heterogeneity among individuals?
2. Get acquainted with the nature of intelligence tests either from psychology of education books or from examining actual intelligence tests.

3. Report on your own experiences with the influence of intelligence testing on life decisions. Listen to the reports of others attempting the same analysis. What seem to be some of the implications concerning the use of intelligence tests in American life?

4. Carry on some careful investigation of the influences of social class, community background, and ethnic backgrounds—including racial backgrounds—on scores in intelligence tests. Take into account such problems as the criticism that tests are not "culture free" or "culture fair."

5. Take advantage of possible opportunities to visit classes which reflect the various categories as to intelligence reported in this chapter. Include special education classes. In what way do these differ from "regular" classes?

6. Interview a teacher involved in special education. Why was he attracted to this area and what does he see as its place in the total educational program?

7. Interview an experienced classroom teacher to get his perception of the differences that exist among children who have collectively been labeled "slow learners."

8. Visit a class where the teacher is working with the gifted. Find out what modern concepts are being used. How is the teacher of the gifted meeting the special needs of the learner?

9. Attempt to get at the "feeling level" with respect to homogeneous grouping by discussing candidly your own reactions to a possible proposal by your instructor that the group hereafter be taught by him in section groups according to intellectual ability.

10. Conduct a panel on such controversial issues as homogeneous versus heterogeneous grouping and questions of acceleration and retention. Attempt to clarify the case for approaches and recommendations.

11. Share your own experiences with others as to similarities or differences between creativity and intelligence.

12. Develop a set of suggestions applying particularly to your own subject field and/or level with respect to developing creativity in students.

13. Develop a list of common sense things you would do in a classroom to compensate for the physical handicaps of young people.

14. Visit social agencies in your community and nearby institutions for juvenile delinquents in order to get some exposure to the problem of juvenile delinquency. Visit court sessions. Talk to community workers and police officials, consult experienced teachers. Attempt to build your own program for combating juvenile delinquency.

15. Invite to class for interaction with your group the most knowledgeable people concerning juvenile delinquency available to you.

16. Talk with a guidance counselor about the problem of the dropout in the schools with which you are best acquainted. Consider with him what the schools might do to retain students. Should they? Is there a case for those who advocate dropping out rather than captivity in programs of "compulsory miseducation"? How should school programs be improved to reduce the desire to drop out?

17. Develop your own summary of how individuals are alike and how different; what commonalities and what diversities exist.

BIBLIOGRAPHY

Association for Supervision and Curriculum Development. *Individualizing Instruction.* 1964 Yearbook. Washington, D.C.: National Education Association, 1964. Person-to-person relationships between teacher and learners. Human potential and how to realize it through individualization and better environment.

Baumeister, Alfred A. *Mental Retardation.* Chicago: Aldine, 1967. To help students and workers in the field apply research findings and theoretical formulations to the appraisal and treatment of mental retardation.

Cruickshank, William M. and Orville Johnson, eds. *Education of Exceptional Children and Youth,* 2nd ed. Englewood Cliffs, N.J.: Prentice-Hall, 1967. Concerning educational and administrative practices currently recommended for exceptional children, as described by nine educators.

Erikson, Erik H. *Identity: Youth and Crises.* New York: W. W. Norton, 1968. An exploration by an outstanding psychologist of the meaning of identity. He considers the problem of identity and identity confusion in creative individuals, contemporary youth in general, and in alienated groups.

Frierson, Edward C. and Walter B. Barbe, eds. *Educating Children with Learning Disabilities: Selected Readings.* New York: Appleton, 1967. The child who needs special education because of learning disorders, not instruction based on mental retardation, emotional disturbance, or visual, speech, or hearing problems.

Gallagher, James J., ed. *Teaching Gifted Students: A Book of Readings.* Boston: Allyn and Bacon, 1965. Readings on appropriate classroom environment and teaching for the gifted.

Gold, Milton, Jr. *Education of the Intellectually Gifted.* Columbus, Ohio: Charles E. Merrill, 1965. Relates theoretical research and demonstration of practices in actual situations to problems of education of the gifted.

Horrocks, John E. *The Psychology of Adolescence.* Boston: Houghton Mifflin, 1962. Widely accepted and used basic textbook in psychology of adolescence.

Johnson, Wendell et al. *Speech-Handicapped School Children.* 3rd ed. New York: Harper 1967. Speech disorders, the speech specialist, possible contributions and roles of the classroom teacher.

Kvaraceus, William C. *Anxious Youth: Dynamics of Delinquency.* Columbus, Ohio: Charles E. Merrill, 1966. An authority skillfully examines delinquency in its many ramifications.

Massialas, Byron G. and Jack Zevin. *Creative Encounters in the Classroom.* New York: Wiley, 1967. The discovery approach as used in the contemporary classroom.

McCandless, Boyd R. *Adolescents: Behavior and Development.* New York: Dryden Press, 1970. A new theoretical treatment of adolescence, including clinical material and case histories.

Reger, Roger, Wendy Schroeder, and Kathie Uschald. *Special Education: Children with Learning Problems.* New York: Oxford University Press, 1968. Concerning children who deviate significantly in a negative direction from the average in their learning patterns or general behavior.

Riesman, David, Nathan Glazer, and Reuel Denny. *The Lonely Crowd.* New York: Doubleday, 1953. An influential book which analyzes the growth of the "other-directed" character tendencies rather than "inner-directed." An important theory to consider in attempting to understand the American character.

Schreiber, Daniel, ed. *Profile of a School Dropout.* New York: Alfred A. Knopf, 1967. Examination of the school dropout problem by many contributors.

Schwebel, Milton. *Who Can Be Educated?* New York: Grove Press, 1968. The case for universal educability based upon a serious national commitment to effective instruction. Central need of education is a new theory and practice to give every child the chance to increase both his capacity and his achievement.

Smith, Robert M., *Teacher Diagnosis of Educational Difficulties.* Columbus: Charles Merrill, 1969. The emphasis is on informal diagnosis—methods which the teacher can use in the classroom every day.

Taylor, Calvin W., ed. *Creativity: Progress and Potential.* New York: McGraw-Hill Book Co., 1964. Fundamentals of a little-known subject—creativity—by one of the contemporary pioneers in the field, calling attention to the area.

Telford, Charles W. and James M. Sawrey. *The Exceptional Individual: Psychological and Educational Aspects.* Englewood Cliffs, N.J.: Prentice-Hall, 1967. An introduction to the problems of exceptional people, including, in addition to the usual categories, the highly creative, the culturally disadvantaged, and the intellectually borderline.

Terman, Lewis M. *Mental and Physical Traits of a Thousand Gifted Children.* Stanford, Calif.: Stanford University Press, 1925. Classic study of the backgrounds of gifted children.

Terman, Lewis M. and Melita H. Oden. *The Gifted Child Grows Up.* Stanford, Calif.: Stanford University Press, 1947. A follow-up on the original study of "gifted children" by the senior author. Reports that the gifted children have, in general, fared well.

Thelen, Herbert A. *Classroom Grouping for Teachability.* New York: A leader in group dynamics deals with the problem of grouping students for maximum results.

Thomas, R. Murray and Shirley M. Thomas. *Individual Differences in the Classroom.* New York: David McKay, 1965. Full focus on the reality of individual differences. Useful categorizations upon which this chapter has drawn.

Tunley, Roul. *Kids, Crime and Chaos.* New York: Dell, 1962. Differs from usual treatments of delinquency in that it is a report on juvenile delinquency throughout the world based on the author's observations abroad.

Waetjen, Walter B. and Robert Leeper, eds. *Learning and Mental Health in the School.* Washington, D.C.: Association for Supervision and Curriculum Development, NEA, 1966. Focuses on the learner and the learning situation.

Young, Milton A. *Teaching Children with Special Learning Needs: A Problem-Solving Approach.* New York: John Day, 1967. Emphasizes the individual differences between children, encourages problem solving and diagnostic testing. Gives the teacher assistance in working with children who have difficulties that interfere with their learning.

AUDIO-VISUAL MATERIALS

Your Child's Intelligence (NEA, 54 fr., Color, Record) Intelligence is discussed; testing for ability and general attitudes is considered.

IQ—Questionable Criterion (Stuart Finley Films, 13 Min.) Shows the utilization of all pertinent information, besides testing, in evaluation. Points out the fallacies and dangers of using one test to identify and categorize the complex human being.

Grouping Students for Effective Learning (Bel-Mort Films, 44 fr., Color) Considers what happens when students are grouped according to age, ability grouping, or flexible grouping.

The Child Beyond—A Series (NCAT, University of Texas) An educational series of 13 programs, semi-documentary in nature, with dramatized interludes and discussions by experts on the exceptional child's areas of difficulty and the avenues of adjustment open to him. Samples are: *The Hurdles too High*—30 Min. *Hear No Evil, See No Evil, Speak No Evil*—30 Min. *Neither Devilish nor Divine*—30 Min.

Exceptional Child—A Series: Individual Differences—Introduction (NET, 29 Min.) A series on aspects of helping exceptional children.

Understanding the Gifted (Churchill Films, 33 Min. color) Uses student participants to point up four primary traits common to the gifted—ability to abstract and generalize, diverse and complex interests, the urge to create, and a well-defined sense of ethics and values.

The Gifted Child (NET, 29 Min.) Explains how these children differ in intellectual, emotional and physical development. Stresses the importance of wholesome home and school activities in meeting the needs and interests of the gifted. Shows negative influences in the home and school. Follows a day in the life of a well-adjusted child.

The Exceptional Child (British Broadcasting Corp., 51 Min.) Studies both the intellectually gifted and the not-so-gifted child. Shows work with children who stammer and with bright, intelligent children who fail to learn to read and write by conventional teaching methods.

Individual Differences—Introduction (National Educational TV, Inc., 29 Min.) Establishes the frame of reference for the remaining programs in the series. Explains that individual differences in children occur in physical, mental and emotional growth and development. Describes and illustrates the special and dynamic problems of the exceptional child.

More Different Than Alike (National Education Association, 30 Min. color) Depicts some unique and creative techniques which provide for individual learning differences. The progress each student is making—a special school for the slow learner—a learning center in which high school students have access to materials and technology for self-instruction—a program of student-planned work schedules and learning projects.

"Keith"—A Second Grader (NET, 23 Min.) From the Four Students Series. The focus is on the student and the purpose is to provide behavioral data for observation and analysis. A typical school day is shown, rather than a series of exceptional incidents.

Dropping Out—The Road to Nowhere, Pt. 1, World Today (Guidance Associates 85 fr., Color, Record.) Dropping Out—The Road to Nowhere, Pt. 2, World Tomorrow (Guidance Associates 85 fr., Color, Record.) Documents that dropouts can expect lower pay and poorer jobs. Points out the rapid disappearance of unskilled jobs and stresses the necessity of education as a job credential in the automated future.

Preventing School Dropouts (California Congress of Parents and Teachers, 29 Min.) Three psychologists discuss factors associated with school dropouts and suggest ways parents, community and school people can help youngsters stay in school.

Mike Makes His Mark (NEA, 29 Min.) Mike hated school and challenged it by making an ugly mark on the front of the school. He found that until he removed it, the mark remained on his conscience.

High Wall (Anti-Defamation League of B'nai B'rith, 32 Min.) Uses a case history involving teenage gangs to present analysis of the kind of background that fosters bigotry and antisocial attitudes.

FIFTEEN

HOW DO SOCIAL PROBLEMS AFFECT EDUCATION?

Why should teachers be concerned about new developments in the social order? Many students of the social foundations of education (comparative education and the history, philosophy, and sociology of education) have answered the question in sober and pedantic terms. But no one has said it better than Harold R. W. Benjamin in *The Saber-Tooth Curriculum,* a satirical fable about imaginary cavemen who developed the first program of education.

THE SABER-TOOTH CURRICULUM

The fable of the Saber-Tooth Curriculum[1] tells of New-Fist, a thoughtful caveman who asked himself what the tribesmen must know in order to live with "full bellies, warm backs, and minds free from fear." He concluded that they had to catch fish with their bare hands, club the little wooly horses, and drive away the saber-tooth tigers with fire. So New-Fist developed a sensible curriculum for the children who lived in the cavemen's country. The curriculum stressed the three fundamentals—fish-grabbing with the bare hands, woolyhorse clubbing, and saber-tooth-tiger-scaring with fire. New-Fist took his children with him as he went about and he gave them an opportunity to practice these three subjects. As the children grew older they had an advantage over other children who had not been educated systematically. So other intelligent members of the tribe imitated New-Fist and the teaching of fish-grabbing, horseclubbing, and tiger-scaring became recognized as the heart of good education.

---

[1] Adapted from Harold R. W. Benjamin's (J. Abner Peddiwell) *The Saber-Tooth Curriculum* (New York: McGraw-Hill, 1939).

The tribe prospered and had adequate meat, skins, and security. The curriculum fitted neatly into the demands of the social order in the cave realm.

But a glacier came down from the north and life in the country of the cavemen changed markedly. The life of the caveman which had once been safe and happy became insecure and disturbing. For the glacier melted and dumped dirt and gravel into the creek which became muddy. It was no longer possible to catch fish with the bare hands because the fish could not be seen in the muddy water. Even the tribesmen who had studied advanced fish-grabbing with their bare hands in the secondary schools and even the university graduates who had studied ichthyology could not grab fish with bare hands.

The melting waters from the glacier made the ground marshy so the little wooly horses went east to the dry open plains, far away from the cavemen's country. However, their places were taken by antelopes who were so speedy no one could get near enough to them to club them. The best trained horse-clubbers of the tribe returned home empty-handed though they used all the techniques which the schools had taught them. But they couldn't club horses when there were no horses left to club.

As a final disruption of paleolithic life and education, the dampness gave the saber-tooth tigers pneumonia and most of them died while the rest crept south to the desert. But with the advancing ice sheet came ferocious glacier bears. These bears were not afraid of fire, could not be driven away even by the best methods taught in the tiger-scaring courses. The tribe was now in deep trouble for there was no fish or meat for food, no hides for clothing, and no security from the hairy death that walked the trails both day and night.

New-Fist had long ago been gathered by the Great Mystery to the Land of Sunset far down the creek. Other intelligent tribesmen devised nets for catching fish, snares for capturing antelopes, and deep pits for trapping bears. They called these new developments "inventions" and the knowledge of these new devices spread throughout the tribe. The tribesmen worked hard at making fish nets, setting antelope snares, and digging bear pits, which were essential to the tribe's prosperity and safety. Meanwhile the schools went on teaching fish-grabbing with the bare hands, wooly-horse clubbing, and saber-tooth-tiger-scaring with fire. So some intelligent tribesmen, whom author Benjamin refers to as "radicals," suggested changes in the school curriculum.

"Fishnet-making and using, antelope-snare construction and operation, and bear catching and killing," they pointed out, "require intelligence and skills—things we claim to develop in schools. They are also activities we need to know. Why can't the schools teach them?"

But most of the tribe, and particularly the wise old men who controlled the school, smiled indulgently at this suggestion. "That wouldn't be *education*," they said gently.

"But why wouldn't it be?" asked the radicals.

"Because it would be mere training," explained the old men patiently. "With all the intricate details of fish-grabbing, horse-clubbing, and tiger-scaring—the standard cultural subjects—the school curriculum is too crowded now. We can't add these fads and frills of net-making, antelope-snaring, and—of all things—bear-killing. Why, at the very thought, the body of the great New-Fist, founder of our paleolithic educational system, would turn over in its burial cairn. What we need to do is to give our young people a more thorough grounding in the fundamentals. Even the graduates of the secondary schools don't know the art of fish-grabbing in any complete sense nowadays, they swing their horse clubs awkwardly too, and as for the old science of tiger-scaring—well, even the teachers seem to lack the real flair for the subject which we oldsters got in our teens and never forgot."

"But, damn it," exploded one of the radicals, "how can any person with good sense be interested in such useless activities? What is the point of trying to catch fish with the bare hands when it just can't be done any more? How can a boy learn to club horses when there are no horses left to club? And why in hell should children try to scare tigers with fire when the tigers are dead and gone?"

"Don't be foolish," said the wise old men, smiling most kindly smiles. "We don't teach fish-grabbing to grab fish; we teach it to develop a generalized agility which can never be developed by mere training. We don't teach horse-clubbing to club horses; we teach it to develop a generalized strength in the learner which he can never get from so prosaic and specialized a thing as antelope-snare-setting. We don't teach tiger-scaring to scare tigers; we teach it for the purpose of giving that noble courage which carries over into all the affairs of life and which can never come from so base an activity as bear-killing."

All the radicals were silenced by this statement, all except the one who was most radical of all. He felt abashed, it is true, but he was so radical that he made one last protest.

"But—but anyway," he suggested, "You will have to admit that times have changed. Couldn't you please try these other more up-to-date activities? Maybe they have some educational value after all?"

Even the man's fellow radicals felt this was going a little too far.

The wise old men were indignant. Their kindly smiles faded. "If you had any education yourself," they said severely, "you would know that the essence of true education is timelessness. It is something that endures through changing conditions like a solid rock standing squarely and firmly in the middle of a raging torrent. You must know that there are some eternal verities, and the saber-tooth curriculum is one of them."[2]

THE MESSAGE OF THE SABER-TOOTH CURRICULUM

In *The Saber-Tooth Curriculum*, Benjamin twitted not only the traditionalists but also the progressives. Though the traditionalists insisted that "the essence of

[2] Harold R. W. Benjamin (J. Abner Peddiwell), pp. 41–44. If you wish to learn more of the perils of the cavemen and of the educational system they developed, you may want to read the rest of *The Saber-Tooth Curriculum*.

true education is timelessness," the progressives did no better when confronted with the new social demands on the cave realm. The progressives simply transferred fish-grabbing with the bare hands from the heated school pool to the banks of the real creek. They described the new approach as creative fish-grabbing. But it was still no longer possible to grab agile and intelligent fish in muddy waters with the bare hands. Despite creative tiger-scaring through waving fire brands before the caged and ancient toothless tigers which were the last of their kind, the giant bears which were unafraid of fire still prowled the trails. But no one in caveman education recognized the threat of the giant bears or even acknowledged their existence.

The message of *The Saber-Tooth Curriculum* is clear. Whatever our philosophies and whatever our methodologies, we in education cannot ignore developments in the social order. If we insist on ignoring social developments, we imperil our society and the people who comprise it.[3, 4]

The glacier comes at Americans today not from the North but from developments in the social order. Today the glacier brings with it the horrors of modern warfare, the deteriorating quality of the environment, and hostile race relations. This chapter considers these three developments in the social order. Obviously, there are other significant developments; but of all social developments, problems of the international setting, of pollution and population, and of race relations are the most critical for our survival.

CONFLICTS IN THE INTERNATIONAL SETTING

The war in Vietnam, possibly the most unpopular war in American history, persisted into the 1970s. A program of acceleration of conflict that marked the Johnson administration was succeeded by a program of gradual withdrawal of troops during the Nixon administration. Fever spots of tension continued to develop across the globe. Hostilities flared between Israel and the Arab world as the Israelis continued to hold the land they had taken after the six-day war of 1967 and as Palestine guerrillas developed raid tactics, including hijacking and dynamiting American and European planes. Nigeria crushed the Biafra rebellion and the world had a preview of the horrors of tribal war and of mass starvation. Yet, though local conflicts persisted and though the major powers supported their favorites with arms and diplomatic encouragement, the world of the early 1970s avoided the feared holocaust of total war.

---

[3] Robert M. Bruker (ed.), *Wakan: The Spirit of Harold Benjamin* (Minneapolis: Burgess Publishing, 1968). If the wit and wisdom of Benjamin appeal to you, you may wish to read this collection of his writings.

[4] Harold R. W. Benjamin, *The Sage of Petaluma* (New York: McGraw-Hill, 1965). This is a semi-autobiographical book, which is purportedly a biography of J. Abner Peddiwell to whom Benjamin attributes *The Saber-Tooth Curriculum*.

Explosion of first atomic bomb, August 16, 1945. Courtesy of Los Alamos Scientific Lab.

DESTRUCTIVE POWER

After more than twenty-five years of research and development of nuclear weapons, the power of the tremendous bomb which destroyed Hiroshima and, in effect, ended World War II in 1945 seems insignificant in comparison to the potential power for destruction possessed by both the Soviet Union and the United States. By the early 1970s the powers of destruction of the major nations are awesome. Sheldon Appleton has summarized some of the facts in *United States Foreign Policy*. He points out that both the United States and the Soviet Union now possess hundreds upon hundreds of thermonuclear weapons. Some bombs have the destructive power of at least fifty megatons and thus have the equivalent of the power of destruction of 50 million tons of TNT. A bomb of this power is 2,500 times as powerful as the famous bomb dropped on Hiroshima and twenty times as destructive as all bombs dropped on Germany during World War II. Appleton points out that existing technology could produce bombs several times as powerful as these. Even a twenty megaton bomb could almost totally devastate 48 square miles with attendant fallout over thousands of additional square miles. President Kennedy once pointed out that full scale nuclear exchange with the weapons in existence during his administration could kill more than 300 million Americans, Russians, and Europeans in less than a single hour. Robert McNamara, Secretary of Defense during the Lyndon B. Johnson administration, once estimated that a Soviet first strike against the

Hiroshima evidenced the destruction the atomic bomb could reap. Courtesy of Atomic Energy Commission.

United States would kill between 130 and 135 million Americans. McNamara added that no conceivable defensive measure could be expected to reduce these fatalities, in the case of an all-out Soviet attack to a level below some tens of millions of Americans.[5]

Nor were nuclear weapons the monopoly of the two superpowers. By the early 1970s, Britain, France, and China had successfully established nuclear power programs. Other countries announcing intentions to develop nuclear weapons, or having access to, and interest in, nuclear power were India, Japan, West Germany, Israel, and Egypt.[6] Commentators pointed out that what historians once called the balance of power might better be termed in the last half of the twentieth century a grim balance of terror based on the capability of major nations to destroy others. Given the nuclear capability of each side, there could only be mutual destruction, rather than any true victor, in a nuclear war.

Yet, as has been historically the case in balance of power world politics, each protagonist watched the other closely and developed whatever extensions of power it could. For instance, as conviction grew in governmental and military circles in the United States that the Soviet Union was extending its missile

---

[5] Sheldon Appleton, *United States Foreign Policy: An Introduction With Cases* (Boston: Little, Brown, 1968), pp. 466–467.

[6] William B. Bader, *The United States and the Spread of Nuclear Weapons* (New York: Western Publishing, 1968), pp. 63–99.

capacity, the United States responded with the beginnings of an anti-ballistic missile system (ABM) to respond to the nuclear warheads. But unlike earlier military authorizations of the post World War II years, the ABM program was approved by Congress only after a substantial fight and after modifications of the original proposal.

On November 2, 1970, the *New York Times* related the findings of the Stockholm International Peace Research Institute, financed by the Swedish government and chaired by the political economist Gunnar Myrdal. The Institute reported that the world's nuclear stockpile amounted to about 50,000 megatons and represented about 15 tons of TNT per person on the globe or about 60 tons of TNT per person in the NATO and Warsaw Pact nations taken together. Military expenditures by the world were approximately equivalent to the total income of the poorer half of the world's population.

By the early 1970s a counterforce to the acceleration of the Southeast Asian war and the expansion of the military establishment developed. The counterforce has many components ranging from absolutist pacifists to those who regard militarism as too expensive, and ranging from destroyers of draft office files to Congressmen appraising priorities. Many movements have contributed to the counterforce, including widespread youth opposition to the war in Vietnam, spearheaded by a small yet influential segment of the youth population which has demonstrated and campaigned against war. One wing of the dissenters took to the streets in the 1967 march on the Pentagon and the struggles on the lakefront of Chicago during the 1968 Democratic National Convention. Another wing of the activist group crusaded through political involvement that took such forms as support of Senator Eugene McCarthy in his unsuccessful bid for the 1968 Presidential nomination and the development and conduct of the October 1969 Mobilization Day. The counterforce against war has also been supported by many older persons, including those who felt that the quality of American life was deteriorating as funds which might have been spent to reduce urban slums, support schools, improve the natural environment, train and employ more blacks, etc., were appropriated for military purposes.

Resistance to war and criticism of expansion of military programs has been supported by difficulties which both the United States and the Soviet Union experienced within their spheres of influence in the early 1970s. The United States has encountered outright opposition or sometimes only half-hearted support from former allies or longtime friends. Among the unfriendly manifestations were demonstrations in South American countries which caused Nelson Rockefeller to reduce his South American itinerary as a representative of the Nixon administration and anti-war demonstrations that greeted Vice-President Spiro Agnew in Australia. Meanwhile, the Soviet Union found itself at odds with another Communist power—China. Mutual vituperation accompanied actual border hostilities.

The result was that, even as the powers of destruction mounted, the efforts to bring annihilating power under control intensified and the attempts to widen areas of mutual understandings increased. Consequently, representatives of the

Many young people hoped they could help effect change through the established political system in the 1968 and 1970 campaigns. Courtesy of Robert Azzi from Nancy Palmer.

Soviet Union and the United States negotiated on arms reduction in Helsinki in 1969 and in Vienna in 1970. Cultural exchanges grew slowly.

POLITICAL ASPECTS

The struggle has had political overtones as well. While many factors entered into the decision by President Johnson not to seek reelection, certainly one powerful factor was the unpopularity among the American people of the war policies of the Johnson administration. While President Nixon's policies of Vietnam War withdrawal and Vietnamization were not supported by all, most Americans—according to polls—thought them steps in the right direction. Another outcome of a shifting political climate with respect to America's role in world affairs was the Nixon doctrine, a declaration that we would help nations confronted with communist aggression but would not supply our own troops to fight on the soil of a nation that was engaged in civil war. Indeed, some feared that the pendulum might have swung from participation in the affairs of the world toward a version of isolationism. But on April 30, 1970, President Nixon

The United Nations. Courtesy of UNATIONS.

announced that American troops had crossed the border of Cambodia. The Vietnam war became a wider Indochina war. Campuses were rocked by protests. President Nixon recognized that the decision involved serious international and domestic political consequences; he promised early withdrawal. By the end of June, 1970, American troops left Cambodia. But the war in Southeast Asia continued.

Keeping peace in this world is a difficult business. Despite the efforts of the United Nations, which stubbornly continued its unspectacular work, revolution and violence continue to haunt a world in which the economic gap between the developed and underdeveloped nations stubbornly increases. The existence of an economic gap coincides with a population explosion characterized by higher birthrates in the underdeveloped nations than in the developed lands. Observers of our society recognize that there is considerable social dynamite lying about any international scene in which the gap between the rich and poor grows wider while birthrates of the poorer people rise.

INTERNATIONAL UNDERSTANDING AND SURVIVAL

That relevant education of American children and youth in the 1970s must deal with international relations and associated problems of war and peace seems self-evident. It is not mere rhetoric to point out that the physical existence of mankind depends on the solution of our international problems. Intelligent decisions in this area quite literally mean the difference between life and death for many human beings. It is essential that all men learn to view themselves and their nations in the larger context of international understanding. Without further elaboration we rest our case for inclusion of international education in the curriculum of American schools.

PROBLEMS OF PEOPLE AND POLLUTION

POPULATION

There are other perils to survival on this planet than nuclear war alone. Though less dramatic than the mushroom cloud of the atomic bomb, the population explosion and the pollution of the surrounding environment imperil mankind.

The population explosion raises the brutal question as to whether there will be sufficient space for man on the planet unless effective population controls are put into practice. The facts of world population growth are hard to live with but they are real. Paul R. Ehrlich presents the facts dramatically:

It has been estimated that the human population of 6000 B.C. was about five million people, taking perhaps one million years to get there from two and a half million. The population did not reach 500 million until almost 8,000 years later—about 1650 A.D. This means it doubled roughly once every thousand years or so. It reached a billion people around 1850, doubling in some 200 years. It took only 80 years or so for the next doubling, as the population reached two billion around 1930. We have not completed the next doubling to four billion yet, but we now have well over three billion people. The doubling time at present seems to be about 37 years. Quite a reduction in doubling time: 1,000,000 years, 1,000 years, 200 years, 80 years, 37 years. Perhaps the meaning of a doubling time of around 37 years is best brought home by a theoretical exercise. Let's examine what might happen on the absurd assumption that the population continued to double every 37 years into the indefinite future.

If growth continued at that rate for about 900 years, there would be some 60,000,000,000,000,000 people on the face of the earth. Sixty million billion people. This is about 100 persons for each square yard of the Earth's surface, land and sea.[7]

The director of the population research center of the University of Chicago, Philip M. Hauser, sums up the world outlook as the world population edges closer to four billion. He says,

The continuation of present birth rates and declining death rates would produce a world population of 7.5 billion by the end of the century. We are almost certain to have a world population of 7 billion by the year 2000 even under the assumption of considerable reduction in fertility in the developing regions of Asia, Africa, and Latin America, an assumption the validity of which has to be confirmed by fact. This means that in the course of the next thirty years there will be about as many added to the population of the world as all of mankind from the beginning of time on this planet managed to generate to this present moment. In the long run, present rates of population cannot possibly persist because they threaten to exhaust space itself. In the shorter run, present

[7] Paul R. Ehrlich, *The Population Bomb* (New York: Ballantine, 1968), p. 18.

growth rates, especially in Asia, Latin America, and Africa, are preventing rapid increases in levels of living and may, between now and the end of the century, generate more not less social unrest, greater not lesser political instability, and more not fewer threats to world peace.[8]

The steepest rates of population increase occur in the poorer and less developed nations. Yet even in the United States population experts are expecting about half again as many residents by the end of the twentieth century. The present United States population is beyond the 200 million mark. The United States birth rate is relatively low compared with other nations (14.4 births versus 9.6 deaths per thousand people).[9] In 1966, Philip M. Hauser and Martin Taitel, of the University of Chicago, wrote "The population of the United States . . . is being projected to exceed three hundred million by the turn of the century."[10] They add that the projections utilize conservative assumptions about the future. The critical one is the birth rate. However, a report of the National Goals Research Staff, released by the White House in mid 1970, indicated that the prediction of 100 million more Americans by the year 2000 will likely prove too high and the increase may be "considerably less."[11]

The population problem in the United States is complicated by the fact that Americans of the year 2000 will live primarily in urban territory. Hauser and Taitel wrote, "By 1980, between 75 and 80 percent of our population may live in urban territory, which would place almost as many persons in urban territory in 1980 as there are in the United States today."[12] What this involves by way of building was also pointed out in 1966 by William L. C. Wheaton, Professor of City Planning and Director, Institute of Urban and Regional Development, of the University of California at Berkeley, who said, "In short, during the next 15 years we must build about as many cities as were created in the first 200 years of this nation's existence. The population of the United States is moving to cities, and primarily to metropolitan areas."[13]

POLLUTION

At the same time that man is overpopulating the nations of the world, he is increasingly polluting his environment. Recognition of the importance of ecology, the science of the relationships between organisms and their environment,

[8] Philip M. Hauser, "Population Explosion—Trends and Implications," *Information Please Almanac, 1970* (Dan Golenpaul Associates, 1969), pp. 53–54.
[9] *Newsweek*, "The Ravaged Environment," (January 26, 1970), p. 36.
[10] Philip M. Hauser and Martin Taitel, "Population Trends—Prologue to Educational Problems," p. 24 in Edgar L. Morphet and Charles O. Ryan, eds., *Prospective Changes in Society by 1980* (Denver: Designing Education for the Future, An Eight-State Project, 1967).
[11] *New York Times*, "Panel Finds Need to Inspire Debate on Nation's Goals," (July 19, 1970), p. 1, 47.
[12] Hauser and Taitel, *Prospective . . . 1980*, p. 41.
[13] William L. C. Wheaton, "Urban and Metropolitan Development," p. 139 in Edgar L. Morphet and Charles O. Ryan, eds., *Prospective Changes in Society by 1980* (Denver: Designing Education for the Future, An Eight-State Project, 1966).

seemed to burst suddenly upon Americans in the 1970s. True, there had been concern for conservation throughout the twentieth century; one American President, Theodore Roosevelt, was largely remembered for his efforts to protect wildlife, halt exhaustion of timber and mineral supplies by private interests, and add lands to public ownership. During the 1930s, the Tennessee Valley Authority (TVA) accompanied public power development with a policy of conservation of natural resources. Popular depression-era writers on economics, such as Stuart Chase, deplored the creation of ravaged lands through the fumes from smelters and condemned the unrestricted gouging of the soil through strip mines.

In the early 1960s, one of the most effective of the pioneers for a better environment was Rachel Carson. Her book, *Silent Spring,* dramatized the threat of the many insecticides which man used to protect his plant life—and which have proven to be lethal poisons to a much wider bird and animal kingdom than bothersome insects. News weeklies reported that she was an alarmist and her message was, at first, deprecated or ignored. But a decade later she was recognized for the wisdom of her warnings.

In the opening pages of *Silent Spring,* Rachel Carson wrote of some future spring season in America when the silence of death would prevail.

Some evil spell had settled on the community: mysterious maladies swept the flocks of chickens; the cattle and sheep sickened and died. Everywhere was a shadow of death. The farmers spoke of much illness among their families. In the town the doctors had become more and more puzzled by new kinds of sickness appearing among their patients....

There was a strange stillness. The birds, for example—where had they gone? Many people spoke of them puzzled and disturbed. The feeding stations in the backyards were deserted. The few birds seen everywhere were moribund; they trembled violently and could not fly. It was a spring without voices.

On the farms the hens brooded, but no chicks hatched. The farmers complained that they were unable to raise any pigs—the litters were small and the young survived only a few days. The apple trees were coming into bloom but no bees droned among the blossoms, so there was no pollination and there would be no fruit.

The roadsides, once so attractive, were now lined with browned and withered vegetation as though swept by fire. These, too, were silent, deserted by all living things. Even the streams were now lifeless. Anglers no longer visited them, for all the fish had died....

No witchcraft, no enemy action had silenced the rebirth of new life in this stricken world. The people had done it themselves.[14]

By the early 1970s, the problem of pollution and attendant deterioration of the quality of the environment had become so widespread that the nation was shocked into action. The combination of difficulties experienced by all Americans with smoke, sewage, noise, garbage, chemical poisoning, and ugliness

---

[14] Rachel Carson, *Silent Spring* (Boston: Houghton Mifflin, 1962), pp. 1–3.

Oil covering the Yorktown, Virginia, public beach after one of several oil spills in 1967. Courtesy of the U.S. Department of the Interior.

suddenly seemed to converge on the national consciousness. The urban environment had especially deteriorated since the earlier conservationists had written and campaigned.

In country areas, pollution spoiled recreational opportunities and vacation enjoyment. Lake Erie was dying; almost every form of life was gone from the lake. The beaches of Santa Barbara, a beautiful resort area, were fouled by oil. The beautiful Ohio of the song of that title became the most polluted river in America. Fishermen cast for trout in rivers speckled with beer cans. Even parks like Yosemite were so crowded by tourists in the summer as to threaten health in camping slums.

But in the urban industrialized areas, pollution destroyed not only the quality of life; it threatened life itself. The Cuyahoga River in Ohio literally caught fire from industrial waste and burned trestles over the river. The Houston Ship Canal became one of the most polluted bodies of water in the United States. In New York City, inversion layers settled down and trapped fumes close to the ground, causing death to some people who had respiratory trouble. Automobiles contributed almost one-half of the two hundred million tons of waste poured into the air each year. Even such cities as Phoenix and Salt Lake City, which America thought of as standing smog-free in the wide open spaces, were hit hard by smog. DDT and other pesticides not only disposed of pests in rural areas but appeared in quantity in human mothers' milk in city areas. A New York City task force reporting to Mayor Lindsay indicated that noise in the city regularly exceeded 85 decibels, which is the level regarded by the medical profession as the threshold above which continuous noise can cause deafness.[15]

Americans of varied social viewpoints agreed in the early 1970s on the necessity of coping with the menace of pollution. Disagreements largely centered

---

[15] *Newsweek,* "The Ravaged Environment" (January 26, 1970), p. 40.

Automobiles cause both traffic and atmospheric problems. Courtesy of The Los Angeles Times.

upon what techniques should be used and upon what combination of bonuses and penalties would prove most effective. Some cynics even suggested that politicians vied with each other in their efforts to reduce pollution; in the 1970s they began using the word ecology as they once used such words as home and mother. A new crusade was clearly underway in American life. Success would not be easy, for America had a long frontier tradition of taking advantage of natural resources and moving on. Not only did America have a frontier and pioneer kind of ethics, it also held firmly to the gospel of progress.

But in the seventies, conservationist-minded Senators like Wisconsin's Gaylord Nelson could say,

Progress—American style—adds up each year to 200 million tons of smoke and fumes, 7 million junked cars, 20 million tons of paper, 48 billion cans and 28 billion bottles.[16]

President Nixon made a commitment in his State of the Union Message of 1970,

The great question of the seventies is: Shall we surrender to our surroundings or shall we make our peace with nature and begin to make reparations for the damage we have done to our air, our land and to our water? . . . Restoring nature to its natural state is a cause beyond party and beyond faction. It has become a common cause of all of the people of this country. It is a cause of particular concern to young Americans because they more than we will reap the grim consequences of our failure to act on the problems which are needed now if we are to prevent disaster later—clean air, clean water, open spaces. These should once again be the birthright of every American. If we act now they can be.[17]

[16] *Ibid.,* p. 34.
[17] President's State of the Union Message, delivered before the Congress of the United States, Washington, D.C., January 22, 1970.

POPULATION, POLLUTION, AND SURVIVAL

Since problems of population and pollution, like international problems, are plaguing man today, and their solution is essential to any improvement of the quality of his existence, American education in the 1970s must deal with such problems. In American schools, study of pollution by children and youth is developing rapidly. Study of population lags behind because of the persistence of objections by some on religious grounds to full consideration of the issues involved. Yet the two problems, pollution and population, are necessarily interrelated in American life and indeed on the world scene too.

RACISM

A third cluster of survival problems confronting Americans in the 1970s centers on racism. True, the problem is worldwide, as blacks in South Africa and Rhodesia as well as Indians and Pakistanis living in Great Britain can testify. But, for residents of the United States, our own domestic problem of racism, largely centered upon white-black relationships but also manifested in society's discriminatory treatment of American Indians, Hispano-Americans, and others, is particularly obvious and acute. In chapter 12, the history of minority group experiences in the United States was briefly sketched. In the present chapter, we will look at the present status of racism in the United States and the strategies for dealing with race relations which are currently proposed and which markedly affect education.

THE NATURE OF RACISM

Racism is essentially the notion that one's own ethnic stock is superior. Racism persists. Yet the concept of race itself has mythological characteristics. *The Columbia Encyclopedia* (second edition) began its entry on race as follows:

... obsolete division of humanity based on criteria of hair texture and color, of skin color, of head shape and other conspicuous physical features. . . . The classification never worked at all, but it had great prestige in the 19th and the early 20th century.[18]

Racism takes the form of denying individuals equal opportunities because of their ethnic stock which is often manifested by a skin color which differs from the majority. Racism becomes institutionalized through policies of discrimination and segregation. For instance, following the Civil War in the United States and despite amendments to the U.S. Constitution, Negroes were segregated by law in many southern states and by custom in many northern states. Through segregation, they were shut away from an equal share in community life. Segre-

---

[18] William Bridewater and Elizabeth J. Sherwood, *The Columbia Encyclopedia*, 2d ed. (New York: Columbia University Press, 1950), p. 1632.

gation to reinforce white dominance took the form of separate schools and colleges for blacks, separate sections in railroad cars, buses, and other forms of transportation, denial of admission to recreational facilities or, if admitted, the provision of a separate section for Negroes in attendance, and even segregation with respect to hospitals, churches and jails.

Since the 1940s the fight against institutionalized segregation and discrimination has been waged on many fronts. In June, 1941, President Franklin D. Roosevelt created the Fair Employment Practices Committee; clauses against discrimination were included in most governmental contracts. In 1948 a directive by President Harry S. Truman called for an end to segregation in the U.S. military forces. In education the historic step away from the institutionalization of segregation and discrimination came in 1954 with the *Brown v. Board of Education of Topeka* decision which declared that segregation was "inherently unequal" and a denial of the protection of the fourteenth amendment. The Civil Rights Law of 1964 was a combining of many of the desegregation efforts. The battle has been waged state by state and in community after community; yet progress toward the elimination of segregation has been slow and grudging in both school and society. Some have grown disillusioned with "deliberate speed" and with the integration goal. By the 1970s, two broad lines of strategy for the improvement of the lot of blacks in the United States had emerged.

STRATEGIES FOR ACHIEVING RIGHTS

One continuing strategy called for the replacement of segregation by desegregation, and the achievement of integration. Desegregation occurs when minority group members are physically present and are accorded nondiscriminatory treatment along with majority group members in some social settings. But integration means more than just physical presence and nondiscriminatory treatment. Integration involves full acceptance of all persons as individual human beings in a variety of social settings such as employment, schools, housing, and the armed forces. Desegregation and integration has been the historic commitment of such groups as the National Association for the Advancement of Colored People and of such Negro leaders as Roy Wilkins, Executive Secretary of the NAACP, Bayard Rustin, a civil rights spokesman who organized effective and orderly marches upon Washington, and Kenneth Clark, a psychologist whose assembling of research was used by the United States Supreme Court in arriving at its decision as to the inherent inequality of segregated schools.

But a new and militant approach to the achievement of the rights of blacks emerged in the late 1960s. It was called black power by its proponents and condemned as black separatism by its opponents. The new approach stressed black awareness and black identity; it called for programs of black studies in colleges and school systems; it supported black control of communities in which blacks lived, rather than integration attempts. Spokesmen include such black organizers as H. Rap Brown and Stokely Carmichael, Black Panther spokesmen such as Bobby Seale and Huey Newton, CORE spokesmen such as Roy Innis, and intellectual leaders such as Eldridge Cleaver and Charles V. Hamilton.

The views of proponents of each of these strategies is set forth below, as stated by Roy Wilkins, defending the strategy of desegregation and integration, and Stokely Carmichael and Charles V. Hamilton, defending the strategy of black power.

Roy Wilkins writes:

To the dismay of at least 95 percent of the Negro-American population, many of the Negro college students to whom nearly everyone looked for new ideas on race advancement have come up with a theory of racial self-segregation.

For all the adult lives of every black American, 40 to 60 years old, the primary goal has been the abolition of obviously unjust racial segregation. No textbooks or philosophical theses are needed to drive this point home. The practical operation of the system is plain enough to a fourth grader. If one separates a minority from the majority culture (and the Negro-American is a distinct and relatively powerless minority), it is easy to build it into a deprived population.

Lily-white politics disfranchises blacks. The latter have no say in the election of men to office, in taxes, in legislation that literally affects their very lives. Lilywhiteism seals off the blacks' living quarters, their recreation, travel, employment, and schools. They are (and have been) ripe for exploitation. The white majority also administers the law and can fasten a criminal label on the black population through convictions and imprisonment.

Aided by the many tentacled communications media, the white majority can build an evil conception into racial policy almost overnight. Heavy tomes by "scholars," textbooks for millions of white children, picture books, tabloid and staid newspapers, magazines, opinion polls, and radio and television all can help create and maintain the net of public opinion that will hobble black people. If one adds the sermons and pastoral advice that can be given each week, to, say, 50,000 congregations and parishes, he can envision and appreciate the enormous anti-Negro machinery. . . .

The separatism called for by a highly vocal minority of Negro-Americans will harm the multiracial, pluralistic society America is seeking to perfect. It is certain to isolate the black population, to the joy of the white segregationist. With its unconcealed aspects of racial hatred and violence, especially its predilection for paramilitary strutting and boasts, it could foreshadow a tragedy in human relations comparable in concept, if smaller in scope, to the hateful Hitler dictatorship.[19]

The case for black control of black communities was equally well argued by Charles V. Hamilton and Stokely Carmichael in *Black Power*.

The adoption of the concept of Black Power is one of the most legitimate and healthy developments in American politics and race relations in our times. . . . It is a call for black people in this country to unite, to recognize their heritage, to build a sense of community. It is a call for black people to begin to define

---

[19] "Black Leaders Speak Out on Black Education," *Today's Education*, 58 (October 1969), p. 32.

The need for black studies became more insistent in the late 1960s. Courtesy of Magnum.

their own goals, to lead their own organizations and to support those organizations. It is a call to reject the racist institutions and values of this society.

The concept of Black Power rests on a fundamental premise: *Before a group can enter the open society, it must first close ranks.* By this we mean that group solidarity is necessary before a group can operate effectively from a bargaining position of strength in a pluralistic society. Traditionally, each new ethnic group in this society has found the route to social and political viability through the organization of its own institutions with which to represent its needs within the larger society. Studies in voting behavior specifically, and political behavior generally, have made it clear that politically the American pot has not melted. Italians vote for Rubino over O'Brien; Irish for Murphy over Goldberg, etc. This phenomenon may seem distasteful to some, but it has been and remains today a central fact of the American political system. There are other examples of ways in which groups in the society have remembered their roots and used this effectively in the political arena . . .

The point is obvious: black people must lead and run their own organizations. Only black people can convey the revolutionary idea—and it is a revolutionary idea—that black people are able to do things themselves. Only they can help create in the community an aroused and continuing black consciousness that will provide the basis for political strength. In the past, white allies have often furthered white supremacy without the whites involved realizing it, or even wanting to do so. Black people must come together and do things for themselves. They must achieve self-identity and self-determination in order to have their daily needs met. . . .

Black Power recognizes—and must recognize—the ethnic basis of American politics as well as the power-oriented nature of American politics. Black Power therefore calls for black people to consolidate behind their own, so that they can bargain from a position of strength. But while we endorse the *procedure* of group solidarity and identity for the purpose of attaining certain goals in the body politic, this does not mean that black people should strive for the same kind of rewards (i.e., end results) obtained by the white society. The ultimate values and goals are not domination or exploitation of other groups, but rather an effective share in the total power of society.[20]

The same division between the desegregation and integration approach and the black power and separatist approach developed in other minority groups. While the majority of Puerto Ricans held to either Commonwealth status or statehood for Puerto Rico and for integrated acceptance into mainland life, a very small minority of Puerto Ricans called for complete independence of the island and for Puerto Rican control of Puerto Rican communities on the American mainland. American Indians were similarly affected; some called for full acceptance of American Indians in American life and others held to increasing Indian control of Indian reservations. Among the Hispanic-Americans, a militant minority called for Mexican-American control of lands which formerly belonged to Mexicans in the American Southwest.

The new militancy had immediate repercussions in the schools. Among those Negroes who supported integration, such as the large body of southern blacks, the struggle in the schools took the form of the attempt to achieve desegregation and integration. In many northern urban areas, the dominant groups were the new black militants who fought for community control, including black teachers and administrators and black boards of education. As black rage mounted, educators found it increasingly difficult to carry on an orderly process of education in ghetto schools.

In the struggle between the two strategies, some observers have attempted to find a middle ground. For instance, some contend that the search for black identity, independence, pride, and power is a necessary phase through which minorities must go. Once power is achieved, they say, the struggle for desegregation and integration can proceed. But others point out that the ends of mankind are shaped by the means used and express skepticism that an integrated America can be reached by following a path resembling the *apartheid* policies of South Africa.

Virgil A. Clift, a student of Negro education in America, writes concerning a middle way in higher education:

The notions of "black separatism" and "black power" on the college campus shock administrators and professors. Yet every major ethnic or religious group makes use of its separate organizations to formulate goals, determine priorities,

---

[20] Stokely Carmichael and Charles V. Hamilton, *Black Power: The Politics of Liberation in America* (New York: Vintage, 1967), pp. 44–47.

and plan strategy. When Catholics, Jews, or Protestants call their special separate meetings for these purposes, it is treated in the press and other media in a salutory fashion. Black students do not understand why they should not be able to separate themselves to determine priorities within the American pluralistic society. "Black power" in terms of developing black leadership within the economic and political system is to employ the same strategy that others do who have power. The term *black* associated with this idea seems to turn off administrators and faculty members. If we lived in a free and open society that did not suppress and oppress black people without power, this would not be the case. It is difficult to admit that schools, universities, churches, and other similar organizations represent institutional power that has frequently been used to dominate and abuse blacks. When they did not dominate and abuse, they condoned it by inaction because they are a part of the system. The black and white higher institutions will have to get their houses in order and begin to play the role they are supposed to play in a free democratic society.

On the other hand, black academic separatism, out of the context of our national history and aspirations in a pluralistic society, can lead to segregated education which does not provide young people with the competencies and skills needed in this highly competitive industrialized society. It is not an either/or proposition. The challenge to students and the university is one of making it possible for the black student to achieve identity and self-esteem while developing essential competencies and skills.[21]

RACISM AND SURVIVAL

Wise decisions as to the best strategy to overcome racism without creating new forms of racism will be crucial for America in the 1970s. A teacher should study the competing approaches carefully in their historical context before arriving at commitment and action. Many social consequences will stem from decisions as to the best ways to overcome racism, judgments which Americans will be making during the 1970s. The welfare of all Americans is involved in the issue, and the decisions made will vitally affect the organization, conduct, and content of American education.

HOW THE SOCIAL ORDER AFFECTS TEACHING

In this chapter we have considered three specific survival problems of Americans in our times: conflicts in the international setting, problems of people and pollution, and the problem of racism. Many other problems also confront the American people. A sampling of additional contemporary problems includes crime, housing, drug addiction, violence, hunger, inadequate job preparation, provisions for the poor, etc. The 1970s undoubtedly will be a period when still

[21] Virgil A. Clift, "Higher Education of Minority Groups in the United States," *The Journal of Negro Education*, 38 (Summer 1969), pp. 301–302.

other problems are added to this already formidable list. So the three selected problems with which we have dealt intensively are only representative of the "glaciers from the north" of which Benjamin wrote in *The Saber-Tooth Curriculum.*

The fundamental reality for the new teacher to remember is that we live in a time of rapid and sweeping social change in which new developments inevitably arise. Some social problems are resolved and new social problems emerge. In a world characterized by rapid and sweeping social change, education must keep up with change or become hopelessly obsolete and irrelevant. If education attempts to ignore social changes, then today's educators, like Benjamin's cavemen, will be teaching the young to grab fish with bare hands, club wooly horses, and scare saber-tooth tigers with fire long after the necessity for such programs has passed and long after it was sensible to carry on such programs. Meanwhile, new developments in the social order will have taken place and new imperatives will be facing Americans.

The schools can ignore developments and imperatives in the social order only at the risk of imperiling society. Teachers can ignore such developments and imperatives only at the risk of their potential contribution—improvement of the lives of human beings—fading into insignificance, irrelevance, and triviality. Schools can only be meaningful institutions if they stay abreast of changes in the social order and teachers can only be meaningful human beings if their teaching recognizes the contemporary social realities.

★   ★   ★

DISCUSSION
1. Talk over the fable of *The Saber-Tooth Curriculum.* Behind the humor, what essentially is the author saying? Can you apply the fable to contemporary education?
2. In *The Saber-Tooth Curriculum,* the author talks about "the glacier from the north." What are some modern equivalents of Benjamin's "glacier from the north?" Describe and discuss the international setting of your times. How does the setting affect education?
3. What is the real purpose of the school in society? Should the school function as a social agent or should it function as a non-committed preserver and expounder of the organized, traditional bodies of knowledge?
4. Should the public school system attempt to accept and *reflect* the tendencies and forces of society or should it set as its major goal the *improvement* of society?
5. Describe the current state of weaponry in America and the world. How has the counterforce against militarism fared? What is the present status of the counterforce to militarism? What is the present political situation in relationship to problems of the war and peace? How have international problems affected presidential politics in the past and presently in the United States?
6. Is the necessity to deal with international relations and associated problems of

war and peace self-evident? To what extent do schools currently deal with such matters? If there appears to you to be a lag, attempt to account for the reasons.

7. What is the significance of the present rate at which the population doubles? What problem does it pose?

8. What are the latest estimates of the population of the United States by the year 2000? What factors influence such calculations? Have there been marked changes in expectancies in the past few years?

9. What do you remember as pertinent lessons you learned in school on conservation or ecology? Is there a need for change in this area? How would you teach it differently?

10. Why was the earlier American pollution problem less crucial than presently? What are some recent illustrations of threats to human life in urban areas through pollution?

11. How has the campaign against pollution mentioned by President Nixon in his State of the Union message of 1970 fared?

12. To what degree are problems of population and pollution being dealt with in today's education? Is one a more popular topic for instruction than the other?

13. What really is the meaning of the word "race"?

14. What has been the history of segregation in the United States? What have been some of the landmarks in the fight against segregation?

15. Discuss major strategies for achieving the minority rights. Summarize the view of desegregationists and black power advocates.

16. Is there a middle way in racial strategy between emphasis on black power and emphasis on uncompromising desegregation?

17. Meet with a close friend, preferably of a different race, and discuss with him or her the issues and problems of racism touched on by this chapter.

18. In what ways has the problem of integration versus separatism manifest itself in minority groups other than blacks?

19. How does the social order actually affect teachers and schools?

INVOLVEMENT

1. Using Benjamin's style and approach, attempt to extend the fable of *The Saber-Tooth Curriculum* through some further experiences of the cavemen.

2. Examine your own subject field and/or level to determine how you could best work on emerging problems of the social order.

3. Identify yourself with a group which follows the strategy which you support in connection with problems of war and peace.

4. Explore how your subject matter field contributes to consideration of problems of international relations.

5. Associate yourself with the work of a political candidate who most closely reflects your own views on war and peace and on international relations.

6. Develop a chart which dramatically portrays growth of population in the world in the last 100 years. Post the chart so that others might become acquainted with the facts.

7. What organizations exist which attempt to cope with pollution problems? If you regard pollution as a major problem, identify the one closest to your own convictions and work with it.
8. Are any candidates for political office particularly active in the fight against pollution? According to your own convictions, identify yourself with such a candidate or a program in the political arena.
9. Set down a list of ways in which teachers of a variety of subjects and levels could educate for better human relations and against racism. Specify the ways in which a teacher at the particular subject and level you plan to teach could foster such programs.
10. After carefully thinking through your strategy for achieving human rights for minorities, associate yourself with some group which represents your convictions.
11. Work with fellow students on campus in the interest of good human relations and in opposition to racism.
12. Talk to a friend or relative who was in school thirty years ago. What does he perceive as the changes in society and culture that have affected education during the last thirty years?

BIBLIOGRAPHY

Allen, Rodney F. and Charles H. Adair. *Violence and Riots in Urban America.* Worthington, Ohio: Charles A. Jones, 1969. Concepts to guide inquiry and to structure evidence about riots and unrest. Theories to generate hypotheses.

Appleton, Sheldon. *United States Foreign Policy: An Introduction With Cases.* Boston: Little, Brown, 1968. A useful study of the development and status of American foreign policy.

Bader, William B. *The United States and the Spread of Nuclear Weapons.* New York: Western, 1968. Focuses on the weapons issue and especially upon the potentiality for destruction of nuclear bombs.

Beggs, David W. and S. Kern Alexander. *Integration and Education.* Chicago: Rand McNally, 1969. The role of education in relationship to the revolution of the American Negro, with a stress on the needs of deprived children.

Benjamin, Harold R. W. (J. Abner Peddiwell). *The Saber-Tooth Curriculum.* New York: McGraw-Hill, 1939. Delightful and satiric fable by a distinguished educator. One owes it to himself to read the book in its entirety.

Bouma, Donald H. and James Hoffman. *The Dynamics of School Integration.* Grand Rapids, Mich.: William B. Eardman, 1968. A look at the problems of school integration by a sociologist, who writes with emphasis on the community, and an educator, who deals with factors in the learning process.

Carmichael, Stokely and Charles V. Hamilton. *Black Power: The Politics of Liberation in America.* New York: Vintage, 1967. Collaboration between a black activist and a black scholar. Presentation of the case for the new militancy in the black community in recent years.

Carson, Rachel. *Silent Spring.* Boston: Houghton Mifflin, 1962. A book which made a difference in American life by calling attention to the dangers to the environment through indiscriminate use of insecticides.

Cleaver, Eldridge. *Soul on Ice.* New York: McGraw-Hill, 1968. Letters and essays written in prison by a militant black leader who seeks identification for himself and his people. A cultural and sociological critique that has relevance for the future of America.

Coleman, James S. et al. *Equality of Educational Opportunity*. Washington, D.C.: U.S. Office of Education, 1966. A survey of more than 500,000 students and 60,000 teachers in 4,000 schools which documents the extent and effects of racial segregation. Classic but seldom read report which contradicts many stereotypes concerning the education of Americans who are poor. Raises questions as to the contribution of schools to society.

Ehrlich, Paul R. *The Population Bomb*. New York: Ballantine Books, 1968. A widely read account of the population problem and its implication for humanity unless the present growth of population is checked.

Ellison, Ralph. *Invisible Man*. New York: Random House, 1946. A comic-tragic soul-searching story of one young black's experiences in self-discovery.

Epstein, Charlotte. *Intergroup Relations for the Classroom Teacher*. Boston: Houghton Mifflin, 1968. Significant and readable book on dealing with intergroup problems with an emphasis upon dramatic vignettes and practical suggestions.

Glock, Charles and Ellen Siegelman, eds. *Prejudice U.S.A.* New York: Frederick A. Praeger, 1969. A series of papers by outstanding academicians and political activists on the nature of prejudice and its impact on education among institutions. A competent review of how prejudice is well rooted in American institutions.

Graham, Hugh Davis and Ted Robert Gurr. *Violence in America*. New York: Bantam, 1969. A report submitted to the National Commission on the Causes and Prevention of Violence. Specialists consider the extent and meaning of violence in America, past and present.

Grambs, Jean D. *Intergroup Education: Methods and Materials*. Englewood Cliffs, N.J.: Prentice-Hall, 1968. A guide to intercultural and intergroup education for those attempting to bring about better human relationships among Americans of varied backgrounds.

Green, Robert L., ed. *Racial Crisis in American Education*. Chicago: Follett Educational Corporation, 1969. Selected readings concerning the subject of racism in American public schools. Suggests solutions to problems of racial imbalance and isolation, and places special emphasis on the urban classroom.

Grier, William H. and Price M. Cobbs. *Black Rage*. New York: Bantam, 1968. Two black psychiatrists look at the potential for violence in the American black.

Kennedy, Robert F. *To Seek a Newer World*. New York: Doubleday, 1967. Robert F. Kennedy's vision, expressed in his own words, of the kind of America he supported and which he did not have the opportunity to realize.

Kvaraceus, William C., John C. Gibson and Thomas J. Curtin. *Poverty, Education, and Race Relations: Studies and Proposals*. Boston: Allyn and Bacon, 1967. Seeking solutions to formidable and challenging problems of American society, stressing obligations to reduce the dual handicaps of poverty and discrimination, and suggesting avenues of strategy in education and teaching for coping with these issues.

Mack, Raymond W., ed. *Prejudice and Race Relations*. Chicago: Quadrangle Books, 1970. Articles from the *New York Times Magazine* on the options before us as seen by leaders of change.

National Advisory Commission on Civil Disorders. *Report of the National Advisory Commission on Civil Disorders*. Washington, D.C.: Government Printing Office, 1968. The Kerner report on the disturbances in the ghettos during the summer of 1967, when rioting and burning occurred.

Stamp, Dudley L. *Land for Tomorrow: Our Developing World*. Bloomington, Ind.: Indiana University Press, 1969. The pressure of population on land and its physical resources.

Urban America, Inc. and The Urban Coalition. *One Year Later*. New York: Frederick A.

Praeger. An analysis of the state of American democracy a year after the Kerner Commission Report which concludes that the nation had moved a year closer to being two societies, black and white, increasingly separate and scarcely less unequal.

Weinberg, Meyer. *Integrated Education*. New York: Glencoe Press, 1968. A reader primarily developed from the magazine *Integrated Education* and dealing with many aspects of the search for equal educational opportunity.

AUDIO-VISUAL MATERIALS

Oral Essays on Education—A Series (NCAT, Michigan State University.) A series of 17 tapes with talks by prominent personalities discussing some aspects of education. Samples are: *Can Education Change*—Margaret Mead—30 Min. *Education in Our American Culture*—Margaret Mead—30 Min. *The Here and Now*—Hubert Humphrey—30 Min. *Pursuit of Excellence*—Arthur S. Flemming—30 Min. *What Price Creativity*—Fred Hechinger—30 Min. *The Public Enterprise*—Henry Steele Commager—30 Min.

The Identity and Dignity of Man (American Association for the Advancement of Science.) A series of discussion sessions on such topics as population and the dignity of man, problems of population control, regulation of behavior, organ replacement, problems with organ repacement, improvement of life through genetic manipulation.

Focus on Behavior: The Social Animal (NET, 30 Min.) Investigates ways man is influenced and changed by society. Shows effects of group pressure to conform in actions and beliefs.

Campus Crossroads (Yale University, 30 Min.) Depicts the orientation given students at Yale University from such countries as Liberia, Egypt, Japan, Ceylon, Brazil, Turkey, Thailand, and Mexico.

Education Under a Thatched Roof (Indiana University, 19 Min.) Demonstrates the preparation and implementation of a unit-team teaching approach at a secondary school in Bangkok, Thailand. Scenes show a unit on sanitation in food being taught to the students, using media, team-teaching, field trips to an outdoor marketplace, instructional materials and other locally available resources.

The Silent Spring of Rachel Carson (CBSTV, 54 Min.) Explains how poisonous and biologically potent chemicals were used with little or no advance investigation of their effect on soil, water, wildlife, and man.

Population Ecology (Encyclopedia Britannica Films, 19 Min. Color) Shows how environmental conditions, such as natural enemies and food factors, can help increase or reduce births and deaths. Discusses how man, with his ability to change environment, has created the birth surplus over death called the population explosion.

Population Explosion (National Film Board of Canada, 15 Min., Color) Discusses factors which have contributed to the imbalance between population and wealth-producing elements in the mid-twentieth century world.

Where is Prejudice (National Educational TV, Inc., 59 Min.) Pictures twelve college students of different races and faiths participating in a workshop to test their common denial that they are prejudiced. Proves that prejudice exists in those who believe themselves to be unprejudiced.

The Victims (Anti-Defamation League: 48 min.) Shows how children develop prejudices. Done with the assistance of Dr. Spock.

Black White Gray (Barker, Thomas B., 4 Min., Color) Symbols illustrate the history of the Negro in society. The film expresses the belief that human beings, regardless of race, are the same.

The Future and the Negro (NET, 75 Min.) Depicts a panel discussion by noted commentators on the future of the Negro, the economic position of the Negro, racism, and the relationship of the American Negroes to Africa. Features Ossie Davis.

The Negro and the American Promise (NET, 60 Min.) Presents Kenneth Clark interviewing James Baldwin, Martin Luther King Jr. and Malcolm X.

Thurgood Marshall—Mr. Civil Rights (Vignette Films, 45 frs., Color) Portrays Thurgood Marshall's leadership in the civil rights movement. Shows how he challenged the "separate but equal" doctrine. The Supreme Court decision to integrate all public facilities.

Society of Bigots—KKK (ABCTV, 26 Min.) Deals with the Ku Klux Klan in the context of President Johnson's charge that it is a "society of bigots." Howard K. Smith covers a Klan rally in the deep south, and interviews the imperial wizard.

War/Peace and the Teaching of Values (Lawrence Metcalf, New York: World Law Fund, Taped lecture, 50 min. The relationships between international understanding and the learner's values.

SIXTEEN

WHAT'S A SCHOOL FOR, ANYWAY?

What's a school for, anyway? It sounds like a simple question. Each of us individually can answer it—to our own satisfaction at least. But trouble develops when others set forth their interpretations of the purposes of education. Try asking your fellow students, friends, neighbors, or family about the goals of education and notice what varying perceptions they present. Place the whole problem in the wider setting of differing cultures and societies, changing social circumstances, and various epochs and eras, and you will have some idea of the complexity of our seemingly simple question.

Of the many possible ways of approaching the matter of purposes, goals, aims, or objectives—terms which we will here use interchangeably pending your more intensive study of philosophy of education—we have chosen three: (1) We will summarize what many thinkers throughout the ages have concluded concerning education. (2) We will report on several studies of the purposes of American education which have been made during the past half century. (3) We will summarize what several outstanding twentieth century American philosophers of education believe. Then, we must leave up to you your decisions on "What's a school for, anyway?"

THINKERS THROUGH THE AGES

SOCRATES (469–399 B.C.)

Socrates the Greek philosopher should strike a responsive chord in many young Americans, for Socrates lived by his principles; there was no hypocrisy in this man. When he became convinced that his responsibility was to discuss ideas with Greek citizens wherever they congregated, he went about Athens applying his dialectic and developing discourses. His dialectical approach was intended to get people to examine their values by clarifying what they meant

Causing others to doubt their assumptions was one of the ideas Socrates believed essential to education. Courtesy of HPS.

by them. ("Justice?" "For enemies as well as friends? In time of war as in peace?") If his pursuit of knowledge necessitated some degree of neglect of his domestic duties, including those to his reputedly shrewish wife Xanthippe, he would neglect his household in the interest of philosophy.

Socrates not only lived by his principles; he died by them after his trial for allegedly corrupting the youth of Athens. Though the oracle of Delphi acclaimed him the wisest man in Greece, Socrates himself felt only that he differed from others in that they thought they were wise and did not realize their own ignorance, while he was acutely aware of his own ignorance.

Socrates thought that knowledge and virtue were esssentially the same. He believed that no man consciously or knowingly did wrong. If virtue was the same as knowledge, then virtue could be taught. Socrates' test therefore became

---

HENRY BROOKS ADAMS *Nothing in education is so astonishing as the amount of ignorance it accumulates in the form of inert facts.*

ARISTOTLE *All who have meditated on the art of governing mankind have been convinced that the fate of empires depends on the education of youth.*

WYSTAN HUGH AUDEN *Unless an individual is free to obtain the fullest education with which his society can provide him he is being injured by society.*

SIR JOHN BUCHAN, BARON TWEEDSMUIR *Education is the only cure for certain diseases the modern world has engendered, but if you don't find the disease, the remedy is superfluous.*

a search for wisdom through his dialectic so that men might achieve right conduct. He was a self-appointed guide to the improvement of his fellow citizens in the intellectual and moral realms. In effect, he was a one-man university.

His pupil, Plato, reported Socrates' discussions in a series of dialogues. For instance, in the *Apology,* Plato presents a defense of Socrates. In the *Meno* he raises the question of whether virtue can be taught. In the *Gorgias* he discusses the nature of right and wrong. Throughout he presents Socrates as thinking with others on the unity of virtue and knowledge and of virtue and happiness. Socrates often preferred to leave people with questions to live with rather than to present them with ready-made answers.

MARK TWAIN (SAMUEL LANGHORN CLEMENS) *I have never let my schooling interfere with my education.*

LOTUS D. COFFMAN *The chief support of an autocracy is an uneducated people.*

JOHN AMOS COMENIUS *Education is the development of the whole man—to be acquainted with all things.*

JAMES B. CONANT *The primary concern of American education today is not the development of the appreciation of the "good life" in young gentlemen born to the purple. Our purpose is to cultivate in the largest number of our future citizens an appreciation both of the responsibilities and the benefits which come to them because they are American and free.*

Socrates, through his discussions, demonstrated his faith in the ability of men to think. He was the embodiment of the educational ideal of reason as he constantly inquired into ideas, and remorselessly probed into uncharted areas of thought. He sought for ideas in the social life of his community and he believed that each man had the potentiality to make a genuine contribution to society. Consequently, he is often regarded as a precursor of the democratic tradition.

PLATO (428–347 B.C.)

The philosopher Plato grew up in a chaotic period when struggles between Athens and Sparta were dividing the loyalties of Greeks. Plato was an enthusiastic, faithful student of the master teacher, Socrates, and the great mentor's influence on his pupil's philosophy was substantial.

But Plato was no democrat. Plato subordinated education, law and order, and human virtue to his ideal conception of a state guided by a timeless Supreme

Pompeian mosaic of Plato with students. Courtesy of HPS.

Good. His ideal society (or state) rejected pure democracy. Plato's utopian state—described in *The Republic*—was predicated on elitism; each man, though possessing equal rights with all others, was to serve the state in the manner for which his individual abilities best suited him. According to Plato the ability to govern, the ability to organize and preserve, and the ability to work and produce are found in all men, but in varying amounts. He categorized the abilities of man into three basic classes: those who were destined to govern, those who were to defend the state, and those who were to perform the menial tasks

---

RALPH WALDO EMERSON *I believe that our experience instructs us that the secret of education lies in respecting the pupil. It is not for you to choose what he shall know and what he shall do. It is chosen and foreordained, and he only holds the key to his own secret.*

EDGAR Z. FRIEDENBERG *Regardless of the uses to which any society may put its schools, education has an obligation that transcends its own social function and society's purposes. That obligation is to clarify for its students the meaning of their experience of life in their society.*

ROBERT FROST *Education is turning things over in the mind.*

of labor. The three classes neatly parallelled the three functions of the state and these, in turn, parallelled three functions of the individual personality. Thus, class structure was characteristic of Plato's ideal state and regarded by Plato as intrinsic to human nature.

> **NORMAN COUSINS** *Education fails unless the Three R's at one end of the school spectrum lead ultimately to the Four P's at the other—Preparation for Earning, Preparation for Living, Preparation for Understanding, Preparation for Participation in the problems involved in the making of a better world.*
>
> **JOHN DEWEY** *Education is life, not preparation for life. . . . The aim of education should be to teach the child to think, not what to think. . . . The idea of education as preparation and of adulthood as a fixed limit of growth are two sides of the same obnoxious untruth.*
>
> **ALBERT EINSTEIN** *The aim of education must be the training of independently acting and thinking individuals, who, however, see in the service of the community their highest life problems.*
>
> **DWIGHT D. EISENHOWER** *In this country we emphasize both liberal and practical education. But too often it is liberal education for one, and a practical education for another. What we desperately need is an integrated, liberal practical education for the same person.*

To Plato, education and society were inseparable. It was the purpose of the educational system to preserve the state by training each man to prepare himself for citizenship to the best of his ability and according to his civic class. An educated elite was to identify the abilities and consequent class of each individual; men were to be trained to accept beliefs and values passed on to them by this elite. According to Plato, a man's civic virtue must be his life's pursuit; he must conduct his life according to established standards of good, evil, truth, knowledge, and reason. Since true understanding of virtue requires a man's total commitment, only the elite who have devoted their lives to the attainment of intellectual and moral truth were qualified to rule wisely and supervise the education of the majority.[1]

In *The Republic*, Plato placed strong emphasis on method of study as the road to proper knowledge. The acquisition of knowledge required intellectual exercise and the use of reason. Education began in the nursery with the telling of fables and fairy stories to children, properly censored to ensure a suitable

[1] Frederick A. G. Beck, *Greek Education: 450–350 B.C.* (New York: Barnes and Noble, 1964), pp. 199–200.

Aristotle with his pupil Alexander. Courtesy of HPS.

moral tone. The gods were always portrayed as models of virtue and incapable of falsehood. In his view of the educational curriculum, Plato included gymnastics for the body and the arts for the soul.

Music and mathematics were essential as far as Plato was concerned in the training of the good Greek citizen; music was taught to develop a sense of rhythm and harmony which he viewed as essential in a responsible citizen, and the basic value of mathematics was its training and sharpening of the intellect. Study of music and mathematics helped one become more efficient in thinking and helped one learn other subjects more effectively and rapidly.

Plato developed several ideas still present in our contemporary educational system: compulsory public education, state sponsorship and support of education, the tradition that education as intellectual discipline was correct for the elite and that useful training was appropriate for the masses, and an authoritarian approach to methodology and curriculum selection.

ARISTOTLE (384–322 B.C.)

Aristotle studied under Plato, became a tutor to Alexander the Great, and opened a school in Athens in which he lectured. He emphasized direct observation of nature and believed that theories must be checked against facts. He constantly looked for the first principles which he regarded as changeless and forming the basis for all knowledge, and he clarified the nature of logical thought and showed how syllogistic reasoning could be an aid to clear thinking. He fostered the pursuit of the life of contemplation, stood for virtue as the mean between the extremes, and strove for rationality.

Therefore, Aristotle's conception of education emphasized the intellectual and cognitive. To Aristotle, the finest citizen was the man who tried to know and understand through speculating, thinking, and contemplating.

Like Plato, Aristotle believed that education for citizens, for warriors, and for leaders should be differentiated. Democracy was not an essential form of government to Aristotle; in fact, he viewed it as a fairly bad form. Man as a political being could fulfill his civic function in an elite society as well as in a democratic society, thought Aristotle.

In later years medieval scholastics were influenced by Aristotle's mode of philosophical inquiry; St. Thomas Aquinas was moved to effect an integration between Aristotelian philosophy and Christian theology. Aristotle's studies in

> **EDWARD GIBBON** *Every man who rises above the common level has received two educations; the first from his teacher, the second, more personal and important, from himself.*
>
> **SAMUEL GOMPERS** *We can advance and develop democracy but little faster than we can advance and develop the average level of intelligence and knowledge within the democracy. That is the problem that confronts modern educators.*
>
> **JOHANN FRIEDRICH HERBART** *The end of education is to produce a well-balanced many sidedness of interest. Morality is universally acknowledged as the highest aim of humanity, and consequently of education.*

rhetoric, logic, ethics and political theory became major ingredients of the classical tradition in education.

JOHANN AMOS COMENIUS (1592–1670)

Comenius was born in 1592 in Moravia in central Europe. He lived and worked amidst the religious and political struggles of the Reformation and the Thirty Years War. In the social struggle, Comenius was Protestant in sympathy and an ordained minister in his sect. During childhood and youth, he attended a typical Latin school; he was disappointed and disillusioned by the traditional, authoritarian approach to learning, the rote memory methodology, and the classical curriculum.

Comenius felt a deep personal relationship with God, and he believed that education should have a Christian orientation. He assumed that God was the author of the natural order of things and that a proper education would be one that followed man's natural development. In his major work, *The Great Didactic*, Comenius developed his ideas on education into a system of universal education based on principles of learning suggested by natural law and the ordering of things as he observed them.[2] He used his convictions concerning the rightness

---
[2] Harry S. Broudy and John R. Palmer, *Exemplars of Teaching Method* (Chicago: Rand McNally, 1965), p. 96.

Comenius and some of his teaching aids. Courtesy of The Bettmann Archive.

of natural law to suggest reforms for school curricula and methodology.

Through his analysis of the principles of natural law, Comenius developed logical timetables for the progression of a young man's education and he argued the case for universal education as a natural human right. He illustrated the importance of effective motivation and methodology through step-by-step graded presentation of one subject at a time and through the realization that "education begins with the universal and ends with the particular."

Comenius developed new textbooks and visual aids for use in the classroom. These were virtually unheard-of innovations in classical and authoritarian schoolrooms. He was influenced by the new science and scientists of his time; he considered science more useful than the humanities, and stressed the practical, useful subjects in the school.

Comenius anticipated the conclusions of modern educators in several areas: a better life as the central goal of education, education in special buildings and in graded groups, and the need for an affectionate, mutually respecting rapport between children and their teachers. He believed that a teacher should be a most influential force in his students' lives and he stressed patience and guidance in the classroom as opposed to strict authoritarianism.

> **ADOLF HITLER** *Universal education is the most corroding and disintegrating poison that liberalism has ever invented for its own destruction.*
>
> **OLIVER WENDELL HOLMES** *Your education begins when what is called your education is over.*
>
> **ROBERT H. JACKSON** *Free public education, if faithful to the ideal of secular instruction and political neutrality, will not be partisan or enemy of any class, creed, party, or faction.*

JEAN JACQUES ROUSSEAU (1712–1778)

Rousseau was born in Geneva, Switzerland. The conduct of his life reflected his philosophical theses, the glorification of nature, natural law, and man's communion with the elements of nature. He was an avowed romanticist, in keeping with the trend of thought sweeping Europe during his lifetime. He claimed that too much civilization, too much society, corrupted man. Social convention directed man away from his natural life and subjected him to artificiality and external standards of conduct, reason, and evaluation. Rousseau insisted that "civilization represented a constant state of war and that it only produced a parasitical aristocracy which had enslaved the common people."[3] Rousseau did acknowledge the state and society as a necessary organization, however, and held that the question of how to maintain and refine the natural freedom of the individual within the boundaries of society was the basic human dilemma.

Rousseau regarded the purpose of education as fostering the natural inward growth of the individual. The basic objective of the school is to foster the natural development of the individual child; everything else is secondary. The schools of his day, however, were largely entrenched in external processes; they were authoritarian, uncreative, and stereotyped.

Rousseau believed that education must deal with life and must teach the child how to utilize his abilities and recognize his potential. School should give the child experience in living, not merely preparation for life. It must train his senses and give him a knowledge of natural objects and forces. He advocated a one-to-one ratio of student and teacher in order that the teacher might know his student well, establish authentic teacher-student relationships, and plan meaningful learning experiences and actions around the needs and interests of the student.[4]

---

[3] Frederick Mayer, *A History of Educational Thought* (Columbus, Ohio: Charles E. Merrill Books, 1960), p. 235.
[4] *Ibid.*, pp. 241–243.

> **IMMANUEL KANT** *The purpose of education is to train children, not with reference to their success in the present state of society but to a better possible state, in accordance with an ideal conception of humanity.*
>
> **JOHN LOCKE** *The attainment of a sound mind in a sound body is the end of education.*
>
> **GEORGE PEABODY** *Education—a debt due from the present to future generations.*
>
> **JEAN PIAGET** *The principal goal of education is to create men who are capable of doing new things, not simply of repeating what other generations have done—men who are creative, inventive, and discoverers.*

Rousseau believed that education should be student-centered, that it should be an action-oriented experience which would develop the individual's ability to manifest the power of his senses, to feel and express emotion, to create, and to utilize his knowledge in practical action for his individual well-being.

JOHANN PESTALOZZI (1746–1827)

Schooled in Zurich, Pestalozzi tried several professions, but was unsuccessful. At Neuhof, he established an orphanage and the remainder of his life was devoted to the care and education of impoverished children.[5] He developed special interests in the underprivileged children of his communities and became dedicated to the ideal of equal education opportunity for all children.

His ideas rest firmly upon his social philosophy[6] and his philosophy was a logical product of the kind of life that he lived. He was a simple, humble man, weak in his abilities to organize, administer, and rule, but powerful in his sensitivity to and awareness of the human condition. The educational ideas of Pestalozzi have much in common with those of Rousseau and Comenius.

Pestalozzi recognized the presence in all men of three basic drives: the primitive impulse, the social impulse, and the ethical impulse. Education, according to Pestalozzi, is the process whereby the ethical impulse triumphs over the others. This belief conflicted with the artificial training common in the schools of his time and favored an inward development whereby the human capacities of love, understanding, and creativity were nurtured.[7] Like Comenius, he emphasized the necessity of pleasant rapport between teacher and student, the need for motivation in learning, and the object lessons which nature can teach us. Noticing that

---

[5] Mayer, p. 265.
[6] Ibid.   [7] Ibid., p. 266.

Pestalozzi's idea of student involvement at the individual ability level has had great effect on education. Courtesy of HPS.

children learn much about their lives and their world naturally if left to their own devices, he channeled his observations into laws of learning and methodology.

> **PLATO** By education I mean that training in excellence from youth upward which makes a man passionately desire to be a perfect citizen and teaches him to rule, to obey, with justice. This is the only education which deserves the name. The other sort of training which aims at acquiring wealth or bodily strength is not worthy to be called education at all.
>
> **WALTER P. REUTHER** We need to move to overcome the deficit in our educational system. Millions of American children are being denied their rightful educational opportunity. All of them made in the image of God—are entitled to an educational opportunity so that they can grow intellectually, spiritually, and culturally, limited only by their own individual capacity. We are robbing our nation of the tremendous creative contribution that these young people will make later in life, because we are denying them their educational opportunity.

He taught geography, for example, by taking walks with the children about the countryside and having them draw maps and construct clay models of what they observed and discussed. He believed in the object lessons of nature as one of the most effective teaching methods. He believed that every child must be free to become involved in learning and develop at his individual ability level.

Each man's knowledge is his power in life, according to this philosopher, and the instincts of the child are much more effective in helping him satisfy his needs than the logic of the adult.

JOHANN HERBART (1776–1841)

Herbart, a German, is an interesting contrast to Rousseau, Pestalozzi, and other progressive or romantic thinkers. He combined the reigning educational theories of the time and advocated a common ground between the authoritarian, classical education prominent in the schools and the student-centered, action-oriented educational ideas of the romantic or progressive thinkers.

> **THEODORE ROOSEVELT** *Education must light the path for social change. The social and economic problems confronting us are growing in complexity. The more complex and difficult these problems become, the more essential it is to provide broad and complete education; that kind of education that will equip us as a nation to decide these problems for the best interest of all concerned. Our ultimate security, to a large extent, is based upon the individual's character, information and attitude—and the responsibility rests squarely upon those who direct education in America.*
>
> **BERTRAND RUSSELL** *The sentiments of an adult are compounded of a kernel of instinct surrounded by a vast husk of education. . . . Throughout education, from the first day to the last, there should be a sense of intellectual adventure.*
>
> **WILLIAM F. RUSSELL** *The defense against a bad idea is a better idea; the defense against propaganda is education; and it is in education that democracies must put their trust.*

Morality and development of character were the fundamental purposes of education, according to Herbart. He advocated a middle-ground approach between freedom and authority. The idea of individual worth and an atmosphere of emotion and creativity must be fostered in the schools, but these must be balanced by reason and by a sense of responsibility and duty to society. He believed in student motivation and involvement in learning activity; but he also believed that students must learn to accept the organization and structure of the subjects as they are presented by their elders, the authorities in society who know best the proper content and structure of knowledge which children and youth must attain. The freedom advocated by Rousseau and others must be combined with the authority essential in good education, for the "natural exuberance (of youth) must meet enough resistance to avert offense."[8] Children

[8] Mayer, p. 273.

must develop self-control and learn to obey, he wrote, for self-control in the interest of common good is essential to character development. Herbart's central maxim was that our minds are formed by the ideas that the world and our teachers impress on us. He felt, therefore, that it was centrally important that teachers employ correct means to attain desirable ends. He felt that he had located the scientific laws of learning and formulated from these a correct methodology for classroom practice. It was based on five basic steps: preparation, presentation, association, generalization, and application. These steps were

> **ERIC SEVEREID** Ours is not an age of reason, but one of anxiety and feelings of frustration. Educators can help in this crisis by substituting courage for fear and intellect for emotion.
>
> **GEORGE BERNARD SHAW** Civilization is dying of what it calls education.
>
> **HERBERT SPENCER** The great aim of education is not knowledge, but action.
>
> **HAROLD TAYLOR** Education is good only as it helps people to enrich and fulfill their lives, both in leading toward personal joy and in leading toward the extension of one's talents into modes of helping other people.
>
> **ARNOLD TOYNBEE** My own guess is that our age will be remembered chiefly for having been the first age since the dawn of civilization in which people dared to think it practicable to make the benefits of civilization available to the whole human race.

supposed to provide the teacher with the definitive answer to the question of how to teach. But Herbart's system was so tightly structured that it tended to stifle the creativity of both teachers and students.[9]

FRIEDRICH FROEBEL (1782–1852)

Froebel's life spanned a period of seventy years in German history. His early years were similar to those of another man of his time, the English romanticist, William Wordsworth. Both of the men spent lonely childhoods; they enjoyed solitary, exhilarating hours in the forests and fields. Each developed a great appreciation for the natural world and formulated theories about the spiritual relationship of God, man, and nature.

Childhood experiences formed the foundation for Froebel's deep religious

---

[9] Mayer, pp. 277–278.

Froebel stressed creativity in his teaching. Courtesy of The Bettmann Archive.

faith which animated his educational ideas. Froebel joined the educators who formulated a theoretical base and practical frame of reference for child-centered education. His beliefs embodied Wordsworth's insight, "The child is father of the man."

He believed that the education of an individual should begin as soon as possible, and he regarded a home united by love as the best educational institution. But according to Froebel, many homes fail in providing love, so the school must take over very early. The early years are the most vital for the development of self-consciousness and determination, as Froebel saw it. He believed that education should be based on the needs of children; one learned about the processes of life, the overall unity of all things, by experiencing them through involvement of the whole person.

Froebel established a kindergarten at Blankenburg where directed play activities for children were designed to prepare them for adult activities. The development of the abilities and talents necessary for the social games and the discovery and analysis of nature and objects were parts of Froebel's kindergarten program. He conceived such experiences as essential to successful, happy adult life.

Froebel's ideas have been described as vague and mystical. He believed in the organized unity of the universe—any given thing is a whole in itself yet part of a larger whole; there is an inter-connected unity of all things and all experiences. He accepted the theory of recapitulation—cultural epochs are relived by each individual during his lifetime; he believed that the developmental process in life, with which he conceived the school as basically concerned, is a swing between opposites, toward a synthesis that unites these opposites at a higher level.[10]

---

[10] Harry S. Broudy and John R. Palmer, *Exemplars of Teaching Method* (Chicago: Rand McNally, 1965), pp. 119–120.

> **GEORGE MACAULAY TREVELYAN** *Education . . . has produced a vast population able to read but unable to distinguish what is worth reading.*
>
> **EARL WARREN** *Today, education is perhaps the most important function of state and local governments . . . It is the very foundation of good citizenship. Today it is a principal instrument in awakening the child to cultural values, in preparing him for later professional training, and in helping him to adjust normally to his environment.*
>
> **DANIEL WEBSTER** *On the diffusion of education among the people rest the preservation and perpetuation of our free institutions.*
>
> **ALFRED NORTH WHITEHEAD** *In the conditions of modern life the rule is absolute, the race which does not value trained intelligence is doomed. Not all your heroism, not all your social charm, not all your wit, not all your victories on land or at sea, can move back the finger of fate. Today we maintain ourselves. Tomorrow science will have moved forward yet one more step, and there will be no appeal from the judgment which will then be pronounced on the uneducated.*

Concerning curriculum and methodology in the school, Froebel believed that the two most important aspects are creativity and freedom. He was especially concerned with problems of creativity; the school's main purpose must be to search for ways of identifying and nuturing creativity. He believed that facts are secondary to experience—memorization should be avoided in the classroom.

FRANCIS WAYLAND PARKER (1837–1902)

Francis Parker was an American educational pioneer of the latter half of the nineteenth century, a time when new social and scientific forces were emerging in America to make an impact on man and his institutions. He was a democratic educator who believed in the sanctity of the individual and his relationship to his fellow man and to mother nature. He takes his place among the ranks of the progressive educators in America and has often been cited for his influence on the teachings of John Dewey, who regarded Parker as the father of modern progressive education.

His educational ideas were clearly influenced by his background of a rural New England childhood, service in the Civil War, and early teaching experiences in Illinois. He became a staunch humanist and a lover of nature; he was also an Emersonian in his distrust of "secondhand book-learning."[11]

---

[11] Merle Curti, *The Social Ideas of American Educators* (Paterson, N.J.: Littlefield, Adams and Co., 1965), p. 377.

> **WOODROW WILSON** *Without popular education no government which rests on popular action can long endure.*
>
> **PAUL WOODRING** *A statement of the aim of education need not be a long list or even a short list; it can be in a single sentence. In a society of free men, the proper aim of education is to prepare the individual to make wise decisions. All else is but contributory.*

Parker condemned conventional education as too bookish, too artificial, and too authoritarian. He saw the formal school as suppressive so he recommended direct study in science through observation and field trips in biology, geography, and nature study. The development of affinity for the natural world was to Parker the key step to individual awareness and basic morality.

In one of his basic works, *Talks on Teaching,* Parker condemned the textbook teacher and the academic curricula and courses of study of many school systems because of their emphasis on fixed quantities of skill and knowledge which seemed to take everything into account except the interests and abilities of the individual teachers and students. He allied himself with Comenius, Pestalozzi, and Froebel in the "learning by doing" concept. He advocated an action-oriented approach to teaching and to formulation of courses of study; the scientific method was essential to him. Spontaneity, student discovery, creativity, individual artistry, nondirected, pleasurable work—all of these were important characteristics in the classroom advocated by Parker.

Parker had the opportunity to put his ideas into effect as superintendent of the Quincy, Massachusetts, public schools from 1875 to 1880. The "Quincy Movement" emphasized informal instruction and eliminated rigid discipline; it stressed the teaching of science and emphasized group activities. Parker applied his ideas further as a supervisor in the Boston schools, as principal of the Cook County Normal School in Chicago, and as founder and principal of the Chicago Institute which became part of the school of education of the University of Chicago.

REPORTS ON THE PURPOSES OF AMERICAN EDUCATION

To this point, the thinking of individuals who have influenced the course of education through the ages has been reported to you. These thinkers often differ from each other in their conceptions of the relative roles of reason and emotion, of freedom and authority, of democracy and elitism, of the individual and society, and of the learner and the teacher. Consequently, their conceptions of the best content and methodology vary. Their basic philosophic assumptions account for their conclusions as to what is good education.

Another approach which might help you to arrive at your philosophy of education is to study outstanding reports on the purposes of education by influential groups of American educators and laymen during the past half century. Below are several such reports which deal with "What's a school for?"

CARDINAL PRINCIPLES OF EDUCATION (1918)

A pioneering report on educational purposes was that of the Commission on the Reorganization of Secondary Education which in 1918 set forth "Seven Cardinal Principles." Unlike earlier reports by other commissions that prescribed amounts of content in the several subject matter fields, the "Cardinal Principles Report" went to the heart of the matter by boldly setting forth purposes for modern schools. Though the Commission specifically refers to secondary education, the recommendations have been found to be applicable to elementary education as well.

1. *Health.* Health needs cannot be neglected during the period of secondary education without serious danger to the individual and the race. The secondary school should therefore provide health instruction, inculcate health habits, organize an effective program of physical activities, regard health needs in planning work and play, and cooperate with home and community in safe-guarding and promoting health interests.
2. *Command of fundamental processes.* Much of the energy of the elementary school is properly devoted to teaching certain fundamental processes, such as reading, writing, arithmetical computations, and the elements of oral and written expression. The facility that a child of 12 or 14 may acquire in the use of these tools is not sufficient for the needs of modern life. This is particularly true of the mother tongue. . . .
3. *Worthy home membership.* Worthy home membership as an objective calls for the development of those qualities that make the individual a worthy member of a family, both contributing to and deriving benefit from that membership. . . . The coeducational school with a faculty of men and women should, in its organization and its activities, exemplify wholesome relations between boys and girls and men and women. . . .
4. *Vocation.* Vocational education should equip the individual to secure a livelihood for himself and those dependent on him, to serve society well through his vocation, to maintain the right relationships toward his fellow workers and society, and, as far as possible, to find in that vocation his own best development. . . .
5. *Civic education* should develop in the individual those qualities whereby he will act well his part as a member of neighborhood, town or city, State, and Nation, and give him a basis for understanding international problems. . . .
6. *Worthy use of leisure.* Education should equip the individual to secure from his leisure the re-creation of body, mind, and spirit, and the enrichment and enlargement of his personality. . . .
7. *Ethical character.* In a democratic society ethical character becomes paramount among the objectives of the secondary school. Among the means for developing ethical character may be mentioned the wise selection of

content and methods of instruction in all subjects of study, the social contacts of pupils with one another and with their teachers, the opportunities afforded by the organization and administration of the school for the development on the part of pupils of the sense of personal responsibility and initiative, and, above all, the spirit of service and the principles of true democracy which should permeate the entire school—principal, teachers, and pupils.[12]

WHITE HOUSE CONFERENCE ON EDUCATION (1955)

Conferences on education are sometimes called by a President of the United States. In 1955 a White House Conference on Education recommended to the President the following aims in education, especially applicable to elementary education:

1. The fundamental skills of communication—reading, writing, spelling, as well as other elements of effective oral and writing expression; the arithmetical and mathematical skill, including problem solving. . . .
2. Appreciation for our democratic heritage.
3. Civic rights and responsibilities and knowledge of American institutions.
4. Respect and appreciation for human values and for the beliefs of others.
5. Ability to think and evaluate constructively and creatively.
6. Effective work habits and self-discipline.
7. Social competency as a contributing member of his family and community.
8. Ethical behavior based on a sense of moral and spiritual values.
9. Intellectual curiosity and eagerness for life-long learning.
10. Esthetic appreciation and self-expression in the arts.
11. Physical and mental health.
12. Wise use of time, including constructive leisure pursuits.
13. Understanding of the physical world and man's relation to it as represented through basic knowledge of the sciences.
14. An awareness of our relationships with the world community.[13]

EDUCATIONAL POLICIES COMMISSION (1935–1968)

As its name implies, the Educational Policies Commission was set up to help define policies for education and to contribute to the resolution of educational issues. Sponsored by the National Education Association and the American Association of School Administrators, and made up of both educators and laymen, the Commission from 1935 until 1968 prepared a series of reports on the issues facing education.

---

[12] Commission on the Reorganization of Secondary Education, *The Cardinal Principles of Secondary Education,* Bulletin No. 35 (Washington, D.C.: U.S. Bureau of Education, 1918), pp. 5ff.

[13] Committee for the White House Conference on Education, *A Report to the President* (Washington, D.C.: U.S. Government Printing Office, April, 1956), pp. 91–92.

As to purposes of education, the Educational Policies Commission in 1938 recommended:

The Objectives of Self-Realization:
The inquiring mind. The educated person has an appetite for learning.
Speech. The educated person can speak the mother tongue clearly.
Reading. The educated person reads the mother tongue efficiently.
Writing. The educated person writes the mother tongue effectively.
Number. The educated person solves his problems of counting and calculating.
Sight and hearing. The educated person is skilled in listening and observing.
Health Knowledge. The educated person understands the basic facts concerning health and disease.
Health habits. The educated person protects his own health and that of his dependents.
Public health. The educated person works to improve the health of the community.
Recreation. The educated person is participant and spectator in many sports and other pastimes.
Intellectual interests. The educated person has mental resources for the use of leisure.
Esthetic interests. The educated person appreciates beauty.
Character. The educated person gives responsible direction to his own life.

The Objectives of Human Relationship:
Respect for humanity. The educated person puts human relationships first.
Friendships. The educated person enjoys a rich, sincere, and varied social life.
Cooperation. The educated person can work and play with others.
Courtesy. The educated person observes the amenities of social behavior.
Appreciation of the home. The educated person appreciates the family as a social institution.
Conservation of the home. The educated person conserves family ideals.
Homemaking. The educated person is skilled in homemaking.
Democracy in the home. The educated person maintains democratic family relationships.

The Objectives of Economic Efficiency:
Work. The educated producer knows the satisfaction of good workmanship.
Occupational information. The educated producer understands the requirements and opportunities for various jobs.
Occupational choice. The educated producer has *selected* his occupation.
Occupational efficiency. The educated producer succeeds in his chosen vocation.
Occupational adjustment. The educated producer maintains and improves his efficiency.
Occupational appreciation. The educated producer appreciates the social value of his work.

Personal economics. The educated consumer plans the economics of his own life.
Consumer judgment. The educated consumer develops standards for guiding his expenditures.
Efficiency in buying. The educated consumer is an informed and skillful buyer.
Consumer protection. The educated consumer takes appropriate measures to safeguard his interests.

The Objectives of Civic Responsibility:
Social justice. The educated citizen is sensitive to the disparities of human circumstance.
Social activity. The educated citizen acts to correct unsatisfactory conditions.
Social understanding. The educated citizen seeks to understand social structures and social processes.
Critical judgment. The educated citizen has defenses against propaganda.
Tolerance. The educated citizen respects honest differences of opinion.
Conservation. The educated citizen has a regard for the nation's resources.
Social application of science. The educated citizen measures scientific advance by its contribution to the general welfare.
World citizenship. The educated citizen is a cooperating member of the world community.
Law observance. The educated citizen respects the law.
Economic literacy. The educated citizen is economically literate.
Political citizenship. The educated citizen accepts his civic duties.
Devotion to democracy. The educated citizen acts upon an unswerving loyalty to democratic ideals.[14]

In 1961, the Educational Policies Commission attempted to define the key purpose of education in *The Central Purpose of American Education:*

The traditionally accepted obligation of the school to teach the *fundamental processes*—an obligation stressed in the 1918 and 1938 statements of educational purposes—is obviously directed toward the development of the ability to think. Each of the school's other traditional objectives can be better achieved as pupils develop this ability and learn to apply it to all the problems that face them. . . . Development of the ability to reason can lead also to dedication to the values which inhere in rationality: commitment to honesty, accuracy, and personal reliability; respect for the intellect and for the intellectual life; devotion to the expansion of knowledge. A man who thinks can understand the importance of this ability. He is likely to value the rational potentials of mankind as essential to a worthy life.

Thus the rational powers are central to all the other qualities of the human spirit. These powers flourish in a humane and morally responsible context and

[14] Educational Policies Commission, *The Purposes of Education in American Democracy* (Washington, D.C.: NEA, 1938), pp. 50, 72, 90, 108.

contribute to the entire personality. The rational powers are to the entire human spirit as the hub is to the wheel. . . .

The purpose which runs through and strengthens all other educational purposes—the common thread of education—is the development of the ability to think. This is the central purpose to which the school must be oriented if it is to accomplish either its traditional tasks or those newly accentuated by recent changes in the world. To say that it is central is not to say that it is the sole purpose or in all circumstances the most important purpose, but that it must be a pervasive concern in the work of the school. Many agencies contribute to achieving educational objectives, but this particular objective will not be generally attained unless the school focuses on it. In this context, therefore, the development of every student's rational powers must be recognized as centrally important.[15]

Not all educators were willing to accept this "central" purpose for modern education. For instance, Theodore Brameld, a spokesman for socially oriented schools, wrote in Phi Delta Kappan:

In the first place, just how central is the central purpose supposed to be? That the nourishment of rational powers is not the *exclusive* purpose of education is evident enough. What is not equally evident from the document is the comparative *importance* of others. . . .

To begin with, where in the entire statement are we challenged to cope thoroughly with such tremendous institutional and cultural alternatives as nationalism and internationalism, capitalism and communism, war and peace, ethnocentrism and cosmopolitanism? Where are we informed that the schools of America share a serious obligation to examine and compare with scrupulous care the precise institutional arrangements which these and other alternatives demand? One or two passages, to be sure, hint at their importance and even imply preferences. In largest part, however, the reader's attention is drawn to the exercise of rational processes which, it is alleged, lead inevitably to the study of such issues.

Yet, even assuming for the moment that rationality is clearly defined (which it actually is not), what guarantee do we have that the schools will then provide opportunity for searching, sustained analysis of the great political, economic, moral, and religious issues of our time? It is very well to hope that they will do so. But the range of opportunities to practice rationality is sufficiently vast (consider only the field of mathematics) to mitigate, if anything, against the possibility. . . .

The paramount innovation that is now required is not . . . chiefly intellectual in its derivation. It stems directly from the crisis that now threatens the survival of mankind.[16]

[15] Educational Policies Commission, *The Central Purpose of American Education* (Washington, D.C.: NEA, 1961), pp. 5, 8, 12.
[16] Theodore Brameld, "What Is the Central Purpose of American Education?" *Phi Delta Kappan*, 43 (October 1961), pp. 10, 11, 14.

IMPERATIVES IN EDUCATION (1966)

Educational organizations often develop statements which are helpful in thinking about the proper purposes of education. For instance, in 1966 the American Association of School Administrators, an organization primarily made up of the superintendents of schools of the nation, suggested some "imperatives in education":

1. *To make urban life rewarding and satisfying.* Urbanization is one of the most pronounced phenomena of the times. People in great numbers are coming to large cities, seeking better jobs, better education for their children, and a better way of life. They come on the crest of a rising wave of human aspirations. . . .
2. *To prepare people for the world of work.* Appropriate education stands squarely between the individual and the job he expects to get. At a time when the gross national product is at an all-time high and when demands for skilled workmen are increasing in many fields, thousands of young people ready to enter the labor market cannot find jobs because they lack the necessary qualifications . . .
3. *To discover and nurture creative talent.* Individually and collectively the people of this country are looking to the schools for a great contribution toward developing the reservoir of creative power needed to meet and deal with challenges arising on the forefront of cultural change. . . .
4. *To strengthen the moral fabric of society.* The basic values which undergird the American way of life and which have guided the actions of people for centuries are being put to a severe test in an era of rapid technological change, social readjustment, and population expansion. The results of this test are most visible where they apply to children and youth. . . .
5. *To deal constructively with psychological tensions.* Psychological tensions have been accentuated by, if they are not an actual outgrowth of, cultural change—change that has placed children and youth in new and vastly different situations. In unfortunate circumstances, these tensions have exploded into violent action; in less visible but equally important instances, they have impaired learning and blemished personalities. . . .
6. *To keep democracy working.* The basic purpose of the school is to develop in all people the skills, understandings, beliefs, and commitments necessary for government of and by the people. This is in essence the responsibility for teaching citizenship—but teaching citizenship under a set of circumstances perhaps more trying than in former years. These circumstances are characterized by urbanization, powerful pressure groups, controversies over civil rights, and increasing interdependence between different parts of the country. . . .
7. *To make intelligent use of natural resources.* In keeping with the basic tenets of democracy, the control and use of natural resources have been entrusted to all the people. The question that now confronts everybody, and the

schools in particular, is whether control of natural resources can continue to be left with the people or whether, because of dramatic increases in their use and misuse, regulatory measures will have to be imposed. . . .

8. *To make the best use of leisure time.* Leisure time was once a luxury for the few. Now it has become a privilege for the many. With each passing decade the amount of leisure time increases through shorter work weeks, unemployment, a longer life-span, labor-saving devices, and customs and legislative action that cause many people to retire while their minds are still active and their bodies still vigorous. . . .

9. *To work with other peoples of the world for human betterment.* Through historical circumstances, a world leadership role has been thrust upon the United States. The hopes of people in other lands are kindled by the ideals and concepts that undergird the American way of life. Because of its strong commitments to maintaining peace; safeguarding the rights of freedom-loving people; and reducing poverty, ignorance, famine, and disease, it becomes increasingly important that the people of this country become familiar with the cultures of other lands and learn how to work in a fruitful manner with people whose customs, values, and traditions differ from their own. . . .[17]

SOME TWENTIETH CENTURY PHILOSOPHERS OF EDUCATION

An additional road to take in finding one's way toward a philosophy of education is to consider the ideas of twentieth century philosophers of education. From the many American philosophers of education, we have selected four: William Heard Kilpatrick, George S. Counts, Boyd H. Bode, and John Dewey. Admittedly, any selection of a few from many names must be somewhat arbitrary. Yet this selection is not capricious, for reading about the views of these four philosophers (or, better still, reading their writings yourself) may help you to understand some of the various directions in which modern philosophers of education lean. Philosophers of education usually recognize that they must take into account at least three referents—the individual, society and values—if their suggestions for content and method are to be sound. Though they avoid claiming that any one factor is sufficient in itself, philosophers of education sometimes lean more heavily on one of the possible referents in developing their views. For instance, Kilpatrick was impressed with the importance of the learner, Counts with the importance of society, Bode with the value question, and Dewey with the interrelations among all three referents.

WILLIAM HEARD KILPATRICK (1871–1965)

William Heard Kilpatrick's career in education began in the latter decade of

---

[17] *Imperatives in Education* (Washington, D.C.: American Association of School Administrators, 1966), pp. 165–173.

the nineteenth century and included more than half of the twentieth century. Kilpatrick has often been described as the leading and most productive disciple of John Dewey. At a time when changing community and family structures were influencing the evolution of the American way of life, Kilpatrick was an educator who stressed the reality of social change and the need for new directions in education.

> *The only way to increase the learning of pupils is to augment the quantity and quality of real learning. Since learning is something that the pupil has to do himself and for himself, the initiative lies with the learner. The teacher is a guide and director; he steers the boat, but the energy that propels it must come from those who are learning. The more a teacher is aware of the past experiences of students, of their hopes, desires, chief interests, the better will he understand the forces at work that need to be directed and utilized for the formation of reflective habits.*[18]

"Learning by doing," "student-centered," "activity-oriented," "pupil involvement," "problem-centered"—these were Kilpatrick's keys to interpreting education. He believed that their implementation would facilitate the updating of educational practices in keeping with the rapidly changing social conditions in America. He explored democratic ideals and ethics and showed how they are emasculated by traditions and by vested interests, and insisted that creative, integrated personalities can be achieved only through genuine sharing of social activities.[19]

Kilpatrick rejected the organization of subject disciplines apart from each other, and denied that the sole purpose of education was to impart knowledge in the traditional, classical sense. In his words, the school should emphasize the development of "desirable, inclusive, character and personality, with especial regard to the dynamic quality of such a character."[20]

At Teachers College, Columbia University, Kilpatrick developed the "Project Method" as a theoretical base with practical implications for the classroom teacher. Kilpatrick believed that we learn what we live; he believed that the school must foster experiences through projects, whereby the student can develop his skills and understandings through actual involvement—group problem-solving, discussion, evaluation, judgment, analysis, etc. To Kilpatrick, education was not the simple storage of random facts and information, but the realistic development of the skills necessary for using information which is important to the learner.

---

[18] Ralph D. Winn, *John Dewey: Dictionary of Education* (New York: Philosophical Library, 1959) pp. 112–113.
[19] Merle Curti, *The Social Ideas of American Educators* (Paterson, N.J.: Littlefield, Adams, 1965), pp. 561–562.
[20] William Heard Kilpatrick, *Philosophy of Education* (New York: Macmillan, 1963), p. 300.

> *The democratic idea of freedom is not the right of each individual to do as he pleases, even if it be qualified by adding "provided he does not interfere with the same freedom on the part of others." While the idea is not always, not often enough, expressed in words, the basic freedom is that of freedom of mind and of whatever degree of freedom of action and experience is necessary to produce freedom of intelligence. The modes of freedom guaranteed by the Bill of Rights are of this nature: Freedom of belief and conscience, of expression of opinion, of assembly for discussion and conference, of the press as an organ of communication. They are guaranteed because without them individuals are not free to develop and society is deprived of what they might contribute.[21]*

Kilpatrick asked questions about the value, meaning, and relevance of the material being studied in the schools. Does the material facilitate the student's growth as a happy, total personality? Does it enable him to pursue a meaningful, productive course, a life good to live? Is the student able to recognize, shape, and seize his opportunities in life to best advantage? In short, can he live life as it is being lived, and improve it persistently and intelligently? In other words, Kilpatrick saw formal knowledge as being of value in the school only insofar as it contributes to the development of improved character and citizenship.[22] While he emphasized the importance of the individual learner, he did not ignore the power of society in shaping human beings. Yet always he returned to the importance of the learner.

"Don't you think that the teacher should often supply the plan?" asks one of the participants in Kilpatrick's dialogue. "Take a boy planting corn, for example; think of the waste of land and fertilizer and effort. Science has worked out better plans than a boy can make." Kilpatrick answers, "I think it depends on what you seek. If you wish corn, give the boy the plan. But if you wish boy rather than corn, that is, if you wish to educate the boy to think and plan for himself, then let him make his own plan."[23]

GEORGE S. COUNTS (1889–)

George Sylvester Counts, born on a Kansas farm, became a student of school and society. Heavily influenced by sociology, he saw education as a social function inevitably conditioned by time, place, and the culture. He saw the school as a force which could help determine the direction of societal change; he became a spokesman for social reconstruction.

---

[21] Winn, *John Dewey: Dictionary of Education*, pp. 40–41.
[22] Harry S. Broudy and John R. Palmer, *Exemplars of Teaching Method* (Chicago: Rand McNally, 1965), p. 150.
[23] Lawrence A. Cremin, *The Transformation of the School* (New York: Alfred A. Knopf, 1961), p. 218.

Counts looked at the social order of the twentieth century and found it inadequate as a means for realizing democratic ideals. Though the social order was characterized by problems of war, an unplanned economy, and racism,

> Education may be defined as a process of continuous reconstruction of experience with the purpose of widening and deepening its social content, while, at the same time, the individual gains control of the methods involved.[24]

Counts found boards of education made up of conservative citizens and dominated by middle-class thinking and found schools either traditional or overly child-centered. So he called for more study of social problems in the schools and asked "Dare the schools build a new social order?"

Counts believed that education should develop individual excellence, strengthen the principles of equality, achieve an economy marked by security and plenty, build a great and enduring civilization, and contribute to the building of a world community. He wrote:

Today a great gulf stands between many of the stubborn realities of our industrial civilization and our customs, loyalties, understandings, and outlooks —between our closely integrated economy and our competitive spirit, between our shrunken world and our tradition of isolation, between our knowledge in almost every field and our ways of life. The task of bringing our minds and our practices in harmony with the physical conditions of the new age is a gigantic and urgent educational undertaking. Indeed, we shall not know peace and serenity until this is accomplished.[25]

Counts was critical of progressive education as having failed to elaborate any theory of social welfare. He called upon progressive education to:

... face squarely and courageously every social issue, come to grips with life in all of its stark reality, establish an organic relation with the community, develop a realistic and comprehensive theory of welfare, fashion a compelling and challenging vision of human destiny, and become somewhat less frightened than it is today at the bogeys of imposition and indoctrination. In a word, Progressive Education cannot build its program out of the interests of children: it cannot place its trust in a child-centered school.[26]

Counts was criticized for supporting indoctrination of liberal or radical answers to social questions. He steadily responded that a degree of indoctrination was inherent in all education and maintained that he supported free inquiry. But he believed that complete neutrality was impossible.

[24] Winn, *John Dewey: Dictionary of Education*, p. 28.
[25] George S. Counts, *The Prospects of American Democracy* (New York: John Day, 1938).
[26] George S. Counts, "Dare Progressive Education Be Progressive?" *Progressive Education*, 9 (April 1932), p. 259.

I believe firmly that a critical factor must play an important role in any adequate educational program, at least in any such program fashioned for the modern world. An education that does not strive to promote the fullest and most thorough understanding of the world is not worthy of the name. Also there must be no deliberate distortion or suppression of facts to support any theory or point of view. On the other hand, I am prepared to defend the thesis that all education contains a large element of imposition, that in the very nature of the case this is inevitable, that the existence and evolution of society depends upon it, that it is consequently eminently desirable, and that the frank acceptance of this fact by the educator is a major professional obligation.[27]

Counts believed that teachers could play a major role in societal improvement:

We must see teaching as the tremendous and difficult task that it is. We must see that it involves nothing less than the guiding of the individual to full maturity and freedom, of inducting him into the most complex and dynamic society of history, of preparing him to assume the heavy duties of managing that society and of transmitting its heritage of liberty unimpaired and even enhanced to his children.[28]

So George Counts, whether at Teachers College, Columbia University, during the 1930s era of the depression, or in his retirement years at Southern Illinois University during the 1970s era of dissent, has been and is a compelling spokesman for those who hold to a social orientation in education.

BOYD H. BODE (1873–1953)

Boyd Henry Bode was another constructive critic of education, but from a different viewpoint than that of George S. Counts. Bode, the son of a midwestern preacher, found that his encounters with Darwin's theory of evolution forced him to reconstruct his religious beliefs. After extensive study of philosophy and initial rejection of the ideas of William James and John Dewey, he decided that the experimental viewpoint of life made the most sense to him.

Bode believed that a fundamental cleavage existed between authoritarian ways of living marked by unchanging absolutist answers to human perplexities in such fields as politics, theology, and economics, and the democratic way of life marked by faith in the intelligence of the common man and a dedication to continuous free inquiry. He held that the essential work of the school was to clarify differences between these ways of living and to examine the consequences of the alternatives.

---

[27] George S. Counts, *Dare the Schools Build a New Social Order?* (New York: The John Day Company, 1932), pp. 11–12 (New York: Arno Press reprint, 1969).

[28] George S. Counts, *Education and American Civilization* (New York: Teachers College, Columbia University, 1952), pp. 460–461.

Bode became a progressive critic of progressive education because, like Counts, he judged the progressive education of his times to be overly child-centered. To Bode, progressive education was at the crossroads. He urged that it take the road toward a free play of intelligence upon man's problems. He

> *Modern life means democracy, democracy means freeing intelligence for independent effectiveness—the emancipation of mind as an individual organ to do its own work. We naturally associate democracy, to be sure, with freedom of action, but freedom of action without freed capacity of thought behind it is only chaos.*[29]

rejected imposition and indoctrination of the social reconstruction school of thought as smacking too much of authoritarianism, albeit of the liberal brand. So he called on education to liberate intelligence and to help each student to clarify his personal philosophy of life. He tested human action by asking whether it resulted in the widening of the area of shared interests, and whether it freed men to think for themselves; he fostered the scientific method.

Bode, rejecting both the overly child-centered school and the social reconstruction viewpoints, became a spokesman for the schools as a force in clarifying alternatives and developing a democratic way of life in which the use of intelligence was prized. His critics claimed that he indoctrinated for the democratic way and attendant democratic values. Bode insisted that he did not indoctrinate and that he asked of students only that they use their intelligence. Their conclusions were up to themselves for, in Bode's phrase, "The gods give no guarantees." Using the Socratic method of dialogue, Bode himself fostered independent thought in his classes at Ohio State University and the University of Illinois through humorous and lively exchange of ideas.

> *Let us admit the case of the conservative: if we once start thinking no one can guarantee what will be the outcome, except that many objects, ends, and institutions will be surely doomed. Every thinker puts some portion of an apparently stable world in peril, and no one can wholly predict what will emerge in its place.*[30]

Bode wrote of democracy:

The democratic school, in brief, is an institution which aims to promote the ideal of "free and equal" by taking proper account of individual differences

---

[29] Winn, *John Dewey: Dictionary of Education*, pp. 18–19.
[30] Winn, *John Dewey: Dictionary of Education*, pp. 13–14.

and by reliance on the principle of community living.[31]

The school, therefore, is clearly under the obligation to show that democracy is a way of life which breaks sharply with the past. It must not merely practice democracy but must develop the doctrine so as to make it serviceable as an intellectual basis for the organization of life. . . .

. . . The school is, par excellence, the institution to which a democratic society is entitled to look for clarification of the meaning of democracy. In other words, the school is peculiarly the institution in which democracy becomes conscious of itself.[32]

The primary obligation of a democratic community to its members is to provide for each the opportunity to share in the common life according to interest and capacity. This is about what is meant by the doctrine of individual differences. Interest is of major importance as an indication of the road along which the initiation of the pupil into the larger surrounding life may best be achieved. But the concept of interest may never be converted into an excuse for permitting the pupil to ignore his responsibilities as a member of his group. . . .[33]

. . . democracy has its own distinctive standard, which has nothing to do with creeds or dogmas, but is guided solely by the requirements of associated living. Democracy places exclusive reliance on empirical methods for determining standards, which is another way of saying that democracy is a name, not for a set of political arrangements, but for a whole way of life . . . our schools . . . have a special opportunity and a special obligation. It is unquestionably not their prerogative to decide which standard or set of standards is to claim our allegiance, but it is unquestionably their obligation to make the younger generation intelligent as to the nature of the choice that has to be made. In order to fulfill this obligation properly, there must be extensive reorganization of subject matter and procedures all along the line.[34]

> Information severed from thoughtful action is dead, a mind-crushing load. Since it stimulates knowledge and thereby develops the poison of conceit, it is a most powerful obstacle to further growth in the grace of intelligence.[35]

---

[31] Boyd H. Bode, *Democracy As a Way of Life* (New York: The Macmillan Company, 1937), p. 82.
[32] *Ibid.*, pp. 94, 95.
[33] *Ibid.*, p. 80.
[34] Boyd H. Bode, "Democracy in a Modern Age," *The Educational Forum*, 15 (January 1951), pp. 141–144.
[35] Winn, *John Dewey: Dictionary of Education*, p. 60.

John Dewey. Courtesy of Photoworld.

JOHN DEWEY (1859–1952)

Though the American philosopher John Dewey was born before Kilpatrick, Counts, and Bode, he lived into his nineties and was their contemporary. John Dewey, professor at Chicago and Columbia, was an extraordinary man. During his long lifetime, he managed to combine several lives. He lived a full life as an individual and father of five children; he was constantly active in social and civic action; he conducted the most famous laboratory school in history. He became a towering figure in philosophy; he left for posterity a legacy of 5,000 pages of articles and 18,000 pages in book form. Dewey was the intellectual inspiration of the progressive movement, though he himself preferred to talk simply of education without any preceding adjectives.

Like other towering figures in American life, John Dewey has had both detractors and disciples. The detractors have frequently condemned him vitriolically, often without bothering to read him. The disciples have sometimes taken one aspect of the broad corpus of his work and identified their selected aspect as the totality of his contribution. A student of education owes it to himself to read Dewey rather than exclusively depend on detractors and disciples; a brief and understandable starting point might be Dewey's *Experience and Education,* followed by the longer and more complex *Democracy and Education.*

Stated perhaps too baldly, Kilpatrick was learner-oriented, Counts was society-oriented, and Bode was values-oriented. But the philosopher of education who came closest to reconciliation of these three emphases was John Dewey who drew freely for his educational theories on psychological, sociological, and philosophical foundations of education. He regarded the individual learner as the starting point in the educational process and thus respected the needs and interests and emotions of children and youth. But he never forgot the necessity of helping people cope with the social problems of their times. He stressed the importance of the development of reflective thought and the use of the scientific method.

Dewey rejected fixed ends and believed that continuous growth was a preferable aim for education. He believed that humans could improve their lives through a continuous reconstruction of experience. For Dewey, the test of an educative experience was whether the learner was led to see himself or some aspect of his world with new meaning.

Contrary to the impression of many, John Dewey did believe in the importance of organized subject matter, which to him represented the "ripe fruitage of experience." He wrote in *Experience and Education:*

> From the standpoint of the educator, ... the various studies represent working resources, available capital. Their remoteness from the experience of the young is not, however, seeming; it is real. The subject matter of the learner is not, therefore, it cannot be, identical with the formulated, the crystallized, and systematized subject matter of the adult; the material as found in books and in works of art, etc. The latter represents the *possibilities* of the former; not its existing state. It enters directly into the activities of the expert and the educator, not into that of the beginner, the learner. Failure to bear in mind the difference in subject matter from the respective standpoints of teacher and student is responsible for most of the mistakes made in the use of texts and other expressions of preexistent knowledge.
>
> ... When engaged in the direct act of teaching, the instructor needs to have subject matter at his fingers' ends; his attention should be upon the attitude and response of the pupil. To understand the latter in its interplay with subject matter is his task, while the pupil's mind, naturally, should be not on itself but on the topic in hand. Or to state the same point in a somewhat different manner: the teacher should be occupied not with subject matter in itself but in its interaction with the pupil's present needs and capacities. Hence simple scholarship is not enough.
>
> ... the problem of teaching is to keep the experience of the student moving in the direction of what the expert already knows. Hence the need that the

teacher know both subject matter and the characteristic needs and capacities of the student.[36]

ARRIVING AT A PHILOSOPHY

Certainly, all possible educational philosophies have not been described in this chapter and all possible answers to "What's a school for, anyway?" have not been explored here. For instance, no attempt has been made to set forth the philosophies of education of various religious denominations. Nor is any single pattern of purposes recommended to the reader. Instead, we have reviewed a range of beliefs from thinkers through the ages, from outstanding commission reports of the past half century, and from twentieth century leaders in philosophy of education. If initial consideration of what a school is for has been encouraged through this introduction to educational philosophy, our purpose in this chapter has been achieved.

DISCUSSION

1. Why is the question "What's a school for, anyway?" a complex problem?
2. Which of the thinkers described under the heading "thinkers through the ages" are closest to your own beliefs? In what ways? Which thinkers do you reject?
3. Attempt to devise some groupings or categories into which the thinkers described might best fit—for instance, elitism versus democracy, reason versus emotion, freedom versus authority, individual versus society, learner versus teacher, etc. Which thinkers resemble each other and which markedly differ from others?
4. Why is the Cardinal Principles of Secondary Education report so significant a milestone in American education? Essentially, How did it differ from earlier reports? Do the Cardinal Principles seem valid to you today?
5. Is the proposal of the White House Conference on Education a useful framework for elementary education? Can you reorder the list in terms of priorities?
6. Are the proposed objectives of the Educational Policies Commission, set forth in *The Purposes of Education,* desirable objectives for education today? How would you modify them?
7. What is your own reaction to the idea that a central purpose is appropriate for American education? Do you accept the view of the Educational Policies Commission or of Brameld? How important is the rational element in education, in your opinion?

---

[36] John Dewey, *Democracy and Education* (New York: Macmillan, 1916), pp. 182–184.

8. The "imperatives in education" were suggested relatively recently. Do you find them still significant for today's schools? How would you modify or fundamentally change the list?
9. What are the fundamental similarities and differences in the views of Kilpatrick, Counts, and Bode? Are the differences among them important? If so, why?
10. In what ways were Dewey's fundamental ideas similar to and different from the three figures just mentioned? Why is Dewey usually regarded by educators as the outstanding philosopher of the four men?
11. Set forth your own viewpoint on "what's a school for, anyway?" In what ways are your views similar to and different from others in your class who have also attempted to summarize their viewpoints?

INVOLVEMENT

1. Turn to histories of education or books contrasting philosophies of education to discover the names of other significant thinkers concerning the purposes of schools. Carry on some investigation into their life work and attempt to write sketches about their backgrounds similar to those in this chapter.
2. Choose a particular philosophical school of thought, study it, and attempt to summarize its implications for education.
3. Ambitiously attempt to set forth your own statement of the purposes of American education. Attempt the same thing for your own field or level.
4. Think of the educational experiences you have had. What seems to have been the purposes of your teachers and your schools?
5. Revisit schools to attempt to see in actual teaching practice the pursuit of some of the purposes of education about which you have read. Talk with teachers involved in instruction about what they believe they are fundamentally attempting to do. Compare this with the statement of the purposes of the individual school which may be available from the school administration.
6. Develop a panel for interchange of ideas on the most desirable purposes of American education today.

BIBLIOGRAPHY

American Association of School Administrators, NEA. *Imperatives in Education.* Washington, D.C.: The Association, 1966. Proposes imperative problems in the educational program which must be revised to meet the necessities of our time.

Archambault, Reginald D., ed. *Dewey on Education: Appraisals.* New York: Random House, 1966. Evaluation of Dewey's theories and issues related to his views.

Arnstine, Donald. *Philosophy of Education: Learning and Schooling.* New York: Harper and Row, 1967. Examines the bases of existing methods and practices and develops proposals for improvement based on a theory of human behavior.

Bayles, Ernest E. and Bruce L. Hood. *Growth of American Educational Thought and Practice.* New York: Harper and Row, 1966. A vigorous and provocative analysis of ideas in American education.

Benson, Charles H., Jr., ed. *Education for What?* Boston: Houghton Mifflin, 1970. Readings reflecting historical and contemporary perspectives, critical and philosophical, on education and teaching.

Bode, Boyd H. *Democracy as a Way of Life.* New York: MacMillan, 1937. Eloquent case for democracy as a way of life characterized by the free play of intelligence on human affairs. A challenge to all absolutisms.

———. *Progressive Education At The Crossroads.* Chicago: Newton, 1938. Reminder to educators that values are essential and child interests are not a sufficient basis for a program.

Broudy, Harry S. and John R. Palmer. *Exemplars of Teaching Method.* Chicago: Rand McNally, 1965. Useful presentations of the approaches of outstanding educators.

Bruker, Robert M., ed. *Wakan: The Spirit of Harold Benjamin.* Minneapolis: Burgess, 1968. A definitive collection of the writings of Harold R. W. Benjamin which are delightful and insightful.

Cahn, Steven M., ed. *The Philosophical Foundations of Education.* New York: Harper and Row, 1970. The contributions which philosophers have made to the study of education. An anthology of historical and contemporary works.

Counts, George S. *Dare the Schools Build a New Social Order?* New York: John Day, 1932. Eloquent case for social reconstruction through the schools plus a criticism of overly individual-centered education.

———. *The Prospects of American Democracy.* New York: John Day, 1938. Overview of the American scene in its historic and contemporary setting. Emphasizes both problems and promise in America.

Dewey, John. *Experience and Education.* New York: Collier-Macmillan, 1938. Critique of American education by Dewey who calls for a balance of foundations of education rather than dependence upon an overly child-centered school.

———. *Democracy and Education.* New York: Macmillan, 1916. Possibly the most famous and most widely read book on education by the distinguished American philosopher.

Gardner, John W. *Excellence: Can We Be Equal and Excellent Too?* New York: Harper and Row, 1961. A distinguished educational statesman presents his views on the need for achieving an excellence which does not sacrifice the American dream of equality.

———. *No Easy Victories.* New York: Harper and Row, 1968. Excerpts from Gardner's varied writing concerning goals for American society. Essentially the book is made up of excerpts from writings and speeches when he served as Secretary of Health, Education, and Welfare.

Kilpatrick, William Heard. *Philosophy of Education.* New York: MacMillan, 1963. The final product of a respected philosopher of education. Recognizes the importance of individuals in a changing society.

Nash, Paul. *Authority and Freedom in Education.* New York: John Wiley and Sons, 1966. Uses the framework of authority and freedom rather than the traditional philosophies of education in order to examine problems of contemporary life.

Thayor, V. T. *Formative Ideas In American Education.* New York: Dodd, Mead, 1965. Philosophies of education, described in concise concepts. Emphasis on educational policy, programs, practices, values, and appraisals in public education.

Venable, Tom C. *Philosophical Foundations of the Curriculum.* Chicago: Rand McNally, 1967. A range of philosophies about the learner, subject matter, process of learning, and teaching agency.

Winn, Ralph B. *John Dewey: Dictionary of Education.* New York: Philosophical Library, 1959. Useful excerpts from the thought of John Dewey.

AUDIO-VISUAL MATERIALS

Your Educational Philosophy—Does it Matter? (Welch Scientific Co., 40 frs.) Presentation of two different philosophies in action, showing the need for a sound philosophy as a frame of reference for work with children.

Plato's Apology—Life and Teachings of Socrates (Encyclopedia Britannica Films, 30 Min. color) A study of Socrates, a man whose influence on the minds of men still endures.

Filmstrip—Comenius (UNESCO, 50 frs.) Use of an illustrated approach to education, an early approach to audio-visual education.

How Do Children Think? (BBC: Roebeck and Co., 30 Min.) Piaget's theory on how children think is discussed. Explanations and examples are given of preconceptual, intuitive, concrete, and formal operations in the process.

Abraham Kaplan (NET, 59 Min.) Abraham Kaplan, professor of philosophy, explains his own immediate background and cultural heritage, his beliefs and attitudes toward teaching and the difference between instruction and education. This film is one of a series of five films from the "Men Who Teach" series showing some of America's inspiring college and university teachers.

Harold Taylor (University of California LA, 30 Min.) Harold Taylor proposes that the capacity to react sensitively to life itself is the foundation upon which all education, in and out of school, should exist. He conveys his concern for the quality of man's personal values.

America's Crises: The Young Americans, Pts. I & II (NET, 59 Min.) A frank questioning of traditional views on sex. Youth's struggle to find a new morality is presented via individual and group interviews.

Youth Forum, NCAT, Deleware Commission of Children and Youth. Sample: What is a relevant education for today?—30 Min.

Youth—The Search for Identity (Current Affairs Films, 46 fr.) The motivations of young people in their search for identity. Points out that the majority of young people are concerned with today's challenges.

SEVENTEEN

WHAT SHOULD THE SCHOOLS TEACH?

A curriculum should carry out the purposes of the school. Just as the seemingly simple question, "What's a school for, anyway?" is complex, the follow-up question, "What should the schools teach?" proves to be more complex than it first appears.

From the standard dictionary definition—"all the courses of study offered by an educational institution" or "a particular course of study, often in a special field"—one would not think curriculum to be an especially complex matter. According to this, the school curriculum could be described by listing all the courses of study or describing particular courses of study offered by that educational institution. Thus an administrator might present to a visitor the curriculum of his school by handing him a heavy bound volume containing the total courses of study or a slimmer volume containing the course of study for a particular subject.

Nor does the matter of curriculum appear particularly complex to many parents and, indeed, to many administrators, teachers, and students. Many people assume that there exists a fixed body of knowledge and skills which all need to master in order to be educated. They assume that in some way (which they do not specify) this body of knowledge and skills has been defined for educators and the public during the ages, has become clear to all and accepted by all, and having been finally established, now constitutes the curriculum for all. They assume that the curriculum is now neatly packaged into fixed and established courses of study.

But these conventional assumptions are flatly contradicted by what we have learned from our study of education. The history of American education testifies to constant change in society and education, rather than to school and society remaining static (chapter 6). The past half century has been a period of controversy over the proper work of the public schools, rather than an era of unanimous agreement (chapter 7). The existence of such nonpublic schools as independent and parochial schools indicates differing conceptions of the functions and programs of schools, rather than monolithic unanimity (chapter 8). A variety of forces influences schools, rather than a making of decisions for all involved by some single authority (chapter 9). Expectations of the teacher's role vary from group to group and individual to individual instead of one role expectation prevailing (chapter 10). Students have different social class and ethnic backgrounds which influence their experiences and their schooling, rather than reflect uniform class, racial, and ancestral backgrounds (chapter 12). Students come to schools from varied community backgrounds—rural, city, and suburban —and their needs are not identical from community to community (chapter 13). Learners differ widely from each other. No ways of grouping can repeal the inexorable law of individuality and replace it with uniform education (chapter 14). Social change is inescapable and rapid and new social problems, including human survival crises, face mankind, rather than society remaining immobile and changeless (chapter 15). The purposes of education are complex and multiple, rather than simple and singular (chapter 16).

Consequently, as to curriculum, varied learning experiences are necessary for individuals from a variety of cultural and community backgrounds in a changing world. A fixed body of skills and knowledge to be mastered by every person cannot be taught or learned. Curriculum opportunities and experiences must change with the growth of knowledge concerning the individual, society, philosophy, and the disciplines. Curriculum cannot stay constant over the ages, established and fixed for all learners, in a world in which knowledge explodes. For students to be educated, they need various and appropriate learning experiences and opportunities. They cannot be well educated by following fixed and inflexible prescriptions-in-advance.

Consequently, contemporary educators recognize that the curriculum is made up of the learning experiences under the control of the school. For instance, Saylor and Alexander say, "Curriculum encompasses all learning opportunities provided by the school. Thus we think of 'the curriculum' and 'the program' of the school as synonymous. In another sense the curriculum of an individual pupil includes the learning opportunities he actually selects and experiences; this is the 'curriculum had.' "[1] Such a definition places the emphasis where it should be, upon the actual learning opportunities offered by the school and the actual learning experiences had by the students. The wider definition also recognizes that a variety of student activities are part of the program of the school. Formerly such activities were regarded as extracurricular, implying something carried on outside the regular, and presumably much more important, curriculum of the school. The broader definition regards student activities— whether the dramatics club, the debate team, the intramural or varsity athletic events, etc.—as "cocurricular," indicating jointness or mutuality with the regular program.

---

[1] J. Galen Saylor and William M. Alexander, *Curriculum Planning for Modern Schools* (New York: Holt, Rinehart and Winston, 1966), p. 5.

WHAT SHOULD THE SCHOOLS TEACH? 415

FIGURE 17.1
Curriculum Influences on the Student

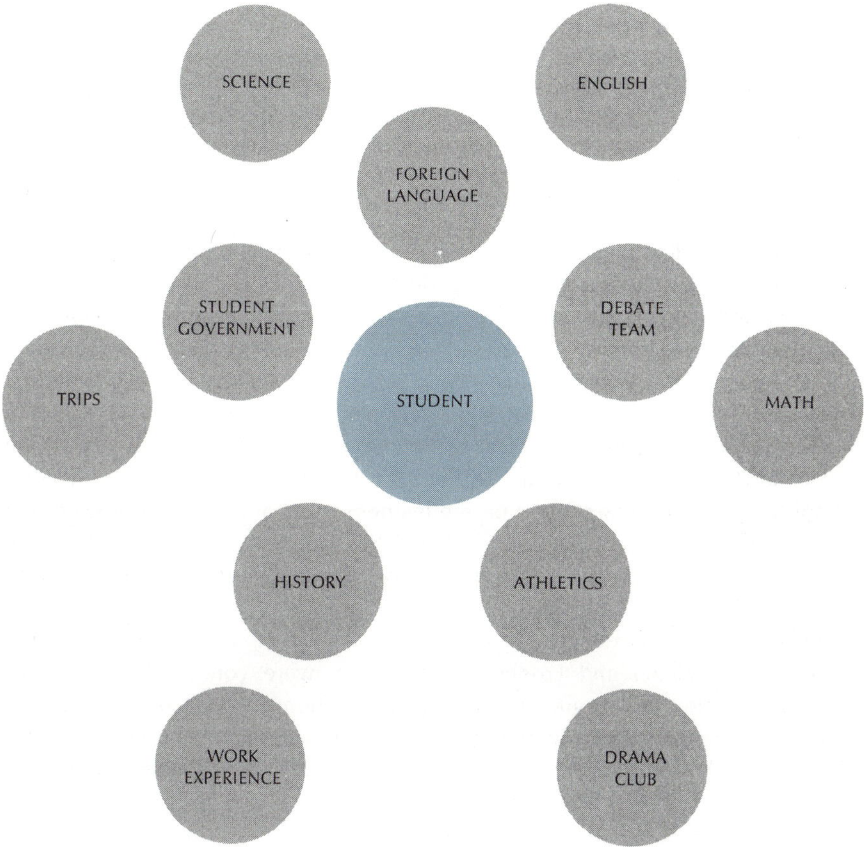

FOUNDATIONS OF CURRICULUM

Curriculum leaders today recognize that the programs of schools must bear some relationship to individual learners, the society in which we live, desirable values, and the disciplines of learning. They differ, to a degree, on the proper combination. Few if any educators turn to one of the above referents in isolation. Yet some curriculum proponents stress one referent or source of the curriculum more heavily than the others. They want to be sure that the particular source they emphasize is sufficiently stressed in determining the best learning opportunities and the best learning experiences for Americans in our times. So some curriculum thinkers remind us of the special importance of the individual learners. Others tend to stress the importance of society in shaping persons. Others remind us of the necessity of values to provide us a sense of direction. Still others emphasize ways in which study of the disciplines can contribute to understanding relationships and ways of inquiry. Consequently, we will examine these four logical referents in curriculum making and the reasons why some curriculum workers regard them as important. We will then describe some combinations of sources which contemporary curriculum leaders recommend to teachers fostering learning experiences in the classroom, to schools providing a total balanced program for learners, and to those providing materials to facilitate learning opportunities and experiences.

NEEDS OF THE INDIVIDUAL LEARNER

In developing learning opportunities, say those who emphasize one referent, stress the individual learner. The individual learner has questions, perplexities, concerns, and tensions which he must resolve; he is thus receptive to education which makes sense to him. The curriculum should meet his needs. The individual learner knows best what he most needs; after all, he is the person with the questions, perplexities, concerns, and tensions. Who can know better than the learner what he needs to learn? Furthermore, who can really teach the learner anything that he doesn't really want to know? Consequently, a good school tries to determine what is on the learner's mind and helps to provide him opportunities and experiences to deal with his interests. The only curriculum which can be meaningful to a learner is the curriculum which holds meaning for him personally.

Belief in the importance of the individual learner has a long ancestry. Comenius, Pestalozzi and Froebel, for instance, were concerned about programs for children and youth. Rousseau, about whom we also read in the last chapter, believed that a child at birth was entirely natural and unspoiled. In his novel, *Emile,* he afforded his fictional child the opportunity to develop natural gifts in an unhampered way. Emile, shielded from the corrupting influences of civilization, learned from inner realization rather than from books. He followed his own interests, learned from many conversations with his tutor, and grew up to be a wise and humane man.

A wing of the progressive education movement—probably the most influential wing—stressed the importance of the needs of the learner. William Heard Kilpatrick, whose philosophy of education was summarized in chapter 16, argued for the importance of the learner.

John Holt sums up the views of contemporary educators who call attention to the importance of the learner and who criticize traditional assumptions as to curriculum:

Behind much of what we do in school lie some ideas, that could be expressed roughly as follows: (1) of the vast body of human knowledge, there are certain bits and pieces that can be called essential, that everyone should know; (2) the extent to which a person can be considered educated, qualified to live intelligently in today's world and be a useful member of society, depends on the amount of this essential knowledge that he carries about with him; (3) it is the duty of schools, therefore, to get as much of this essential knowledge as possible into the minds of children. Thus we find ourselves trying to poke certain facts, recipes, and ideas down the gullets of every child in school, whether the morsel interests him or not, even if it frightens him or sickens him, and even if there are other things that he is much more interested in learning.

These ideas are absurd and harmful nonsense. We will not begin to have true education or real learning in our schools until we sweep this nonsense out of the way. Schools should be a place where children learn what they most want to know, instead of what we think they ought to know. The child who wants to know something remembers it and uses it once he has it; the child who learns something to please or appease someone else forgets it when the need for pleasing or the danger of not appeasing is past. This is why children quickly forget all but a small part of what they learn in school. It is of no use or interest to them; they do not want, or expect, or even intend to remember it. The only difference between bad and good students in this respect is that the bad students forget right away, while the good students are careful to wait until after the exam. If for no other reason, we could well afford to throw out most of what we teach in school because the children throw out almost all of it anyway.[2]

Today many young people believe that schools fail human beings. For instance, a group of high school students from Montgomery County, Maryland, presented analysis of their own schooling to their Board of Education. They began with the comment that "It is quite safe to say that the public schools have critically negative and absolutely destructive effects on human beings and their curiosity, natural desire to learn, confidence, individuality, creativity, freedom of thought and self respect."[3] The students then proposed a series of reforms including a complete rescheduling of the curriculum, voluntary seminars organized by the students, student involvement in choosing teachers, and the elimination of letter grades.

Several angry and earnest books testify to the failure of schools to relate to students as individual persons. Jonathan Kozol titled his book *Death at an Early Age* and amplified the title in his subtitle, *The Destruction of the Hearts and Minds of Negro Children in the Boston Public Schools.*[4] Kozol was dismissed from the Boston schools for deviating from the fourth grade course of study, especially by using a poem by Langston Hughes which was not on the list of approved publications.

Herbert Kohl describes in *36 Children* his work in creative writing with a class of eleven-year-old Negro children. Yet in following up the children after their meaningful year with him Kohl found, "Robert is not the only one of the 36 children who is now close to being a dropout—John, Margie, Carol, Sam—I stopped searching, don't want to know the full extent of the misery and tragedy

---

[2] John Holt, *How Children Fail* (New York: Pitman, 1964), pp. 174, 175.
[3] Ronald and Beatrice Gross (eds.), *Radical School Reform* (New York: Simon and Schuster, 1970), p. 147.
[4] Jonathan Kozol, *Death At An Early Age* (Boston: Houghton Mifflin, 1967).

of the children's present lives. Recently one of the kids told me: Mr. Kohl, one good year isn't enough . . ."[5]

James Herndon in *The Way It Spozed to Be*, a record of a year in a metropolitan ghetto school, writes:

> Sitting in a classroom or at home pretending to "study" a badly written text full of false information, adding up twenty sums when they're all the same and one would do, being bottled up for seven hours a day in a place where you decide nothing, having your success or failure depend, a hundred times a day, on the plan, invention and whim of someone else, being put in a position where most of your real desires are not only ignored but actively penalized, undertaking nothing for its own sake but only for that illusory carrot of the future—maybe you can do it, and maybe you can't, but either way, it's probably done you some harm.[6]

Nat Hentoff in *Our Children Are Dying* documents the spirited struggle by Elliot Shapiro, a farsighted and sensitive New York City principal, for a curriculum which makes sense to young people.[7]

As a challenge to the curriculum which fails to recognize the importance of the learner, some educators have founded or conducted their own schools. Currently the most famous is Summerhill, founded in England by A. S. Neill. At Summerhill, the children come to school only when they wish to. Yet, paradoxically, when they do attend classes, the curriculum is relatively formal.[8]

George Dennison conducted an "alternative" school in New York City described in *The Lives of Children;* he believes that:

> . . . the business of a school is not, or should not be, mere instruction, but the life of the child.
>
> This is especially important under such conditions as we experience today. Life in our country is chaotic and corrosive, and the time of childhood for many millions is difficult and harsh. It will not be an easy matter to bring our berserk technocracy under control, but we can control the environment of the schools. It is a relatively small environment and has always been structured by deliberation. If, as parents, we were to take as our concern not the instruction of our children, but the lives of our children, we would find that our schools could be used in a powerfully regenerative way. Against all that is shoddy and violent and treacherous and emotionally impoverished in American life, we might propose conventions which were rational and straightforward, rich both in feeling and thought, and which treated individuals with a respect we do little more at present than proclaim from our public rostrums. We might cease thinking of school as a place, and learn to believe that it is basically relationships: between children and adults, adults and adults, children and other children.[9]

---

[5] Herbert Kohl, *36 Children* (New York: The New American Library, 1967), p. 206.
[6] James Herndon, *The Way It Spozed To Be* (New York: Simon and Schuster, 1965), p. 188.
[7] Nat Hentoff, *Our Children Are Dying* (New York: Viking, 1966).
[8] A. S. Neill, *Summerhill* (New York: Hart, 1960).
[9] George Dennison, *The Lives of Children* (New York: Random, 1969), p. 6–7.

A teaching intern from the Teacher Corps establishes warm relationships with students. Courtesy of Paul Conklin from the Teacher Corps.

Educators like George Dennison who are concerned for the lives of individual learners also emphasize the importance of affective (emotion-related) education rather than cognitive (intellect-related) education alone. For instance, Dennison says,

> My purpose is not to castigate the bureaucrats, but to recall parents and teachers to an awareness of one crucial truth, a truth that should be, but is not, the gut-wisdom of everyone: that in humane affairs—and education is par excellence a humane pursuit—there is no such thing as competence without love. . . .
>
> In naming love as the necessary base of competence in humane affairs, I am referring not only to the emotion of love, nor just to the moral actions and feelings that belong to caring, but to loving and caring in the very generalized, primitive sense in which they constitute a background condition of life, as we say of young children that they live "as if in love," and as adults, when they are simplified by disasters and extreme demands, reveal a constructive energy and compassion which are obviously generalized and basic.[10]

MEETING SOCIAL DEMANDS AND LEARNING ABOUT SOCIAL REALITIES

Some educators emphasize that learning opportunities and learning experiences for children, youth and adults are heavily influenced by the surrounding society. Exponents of this view stress the importance of the total environment—the family, the neighborhood, the community, the nation, and indeed, the world—in determining the educational task. Though the socially oriented recognize the importance of individual learners, they point out that individuals must learn in a society.

Historically, many educators have stressed the importance of adaptation or accommodation to the society that surrounds the learner. Such curriculum

---

[10] *Ibid.*, pp. 275–276.

workers often use terms such as "acculturation" and "socialization" in describing the necessity of students adjusting to social demands upon the individual. For instance, immigrant children were asked to acculturate and become "socialized" (not a radical term) to the demands of the new society which they were experiencing. Sometimes supporters of meeting societal demands emphasize "good citizenship"; by this they have often meant conformity to societal values and demands. Thus, those who emphasize social demands tend to stress keeping things as they are through an educational program emphasizing the demands which society makes upon the people who live within the nation. Such thinkers provide a conservative emphasis in a time of change.

Though historically the emphasis of those who stress society has been placed on societal demands, today the demands of the socially oriented have largely shifted to emphasis on changes which must be made in society. Today many socially oriented thinkers stress the need for human beings to cope with the urgent social realities of the times. If people's lives are to be improved, they say, social problems must be studied, understood, and acted upon. Some add that a socially oriented curriculum is necessary if mankind is even to survive.

Consequently, those who see an important function of the school as illumination of the social realities of our times advise educators never to minimize the importance of mankind's dilemmas as the proper content for study. They want schools to include emphasis on the real and urgent problems which heavily influence the learner's life. They advocate learning about and acting upon international problems such as the threat of nuclear war, ways to achieve a viable peace, relations among nations, problems of imperialism and colonialism, and the gap between developed and underdeveloped nations. They believe that racism is a menacing problem and that black-white relations in America threaten the social order. They call for the study of possible solutions, such as desegregation and integration or black identity and community control; they stress the importance of building democratic human relationships. They point to the need for study and action upon pollution; the population problem must be faced squarely, they say. Making the cities livable is a major challenge; the study of the economic system and of consumer education is needed. They call for more knowledge of government and its operation at all levels from local to federal. They ask for realistic study of communication and the agencies of public information.

Occupational information and training are of high importance to them. Side by side with general education concerning the social realities of our times, they would have specialized education by which young people could prepare themselves for socially useful work. In short, this socially conscious school of thought calls the attention of educators to the world outside the classroom windows, in the total surrounding environment which confronts the individual.

The voice of the social realities school of thought is heard particularly during periods of crisis. The 1930s, for example, were a time of economic depression unprecedented unemployment, and the shattering of customary life patterns of Americans of all social classes. In the same decade, Hitler came to power in

Germany, the Nazi conquest in Europe began, and World War II opened. In the United States, proponents of a social reconstruction school of thought cried out for an education which came to grips with such problems. It was during this period that George Counts, whose view was summarized in chapter 17, asked eloquently, "Dare the schools build a new social order?"

When the nation threw its energies into World War II with solid support from a citizenry that conceived fascism a genuine threat to American democracy, less was heard from the supporters of social reconstruction. In the Eisenhower years which followed, *Time* magazine characterized youth as "the silent generation"; the 1950s decade was not a propitious era for those who advocated focusing upon social problems. But in the 1960s as the revolt of blacks accelerated and as the war dragged on in Vietnam, concern for dealing with social problems again mounted.

Some educators count upon the schools to contribute to social understanding. For example, in 1970 Theodore Brameld, a veteran social reconstructionist, proposed as a normative model that "a minimum of one-half of the entire time devoted to the curriculum be spent outside the classroom—in the laboratory of direct participation with people and institutions, and always with the close support of teacher-consultants equipped to deal with whatever situations or issues have been selected for analysis and prognosis."[11] He said,

> The structure of the curriculum may be symbolized . . . in the form of a moving 'wheel.' The 'rim' is the unifying theme of mankind—its predicaments and its aspirations. The 'hub' is the central question of any given period of learning (perhaps extending over one week, perhaps a semester), while the 'spokes' are the supporting areas of concentrated attention that bear most directly upon each respective question. The 'spokes' may thus be termed 'courses' in art, science, foreign language, or any other pertinent subject or skills. But these are not to be construed as *mere* courses. At all times they are as supportive of the 'hub' as it is of them.[12]

But some observers of American life are sweepingly condemnatory of the entire "system" or "establishment." Paul Goodman's view, for instance, is apparent in two of his books on education, *Growing Up Absurd* and *Compulsory Miseducation*.

> Now the organized system is very powerful and in its full tide of success, apparently sweeping everything before it in science, education, community planning, labor, the arts, not to speak of business and politics where it is indigenous. Let me say that we of the previous generation who have been sickened and enraged to see earnest and honest effort and humane culture swamped by this muck, are heartened by the crazy young allies, and we think that perhaps the future may make more sense than we dared hope.[13]

---

[11] Theodore Brameld, "A Crosscutting Approach to the Curriculum: The Moving Wheel," *Phi Delta Kappan* (March 1970), p. 347.   [12] *Ibid.*, p. 348.
[13] Paul Goodman, *Growing Up Absurd* (New York: Alfred A. Knopf, 1960), p. 241.

Theodore Roszak, a professor of history, condemned "the educational establishment" and "compulsory schools" in a talk to the Association for Supervision and Curriculum Development Conference in 1970. Roszak views compulsory public schooling as a pedagogical fad destined to become the iron social orthodoxy of all industrial and industrializing societies. He believes the educational establishment, designed to serve the purposes of society, has been successful in the development of scientists and technicians necessary to this industrial way of life. He thinks educators must "let the students go" to bring about the kind of man needed for tomorrow's world. Educators should help children and youth escape from the snares of the system. "Once we stop forcing *our* education on the children, perhaps they will invite a lucky few of us to participate in *theirs*." He supports the "voluntary" school where the teacher teaches insofar as the student authorizes.[14]

Such authors are definitely critical of the system and the establishment. But their concern seems to be more for freeing the young for alternative ways of learning, such as learning through travel and on jobs, than for changing the curriculum of the schools to open wider opportunities for dealing with social realities.

The most vigorous spokesmen for dealing with the socially significant in schools and colleges are some among the young people engaged in dissent. Many contemporary black young people have contributed to setting up programs of black studies; the programs range from conventional historical exploration of the black heritage to radical training for social action on behalf of rebellion in the black ghettos. A substantial number of white students, many of them from middle-class suburban schools, have also criticized the current curriculum as out of touch with the great changes in American life. They ask for more study of war, racism, pollution, population. They oppose a curriculum containing much academic material which has little or no connection with the problems of contemporary American life. So they call for curricular change.

However, as with adults, some among dissenting young people despair of change through the school and focus on fighting what they conceive to be the repressiveness of both the school and society. One such student, Steve Wasserman, seventeen years old, of Berkeley High School in Berkeley, California says:

. . . . we developed a program that we feel speaks for the real needs of Berkeley High students. One of the basic points of the program concerns the exercise of our rights; the right of free speech, the right to leaflet, the right to have independent newspapers, the right to assemble and organize ourselves for our own needs, the right to take political action in our own interest without penalty, the right to do these things without administrative restrictions, interference or approval.

Another point in our program concerns our commitment to struggle against

---

[14] "San Francisco: Everybody's Favorite City(?)" *News Exchange,* Association for Supervision and Curriculum Development, NEA, vol. 12 (June–July 1970), p. 4.

Student protest in the high schools. Courtesy of Howard Petrick from Nancy Palmer.

racism, the racism that is institutionalized in the school system, in others and in ourselves.[15]

Wasserman then adds, "We are going to begin implementing our program—and begin breaking the law."[16] Thirteen-year-old Jim Gardner of Intermediate School 44 in New York agrees, "We strain to move aside the dead weight of authority blocking our path, but are either overcome by the bureaucracy, or forced to use violent means."[17] If curricula based on social realities were developed, such revolutionary young people might work within the system for improvement of American life.

DEVELOPING HUMANE VALUES

A third emphasis that some consider the best learning opportunities and experiences for children, youth, and adults stresses the central role of values in human life. On this logic, the basic questions fundamental to education deal with right and wrong, good and bad, desirable and undesirable. The task of education is in large part to help the individual arrive at a pattern of values which gives meaning to his life. One does not indiscriminately gratify all needs; certain

---

[15] Ernest Dunbar, "Trouble: The High School Radicals," *Look* (March 24, 1970), p. 73.
[16] *Ibid.*   [17] *Ibid.*

needs are selected by educators as appropriate for gratification through the school. The gratification of these needs involves some sense of direction, of orientation, of philosophy. The truly crucial questions as to needs are concerned with the direction toward which the need leads. Similarly, the crucial question for a society confronted by social problems is to determine guiding values or philosophy. For instance, studying about riots does not help us to determine whether society needs more policemen or more militants, whether society needs more repression or an improved environment. Only our values help us with such questions, they argue.

The viewpoint that development of a philosophy of life is the central task of education has a long history. The Greek philosophers, Socrates, Plato, and Aristotle, regarded philosophy as basic to education. Through the ages, religious groups have founded schools to instruct the young in the values of the way of life represented by the church; this has been an historic justification for Roman Catholic education. In the American colonies, as we have seen, Puritans established schools primarily so that the people learned to read the Bible, which was regarded by the Puritans as the basic source of morality and philosophy of life.

In twentieth century America educators also have spoken up for a value-oriented and value-clarifying education. Accepting that the task of the secular school in America was the development of humane values, Boyd H. Bode (whose work was summarized in chapter 16), proposed that schools constantly clarify the conflict between authoritarian and democratic ways of living. Bode believed that the value of curriculum content was to be judged by the extent of its contribution to this objective. To Bode, the primary value characteristic of a democratic way of life was the use of the method of intelligence. He called for unremitting application of intelligence to a wide array of human problems. He regarded the work of the school not as the imposition of any single value pattern but the unremitting clarification of alternatives.

Lawrence E. Metcalf and Maurice P. Hunt have applied Bode's view to social problems. They believe that the task of the school is to help young people clarify their values with respect to "closed areas" in American discourse, such areas as communism and capitalism, sex and drug addiction, revolution and student dissent, etc. In an article they recently proposed "that the schools incorporate in their curriculum a study of an important social movement, rejection by youth, and that this study emphasize examining, testing, and appraising the major beliefs caught up in this movement."[18] They add, "A curriculum that would assist young people in an examination of their basic assumptions about society and its improvement must deal with values and social policies."[19]

This approach is attractive to those who believe improvements must be made within the going system. But some revolutionary students reject any study of values. They disagree with those who believe that democratic ends require the use of democratic means. They prefer intuitive rather than rational thought. One

---

[18] Lawrence E. Metcalf and Maurice P. Hunt, "Relevance and the Curriculum," *Phi Delta Kappan*, 51 (March 1970), p. 359.
[19] *Ibid.*, p. 360.

wing of current youth dissent deprecates values and regards goals as illusory. Followers of this view believe that a revolution must come first. The time for talking about goals and the building of a new society is after the overthrow of the establishment, they say.

Some who stress the importance of values believe that the application of values to social problems is only part of the philosophical task of the curriculum. To them, the crisis of our times is a crisis in values which affects all areas of human life. The basic questions deal with the significance and purpose of life itself. They believe there must be concern not only for the public sphere but also for the private sphere. Value-oriented educators of this persuasion often stress the humanities, including literature, the arts, music, etc. They call on schools to deal with the recurring questions of truth, beauty, justice, freedom, etc. Joseph Wood Krutch said:

> The humanities . . . include every sort of consideration of those human concerns which cannot be treated experimentally and usually cannot be measured—such as right and wrong, the ugly and the beautiful, the nature of happiness, the characteristics of the good life, and so forth—all of which, as soon as they are enumerated, are seen to be the things with which most men are more immediately concerned than with the facts established by science.
>
> Justice Oliver Wendell Holmes once said that science tells us a great deal about things that are not very important; philosophy a little bit about the things which are extremely important . . .
>
> The humanities prove nothing because the things with which they are primarily concerned are not susceptible to scientific proof. But the humanities can and do *carry convictions,* and they are able to do so because they describe human life in terms which we recognize as true to our own inner experience . . .[20]

STRUCTURE OF THE DISCIPLINES

A fourth referent in considering the opportunities and experiences which should constitute the school curriculum is the study of the disciplines. The historical experience of mankind with respect to knowledge has resulted in a division of knowledge into broad categories which, in turn, can be divided into disciplines. The broad categories of knowledge today are the sciences, mathematics, the social sciences, the humanities, and the arts. In turn, the broad category of sciences can be broken down into the disciplines of psychology, biology, chemistry, physics, astronomy, botany, etc. The broad category of mathematics can be broken down into such disciplines as algebra, geometry, calculus, etc. Similarly, the social sciences can be broken down into history, geography, political science, sociology, economics, anthropology, etc. The humanities embrace literature, philosophy, etc. The arts include music, fine arts,

---

[20] Joseph Wood Krutch, "A Humanist's Approach," *Phi Delta Kappan* (March 1970), pp. 377–378.

industrial arts, etc. Study of the disciplines comprising the broad categories is required if one is to become educated, say the proponents.

Supporters of study of the structure of the disciplines are critical of the conventional subject matter approach. They believe that current study of subject matter too often takes the form of acquiring miscellaneous and unrelated facts and results in a smattering of knowledge which is inadequate for a true understanding of the disciplines. Instead, they ask for a study of the *structure of the disciplines*. By this they mean understanding the major concepts in a discipline, seeing the relationships of these concepts with each other, and understanding the particular methods of inquiry which are used in that particular discipline. In effect, they advocate that students study geography so that they learn to think like geographers, study mathematics so that they learn to think like mathematicians, study biology so that they learn to think like biologists, etc. According to those who would emphasize structure, such mastery of a variety of disciplines results in the educated person.

Though the study of organized subject matter is old and long established, the idea of studying the structure of the disciplines is relatively new. The major spokesman for the idea in our times is Jerome Bruner of Harvard University, a psychologist who describes his ideas on curriculum in *The Process of Education*.

> ... the curriculum of a subject should be determined by the most fundamental understanding that can be achieved of the underlying principles that give structure to that subject. Teaching specific topics or skills without making clear their context in the broader fundamental structure of a field of knowledge is uneconomical in several deep senses. In the first place, such teaching makes it exceedingly difficult for the student to generalize from what he has learned to what he will encounter later. In the second place, learning that has fallen short of a grasp of general principles has little reward in terms of intellectual excitement. . . . Third, knowledge one has acquired without sufficient structure to tie it together is knowledge that is likely to be forgotten.[21]

The ways in which scholars conduct inquiry differ from discipline to discipline, proponents say. For instance, a mathematician uses different tools and methods of approaches to inquiry than does a historian. In *Realms of Meaning*, Philip H. Phenix says,

> Each discipline has characteristic methods of investigation that distinguish it from other disciplines. By describing the way men of knowledge in a particular field of scholarship go about their professional task, these methods in fact define the discipline.[22]

During the decade which immediately followed the Sputnik anxiety in American education (a period during which heavy emphasis was placed upon separate subjects and less attention was paid to general education), the structure of the

---

[21] Jerome S. Bruner, *The Process of Education* (Cambridge, Mass.: Harvard University Press, 1960), p. 31.
[22] Philip H. Phenix, *Realms of Meaning* (New York: McGraw-Hill, 1964), p. 332.

disciplines approach was popular. The scholars developed curricular programs and projects and reconstructed the separate fields. For instance, Zacharias, with his Massachusetts Institute of Technology colleagues, reconstructed instruction in the field of physics and developed the PSSC physics program. Arnold Grobman and his associates at Boulder, Colorado, developed through the BSCS study three versions of biology textbooks. New mathematics programs were developed at outstanding universities. After the revision of the National Defense Education Act of 1964, scholars in the social sciences developed projects in such fields as sociology and geography. Additional science projects took the form of CHEMS and CBA chemistry, ESCP earth science and others. It is commonly recognized that such developments often eliminated the obsolete from subject fields and resulted in the inclusion of new content. In the better of the projects, principles, relationships, and processes of inquiry were stressed.

By the 1970s, the disciplines proposal, which had ridden high throughout the early sixties, seemed to have passed its zenith. Scholars too were increasingly recognizing the necessity for education related to current social problems. For instance, R. Thomas Tanner, of the department of science education at Oregon State University wrote, "The subject matter developed during the past 13 years may very well constitute a much-improved curriculum in science per se, but it does not go very far beyond science concepts in exploring the societal implications of the scientific enterprise, the interactions of science with society, culture, and human values. Scientists and science educators are beginning to express grave concern over this deficiency in the new status quo of science education.[23] Tanner goes on to propose some urgently needed themes related to the quality of the deteriorating environment; he calls for a multidisciplinary team approach to these problems involving social studies teachers and other educators rather than depending on science or the separate scientific disciplines alone.

ONE SOURCE OF CURRICULUM—OR SEVERAL

In the continuing quest for a relevant curriculum, the question naturally arises as to whether the curriculum should be built on some combination of the sources proposed, the referents just described. Most current curriculum leaders suggest varying combinations of sources. For instance, Arthur W. Foshay, who brought the disciplines proposal to the national convention of the Association for Supervision and Curriculum Development in his 1961 presidential address, has offered what he terms, in a phrase borrowed from Jonathan Swift, "a modest proposal." Foshay depends upon three sources: the child (the needs of the individual learner school of thought), society (the social realities school of thought), and the disciplines proposal (the structure of the disciplines school of thought).

[23] R. Thomas Tanner, "The Science Curriculum: Unfinished Business for an Unfinished Country," *Phi Delta Kappan*, 51 (March 1970), p. 353.

Lawrence E. Metcalf and Maurice P. Hunt support a curriculum based on social realities and examination of values. They say,

> A relevant curriculum is sometimes defined as one addressed to the personal problems of youth. This is not good enough. It is more relevant to engage young people in the problems of the larger culture in which many of their personal problems have their origin. The culture of most significance to the young consists of those aspects that are problematic—that is, the large conflicts and confusions which translate into the conflicts and confusions of individuals.[24]

The writer of this book has proposed a general education supplemented by vocational education and study of the special disciplines. He says:

> Reassessment of the social setting indicates that there do exist fundamental problems for study by youth which cut across disciplines and which form the heart of problem-centered general education. Such centers of experience are derivative from social realities and grow out of the social foundations of education. They reflect the personal-social needs of learners and grow out of the psychological foundations of education. They offer opportunity for the full development of democratic values, including the key value of use of intelligence, and they stem from the philosophical foundations of education. Reassessment of current social trends and forces reaffirms that such interdisciplinary problems are real, vital, and inescapable for study by the young. A moratorium on dealing with such problems might inhibit long-range individual and societal growth. . . .
>
> Along with the general education of the core curriculum, the specialized education of study of separate subjects for vocational or pre-vocational purposes has long been accepted.
>
> There also exists a "third force" in the curriculum today, mastery at appropriate levels of student maturity of the structure or relationships which characterize the separate disciplines. . . .
>
> Perhaps we can achieve a broader and better curriculum which does not force us to choose among potentially and mutually complementary desirable approaches. To this writer, after reassessment, it seems that what is needed is a general education which focuses on vital problem areas. . . . A specialized education is needed which enables young people to prepare themselves for vocations. Needed is a third force in education, whether regarded as general or special education, which gives those for whom the experience will be meaningful the opportunity to think about separate organized disciplines as specialized scholars think about them.[25]

Arno A. Bellack proposes a synthesis of structure of the disciplines with a social problems approach. He says:

---

[24] Lawrence E. Metcalf and Maurice P. Hunt, "Relevance and the Curriculum," *Phi Delta Kappan,* 51 (March, 1970), p. 361.
[25] William Van Til, "What Knowledge Is of Most Worth?—A Reassessment," *The High School Journal,* 48 (February 1965), pp. 337–338.

... problems in the world of human affairs do not come neatly labeled "historical," "economic," or "political." They come as decisions to be made and force us to call upon all we know and make us wish we knew more. It was concern for broad cultural and moral questions that go beyond the boundaries of any one discipline that led the progressives to urge that students have the opportunity to deal with them in all their complexity. They proposed a new curriculum, one centered on the problems of youth and broad social issues and drawing upon the academic disciplines as they become relevant to the problems under study. . . .

Giving students an opportunity to grapple with broad social and cultural problems was basically a promising innovation. But at the same time one is forced to recognize that problem solving on such a broad base cannot be pursued successfully without growing understanding of the fields of knowledge on which the problem solver must draw.

Recognizing then the value in systematic study of the fields of knowledge and the importance of developing competence in dealing with problems and issues that are broader than those of any one field, the question arises of why opportunities for both types of activities should not be included in the program of all students. One might envision a general education program that would include basic instruction in the major fields. . . . (the natural sciences, the social sciences, mathematics, and the humanities), together with a coordinating seminar in which students deal with problems "in the round" and in which special effort is made to show the intimate relationships between the fields of study as concepts from those fields are brought to bear on these problems. Such a seminar would also furnish excellent opportunities to help students become aware of the different modes of thought and various types of language usage involved in dealing with problematic situations and the necessity for making clear distinctions among them.[26]

THE NEW TEACHER'S SEGMENT OF THE TOTAL CURRICULUM

As a new teacher considers what a school should teach, he must take into account such logical referents or sources for a curriculum made up of learning experiences as those described in this chapter. He might well think through the pros and cons of placing emphasis on one or another referent or the desirability of balance among several.

When he has done so, he must face the fact that the level on which he has chosen to teach and/or the broad field of the curriculum he has chosen to emphasize—whether social studies, language arts, sciences, mathematics, world languages, physical education, or the several art fields—are segments of the total curriculum. So the questions of foundations of curriculum eventually come

---

[26] Arno A. Bellack, "What Knowledge is of Most Worth?" *The High School Journal*, 48 (February 1965), pp. 330–331.

home to him at his chosen level and/or broad field. So far as he can influence the learning experiences of children, youth or adults—and teachers can influence those learning experiences more than the new teacher realizes—what sources or referents will he stress? The individual learner? The social realities of the times? Values? The structure of the disciplines? Some balance among several sources? His basic theoretical assumptions will be the shapers of his practice. The new teacher's decisions, even though tentative, will influence the learning experiences which constitute that small part of the curriculum of the totality of American education for which he is responsible. His judgments as to proper stress and balance will make a difference to the human beings whom he is educating— and make a difference to himself as both a person and a teacher.

★   ★   ★

DISCUSSION
1. What are the traditional assumptions about the curriculum which are contradicted by the earlier chapters of this book? What are some necessary characteristics of a curriculum in a changing world?
2. What is a useful definition of curriculum, according to contemporary educators? How does this definition differ from the conventional dictionary definition? What are the possible referents or sources upon which educators draw in their curricular theories?
3. What are the arguments for emphasizing the needs of the individual learner in a desirable curriculum? Who supports these arguments? How strong does the case for meeting the needs of the learner seem to be to you?
4. What is the meaning of affective education? Cognitive education?
5. What are the two major different interpretations of social demands? Which one seems more important to you? What types of social problems lead some thinkers to emphasize social realities in contemporary American education?
6. What is the meaning of social reconstructionism? Do contemporary social reconstructionists differ from contemporary critics of "the educational establishment" and "compulsory schools"? Would a curriculum based on social realities lead to revolution or avoid revolution in America?
7. What is the case for emphasizing values in a curriculum? What is the history of this approach? What form does value emphasis take in secular American education?
8. How are the viewpoints of value emphasis and recognition of social realities sometimes fused? How do values relate to the humanities?
9. How does the structure of the disciplines approach differ from formal education?
10. What is the meaning of study of the structure of the disciplines? What disciplines are involved? Does the number of disciplines complicate the problem of providing for study of the structures of disciplines?
11. What are some of the major projects in subject matter fields in recent American education? What are their strengths and weaknesses?

WHAT SHOULD THE SCHOOLS TEACH?

12. Why is there a possibility that the "disciplines proposal" has passed its zenith? What educational problems appear to be engaging curriculum makers during the 1970s?
13. Should a curriculum be based on a single source or referent? Why or why not?
14. What are the proposals of some educators for possible combinations of sources or referents?
15. How does the question of curriculum referents or sources affect classroom teachers? What sources or referents seem most significant to members of your class? To you?
16. What courses in high school that you were required to take have continued to seem irrelevant and unnecessary to you? Why?

INVOLVEMENT

1. Recheck the preceding chapter on purposes of education and identify the historical figures and arguments cited which would support one or the other of the referents or sources for curriculum or support some combination of them.
2. Several books by new teachers about their experiences were mentioned in this chapter. Each individual in the class might read one such book and report to the group as a whole.
3. Develop a compilation of significant social problems. Categorize them. If one used an interdisciplinary approach to education, what disciplines would he draw on for the solution of such problems?
4. Assume the existence of a curriculum divided into major subject matter areas. Attempt to allocate contemporary social problems to the most likely areas for purposes of study.
5. Describe some possible approaches to social problems based on Theodore Brameld's model of the moving wheel.
6. Learn more of the viewpoint of critics of contemporary education such as Goodman, Roszak, Friedenberg, etc. by reading and reporting on their views.
7. Read the views of revolutionary young people as contained in contemporary anthologies. Report to the class on these views and analyze their work. Invite a young person representative of these views, along with an opponent of these views, to class for a discussion session.
8. Trace the development of education based on values throughout the history of American education. Determine what forms value education took at varying times.
9. Analyze the possible contributions of the various humanities to value education. Observe the teaching of humanities in schools to determine whether teachers are taking advantage of opportunities for value education inherent in the humanities.
10. Attempt to analyze the discipline you know best as to its structure and especially its methods of inquiry. Attempt to set forth some of the major concepts of the discipline you know best. Compare your results with those of students studying other disciplines to learn more of different tools, methods and approaches in varying fields.
11. In the field with which you are most familiar, what have been the major projects during the past decade? Become familiar with the nature of these projects.
12. Attempt to put yourself into the place of any thinker in education described in the previous chapter. What might he say about the referents or sources for the cur-

riculum proposed in the present chapter? Attempt to set down his view. Compare your product with that of others in the class who are attempting the same thing.

BIBLIOGRAPHY

Barlow, Melvin, ed. *Vocational Education. Sixty-fourth Yearbook of the Society for the Study of Education, Part I.* Chicago: University of Chicago, 1965. Chapters on phases of vocational education in the United States, including the impact of federal legislation and policies.

Bruner, Jerome S. *The Process of Education.* Cambridge, Mass.: Harvard University Press, 1960. An important book which supplies a theoretical foundation for the curriculum approach stressing the structure of the disciplines. Deals with structure, interest, intuition, and readiness.

———. *Toward a Theory of Instruction.* New York: Norton, 1968. An implementation of Bruner's ideas concerning the structure of the disciplines as an approach to instruction.

Crary, Ryland W. *Humanizing the School: Curriculum Development and Theory.* New York: Alfred A. Knopf, 1969. Analysis of school experience from a humanistic point of view. Includes materials on dropouts, the urban crises, black-white relations, etc.

Dennison, George. *The Lives of Children: The Story of the First Street School.* New York: Random House, 1969. Vigorous and forthright account of the creation, program, and demise of an "alternative" school.

Goodlad, John I., Renata Von Stoephasius, and M. Francis Klein. *The Changing School Curriculum.* New York: Georgian Press, 1966. Section I is intended to provide a summary of the shaping forces, the characteristic features, and what the writers consider to be the major strengths and weaknesses of current curriculum reform. Section II describes most of the major projects—such as mathematics, physical and biological sciences, social science, humanities, health education and related educational programs and activities. Section III discusses some problems and issues within a larger context, including aims and objectives, organization, evaluation, and instruction.

Goodman, Paul. *Compulsory Miseducation.* New York: Horizon Press, 1964. Vigorous criticism of the American educational system which maintains what Goodman condemns as "compulsory miseducation."

———. *Growing Up Absurd: Problems of Youth in the Organized System.* New York: Random House, 1960. A vigorous and controversial book by a social critic of education who sees the schools, within the total system, as contributing to the angers and confusion of contemporary youth in a society that offers little to the young.

Gross, Ronald and Beatrice Gross, eds. *Radical School Reform.* New York: Simon and Schuster, 1969. Selected readings reflecting the range of radical thought and practice in public education, emphasizing significantly different schools.

Hentoff, Nat. *Our Children Are Dying.* New York: Viking, 1966. An account of the gallant efforts of a competent and sensitive principal in a New York City slum school, as reported by a skillful journalist.

Herndon, James, *The Way It Spozed To Be.* New York: Simon and Schuster, 1965 Account by a west coast teacher of experiences, while working in a school attended largely by blacks.

Holt, John. *How Children Learn.* New York: Pitman, 1967. A constructive proposal for an educational system which is more oriented to the needs and perplexities of students and less subject matter oriented.

———. *How Children Fail.* New York: Pitman, 1964. A view as to what is wrong with the educational system which emphasizes that schools are frequently indifferent to the real problems and needs of young people.

———. *The Underachieving School.* New York: Pitman, 1969. Short articles by the author developing his theory that schools should be less authoritarian and more child-centered.

King, Arthur R., Jr. and Brownell, John A. *The Curriculum and the Disciplines of Knowledge.* New York: John Wiley and Sons, 1966. An explanation of the structure of disciplines emphasizing intellectual development as the basic goal.

Kohl, Herbert. *Thirty-Six Children.* New York: New American Library, 1967. Eloquent account of a young teacher's experience in shifting from unrealistic approaches to a vital individual-centered program. Particular emphasis upon experiences in writing and with mythology.

Kozol, Jonathan. *Death at an Early Age.* Boston: Houghton Mifflin, 1967. A blunt account of "the destruction of the mind and spirit of Negro children in the Boston public schools." A young teacher's graphic descriptions of his experiences as a substitute teacher.

Lynd, Robert S. *Knowledge for What?* New York: Grove Press, 1964. A classic plea for social significance in education and for knowledge which is genuinely relevant.

Neill, A. S. *Summerhill: A Radical Approach to Child Rearing.* New York: Hart, 1960. A fascinating account of an English school which stresses the freedom of children to establish their own educational pace yet which provides a formal curriculum when they decided to attend classes. A significant book which has resulted in many imitations of Summerhill being established in America and England.

Nelson, Lois N., ed. *The Nature of Teaching.* Waltham, Mass. Blaisdell, 1969. Readings on the logic and strategies of instruction. Stresses thought processes, inquiry, and discovery.

Oliver, Donald W. and James P. Shaver. *Teaching Public Issues in the High School.* Boston: Houghton Mifflin, 1966. Focus on the teaching of controversial issues as the heart of a meaningful curriculum.

Patterson, Franklin. *High Schools for a Free Society.* Glencoe, Ill.: Free Press, 1960. Pungent criticism of the curriculum practices of the 1950s and 1960s and a call for a problems-centered approach to curriculum.

Phenix, Philip H. *Realms of Meaning.* New York: McGraw-Hill, 1964. Accounts of how the various disciplines use differing forms of inquiry and varying procedures.

Smith, B. Othanel, William O. Stanley, and J. Harlan Shores. *Fundamentals of Curriculum Development,* rev. ed. New York: Harcourt, Brace and World, 1957. A classic curriculum book advocating emphasis upon social problems and an attendant social reconstruction of society.

AUDIO-VISUAL MATERIALS

Revolution in the 3 R's (Three M Company, 60 Min.) An ABC-TV film on the Summerhill technique, the Montessori method, the 'new math' programs, etc.

Make a Mighty Reach (IDEA, 28 Min., Color) This film deals with school improvement through innovation.

Summerhill (National Film Board of Canada, 28 Min. color) Visits England's Summerhill, founded by A. S. Neill forty-five years ago to prove that students can make decisions about their studies without lessening the quality of their education.

Education for Cultural Reconstruction (NET, 29 Min.) Theodore Brameld defines cultural reconstruction. He elaborates on the reconstructionist viewpoint.

The Classical Realist Approach to Education (NET, 29 Min.) from the Philosophies of Education Series. Defines classical realism and discusses the theory's basis in the 'natural law.' Shows the application of the theory in a physics class.

An Experimentalist Approach to Education (NET, 29 Min.) from the Philosophies of Education Series. H. Gordon Hullfish elucidates the experimentalist viewpoint, answers objections, and comments on a film sequence of a progressive classroom.

How Can the Curriculum for Individualized Education be Determined? (Special Purpose Films, 35 Min.) Presents John Goodlad in a discussion of curriculum for personalized instruction. He considers academic content, teaching skill and school organization.

As the Twig is Bent (EBEC, 26 Min.) Film focuses on two different approaches to education, "the curriculum centered" approach and the "learning process centered" method. Two kindergarten classrooms are shown.

Deciding What to Teach (Guidance Associates, Harcourt, Brace and World, 107 frs., Color, Record) Discusses four sets of problems related to deciding what to teach—making decisions, establishing priorities, selecting content and balancing the program.

Drug Abuse: Everybody's Hang-Up (Smith, Kline & French: NEA, 12 Min. color) Dramatically depicts the problem of drug abuse among young people. For stimulating discussion by students, teachers, parents, administrators and community groups.

Marijuana (Scott, Richard S. and Max Miller, 34 Min. Color) Discusses the physical dangers and emotional dependency in relation to marijuana. Examines legal aspects. Interviews users and non-users. Narrated by singer Sonny Bono.

Teaching Public Issues: Developing a Position (American Education Publications, 38 Min.) The teacher tries to help students develop justification and reasoning when making a stand on an issue. Opposing views of the American Revolution were used for this film. The students argue whether or not violent protest is justified and they examine their own positions on the topic in relation to historical and contemporary analogies.

Teaching Public Issues: Discussion Techniques (Amer. Educ. Publications, 30 Min.) Illustrates different kinds of teaching and class activities including Socratic debate, small group discussion, deliberate discussion, and role playing.

How the Historian Decides What is Fact (Holt, Rinehart, and Winston, 25 Min.) Demonstrates the inquiry method of teaching students. How the historian decides what is a fact in the study of history.

Resources for Learning (McGraw-Hill, 23 Min., Color) Shows the range of traditional and new educational media available to schools and draws implications regarding their use for the improvement of education. Illustrates the effective contributions that a variety of media can make to the basic patterns of teaching and learning, large group presentations, small group interaction and independent study.

Experiment in Excellence (McGraw-Hill, 54 Min.) Examines educational methods such as team teaching, speed reading, language laboratories, and advanced placement programs. Emphasizes the value of the teacher in providing individual attention.

Focus on Change (NEA, 89 fr., Color) Designed to stimulate thought and action to achieve improvements in school programs.

The Quiet Revolution (National Education Association, 28 Min. color) Depicts a variety of staffing patterns in schools that have initiated team teaching, nongraded elementary programs, flexible scheduling and other innovations.

EIGHTEEN

HOW DO CURRICULUM CONTENT AND ORGANIZATION CHANGE?

The curriculum is not static. It may not change rapidly enough to satisfy those who want reform, but it does change. For instance, the curriculum of your college is a far cry from the seven branches of learning which made up the liberal arts curriculum of the Middle Ages: the trivium—grammar, logic, and rhetoric—and the quadrivium—arithmetic, geometry, astronomy, and music.

CHANGING CURRICULUM CONTENT

PROCESSES

In American education, one standard approach to changing the curriculum has been to call together a group of experts in a particular subject. The specialists include college professors who convene, confer, and develop a new course of study which usually lists topics to be studied and specific approaches, and provides updated bibliographies of teaching materials. This approach sounds logical, but it has been found that teachers are more likely to use new materials when they have helped develop them; courses of study prepared by outside experts are often filed and forgotten.

Consequently, a major step in curriculum development during the past fifty years has been the increased involvement of teachers in preparing curriculum materials. Teachers have been added to course of study committees as active participating members. They have also played an especially important role in developing resource units for a topic or a problem area. Unlike a course of study which usually prescribes what is to be taught, a resource unit lists many suggestions and allows the teacher considerable freedom of choice among learning experiences. Resource units often include an analysis of the problem or topic, a listing of teaching materials, and a variety of possible learning activities. From the resource unit, teachers select the most appropriate activities and materials for a particular class.

Some school systems try to maintain system-wide curriculum uniformity, but others use a "broken-front" approach, in which the individual school is central in curriculum revision. In the latter approach, within a particular school a committee of teachers might work on the curriculum of a certain grade level. Or a committee might tackle a broad area, as social studies or science. Committee work in the different schools may be coordinated by a system-wide committee led by members of the central office staff, yet each school usually has a great deal of freedom to develop its own program.

During the 1960s, sponsors of the new curriculum projects, particularly in science and mathematics, developed a more sophisticated approach to curriculum construction. They involved subject-matter experts, specialists in the psychology of learning, and public school teachers. Content and methods often were tested on some elementary or secondary school students before more extensive field trials in the schools; programs went through several preliminary versions before formal publication.

The result was often a course package including one or more textbooks, supplementary materials in the form of pamphlets, films, or recordings and comprehensive manuals to guide the teacher. Summer institutes were frequently held to train teachers in the use of such materials. The project approach provided teachers with specific materials and techniques developed by specialists, otherwise inaccessible to teachers. Yet the approach was criticized as converting the teacher into a mechanic who used generalized expert-prepared materials without sufficient adaptation to local conditions. Despite increasing centralization in American life, many educators continued to value local control of schools to insure that the curriculum would be adapted to community needs and to the needs of particular groups of learners.

Although many educators participate in the process of change of curriculum content, candor and realism compel us to recognize that the motivation for change usually comes from changes in society as a whole. Educators may theorize about the ideal curriculum, but when a significant social change generates a demand for educational change, the schools change, however grudgingly and reluctantly. Educational history records many instances in which particularly threatening social problems are referred to the schools for solution.

In the 1930s, the economic and international crisis led to an increase in socially oriented materials in the programs of schools. World War II in the 1940s led to the adaptation of school programs to wartime demands. In the 1950s, the schools reacted to the national fear that the United States might be second to the Soviet Union in the space race. This persisted into the early 1960s; emphasis was placed on strengthening programs in science, mathematics, and modern languages, supported by federal funds to realize American national purposes. But the later sixties saw a rediscovery of poverty in America and emphasis shifted to the education of disadvantaged youth, supported by philanthropic and government funds.

Confrontation of police and parents over local control of the schools. Courtesy of Ernest Baxter from Black Star.

In the 1970s, confronted by angry youth and dissenting blacks and the dismay of the silent majority at crime, bombings, and incipient revolution, American society again looks to the schools for help. Such approaches as black studies, free universities, free choice curricula, and problem-centered programs are developing. In the early 1970s, national concern also is aroused by sharp increase in the use of drugs by both the college and high school population. Especially in the large cities, then in the suburbs and smaller cities, and finally in rural areas, courses and programs concerning drug abuse have been added to the curriculum.

As we know from chapter 9, influence is brought to bear on the curriculum by many agencies and institutions: local school boards, state departments of education, state legislatures, accrediting agencies, college committees that set entrance requirements, university projects, philanthropic foundations, pressure groups, etc. With the growth of activism and various forms of protest in recent years, a powerful new change agent has been added: curriculum demands.

CHANGING THE CURRICULUM THROUGH DEMANDS

Demands may be by students and ethnic groups, by organizations or individuals. They may be minor or they may require sweeping changes. When curriculum demands are made, the authorities are informed that certain changes must be made now—or else. "Or else" may take the form of sit-ins, strikes, boycotts, or even violence and destruction. Such demands often are labeled "non-negotiable" but they may actually be negotiated as meetings of the conflicting parties proceed. Sometimes, after discussion, immediacy too is replaced by flexibility as to time of implementation. Yet in all curriculum-making through demands, there is implicit some degree of threat or coercion unless action is taken swiftly.

Supporters of curriculum-making through demands point out that existing establishments, whether governments or schools, are notoriously unready to change and exasperatingly deliberate in the operation of their change mechanisms. They say that the only way to speed up the glacial pace of curriculum change is to confront an institution with a set of demands, for only through necessity will an institution modify its customary program. For example, black studies programs in high schools and colleges have come about largely through the technique of making demands. Confrontation tactics have resulted in increased student participation in secondary and higher education and increased opportunities for students to influence the curriculum.

Opponents say that curriculum-making in response to demands creates an anarchic situation, a chaos in which forces which have the most power reign temporarily in an eternal "king of the hill" type of struggle. Discussion is bypassed; when confrontation becomes the way of making curriculum change, the democratic process may be violated.

Precipitate decisions made in response to urgent demands also may result in inadequate programs. Hasty action may help the group pressing the demands but may ignore or hinder the welfare of those who are not represented. As the old saying puts it, "the squeaking wheel gets the grease."

Carl Sandburg the poet and Jimmy Durante the comedian are not known as authorities on curriculum change. Yet two of their characteristic phrases are extremely pertinent to curriculum-making. In *The People, Yes,* Carl Sandburg said, "Everybody knows more than anybody." In television appearances Jimmy Durante said, "Everybody wants to get into the act." Many educators recognize that everybody knows more than anybody and that everybody wants to get into the act. The schools belong to the people and educators have no monopoly on the wisdom needed to bring about worthwhile curriculum change. Yet educators are the professionals in this field and must play vital roles both as participants and as leaders.

One of the educational tasks for the seventies is to develop ground rules to insure the widest possible participation by many in curriculum-making. Educators must improve the democratic processes and foster responsible participation by those affected by curriculum decisions. Rather than abdicate their curricular responsibilities, educators must learn to exercise their responsibilities in a setting in which all the people—not simply one of the segments of the people—establish the basic policies.

CHANGING CURRICULUM ORGANIZATION

Societal demands often bring about change in curriculum content, but how content is organized and taught usually is left to the educational experts.

NONGRADED SCHOOLS

For instance, a widely approved organizational innovation of the 1960s was the nongraded school. Essentially the nongraded idea is to establish classes on some basis more educationally justifiable than mere age or year in school. The aim is to individualize instruction and eliminate the trappings of grade level school organization, such as annual promotion from grade to grade. Typical primary nongraded programs mix students who might ordinarily be labeled first, second, or third graders.

Robert Anderson and John Goodlad in their book, *The Nongraded Elementary School*, describe in detail a nongraded approach for elementary schools. Sidney P. Rollins, architect of a well-known nongraded junior-senior high school program, described the nongraded school as follows:

1. In the graded school a year of progress in a subject usually corresponds to a year in school, while in the nongraded school a child may progress through more or less than a year's work in a subject. In the graded school subject matter tends to be organized in terms of a year of work, while in the nongraded school subject matter is organized in terms of longer periods of time . . .

2. In the graded school a pupil is expected to progress "of a piece"; that is, he is expected to advance at a standard pace in all areas of development, while in the nongraded school differences in the potential of a given youngster are recognized; he may progress quickly through one subject field and more slowly in others. Conceivably, he may be working at as many different levels as there are subjects. . . .

3. In the graded school a pupil's progress is measured in terms of his ability to "cover" a given amount of content, while in the nongraded school the measure of progress is the pupil's own achievement. In the graded school unsatisfactory progress in a subject requires repetition of the year's work. Failure is the ultimate penalty; fear of failure constitutes a primary extrinsic motivation. In the nongraded school pupils are given whatever time (within limits) they need in order to learn the material. At the end of a semester or a year the child does not fail, and does not repeat, he is given recognition for whatever progress he has made and then is permitted to continue on from there. . . .

4. In the graded school, because there is a specified amount of content that must be learned in a given amount of time, pupils within each class must progress at approximately the same speed, while in the nongraded school pupils within each class are given an opportunity to progress at their own speeds. As each week or quarter or semester terminates, each pupil is rescheduled on the basis of his progress during the previous week, quarter, or semester. Even daily rescheduling presently is feasible. . . .

5. In the graded school pupils are evaluated in terms of how well they appear to have mastered the material specified for their grade, while in the nongraded school a pupil is evaluated in terms of the quality of learning and the quality of content that has been learned. The principal criterion for evaluating the pupil is the pupil himself. Such pupils progress at their own rates of speed, and since they are not permitted to progress until some evidence of mastery is available, it is not necessary for any pupil to fail. . . .

6. In the graded school apt pupils are occasionally offered something called "enrichment." The child is offered additional work at the same sequential level as less apt pupils. In the nongraded school apt pupils are encouraged to move ahead regardless of the grade level of the work. There is no fear of encroaching upon the domain of the next teacher because nongraded schools are oriented in terms of the pupil's own progress, not in terms of private teacher-empires. . . .
7. In the graded school pupils are "promoted" at the end of the year, while in the nongraded school there is considerably more flexibility of pupil movement. Pupils can shift from one group to another at almost any time. . . .
8. In the graded school there exists a tendency to use a single text, because all pupils are expected to cover a specified amount of content in a specified length of time, while in the nongraded school the flexibility of pupil movement tends to encourage use of a broader range of source materials. Once pupils are encouraged to progress at their own rates, and to explore areas of interest, a single textbook is inadequate. . . .[1]

A somewhat different nongraded approach is advocated by B. Frank Brown. Brown describes as follows the nongraded approach of the high school of which he was once principal:

Youngsters at Melbourne High School have been reclassified in line with their level of achievement and assigned to fluid learning situations in each subject on the basis of their needs. Through selective acceleration, some students begin college level work when they arrive as tenth-graders. By the same token, some students in the twelfth grade receive greater amounts of remedial work in areas in which their achievement is below standard.

The plan for continuous learning at Melbourne accommodates youngsters by placing them in temporary learning situations from which they can move at any time. These *ad hoc* learning arrangements are called phases. A phase is a stage of development with a varying time element. One student may remain in a low phase indefinitely; another may progress rapidly into higher phases.

When students enter Melbourne High School they are sorted on the basis of nationally standardized achievement tests. They are then clustered into a new spectrum in line with their various aptitudes and abilities.

Phase 1—Subjects are centered around remedial work.

Phase 2—Subjects are concerned with basic skills.

Phase 3—Subjects are designed for students seeking an average education.

Phase 4—Subjects are available for students desiring education in considerable depth.

Phase 5—Subjects are open to students who are willing to assume responsibility for their own learning and plan to go far beyond the boundaries of a single course.

Phase Q—Students whose creative talents are well developed in special areas

---

[1] Sidney P. Rollins, *Developing Nongraded Schools* (Itasca, Ill.: F. E. Peacock, 1968), pp. 12–16.

should give consideration to this "Quest" phase of the curriculum. This is an important dimension of the phased organization designed to give thrust in the direction of individual fulfillment. In this phase a student may research an area in which he is deeply and broadly curious, either to develop creative powers or in quest of knowledge. A student may spend from one to three hours a day in Quest.

Phase X—Non-academic subjects which do not accommodate student mobility; e.g. typing, physical education. These subjects are ungraded but unphased.[2]

Exponents of nongraded schools point out that numerous teaching-learning problems have been created by the "lock-step" graded approach to curricular organization. Students have been evaluated and ranked in their achievement by comparison with other children of the same chronological age who were exposed to the same material for the same length of time. Students have lost out in important subject areas because they missed instruction on crucial days and teachers had to move on for the good of the group. Students with cultural deficiencies, but eager to learn, have been inhibited in their work by more aggressive or talented students in their age groups. In short, individuals were expected to adjust to the common standards and goals characterizing a particular grade level.

Successful implementation of a nongraded curriculum eliminates most of these problems. But additional responsibility for fostering *learning* falls upon the teacher.

If you teach in a nongraded system, you will probably be less concerned with common standards and uniform performance of the group (and the inevitable inability of certain individuals to meet them) and more concerned with the relevance and value of your teaching to the individual learner. You may provide for the individual needs of slower students without the feeling of futility which often accompanies the realization that the student is so far behind that he will never catch up. In the same manner, slower students may be more readily motivated because they do not experience this feeling of futility in their attempts to catch up.

The threat of failure in the graded system is a coercive device many teachers depend upon. Elimination of failure in the nongraded school will deprive the new teacher of this inducement. He will have to be more original and innovative in his methods and demonstrate more understanding of learning. Initiative and resourcefulness will be called for if the teacher of the nongraded class is to develop logical sequences for instruction, since existing textbooks and curricular aids are primarily organized for the graded program. An English teacher, for example, must have a thorough knowledge of the structure of language and composition in order to permit the student to attain particular understandings and skills sequentially as the student moves through the phases of a nongraded program.

[2] B. Frank Brown, "The Non-Graded High School," *Phi Delta Kappan*, 44 (February 1963), p. 207.

Left: Courtesy of Joe DiDio from NEA. Right: Courtesy of George S. Zimbel from EFL.

TEAM TEACHING

Another frequently accepted innovation of the 1960s was team teaching. J. Lloyd Trump, of the National Association of Secondary School Principals, focused national attention on this conception through a study supported by the Ford Foundation and carried through by NASSP's Commission on the Experimental Study of the Utilization of the Staff in the Secondary Schools. In 1968, Trump, writing in cooperation with Delmas F. Miller, summarized team teaching as follows:

The term "team teaching" applies to an arrangement in which two or more teachers and their assistants, taking advantage of their respective competencies, plan, instruct, and evaluate in one or more subject areas a group of elementary or secondary students equivalent in size to two or more conventional classes, using a variety of technical aids to teaching and learning through large-group instruction, small-group discussion, and independent study. If one of the foregoing ingredients is missing, the result is *not* team teaching. It may be "cooperative teaching," "rotation of teaching," "utilization of teacher aides," or something else—but it is not team teaching.

The members of a given team may come from one subject department or grade level in the school or from several subject or grade areas. Although present research does not favor one kind of team over the other, we prefer teams that cut across subject lines. Such teams tend to plan instruction that recognizes better the interrelatedness of subject content. (In this regard, teaming has some of the same objectives as the core or common learnings curricular approach.) Teachers still work primarily in their specialties, even with special interests within their subject fields, but they benefit from working in group activities with colleagues in other subject fields. Of course we have seen excellent as well as ineffective teams of all types. The organization itself does not produce the goals of team teaching.

The individual needs opportunities for varied educational groupings and experiences. Courtesy of DeWys.

A team preferably includes older, more experienced teachers as well as beginners and less experienced ones, each benefiting from contact with the others. The team should select a leader to preside at planning and evaluation sessions. However, formalizing this position too much, or paying extra salary to the leader, may inhibit achievement of team teaching goals. The position of team leader is not analogous to that of a department chairman.[3]

If you teach as a team member, you may find the fishbowl qualities of team teaching difficult to live with at first. Some new teachers prefer the isolation of the self-contained classroom to the demands placed upon them by the sharing of the teaching team; they prefer to carry on their trial-and-error experimentation in private. As a neophyte, however, you may profit considerably from a close, cooperative relationship with experienced teachers. The cooperative approach may offer many opportunities for you to refine your techniques and develop more creative methods sooner than you might in isolation. You may find satisfaction in the greater varieties of small-group instruction offered by team teaching and the resultant opportunities to help individual pupils develop at their own rate.

Certainly in a team teaching situation your time and efforts should be used more advantageously. The well-organized team allows the teacher to specialize in areas of particular ability and interest. Teams sometimes include teaching aides or paraprofessionals to assist in the many time-consuming, often nonprofessional, tasks which are necessary in teaching and thus assistants may be available to help you grade papers, prepare tests, arrange physical facilities, and maintain student records.

To be effective in team teaching, you must be competent and self-assured, unafraid to expose your knowledge and your ideas to the scrutiny of fellow

---

[3] J. Lloyd Trump and Delmas F. Miller, *Secondary School Curriculum Improvement: Proposals and Procedures* (Boston: Allyn and Bacon, 1968), pp. 318–319.

teachers and laymen. You must believe in the objectives of the team approach and its ability to improve instruction. You must respect the teachers with whom you will work on the team, for a spirit of cooperation, mutuality, and willingness to work together is essential to the successful teaching team.

The support of administration is important to effective team teaching. Unfortunately, the development of team teaching has been handicapped by the fact that administrators and school boards may adopt the large lecture groups as a means of saving money, while neglecting small discussion groups and independent study.

CORE CURRICULUM

The core curriculum, like the interdisciplinary team program, emphasizes the interrelatedness of all human knowledge. It goes even further, however, abandoning arbitrary subject matter divisions to deal directly with human problems in all their complexity. Taught either by one teacher or by a team, a secondary-school core class usually lasts two or three periods each day and may be listed on the schedule as "core," "common learnings," or "general education." Similar problem-centered studies are often called "experience units" in elementary schools.

Interdisciplinary courses have long been popular at the junior high or middle school level, and are increasing in the senior high schools. Most core programs take the place of separate classes in social studies and language arts. The two major variations of core are described as follows by Gordon F. Vars:

In *structured core* the students explore broad "problem areas" or "centers of experience" that are specified in advance by the staff. These areas or centers are categories of human experience that embrace both the personal problems, interests, and needs of students and the problems confronting contemporary society. In emphasis they range from those heavily weighted with adolescent concerns, such as "Personality Development" or "Problems of Family Living," to those that emphasize broader social issues, such as "Intercultural Relations," or "Problems of World Peace." Within these areas, students and teachers cooperatively develop learning units focused on specific problems identified by members of that particular class. The problems areas and illustrative learning units below were developed by Jean V. Marani, supervisor of interns in the public schools of Sarasota, Florida. (See Table 18.1)

To aid in teacher-student planning, many schools provide resource units or guides that explore the ramifications of a problem area, suggest objectives, list possible learning activities and instructional materials. From these a teacher and his students can select or develop learning experiences they deem most appropriate. In preparing resource units, staff members may be joined by parents, students, university consultants, and other knowledgeable people.

In *unstructured core*, students and teachers are free to study any problem that they consider worthwhile. To be sure, classes usually rule out topics that they have studied before, that interest only a minority of the students, or for which the school and community provide insufficient learning resources. In some cases criteria such as these are defined in advance by the staff; at other times they are developed cooperatively by teachers and students.

Units studied in unstructured core may fall within the same problem areas or centers of experience as those of a structured core program. Often as not, however, they may cut across or combine several areas. Consider, for example, the class that started out to study boy-girl relations, became concerned with the problem of juvenile delinquency in the local community, and ended up spear-heading a community-wide effort to provide wholesome recreation for young people.

TABLE 18.1

Suggested Problem Areas for a Junior High School Core Program that Replaces English and Social Studies

PROBLEM AREA	ILLUSTRATIVE LEARNING UNITS
	GRADE SEVEN
1. Education and School Living	Orientation to Junior High School
	What Are My Talents?
2. Self-Understanding	Growing Up
	How to Make Wise Decisions
3. Living in the Community	The Outlook for Teenagers in Sarasota
	How Florida Meets the Problems of a Growing State
4. Economic Understanding	How Our Natural Resources Are Utilized
	Business Around the World
5. Intercultural Understanding	Teenagers Around the World
	Understanding Our Asian Neighbors
	GRADE EIGHT
1. Education and School Living	Orientation
	How to Study
2. Personal-Social Relations	Achieving Maturity
	Boy Meets Girl
3. Democratic Government	Documents of Democracy
	Our Old World Heritage
	The Beliefs of a Democratic People
4. Vocational Preparation	Planning for High School
	Vocational Orientation
5. Relationships with Minority Groups	The Negro's Role in Our Society
	Religions of the World
6. Intercultural Understanding	Men and Achievements of the 20th Century
	The U.S.'s Rise to World Leadership

	GRADE NINE
1. Education and School Living	Assessing My Potential
	Our Educational Future
2. Personal-Social Relations	How to Deal with Juvenile Delinquency
	Youth's Status
3. Healthful Living	The Community Health Program
	Healthful Products
4. Economic Understanding	My Role as a Consumer-Producer
	Money Management
	World Economic Systems
5. Democratic Government	Comparative Governments
	The Citizen's Role in Policy Making
6. Intercultural Understanding	The World's Resources
	Ways of Achieving Peace

Gordon F. Vars (ed.), *Common Learnings: Core and Interdisciplinary Team Approaches* (Scranton, Pa.: International Textbook Co., 1969), pp. 8–9. Listing of problem areas and illustrative learning units developed by Jean Marani Graetz, supervisor of interns in public schools of Sarasota, Florida.

In addition to work on broad problems or topics, students in all types of block-time classes spend a good deal of time developing their communication skills, reading for enjoyment, carrying out homeroom-type activities, discussing current affairs, solving problems of interpersonal relations and the like.[4]

If you teach in a core program, you must be willing to help students work on selected problems. The quest for solutions may involve several subject fields. The fields may not always fall within the areas which you know best. For instance, problems may cut across such broad fields as language arts and social studies. They may interrelate science and mathematics. Reports by students may employ arts media. So core teaching requires versatility on your part; the broader your liberal arts education the better your perparation for core teaching will be. Narrow subject specialists had best not apply!

COMPUTERIZED MODULAR SCHEDULING

Innovations such as nongrading, team teaching, and core curriculum often create problems in scheduling students. Consequently some schools now use computers for modular scheduling. A module is a unit of time, shorter than the usual class period, that is used as a building block in creating a daily schedule. A pioneer in computerized scheduling was Marshall High School in Portland, Oregon. Its principal describes faculty participation in schedule-making:

[4] Gordon F. Vars (ed.), *Common Learnings: Core and Interdisciplinary Team Approaches* (Scranton, Pa.: International Textbook, 1969), p. 9.

... the staff of each department at Marshall High School was asked the basic question, "How would you like to teach your course next year without the limitations of a conventional schedule?" From the answers given, course structures, teacher team assignments, and room utilization needs were projected. The faculty members were encouraged to think in terms of large- and small-group instruction and various forms of laboratory groups, together with independent study for all students. From the teacher recommendations, the decision was made to divide the school day into 21 twenty-minute modules, or periods of time. Thus, a large-group presentation might be two modules, or forty minutes, less four minutes passing time, and a lab meeting might be as long as five modules, or 100 minutes. Any multiple of these short time blocks could be requested in order to satisfy the needs of the students and of the particular activity taking place in the course.[5]

If you teach in a school which uses modular scheduling, you will participate in decision-making as to the length of your teaching periods. You will have to think through whether your grade level or subject and your characteristic teaching style are best served by sustained periods or shorter periods, by daily instruction or less than five meetings weekly, by large- or small-group work—or by some combination among these. For instance, a physical education teacher may prefer three 100-minute sessions weekly to five 60-minute sessions. A social studies teacher may prefer one long session of 60 minutes for large-group work and the rest of his time in 40 minute blocks for small-group work. A science teacher may prefer two long laboratory sessions and one shorter class meeting.

INDEPENDENT STUDY

Modular scheduling facilitates another valuable innovation, independent study by students. Petrequin says of the Marshall High School experience:

Proceeding with our working definition that independent study will mean the constructive use of unscheduled time, we can describe the four basic activities in which a student may participate during this time. First, a student often does his regularly assigned classwork; second, the student may become involved in an extensive or intensive extension of his regular class assignment—more likely than not, a student would be given "extra credit" for this type of work; third, a student might be engaged in an independent-study project; finally a student could participate in an enrichment experience. Although the term "enrichment experience" seems a bit unwieldy for a description, it is an appropriate one, for it does suggest the nature of the activity. . .

Although a student is often engaged in a variety of activities during his unscheduled, independent-study time—he may study in the library or any one

---

[5] Gaynor Petrequin, *Individualized Learning Through Modular-Flexible Programming* (New York: McGraw-Hill, 1968), p. 3.

TABLE 18.2

A Sample for Modular Scheduling

PAUL ADAMS JR. HIGH SCHOOL SPRING 1970

PAUL ADAMS JR. HIGH SCHOOL SPRING 1971

NAME: KEITH, KAREN MAE CODE: 3B83 GR SCH: 13 SEX: F HOMEROOM: 413 GRADE: 7

MOD	TIME	MONDAY	TUESDAY	WEDNESDAY	THURSDAY	FRIDAY
	8/35	HOMEROOM	HOMEROOM	HOMEROOM	HOMEROOM	HOMEROOM
1	8/45	MUSIC ROOM 201 TEACHER BOYD				
2	9/14		MATH R ROOM 304 TEACHER LANE		MATH R ROOM 304 TEACHER LANE	
3	9/43			HEAL R ROOM 201 TEACHER KYLE		HEAL R ROOM 201 TEACHER KYLE
4	10/12					
5	10/41	MATH R ROOM 419 TEACHER WILLIAMS		MATH R ROOM 419 TEACHER WILLIAMS		MATH R ROOM 419 TEACHER WILLIAMS
6	11/10	MATH R ROOM 419 TEACHER WILLIAMS	SOC S S ROOM 201 TEACHER MADISON	MATH R ROOM 419 TEACHER WILLIAMS	SOC S S ROOM 201 TEACHER MADISON	MATH R ROOM 419 TEACHER WILLIAMS
7	11/39					
8	12/08	SOC S S ROOM 219 TEACHER MADISON	MUSIC ROOM 504 TEACHER BOONE	SOC S S ROOM 219 TEACHER MADISON	MUSIC ROOM 504 TEACHER BOONE	SOC S S ROOM 219 TEACHER MADISON
9	12/37	SOC S S ROOM 219 TEACHER MADISON	MUSIC ROOM 504 TEACHER BOONE	SOC S S ROOM 219 TEACHER MADISON	MUSIC ROOM 504 TEACHER BOONE	SOC S S ROOM 219 TEACHER MADISON
10	1/06		HEAL R ROOM 107 TEACHER KYLE		HEAL R ROOM 107 TEACHER KYLE	
11	1/35		HEAL R ROOM 107 TEACHER KYLE	ENG S ROOM 207 TEACHER PAYNE	HEAL R ROOM 107 TEACHER KYLE	ENG S ROOM 207 TEACHER PAYNE
12	2/04	ENG S ROOM 207 TEACHER PAYNE	ENG S ROOM 304 TEACHER CASE	ENG S ROOM 207 TEACHER PAYNE	ENG S ROOM 304 TEACHER CASE	ENG S ROOM 207 TEACHER PAYNE
13	2/33	ENG S ROOM 207 TEACHER PAYNE	PHY ED ROOM 102 TEACHER SWANSON		PHY ED ROOM 102 TEACHER SWANSON	
14	3/02		PHY ED ROOM 102 TEACHER SWANSON		PHY ED ROOM 102 TEACHER SWANSON	
15	3/31		PHY ED ROOM 102 TEACHER SWANSON	HOMEROOM	PHY ED ROOM 102 TEACHER SWANSON	HOMEROOM

of the seven resource centers, confer with teachers or his fellow students, practice on a musical instrument, work on an independent-study project, listen and respond to language tapes—there is a good possibility that he may include an enrichment experience. Enrichment experiences include an array of specialty courses, unique training activities, class auditing on a formal or informal basis, and special programs that are available to the students because of the flexibility of our scheduling system.[6]

If your school utilizes independent study, you may find it an effective but a demanding method. In a school using independent study, you may be expected to direct laboratory work or conduct seminars on topics important to students. You may be expected to confer with independent study participants on a regular basis to give direction and check progress. You will undoubtedly spend many hours reading and evaluating project reports which students submit to you. Your work during independent study hours will certainly not be routine.

RELATION OF ORGANIZATION TO CONTENT

Innovations in curriculum organization may lead to better utilization of manpower and greater efficiency in operation. Sometimes, as in the case of core programs, they affect curriculum content. Usually, however, organizational changes relate more to effective management of time, teachers, and students, rather than to what is taught. Educational innovations related to management usually may be adopted with less community controversy than changes in content. For instance, the addition of sex education or black studies in a curriculum at the elementary, secondary, or college level is likely to arouse more community controversy than the introduction of team teaching or modular scheduling.

DISCUSSION
1. What are the processes customarily used in changing the curriculum? What has been learned from such processes and consequently, what changes in curriculum development have taken place relatively recently?
2. Where does the motivation for curriculum change as to content usually originate? Can you illustrate?
3. What is the case for and against changing the curriculum through demands by individuals or groups? What processes must be developed if curriculum-making by demands is not to prevail?
4. What essentially is a nongraded school? What are its advantages and disadvantages?

[6] Ibid., p. 66.

5. Imagine yourself in a school situation in which nongrading is prevalent. How would your work be different from your anticipated work in a more conventional school?
6. What essentially is the nature of team teaching? What are its advantages and disadvantages? Imagine yourself teaching in a team teaching situation. How would this be different from teaching in a more usual situation?
7. How does team teaching threaten the traditional teacher?
8. What is the meaning of the core curriculum? Of the sources or referents described in the last chapter, which are most likely to be used in core curriculum approaches? Which less likely?
9. What is the difference between structured and unstructured core?
10. If you taught in a core program, how might this experience be different from teaching in a more conventional school program? What kind of educational background and experiences would be maximally useful to you in teaching in a core program?
11. What is the meaning of modular scheduling? In modular scheduling, what is the role of the human being in supplying ideas and the computer in supplying programs?
12. What do you see as the value of having modular scheduling at the high school level? Do you see any problems or possible losses?
13. How might your work as a teacher be different if you taught in a school characterized by modular scheduling?
14. Were there any features of a "core" approach, ungradedness, modular scheduling, etc., in your school experience?
15. What is the future of independent study? Do you see many advantages or limitations of this approach?
16. How would your work be different if it included substantial relationships to independent study?
17. Why are matters of content change often more controversial than matters of organizational change?

INVOLVEMENT

1. Investigate a curriculum project related to your subject field or level and report upon it to the class as a whole.
2. If changes in curriculum through demands take place in your community, attend such meetings as an observer. Note any desirable or undesirable features of this approach in action.
3. Learn of the location of a nongraded school and visit classes on several levels. Talk with the teachers about advantages and disadvantages of this approach.
4. After visiting a school in which team teaching takes place, interview several members of a particular team for their perceptions of their responsibilities.
5. A core or block of time program may be found on the junior high school level in your own or a neighboring community. If so, visit such a program. Compare the approaches you observe with those described in this chapter.
6. Draw up a chart for a proposed core curriculum from the seventh through the twelfth grades characterized by learning units which seem most important to you at this time in American life and at varied stages of the learners' development.

7. If a nearby school uses computerized modular scheduling, visit to learn both about the machinery involved and the resultant program. Note the differences in utilization of modules by teachers in subject fields.
8. Observe independent study as it takes place in a school situation. What types of students seem to use this opportunity well? Why do some do badly?
9. Observe any situations of curriculum change in local schools to test the validity of the generalization that content changes are more controversial than organization changes.

BIBLIOGRAPHY

Alberty, Harold B. and Elsie J. Alberty. *Reorganizing the High-School Curriculum,* 3rd ed. New York: Macmilan, 1962. A classic in curriculum which sets forth the case for an approach centered upon the needs of the learner and democratic values. Advocates and describes the uses of the core curriculum.

Alexander, William M., Vynce A. Hines, et al. *Independent Study in Secondary Schools.* New York: Holt, Rinehart, and Winston, 1968. A guide to the technique of independent study by students under teacher direction.

Allen, Dwight and Keith Ryan. *Microteaching.* Reading, Mass.: Addison-Wesley, 1969. An introduction to microteaching and a progress report on how far it has come to date.

Beggs, David W., III, and Edward G. Buffie, eds. *Nongraded Schools in Action.* Bloomington, Ind.: Indiana University Press, 1967. Accounts of the purposes and programs of a variety of nongraded programs.

Broudy, Harry S., B. Othanel Smith, and Joe R. Burnett. *Democracy and Excellence in American Secondary Education.* Chicago: Rand McNally, 1964. A proposal for a single-track, nongraded high school with a curriculum devoid of electives.

Brown, B. Frank. *Education by Appointment: New Approaches to Independent Study.* New York: Parker Publishing, 1968. A provocative book on independent study, tracing its beginnings, patterns, and describing the "quest" curriculum.

——— *The Nongraded High School.* Englewood Cliffs, N.J.: Prentice-Hall, 1963. Description of a Florida high school administered by the author during a period of change in the composition of the student body and of experimentation with the nongraded school and other innovations.

Crosby, Muriel. *Curriculum Development for Elementary Schools in a Changing Society.* Boston: Heath, 1964. Competent suggestions on the development of the curriculum in elementary schools by an experienced school administrator and educational theorist. Chapters on broad curricular fields and stress on human relations needs and problems.

Eurich, Alvin C. *Reforming American Education.* New York: Harper and Row, 1969. Defines the "innovative" spirit in education and develops the thesis that the innovative approach is the most promising strategy for improving education to meet the needs and challenges of a changing society.

Goodlad, John I. and Robert H. Anderson. *The Nongraded Elementary School,* New York: Harcourt, Brace, and World, rev. ed. 1963. The case for the nongraded elementary school as the best form of organization for challenging learners of widely varying abilities, attainments, and interests.

Gross, Ronald and Judith Murphy, eds. *The Revolution in the Schools.* New York: Harcourt, Brace and World, 1964. Reports by pioneering educators, behavioral and social scientists, and practicing teachers on the nongraded school, team teaching, new concepts in learnings, etc.

Hanslovsky, Glenda, Sue Moyer, and Helen Wagner. *Why Team Teaching?* Columbus, Ohio: Charles E. Merrill, 1969. Can be used as a "how-to" book listing ways to prepare for and begin team teaching.

Heathers, Glen. *Organizing Schools Through The Dual Process Plan.* Danville, Ill.: Interstate Printers and Publishers, 1967. This book contains the results of an experiment to reorganize elementary and middle schools, combining graded and nongraded instruction in a semi-departmental framework.

Hillson, Maurie and Joseph Bongo. *Continuous Progress Nongraded Education: Inventions, Innovations, and Implementations.* Chicago: Science Research Associates, 1970. A handbook for effecting a flexible nongraded system characterized by individual instruction.

Johnson, Robert H. and John Joseph Hunt. ℞ *For Team Teaching.* Minneapolis: Burgess, 1968. Outlines the need for team teaching from the teachers' viewpoint and the need for administrative support.

Kohl, Herbert R. *The Open Classroom.* New York: Random House, 1970. The author of *36 Children* reports on ways to achieve some of the goals which he envisioned in his earlier book. The emphasis is upon techniques to use to prevail against the rigidities of the traditional classroom and traditional administration.

Michaelis, John U., Ruth H. Grossman, and Lloyd F. Scott. *New Designs for the Elementary School Curriculum.* New York: McGraw-Hill, 1967. Emphasis upon new developments in elementary curriculum by the senior author, a well established social educator, and his collaborators.

Petrequin, Gaynor. *Individualized Learning Through Modular-Flexible Programming.* New York: McGraw-Hill, 1968. Practical insights on how a school used programming through computers and fostered individualized learning, by the principal of the school involved.

Rollins, Sidney P. *Developing Nongraded Schools.* Itasca, Ill.: F. E. Peacock, 1968. A rationale for the establishment of nongraded schools, followed by a theoretical, the applied presentation of curriculum, teacher roles, administration, physical environment, and teacher training for nongraded schools.

Saylor, J. Galen and William M. Alexander. *Curriculum Planning for Modern Schools.* Chicago: Holt, Rinehart and Winston, 1966. Process and procedures in curriculum planning, including proposals for bases for curriculum planning and for the organization of the curriculum and instruction.

Trump, J. Lloyd and Dorsey Baynham. *Focus on Change: Guide to Better Schools.* Chicago: Rand McNally, 1961. Historically important report on utilization of staff based on NASSP study which fostered team teaching.

Trump, Lloyd and Delmas F. Miller. *Secondary School Curriculum Improvement: Proposals and Procedures.* Boston: Allyn and Bacon, 1968. The sponsor of team teaching and a competent secondary educator collaborate on the development of innovations in curriculum to meet the changing needs of individual students.

Vars, Gordon F. *Common Learnings: Core and Interdisciplinary Team Approaches.* Scranton, Penn.: International Textbook, 1969. Approaches to common learnings by a leader in the development of practices in the core curriculum.

Waskin, Yvonne and Louise Parrish. *Teacher-Pupil Planning for Better Classroom Learning.* New York: Pitman, 1967. A how-to book for teachers who believe that cooperative planning with pupils is part of the key to meaningful classroom experience.

AUDIO-VISUAL MATERIALS

How Can You Apply Team-Teaching and Non-grading to Your School? (Special Purpose Films, 35 Min.) Outlines the kinds of decisions which the school principal and teacher must make to apply team teaching and nongrading techniques. Gives examples involving peer group composition and variables of teaching style.

Why Are Team-Teaching and Non-Grading Important (Special Purpose Films, 49 Min.) Presents John Goodlad as he explains how team teaching and nongrading help to bridge the gap between the problems of school organization and individual learning differences.

The Improbable Form of Master Sturm (IDEA, 14 Min., Color) Deals with the nongraded school and concern for individual differences in students. The school shown has practiced nongradedness for ten years.

Non-Graded Education for the Modern Elementary School—A Series (Eye Gate House, Records) Introduces and explores concepts inherent in nongraded education. Discusses objectives, groupings, and orientation. Samples are: *Effecting the Change to a Non-Graded Program* (43 fr.) *Non-Graded Education—An Overview* (111 fr.) *Question of Grouping for a Non-Graded Education Within the Non-Graded School* (43 fr.)

Team Teaching on the Elementary Level (Bailey Films, 13 Min., Color). Discusses the purposes and methods of team teaching. The method in use on an elementary level in an experimental project.

High School Team Teaching: The Ferris Story (Bailey Films, 26 Min., Color) A springboard for further investigation and study by groups interested in team teaching and flexible scheduling.

Characteristics of a Core Program (Columbia University Teachers College, 20 Min.) Describes the characteristics of the core program at the junior and senior high school levels.

Critical Moments in Teaching: Walls (Holt, Rinehart and Winston, 11 Min., Color) A young high school teacher has tried to expose his high school class to independent study. All have failed to do assignments on their own. How can he make them respond?

Individualizing in Duluth (Audio Productions Education Service, 12 Min., Color) Shows how a Duluth, Minnesota, school teacher leads his class into individualized study of a subject.

Resource Center (Stanford University, 28 Min., Color) Dwight Allen presents the functions and uses of resource centers for students in various academic areas, and discusses the staffing and administration of such centers.

Differentiated Teaching Staff (Stanford University, 28 Min. color) Dwight Allen discusses an approach to teaching which emphasizes a range of teacher competencies in a variety of staff positions.

PART FOUR

THE NEW TEACHER

NINETEEN

WHAT DOES THE NEW TEACHER WORRY ABOUT?

A teacher, like every other human being, is bound to have understandable and natural insecurities, especially when he is just beginning to test his ideas about teaching. He must learn to relate positively and effectively to a variety of individual personalities who are new to him: the children or youth who are assigned to his care, their parents or guardians, and his professional associates who may have a profound influence on his career.

Even if one is a successful teacher with many years of experience, he can never rest secure in predictable patterns of behavior; the good teacher is forever searching for better ways of planning and organizing his work and of developing relationships with others. So most worries of the new teacher are not unique to him (though he may feel that they are); they emerge whenever and wherever human beings come together in purposeful groups.[1] They usually have to do with identifying, clarifying, and achieving group goals, and with maintaining a psychological climate of warmth and mutual respect that encourages participation and responsible behavior by group members.

High on the list of a new teacher's concerns are worries about discipline; students with problems; how to provide a variety of methods and materials so that individual differences can be met; confrontations of all kinds. We will attempt in this chapter to deal with these particular worries which grow from his relationships with children and youth, whether the school is public or nonpublic; elementary, secondary, or college; urban or rural; set in a wealthy suburb, a middle-class neighborhood, or an impoverished slum.

---

[1]Findings from inquiry into group processes and group dynamics, a relatively young twentieth century field, are of considerable value to educators. See:
  Dorwin Cartwright and Alvin Zander (eds.) *Group Dynamics* (New York: Harper, 1960).
  Herbert A. Thelen, *Classroom Grouping for Teachability* (New York: Wiley, 1967).

DISCIPLINE

Clearly, discipline is one of the major worries of the new teacher. And little wonder. On the success of his efforts to build relationships of warmth, respect and trust will depend the quality of his control, the excellence of his teaching, and the opportunity for students to grow.

Too often the new teacher sees discipline and control as processes separate from teaching; instead they are at its very heart. Control is the by-product of the teacher's relations with each student as an individual and with the group as a whole. The new teacher often asks himself whether his relations with students should be permissive or authoritarian. Neither a laissez-faire nor an authoritarian approach to classroom control can create the climate that is necessary for the development of the kind of human relationships necessary for growth. As early as 1939 Kurt Lewin, Ronald Lippitt and Ralph White conducted an experiment on the reaction of a boys' club to different kinds of leadership: laissez-faire (permissive), authoritarian and democratic. The results are impressively in favor of the democratic, which is characterized by respect for individuals, careful explanation of goals and methods and cooperative planning for work.[2]

PERSONALITY PATTERNS AND DISCIPLINE

The personality of the teacher will have much to do with the kind of relationships he develops with students and the nature of his control. A new teacher may well ask himself whether his special life style will permit him to develop an effective classroom control. Can the new teacher be himself? Or must he basically change his life style and play an unfamiliar role while teaching?

Some educators counsel the new teacher to be completely himself and to follow the style with which he is most comfortable, whether it is open or restrictive, relaxed or taut, permissive or authoritarian. Others counsel the new teacher to begin with tight patterns of control, then gradually loosen certain ones, a practice satirically described as "never smile until Thanksgiving." But there is a middle way in which a new teacher may maintain his basic life style and be himself, yet watch with a critical eye to see the consequences of his behavior and change his ways of working with others when those ways are ineffective.

For example, though he may be inclined to be open, permissive, and informal, the new teacher might well consider whether to allow students to call him by his first name in classroom situations. He might ask himself whether any gains from first-naming are negated by losses such as overly casual student attitudes

---

[2] See R. Lippitt and R. White, "The Social Climate of Children's Groups," pp. 485–506 in Barker, Kounin, and Wright (eds.), *Child Behavior and Development* (New York: McGraw-Hill, 1943). The study has since been rewritten and published as *Autocracy and Democracy* by the original authors (New York: Harper and Bros., 1960).

Teacher and class enjoy a good laugh together. Courtesy of DeWys.

toward him as a teacher and resentment or amusement among the young that an older person should consider himself a peer. Similarly, however closed, restricted, and formal his life style may be, the new teacher must consider the saving contribution which humor makes to a classroom situation. He might ask himself whether some light-hearted words might result in occasional avoidance of trouble.

No one except possibly a gifted actor can successfully maintain a role that is not his, save at the price of great strain; a danger always exists that he will drop the role under tension and revert to his own way. So as to discipline, the best bet is to be oneself, rather than attempt to be an actor, yet modify one's ways of relating to students through self-criticism and recognition of effective approaches to control. The result should be greater respect for the new teacher as an individual. Young people and children value honesty and sincerity and willingness to be realistic; they readily detect phoniness.

There is no single teaching pattern which guarantees success with all students. Some students particularly appreciate and respect the teacher who closely identifies with the problems and concerns of class members. Others appreciate and respect the teacher who is apparently more interested in the content he is teaching than in the individual personalities in the class. And some students equally respect both types.

However, followers of the perceptual school of psychology fostered by Carl Rogers, Earl Kelley, Abraham Maslow, and Arthur Combs, believe that some

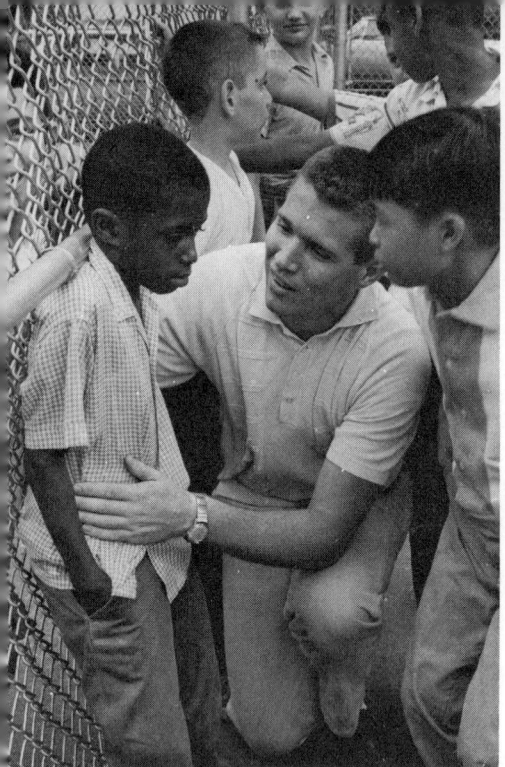 

Discipline can be maintained with compassion and care. Left: Courtesy of Lisl Steiner from Teacher Corps. Right: Courtesy of VISTA.

personality patterns are preferable to others. They call for fully functioning and self-actualizing persons. By way of definition, they say that the fully functioning, self-actualizing personality thinks well of himself and of others, and therefore sees his stake in others. He sees himself as part of a world in movement—in process of becoming. Seeing the importance of people, he develops and holds human values. He knows no other way to live except in keeping with his values.[3]

Carl Rogers sees the fully functioning person as a human being in flow, in process, rather than as having achieved some state. To him such a person is sensitively open to all of his experience. He experiences in the present, with immediacy. He permits his total organism to function freely in all its complexity in selecting from many possibilities the behavior which will be most genuinely and generally satisfying.[4]

Arthur Combs says that the truly adequate self-actualizing person is one who has "a positive view of self, identification with others, openness to experience and acceptance, and a rich and available perceptual field."[5] Elaborating upon these characteristics Combs says:

1. Extremely adequate, self-actualizing perons seem to be characterized by

---

[3] Earl C. Kelley, "The Fully Functioning Self," pp. 18–20 in *Perceiving, Behaving, Becoming* (Washington, D.C.: Association for Supervision and Curriculum Development, 1962).
[4] Carl Rogers, "Toward Becoming a Fully Functioning Person," pp. 31–32 in *Perceiving, Behaving, Becoming* (Washington, D.C.: ASCD, 1962).
[5] Arthur W. Combs, "A Perceptual View of the Adequate Personality," p. 51 in *Perceiving, Behaving, Becoming* (Washington, D.C.: ASCD, 1962).

The teacher adapts the form of discipline to the particular child and circumstances. Courtesy of Jules Zapon from DPI.

an essentially positive view of self. They see themselves as persons who are liked, wanted, acceptable, able; as persons of dignity and integrity, of worth and importance. This is not to suggest that adequate people never have negative ways of regarding themselves. They very well may. The total economy of such persons, however, is fundamentally positive. They see themselves as adequate to deal with life.[6]

2. The feeling of oneness with one's fellows produces in the truly adequate person a high degree of responsible, trustworthy behavior. There is reason for this response. When identification is strong, one cannot behave in ways likely to be harmful or injurious to others, for to do that would be to injure one's self. As a consequence, adequate persons are likely to manifest a deep respect for the dignity and integrity of other people and a strong sense of justice and moral probity.[7]

3. Truly adequate persons possess perceptual fields maximally open to experience. That is to say, their perceptual fields are capable of change and adjustment in such fashion as to make fullest use of their experience. Truly healthy persons seem capable of accepting into awareness any and all aspects of reality. They do not find it necessary to defend themselves against events or to distort their perceptions to fit existing patterns. Their perceptual fields are maximally open and receptive to their experiences.[8]

4. The truly adequate person must also be well informed. . . . One need not

---

[6] *Ibid.*, p. 51.   [7] *Ibid.*, pp. 54–55.   [8] *Ibid.*, p. 56.

know everything to be adequate, but one must certainly have a field of perceptions, rich and extensive enough to provide understanding of the events in which he is enmeshed and available when he needs them. Adequate people have such perceptual fields. This does not mean that their perceptions are necessarily of an abstract, intellectual character or gained solely from formal schooling. Rich perceptual fields may be derived from quite informal sources through firsthand involvement in human relations in business, in recreation, or in performing a trade or occupation.[9]

What are the implications of the self-actualizing personality for the problem of discipline? The self-actualizing teacher encourages good discipline by showing that he is interested in the individual young person and his welfare. Such a teacher is willing to listen to a young person while reserving or at least not indicating judgment. Such a teacher gives the young person direct evidence that he is liked. He builds mutual trust; he looks hard for ways in which a young person can succeed. He behaves in ways which young people regard as fair. When he makes a mistake, he does not hesitate to say, "I made a mistake; I'm sorry." He has inner security and does not constantly feel personally threatened by misbehavior. He is often able to rally leaders to his side in emergency situations and to avail himself of the group pressure which students themselves can bring to bear. Yet, he does not allow group pressure to get out of hand and become punitive. Because of feeling secure, he can maintain a sense of humor. In time, such a teacher may master the delicate combination of being objective enough to look clinically at a class and its members and at the same time maintain humane concern for and involvement in the welfare of both individuals and the total class.

The self-actualizing teacher will avoid temptations to maintain discipline through techniques which in actuality often lead to open resentment and rebellion. A self-actualizing teacher will not ridicule either the individual or his family. He will avoid sarcasm. He will not try to command the situation through hollering; he won't filibuster through talking incessantly. Such a teacher will not depend upon idle threats or inflict degrading punishments, nor will hold grudges or bar students from making fresh starts with a new day or new term. The sensible teacher will avoid punishing indiscriminately a whole class through, for example, keeping everyone after school. He will avoid talking down to the pupils just as he will try to avoid talking over their heads. He will avoid "taking everything personally," that is, seeing all misbehavior as a personal affront to him and his dignity.

Perceptual psychologists believe that a positive attitude toward oneself and toward others does help with respect to discipline. For self-acceptance is a prerequisite to accepting others. Self-understanding is a prerequisite to understanding others. As Rolf Muuss has pointed out, " 'Thou shalt love thy neighbor as thyself' seems to contain a deep psychological insight in this respect . . ."[10]

---

[9] *Ibid.*, pp. 59–60.
[10] Rolf E. Muuss, "First-Aid for Discipline Problems," *Discipline in the Classroom* (Washington, D.C.: National Education Association, 1969), p. 16.

Whether good relationships and desirable conditions for learning are achieved depends largely on the teacher's faith in himself, the richness of his feeling life, his intellectual power, his fairness and honesty, his awareness of what is happening in the class (a new teacher is often so concentrating on himself that he can't see the class or the individuals in it), his refusal to vent any frustration by cutting and sarcastic language, his refusal to gain personal satisfaction in exercising power over others, and his willingness to alter his carefully prepared plans in the light of new and pressing needs for change. If this seems a high order, it is! Teaching is a field that tests your capacities as a human being.

THE CURRICULUM AND DISCIPLINE

Behavior problems that challenge the relationships between teacher and child often grow out of a curriculum which does not make sense to the learner. When the academic content bears no relationship to the needs or the experience or the world of the learner, the classroom can become a breeding place for rebellion. It is not simply that the content is too hard or too easy, though this may sometimes be the case. The problem is often that the curriculum experiences are trivial and academic. They are unrelated to the learner's needs, irrelevant to the social realities which surround the learner, lacking in relationship to values, and inadequate in developing concepts and stimulating inquiry. In other words, sometimes the real villain with respect to discipline is a curriculum which does not take into account the background of the learner nor provide a wide variety of activities in which each child may satisfy his special need or interest.

If young people are deeply absorbed in their work and enjoying the activities which the school provides, they are less likely to create discipline problems. To achieve high absorption, careful and systematic planning of classroom experience is necessary. Such planning can only be successful if the teacher knows the general background and experiences of the young people who make up the class and if he comes to know the backgrounds and experiences of as many individuals as he possibly can. Useful experiences for a college-oriented and sometimes intellectually self-motivated group of upper-middle-class students, may not be helpful when they are provided for an occupation-oriented and sometimes intellectually less motivated group of the upper-lower-class young. So-called "bad" language, including profane or obscene four-letter words, may represent genuine defiance in an upper-middle-class suburb but may represent the only known way of expressing a particular idea in a lower-class area.

The ingenious teacher finds ways of relating content to the needs and interests of young people. Sustained classroom activities may work with some individuals whereas varied activities and methods may be better for pupils who have a short attention span, difficulty in learning through symbols, and who need stimulation through experiences enriched by seeing, hearing, and touching. The teacher keeps an eye on the level of communication and tries to combine adequate understanding with sufficient challenges; he uses a variety of methods and materials.

The successful teacher also arranges the immediate setting to get the best

"Better discipline will prevail when learning experiences relate closely to the present interests and needs of children . . ." Courtesy of Paul Conklin.

results. He checks the classroom environment for temperature, ventilation, and light; he tries to create a surrounding environment appropriate to his particular subject or grade level. He may have materials about the room such as an aquarium, separate corners for science, art, or reading, books on hobbies, charts, and bright posters to tempt children to explore and think. The teacher may strategically space work centers throughout the classroom to make the room a workroom and to prevent children from clustering in overly large groups and to reduce the time that the teacher stands in front of the room. Time is provided for getting out materials and restoring them. A room left in a disorderly state is an invitation for the new occupants to engage in disorderly behavior.

Some teachers hesitate to plan with students because of fear of disorderly behavior. Actually, the reverse is more frequently the case—undesirable behavior often grows out of lack of sharing in planning with the result that the student sometimes does not understand the work that is going on and cannot find his place in the process. In today's schools, there is less likelihood of the emergence of discipline problems if students have a say in the development of ground rules. There is less chance of disorderly conduct if the content itself is developed cooperatively with young people through the process of teacher-pupil planning. Today's young people often rebel against rules which they have not been allowed to participate in developing.

There is reluctance among even experienced teachers to plan cooperatively with students. Some of this comes from a misunderstanding of the kind of opportunities which the curriculum presents for choices. There are many, many situations in which students at any age can be involved in making decisions which affect them. Students can plan together for the details of a field trip including deciding on the standards of conduct that are to be observed; identifying the purposes of the excursion; suggesting what to see, hear, or do; building the criteria for judging the effectiveness of their experience; and evaluating the trip. In preparing to hear a speaker, watch a film or filmstrip or hear a recording, the class may list and present the questions to be asked and judge how adequately they were answered. Students can set up standards for classroom behavior and check from time to time to see whether they are still effective guides to conduct. Students may compose a list of activities which may be pursued when required work is finished and be responsible for carrying through such activities. Such participation is essential for learning. In *The Authentic Teacher* Moustakas points out three conditions for growth in the individual: freedom to be, choice and the capacity to choose, and responsibility and self-confirmation.[11]

The introductory article of a pamphlet published by the National Education Association notes the close relationship between student behavior and significant learning experiences,

Better discipline will prevail when learning experiences relate closely to the present interests and needs of children who see the use of what they are learning. Better discipline will prevail when learning is related to the social realities which surround the child. Better discipline will prevail when we practice what we preach as to respect of personality. Better discipline will prevail as we develop active student participation, creative contributions, social travel, and all else that fosters significant experience. Better discipline will grow out of a better curriculum in a better setting.

You may know a little Jimmy who is a discipline problem despite an apparently meaningful curriculum. So do I. But in our concern for nonconforming little Jimmy, let us not neglect improving the environment of millions of Jimmys through gearing our curriculum to the lives of the young and avoiding needless disciplinary struggles.[12]

---

[11] Clark Moustakas, *The Authentic Teacher* (Cambridge, Mass.: Howard A. Doyle, 1966), pp. 9–12.
[12] William Van Til, "Better Curriculum—Better Discipline," p. 1–2 in *Discipline in the Classroom* (Washington, D.C.: National Education Association, 1969).

STUDENTS WITH PROBLEMS

Let us now look more closely at ways of dealing with nonconforming Jimmy, the individual "problem" student. As the poet Robert Burns has pointed out, "The best laid plans o'mice and men gang aft a-gley." Even the best of teachers encounter discipline problems with particular individuals, however self-actualizing the teacher's personality may be or however relevant the curriculum to the learners' life experiences.

How should a teacher work with a troublemaker who is acting alone or in concert with fellow troublemakers? The first necessity is to deal with the immediate problem so that the class may continue its work and not disintegrate into disorder. Only rules of thumb can be used here; sometimes the best approach is to ignore the problem for the moment, sometimes it may be necessary to check it then and there, or even to remove the disturber from the classroom situation, though this often proves to be a defeating experience.[13]

But as soon as possible, any action should be followed by a talk with the individual and a realistic analysis of the problem confronting the new teacher. The immediate incident may be the focus. However, the perceptive teacher soon tries to determine causation and patterns. To learn still more about the individual student, the teacher may turn to cumulative records or the experiences of other teachers with the individual. Some authorities recommend going to such sources prior to disturbances in order to spot potential troublemakers in advance. But there is a danger that such a procedure may result in a judgment of guilty prior to any offense being committed. One needs also to be sure that he responds only to those recorded comments that are objective descriptions of behavior.

A combination of discussing the situation with the student and reviewing the student's past history through reading records and consulting former teachers should help the new teacher to diagnose what is basically wrong. In some situations a few words may be all that is needed to result in renewed efforts to build trust and respect on the part of both teacher and student. In other situations, the problem may be much more complicated. Sometimes it is a reflection of accepted social class patterns, such as foul language or toughness on the part of a youth influenced by lower-lower-class life patterns. Sometimes the behavior incident grows out of deep unmet personality needs of the student; for example, hunger for group attention or for approval. Sometimes the negative classroom behavior has to do with racial antagonism. Sometimes the disturbance may grow out of economic factors, such as lack of money to join the group at the drugstore after school or envy of someone's new clothes. Sex differences in negative behavior may be found; in general, girls tend to be more fearful and suspicious and more inclined to tears, while boys tend to be more overtly hostile and destructive.

No single prescription can apply to all cases. In each situation, the teacher must use his own judgment and, always conscious that troublesome pupils are

---

[13] Katherine La Mancusa, "Now Enter Billy Bully," *We Do Not Throw Rocks at the Teacher* (Scranton, Pa.: International Textbook, 1966), pp. 51–57.

really troubled pupils, attempt to do whatever good sense would suggest in the particular setting. Nor is the teacher completely alone in meeting such situations. Principals are sensitive to behavior problems in classrooms and can often aid the new teacher. A good supporting staff can be helpful. The number of guidance counselors in schools is growing. Increasingly schools have relationships with outside agencies, such as mental health centers and guidance clinics. The perceptive new teacher will take advantage of such facilities when they exist. Professional therapy is not the province of the teacher, but in most cases teachers can provide an environment which is non-threatening and to which insecure or lost individuals may respond.

In schools in which mutual trust among faculty members is characteristic, conferences with other teachers should help. Staff discussion meetings may deal with individual students who baffle their teachers. In most situations, teachers, nurses, administrators, and counselors are essentially on the side of new teachers and willing to try to help. Nor should conference with parents be minimized as one technique in working out solutions to behavior problems. For every parent who proves impossible (as perceived by the teacher) in a conference, there are many others who, greeted with tact and without a patronizing attitude, will be enormously helpful to the teacher.

INDIVIDUAL DIFFERENCES AND VARIED METHODOLOGIES

Another worry of the new teacher is how to deal with individual differences, which, as we know from an earlier chapter, are inevitable among human beings —differences in intellectual abilities, capacities for creativity, handicaps, and social attitudes.

Perhaps the best advice for the new teacher is that he continue to learn about individual differences among human beings and to explore various methods which he can use in his particular subject field or at the particular level—elementary, secondary, or college—at which he has chosen to work. Obviously the new teacher cannot provide for individual differences if his sole techniques are those he has too frequently been exposed to in his own learning experiences—lectures or question-and-answer recitations. The lecture is, by definition, aimed at the class group as a whole and usually is directed to the average student. Question-and-answer recitations provide for little more variation. Though a harder question may be asked of the more intellectually able student and an easier question may be asked of the less intellectually able, the teacher is aware that others are listening to the responses and that the recitation must be geared to the average or middle group. So if the teacher confines himself simply to such mass-education approaches as the lecture and the recitation, he will be unsuccessful in adapting his instruction to individual differences.

The new teacher might well focus on methods which have promise for differentiation. For instance, he might work with small groups within a class. In good modern schools, committees of students often carry on studies which illuminate problems or topics that are the concern of the whole class. In this case committees report to the group as a whole, working out a wide variety of presentations: a panel, a dramatic skit, a radio program, an interview, a mural, a chart, a map, or even a dance. Within such committees some students make a more significant contribution than others. Members are encouraged to go as far as they can and to contribute at the highest level they can reach.

Another teaching technique is the use of extensive individualization. Children and young people can be encouraged to work independently on their own, on topics or problems of greatest interest, geared to individual ability. Individual reports may be made to the class as a whole; more than likely the teacher may simply help the individual find materials and consult with him on his progress. Independent work can flourish in schools organized to provide both teachers and students with time for such activity. Schedules which provide for individual work in laboratories, art rooms, libraries and for face-to-face conferences with teachers are more challenging than the old classroom organization of set periods and inflexible scheduling.

Meeting individual differences may often be achieved through using media to which individuals particularly respond. Some learn a good deal from resources with visual and auditory appeal—films, television broadcasts, radio programs, recordings, and filmstrips. Some gain particularly from panels, symposiums, and debates; others learn better through field trips, social travel, and community participation.

Educational technology is also in the process of providing aids to individualization. Programmed instruction is geared to the individual learner who works at his own program and proceeds at his own pace. Computer-aided instruction, currently in its infancy, provides an even more sophisticated approach to individualized learning.[14]

Obviously such brief mention of possible techniques cannot substitute for the information on methods and materials which can be acquired in courses in general methods and courses in special methods of teaching. If the prospective teacher takes advantage of the opportunities which his future courses should provide him, he will learn the materials and methodologies that will markedly reduce his insecurity concerning ways of providing for individual differences.

Skill in using varied methods and materials should be accompanied by deep concern for motivating students. The new teacher must constantly provide stimulating experiences in which subject matter becomes a resource for new insights into human behavior, new pleasures in living, and a means of developing new skills, whether intellectual, social or manipulative. When he finds students who do not respond to the curriculum, his responsibility is to attempt to find out why. Is the problem a matter of reading skill? Are physical factors, such as

---

[14] Don D. Bushnell and Dwight W. Allen (eds.), *The Computer in American Education* (New York: John Wiley and Sons, 1967).

John I. Goodlad, John F. O'Toole, Jr. and Louise L. Tyler, *Computers and Information Systems in Education* (New York: Harcourt, Brace & World, 1966).

Paul I. Jacobs, Milton H. Maier, and Lawrence M. Stolurow, *A Guide to Evaluating Self-Instructional Programs* (New York: Holt, Rinehart and Winston, 1966).

eyesight, involved? Is the student exhausted because of some environmental circumstance? Does the classwork seem irrelevant to the student?

Different responses are called for by different situations. If the problem is reading, then remedial reading is called for. If the problem is physical—such as eyesight—the cooperation of the nurse and the family is needed. If the problem is exhaustion, investigation of the family situation and cooperation with school or community social work agencies are required.

If the problem is curriculum relevance, close examination of one's own approaches as a teacher is called for. Is subject matter becoming an end in itself, with the growth of children and youth secondary? Can the content be adapted so as to contribute to the lives of students? Can more concrete illustrations be used? Can applications be stressed? Can a conception of possible future uses be built, especially uses for living a better life? Can more able students help others perceive greater relevance? Has the new teacher begun where the learners are? After all, there is nothing more useless to a student than an answer for which he doesn't have a question! Of what use is a solution for which a student does not have a problem?

General psychology and psychology of education courses for teachers in training can be particularly useful in helping the new teacher to become more competent in motivating students. The beginning of wisdom on motivation is to motivate oneself to learn more about motivation!

CONFRONTATION

Until recently the worries identified so far would have constituted the major problems arising in the context of teacher-student relations. But in the 1970s, a technique of social action borrowed from college campus dissent and from black protest has appeared in American high schools, junior high schools, and even a few elementary schools—the technique of confrontation. Confrontation can be variously defined. For our purposes, it means confronting authorities with demands for changes accompanied by explicit or implicit threats of disruption if the demands are not met, usually within a specified time. Confrontation does not proceed through the normal processes of communication or the usual channels of action (or perhaps inaction); the usual processes may have been tried and found wanting or simply bypassed. Confrontation may or may not take the form of violence.

Protest is a wider term than confrontation. Protest may take place through the normal processes of communication and customary channels of action in a school. It may also take the form of confrontation. Before condemning all student protest and confrontation, one should take into account that the United States was established through a protest which eventually took the form of a confrontation—the American Revolution. Such rights as freedom of speech, freedom of the press, and the right of the people peaceably to petition their government are built into the Bill of Rights as legal channels for protest.

The days of dictating policy to students seem to have passed. Courtesy of Howard Petrick from Nancy Palmer.

According to a survey of more than 1,000 public and private schools reported by the National Association of Secondary School Principals in 1969, the majority of secondary schools were then experiencing protest activities of some sort. Nor was protest confined to the senior high school. Fifty-nine percent of the senior high school principals reported protest activities and, contrary to expectations, almost as many junior high school principals (56 percent) reported protest activities. City schools and suburban schools were the major focus of protest with a rate of 67 percent. In rural areas, the rate dropped to 53 percent, yet even in rural America the majority of secondary schools were experiencing protests.

What were the students unhappy about? At the head of the list were dress and hair regulations. One-third of the principals reported objections to the dress code. One-quarter of the principals reported conflicts over hair lengths and styles. Other matters drawing protest included smoking rules, the conduct of the cafeteria, assembly programs, choices of speakers, censorship and regulation of school papers, the matter of underground papers or pamphlets, and scheduling of such events as sports and social occasions. Problems in the area of race relations were reported by only ten percent of principals. But when racial problems occurred they tended to be characterized by substantial anger, hostility, and sometimes violence. A major object of sharp dissatisfaction was the school program itself. Forty-five percent of the principals cited student protests related to teachers—quality of teaching, assignment of teachers, lack of freedom to choose teachers; to the content of the curriculum; to groupings in classrooms; and to schedules, homework, grades, and examinations.[15]

Who are the leaders of white and black student activism? In *Protest in Black and White*, David A. Kukla sums up some insights from recent research. He says:

... the young white rebels come from "the best" families. They digested the fundamental values of such a home: emphasis on human relationships, honesty, and concern for the rights of others. Thinking of themselves as unique, they became involved with the established patterns for success, but eventually were disillusioned. Perhaps the key to understanding the motivation of these students is that they feel personally responsible for the evils in society. And their goal is to use any means to correct those evils ...

A substantial number of black student leaders cannot be considered deprived. They are sons and daughters of middle-class and even affluent parents. They are also bright and aggressive, sometimes being pushed to make demands by their black "brothers and sisters" outside the schools.

Kenneth Keniston has pointed out that the black student revolt "involves the extension to more and more people of economic, political and social rights, privileges and opportunities originally available only to the aristocracy, then to the middle class and now to the white American worker." As affluence spreads in the United States, it is becoming more and more outrageous that poverty still exists here. Thus, the black students are less willing to compromise with the white establishment. Our process of change is too cumbersome for them; and they feel that "moderate reforms" are merely stall tactics catering to prejudice or, at best, to indifference. ...

The same characteristics of college student radicals are manifest in the demands of high school students across the country. The stress on self-identity, the rights of minorities, and distrust of centralized authority are the pivotal cause of the revolution in these schools.[16]

In a four-month period from November 1968 through February 1969, Alan F. Westin reported 361 disruptive cases in junior and senior high schools which he classified as follows: racial 132; political, including Vietnam, 81; against dress regulations, 71; against discipline, 60; for education reform, 17.[17] Newsweek says of 1969, "Last year some 6,000 'incidents,' ranging from racial strife through political protest to arson attempts, were registered in the nation's public high

---

[15] "Survey Finds Dissent Moving Into Lower Grades," *Education USA* (Washington, D.C., National Schools Public Relations Association, March 10, 1969), p. 151.
[16] David A. Kukla, "Protest in Black and White," *The Bulletin of the National Association of Secondary School Principals* (January 1970), pp. 75, 76, 79.
[17] "High Scool Unrest Rises, Alarming U.S. Educators," *New York Times* (May 8, 1969), pp. 1, 30.

schools."[18] A sampling of headlines from the *New York Times* for the year 1969 and limited to the metropolitan New York area alone includes; "Guards Assigned to Erasmus High: Move Follows Tying Up of Teachers by Radical Gang"; "Newark Schools Get Guard Corps"; "Students Battle in Jersey School"; "Forty Policemen Guarding Jackson High"; "100 Black Pupils Rampage in New Brunswick School"; "Great Neck High Has a Competitor: A Student-Run 'Free School' Reflects Unrest in Suburb"; "50 Patterson Students Arrested"; "Fires Set at Williamsburg School in New Disorders"; "City High Schools Ordered to Name Security Officer"; "Right of Peaceful Student Dissent Is Affirmed by City School Board."

All teachers have the potential to reduce or eliminate the causes of student dissent, through involving students in a genuinely democratic process, characterized by respect for each individual whether teacher or student; by more teacher-pupil planning in classes; more relevant curriculum; more emphasis upon varied ethnic studies in the curriculum; and more opportunities for students to express themselves.

The new teacher may be able to make a special contribution since he is usually closer in age to the junior and senior high school student than is the typical teacher. He has a strategic opportunity to serve as a middleman or moderator or advisor in student dissent. For example, he is often acutely aware of problems arising from dress codes; he himself may have experienced the impact of such restrictions in schools or colleges he has attended. Thus he might be particularly helpful on a committee on dress codes. James E. Allen, Jr., former United States Commissioner of Education, in a letter to all school superintendents on September 9, 1969, wrote, "If dress codes are believed necessary, they should be established with student and parent participation and should respect a student's self image, allow for differences and promote intergroup respect rather than conformity to a single value system with its implied superiority."[19]

The new teacher might be a helpful participant in committees with student membership which have responsibility for drafting improved disciplinary regulations. He might be helpful in removing grievances, such as discrimination in selecting students for recognition in student government, in athletics and honor societies, and in determining membership in clubs organized to serve special needs. He might even become an unofficial ombudsman or liaison person between students and staff, though these are difficult and demanding roles.

As he works with students who are reaching out for greater involvement in the world of school and community life, the new teacher must be always aware of the changes that are necessary if institutions that deal with human values and human needs are to be remade and revitalized. In her contribution to *Student Unrest: Threat or Promise*, Maxine Greene counsels those who teach:

It is not really hard to understand the disenchantment of our students. It is not even hard to understand their objections to the traditional teacher-student arrangements, their resentment of the authority which seems to inhere in the

---

[18] "What's Wrong with the High Schools?" *Newsweek* (February 16, 1970), p. 65.
[19] "Student Role Urged to Avert Disruption," *New York Times* (September 10, 1969), p. 17.

very presence of a person standing in front of a classroom and addressing people who, in their very willingness to sit and listen, are accepting inferior roles. We need to be as imaginative as we can about the protest, as empathetic as we can. And we need continually to concern ourselves with creating the kinds of conditions and learning situations in which students feel that we welcome choosing and involvement and making sense in an open world. To do this, we have to think about restoring to the young a sense of potency even as we try to communicate the values of competence, the excitement of patterning, of mindfulness.[20]

DIMINISHING YOUR WORRIES

These then are some of the things which the new teacher worries about—maintaining discipline, helping individual students who have problems that disturb the class and/or prevent them from learning, providing for individual differences through a wide range of resources and methods, and dealing with confrontation. There are no easy answers which will completely eliminate such worries. There are no panaceas that supply infallible prescriptions to solve such problems.

The new teacher must explore for answers, whether independently, through organized courses, or in interaction with experienced teachers and administrators. Fortunately, the more the new teacher learns and the more his abilities grow in coping with any one of his worries, the more his other worries should diminish. For instance, the more the new teacher can skillfully deal with individual differences, the more likely he is to have rapport with students and the less likely he is to have discipline problems. The problems considered in this chapter are interrelated, and the overcoming of one helps in the conquest of the others.

DISCUSSION
1. What is your opinion of the major worries of individuals planning to enter teaching? What are some of your own major worries in this connection?
2. What is the meaning of discipline? Does it differ from "control"?
3. What is the case for "being one's self" in matters of discipline? What are the cases for the alternatives?
4. What are some of your personal experiences with school discipline? Interpret these experiences in light of what you now understand about teachers and teaching.

[20] Maxine Greene, "The Spectrum of Disenchantment," *Student Unrest: Threat or Promise* (Washington, D.C.: Association for Supervision and Curriculum Development, NEA, 1970), pp. 32–33.

5. In what specific ways have teachers you have respected dealt with discipline problems in their classrooms?
6. What is the essence of the fully functioning self-actualizing personality?
7. What are the implications of the self-actualizing personality theory for the problem of discipline?
8. Is it ever legitimate in the classroom for teachers to be angry, irritated, or hostile? If so, why? If so, when?
9. How would you describe your philosophy of discipline to a group of parents whose children were in your classroom?
10. Whom do you remember as being a particular problem to one of your teachers? What insights do you now have into what caused him to become a problem and into the teacher's method of handling the problem?
11. What are some possible approaches in dealing with the individual problem student? What resources does the teacher have to call upon?
12. What do you see as the role of a classroom teacher in dealing with an emotionally disturbed child?
13. What is the relationship between curriculum content and instructional methodology and the problem of discipline? Is it likely that planning with students will lead to better or poorer discipline?
14. What are some characteristics of methodologies which provide for individual differences? What techniques seem to you most promising?
15. What are some key factors in motivating students?
16. Why is readiness on the part of the pupil so significant for learning?
17. What is the meaning of confrontation? How does it differ from protest? How widespread is contemporary student protest and confrontation? What do you think are the implications of protest and confrontation?
18. What are the major grievances of dissenting students? From your experience, are some of these grievances valid? Can you visualize any contributions which you can make to dealing constructively with protest and confrontation as a new teacher?
19. How are the worries of teachers interrelated? In what ways does dealing with one problem aid the teacher in dealing with an allied problem?

INVOLVEMENT
1. Conduct a survey among class members about their worries as they contemplate becoming a teacher. What proves to be the most usual worry?
2. Try role playing in a series of discipline situations. (One student plays the role of a teacher, another the principal, another a parent, another an administrator, etc. A discipline situation is described in general and the actors improvise their lines and response).
3. Visit a school and observe the interaction in a class. What ways does the teacher use to exercise control? Are they verbal or nonverbal? Are they threatening, punishing, praising? What appears to be the climate of the classroom—laissez-faire, dictatorial, or democratic? Why?

4. Try the role of a fully functioning self-actualizing person by earnestly and consciously attempting to follow this pattern for a period of time. Note whether you encounter any unusual responses from people who are not aware of the nature of your attempt.
5. Try various possible approaches to discipline with young people with whom you have some relationship through family, organizations, etc. Note what seems to succeed with them and speculate on why.
6. Attempt to develop a characteristic curricular experience in your field of specialization. Speculate on whether or not certain discipline problems might or might not occur under these circumstances.
7. Relate these concepts to discipline:
    security   recognition
    responsibility   belonging
8. Present a case study of a problem student observed by you in schools. Discuss possible approaches to such an individual.
9. Visit a classroom. Keep a time diary to determine the percentage of time you observe the teacher doing the talking. How much time is given to students' talking? To quiet study?
10. List some of the possible methodologies to provide for individual differences which you could use in a class you might teach. Share these with other students. Which techniques seem best? At which level or in which subject fields? Are there common denominators?
11. Practice making anecdotal notations about children as you observe them at work. Share these with another student and criticize one another's work.
12. Prepare a personal file of sources for instructional materials. (See audio-visual suggestions in this book.)
13. Visit a school and observe a class for an hour. What teaching methods are used? How much time is taken by each method? What materials are used? How are they used?
14. Observe situations in which educational technology is used to see whether individual differences are truly provided for and to assess the general atmosphere surrounding the work of students.
15. In your estimation, how will the use of instructional devices such as teaching machines and programmed books alter elementary school objectives?
16. Conduct your own study of the incidence of confrontation in schools and the apparent causes.
17. Define some of the contributions you hope to make in dealing with confrontation and protest activities in schools in which you will be teaching. Analyze your own strengths and weaknesses as a mediator.

BIBLIOGRAPHY

Bernhardt, Carl L. *Discipline and Child Guidance.* McGraw-Hill, 1964. Utilization of the accumulating knowledge of child development to formulate principles and a point of view about discipline.

Birmingham, John. *Our Time Is Now.* New York: Praeger, 1970. Students speak out on topics which concern them, such as civil rights and student rights.

Clark, Donald H. and Gerald S. Lesser. *Emotional Disturbance and School Learning: A Book of Readings.* Chicago: Science Research Associates, 1965. A sampling of the literature to help the reader in coping with emotional disturbance in relation to school learning.

Combs, Arthur W., ed. *Perceiving, Behaving, Becoming.* Washington, D.C.: Association for Supervision and Curriculum Development, National Education Association, 1962. The case for the humanistically inclined perceptual school of psychology and its applications to the development of children and youth.

Donahue, George T. and Sol Nichtern. *Teaching the Troubled Child.* New York: Free Press, 1965. Insights gained in the Elmont project concerning the education of emotionally disturbed children.

Dreikurs, Rudolf. *Psychology in the Classroom,* 2nd ed. New York: Harper and Row, 1968. A practical manual on dealing with behavior problems and learning deficiencies.

Gnagery, William J. *The Psychology of Discipline in the Classroom.* New York: Macmillan, 1968. Findings in discipline research with authentic incidents from classroom situations.

Hart, Richard L. and J. Galen Saylor, eds. *Student Unrest: Threat or Promise?* Washington, D.C.: Association for Supervision and Curriculum Development, NEA, 1970. Papers contributed by theorists and practitioners at an ASCD conference on student unrest.

Henderson, George and Robert F. Bibens. *Teachers Should Care.* New York: Harper and Row, 1970. Teaching as a process of human relationships with an emphasis upon the apprehensions that new teachers feel as they begin their work.

Hook, Sidney. *Academic Freedom and Academic Anarchy.* New York: Cowles, 1970. Extremism on university campuses. A condemnation of academic anarchy.

Hymes, James L. Jr. *Behavior and Misbehavior: A Teacher's Guide to Action.* Englewood Cliffs, N.J.: Prentice-Hall, 1955. A guide for the teachers to encourage thoughtfulness and wise action, good for children and for society.

Keene, Melvin. *Beginning Secondary School Teacher's Guide: Some Problems and Suggested Solutions.* New York: Harper and Row, 1969. A guide designed to give practical help to the college student-in-training for either junior or senior high teaching. Specific problems are identified and possible methods of dealing with these problems outlined.

Kenniston, Kenneth. *Young Radicals: Notes on Committed Youth.* New York: Harcourt, Brace and World, 1968. Observations on young radicals who are new leftists with a deep commitment to community organizing and peace work as a part of a broader objective of social change.

Klein, Alexander, ed. *Natural Enemies???* New York: J. B. Lippincott Company, 1969. A lively compendium of a very wide variety of views on the younger generation and its interrelationships with elders. Almost any conceivable view can be found in this varied compendium.

La Mancusa, Katharine C. *We Do Not Throw Rocks at the Teacher.* Scranton, Penn: International Textbook, 1966. A recent, light-hearted and delightful book devoted to the teacher goal of establishing classroom control and/or discipline.

Libarle, Marc, and Tom Seligson, eds. *The High School Revolutionaries.* New York: Random House, 1970. High school radicals speak for themselves.

Lifton, Walter M. *Working with Groups: Group Process and Individual Growth,* 2nd ed. New York: Wiley, 1966. The theory and practice of group dynamics.

Lippitt, Ronald et al. *Understanding Classroom Social Relations and Learning.* Science Research Associates, 1967. Specialists on human relations help teachers with implementation of their discoveries.

Long, Nicholas J., William C. Morse, and Ruth G. Newman, eds. *Conflict in the Classroom: The Education of Emotionally Disturbed Children.* Belmont, Calif.: Wadsworth, 1965. Topics such as the viewpoint of the emotionally disturbed child and better programs and schools for such children.

Mead, Margaret. *Culture and Commitment.* New York: Doubleday, 1970. Lectures by the distinguished anthropologist which holds that everyone born before World War II is an immigrant in time struggling against unfamiliar conditions of life in a new era and that today's young generation is akin to a first generation born into a new country. Like all of Mead's work, lively, provocative, discussion-rousing.

Moustakas, Clark. *The Authentic Teacher.* Cambridge, Mass.: Howard A. Doyle, 1966. A competent scholar of human development helps with respect to discipline, control, teacher personality, etc.

Shumsky, Abraham. *In Search of Teaching Style.* New York: Appleton-Century and Crofts, 1968. The teacher is a person threatened by changes and challenged by the need to change. A book about the teacher and his experiences as he searches to improve his teaching style.

Thomas, George and Joseph Crescimbeni. *Individualizing Instruction in the Elementary School.* New York: Random House, 1967. Elementary education with particular emphasis on the role of the individual.

Verville, Elinor. *Behavior Problems of Children.* Philadelphia: Saunders, 1967. Clinical child psychology to help the student understand behavior problems and to take part in their prevention and treatment.

Watson, Goodwin, ed. *Change in School Systems.* Washington, D.C.: National Training Laboratories, National Education Association, 1967. A human relations oriented book which stresses the contribution that group processes and group dynamics can make in the interests of educational change.

Webster, Staten W. *Discipline in the Classroom: Basic Principles and Problems.* San Francisco: Chandler Press, 1968. A frame of reference for understanding problem behavior plus case reports of student behavior problems.

AUDIO-VISUAL MATERIALS

The Idea of the City (Behavior Modification in the Classroom, University of California, Extension Media Center, 24 Min., Color) Discipline problems with students resulting from inattentiveness, distraction of class and daydreaming in the classroom are handled with a positive psychological approach. Reprimand responses to bad behavior are replaced with rewards and repeated praise for good behavior.

Motivation, a Key to Achievement (Popular Science, 40 fr., Color) Stress on the importance of motivation.

Critical Moments in Teaching—Backfire (Holt, Rinehart, and Winston, 10 Min., Color) A classroom scene in which a problem in individual student motivation develops through poor teaching techniques. Provides background for discussion of problems related to motivation and learning.

Interaction in Learning (NET, 29 Min.) Types of social interaction that arise during the school years are presented showing the importance of this type of contact to shape a more positive self-concept.

Critical Moments in Teaching: Less Far Than the Arrow (Holt, Rinehart, and Winston, Inc., 8 Min., Color) The teaching problem of motivating a class in a secondary school.

Glasser on Schools (Dave Bell Assoc., 18 Min., Color) Dr. William Glasser discusses his 'no fail' educational philosophy and the principles which he thinks should be applied to teach people how to learn rather than how to fail.

Critical Moments in Teaching: A Child Who Cheats (Holt, Rinehart and Winston, 10 Min., Color) A girl who is "average" begins to make scattered high test scores. Most of these scores are the same as those of the child who sits next to the girl. The teacher is faced with a problem of what to do about this situation.

Critical Moments in Teaching: I Walk Away in the Rain (Holt, Rinehart and Winston, 11 Min., Color) A young high school student does only what is necessary to get by, even though he is capable of doing quite well. The problem is to get this boy to work up to his potential.

Counseling Discipline Cases (Psychological Cinema Register, 20 Min.) A counselor explores reasons for school absences and works with a student who is frequently absent and has forged an excuse.

Critical Moments in Teaching: Image in a Mirror (Holt, Rinehart and Winston, 9 Min., Color) An elementary child is convinced she is going to fail. Even though she makes excellent grades she still lacks self-confidence. How may the teacher deal with this problem?

Providing for Individual Differences (Iowa State Teacher's College, 23 Min.) Illustrates ways various teachers from elementary through high school deal with differences in the way children learn.

Finding Out (BBC: Roebeck and Co., 30 Min.) Primary children are encouraged to handle objects, ask questions, and design experiments. Methods of teaching and learning in the primary school are discussed.

Looking at Teaching (Colonial Films, 73 frs., Color) Illustrates the relationship between the teacher and student, showing that the instructor must adjust to the learner's initial behavior and learning ability. Discusses the subjects of preplanning, motivation, involvement and testing as they relate to the teaching and learning process.

Learning and Teaching (Bel-Mort Films, Color) Asking Questions, 44 fr. Determining Students Grades 43 fr. Explaining 49 fr. Grouping Students for Effective Learning 44 fr. Instructional Materials 44 fr. The Logical Dimension in Teaching 49 fr. The Measurement of Learning Pt. 1—47 fr. The Measurement of Learning, Pt. 2—47 fr. The Measurement of Learning Pt. 3—45 fr. Methods of Teaching, Pt. 1—An Overview 45 fr. Methods of Teaching, Pt. 2—Teaching Types 43 fr. Methods of Teaching, Pt. 3—Selected Quotations 49 fr. Pictures and Words, Pt. 1—Pictures 49 fr. Pictures and Words, Pt. 2—Words 52 fr. Planning a Unit 44 fr. Reading a Cross Section 43 fr. Teaching Science, Photosynthesis 43 fr. Transfer of Learning 46 fr. A series of filmstrips on teaching methods and procedures.

TWENTY

WHAT IS THE WORK OF THE NEW TEACHER?

Variety, which the poet William Cowper called "the very spice of life," is characteristic of teaching and education. The two million plus American teachers are individual persons. They work on a variety of levels—preschool, nursery school, kindergarten, elementary, junior high, senior high, college, university, and adult, each with its characteristic mode of operation. There is a considerable range in their salaries and their organizations are numerous. Most teach in the public school system while some work in independent private schools or religiously sponsored schools.

Variety characterizes the learners. Students of varied classes and ethnic groups come to schools from communities which are rural, city, or suburban. Like teachers, each learner is an individual personality.

Varied social forces make their impact on education. Conceptions of the purposes of a school differ. Curriculums are derived from several sources. Various ways of organizing the curriculum are proposed and adopted.

Consequently, generalizations concerning the work of the American teacher must be made with the recognition that a wide range of differences exists which is not indicated by deceptive averages. Forewarned, let us approach our generalizations about the work of the teacher with caution. In the school in which you will teach, things may be quite different. We will begin with facts about number and size of your classes, co-curricular activities, homework, and other characteristic duties. Then we will look at your tools—textbooks, the library, audio-visual and new instructional technology resources. Then we will consider your community relations, including parent-teacher meetings, parent conferences, and community participation.

A Project Head Start preschool—group play for social development. Courtesy of Morton R. Engelberg from Head Start.

CLASSES AND RELATED RESPONSIBILITIES

NUMBER OF CLASSES

The number of classes that you might teach varies according to the level in which you teach. In general, if you are a preschool, kindergarten, or elementary school teacher, you will work with a single class. If you teach in junior or senior high school, college, or graduate school you will usually work with several classes. If you are in adult education you will sometimes teach a single class and sometimes teach several sections of the same course.

The typical preschool, kindergarten, or elementary school teacher stays with a single class from the beginning of the school day to its end. (However, a number of elementary schools use some degree of departmentalization; teachers meet several classes in their subject area daily, as is done in high school.) If you teach in a self-contained class on one of the childhood levels, you will find your free time limited. However, team teaching may include time for joint planning with other teachers and usually does allow you some flexibility in time use. Sometimes a teacher has an aide. Otherwise, as a preschool, kindergarten, and elementary school teacher, you will depend for free time largely on recesses in which one or more teachers may be in charge of a large group or on the occasional conduct of a class by a special teacher of music, physical education, or art.

If your level is junior high school you will find that the typical junior high school operates on either a six- or seven-period day. Eight out of ten junior high schools follow this pattern. A few schools have a program of fewer than six periods a day and schools with eight-period days are increasing as the curriculum of the junior high becomes crowded with more subjects.[1] In most cases a junior

[1] William Van Til, Gordon Vars, and John M. Lounsbury, *Modern Education for the Junior High School Years* (Indianapolis: Bobbs-Merrill Company, 1967), p. 63.

Audio-visual materials aid in teaching and learning. Courtesy of Fred Kaplan from Black Star.

high period averages 50 minutes, exclusive of time for passing from one class to another. So as a typical junior high school teacher you will probably teach five or six classes and have one period free. ("Free" should not be taken too literally; during a so-called free period teachers often hold conferences, mark papers, prepare for classes, fill out forms, or catch up on what is happening about the school.)

The senior high school day is also conventionally divided into equal periods. The senior high school teacher too usually has one period free. However, as computerized scheduling develops and senior high school programs increasingly are fitted to the needs of the individual student, the faculty too has a variety of teaching assignments and corresponding variety in unscheduled time.

On the college level, the American Association of University Professors, the major organization of college and university teachers, recommends a maximum undergraduate teaching load of twelve hours per week. The AAUP indicates that no more than six course preparations during the academic year should be scheduled. The AAUP suggests as a preferable undergraduate pattern a teaching responsibility of around nine hours per week and fewer course preparations. Junior or community colleges usually follow the former pattern of twelve hours a week or indeed, sometimes more, and so do many private and public four-year colleges. Staffs of the four-year colleges which are actively working toward excellence sometimes achieve the preferable pattern of nine hours of undergraduate instruction. On the graduate level, the AAUP suggests a teaching load of nine hours per week but regards six hours as preferable.[2]

The workload in higher education is often misunderstood by the public. A classic story told in academia concerns the testimony of a college president to a rural-dominated legislature. The college professor testified that in his institution the average workload for a professor was 11 hours; a rural legislator

---

[2] Statement on Faculty Workload, *AAUP Bulletin* (Spring 1970), p. 31.

The typical elementary school teacher stays with a single class for the entire school day. Courtesy of Paul Conklin.

appreciatively commented that 11 hours represented "a purty good working day," which was almost as long as his own. As a contribution to more accurate interpretation, the American Association of University Professors suggests that workloads described in hours per week of formal class meetings misrepresent the true situation.

The teacher normally spends far less time in the classroom than in preparation, conferences, grading papers and examinations, and supervision of remedial or advanced student work. Preparation, in particular, is of critical importance . . . not only preparation for specific classes or conferences, but that more general preparation in the discipline, by keeping up with recent developments and strengthening his grasp on older materials, without which the faculty member will soon dwindle into ineffectiveness as scholar and teacher.[3]

The number of classes taught in adult education is conditioned by the fact that, for most adult educators, this field is not a full-time field of employment. Typically an adult educator teaches a single course which represents the individual's specialty. Sometimes this course is taught in several sections; rarely does the adult educator teach several courses that are different from each other during the semester or other period of student enrollment.

SIZE OF CLASSES

In classes at the preschool, kindergarten, and elementary school levels, there is considerable variation as to number of students enrolled.

Preschool education is still relatively new in America and it is rapidly burgeoning. Consequently, it is hard to strike an average among classes, since little solid information is available. Class size ranges from a handful of tots

[3] *Ibid.*, p. 30.

Learning a foreign language requires much individual attention. Courtesy of Ron Sherman from Nancy Palmer.

taught in a home or community agency or former store while their mothers work in business or industry, to many children gathered together in a more school-like setting. In 1966–67 the average public-supported nursery school enrolled about eighteen students in a typical class.[4] The average public school kindergarten class was somewhat larger—approximately twenty-six in 1967–68.[5]

In the representative public elementary school, the number of students per class was about twenty-eight in 1968.[6] Classes in independent private schools tend to be smaller and classes in typical parochial schools tend to be larger than classes in the typical public school at both elementary and secondary school levels.

In the junior high school, a 1967 NEA study of 128 large public school systems showed that the median class size varied as to subject areas. The largest classes were found in physical education, thirty-eight, with music next in size, thirty-five. Relatively small class sizes prevailed in industrial arts—twenty-four. The rest of the junior high school classes were comparable in size, ranging from twenty-seven in foreign languages to thirty in social studies.[7]

The same 1967 study revealed generally smaller high school subject area classes. Physical education classes were the same, thirty-eight, and music classes were larger, thirty-eight, but in every other subject area the medians reported were one to two smaller than junior high school classes.[8]

In considering the average number of students in an elementary or secondary school class, one must take into account the growth of team teaching and non-

---

[4] NEA Research Division, *Nursery School Education, 1966–67*, Research Report 1969–R6 (Washington, D.C.: The Association, 1968), p. 26.
[5] NEA Research Division, *Kindergarten Education in Public Schools, 1967–68* (Washington, D.C.: The Association, 1969), p. 24.
[6] "Class Size: Attitude and Action," *NEA Research Bulletin* (December 1969), pp. 115–116.
[7] "Class Size in Large School Systems," *NEA Research Bulletin* (October 1967), p. 79.
[8] *Ibid.*

graded classes. Situations in which three teachers work with perhaps seventy students in a team teaching, and/or nongraded organization especially in the primary, upper elementary, and junior high school are increasing.

On the college level, there is indeed wide variation. Classes range from small and comfortable seminars of perhaps a half dozen or a dozen students to giant introductory courses with enrollments in the hundreds. Faced with the recent increase in college enrollments, some universities have adopted television instruction for hundreds of students, supplemented by occasional discussion groups of moderate size. So wide is the range that to quote averages would tend to be misleading.

On the graduate school level, a wide range in size persists, though the range is somewhat narrower than on the undergraduate level. As a fifth year of study for teachers has become increasingly required for professional preparation, masters' degree classes have increased in size. Though doctoral programs are on the increase in American universities, the universities have so far managed to keep class sizes down.

Teachers prefer fewer students in their classes. They point out that with relatively smaller numbers they can achieve greater individualization and may pay more attention to individual differences. They say that better discipline can be maintained. Yet research studies to date concerning the relationships of class size to effectiveness of instruction are ambiguous in their results. Evidence as to whether improvement is related to reduction of class size is conflicting and confusing. However, in the drive for better working conditions and higher quality in education, it is predictable that teachers will continue to seek public support for smaller classes. It is also likely that the public will continue to resist smaller classes because of additional costs.

Sometimes in a community characterized by a housing boom or in a "federally impacted" area in which military or other government installations have been built, size of classes has increased sharply and swiftly. Such emergencies sometimes have triggered teachers' and administrators' ingenuity and resulted in more use of technological aids and new ways of utilizing staff and grouping students. More often they have resulted in a decline in effectiveness of teaching until building caught up with enrollment expansion.

CO-CURRICULAR ACTIVITIES

Co-curricular activities are a part of the teacher's work, especially in secondary schools and occasionally in colleges. Though the co-curricular program in junior and senior high schools is no longer regarded as extracurricular, for teachers the program involved is extra in that it is not part of the regular class load. However, teachers often approach co-curricular activities with anticipation, since many such activities reflect their own interests and hobbies. Sensible school administrators schedule teachers for co-curricular activities related to individual hobbies and interests when this is possible. A new teacher interested in dramatics may find himself the director of the annual school play; a new teacher with an interest or background in debate may find himself coach of the debate team. When a co-curricular program is highly varied, new teachers may find that even unusual hobbies may be reflected in the program. Quite literally, the range may be from A to Z, from an archery club to a zoology group. Yet sometimes as a new teacher you may be saddled with an unwanted club that no other teacher wishes to sponsor.

The co-curricular program of the school is usually more informal than the regular class program. Consequently, one of the rewards for you as a new teacher is coming to know students who share your interests in a relaxed, informal, non-compulsory situation. Interpersonal relationships are advanced as students proceed at their own pace. A new teacher sometimes learns from co-curricular activities some techniques to make regular classroom instruction livelier and more informal. The rewards of co-curricular activities to the teacher are often financial as well. A 1970 NEA study reported that of 1,142 1969–70 salary schedules surveyed, 489 (or 42.8 percent), paid supplements for directing certain extracurricular activities. Although athletic activities dominate the supplementary salary picture, various nonathletic activities such as dramatic events, the school newspaper and yearbook, and vocal musical events are also well represented.[9] In general, the typical junior and senior high school teacher sponsors one major co-curricular activity each semester.

HOMEWORK

Some teachers also have another out-of-class activity—the homework they assign which must be read, graded, etc. The extent of homework in American schools varies from level to level. Homework, in the sense of required activities and studies after the student has returned home from school, is not characteristic of preschool, nursery school or kindergarten education and is frowned upon by most elementary school educators. Critics of homework point out that the success or failure of home study depends heavily upon the home environment and the interests and educational background of parents. Children generally perform homework adequately when the parents are inclined to supervise and guide the child. But children from home environments in which parents are uninterested in schooling often have trouble doing homework. Instead, many early childhood and elementary school educators advocate guided study in school characterized by supervision and follow-up.

In the junior high school and middle school, homework increases. At the high school level homework is taken for granted as a part of the program. James B. Conant, for example, assumes the desirability of homework in his recommendations for secondary education. Colleges almost universally require substantial homework, ranging from daily preparation to term papers supposedly prepared over the period of an entire semester.

---

[9] National Education Association, Research Division, *Salary Schedule Supplements for Extra Duties, 1969–70*, Research Report 1970–R4 (Washington, D.C.: The Association, 1970) p. 6.

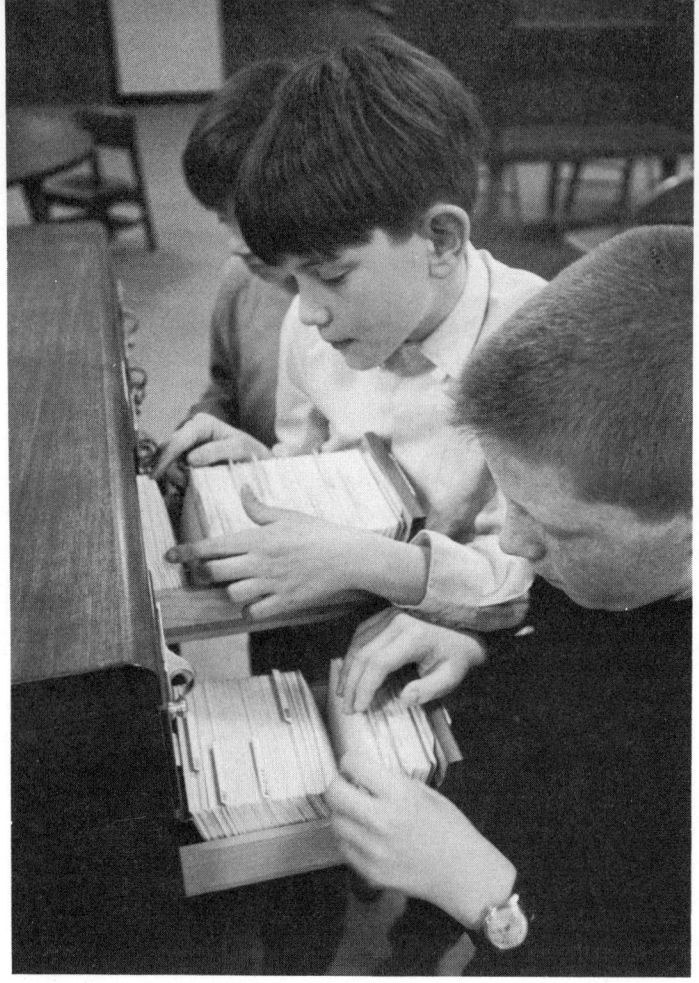

Learning how to use the library efficiently is one of the essentials in education. Courtesy of DeWys.

Homework is usually heaviest in such academic areas as mathematics, languages, and the sciences and is usually lightest in the arts. Unfortunately, teachers usually assign only a common or unitary assignment, rather than individual assignments. One study has shown that 90 percent of assignments made were entirely teacher dominated, although another study indicated that most students preferred assignments resulting from joint planning by both teacher and students.[10]

If a teacher or professor decides to assign homework, he also assumes a responsibility—that of reading the homework, returning it promptly, and using it for educative purposes. There are few more disillusioning experiences for students than carefully preparing homework and then finding that their efforts are ignored or returned long after any possibility for reinforcement is likely. So you as a good teacher have a responsibility for avoiding homework that is mere drudgery and unrelated to the student's needs.

---

[10] Cited by Wayne H. Holzman, "Study," *Encyclopedia of Educational Research*, 4th ed., p. 1390.

Those who support homework feel that it results in the application of recent learning; what has been learned is immediately reinforced. An additional value proposed for homework is the opportunity for the student to find new ideas that might not be encountered in the regular program. It is also argued that memorization can better be done in the students' free time than in the concentrated class time. This reasoning is, of course, doubted by those who are skeptical of the values of memorization and who regard as hypocritical any argument that memorization takes up too much valuable instructional time.

Perhaps the best homework you can assign is that which provides lively learning experiences based on classroom living. Such homework may relate to reading newspapers, listening to television programs, or attending a movie. It may involve reading of materials drawn from the library; it may be based on attendance at a concert, a play or a forum. Homework need not always be textbook exercises. It can be long-term rather than daily.

Homework is heavier in times when schools are under pressure from society to produce results, as during the Sputnik era.[11] Homework demands are relaxed when society is more permissive or when out-of-school activities such as student employment or community participation by students are regarded as important.

Until class time and activities are seen as individualized and student-paced, you, as a beginning teacher, will find homework in most schools the flat, uninteresting drag you recall. Will you be among those striving to replace this kind of fare?

SHARING OTHER CHARACTERISTIC SCHOOL DUTIES

Teaching your own classes is not your only activity as a teacher. Nor are activities related to preparation for classes or marking papers your only out-of-class activities. In most schools from preschool through secondary levels there are additional duties, including lunchroom duty, playground or recess supervision, responsibilities in connection with study halls, supervision of corridors and halls, and a variety of paper work. Teachers sometimes remark that they have little time to teach. In an effort to reduce the volume of such responsibilities, perceived by teachers as essentially routine and nonprofessional, a new group of workers has been employed by schools. Educators are finding that the new staff increasingly goes beyond routine work and plays a useful personal role in the education process by working with individuals and small groups. Students are gaining from relationships with a variety of adults.

Titles for the new personnel vary. The most popular terms are teacher aides and paraprofessionals. The new workers free teachers for greater concentration on teaching activities and individual needs; they often enable the teacher to introduce more creativity into his work. Unfortunately, sometimes the new workers conflict or compete with the established teacher corps. Because of such

---

[11] Robert Fleming and Ronald C. Doll (eds.), *Children Under Pressure* (Columbus, Ohio: C. E. Merrill, 1966).

situations, teacher unions and teacher associations have sometimes viewed the new workers with a degree or reserve and even opposition.

The numerous occasions on which teacher aides and paraprofessionals have proven to be helpful to the teacher have resulted in a steady decrease in opposition by teachers and their organizations to new patterns of staff utilization. In 1970 the American Federation of Teachers (AFT) in New York launched a campaign to organize paraprofessionals for higher pay and benefits. Particularly in schools in underprivileged areas, paraprofessionals and teacher aides recruited from the local community and often from minority groups have made significant contributions to effective education. In Pittsburgh for instance, neighborhood mothers worked in black areas. In New York City, the Public Education Association encouraged unpaid volunteers to foster remedial work. Such helpers frequently know neighborhoods intimately and students personally.

The utilization of teacher aides and paraprofessionals is on the increase. A task force of Associated Organizations for Teacher Education, chaired by an active school superintendent, says in a preliminary working paper:

... A 1970 survey of eighteen of the large city school systems revealed that all employ adult paraprofessionals, with the greatest number being used at the elementary level. These paraprofessionals are handling clerical activities as well as classroom supervision in the absence of a teacher. In most instances the paraprofessional is not licensed by the state.

TABLE 20.1

The Teacher's Working Week

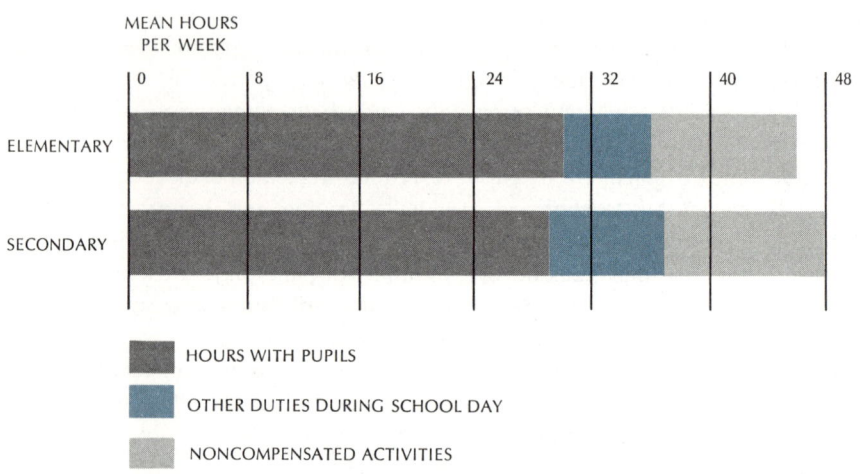

NEA Research Division, *The American Public School Teacher,* 1965–66, Research Report 1967–R4 (Washington, D.C.: The Association, 1967), p. 27.

... We cannot "scratch off" the adult generation as we work for and with the younger generation. We must develop and utilize promising adult resources of the city, however "uncredentialled" they may be, both for what this can mean for them and what they in turn can mean for the strengthening of positive hope and resolve in reshaping curricular and institutional patterns for education in the city ...

The concept of *the* teacher—i.e., one person alone within a self-contained classroom, trying to interact effectively with from twenty to forty students—is gradually being supplanted by the concept of a teaching team composed of persons of widely differing competencies, training and life experiences. The team may include not only the teacher as diagnostician, leader and participant, but also other professionals such as curriculum specialists and paraprofessional school workers, the latter serving at various levels of responsibility depending upon the needs of the situation and their own degree of competence. The team may occasionally include volunteers or older students in a "youth-teaching-youth" program.[12]

In *A Learning Team: Teacher and Auxiliary,* the authors propose that the goals of a team made up of teachers and auxiliaries should be:

... first to establish rapport and mutual trust between school, home and child; then to create a learning environment in the school which is rich, varied and alive; next, to analyze each student's behavior within the environment so as to identify his needs, his interests, his anxieties, his goals—conscious and unconscious—his learning style, his modes of attacking a problem, and his apparent feelings toward self and others. The final step in the process is to restructure the environment, while providing the medley of supportive services that are needed, as the learner meshes his strivings to an educational task which is consonant with his goals, and at the same time replete with opportunity for his growth and development.[13]

Your introduction into teaching would be still more significant if it could include experience comparable to those of an aide or paraprofessional, culminating in an internship. You would come to know and appreciate the team approach to the teaching-learning situation. You might check into any local possibilities of your participating in a team as part of your teacher preparation program.

---

[12] Report and Recommendations of the Task Force on Preparation of Educational Personnel for the Inner City: Professional and Paraprofessional (Washington, D.C.: Associated Organizations for Teacher Education, February 1970), pp. 1–2, 5–6 (mimeographed).

[13] Gordon J. Klopf, Garda W. Bowman, and Adena Joy, *A Learning Team: Teacher and Auxiliary* (Bank Street College of Education for the United States Office of Education, 1969), p. viii.

THE TOOLS OF THE TRADE

THE USE OF TEXTBOOKS

The use of textbooks for the grade level or the courses which you will teach constitutes a crucial problem to you as a new teacher. It is not that textbooks for your use will not be available; in all but a small fraction of contemporary schools, textbooks will be readily available though they may not always be most appropriate or most up-to-date or even best suited to your class's reading level. Nor is it that the process of obtaining them is difficult; in the large majority of school situations (but not in all) textbooks will be ready and waiting for you. Yet despite the existence and easy availability of textbooks for your grade level or courses, the use of textbooks involves problems for you which are likely to test the high resolutions you have made as to the kind of teacher you will be. You have a choice as to whether your textbooks will dominate the content, methodology, and total approach of your teaching.

As you look over the textbooks supplied, there may be powerful forces at work urging you toward becoming the type of traditional teacher who rarely deviates from the text adopted. Your own natural nervousness in an unfamiliar situation will encourage you in this direction, as will your insecurity about your ability to translate into practice your own ideas about education which you formulated in college courses, student teaching, and discussions with friends. Another force takes the form of the attitudes of some experienced teachers who may advise you to take the easy way out by simply following any textbook provided. It may even occur to you that the administration of your school and system by the very act of supplying you with textbooks is implicitly advising you to teach the textbooks. And, frankly, a beginning teacher has little leeway in choosing texts or ordering alternatives.

While your situation is by no means as serious as that of Faust who sold his soul to the Devil, you may feel that there are some similarities! The easy way would be to forget your resolutions and what you may have learned and to allow your textbooks to completely dominate your teaching. You can find many arguments to support this position: the textbook was presumably written by an authority who knows the subject intimately; the activities suggested by the textbook writer may be better than any you could devise; with increasing investment in production, textbooks presumably grow better and better.

The harder way is to use your textbooks as tools, not as your sole instruments in the struggle to achieve your educational goals. If you take the harder but more challenging way, your textbooks will be one among several tools you use. To the extent that your textbooks are useful in developing the best possible education for each student, you will use them; to the extent that other media or approaches are appropriate, you will select them. The backgrounds of students should be taken into account in deciding on the appropriateness of the content of the textbooks; if textbooks do not fit the students, alternative materials should be used. More materials than the textbooks alone are usually available to the classroom teacher. Many modern school administrators would prefer that you use your textbooks selectively rather than slavishly; such principals and supervisors may help you devise multi-resource lessons.

Concerned teachers approach decisions about the use of textbooks with care and deliberation. You might carefully appraise the teaching situation in which you find yourself, including student backgrounds, community expectations, school practices, administrative viewpoints, etc. You will discover that some textbooks fit well into your plans. You will find that other textbooks are useful as resources to supplement and extend your teaching. You might find still other textbooks which, in your situation, should be avoided or minimized, to the extent that you can avoid them or minimize their use. Frequent student-teacher evaluations might help you develop varied ways of using your available textbooks. Seek the aid of an experienced teacher or librarian to check on the existence of other media and materials.

Some may advise you that to follow a text doesn't make you a traitor to ambitions growing from pre-teaching experiences. They may regard the Faustian analogy as overly dramatic. They may suggest that you begin conservatively by using your textbooks and branch out only as you develop more confidence. On the other hand, how we begin sometimes determines where we end up. Robert Frost said it well in "The Road Not Taken:"

> Two roads diverged in a wood, and I—
> I took the one less traveled by,
> And that has made all the difference.[14]

LIBRARY, AUDIO-VISUAL, AND NEW TECHNOLOGY RESOURCES

You have many resources to use imaginatively in libraries, audio-visual centers, and technological collections. Your own teaching style can be heavily influenced by the availability of library resources. Very early in your acquaintance with a new school, you might become familiar with both the school and the public library holdings related to your grade level or subject area. In most cases, librarians are on your side and are interested in the use of their facilities and eager to help you become familiar with their procedures. Certainly, you will realistically appraise the reading levels of your students, for little good can come from using library materials which are beyond the grade, interest, or intellectual level of the students you teach. As you consider what your students should read, you might well use existing bibliographies rather than always start from scratch. Again, the librarian's professional help can be useful to you.

Today schools vary widely in availability of audio-visual materials. Some schools have a learning resources center which may be an integral part of the library; some have little or nothing at the school or even district centers. But even such schools often have access to state or university depositories of films,

---

[14] Robert Frost, *The Complete Poems of Robert Frost* (New York: Henry Holt, 1949), p. 131.

filmstrips, film loops, and recordings. Of course, the use of such resources requires ordering weeks or even months in advance and thus the spontaneity that comes with easy availability is diminished. Yet, with advance planning, teachers in schools lacking learning resources centers can still make good use of audio-visual materials.

There are hurdles other than availability to overcome in using audio-visual materials. One obstacle may lie within yourself—the possible inclination to view the showing of a film or the playing of a record or tape as an opportunity to relax from the none too easy business of teaching. It takes some self-discipline to recognize that a film or a tape or a record should be previewed before it is used or, should this not prove possible, that careful descriptions of the content of the material should be studied in advance of screenings or listening sessions. It takes some self-discipline to recognize that one must be selective about audio-visual materials, using them when they are appropriate and for purposes which should be clear to the teacher, and which ought to be made clear to the learner.

Too, students who constantly encounter records, television, drive-in movies, etc., in their environment outside of school have often developed habits of only partially paying attention to the audio-visual aids. It may take some effort to get students to listen attentively and to watch carefully if material is less exciting than skillful mass media productions. If the teacher suggests things to look for and questions or problems to have in mind before presenting the audio-visual program and follows the presentation with discussion, the outcome may be better communication and consequently better learning.

The availability of new teaching technology in American schools also varies widely. In a growing number of schools, television of several types is accessible. In some schools, the only available television programs are those that happen to be broadcast by the major commercial networks. While some of these may well be germane to your purposes as a teacher, most of them, including the better documentaries, plays, and news programs, occur during evening hours. Given the wide access to television that American young people currently have, the teacher might well request or require listening to a selected program for follow-up consideration in class the next day.

In addition to commercial programs, some schools have access to and make use of television broadcasts from educational television stations. *Sesame Street* is an example of an effective educational television program developed for the very young child. Then, too, some school systems have their own closed circuit broadcasts directed to certain grade levels or subject areas; a few schools prepare their own television materials. Whatever the approach, the new teacher will soon learn of it because staff members, including audio-visual personnel, are usually interested in wide dissemination.

A minority of schools also employ programmed instruction in the form of so-called teaching machines, or, less frequently, in the form of computer-assisted instruction. Again, there is seldom a problem of learning about the existence of such resources; there is a greater problem of learning to use them well to meet the needs of students. Your own college may use machines for instruction;

if so, observe their use or abuse. Sometimes machine instruction is planned for a class as a whole; sometimes machines supplement the learning requirements of individuals. In most cases, the school leaders find it necessary to supply in-service training for both experienced and new teachers with respect to available educational technology. You might get a headstart by including audio-visual instruction in your total undergraduate program and experiment with it during pre-service experiences. The industrial revolution in education is here to stay. The new teacher should learn to use the new machines constructively without allowing the curriculum to be dominated by too arbitrary and rigid use of programmed materials, ETV, and curriculum packages (some of which are advertised as "teacher proof").

EQUIPMENT AND SUPPLIES

As a new teacher, you will soon discover the inevitable and potentially highly helpful "office." The secretaries and assistants who maintain school offices are your resources for information on a variety of equipment and supplies, whether they take the slight form of a pencil or the bulky shape of an overhead projector. These clerical workers follow procedures developed by the system or the individual school so any basic questions and certainly any complaints or proposed procedural revisions should be channeled to administrators, including department chairman or supervisors. Learning the established routines for equipment and supply use early and heeding these procedures should put the new teacher in the good graces of those who preside over offices and make life easier for the teacher in quest of equipment and supplies. Nor should the importance to you of the custodian be forgotten; he is a good man to have on your side when the time comes for moving furniture, rearranging desks, or even when frantically hunting at the last moment for a piece of chalk.

PARENT AND COMMUNITY RELATIONS

PARENT-TEACHER MEETINGS

One type of teacher-community relationship is through the meetings of parent-teacher organizations. Though attendance at parent-teacher meetings is seldom compulsory for teachers, most schools heartily encourage teachers to be present. Attendance at such meetings and participation in activities of the association can provide the new teacher with a rudimentary introduction to the community where he works.

Some parent-teacher organizations are independent of national organizations and are autonomous bodies associated with a single school or single district. Other parent-teacher organizations are part of the National Congress of Parents and Teachers. The latter group is also organized along state lines. The national organization, popularly termed PTA, states its purposes as follows:

1. To promote the welfare of children and youth in home, school, church, and community.
2. To raise the standards of home life.
3. To secure adequate laws for the care and protection of children and youth.
4. To bring into closer relation the home and the school, that parents and teachers may cooperate intelligently in the training of the child.
5. To develop between educators and the general public such united efforts as will secure for every child the highest advantages in physical, mental, social and spiritual education.

The new teacher is not usually called upon to make any particular contribution to his first parent-teacher meetings. You will probably do little more than be recognized when introduced to the group as a new teacher. Therefore, you should have abundant opportunities to learn not only from the formal program of the meeting but also from its implications. A parent-teacher meeting affords you the opportunity to speculate, for example, on which parents attend and which do not. Are any groups of parents conspicuous by their absence? Or presence? Are the attendants at the meeting representative of the students in your class or classes? Is attendance skewed toward the more prosperous and economically influential parents? Is attendance representative of the distribution of your classes in terms of racial, nationality, and religious dimensions? Which parents set the tone for the meeting? Is the meeting the creation of the school administration or of the parents or of both groups jointly? Careful observation of such meetings can make some contribution, however elementary, to your understanding of the locus of power in your school and community.

The new teacher can also learn from the substantive content of the meeting. Does the meeting deal with the real problems of the children or youth whom you have come to know through your classes? Or does it deal with peripheral matters? Is the meeting concerned with shadow rather than substance through emphasis placed upon formalities and rituals? What else could the meeting focus upon? The parent-teacher meeting is often a reflection of the parents' and the community's conception of and commitment to education.

The attitudes of his colleagues and administrators toward the meeting should also be of interest to the perceptive new teacher. Do teachers welcome the meeting or do they attend grudgingly, if at all? Do they see such meetings as significant and useful? Does the administration regard the occasion as an opportunity for genuine sharing? Or does it apparently fear such meetings? Does the administration manipulate the meeting to reinforce the present school programs by simply acquainting parents with the status quo rather than regard the meeting as an opportunity for parental suggestions and possible program improvements?

The first active role the new teacher is likely to play in a parent-teacher organization will come sometime during the school year when a meeting attended by parents takes the form of a program of visitation of individual classrooms accompanied by discussions with teachers. As a new teacher you may be fearful of such occasions, for you recognize that they might bring to light not only your successes but also your failures—and you will probably have both. However, a new teacher might use the occasion to describe his program and purposes and, when appropriate, to ask for the kind of cooperation from parents he most needs. He would be well advised to try to differentiate between that part of the visit with parents which deals with the experience of the class as a whole and those inevitable parent-requested conferences about the progress of individual students. To discuss individual students in the larger parent meeting is clearly a dubious practice, even when a parent urges or invites the new teacher to do so.

CONFERENCES WITH PARENTS

While parent-teacher meetings are obviously useful to the teacher, individual parent conferences often supply him the clues he needs to be more effective with young people. Whether a parent actively seeks a conference is often largely a function of the parent's social class. For instance, most upper-middle-class parents will not hesitate to request a conference with a teacher, particularly when disturbed about some aspect of the school program or the student's progress. The lower-class parent may also be concerned about the program or the child but will usually not request a conference; such a parent often feels uncomfortable or out of place in a typical school atmosphere. But, whether a conference is parent- or teacher-initiated, the new teacher must demonstrate a reasonable amount of skill in human relations. Teacher sensitivity can convert the possible initial discomfort of the meeting into a constructive and cooperative relationship. College experience in the behavioral sciences, as well as out-of-school activities in programs such as Head Start and youth work, can prepare the teacher to deal skillfully with parents and their concerns.

The problem of knowing how to act and what to say, however, is really secondary to the problem of obtaining parent conferences with those parents who never request them, such as parents from disadvantaged backgrounds. Somehow the new teacher has to find a way of getting in touch with the parent who does not volunteer to come to school to meet him. Sometimes a request for the parent to confer at the school is in order. The new teacher, however, would be well advised to recognize that for many parents such an invitation is a summons and a potential threat. Some parents find that the invitation conflicts with their working hours or responsibilities to children not yet in school. If they come at all, they may have their defenses up.

The new teacher may find that the better way to communicate is, by careful prearrangement, to visit the parents at home. Sometimes this is easily arranged; at other times because of parental reluctance, embarrassment at poor home conditions, poverty, or occasionally because of the high crime rate in a neighborhood, arrangements may prove difficult. But, when made, such home visits are often rewarding; new insights come to a teacher when he visits the home which day after day has been contributing to a student's experiences, whether positively or negatively.

COMMUNITY PARTICIPATION

One of the most realistic approaches to understanding the school's community is to work actively in that community as a participating citizen. The range of possibilities is as wide as your interests, concerns, and hobbies. Some recreation-oriented teacher-citizens participate through the programs of Y's, whether YMCA, YWCA, YMHA, etc. Some manage Little League baseball teams or organize youth hostels. Some work in neighborhoods through their churches. Some socially conscious teacher-citizens work with community centers or settlement houses. Some become involved in community action campaigns, such as fair housing programs or community fund drives. Some participate in political action through working with political groups. In all such cases, the teacher-citizen becomes a contributor, sharing in at least a segment of the total community life.

In his community activities, the teacher has the responsibility to continuously make it clear that he is proceeding as a citizen rather than as a spokesman or a representative of the school as an institution. Two classifications of rights and responsibilities of the American teacher should be clearly differentiated. As a teacher of children and adolescents, a teacher has certain rights and responsibilities. His rights include freedom to teach so that young people may learn; his responsibilities include living by a professional code of ethics and the fostering of the use of intelligence by students. As a citizen of the United States, the individual who is a teacher also has certain rights and responsibilities. A teacher not only *may* participate in the common life as a citizen, but to be a truly democratic citizen he *must* participate. He must run the risk of reaching a conclusion on race relations or foreign policy or the economy or any other controversial issue which does not happen to be the majority position of that moment. Active citizenship always involves the possibility that one may espouse unpopular causes as well as majority beliefs.

The new teacher should not assume, however, that his claim to citizenship or to freedom to teach will go completely unchallenged. It is possible that frequent peer and/or community pressures will be felt to restrict teacher activities both within and without school. Evidence to support this assertion is, unfortunately, all too readily available.

Jonathan Kozol in *Death at an Early Age* tells of his dismissal from the Boston schools for refusing to restrict his classroom reading and reference material to a list of approved publications. School authorities and certain community elements particularly objected to his use of the poem "Ballad of the Landlord" by Langston Hughes with his fourth grade class.[15]

In the 1969–70 school year, five Plainfield, Indiana, teachers wore black armbands to school on October 1969, Vietnam Moratorium Day. In the words of the school board, any teacher who identified himself with "any controversial movement" on school time could be declared "guilty of misconduct and insubordination."[16] The teachers challenged the policy statement with a suit before the

---

[15] Jonathan Kozol, *Death at an Early Age* (Boston: Houghton Mifflin, 1967), pp. 225–232.
[16] "Patriotic Town Is Angry Over Teachers' Protest," *New York Times* (May 29, 1970), pp. 31–32.

federal district judge in Indianapolis. After a preliminary hearing indicated they had no hope of winning without going through the drawn-out procedure of an appeal, all five teachers notified the school board they would not be returning in September.

A teacher in Mayer, Arizona, was accused in 1968 by a disgruntled former student of supplying marijuana to a minor, a felony which upon conviction carries a ten-year to life imprisonment penalty in Arizona. She was arrested and community opinion (encouraged by her nonconformity—she was an avid racing fan and often played pool at a local tavern) quickly hardened against her. Although she was completely exonerated, she learned the bitter lesson that a teacher can be at the mercy of resentful pupils and a conventionally minded community.[17]

In some southern states which have resisted desegregation, black educators often were overtly discriminated against when jobs were reassigned. Representative of this group was Fred McCoy, a principal of an all-black elementary school in Natalbany, Louisiana, who was reassigned to teach a fourth grade class in the mornings and do janitor chores in the afternoon.[18]

Of course, teachers are not completely without protection in such cases as have been mentioned. Actions by school authorities, if arbitrary, can be contested in the courts. To aid teachers in such expensive and time-consuming cases, the NEA, for example, maintains the DuShane Emergency Fund to provide teachers with financial and legal assistance when their rights are challenged. Also, teachers have increasingly moved toward negotiated agreements with school boards which detail their professional rights and responsibilities. The struggle for teacher rights is a continuing battle in which you, the new teacher, might well enlist.

The authentic American tradition is that the citizen has a right to hold his point of view and to defend it through legal means. Once we accept any doctrine that educators as citizens do not have the same rights and privileges as do other American citizens, we open the way to the application of a variety of illegitimate pressures upon individual teachers.

PROBLEMS AND HELPS FOR THE NEW TEACHER

In your first year of teaching you may encounter formidable problems partially because of the practices of your school system. Or you may encounter substantial sympathetic help through these same procedures. You may even encounter some strange mixture of both.

The operational practices of many school systems often contribute to the difficulties of the beginning teacher. Some school systems, particularly in the large metropolises, have established the tradition of assigning the newest and

---

[17] Elisabeth Keiffer, "The Trial of Elaine Murphy," *Good Housekeeping* (May 1969), pp. 12–28.
[18] "The Bad Side of Integration," *Time* (July 13, 1970), p. 32.

therefore least experienced teachers to the most difficult teaching situations, those in the slums and the ghettos which are rife with social and educational problems. It is usually neither malignancy nor stupidity which accounts for this type of assignment. Openings for teachers annually are usually more frequent in disadvantaged areas. Teacher transfers from such areas often take place when the teacher, after achieving tenure, may be offered the option of teaching elsewhere and chooses an area nearer home or in a less trouble-prone neighborhood. True, many teachers, given the choice, remain in the difficult or disadvantaged situation; they accept the challenge of contemporary education or they like the work. But a larger number of teachers move out of the ghetto or slum school when the opportunity occurs.

In the particular school in which the new teacher works, he sometimes is assigned a class or classes unwanted by experienced staff members. Again, while there are many teachers who enjoy the challenge of working with relatively low ability groups, most teachers, given a choice, choose the average or above-average section. Thus the new teacher, despite inexperience, finds himself frequently facing the difficult task of working with low-ability students who are often less motivated to school achievement.

There are even situations in which new teachers unfairly are assigned excessive after-hours duty, older textbooks, etc., though such situations are clearly discrimination by administrators who practice favoritism toward experienced teachers. Fortunately such practices are rare.

Yet there exist systems which use procedures which provide substantial help to the new teacher. (Paradoxically, some systems both provide help to new teachers through positive procedures and contribute to the difficulty of new teachers through negative operational procedures!) Such help may be informal through friendship and earnest advice; it may be formalized through pre-school meetings for new teachers, regular meetings throughout the school year, conferences with principals and supervisors, readiness to help in emergencies, etc. There are schools in which the staff leans over backward to be helpful to the new teacher. His in-service education may be co-sponsored both by the school system and a local university. He may be given a lighter load than experienced teachers. Though he will inevitably encounter problems, he has much within the existing system going for him. For some new teachers, the transition to actual teaching may be eased by a teacher-education program which carefully inducts the new teacher into teaching not only through classroom instruction but through multiple opportunities for observation, participation, work as aides, helpful student teaching, periods of internship, etc.

Inevitably there are dropouts from teaching as from study. The majority of teachers work through the problems which a first year in any occupation or profession presents and come back for more of the combination of joyous achievement and painful frustration which teaching often involves. Good teaching can make a change in the lives of human beings, and a good teacher, whether experienced or inexperienced, knows it and persists.

★   ★   ★

DISCUSSION

1. What are the advantages and disadvantages of working with a single class throughout the day, rather than different classes for shorter periods throughout the day?
2. Discuss the kinds of knowledge an elementary school teacher should possess in order to teach in a self-contained classroom.
3. List what you consider to be the advantages of organizing subject matter for elementary schools on some basis other than separate subjects.
4. What co-curricular activities do you feel you are qualified and prepared to sponsor? Why do you feel that these particular activities are important to students?
5. What types of activities do you think should be conducted by teachers with no extra compensation? with extra compensation?
6. What has been your own experience in respect to homework during your years of schooling? Do you believe it has made a significant contribution to your learning? What is the case for or against assigned homework?
7. Should different homework policies prevail at different levels of the educational ladder? Are some types of homework more beneficial than others? What types?
8. How would you like to see children and youth spend their after-school time? What role should homework play?
9. Defend the position that daily homework is a necessary part of a student's school experience.
10. What are some of the relatively routine responsibilities of teachers about which educators complain? Which of these can be allocated to assistants and which are inevitable characteristics of the choice of education as a field of work?
11. What do you believe should be the position of the teaching profession in relation to the use of paraprofessionals?
12. How does an assistant sometimes unwittingly handicap a new teacher? What are some of the ways in which a new assistant consciously attempts to help a new teacher?
13. Under what circumstances might a teacher adhere closely to a textbook? Under what circumstances might she deviate, even to the point of abandoning the textbook? What other tools of the trade are available to teachers?
14. How might a new teacher most readily become familiar with library, audio-visual, and technological resources? What are some benefits from using such resources with students? What are some cautions to be observed?
15. What are the most frequent uses of television in American schools? To what extent has educational technology other than television been adopted in American schools?
16. What are some of the ways in which the teacher might come to understand the community in which he or she works?
17. What are the functions of parent-teacher meetings? What kinds of parent-teacher meetings are most effective? Least effective? What can one learn from attendance at the parent-teacher meeting if one is a new teacher?
18. How can parent conferences be made useful for all involved, including students, teachers, and parents? What approaches to the conference might be most workable?

19. What alternatives does a teacher have when a parent is unwilling or unable to come to school? Do you see possible problems in visits to students' homes?
20. What is your own view on what teachers as a professional group and a teacher as an individual should do under circumstances of attempted restriction of rights? What protection do teachers have in such cases?
21. What is your opinion as to how a successful first year of teaching might be fostered by both school systems and the new teacher?

INVOLVEMENT

1. Check into research on the relationship between class size and the effectiveness of learning. Does the evidence seem conclusive to you?
2. Spend an afternoon with the extracurriculum of a typical junior or senior high school. Then attempt to generalize on the importance or lack of importance to the students and teachers involved. Do you observe any instances of gain to individuals?
3. Review your own experiences as a student with homework. How do these compare with the experiences of other students in your group?
4. Interview an intermediate elementary student, a junior high student, and a senior high student to determine the type and amount of homework they are expected to complete in a week. What are their reactions as to the importance and helpfulness of these assignments?
5. Visualize a typical homework assignment which you might make in your subject field and at the level of instruction at which you will teach. How important is your proposed assignment? How creative? Could it have been done within supervised study time in class?
6. Interview a teacher on the amount of time he teaches and the amount of time which is given to activities he regards as routine. What suggestions does he have for reduction of routine work? What attitudes does he take toward aides or paraprofessionals?
7. If paraprofessionals work in the schools which you visit, interview several about the nature of their work. Determine whether they have particular grievances. Ask them what aspects of their work give them most satisfaction.
8. Examine several textbooks which you might use in your future teaching. Ask yourself how you might most effectively use such textbooks; supplementary resources. Look particularly at proposed activities, which are usually found at the end of chapters.
9. Develop a plan for teaching for approximately a week which leans heavily on the best of the textbooks which you have examined. Develop a teaching plan for a week which almost completely avoids the use of a textbook. Note how much time preparation of each plan took. Ask yourself which plan seems most valuable for learning by students.
10. Examine a textbook on the adoption list in the state and in the subject or on the grade level in which you plan to teach. What are its strengths and weaknesses in light of what you expect to teach in that particular area?
11. Build a bibliography for future use in your teaching. Obtain the help of a librarian in doing so.

12. The next time you see a classroom film, ask yourself what questions you would have raised before showing the film and what discussion you would foster after student viewing.
13. If a school in your vicinity is notable for its use of technology, visit it and become acquainted with the resources and their uses.
14. Attend a parent-teacher meeting as an observer. Follow the suggestions contained in this chapter in observing what is said in the meeting and perhaps what is unsaid.
15. Obtain whatever catalog of films you are most likely to use in your own teaching in the community in which you tentatively plan to teach. Check off the films which you would most likely use in your particular field of instruction.
16. Check with parents of children and youth of school age who are among your acquaintances as to the extent of their relationship to the schools through parent-teacher meetings, conferences with teachers, etc. Ask them about the kinds of relationships they would like to have with the schools attended by their children.
17. Establish your own relationship with the community through some organizations or groups which fit your patterns of interest or conviction.
18. Follow closely cases of infringement of teacher rights or freedom to teach. When it seems appropriate, play a role as a citizen in such incidents.
19. Determine what the school or school system in which you hope to teach does to help teachers in their first year of teaching. Inquire too of assignment policies as they apply to first-year teachers.

BIBLIOGRAPHY

Anderson, Robert H. *Teaching in a World of Change.* New York: Harcourt, Brace and World, 1966. Helping students to be aware of the changes they will face, of the forces behind those changes, and the opportunities those changes offer. Suggests that each teacher evaluate the proposed innovations and adapt them to the special characteristics of his own pupils, and decide which innovations to accept and which to reject.

Auerbach, Aline B. *Parents Learn through Discussion: Principles and Practices of Parent Group Education.* New York: John Wiley and Sons, 1968. Helpful on ways in which parents can learn about schools and how teachers can interrelate with parents through discussions.

Battle, J. A. and Robert L. Shannon, eds. *The New Idea in Education.* New York: Harper and Row, 1968. Anthology on developments in education, including several contributions by the authors. Focuses on ideas about what learning is, its ends and means.

Beauchamp, George A. *Basic Dimensions of Elementary Method.* Boston: Allyn and Bacon, 1965. Basic dimensions as a point of departure for examining the instructional process.

Black, Hillel. *The American Schoolbook.* New York: Morrow, 1967. A lively and controversial critique of the American textbook, its uses and misuses.

Dale, Edgar. *Audio-Visual Methods in Teaching,* 2nd ed. New York: Holt, Rinehart and Winston, 1965. A comprehensive and widely accepted textbook in a field of growing importance. Discusses theory and utilization of instructional materials.

DeBernardis, Amo. *The Use of Instructional Materials.* New York: Appleton-Century-Crofts, 1960. A guide to the teacher in the use of a wide variety of teaching aids and suggestions as to how they may be used in the classroom.

Fleming, Robert and Ronald C. Doll, eds. *Children Under Pressure.* Columbus, Ohio: Charles E. Merrill, 1966. Earnest and eloquent case for less pressure on children, despite adult anxieties. Documentation of harmful affects of undue pressures.

Glaser, Robert, ed. *Teaching Machines and Programed Learning, II: Data and Directions.* Washington, D.C.: Department of Audio-visual Instruction, NEA, 1965. Assessment by leading scientists and practitioners in the field.

Goodlad, John I., ed. *The Changing American School.* Sixty-fifth Yearbook of the National Society for the Study of Education, Part II. Chicago: University of Chicago Press, 1966. A yearbook which includes consideration of innovations emerging in American education and descriptions and analysis of proposals for change, with appraisals.

Inlow, Gail. *The Emergent in Curriculum.* New York: John Wiley and Sons, 1966. Assesses current innovations in curriculum against a background of traditional practices. Deals with organizational approaches, such as team teaching, and technological approaches such as television and programed learning.

Klopf, Gordon J., Garda W. Bowman, and Adena Joy. *A Learning Team, Teacher and Auxiliary.* Bank Street College of Education for the United States Office of Education, 1969. Philosophy and practice of collaboration by varied educators in a learning team, implying aides, paraprofessionals, etc.

Lange, Phil C., ed. *Programmed Instruction.* Sixty-sixth Yearbook of the National Society for the Study of Education, Part II. Chicago: University of Chicago, 1967. Principles and theories in the field as related to the learning behavior of students.

Noar, Gertrude. *Teacher Aides at Work.* Washington, D.C.: National Commission on Teacher Education and Professional Standards, NEA, 1967. Report on the use of teacher aides in schools. New staffing concepts so that nonprofessionals can contribute to the improvement of education and make the teacher's job more manageable.

Samalonis, Bernice L. *Methods and Materials for Today's High Schools.* Cincinnati: Van Nostrand Reinhold. 1970. A practical methods textbook for secondary education.

Schrag, Peter. *Voices in the Classroom.* Boston: Beacon, 1965. A report by an able journalist on schools he visited throughout the nation.

Schueler, Herbert, Gerald S. Lesser, and Allen L. Dobbins. *Teacher Education and the New Media.* Washington, D.C.: The American Association of Colleges for Teacher Education, 1967. Closed circuit television, video-tape recordings, and 8 mm. films.

Stout, Irving W. and Grace Langdon. *What Research Says to the Teacher: Parent-Teacher Relationships.* Association of Classroom Teachers of the National Education Association. Washington, D.C. NEA, 1968. Concise, valid, and up-to-date summaries of educational research findings and their implications for teachers in the area of relationships with parents.

Working With Parents. Published by National School Public Relations Association in Cooperation with the Association of Classroom Teachers Department of the National Education Association, 1968. How a teacher becomes an interpreter, building a foundation of public support of the school by developing relationships with parents.

AUDIO-VISUAL MATERIALS

How the Student Council Solves a Real Problem (Educational Filmstrips, 52 fr., Color) Stresses the role of the sponsor as a guide to the student council.

Resources for Learning (McGraw-Hill Textfilms, 20 Min. Color) Educational media in a broader perspective with respect to their services in the teaching-learning process. The profusion of media available to education and the changes taking place in patterns for teaching and learning.

Television Techniques for Teaching (San Diego Area Instructional Television Authority, 23 Min. Color) Demonstrates some practical approaches to utilizing television in the classroom.

Wonders Never Cease (NEA, 27 Min.) An overview of audio-visual materials in education, including electronic computers. Stresses that such materials are aids to the teacher and are not replacements for him.

Programming is a Process—An Introduction to Instructional Technology (University of Illinois, 32 Min. color) Introduces viewers to the basic process of instructional technology—programming an instructional sequence for maximum student learning. The steps of the programming process, applicable to all media, are described as a means toward instruction.

The Film and You—Using the Classroom Film (Bailey Films, Inc., 14 Min. color) Explains how the motion picture is an effective instructional aid in the classroom. Shows how a sixth grade teacher prepares her class for the film showing and how she devises relevant follow-up activities.

Television in your Classroom (Illahee Group, Puget Sound Instructional TV Association, 44 frs. Color, Record) Outlines five basic elements of effective instructional television utilization—importance of study guides, the proper adjustment and placement of the classroom television set, the role of positive teacher attitude, the significance of effective follow-up activities and the distinct usefulness of evaluation and feedback by the classroom teacher.

The Teacher and Technology (Ohio State University, 49 Min.) Programs which illustrate the role of the educational media specialist in applying technology to the problems of large numbers of students, or of individual instruction.

Computer in the Classroom (Rand Corp., 13 Min.) Depicts by candid photography a group of gifted ninth and tenth graders as they respond to a summer course devoted to practice at a computer. Programming, flow charting, testing, and explanations of computer circuiting and computer chess.

School Libraries in Action (North Carolina Department of Public Instruction, 17 Min., Color) Presents school library practices in North Carolina, the role of the librarian, and how skills necessary for the efficient use of library resources are developed by children.

Telling the PTA Story (Eye Gate House, Inc., 46 frs., Color) Details the PTA's objectives.

TWENTY-ONE

WHAT ABOUT EVALUATION AND GUIDANCE?

Since all teachers must both appraise and help students, the work of the new teacher calls for some acquaintance with two specialized fields which are important in teaching—evaluation and guidance. Ideally, the new teacher should study these fields in courses taught by specialists in the fields, for each involves important substantive content for the classroom teacher. Here, we will at least open up some issues and sketch some background for consideration by the new teacher concerning evaluation and guidance.

EVALUATION AND MEASUREMENT

THE PROCESS OF EVALUATION

Evaluation is a process of determining the value or worth of something through examining, judging, appraising, estimating, and measuring. Thoroughgoing evaluation in education includes (1) identifying the purposes of education, (2) gathering data and evidence to show whether the purposes are being achieved, (3) interpreting the evidence and data gathered, and (4) making the changes called for by the interpretation. As we have already seen from chapter 16, the determination of purposes of education is no simple matter; it is marked by substantial conflict in viewpoints. Gathering and interpreting data and evidence presents technical problems and making changes based on evaluation is difficult. Yet it makes little sense to educate people without determining whether the education they have experienced produces effective results.

In attempting to evaluate, educators have developed a variety of formal and informal measurements. Measurement is only part of the total process of evaluation and tests are one way of measuring. In ancient China examinations were used to select civil servants, and in European universities during the Middle Ages examinations for both professors and students were common. In the United States, Horace Mann campaigned for written rather than oral examinations in school districts in Massachusetts.

Late in the nineteenth century, Joseph M. Rice, a pediatrician and a muckraking journalistic crusader for better schools, called for reforms in education to be based on data gathered through objective tests. At the close of World War I, Edward Thorndike developed many techniques for objective testing and popularized this approach to testing. In the twentieth century Ben D. Wood fostered cooperative test development and programs, encouraged state-wide surveys of achievement through tests, and pioneered in electrical equipment to score tests.[1]

EVALUATION INCLUDES APTITUDES AND INTERESTS

Today educators are concerned with aptitudes, interests, personality, and values, as well as with so-called objective and other tests of academic achievement. For instance, educators use aptitude tests in an attempt to learn more of the individual's potential to master a specific series of skills, such as skills in algebra or modern languages, in verbal reasoning or numerical ability, or in clerical or mechanical abilities. Critics believe that aptitude tests are better at predicting potential failure than potential success. Such critics say that past performance is a better predictor of aptitude than a paper and pencil test.

Contemporary educators also use attitude inventories to attempt to identify specific personality problems or areas in which the individual is maladjusted. Such inventories or check lists include the Minnesota Counseling Inventory, the California Personality Test, the Mooney Problem Check List, the Science Research Associates Youth Inventory, the Adjustment Inventory of Stanford University and the Minnesota Multiphasic Personality Inventory (used primarily with adults and college students).

Personality instruments sometimes come under fire from psychologists and educators. Some groups of parents, especially those representing strongly conservative views on school and society, criticize some personality inventories as an invasion of privacy which uses the prestige of science and the sanction of research to justify offensive probing into the personal and private affairs of young people and their families. Supporters of personality tests respond that skilled teachers and counselors will use the findings with discretion and for the personal development of the young person. Some specialists in counseling point out that there is no real evidence that personality questionnaires can be used for personal development; they say that non-test devices, such as private conferences, personal history questionnaires, autobiographies and biographies, diaries and logs, supplemented by sociometric methods and staff reports, can be more useful in helping the young person with his personal perplexities. Also, tests can be faked. For instance, Merle M. Ohlsen says:

[1] Robert L. Ebel, "Measurement in Education," *Encyclopedia of Educational Research*, 4th ed., p. 778.

One does not have to be a tests and measurements expert to discover why most personality questionnaires used in the schools fail to identify children needing special help. If one takes his favorite personality questionnaire, reads the directions, and responds to the items, he will discover that he is able to present whatever picture of himself he wishes to present. This is true for pupils, too. What a pupil tells a staff member about himself through use of the questionnaire will depend on his awareness of his problems, his ability to see the similarity between his problems and those presented in the questionnaire, his ability to understand the statements made, and his willingness to report his problems to those who will see the test results. Whether pupils can, or are willing to, trust those who will see their responses, and whether they can face their problems, will also determine how they respond to the test.

All in all, other sources of information prove more helpful than personality questionnaires.[2]

Interest inventories are also used to determine the likes and preferences of students for vocational guidance purposes. For instance, two long established interest inventories are the Strong Vocational Interest Blank for Men and the Kuder Preference Record-Vocational. The argument for the use of such interest inventories with fifteen- or sixteen-year-olds is that they may be used to identify occupations from which clients may obtain job satisfaction. Critics of interest inventories claim that too early use of data and too specific application to occupations may tend to oversimplify the complex matter of occupational choice. However, as Ohlsen has pointed out, a counselor can note the problems critics cite and still find interest inventories useful in helping young people identify groups of activities in which they have interests.[3]

Since the administration of intelligence and aptitude tests and attitude and interest inventories is usually conducted by means of a school-wide or system-wide testing program, the new teacher normally first encounters his problems of measurement and evaluation in connection with tests of achievement in his or her class.

TESTS OF ACHIEVEMENT

Lively controversy surrounds the use of various tests of achievement at grade levels and in subject fields. For instance, there is considerable disagreement as to the desirability of using objective instead of essay tests.

Teacher supporters of objective tests defend true-false, multiple-choice and similar tests because of their convenience and economy; they claim that they provide scores which are precise and objective. Defenders of essay tests claim that essays provide for a demonstration of a variety of reasoning and communication skills that objective tests cannot measure. In turn, the defenders of

---

[2] Merle M. Ohlsen, *Guidance Services in the Modern School* (New York: Harcourt, Brace & World, 1964), p. 255.
[3] *Ibid.*, p. 293.

objective tests point to the difficulty of appraising essay tests as shown by the wide variety of judgments of essays by presumably qualified readers.

But sponsors of objective tests have their critics too. Banesh Hoffmann, for instance, is particularly critical of multiple-choice tests. He claims that the brighter students often see in the so-called "incorrect responses" some answers which are more creative and intelligent than the responses which the test-maker considers correct. So Hoffmann writes articles against objective testing with such titles as, "Tyranny of Multiple-Choice Test"[4] and "Psychometric Scientism"[5] and a book titled *The Tyranny of Testing*.[6] Defenders of multiple-choice tests claim that Hoffmann's evidence is insufficient and that miskeying or indeterminancy in responses is far less frequent than he claims. Nor do the supporters acknowledge that objective testing is a kind of guessing game, for they believe that a sufficiently long objective test avoids any impairment of the score that might be caused by guessing.

Standardized achievement tests are often used at the beginning of a school year to determine where students stand in achievement as a new school year begins. The tests can then help the teacher plan to identify and meet the student's needs and learning problems. The results of standardized tests also provide answers to parents' questions about their children's standing. Parents are often supporters of standardized testing because it helps them know how their children are doing as compared to national norms.

Standardized achievement tests come under fire from critics who charge that teachers often teach simply what the tests attempt to measure. Teachers are said to concentrate on instruction intended to enable the student to pass such tests as the Regents examinations of the State of New York, a state-wide testing program that has been in existence more than a century. Yet despite such criticisms, standardized testing prospers and proliferates. A major organization in the field is Educational Testing Service of Princeton, New Jersey. Educational Testing Service not only constructs, administers, scores, reports, and analyzes tests; it also carries on research concerning testing and other educational matters.

Yet many teachers use their own teacher-made tests in their classes in addition to or as a substitute for a variety of standardized tests. They argue that the teacher knows best what he is attempting to achieve and can best devise the particular test that tells him and the students whether results are being obtained. In other words, they feel that their own tests can be tailor-made to fit the needs of the pupils. Supporters of objective testing, however, doubt the individual teacher's competence in test-making. They point out that some tests are homemade in the worst sense. But it is probable that most of the tests used in classrooms are made by the teachers themselves.

Meanwhile, some educators and, apparently, a growing group of students believe that tests of all types, whether standardized or teacher-invented, are overused in American classrooms. They see tests as handicaps to effective learn-

---

[4] Banesh Hoffmann, "Tyranny of Multiple-Choice Test," *Harper's* (March 1961), pp. 37–44.
[5] ———, "Psychometric Scientism," *Phi Delta Kappan* (April 1967), pp. 381–386.
[6] ———, *The Tyranny of Testing* (New York: Crowell-Collier, 1962).

ing, and as sources of confusion, frustration, and hostility on the part of students. They point out that in a world in which nothing succeeds like success, nothing fails more dismally than failure—and it is the fate of the less academically able students to be constantly confronted with failure on tests. The sponsors of perceptual psychology, like Earl Kelley, are particularly critical of the destructive effects of an excessive use of tests on human personality.

In the later 1960s when a national assessment program was proposed, critics such as Harold Hand of the University of Illinois opposed national assessment. He feared that the result would be a rigid national testing program similar to that used by ministries of education in European, African and Asian countries and foresaw damaging social consequences to education.[7] The Association for Supervision and Curriculum Development has also viewed national assessment as a step toward federal control of education and a uniform national curriculum. The sponsors of national assessment say that they are simply attempting to provide data through national assessment on the attainment of groups in different regions, residential environments, economic status, and age ranges. They compare the data they gather to the economic information needed to achieve a better economic order in the country.

In July 1970 the National Assessment of Educational Progress reported on national results in science and citizenship, two of ten subject areas in the survey. Through tests, measurements and interviews, about 100,000 people between the ages of 9 and 35 were sampled in these two areas. Among the findings of the federally supported survey was "that the knowledge and learning skills of students and young adults are greater when 'textbook' information is reinforced by practical experience."[8] To minimize the accusation that national assessment could lead to curriculum uniformity, the National Assessment of Educational Progress reported results and encouraged readers to reach their individual conclusions; it avoided presenting highly specific recommendations for national curriculum changes.

In the debate on whether schools test too much or not enough, the public is split, though public opinion leans in the direction of support of more testing. A 1965 Gallup poll showed that 48 percent of the adults in the United States favored the use of a standard examination nation-wide for the granting of diplomas.[9]

STANDARDS FOR GRADING

Perhaps even more controversial than testing is the question of grades, whether on assignments, examinations, or courses. (The word "mark" usually

---

[7] Harold C. Hand, "National Assessment Viewed as the Camel's Nose," *Phi Delta Kappan*, 47 (September 1965), pp. 8–13.
[8] "Learning + Experience = Knowledge, Survey Shows," *The New York Times* (July 8, 1970), p. 1.
[9] American Institute of Public Opinion, "Standard Nation-Wide Examination to Qualify for School Diploma?" Gallup Poll Reports, The Institute, 1965.

applies to grades recorded for courses, rather than to grades on examinations and assignments.) In general, there are three viewpoints: (1) grading by comparison, (2) grading by achievement of individual potential, (3) abolition of grades.

Supporters of grading by comparison believe that pupils should be graded or ranked on assignments, examinations, or courses in comparison with other pupils. Implicit in this assumption is the belief that some kind of standard should be established and that those who achieve beyond this standard should receive marks above the average while those who achieve below the presumed standard should receive lower than average marks. Yet proponents of this view sometimes have difficulty in defining exactly what the chosen standard actually is.

Since the standard must be in relationship to the performance of some other group, the question arises as to which of several groups to use as a standard.

1. Should a national group of a given grade or age be used as a standard for grading performance? If a national standard were used in the United States, the vast majority of students in the slums would be graded somewhere between failure and below average, whereas the majority of students in suburban areas would be graded somewhere between success and above average.

2. Should the mark be based on some smaller unit for comparison, as the community or the school itself? But schools differ as to social class and local factors within a community. If the grade level of a given school is the unit used, problems arise when there are several classes at the same grade level or in the same subject area. What should be done about groups which are sectioned in terms of ability? Should all "fast" sections have a heavy preponderance of high grades and all "slow" sections have a heavy preponderance of low grades and failure? What happens then to the motivation of less able students who are constantly deprived of opportunities for success as measured by grades? If an honors group must demonstrate extremely high accomplishment to receive a high grade, does this penalize such students and reduce their motivation to enroll in an honors group?

3. So a third proposal is to judge to comparative performance of the individual in his own class. The teacher assumes that he knows what a desirable standard or average for his class is and he grades accordingly. Some students receive high grades and some lower grades, depending on academic achievement alone. No consideration is given to the individual's effort or potential. Some criticize this approach as unfair and inhumane.

4. Another possibility in judging performance is to depend on the teacher's idea of what is, in general, typical for the age level or grade or subject. But estimations of what is typical in general vary widely from teacher to teacher. No clear reference group is involved because individual teacher's standards are vague and indefinable.

An alternative to grading based on the comparison of the individual with some group, whether national, school-wide, class, or "typical" of children and youth everywhere, is grading the student on the basis of his own achievement of his potential. In this system of grading the student who proceeds at his maximum capacity receives the better marks. The student who is achieving less than he is capable of achieving receives lower than average marks. The student who is proceeding normally presumably receives an average mark.

The approach to grading on the achievement of potential is defended as opening up the possibility for success to each student. After all, the student is not being graded on someone else's ability—he is being graded on the basis of his own achievement in relationship to his potential. But opponents of this form of grading ask how is the teacher to know whether the student is living up to his potential? Can the teacher really assess this? Some point out that there is a danger that students will be marked high if they are docile, compliant, dutiful, and industrious, and marked low if they are unruly and skeptical, or perhaps creative and original! Still other critics point out that the world is essentially competitive and that grading on the basis of individual achievement might be socially misleading to pupils, and thus in the long run no help to them at all. The academically weak student who tries hard might discover that only the school, not the competitive world, regards him as "A." The brilliant student who does not live up to his potential might be cheated or handicapped by "C's" interpreted as evidence of low ability by college and graduate school admissions officers.

SYMBOLS IN GRADING

In both grading by comparison and grading by the achievement of one's potential, symbols are used to represent marks for the course. A mark is "(1) a single summary symbol, (2) covering achievement in some substantial segment of the educational enterprise, (3) given by an instructor, (4) for purposes of record and report."[10] A mark is often largely derived from previous grades or scores.

The most frequent symbol system used in marking in American schools is A, B, C, D, and F (for some reason, E is usually neglected), sometimes accompanied with modifiers in the form of plus or minus. This system is largely used on the junior and senior high school levels; numerical grading is its nearest competitor. On the elementary school level, marking according to "S" for satisfactory and "U" for unsatisfactory has gained some ground, especially in the kindergarten and primary grades. School systems exist in which all three approaches may be used. For instance, the primary teachers may mark on the basis of "S" and "U," the upper elementary school teachers may use the alphabetical marking system, and the secondary school teachers may use the numerical approach.

CRITICISMS OF GRADING

Fundamental challenges to grading and marking come from those who would abolish the symbol system of marking in education. These opponents say that marks are extremely inaccurate as a judgment of competence; marks differ from teacher to teacher, from school to school, subject field to subject field, commu-

---

[10] Robert L. Thorndike, "Marks and Marking Systems," *Encyclopedia of Educational Research,* 4th ed., p. 759.

nity to community. Marks, it is argued, focus the attention of both teacher and learner on tests and examinations; they cause both teacher and learner to ignore the major objectives of the educational program. Marks, argue the critics, are no way of communicating with parents about a child; to do so requires all of the letters of the alphabet arranged into words, phrases, sentences and paragraphs! A single letter such as "B" alone tells the parent (and the child) very little about his work. The standard marking system is too cold and impersonal to build good relationships between school and home. The communication goes in one direction only, from the school to the home which presumably simply absorbs the information.

Marks, continue the more aggressive of the critics, threaten the welfare of some children by constantly reminding them of their failures. They support a rugged individualism and dog-eat-dog attitude on the part of the student. They distort what the school is actually attempting to do in the way of building humane values. Pressures for high marks on courses and good grades on assignments and examinations lead to cheating and lack of honesty.

ALTERNATIVES TO GRADING

The critics of current marking systems call instead for what they conceive as better communication concerning a student's progress. They are frequently

TABLE 21.1

Methods Used by Elementary and Secondary Teachers to Report Pupil Progress to Parents*

METHOD USED	ELEMENTARY	SECONDARY
A report card with a classified scale of letters	71.6%	83.1%
A scheduled conference with the parents	59.9	20.0
A written description of the pupil's performance	24.3	10.4
A report card with a classified scale of numbers	10.0	8.8
A report card showing percentage grades	2.4	10.0
A report with either pass or fail	8.2	2.6

* Compiled from a nation-wide sample survey.
"Reporting Pupil Progress," *NEA Research Bulletin* (October 1969), p. 75.

proponents of conferences between teachers and parents. In a conference, two-way communication exists and the teacher can learn from the interaction. Parents can learn ways of being helpful at home in the interest of better learning by the young person. Both the program and the potential of the individual student can be considered in a situation which is flexible and adaptable.

Skeptics concerning dependence upon conferences point out the amount of time they require. Teachers have so many students, they say, that they simply do not have time for conferences. Nor are all teachers qualified to carry on an effective conference with parents. Nor will parents wish to come to school for conferences year after year. On the junior and senior high school levels, conferences with several teachers would be necessary. In addition, say the doubters, teachers do not really know their students well enough to hold a conference with parents, since many teachers are essentially subject-oriented and have only vague impressions of the individual pupil's personality.

Another proposal by those who oppose the current marking system is the writing of letters by teachers to parents concerning the progress of the child. Such a letter usually describes both the general work of the class and the individual performance of the individual student. Teachers in schools using reporting through letters have set aside long weekends approximately twice a year for the writing of such communications to parents.

Again, the critics raise the factors of time and teacher abilities in communication. They also point out that a letter is not a two-way communication and that some of the flexibility claimed for the conference approach is lacking. After a while, say the critics, the teacher begins to write the same letter over and over with only minor revisions and thus individualization in communication is not achieved.

Confronted with such criticisms, the exponents of abolition of the marking system often either stand firm on advocacy of conferences and letters or settle for expansion of report cards. Expanded report forms provide an opportunity to say more about a student than can be conveyed through the brief symbol. For instance, categories as to achievement and attitudes may be spelled out and the teacher has an opportunity to check specific factors in several categories. The proponents feel that such an expanded report is much more useful than a few symbols. From such check lists the teacher may develop a profile of the young person which should be useful to the parents. Again, the critics cite the factor of time and point out that teachers often do not know students intimately and consequently react to them with generalized approval in all categories producing a positive or "halo" effect or, on the other hand, with generalized disapproval in all categories.

In answer to the above criticisms, the opponents protest, oftentimes impatiently, that the criticisms are essentially expedient. If the problem is time, the proper solution is to provide the teacher with more time to make conferences, letters, and reports meaningful, rather than to insist upon the inanity of brief symbols. If the problem is money, the community had best provide it, rather than sanction a system of grading which is fundamentally harmful. If the problem is teachers knowing the students, then class size should be reduced and the emphasis should be placed upon individualization in instruction. The proponents of marks regard such proposals as Utopian.

SOCIAL SIGNIFICANCE OF GRADING

The new teacher will probably encounter continuing controversy concerning marking and grading as he works with fellow teachers, administrators, parents, students and community members. In some schools or systems, grading has become a focus of community controversy. Practices as to grading and marking are deeply established in American schools and society. When the grading system is changed in an American school, other factors operating in the institution are also affected, such as ground rules for reward and punishment. Some community citizens perceive changes in or abolition of marking as a threat to the competitive social system which they support. Thus changes in grading appear to some subversive and un-American. Consequently, to change a marking system involves considerable social engineering.

GUIDANCE AND COUNSELING

THE NATURE OF GUIDANCE AND COUNSELING

In the school setting, guidance is the cooperative effort of the counselor and his colleagues to further a child's normal development and help him recognize his problems and improve his adjustment as he moves through school. Counseling is one of several guidance services provided by the best schools.

Ohlsen describes eight possible guidance services:

Counseling services are needed when a reasonably well-adjusted pupil encounters problems that he cannot solve either by himself or with the assistance of such important other people as parents or teachers. . . .

The *child study* service is needed: (1) to determine a pupil's readiness for a school experience or a next phase in the school program—e.g., to begin formal instruction in reading; (2) to help pupils and their teachers determine whether the pupils are making satisfactory progress in their school work; (3) to identify and to diagnose learning problems and to plan appropriate remedial programs for individuals; (4) to identify pupils for special programs involving exceptional children, including both the gifted and the talented as well as the various types of handicapped children; (5) to help individuals discover what they feel they need to know about themselves in order to make intelligent educational and vocational plans; (6) to help pupils to identify and to cope with those distracting and disturbing forces which are interfering with efficient learning and healthy living.

Orientation is designed to help pupils prepare for and adjust to new situations as they progress through the schools—e.g., from home to kindergarten, elementary to junior high school, and senior high school to college or to employment.

The *information service* is a cooperative effort of teachers, counselors, and librarians to obtain appropriate materials, to organize them for the pupils' most efficient use, and to help pupils understand the significance of the materials for them when they cannot do so by themselves. The need for educational and vocational information is obvious. Social information is needed, too. As children grow up, their questions suggest that they want and need a great variety of information.

Educational and vocational planning is especially important in the United States where we have a strong tradition that every man has the right to choose his life work. To choose well a pupil must understand his abilities, aptitudes, and interests, and be familiar with vocational opportunities available to him. He also must be able to relate this information to his perception of himself and to his other important life goals. Similar knowledge of himself and of the opportunities available to him is needed to make intelligent educational plans. For most students these are difficult decisions, and for many the assistance of well-qualified counselors is needed.

Job placement can help a student avoid drifting into a job, often obtained with the assistance of friends and relatives, that has little or no relationship to his most salable skills. For best vocational placement, most youngsters need assistance in identifying and in developing their salable skills, in identifying appropriate jobs for these skills, and in selling themselves to a prospective buyer.

A good *follow-up service* can provide a high school's students with helpful information on what they may expect when they leave school, and provide the staff with suggestions that they can use to improve the school's program. Both types of information are needed by every school.

A carefully planned program for *leadership and social development* provides for the identification and training of prospective leaders, encourages school activities which provide leadership experience, and assists in the development of meaningful social and extra-class activities. It also enlists pupils' assistance in planning and developing meaningful social experiences.

Except for educational and vocational planning, job placement, and follow-up services, which are not essential for most pupils below grade seven, the basic services described above are needed by all youth.[11]

THE TEACHER'S RESPONSIBILITY FOR GUIDANCE

The teacher has a responsibility to further the student's normal development, to help the student recognize his problems, and to improve his adjustment. Again and again, teachers are called upon for informal guidance in both academic and social situations as problems of students arise and as students' perplexities become apparent to teachers.

The teacher's responsibility for more formal guidance, including counseling, varies in practice from level to level. Counseling is an accepting, trusting relationship between a counselor and one or more clients. Within this relationship clients learn to face, express, and cope with their problems, identify alternative solutions, develop the courage and self-confidence to act, and change their behaviors. Students and staff must perceive the counselor as a non-judgmental, trustworthy confidant. Failure to provide such a safe environment in which youth can solve their problems and develop their relationship skills, as well as the

---

[11] Merle M. Ohlsen, *Guidance Services in the Modern School* (New York: Harcourt, Brace & World, 1964), pp. 18, 19, and 20.

The teacher and the counselor work together for the benefit of students. Courtesy of Ron Sherman from Nancy Palmer.

schools' and colleges' failure to provide meaningful participation in solving real social problems, accounts for much of dissident youth's hostile reactions today. They also are saying to teachers, "Merely tolerating us isn't good enough. We want our teachers to care, too, and to help us develop as persons as well as scholars."

Every teacher should exhibit genuine concern for every pupil and be concerned about his general development. But the teacher is not a counselor. Though he does not have the preparation to do counseling, he can and should encourage his pupils to talk to him privately, assess pupil growth, foster growth, and provide appropriate educational, personal, and social information.

At some educational levels the professional help of counselors is currently available; at others, the professional help of counselors hardly exists, though it is steadily growing. With respect to guidance, the preschool, nursery school or kindergarten teacher is still almost always on her own and without the aid of counselors; guidance help, if available, comes from community agencies or school psychologists. The elementary school teacher is also largely dependent upon her own resources, even though elementary school counseling is rapidly increasing. According to one estimate, in 1965 there were between 2,000 and 3,000 elementary school counselors in the United States. Yet if a ratio of one counselor to 600 children in schools were achieved, approximately 54,000 counselors would have been employed in elementary schools in the 1969–70 school year.[12]

[12] Harold F. Cottingham, "Counseling—Elementary Schools," *Encyclopedia of Educational Research* 4th ed., p. 230.

TABLE 21.2

Educational Characteristics of the Civilian Labor Force 25 and Over

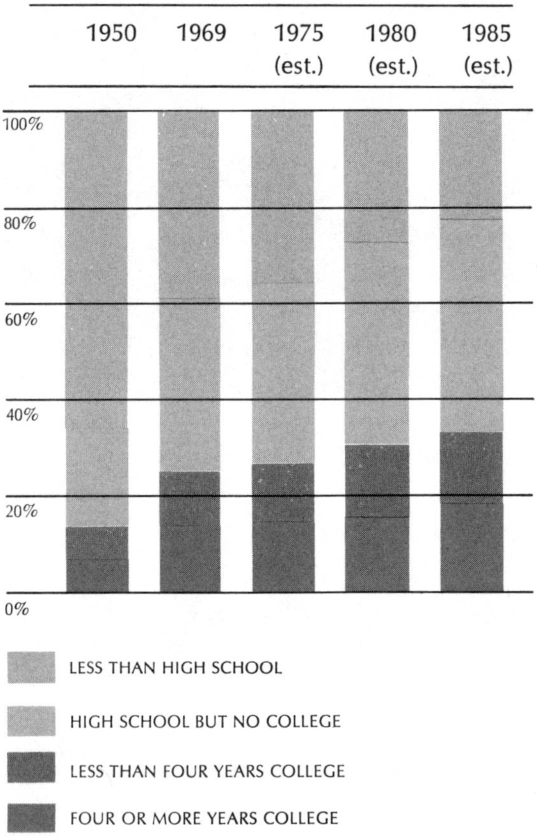

	1950	1969	1975 (est.)	1980 (est.)	1985 (est.)

LESS THAN HIGH SCHOOL

HIGH SCHOOL BUT NO COLLEGE

LESS THAN FOUR YEARS COLLEGE

FOUR OR MORE YEARS COLLEGE

Bureau of Labor Statistics

Ohlsen comments:

Most educators recognize the importance of the elementary school teacher's role in furthering children's normal social, emotional, and intellectual development; increasing their desire to learn; maximizing their independent learning; helping them learn to understand and accept themselves, including what they have a right to expect from themselves; helping them learn to accept and relate to classmates; and helping them discover and develop special interests, abilities, and aptitudes. These goals can best be accomplished with the consulting help of a competent elementary school counselor.

Sometimes a counselor can provide this help best by observing a child in the classroom in order to assess the others' impact upon the child and the child's impact upon others, including the teacher. For other teachers the best assistance is provided in individual sessions. For still others their needs can be best served

A counselor helps the student learn how to write job applications as part of a job-upgrading program. Courtesy of Arthur Leipzig from Ford Foundation.

in groups. For teachers who are helped by such consultation, certain common ingredients seem always to be present: the teacher perceives the relationship as a safe one in which he can participate in his own development; participation is voluntary; the counselor does not function as an evaluator; and the relationship is a mutual one—each giving and receiving aid. It is safe for a participant to admit his problems and his efforts to change are reinforced by the other person or group members.[13]

Specialized help from counselors on the high school level has been more frequently available to students. For instance, in 1965, 41,000 people were engaged in counseling in American secondary schools. Some of these were part-time workers so the full-time equivalent of counselors was 31,000 people and the number of counselors as compared to pupils was 1 to 507. Yet on the high school level such educational statesmen as James Bryant Conant and such leaders in guidance and counseling as C. Gilbert Wrenn were recommending a 1 to 300 ratio.[14]

---

[13] Merle M. Ohlsen, "Elementary School Counseling," *Contemporary Education* (November Supplement, 1969), p. 10.
[14] Martin Katz, "Counseling—Secondary Schools," *Encyclopedia of Educational Research*, 4th ed., p. 248.

An estimate as to the number of college counselors in 1966 was 2,500; the approximate ratio for four-year institutions was one counselor for 2,000 students.[15] Most institutions had a chief student-services officer who usually held such a title as Dean of Students, Dean of Student Affairs, or Dean of Student Services.[16] In most colleges and universities student personnel services are coordinated by one of the above or by a Vice President for Student Affairs. These services include counseling, testing, student activities, student government, leadership development, housing, health, and placement. Usually each one of these services is administered by a specialist in the area. The larger of the universities had counseling centers on the campus. Graduate students could usually use such campus facilities and resources.

So despite the growth of counseling encouraged by increased support of the federal government throughout the decade of the 1960s, teachers still retained a substantial responsibility for guidance—the whole responsibility when counselors were lacking and a shared responsibility when counselors were present in schools or colleges.

When teachers share a responsibility for guidance with counselors, perplexing questions frequently arise. What is the responsibility of the teacher? What is the responsibility of the counselor? To some, the question is not an issue; they believe that guidance and education are one and the same and that all counselors are teachers and all teachers are counselors. This position is frequently taken by those who hold a broad concept of the functions of the teacher. On the other hand, some think that the special province of counselors is to help pupils to choose among the possible courses of action open to them. According to this point of view, the guidance function emphasizes decisions, goals, value judgments, and plans, whereas instruction is a matter of acquiring knowledge, skills, facts, concepts, etc. Obviously this is not a satisfactory description of instruction from the point of view of those who hold that instruction should meet the needs of the individual learner, or throw light on the social realities of the times, or develop value judgments, or all three.

A sensible resolution of the question of the responsibility of the teacher and the responsibility of the counselor is to recognize that, though school counselors are educators, they perform specialized services which require specialized knowledge and skills different from (but not better than) teachers. The counselor's role stresses helping relationships. A good counselor works with students on problems on which they want help. He helps students come to know themselves. He helps them locate and appraise information about opportunities available to them. He helps them to learn to make decisions. He consults teachers, administrators and parents as he works. In short, the effective counselor *counsels.*

In the present state of education the counselor needs all of the help from teachers he can obtain with respect to guidance and counseling. On the secondary school level, for instance, the counselor often finds himself busy helping

---

[15] Ralph F. Berdie, "Counseling—College and University," *Encyclopedia of Educational Research,*" 4th ed., p. 220.   [16] *Ibid.,* p. 219.

students with their choices of college and their planning of high school programs. It is usually his responsibility to counsel low achievers and to counsel on subject matter difficulties. Project Talent found that "adjustment counseling was practiced regularly in a majority of the schools only insofar as it pertained to students' problems with teachers (thus perhaps overlapping the academic area); counseling on personal and family problems, or on relations with classmates, took place regularly in only about a third of the schools."[17] Counselors, like teachers, find themselves engaged in a variety of activities such as clerical work, supervising study halls, scoring tests, etc., and are unable to give as much time as they would wish to their central activity, which they describe as "counseling students." A study by C. Gilbert Wrenn during the 1960s showed that only about one-third of the full-time counselors on the secondary school level were able to spend as much as half of their time with this basic and distinctive activity.[18]

In order to protect school counselors from being assigned duties which damage their relationship with students and staff and to allow more time for essential professional duties, American School Counselors Association (1967) published a carefully prepared job definition. These duties stress the counselor's helping relationships: counseling students concerning the problems with which they want assistance, helping students to get to know themselves, helping them locate and evaluate information concerning the opportunities available to them, helping them learn to make decisions and learning to act upon their decisions.

The understanding and support of teachers and administrators is essential for counselors to implement their professional role. Counselors must win the confidence of the students and staff—an essential in counseling students and in functioning as a consultant for colleagues and parents. Though personal counseling is not provided in all schools, youth recognize the need for it. However, young people, and especially dissident youth, can accept it only from those who are unequivocal confidants.

THEORIES OF GUIDANCE AND COUNSELING

Since guidance is a necessary part of the work of the teacher, the new teacher should familiarize himself through specialized reading and courses with the major current theories of counseling: psychoanalytic theory, behavior theory, trait-factor theory, and client-centered counseling. Psychoanalytic techniques are seldom used by counselors in schools, although Freudian theory is sometimes helpful to teachers in understanding personality. Behavior theory is used more frequently in clinics than schools, though it is developing in some schools. The two theories which have had wider use in schools are trait-factor theory and client-centered counseling.

---

[17] Martin Katz, "Counseling—Secondary Schools," *Encyclopedia of Educational Research*, 4th ed., p. 243.
[18] C. Gilbert Wrenn, *The Counselor in a Changing World* (Washington, D.C.: American Personnel and Guidance Association, 1962), p. 114.

Counseling grew out of the vocational guidance movement of the early twentieth century. One student of the movement reports that counseling "was fathered by economics" (through the growth of technology and the division of labor), "mothered by ideologies" (through interpretations of democracy which stressed reform and humanitarianism), "housed largely in secondary schools" (though it had started in a settlement house), and "befriended by psychology" (particularly through measurement and clinical work). In any case, counseling in secondary schools initially stressed correct, wise, and right choices so that the student would be guided into the "right occupation." To predict the "right occupation," the counselor had to discover the key traits of the student. But the occupational plans of students change. Their choices of careers do not remain consistent. The trait-factor theory in which the counselor diagnoses the student's interests and aptitudes, furnishes information on jobs, and relates the student's traits to job requirements did not seem adequate to some theorists.

Carl Rogers, whose views we mentioned in chapter 19 in connection with perceptual psychology, was a pioneer in client-centered counseling, originally called nondirective counseling. Rogers emphasized that individuals change and have the capacity to change. He believed that attitudes and emotions often became blocks to the individual's acceptance of himself and thus kept him from solving his problems rationally. Consequently, Rogers stressed self-acceptance so that the individual might grow and become a self-actualizing personality. Counselors who follow the Rogers' viewpoint depart from a clinical method stressing analysis, synthesis, diagnosis, prognosis, counseling or treatment, and follow-up. Doubtful of too much measurement and prediction, the client-centered counselor stresses personal relationships between counselor and student and tries to develop a warm and permissive atmosphere which does not threaten the student. Emphasis is on spontaneity and mutual trust rather than on techniques. As the title of a widely read yearbook of the Association for Supervision and Curriculum Development puts it, the emphasis today is on "perceiving, behaving, becoming."

GUIDANCE AND EVALUATION ARE INESCAPABLE

The teacher is a guidance worker too. He tries to understand the behavior of students and identify their problems. In his own way, he tries to be helpful to them as to vocational planning, educational decisions, and personal problems. He tries both to create an accepting environment for growth through the schools and to help parents with the needs of their children. He tries to help a student develop values, appraise himself, develop a healthy self-concept, make choices, and achieve his potential. Guidance is an inescapable aspect of the teacher's work.

However, without the help of a qualified counselor the teacher is limited in what he can do. With the help of a qualified counselor, the quality of the teacher's services can be improved by the addition of the counselor's specialized services.

Equally inescapable is evaluation. Evaluation today is not limited to the field of academic achievement alone; it also embraces attitudes and interests. Contemporary controversies over testing include not only the continuing debate between advocates of objective tests and those who support such tests as essay examinations; today testing in American schools, whether standardized achievement or teacher-developed, is regarded by some critics as excessive. Grades and marks are also under fire; newer ways of reporting progress—check lists, conferences, and letters—are proposed. Proponents of grades and marks are forced to clarify which groups they propose to use when they make comparisons. Recognition grows that testing and grading programs are not simply matters for technicians but, instead, have significant social implications in American life.

DISCUSSION

1. What are the several phases involved in evaluation? How is evaluation different from measurements? Are there ways of measuring other than testing?
2. What are the various methods that you as a teacher will use to evaluate the progress of your pupils? Which of these methods will be completely objective?
3. Why do schools use interest inventories? Attitude appraisals? Personality inventories? Are these matters any of the school's business?
4. Why are personality instruments frequently considered invalid? What arguments support their use?
5. Should the same achievement or aptitude test series be used throughout all grade levels? Why or why not?
6. What are your arguments in favor of the use of teacher-made tests? In opposition?
7. What are the uses and abuses of tests and grades?
8. Do you believe performance should be graded in relation to national norms, group norms, or individual norms? Defend your position.
9. What grading procedure do you intend to use with your classes?
10. What is your own viewpoint on the use of symbols in grading as contrasted to more substantial reports? What alternatives to symbols do we usually have?
11. Why does a change in a marking system frequently prove controversial? Is there a relationship between grading and marking and an American social system characterized by competition?
12. What are the major guidance services of a good school? Which of these are you aware of from your own experience as a high school student?
13. What are the teacher's and counselor's guidance roles? How might their respective areas of responsibility best be defined?

14. What are the major theories currently being used in school counseling? Do you see any advantages or disadvantages in any of these theories?

INVOLVEMENT

1. Compile a useful list of intelligence, achievement, and personality tests that you can use as an elementary teacher. Be sure to include the title, authors, publishers (with addresses). Indicate opposite each test its principal use.
2. Explore with your class the various personality and interest inventories members may have experienced. Is there any evidence from accounts of these experiences of "faking" or "beating the tests"?
3. Using a familiar class level and subject matter for illustrative purposes, cite the major arguments supporting the contention that pupil evaluation is most successful when based on limited, well-defined educational objectives.
4. Write several specific objectives in your area of specialization and have other class members criticize them.
5. According to class members, do tests of achievement constitute valid instruments for college admission, for decisions on whether one passes courses, etc.? Explore the implications of opinions by class members.
6. List outcomes in your teaching area that could not be measured by an (a) oral test (b) essay test (c) short-answer tests.
7. Consider your own college or university's grading policies. To what extent do they seem sound or unsound? If a consensus exists in your class, communicate it to the administration of your school.
8. Discuss the matter of grades and marks with an experienced teacher. What are his reactions to the various points of view expressed in the chapter?
9. Visit a community agency which engages in counseling with school-age children and youth. What training do such counselors have? What relationships do they have to the schools?
10. Interview elementary and secondary school counselors. How do they see their role in relation to their student clients and the other school personnel?
11. Spend a day with a classroom teacher. In what ways does he or she use counseling skills in deaing with all the personal relationships in which he or she is involved?
12. Interview the personnel director of a school system. What does he or she see as the role of the school counselor? How does he or she evaluate the relative success of the counselors in the system?

BIBLIOGRAPHY

Ahmann, J. Stanley and Marvin D. Glock. *Evaluating Pupil Growth,* 3rd ed. Boston: Allyn and Bacon, 1967. A helpful book on purposes and procedures in evaluation.

Bentley, Joseph C. ed. *The Counselor's Role: Commentary and Readings.* Boston: Houghton Mifflin, 1968. The roles of the counselor, as viewed by specialists.

Boy, Angels V. and Gerald J. Pine. *The Counselor in the Schools: A Reconceptualization.* Boston: Houghton Mifflin, 1968. A framework of phenomenology, humanistic psychology, existential thought, and client-centered counseling theory.

Faust, Verne. *The Counselor-Consultant in the Elementary School.* Boston: Houghton Mifflin, 1968. Deals with elementary school counseling as a profession in its own right and develops a human behavior rationale for the counselor's role.

Grobman, Hulda. *Evaluation Activities of Curriculum Projects.* Chicago: Rand McNally, 1969. The context of curriculum evaluation, what to evaluate, whom to evaluate, how do we evaluate, and some reasonable expectations from evaluation of projects.

Gronlund, Norman E. *Measurement and Evaluation in Teaching.* New York: Macmillan, 1965. Principles and procedures of the evaluative process including objectives, instruments, and using results.

Gronlund, Norman E. *Constructing Achievement Tests.* Englewood Cliffs, N.J.: Prentice-Hall, 1968. For teachers and prospective teachers to assist in the construction of achievement tests which measure clearly defined learning outcomes in harmony with instructional objectives.

Hansen, James C. and Richard R. Stevie. *Elementary School Guidance.* New York: Macmillan, 1969. A behavioral approach to the concept of elementary school guidance, the function of various pupil personnel specialists, and the services provided within a guidance program.

Hoffmann, Banesh. *The Tyranny of Testing.* New York: Crowell-Collier, 1962. Militant and vigorous condemnation of what the author conceives as the abuses of testing.

Johnson, Mauritz, Jr., William E. Busaker, and Fred Q. Bowman, Jr. *Junior High School Guidance.* New York: Harper and Brothers, 1961. Historical, philosophical, and administrative backgrounds concerning guidance in the junior high school.

Linden, James D. and Kathryn W. Linden. *Tests on Trial.* Boston: Houghton Mifflin, 1968. For the test consumer in search of information about tests and testing. A resource which provides data on selected tests in common use.

Lindzey, Gardner and Calvin S. Hall, eds. *Theories of Personality: Primary Sources and Research.* New York: John Wiley and Sons, 1965. The readings provide further insight into such major thinkers as Freud, Jung, and Allport and afford the reader an opportunity to evaluate and compare their contributions.

McClary, George O. *Interpreting Guidance Programs to Pupils.* Boston: Houghton Mifflin, 1968. To stimulate actions and activities which will encourage pupils to make more and better use of guidance services.

Miller, Carroll. *Guidance Services: An Introduction.* New York: Harper, 1965. Material on guidance principles and techniques.

Ohlsen, Merle M. *Guidance Services in the Modern School.* New York: Harcourt, Brace and World, 1964. A comprehensive and definitive book on guidance services for those who conduct such services and those who relate to them.

Sachs, Benjamin M. *The Student, the Interview, and the Curriculum: Dynamics of Counseling in the School.* Boston: Houghton Mifflin, 1966. Resources which teachers and counselors must use in meeting needs of individual students. An attempt to decrease the distance between teacher and counselor.

Sodola, Quentin and Kahmer Stordal. *Basic Educational Tests and Measurements.* Chicago: Science Research Associates, 1967. The theoretical and applied concepts essential to an understanding of educational measurement.

Smith, Fred and Sam Adams. *Educational Measurement for the Classroom Teacher.* New York: Harper and Row, 1966. The use of teacher-made and standardized tests as tools of instruction in teaching.

Steffler, Buford. *Theories of Counseling.* New York: McGraw-Hill, 1965. Descriptions of the major positions with regard to counseling, as distinguished from psychotherapy, that are now determining the form that this expanding activity is taking.

Wilhelms, Fred T., ed. *Evaluation as Feedback and Guide.* Association for Supervision and Curriculum Development, NEA, 1967. Evaluation should provide feedback and guidance for all of education. Endorses a new approach to replace marking and grading.

AUDIO-VISUAL MATERIALS

Evaluation (Vimcet Associates, 45 frs., Color, Audio Tape) How the efficacy of instructional efforts is to be judged. Pre-assessment, test design and data interpretation.

Selecting an Achievement Test (Educational Testing Service, 14 Min.) Outlines criteria to follow in the selection of achievement tests, such as content validity, relevance for a given course and proper balance of materials included.

What's the Good of a Test? (Journal Films, 12 Min., Color) Describes how to use tests, what tests measure and how to prepare for and take a test. Explains and illustrates composition or essay questions, objective questions and standardized tests.

Determining Student Grades (Bel Mort Films, 43 frs., Color) Uses drawings to analyze student competitive grading, grading a student against his ability to learn, and attempts to combine the first two approaches.

Report Card (Holt, Rinehart and Winston, 12 Min., Color) An open-ended film which examines the problem of the basis on which students should be graded.

As They Grow—Elementary Guidance—New Dimensions in Meeting Pupil Needs, A Series (Guidance Associates, 52 fr., Color, Record) Provides insights into elementary guidance systems. Examines the role of the guidance counselor.

Elementary Classroom Guidance (BFA, 85 fr., Color, Record) Emphasizes well set-up classrooms and the proper use of cumulative records to help guide primary children through their learning experiences.

Role of the Counselor in the Secondary School (Guidance Associates, 77 fr., Color, Record) Probes functions of the secondary school counselor, such as interaction with teachers and parents, assistance with career and course selection, record keeping and interpretation.

Challenge of Change: The Case for Counseling (NET, 29 Min., Color) A view of the guidance process in schools and the individuals who should be involved.

Your Child's Mental Health (NEA, 72 fr., Color, Record) Discusses the importance of a healthy mental outlook and factors that could cause mental problems.

TWENTY-TWO

WHAT WILL THE SCHOOLS OF THE YEAR 2000 BE LIKE?

For many, the year 2000 may seem quite distant. But a person born in 1951 will be 49 years old in that year, and a person born in 1954 will be 46. While these may not be the most eagerly anticipated birthdays in a person's life, they do represent the middle, rather than the old age years. Neither the person born in 1951 nor the one born in 1954 will reach today's usual age of retirement, 65, until near the end of the second decade of the century. So, should you choose teaching as your career, the year 2000 will represent perhaps the most productive segment of your career. You should be near the top of your form, professionally speaking, in the year 2000. It is, in reality, that *near*, rather than that *distant*.

What might education and society be like in the year 2000? Some may regard such questions as both foolish and fruitless, saying that the future is impossible to predict. To support their contention, they cite earlier efforts of intellectuals to define the future, including the Utopian dreams developed throughout the ages, from those of Plato to those of Edward Bellamy, and the Inferno-like predictions of Dante, H. G. Wells, Aldous Huxley, and George Orwell.

In the 1970s it is quite evident that neither the Utopian dream nor the predicted Inferno has materialized, and that neither Heaven nor Hell has yet prevailed. For reasons such as these, some scholars believe that speculating about the future is no more reputable than consulting the astrologer, and that it is about as reliable as the predictions contained in the farmer's almanac.

Yet speculating on (or attempting to identify probable characteristics of) the future today is conducted differently from the tradition of prophesying Utopias or Infernos. Scholars today have better tools for use in speculating on the future than their predecessors. Consequently many reputable scholars are today engaged in "futurism," and have developed some noteworthy analyses of "future states."

The American Academy of Arts and Sciences devoted the Summer 1967 issue of *Daedalus* to a report by the Academy's Commission on the Year 2000. In this publication, outstanding scholars, primarily physical and behavioral scientists and some humanists, presented papers relating to various aspects of the future, and interacted with each other.[1] *The Year 2000*, by Herman Kahn and Anthony J. Wiener, provides a comprehensive fact base for making assumptions about the future.[2] A versatile social scientist, Donald N. Michael, specifies the dangers which lie ahead for "the unprepared society."[3]

Many educators are also playing a role in contemporary speculation on the future. In an earlier chapter of this book (chapter 2), you were introduced to *The High School of the Future*.[4] Harold Shane has contributed insightful articles in *Phi Delta Kappan*, "Future Shock and the Curriculum,"[5] and "Future-Planning and the Curriculum."[6] The author of this book has written *The Year 2000: Teacher Education*[7] upon which he will also draw in this chapter.

Especially helpful to educators are the publications that were prepared by a project in eight western states called *Designing Education for the Future*. Highly important to new teachers are three volumes in the series which deal with prospective changes in society, the educational implications of these changes, and emerging teacher education.[8]

Some of the more promising efforts relating to probable futures differ from the types of prophecies used to describe the Utopias and the Infernos in that they incorporate the concept that various kinds of futures are possible. Today's scholars are therefore concerned with describing *alternative futures,* rather than with describing a single predefined future.

Kenneth E. Boulding, a distinguished economist and student of society, provided a valuable insight concerning the importance of the idea of *alternative*

---

[1] *Daedalus*, 96 (Summer 1967).
[2] Herman Kahn and Anthony J. Wiener, *The Year 2000: A Framework for Speculation on the Next Thirty Three Years* (New York: Macmillan, 1967).
[3] Donald N. Michael, *The Unprepared Society: Planning for a Precarious Future*, 10th John Dewey Society Lecture (New York: Basic, 1968).
[4] William M. Alexander (ed.), *The High School of the Future: A Memorial to Kimball Wiles* (Columbus, Ohio: Charles E. Merrill, 1969).
[5] Harold Shane, "Future Shock and the Curriculum," *Phi Delta Kappan*, 49 (October 1967), pp. 67–70.
[6] Harold G. Shane and June Grant Shane, "Future-Planning and the Curriculum," *Phi Delta Kappan*, 49 (March 1968), pp. 372–377.
[7] William Van Til, *The Year 2000: Teacher Education* (Terre Haute, Ind.: Indiana State University, 1968).
[8] Edgar L. Morphet and Charles O. Ryan (eds.), *Prospective Changes in Society by 1980*, Designing Education for the Future, Number 1 (New York: Citation Press, 1967); idem, *Implications for Education of Prospective Changes in Society*, Designing Education for the Future, Number 2 (New York: Citation Press, 1967); Edgar L. Morphet and David L. Jesser (eds.) *Preparing Educators to Meet Emerging Needs*, Designing Education for the Future, Number 7 (New York: Citation Press, 1969).

futures with his concept of "system breaks."[9] System breaks refer to discontinuities, surprises, turning points, or sudden changes in the characteristics of a system—all of which are unpredictable or only partially predictable in advance.

If system breaks are distinct possibilities (and past history has repeatedly demonstrated that they do occur), then those who are concerned with forecastiing probable futures cannot assume that present trends will continue and that the future will simply be an extension of the present. Such scholars must also include provision for the possible futures that may exist as a result of system breaks. On the basis of all pertinent information, the futurist sets forth or forecasts the future (or futures) most likely to emerge.

Since in contemporary futurism alternative futures are set forth and considered, speculation on the future can be an important aid in clarifying alternative courses of action in the present. In other words, futurism can help modern man, including educators, to confront their present problems squarely and to systematically plan for feasible solutions. Contemporary futurism is not a form of escapism. It is a procedure that tends to force man to face realities.

POSSIBLE SYSTEM BREAKS AND THEIR CONSEQUENCES

Because of the nature of system breaks, it cannot be predicted when they will occur. Scholars can indicate, however, that they *may* occur at some point in time. This was true in the case of the discovery of ways of harnessing nuclear energy, and in the development of materials designed to increase agricultural production. System breaks of this nature have occurred in the past. System breaks, of the type listed in the sampling below, *may* occur in the future:

Developments in automation and cybernation may increase production to an unimaginable high, and at the same time make possible more leisure time than may now be thought possible.

Developments in communications (especially in laser technology) may make possible virtually exponential increases in man's ability to communicate with fellow men throughout the world.

Developments in oceanography may make possible whole new sources of food.

Developments in energy sources may result in "clean," nonpolluting fuels.

Developments in medicine, geriatrics and biochemistry may result in discovery of techniques whereby the education of a person may be facilitated through drugs, chemicals, and transplants.

System breaks of the type described above are potentially beneficial. Other types of system breaks related to the development of nuclear weaponry, poisonous and nerve gasses, environmental pollutants, famine, overpopulation, and social imbalances are, of course, potentially harmful. But regardless of

---

[9] Kenneth E. Boulding, "Expecting the Unexpected: The Uncertain Future of Knowledge and Technology," *Prospective . . . 1980,* p. 203.

possible consequences, system breaks, if and when they occur, will cause the role of education to change dramatically. Consider the following implications for education of the five potential and beneficial system breaks described above:

If, in the year 2000, the average worker only had to devote 20 hours per week to his task, the educational system would have to place major emphasis upon *leisure-time* experiences, rather than upon *work-experience* activities.

If, in the year 2000, it is possible and feasible to converse, through both audio and video media, with people throughout the world, the educational system would have to place much emphasis upon "human-to-human" aspects of education.

If, in the year 2000, production of new sources of foodstuff from the oceans proves to be economical and feasible, the educational system will have to provide entire new curriculums devoted to "marine agriculture."

If, in the year 2000, nonpolluting energy sources are available at reasonable costs, industry will be able to produce, at an even greater rate than at present, goods for all people, and mass transportation facilities will be available to virtually everyone. The educational system will have to assume major responsibility for the development of people who are capable of using such goods and facilities in the most advantageous manner.

If, in the year 2000, it is possible to induce or facilitate learning through drugs, nerve stimulants or transplants, the educational system would have to include not only persons trained in the educative process, but persons trained in medicine, biochemistry, and applied psychology as well.

It may well be that by the year 2000 none of the types of system breaks described here will have occurred. On the other hand, it is entirely possible that at least several will have taken place. An even more likely possibility exists that portions or segments of the developments described above will have occurred.

Obviously, all system breaks are not always pleasant to contemplate. Here are a sampling of horrible possibilities:

1. The potentiality exists of nuclear war which would create global devastation through reducing much of the world to rubble; such a war would exterminate many human beings.

2. The potentiality exists of worldwide famine accompanied by the poisoning of air, land, and water through a combination of an unchecked population explosion and an unstemmed pollution of the earth's natural resources.

3. The possibility exists of a social revolution taking the form of anarchy in a society in which the establishment wages war but is unable to cope with domestic social problems and in which the poor, the black, and the young destroy the social institutions.

If any of these system breaks prevailed, what would education be like in the year 2000?

If the year 2000 saw the United States participating in a global nuclear war, schools would be converted into hospitals and refugee centers. To the extent that education was maintained, the attempt would be to develop manpower for the war effort and ingenuity to insure national survival. As to values, the schools would probably teach unquestioning loyalty to our side.

If overpopulation and pollution prevailed, human beings would be so busy averting famine and environmental disasters that all available young people would be working for survival. The schools might be used simply as assignment centers for needed jobs.

If the year 2000 were a time of a revolution characterized by anarchy, the schools, as a representative of social authority, would be occupied by mobs, and destroyed by burning and vandalism. New versions of education would take place in nonschool settings.

You may well point out that such extreme scenarios are unlikely. You may be quite right that these are unlikely alternatives. We hope so. Yet possible system breaks, even as drastic as these, must be taken into account as we speculate on the future and must influence our own planning today toward desirable futures.

Rather than such extreme system breaks as those described above, the year 2000 may be a time when such tendencies are overcome or at least contained by the going system. For example, war may have been eliminated or may take the form of small regional "brushfires," readily contained. Problems of overpopulation and pollution may have been conquered or worldwide effective famine-relief systems and emergency approaches to particular environmental problems may have been put into effect. The causes of anarchic revolution and social imbalance may have been overcome as ghettos and wars are eliminated and effective education and meaningful employment prevail or the social structure may prove resilient enough to contain a continuing degree of violence and social anger. Should any of these developments take place, there would be substantial changes in American society but not sharp system breaks.

THE MOST LIKELY AMERICAN SOCIETY OF THE YEAR 2000

If we assume that substantial social changes—based on prevailing trends rather than on major system breaks—will take place in the United States between now and the year 2000, we can speculate on the American society most likely to exist at that time. Obviously, there is no inevitability in the trends described here; they are simply statements of the way things appear to be going.

So we will make the assumption that in the year 2000 the United States will still exist as a nation and as a major world power. By that time the states of the Union may number 52 instead of 50, should Puerto Rico and perhaps the Virgin Islands be admitted.

The United States of the year 2000 will be more heavily populated than is the United States of the early 1970s; current estimates place the probable American population from 280 to 300 million at the turn of the century. This population will live primarily in urban areas. A report of the National

Goals Research Staff, *Toward Balanced Growth: Quantity with Quality,* issued in 1970, predicted that by the year 2000, 70 percent of the population of the United States will live in twelve metropolitan areas.[10] By 2000, several metropolitan areas will have agglomerated into three megalopoli, in which will be found almost half of the American people. According to Kahn and Wiener, these urban complexes will be Boswash (the Boston to Washington complex), Chipitts (the Chicago along the Great Lakes to Pittsburgh complex), and Sansan (the San Diego to Santa Barbara—eventually San Francisco—complex).[11]

FIGURE 22.1

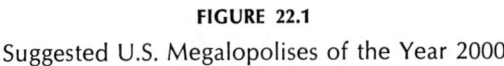

Suggested U.S. Megalopolises of the Year 2000

Herman Kahn and Anthony J. Wiener, "The Next Thirty-Three Years: A Framework for Speculation," pp. 73–100 in Daniel Bell, *Toward the Year 2000: Work in Progress* (Boston: Houghton Mifflin, 1968).

The futurists expect that the United States will have a substantially higher gross national product (GNP) than it now has (932 billion in 1969, according

---

[10] *New York Times,* "Panel Finds Need to Inspire Debate on Nation's Goals" (July 19, 1970), pp. 1, 47.
[11] Herman Kahn and Anthony J. Wiener, "The Next Thirty Three Years: A Framework for Speculation," *Daedalus* (Summer 1967), pp. 718–719. See also Kahn and Wiener, *The Year 2000,* pp. 61–62.

to the National Goals Research Staff) and even more important, that it will have a substantially higher GNP per capita (or person). According to the President of Resources for the Future, "A two-thirds increase in GNP in the next 15 years seems altogether reasonable."[12] Kahn and Wiener say, "The surprise-free United States economic scenario calls for a $1 trillion economy in 1975, $1.5 trillion in 1985, about $3 trillion in the year 2000."[13] In general, those who comment on gross national product in the year 2000 assume that it could range from double to three and a half times the 1965 figure (calculated in terms of 1965 dollars rather than inflationary dollars).

The increase in the GNP described above is related to the predicted further increase in scientific knowledge and technological development in the United States. Productive power in the year 2000 will be increased by continued growth in computer technology, and by further automated, cybernated, and electronic expansion.

As the United States continues to develop, it (paradoxically) is expected to follow both centralizing and decentralizing tendencies. The United States has developed as "a national society," depending heavily upon centralization in government, in mass media, and in modern transportation.[14] Yet at the same time there may well be an expansion or extension of "creative federalism," with governmental power delegated to states, regions, and localities. A leading political scientist has predicted that: (1) all governments will continue to grow; (2) sharing will increase; (3) the states will have to act with great vigor to maintain their traditional position in the governmental structures; and (4) localities will have to struggle for policy control—as distinct from administrative control—of new programs.[15]

The nature and role of work will be influenced by the probability of plenty in the American society of the year 2000, with problems of production largely solved because of (1) the ability of Americans to combine industrial facilities with a good geographic location, (2) a substantial resource base, and (3) a constantly innovating technology. As a result there likely will be different work patterns among the population. Many, perhaps most, Americans will work about a thirty to thirty-two hour week.[16] Colm points out that hours of work which were about thirty-eight and a half per week in the late 1960s by 1980 may become approximately thirty-six hours. "In addition it may become common to have a sabbatical for labor; that is, a period in which a worker, after several years of work may need retraining or additional training, travel, or to pursue some other activity of his choice."[17] But while the employed worker is working his

---

[12] Joseph L. Fisher, "Natural Resource Trends and Their Implications," Prospective . . . 1980, p. 9.
[13] Kahn and Wiener, The Year 2000, p. 167.
[14] Daniel Bell, "The Year 2000—The Trajectory of An Idea," Daedalus (Summer 1967), p. 643.
[15] Daniel J. Elazar, "The American Partnership: The Next Half Generation," Prospective . . . 1980, pp. 111–115.
[16] Kahn and Weiner, The Year 2000, p. 175.
[17] Gerhard Colm, "Prospective Economic Developments," Prospective . . . 1980, p. 92.

shorter work week, the unequipped or unemployable or unable population may not be working at all and may be supported at a subsistence level in a welfare-oriented state. Meanwhile a leadership group, holding specialized key positions by virtue of their intellectual capabilities may be overworking themselves because of a combination of forces, factors, and drives. Key personnel will work hard for reasons of prestige, status, increased income, and a sheer desire to accomplish and lead. The leisure-time problems and needs of each of these groups—the employed workers, the unemployable population, and the specialized leaders—will obviously be very different each from the other.

Meanwhile, the knowledge explosion will continue its convulsive leaps, and full utilization of knowledge sources will become essential for anyone who aspires to leadership and social regard.

One of the most fascinating areas for speculation is the question of goals or directions for American society in the year 2000. It is difficult to extrapolate curves into the future as to norms and values. Yet if we do so, the likelihood is that America will move from the older established tradition of stressing hard work, thrift, and spare living and toward a more leisure-oriented, free-spending and hedonistic pattern of living. One can already see indications of this direction in books on contemporary youth such as *The Age of Aquarius*.[18] One might even speculate that of the familiar trilogy of the Declaration of Independence, "life, liberty, and the pursuit of happiness," the latter may come into its own.

The rights to life and liberty will probably be taken for granted; these will be expected by the population as a matter of course, even though struggles relating to the latter may take place, primarily in resistance to invasions of privacy and impersonal bureaucratic controls. But it may well be that the pursuit of happiness will be of paramount concern to a pleasure-seeking America. In the society of the year 2000 there may be time available for members of that society to enjoy life—to engage in avocational activities, travel, cultural enrichment, and other self-renewing activities.

Willis Harman, Director of the Educational Policy Research Center at Stanford, has perceptively examined possible futures, and has suggested that the United States, as a nation, will have to choose between two basic alternative types of society. One alternative would appear to be a militaristic, police-state society, or, as he phrases it, a "garrison state"; the other would be a more humanistic society, or in Harman's term, a "person-centered society."[19] Other thinkers such as Kahn and Wiener see a basic long-term multifold trend toward "increasingly sensate (empirical, this worldly, secular, humanistic, pragmatic, utilitarian, contractual, epicurean, or hedonistic) cultures."[20]

---

[18] William Braden, *The Age of Aquarius: Technology and the Cultural Revolution* (New York: Quadrangle Books, 1970).
[19] Willis W. Harman, "The Nature of Our Changing Society: Implications for Schools," unpublished paper (Eugene, Ore.: ERIC Clearinghouse on Educational Administration, October 1969).
[20] Kahn and Wiener, "The Next . . . Years," p. 706.

Osaka Exposition, 1970. Courtesy of UPI.

Commentators on future American society tend to agree that it will not be a Utopia by the year 2000. Just as Americans of the early 1970s had their problems relating to war and peace, integration and desegregation, poverty and affluence, urban ghettos and suburban enclaves, and alienated youth and conservative middle-age, so also will the citizens in the year 2000 be faced with problems that are somewhat similar in nature, including obsolescent housing, organized crime, environmental pollution, and difficult intergovernmental relationships. Harman has pointed out that a serious gap exists between our *professed values* (what we say we believe) and our *operative values* (what our actions demonstrate our real beliefs are). The degree to which society and education will be able to resolve or alleviate those social problems of 2000 will depend, in no small measure, on whether this gap in values can be narrowed.

In summary, many scholars are suggesting that the most predictable and probable forces and factors that will have shaped American society by the year 2000 will be these:

1. The continuance of the United States as a nation and as a world power
2. An expanded U.S. population estimated at 300 million
3. Increased urbanization
4. Increase in urban megalopolitan complexes containing almost one-half of the people
5. A markedly higher gross national product
6. Continued expansion of scientific knowledge and technological development—especially in computerized, automated, cybernated, and electronic areas
7. An increasingly national or centralized society concurrent with an increasingly decentralized society
8. Less working time for the ordinary worker; unemployability for the untrained or unable; hard work by the leadership group

9. Expansion of the knowledge explosion
10. Expansion of the pursuit of happiness goal in American life as hedonism increasingly replaces puritanism
11. The continuance of social problems
12. A delay in the arrival of either Utopia or Inferno

THE MOST LIKELY AMERICAN EDUCATION IN THE YEAR 2000

In order to examine the probable educational system of the future, one must begin with population and its distribution. Which levels of the educational ladder will be characterized by sharp population increases and which will simply hold their own? The predictions given below are cautious, and are limited to the years until 1980.

The increase at the elementary school level should be the most manageable of all increases. In the United States, elementary education for all of the children of all of the people, with negligible exceptions, has already been achieved. Hauser and Taitel predicted in 1966 that by 1980 "enrollment may increase by over four million or by only twelve percent. This is approximately an average of one percent per annum, an easily managed rate."[21]

At the secondary school level, we have not yet achieved secondary education for all of the youth of all of the people. The dropout rate for the nation is still almost one out of three students. A major problem facing secondary education, therefore, is to absorb as many as possible of those who now drop out, in addition to those who enter high school as a result of population growth.

The largest increase in terms of percentages should occur at the college and university levels. In the 1950s there was a 61 percent increase in college and university enrollment. The first half of the 1960s saw a 60 percent increase. Still another 61 percent increase is expected over the span from 1965 to 1980.[22] Community colleges will especially increase their enrollments. Open admission policies in city colleges and state universities will also account for much of the anticipated enrollment growth. Upper undergraduate years and graduate years will reflect increased enrollments too; however these increases should be less sharp than the prospective increases at the level of the first and second years of higher education.

If the projected increase in the gross national product materializes, Americans can clearly afford to support education adequately out of that expanded gross national product. Whether Americans will choose to spend their money for education, however, is another matter. On the side of the probability of increased support is the increasing recognition that knowledge is power, that education is the indispensable key to leadership and that education (as we indi-

---

[21] Philip M. Hauser and Martin Taitel, "Population Trends—Prologue to Educational Programs," *Prospective . . . 1980*, p. 52.
[22] *Ibid.*, pp. 52–53.

Experiment in urban housing. Courtesy of Man and His World (Montreal).

cated in our chapter on "Where Does the Money Come From?") is of great value in the economic development of the nation.

On the other side of the ledger is the very real possibility that revolutionary assaults on universities may result in social repression and accompanying budgetary slashes for higher education. Indeed, a minority of students may bring about a system break of anarchy by destroying the universities and other social institutions. A different system break is predicted by Michael Young in his fascinating *Rise of the Meritocracy, 1870–2033*.[23] Young foresees so much emphasis on the training of an intellectual elite at the social controls that the masses will revolt by the year 2000.

In a nation that can afford education and has established its value to society, the likelihood is that there will be continuing support for the various types of resources—human, technological and physical—that will be needed in the educational system.

Students in the year 2000 may have little contact with teachers who view their role as only that of imparting knowledge. Instead, students—learners—may be interacting meaningfully with teachers who perceive their role to be that of *facilitators* of learning, and who will be constantly guiding the student toward that end. Meaningful methods or techniques for motivating learning, utilizing ability and evaluation as guides, may be the cornerstone of the teaching-learning process.

[23] Michael Young, *The Rise of the Meritocracy, 1870–2033* (Toronto: Random, 1959).

If the above developments take place, students will view methods of accumulating relevant information in a meaningful context as being of far more significance than the "old fashioned" concept of memorization of data, so characteristic of many twentieth century schools. They will rely heavily on information storage and retrieval banks, and will be concerned primarily with *how* to locate and utilize needed information.

Kahn and Wiener have surmised that "computers will also presumably be used as teaching aids, with one computer giving simultaneous individual instruction to hundreds of students each at his own console and topic, at any level from elementary to graduate school."[24] Richard L. Shetler has provided an even more dramatic portrayal:

> Just imagine the staggering possibilities of having all the world's great libraries, the accumulated knowledge of mankind, at your fingertips, of being able to select from them the information that is desired, and at the same time having a machine that can analyze, sift, integrate and calculate for us.[25]

As to curriculum, the likelihood is that curriculum-making will increasingly be done by federations of professionals. Groups of educators, including liberal arts specialists in disciplines but also increasingly specialists in the foundations of education, in various media, and in curriculum, will develop concepts and create materials to implement their ideas. Instead of a single curriculum design for a field, such as PSSC physics, it is likely that there will be multiple designs offered to schools through research and development laboratories. Yet the curriculum change problem of obtaining sufficient teacher involvement and participation will probably persist as curriculum-making moves more and more into the hands of experts.

Though the National Education Association and the American Federation of Teachers may be effectively merged long before the year 2000, the number of educational associations will probably grow larger with the growth of specializations and the necessity for the representation and the professional information which such associations can provide. Some foresee the development of super-organizations similar to holding companies to relate specialized educational groups to larger concerns.

By the year 2000, the teacher in the self-contained classroom may well be obsolete. Already, increased numbers of supporting personnel are coming into education. The available technology is expanding. Specialization is increasing. By the year 2000, a coordinating teacher may take for granted the presence of a supporting staff including secretarial workers, teacher aides, instructors and assistant teachers. The help of technicians, evaluators, and researchers may be available to teachers. If so, the role of the coordinating teacher will increasingly be that of "the master of the mix," as O.K. Moore, the creator of the talking typewriter, has phrased it. "The mix" upon which the teacher would draw would

---

[24] Kahn and Wiener, *The Year 2000*, p. 90.
[25] Richard L. Shetler, "Major Problems of Society in 1980," *Prospective . . . 1980*, p. 266.

Education of the future may include studying at home with a computer. Courtesy of Arthur Schatz for Life © Time Inc.

include readily accessible libraries of books, television programs that could be replayed, films, sound tapes, computer consoles, etc. Such a teacher would also utilize field trips, independent study, guests and visitors for instructional purposes.

One might even speculate that the teacher of the future will divide his six-hour working day into approximate thirds. One third might be spent in the classroom (or community or laboratory) in supervising or facilitating learning of a particular discipline or interdiscipline. Another third might be spent working with the staff members as they coordinate and plan future learning experiences. The final third might find the teacher engaged in some particular specialty, such as individual therapy, conducting analysis groups for discussion of values, preparing television presentations or tapes, working with specialists in programming computers, developing evaluation techniques and tests, etc.

Management of the individual school may be correspondingly complex. In the future it might be shared by an administration specialist and a curriculum specialist. The latter might work on program while the former might be concentrating on community relationships and the coordination of the total enterprise through managerial and political skills.

Brickell visualizes the changing roles of teachers and administrators as follows:

The present role of teacher will gradually evolve into a cluster of roles encompassing such discrete functions as team leader, formulator of detailed objectives, instructional sequence planner, script writer, presenter of information, evaluator of pupil responses and designer of supplementary pupil experiences. The new administrative and supervisory specialties will include position titles such as Specialist in Outside Developments, Supervisor of Professional Training, Director of Equipment Acquisition and Maintenance, Chief of Materials Production, Program Assessor, Coordinator of Temporary Personnel Assignments, Professional Librarian, and Travel Officer. We can anticipate that an Assistant Superintendent for Development and Training will cap off the pyramid of such positions in the central office of the school system.[26]

Yet Brickell also says, quite possibly with tongue in cheek, "Very probably (I regret to assume) if one opens the door to a typical 1980 classroom and walks inside, the teacher will be standing up front talking."[27] This could very well be true in the year 2000 as well.

A fundamental change for the student as to schools may be that he will not need to go to school so often! For, in addition to schools, students will have opportunities for learning through home information centers. A home learning and information center might include "video communication for both telephone and television (possibly including retrieval of taped materials from libraries or other sources) and rapid transmission and reception of facsimiles (possibly including news, library materials, commercial announcements, instantaneous mail delivery, other print outs)."[28] While home learning and information centers may turn the student's steps homeward, the development of extended recreational facilities of schools may turn his steps schoolward. Just as college campuses have developed student unions, gymnasiums, natatoriums, and the like, elementary and secondary schools may develop expanded recreational facilities as part of master plans for the improvement of the environment surrounding youth.

Again we might sum up the *most likely* American pattern of education *if* the *most likely* American society of our earlier projection actually prevails. (All bets are off if major system breaks take place.) In such a society, the typical school would reflect the following influences and characteristics:

1. The elementary school population would increase to a minor degree; the secondary school population would increase substantially but less rapidly than in recent decades; college and university enrollments would sharply increase.
2. The typical school would be an urban school.
3. About half of the nation's children and youth would go to schools in megalopolitan complexes such as Boswash, Chipitts, or Sansan.
4. A markedly higher gross national product would be potentially available for educational support and thus the school would have potentially sufficient funds to build needed facilities, to buy needed supplies and equipment, and to pay teachers a substantial wage.

---

[26] Henry M. Brickell, "Local Organization and Administration of Education," *Implications for Education of Prospective Changes in Society,* Designing Education for the Future (New York: Citation, 1967), p. 227. [27] *Ibid.*, p. 216.
[28] Kahn and Wiener, "The Next . . . Years," p. 714.

5. The schools would make use of computer technology not only for purposes of scheduling but also for instruction through an elaborate electronic network.
6. Schools would depend heavily on a curriculum-making process developed through national curriculum projects engaging a wide variety of experts.
7. Educational organizations would proliferate.
8. A coordinating teacher would be a key person in an educational program involving paraprofessionals, clerical workers, researchers, computer specialists, and audio-visual technicians.
9. A teacher would teach, coordinate staff members, and engage in an individual educational specialization.
10. Management of the individual school would be shared by an administration specialist and a curriculum specialist.
11. In addition to the school's extensive facilities for storage and retrieval through material centers, computer technology, and library materials, students would have access to home information centers containing substantial technology.
12. Recreational facilities in relationship to the schools and as part of the total environment would be markedly expanded on both the elementary and secondary levels.

What would be the crucial life decisions which students would be making in such schools? In the kind of society we have envisioned for the year 2000, in which neither Utopia nor Inferno prevails, students would be attempting to meet their needs through rich and diversified educational opportunities. They would also be dealing with the crucial human problems which pose difficulties as to survival of their society. They would be engaged in vigorous discussion of value choices, including decisions on the better ways of using leisure in a period providing many competing opportunities; they would also be considering the fundamental value question of how a man should best live his life.

As social scientist Jack Allen says:

Certainly in this period of accelerating change we should find no difficulty in supporting John Dewey's credo of a nonstatic education for a nonstatic world and in voicing with Whitehead the dangers inherent in an education designed to produce fixed persons for fixed duties. Translating such observations into the realm of instructional strategies, it becomes increasingly apparent that the educative process needs to shift its basic premise from a concept of *teaching* to one of *learning*. The responsibility of educational personnel—managers, instructional professionals, paraprofessionals—is to provide an environment in which individuals and groups can learn more efficiently and effectively. . . .

How to make choices, how to alter our perceptions, how to respond to new realities—these are problems each of us must handle with reasonable effectiveness lest we join the ranks of the obsolete.[29]

★ ★ ★

[29] Jack Allen, "The Revolution of Our Time," *Issues Today*, 2 (April 1, 1970).

DISCUSSION

1. How old will you be in the year 2000? Others in your family, among your associates, among the younger people you know? When presumably would you retire if the retirement age remains approximately 65? How near is the year 2000 to you?
2. What other system breaks than the ones mentioned by the author do you see as conceivable by the year 2000? Do you believe that anyone can possibly conceive all the potential ones? Why or why not?
3. Discuss with class members their estimate of the most likely system breaks. Consider the question of whether human beings can influence system breaks or whether system breaks are inevitable.
4. What have been some of the classic Utopian speculations? Infernos? How does today's "futurism" differ from such past speculation? What is the significance of the concepts of "alternative futures" and "system breaks?"
5. Read some of the Utopias and Infernos and check the author's visions with your own value preferences. Do they jibe?
6. What are your opinions on the general directions of norms and values in American society? What evidence is there for and against the "pursuit of happiness" hypothesis?
7. What are the outstanding characteristics of the most likely American society of the year 2000? Why is the matter of population a key factor?
8. How would you rephrase the probable characteristics of the "most likely American society of the year 2000"? What type of society would you prefer, if any, to the society envisioned here?
9. What can an individual human being do to influence the future?
10. What might education be like in the year 2000? What seems most likely to you? Can you relate your projection to social forces and trends?
11. Do you see any particular advantages or disadvantages in the education you have projected for the year 2000? How does your projection differ from that in this chapter? Can you differentiate what you expect education to be and what you would like education to be?
12. After your careful thinking during this course, what do you see as changes in the educational system, including teacher education, that could better prepare you to be a teacher in the year 2000?
13. What can you do to bring about the type of future education you support? You individually? You collectively with others?

INVOLVEMENT

1. Examine the issues current in news magazines and in TV reports and discussions. What predictions for the future do you see in these presentations? Do these predictions have any bearing on education in America?
2. Write out your own projection of the most likely future society and the most likely future education, using the year 2000 as a target year. Compare your projections with those of others in your group.
3. Carry on your own independent program of reading as to contemporary "futurism."

4. Initiate a group of people particularly interested in "futurism." Meet regularly outside of class to discuss alternative futures and how human beings might influence them for the better.
5. Involve two or three high school students (friends or neighbors) in a discussion of what they believe good education should be like in the future. Do they consider education as a road to a "better life"?
6. Attempt to envision some of the technological media which may be characteristic of the year 2000. Compare what you envision with technological media with which you have become familiar through visits or through your own college or university.
7. Consider the possible specialization which you might follow in future years. What could be done now to move in the direction of such specialization? Should you attempt to do so? Compare your proposal with those of others.
8. What is your own preparation for teaching in the society and education contemplated for the year 2000? What could you do now or in the immediate future to improve your preparation? Or is any preparation for the future completely unthinkable? Take whatever action seems indicated by your answers.

BIBLIOGRAPHY

Alexander, William M., ed. *The High School of the Future: A Memorial to Kimball Wiles.* Columbus: Charles E. Merrill, 1969. A useful and provocative volume in which an earlier book by Kimball Wiles serves as the point of departure for speculation on the high school of the future by nineteen educational leaders.

Braden, William. *The Age of Aquarius: Technology and the Cultural Revolution.* Quadrangle Books, 1970. A brilliant and vigorous book which looks at the America emerging from the contemporary black, student, and women's movements of our times.

Bushnell, Don D. and Dwight W. Allen, eds. *The Computer In American Education.* New York: Wiley, 1967. A description of the present and potential place of computer technology in American education.

Cohen, Arthur M. *Dateline '79: Heretical Concepts for the Community College.* Beverly Hills, Calif.: Glencoe Press, 1969. The future of the community college as it organizes its curriculum and instructional procedures to serve future students.

Eurich, Alvin C., ed. *Campus 1980: The Shape of the Future in American Higher Education.* New York: Delacorte, 1968. To bring closer together the present plans for change in higher education and future probabilities on the campus and in the nation.

———. *High School 1980: The Shape of the Future in American Secondary Education.* New York: Pitman Publishing Corporation, 1970. Projections by a group of specialists on the shape of things to come in the American high school.

Fields, Morey R., ed. *Frontiers in Education.* New York: Center for Applied Research in Education, 1967. A collection of papers on various types of educational frontiers and the results of basic and applied educational and psychological research.

Foreign Policy Association. *Toward the Year Two Thousand Eighteen.* New York: Cowles, 1968. A look ahead in the area of foreign policy by an organization specializing in education on foreign affairs.

Henderson, Algo D., ed. *Higher Education in Tomorrow's World.* Ann Arbor, Mich.: University of Michigan, 1968. Report from an international conference on higher education in tomorrow's world which deals with the future situations and presents a manifesto for the future.

Hirsch, Werner Z. *Inventing Education for the Future.* San Francisco: Chandler, 1967. Papers by scholars on educational innovations, ways of studying the future, specific innovations, and prospects and strategies for change.

Huxley, Aldous. *Brave New World Revisited.* New York: Harper and Brothers, 1958. A follow up on Huxley's novel *Brave New World* which points out how fast the world has moved toward the grim prophesies of the novel. He deals with overpopulation, over-organization, propaganda, the arts of selling, brainwashing, chemical persuasion, as well as with education.

Kahn, Herman and Anthony J. Wiener. *The Year 2000: A Framework for Speculation on the Next Thirty-Three Years.* New York: MacMillan, 1967. A highly useful assemblage of factual data and speculative theories in the year 2000 by two perceptive leaders in "futurism." An indispensable source book.

Keppel, Francis. *The Necessary Revolution in American Education.* New York: Harper and Row, 1966. The former United States Commissioner of Education describes the changes in American education which he believes necessary.

Leonard, George B. *Education and Ecstasy.* New York: Dell, 1968. Optimistic future-oriented book stressing both the use of mechanical devices and an affective-oriented education.

Michael, Donald N. *The Next Generation.* New York: Random House, 1965. An extremely perceptive speculation on the future of today's youth in the world of the next twenty years by a versatile social scientist who examines probable tendencies in today's environment.

Morphet, Edgar L. and Charles O. Ryan, eds. *Implications for Education of Prospective Changes in Society.* Denver: Designing Education for the Future, An Eight-State Project, New York: Citation Press (no. 2), 1967. A useful book by a variety of educational leaders who attempt to apply societal implications to the future of education.

———. *Planning and Effecting Needed Changes in Education.* Denver: Designing Education for the Future, An Eight-State Project, New York: Citation Press (no. 3), 1967. A book largely by specialists in administration describing ways of putting into effect changes which the Project has envisioned through earlier publications. Important particularly for administrators though not as imaginative as some contemporary projections.

———. *Prospective Changes in Society by 1980.* Denver: Designing Education for the Future, An Eight-State Project, New York: Citation Press (no. 1), 1967. An important book which brings together essays by American leaders on anticipated developments in American life in the years ahead. For instance, the volume contains the perceptive theories of Kenneth E. Boulding who describes the concept of the "system break."

National Association of Secondary School Principals, *The Coming Crisis in Secondary Education.* The Bulletin of the National Association of Secondary-School Principals. Volume 49. Number 298. February, 1965. A challenging criticism of secondary education by Ivor Kraft, followed by reactions from fourteen experts in the field. A stimulating collection of ideas and challenges concerning secondary schools of the future.

Toffler, Alvin. *Future Shock.* New York: Random House, 1970. Stresses the drastic adjustments and consequent shocks to people in today's world as the future becomes a reality.

AUDIO-VISUAL MATERIALS

The Futurists (CBSTV, 25 Min., Color) Analyzes some of the physical, social and economic problems which will face the world today and in the future. Ten leaders in world government, science, technology, and sociology give their views. Narrated by Walter Cronkite.

Schools for Today and Tomorrow (Aegis Productions, 15 Min., Color) Shows new concepts in classroom design and teaching methods.

The Communications Explosion (CBS: McGraw-Hill, 25 Min., Color) One of the 21st Century Series. Communications of the present and predictions as to the future are presented. The economic and technical possibilities of direct communication are described.

Your Child and the World of Tomorrow (National Education Association, 76 frs., Color, Record.) Considers the nature of the changes that will occur over the next twenty years, discusses the need for new educational programs and describes the type of home environment that will help young people cope with the world of tomorrow.

TWENTY-THREE

IS TEACHING FOR YOU?

Now is the time to review a basic decision. Is teaching for you?

Throughout the earlier chapters of this book, we have urged you to make important subordinate decisions concerning teaching. For instance, why teach? At which educational level? Who else teaches in American schools? Are salary and status important to you? What educational organizations do you incline toward? We also asked you to consider advantages and disadvantages of teaching in public, independent, and parochial schools. We raised questions about who is in charge in American schools, what is expected of teachers, and where the money comes from. We sketched social, psychological, philosophical, and curricular foundations of education. We asked, what does the new teacher worry about? What is the work of the new teacher? How about evaluation and guidance? What will the schools of the year 2000 be like? Your thinking, however tentative, on all such matters should contribute to your basic decision—is teaching for you?

TIME FOR A DECISION

We could supply you some check lists to guide your decision-making. But we won't, because we believe it is better for each one of you to make your own list. We will suggest a process for making your basic decision, tentative or firm, whether or not to become a teacher.

Build a list of factors you intend to take into account as you decide whether teaching is for you. For instance, you might ask yourself what you really want in your future work and, indeed, in your life. Be completely honest with yourself. Pull no punches. Show the list to no one. Or show the list only to the person (or persons) who shares your most important decisions with you. Then take your list and check each item on whether it leads you as an individual toward or away from teaching. You might use a five point scale: (1) heavily toward, (2) somewhat toward, (3) neutral, (4) somewhat away, (5) heavily away.

One category in decision-making will probably prove to be your own goals. Do you want to make a difference in the world? If you do, jot down this goal unashamedly. Say it your own way. If this goal is not important to you, skip it. Do you want to work with people? If so, list this in your own words. Do you want to communicate the excitement of some content or some ideas that have set you on fire? If so, say it out. Do you want to help people cope with their problems? Or help them lead more meaningful lives? What are your other goals with respect to your work and your life? Now use your five point scale in making your own personal interpretation as to whether your goals lead you to or away from teaching.

Try the same approach as to your own life style. Are you somewhat individualistic? Are you group-inclined? Do you generally go along with life as it is lived around you? Do you struggle against things as they are? Are you often a leader? Are you usually a follower? Are you a good student? Are you not particularly inclined to intellectual matters?

Try the same approach with respect to the economic aspects of the teaching profession, including money, tenure, security, vacations, etc. For instance— having a good deal of money is important to me. A moderate living standard satisfies me. I couldn't care less about money. Economic security is important in my thinking. I simply can't think in terms of security or tenure. I must admit the long summer vacation is important to me. Think of related statements and put them down. Then judge the relationship of these welfare-related factors to teaching.

Give yourself your own personal version of merit rating in the form of a self-appraisal. Who am I? What do I do well? How do I relate to people? What are my personality characteristics? How is my health? Am I relatively stable emotionally? Am I resourceful and adaptable? Cooperative? Translate the questions into positive descriptive statements about yourself. How does this self-appraisal (which should neither be overly generous nor overly condemnatory) relate to teaching? Do aspects of your self-appraisal lead you to or away from teaching?

We suggest nothing as simplistic as just totaling up your score. Instead we suggest that you take a long look at the total profile of yourself with respect to teaching which you have devised.

Here are illustrative sets of factors jotted down by three hypothetical individuals. Read over these sets and ask yourself how you would check them on a five point scale if you happened to be Ann, Zelda, or Tony (who, indeed, might check them differently from you). Even more important, write down your own list and check it as to which items lead you toward and which move you away from teaching.

ANN

I really like to work with people.
I genuinely like kids and I think they like me.
I intend to get married.

I think I am both an individualist and a person who likes to work with others in groups.
I like to vacation in new places, though I like my home community and hope I'll work here.
My major hobbies are tennis, theater, and movies.
A moderate standard of living is all I need; keeping up with the Joneses is not for me.
I couldn't care less about security or tenure.
People see me as patient and tolerant (perhaps I am not as much so as they think).
I would like to be a "self-actualizing" person and at least I'm trying.
I think people like me and I generally like them except for certain weirdos.
I think I'm resourceful when new problems come about.

ZELDA

In all honesty, I am mostly concerned about me, not other people.
When it's all over, I want to say that I have really lived.
Above all I want to travel widely and often.
I put a good deal of emphasis on clothes.
I want to live as an individualist in one of the colorful cities of the world.
Let's face it, I need money to enjoy life.
Security is for the birds.
I think I could do my job well, whatever it might be, but I would never let it become overly important to me.
Emotionally, I'm often up or down.

TONY

There is a lot wrong with things as they are and I propose to help change them.
People do not pay attention to the humanities in this practical science-oriented world.
I read a good deal and have been called a "culture-vulture."
However, I don't believe in the ivory tower; I think that human beings should also act.
I would like to write a book—some time I might.
I would like to help people to see potential in literature for the enjoyment of life.
At this stage I don't think I really care much about money.
Ditto security and tenure.
I get along all right with people, particularly people who have something important to say. I'm impatient with idiotic people.
I believe I am a hard worker.
I get angry too often, particularly at things as they are.
I'm more of an individualist than a collectivist.

With or without the suggested self-analysis inherent in such a check list, some of you have concluded or will conclude that you are not going to be a teacher. To you, we wish good luck in whatever your chosen work proves to be. Possibly a few ideas about education which you may have acquired in reading this book will be helpful to you. Possibly you will be a better parent for knowing more about education through American schools. You might even be a better citizen through understanding one of mankind's central activities, the education of the young. Perhaps you will be a more constructive critic of education and a more vigorous supporter of good schools than you would have been without the experience of reading this book.

TO THOSE WHO WILL TEACH

Some of you have already decided or will decide soon that teaching is for you. If so, we suggest that you be a good teacher. Be a good one because you owe it to yourself to be competent in whatever you do. Be a good one because only good teachers will be needed in the 1970s. Be a good one because you owe it to children and youth. Be a good one because you are being entrusted with a tremendous responsibility by your fellow men. Take seriously and carefully your steps toward becoming a good teacher.

UNDERGRADUATE EDUCATION

Step one toward becoming a teacher is an undergraduate education which combines sound general education with effective teacher education and which eventuates in a bachelor's degree. In all likelihood, you already know the particular combination used in your own college or university and can state the requirements involved. (If you don't know them, we suggest that you stop reading right now and turn to the college catalogue!) But to get the most out of whatever pattern is used at your school, take advantage of formal and informal sources of information which exist concerning getting the best possible education at your institution.

Formal sources include your advisor—how long has it been since you talked with him? If by some chance you don't happen to have an advisor, a trip to the dean's office will soon remedy that deficiency. Formal sources also include your professors, past and present, and the courses in which you are enrolled.

Informal sources include the student grapevine which often suggests professors and courses which are indispensable as well as, sadly enough, professors and courses to be avoided if at all possible. Informal sources include the activities of the Student Education Association which probably exists on campus; the program may offer you ideas and information on education not readily available in the standard education courses.

CERTIFICATION

Step two in becoming a teacher is to be sure that your program leads you to certification to teach. Certification for teaching, like certification for any other profession including law, medicine, nursing, etc., has a long history and is a subject of controversy. Ideas vary widely as to desirable certification practices. In education as in other professions, opinions range from the view that any college graduate can teach anything regardless of patterns of preparation, over to advocacy of rigid prescriptions of unalterable requirements. Opponents of certification requirements often dramatically point to an eminent leader in some field of study and declare that in such-and-such a state in this nation he would not be allowed to teach in public schools without further courses—to which proponents of certification retort hotly that such a leader must know more than subject matter to teach children and youth effectively in contemporary public schools. The controversy is lively and worth your attention.[1]

For your immediate purposes, however, what you need most is clear and reliable knowledge of the requirements for certification at the subject field and/or level in the state or states in which you propose to teach. To help you, we have included Table 23.1. Look up the practices of your own state as to elementary school or high school minimum requirements.

But facts are fleeting and certification requirements change so you should be aware that a booklet entitled *Requirements for Certification: Teachers, Counselors, Librarians, Administrators for Elementary Schools, Secondary Schools, Junior Colleges* is published annually under the direction of Robert C. Woellner and M. Aurilla Wood. You should know also that the report summarized in Table 23.2, *A Manual on Certification Requirements for School Personnel in the United States* is published every three years by the National Education Association.[2]

Even so, you should write to your own State Department of Education (or Public Instruction) for the latest certification data concerning your subject field and/or level. In addition, you should talk to your advisor and if your school has an office devoted to certification, use it for your purposes.

It makes good sense for you to be certain on certification matters if you intend to teach in the public schools. The era of "limited" certification—emergency or substandard or conditional permits to teach—is over; though one in seven teachers taught on such permits just after World War II, today less than one in twenty teachers do so and they are under pressure for full certification. Though certification for teaching in parochial and independent schools is regu-

---

[1] Margaret Lindsey (ed.), *New Horizons for the Teaching Profession* (Washington, D.C.: National Education Association, National Commission on Teacher Education and Professional Standards, 1961); James D. Koerner, *The Miseducation of American Teachers* (Boston: Houghton Mifflin, 1963); James Bryant Conant, *The Education of American Teachers* (New York: McGraw-Hill, 1963); Robert M. Weiss, *The Conant Controversy in Teacher Education* (New York: Random, 1969).

[2] *A Manual on Certification Requirements for School Personnel in the United States* (Washington, D.C.: NEA, 1970).

lated only in a minority of states, the most probable direction that such schools will take is toward greater emphasis on certification.

Throughout this book we have called your attention to the changing supply and demand situation as to teaching in the early 1970s. Not everybody who wants to teach may be able to find a position in education in the years immediately ahead, for the annual supply of potential beginning teachers is increasing while the demand for additional teachers is decreasing. Even certification will not guarantee your employment as a teacher. But through a careful application of certification procedures to your own situation, you can increase your chances of being employed in the particular type of post you most want.

For one thing, you should look carefully at the most up-to-date information you can obtain on the distribution of opportunities to teach at the present time. You will find that some fields are marked by higher supply and lower demand than others and, conversely, some are characterized by lower supply and higher demand. For instance, there was in 1970 a critical shortage of mathematics, science, industrial arts and vocational education teachers in the secondary schools, whereas there is, in general, an adequate supply of secondary school teachers of foreign language (especially French), social studies, and men's (not women's) physical education. There was in 1970 a low supply of special education teachers in both elementary and secondary education. Remember that these were national estimates and that the situation in your state, or, indeed, your community, may vary substantially from the above.

But, you may point out plaintively, you can't completely shift your specialization at this stage of your career. This is certainly true for most of you though it is not necessarily true for all. Some schools of education offer programs to help teachers modify their present patterns, such as summer workshop opportunities for teachers of regular elementary classes to become teachers of special education.

Yet what many potential beginning teachers can do, if they find themselves in currently crowded fields, is to increase the scope of the classes they are qualified to teach. This can be done by (1) minoring in a subject field which is in higher demand than one's major, and (2) broadening one's major field. Take social studies on the secondary school level as a possible illustration of a field marked by surplus supply. A minor in language arts or industrial arts might increase your availability for a position you particularly want. A broad background in several fields of the social studies, certainly including history, would be preferable to an endorsement only in economics and sociology. Other illustrations of the advisability of broadening backgrounds include the case of the speech teacher who would be more in demand if certified to teach English language arts and the case of the biology teacher who would find himself in an excellent position to choose among possible posts if he majored broadly in the sciences with mathematics as his minor. A realistic chart from a booklet of advice to teachers recently issued by a middlewestern university supplies more possible combinations. (See table 23.2 on page 556.) Check it against similar advice available from your own college.

TABLE 23.1
Minimum Requirements for Lowest Regular Teaching Certificates by States and Territories*

	ELEMENTARY SCHOOL			HIGH SCHOOL		
STATE	DEGREE OR NO. OF SEMESTER HOURS REQUIRED	PROFESSIONAL EDUCATION REQUIRED, SEMESTER HOURS	DIRECTED TEACHING REQUIRED, SEMESTER HOURS	DEGREE OR NO. OF SEMESTER HOURS REQUIRED	PROFESSIONAL EDUCATION REQUIRED, SEMESTER HOURS	DIRECTED TEACHING REQUIRED, SEMESTER HOURS
Alabama	B	27	6	B	21	6
Alaska	B	24	C	B	18	C
Arizona	5[a]	24	6	5[a]	22	6
Arkansas	B	18	6	B	18	6
California	B[b]	AC[b]	AC[b]	B[b]	AC[b]	AC[b]
Colorado	B	AC	AC	B	AC	AC
Connecticut	B	30	6	B	18	6
Delaware	B	30	6	B	18	6
D.C.	B[e]	15	C	5[e]	15	C
Florida	B	20	6	B	20	6
Georgia	B	18	6	B	18	6
Hawaii	B	18	AC[d]	B	18	AC[d]
Idaho	B	24	6	B	20	6
Illinois	B	16	5	B	16	5
Indiana	B	27	8	B	18	6
Iowa	B	20	5	B	20	5
Kansas	B	24	5	B	20	5
Kentucky	B	24	8[e]	B	17	8[e]
Louisiana	B	24	4	B	18	4
Maine	B	30	6	B	18	6
Maryland	B	26	8	B	18	6
Massachusetts	B[f]	18	2	B	12	2
Michigan	B	20	5[g]	B	20	5[g]
Minnesota	B	30	6	B	18	4
Mississippi	B	36	6	B	18	6
Missouri	B	18	5	B	18	5
Montana	B	AC	AC	B	16	AC
Nebraska	60[h]	8	3	B	AC	AC
Nevada	B[i]	18[j]	6	B	20	6
New Hampshire	B	30	6	B	18	6
New Jersey	B	30	6[k]	B	21	6[k]
New Mexico	B	24	6	B	18	6
New York	B	24	C[l]	B	12	6[l]
North Carolina	B	24	6	B	18	6

IS TEACHING FOR YOU?

State						
North Dakota	B	16	3	B	16	3
Ohio	B	28	6	B	17	6
Oklahoma	B	21^m	6	B	21^m	6
Oregon	B	20	–^{n}	B^o	14	–^{n}
Pennsylvania	B	AC	6–12^p	B	18	6–12^p
Puerto Rico	68^q	53^q	6^q	B^q	29^q	5^q
Rhode Island	B	30	6	B	18	6
South Carolina	B	21	6	B	18	6
South Dakota	60^r	15	3	B	20	6
Tennessee	B	24	4	B	24	4
Texas	B	18	6	B	18	6
Utah	B	26	8	B	21	8
Vermont	90	18	6	B	18	6
Virginia	B	18	6	B	15	6
Washington	B^s	AC	AC	B^s	AC	AC
West Virginia	B	20	6	B	20	6
Wisconsin	64^t	26	5	B	18	5
Wyoming	B	23	C	B	20	C

LEGEND: — means not reported. AC means approved curriculum; B means a bachelor's degree of specified preparation; 5 means a bachelor's degree plus a fifth year of appropriate preparation, not necessarily completion of the master's degree; C means a course.

* Professional requirements listed are the basic requirements for degree or lowest regular certificates. Some variations from the professional requirements as stated in this table may be found in the requirements for specific certificates.

a Standard certificates: master's degree of 30 s.h. of graduate credit. Temporary certificates: bachelor's degree and completion of an approved program; valid for five years only.

b Under the approved-program approach for elementary and secondary teacher certification, California will accept the number of semester hours for the major, minor, professional education, directed teaching, and general education as required by the preparing institution for the completion of its approved teacher education curriculum. However, professional education is not acceptable for a credential major or minor. Four years of preparation (bachelor's degree) is the minimum requirement for initial elementary or secondary certification; a fifth year is required for the permanent certificate.

c Bachelor's degree for elementary and junior high school; master's degree for senior and vocational high.

d Not included in Columns 3 and 6.

e A teacher who has taught successfully for four or more years is required to take only 4 s.h. of practice teaching or a seminar of 4. A teacher who has had two years of successful experience may take a seminar dealing with professional problems instead of the 8 s.h. in practice teaching.

f Completion of the bachelor's degree or graduation from an approved four-year normal school.

g Total of 8 s.h. of laboratory experience, 5 of which must be student teaching.

h Provisional teaching certificates are issued for specifically endorsed grades, subjects, fields, and areas in designated classes of school districts upon evidence of partial completion of an approved teacher education program, generally at least 60 s.h., including specified amounts of general and professional education. Effective September 1, 1972, elementary teachers in accredited schools must hold a certificate based on degree preparation.

i A temporary certificate will be issued on completion of 96 hours in a program leading to the bachelor's degree.

ʲ For a five-year nonrenewable certificate. The holder must establish eligibility for a regular five-year certificate, the requirement for which is 30.
ᵏ The practice-teaching requirement is 150 clock hours, 90 of which must be in actual classroom teaching.
ˡ One year of paid full-time satisfactory teaching experience on the level for which certification is sought may be accepted in lieu of college supervised student teaching but only when such experience carries recommendation of the employing school district administrator.
ᵐ For the standard certificate; for the temporary certificate, the requirement is 12.
ⁿ Required, but there is no specific hours requirement.
ᵒ Provisional certificate only; for standard certification, a fifth year must be completed within five years after provisional certification.
ᵖ Minimum 6, maximum 12.
ᵠ Puerto Rico did not report for 1970. Requirements shown are carried over from the 1967 Edition of this report.
ʳ All teachers in independent school districts must have a certificate based on a bachelor's degree. The 60-hour certificate has very limited validity. It will seldom be used after July 1, 1970; none will be issued after July 1, 1972.
ˢ Provisional certificate only; for standard certification, a fifth year must be completed within six years after provisional certification.
ᵗ Bachelor's degree must be completed within seven years. Such certificates apparently are issued only to graduates of two- or three-year programs in state or county colleges and will not be issued after 1971–72. Effective with the 1972–73 school year, the bachelor's degree will be the minimum requirement for initial certification.

Source: T. M. Stinnett, *A Manual on Certification Requirements for School Personnel in the United States* (Washington, D.C.: National Education Association in Cooperation with the National Association of State Directors of Teacher Education and Certification, 1970).

OBTAINING YOUR FIRST POSITION IN EDUCATION

So you find yourself well on the way to completion of your undergraduate education and to meeting some pattern of certification requirements. You try your hand at student teaching and you like the experience. The time for securing your first teaching position then draws nearer. How to proceed?

Obviously, you begin with your preferences plus qualifications. Level? Subject field or fields? Public, independent, parochial? Any preferences (social or antisocial) as to social class or ethnic group backgrounds? Rural, urban, or suburban? Region? State? Community?

Have you taken into account that education is far more extensive than the field of teaching in American schools? Obviously, some positions will require more experience and training than you now have, such as a superintendency, a principalship, supporting central office staff positions, etc. But how about working for professional organizations or teacher unions? State departments of education and federal agencies? Educational publishers or burgeoning educational technology or educational television? Agencies specializing in youth work, in recreation, etc.? Domestic programs like VISTA? And the world of international education—Peace Corps, American Dependent Schools Overseas, Agency for International Development? In education, it's a wide wide world.

A teaching intern faces her first class. Courtesy of Jack Mitchell from DPI.

Perhaps you have a headstart. For instance, you may have done your practice teaching in the school in which you would like to teach. You may even have graduated from the school in which you would like to teach!

But most new teachers have no head start; they use the services of the college or university placement bureau for which there is usually no charge. As you fill out the various blanks and forms provided by your placement bureau, try hard to communicate to the prospective reader who you uniquely are and what you uniquely can contribute. Most placement forms ask you to supply references; they are essential and are not to be minimized. If possible, provide references from people in varied walks of life but certainly include one or more professors who know you quite well. But experienced employers are apt to assume that your references will speak favorably of you (after all, that is why you suggested these endorsers), so they will look long at other phases of your papers. They will be interested in how well you worked in your student teaching assignment. They will study your responses to whatever opportunities the forms afford you to talk about yourself and your ideas; many placement forms supply you a blank candidate's page for you to fill out. As he reads your papers, a prospective employer often asks himself, "Is this candidate right for us? Do I want to learn more about him or her through more correspondence or through a personal interview?" Then, at some point, he places your credentials in some grouping which conveys to him "promising—follow up" or "middling" or "reject" and turns to the next set of papers. By then you have had your opportunity to present yourself to him for initial acquaintance; the "promising" grouping will be followed up through interviews.

With the teacher's aid, a child grows and learns. Courtesy of Jonathan King from EFL.

A good placement officer will do his best to bring your credentials to the attention of school administrators. The higher the demand for teachers and the lower the supply, the more the administrators consult the placement bureau. Conversely, in times of high supply, the administrator is less likely to encounter your particular papers. In either case—and especially in a situation of high supply and low demand—much of the initiative rests with you. You are the person who should be writing to the school system or school in which you would like to work, describing what you have to contribute and suggesting that the administration acquire your credentials from the placement bureau at the college or university. Shun misspellings and grammatical errors like the plague; the excuse of "too busy to proofread" is quite unpersuasive to your reader and reproducing machines will impersonally duplicate and perpetuate your errors from now till eternity.

As to interviews, both naturalness and empathy are recommended. Be yourself, yet also put yourself into the interviewer's place; he genuinely wants to know you well and wants to make no mistake concerning you. What can you tell him that will help him make a sound decision? As the interview develops, you might even quietly ask yourself whether you would employ you if you were the interviewer!

In addition to the placement bureau, there are other avenues for placement which you might use. Some state departments of education and some teacher associations maintain placement agencies—your placement office will know if this is the case in your vicinity. Commercial placement bureaus also exist; of course such services usually make a charge for registration and collect a com-

VISTA volunteer in poor rural area. Courtesy of Joan Larson from OEO (VISTA).

mission from your first year's salary. The United States Employment Service also maintains local and state offices.

Some of you will be appointed to posts you hoped to get. But the fact remains that others will not get the particular posts that they most wanted. Some may have to settle for alternatives. For instance, let us return to Ann, Zelda, and Tony. Perhaps Ann may not get the elementary school position in the community she grew up in, despite her hopes. (But the result might be a broadening of Ann's horizons as she finds a post in a preschool program in another state.) Perhaps Tony won't get the position teaching the humanities in the upper-middle-class suburb to which he applied. (But maybe Tony will prove to be a good teacher of humane values in an inner-city situation or in a rural area; the book he has promised to write some day may be improved by his broader framework of experiences.) Maybe Zelda won't get a post in a glamour city like San Francisco. (But maybe teaching is not Zelda's cup of tea anyway—so perhaps it's just as well.)

ONLY THE BEGINNING

When the day comes for you to teach your first class, your advanced education will also begin. For true education is continuous and never-ending. Not only will you learn from experience; there will be many informal and formal opportunities for your further education.

Informal opportunities include your own reading and viewing. Whatever

TABLE 23.2

Suggested Subject Area Combinations
To Increase Job Opportunity

SUBJECTS	SUGGESTED COMBINATIONS
English Speech Journalism French German Latin Spanish	1. Other subject areas in this block tend to make good combinations. 2. Speech or journalism majors might consider a combination with English to expand job opportunity. 3. Foreign language majors might consider a combination with English or perhaps another foreign language. 4. English and library science often make a good combination.
Biology Chemistry Earth Science General Science Physics Math	1. Science majors with no minor should attempt to secure certification in two or more science areas in this block. 2. Science majors certified in only one or two areas might consider a combination with math. 3. Math majors do not need a minor area; however, increased opportunity may result for people certified to teach chemistry or physics.
Social Science Economics Geography U.S. History World History Political Science Sociology P.E.	1. Social science majors should attempt to secure certification in at least four areas in this block if they do not have another subject area. 2. Social science majors with less than four areas might consider a minor area in math, English, or any other subject area in greater demand.
Men's P.E. Women's P.E.	1. Preparation in another teaching area may be critical to securing a teaching position for boy's P.E. candidates. Math, industrial arts, and English appear to be good subject combinations. 2. A teaching area for girl's P.E. majors is not as critical as for boy's P.E. Students are encouraged to secure an area major which would permit teaching at both the elementary and secondary level.
Business Ed.	1. Shorthand appears to increase job opportunity in many areas.
Art Industrial Arts Special Ed. Home Economics Music Library	1. No subject combinations appear to be necessary at this time. 2. Certain areas in this block make good combinations with subject areas in the above blocks.

Teacher Supply/Demand (Terre Haute, Ind.: Indiana State University), p. 6.

relates to the individual, to society, and to values—whatever relates to psychological, social, and philosophical foundations—should be grist for your mill, whether encountered through books or films or television. The printed word alone as to education is voluminous and embraces professional and trade books, popular and professional magazines, pamphlets and journalistic columns. Be sure to include new books about school and society which are the subject of lively discussion among informed people. For instance, two late 1970 books widely read by the well-informed were Charles E. Silberman's case for open, informal teaching, *Crisis in the Classroom*,[3] and Charles A. Reich's advocacy of a new "consciousness" in *The Greening of America*.[4]

Formal opportunities include in-service education. A major enterprise of school systems is the improvement of the work of teachers. You will encounter in-service education first in the form of an orientation program for new teachers which customarily takes place prior to the opening of schools in the fall. The scope of such in-service sessions for orientation range from lectures on ideas by consultants to the homely details of setting up one's classroom in readiness for students. Many school systems often continue orientation sessions for teachers throughout the academic year. In the better of these programs, new teachers have opportunities to present their problems for discussion and interaction among themselves and for expert advice from experienced staff members. In addition, school systems today provide in-service sessions for all teachers. The focus may be upon acquaintance in broad terms with organizational innovations and curriculum content changes or the focus may be on a particular problem or approach upon which the school system is concentrating. For instance, a school system may concentrate in a given year on case studies of children, or meeting the problem of drug addiction, or revising the social studies program, etc.

Formal opportunities also include graduate work. As five years of higher education for teaching becomes increasingly taken for granted, teachers will either defer beginning to teach in favor of continuing into a fifth year of preparation or will continue their formal education during summers, late afternoons, and occasional evenings while being fully employed as teachers. In either case they will probably study for and obtain a master's degree. Most teachers who work toward master's degrees concentrate on the levels and/or subjects they are currently teaching. But the new teacher should also recognize that the master's degree program can also help him to move toward some specialization in education which now attracts him. True, doctoral level study is required increasingly for full opportunities in such specializations as school superintendency, the principalship, and the curriculum director's post. Yet many educators begin their preparation for such positions at the master's degree level and many other central office posts than these are open to people who specialize in such fields as supervision or audio-visual education on the master's degree level. Conse-

---

[3] Charles A. Silberman, *Crisis in the Classroom* (New York: Random House, 1970).
[4] Charles A. Reich, *The Greening of America* (New York: Random House, 1970).

quently new teachers often combine study for greater competence in their teaching field with at least a beginning on specialization in some administrative, curricular or supervisory responsibility.

So your education in the field of education is still in its initial stages. Through these pages, an attempt has been made to introduce you to education. But an introduction is only a beginning. For you as an educator, there is much more to know, many more experiences to be had, much more living to do. May you learn much, experience widely, and live well in your years as an educator! For yours is a career field where the action is and where human beings can make a difference.

★ ★ ★

DISCUSSION
1. As you have made important subordinate decisions concerning teaching while reading the earlier chapters, which ones of these decisions were especially important to you? Why?
2. What are some of the factors which you would advise individuals to take into account as they decide whether teaching is for them? Which of these factors seem most important to you?
3. What might be the value of a book like this one for an individual who decides not to teach? Dead loss? Some possible gain? Substantial gain?
4. What is the combination of general education and teacher education which characterizes the college or university in which you are now enrolled? What criticisms do you have of the combination? What suggestions do you have for improvement?
5. What is the argument for certification of professional people? Are there occasional excesses with respect to certification? What is your own view on certification?
6. How can a teacher who is looking for a first position in teaching or who contemplates a transfer from a present position best utilize placement offices, employment agencies, etc?
7. What type of in-service program seems to you to be potentially most helpful to new teachers?
8. What is your own thinking concerning a fifth year of preparation? What are your own plans in this connection?
9. Why educate? Why teach?

INVOLVEMENT
1. If you have not already done so, build the list of factors you intend to take into account as you decide whether teaching is for you. Check it and examine the resultant profile. What seem to be some possible implications for you?
2. Put yourself in the place of Ann, Zelda, and Tony and check their list as you think they should. Do any implications for their possible careers emerge?

3. Carry on a careful investigation of the certification requirements which affect you and the steps you should take to achieve certification. Share your findings with others to make sure that you have not overlooked any important matter.
4. Investigate carefully the current situation with respect to supply and demand particularly as it affects you. In so doing, call on whatever sources of help you need, such as state department of education sources, teacher association and union sources, local university resources, etc.
5. Try your hand at a preliminary draft of your placement papers. Check this with friends and associates to get their reactions. Make changes and improve your first draft of your papers.
6. Widen your horizons on possible positions in education through reading up-to-date sources on current careers for those contemplating work in the broad field of education. Role play an interview with an administrator who is supposedly considering you for a post in his school or system.
7. Gather information from universities in which you might study for a master's degree. Contrast and compare the various patterns of programs, requirements, etc.
8. Take a long look with other students at the many further ways you can acquire competency in education following the conclusion of the introductory course in which you are enrolled.

BIBLIOGRAPHY

Adams, Don and Robert M. Bjork. *Education in Developing Areas.* New York: David McKay, 1969. Contrasts between developed and underdeveloped societies. The role and problems of education in the development of nations.

Barr, Richard H. and Betty J. Foster. *Statistics of Public Elementary and Secondary Day Schools.* Washington, D.C.: U.S. Department of Health, Education and Welfare, Office of Education, 1970. Basic statistics on pupils, teachers, instruction rooms and expenditures as of Fall 1969.

Biegeleisen, Jacob I. *Careers and Opportunities in Teaching.* New York: E. P. Dutton, 1969. Informal overview of teaching opportunities at levels ranging from very young children to college and university and including teaching careers abroad.

Conant, James B. *The Education of American Teachers.* New York: McGraw-Hill, 1963. A two-year study of teacher certification policies and teacher training programs which raises questions on who is responsible for the education of teachers, who ought to be responsible, and how institutions preparing teachers should conduct their programs

Hodenfield, G. K. and T. M. Stinnet. *The Education of Teachers: Conflict and Consensus.* Englewood Cliffs, N.J.: Prentice-Hall, 1961. A summary report on national conferences at which scholars from the liberal arts and professors of education dealt with existing conflicts, established common objectives, and clarified responsibilities in the preparation of American teachers.

Koerner, James D. *The Miseducation of American Teachers.* Boston: Houghton Mifflin, 1963. An indictment of the quality of professional education, and programs of teacher education, and the faculties held responsible.

Stinnett, T. M. *A Manual on Certification Requirements for School Personnel in the United States.* Washington, D.C.: National Commission on Teacher Education and Professional Standards, NEA 1970. A comprehensive book on certification requirements for each state, on how to get a teaching position at home and abroad. Lists 1,199 education institutions and the programs for which they are approved.

Unruh, Adolph, and Harold E. Turner. *Supervision for Change and Innovation.* Boston: Houghton Mifflin, 1970. General discussion of supervision with demonstration of the theories presented. In-service education is fully described.

Woodring, Paul. *A Fourth of a Nation.* New York: McGraw-Hill, 1957. A review of movements, trends, dilemmas, and debates in education, including proposals for reform in teacher education.

AUDIO-VISUAL MATERIALS

Preparing to Teach (American Council on Education, 56 fr.) Preparation for the teaching profession in a typical American teacher education institution.

The Teacher Prepares (Protestant Film Commission, 56 frs.) Tells the story of a teacher who overheard two children talking about her poor teaching. Outlines the specific ways by which she overcame the situation.

The Teachers (San Fernando Valley State College, 49 Min.) Follows the activities and reactions of a group of teachers and administrators during a six-week institute in which they took field trips, lived for five days in a poverty area and spent a week in intensive interaction at a conference center.

The Workshop Process (UCLA, 12 Min.) Organization, operation, and evaluation of a teacher's workshop developed in the Montebello School District in California. Stages in planning, and the outcomes.

Helping Teachers to Understand Children, Part 2 (United States National Audiovisual Center, 25 Min.) Describes a summer workshop at the Institute for Child Study of the University of Maryland. The forces that affect a child's personality, his approach to other children and to his studies.

INDEX

Ability grouping, 331
Abolitionists, 282
Abraham, Willard, 21
Academy, 41, 137, 146, 177, 178
Acceleration, 332–333
Acceptance, 340, 345, 462
    self, 462, 520
    and integration, 367
Accommodation policy, 282
Accountability, 213
Accreditation, 176
Acculturation, 420
Achievement: need of, 344, 345
    of potential, grading by, 509–510
    tests of, 506–508
Activism, social and political, 50–51, 77, 208–209, 307, 313, 358, 360, 469–473
    See also Protest, youth
Adair, Charles H., 374
Adams, Bill, 125
Adams, Don, 559
Adams, Henry Brooks, 379
Adams, Sam, 21, 523
Adjustment Inventory, 505
Adler, Mortimer, 4
Administration: board of education, 197–200
    central office and supervisory staff, 202–204
    changing role of, 537–538
    college and university, increased student participation in, 52
    discrimination against new teachers by, 498
    expectations of teachers by, 223–225
    responsibilities of, 41, 225
    school principal, 205–206, 211–212
    school superintendent, 200–202

Adult education, 52–54, 267, 482
    teachers in, 56
Advanced placement program, 179
Aesthetic expression, 34, 41
Affection, need for, 340, 345
Affective learning, 33, 78, 419
Age: of elementary and secondary school teachers, 68–69
    for school entrance, 29
Age of Aquarius, The (Braden), 532
Aggression, 337–342
Agnew, Spiro, 358
Agricultural Extension Service, 253
Agriculture: decline of, 302
    marine, 528
    mechanized, 295–296
    vocational, 300
Ahmann, J. Stanley, 522
Ahmann, Matthew, 190
Aiken, Wilford M., 156n
Alabama, school expenditures in, 250
Alberty, Harold B. and Elsie J., 451
Alcatraz Island, 280
Alcoholism, 280
Alcott, Bronson, 4
Aldrin, Edwin, 6
Alexander, S. Kern, 374
Alexander, William M., 45n, 59, 414n, 451, 452, 526n, 541
Alienation: of blacks, 308–309
    of Indians, 280
    of lower classes, 308–309
    of youth, 271
Allen, Dwight W., 451, 453, 541
Allen, Jack, 539
Allen, James E., Jr., 472
Allen, Rodney F., 374
Allen case, 189
"Alternative" schools, 167, 179, 180, 418

American Academy of Arts and Sciences, 526
American Association of School Administrators, 157, 395
American Association of University Professors, 481
American Educational Research Association, 116
American Federation of Teachers, 104, 105, 536
    Bill of Rights of, 102, 121–122
    membership in, 74, 107, 108
    political activity in, 77
    possibility of merger of NEA and, 113–114
    publications of, 106
    struggle between NEA and, 106–114
American Revolution, 434, 469
American Teacher (AFT), 106
Amherst College, 47
Analysis: of experiences and values, 43–44
    self, 55, 544–547
And Madly Teach (Lynd), 160
Anderson, Archibald W., 48n, 291
Anderson, James G., 215
Anderson, Margaret, 320
Anderson, Robert H., 439, 451, 501
Anderson, Sherwood, 298
Anti-ballistic missile (ABM) system, 358
Anti-Poverty Bill, 164
Apology (Plato), 380
Appalachia, 162, 279, 296–297
Appleton, Sheldon, 356–357, 374
Apprentice training, 131
Approval, need for, 345
Aptitude tests, 505
Aquinas, St. Thomas, 384
Archambault, Reginald D., 410
Arden, Eve, 67
Area Redevelopment Act, 254
Area superintendent, 203
Aristotle, 4, 177, 379, 383–384, 424
Armstrong, Neil, 6
Arnstine, Donald, 410
Ashton-Warner, Sylvia, 84
Assimilation in American Life (Gordon), 278
Assistant principal, 223
Assistant superintendent, 203, 224
Association for Supervision and Curriculum Development, 116, 508
Atlanta Compromise, 144
Attendance, school: compulsory, 32
    expansion of, 16–17, 26
    median, of Mexican-Americans, 288
    See also Enrollment figures
Attitude inventories, 505
Auchincloss, Louis, 67
Auden, Wystan Hugh, 379
Audio-visual director or coordinator, 203
Audio-visual materials, 22, 62–63, 85, 125, 150–151, 174, 194, 217, 239, 263, 293, 322–323, 350–351, 376–377, 412, 433–434, 453, 477–478, 502–503, 524, 542–543, 560
    use of, 468, 491–493
Auerbach, Aline B., 501
Authentic Teacher, The (Moustakas), 465
Automobile, influence of, 296

Bachelor's degree, 69, 87, 89, 91
Bader, William B., 357n, 374
Bailey, Stephen K., 196, 215
Bailyn, Bernard, 149
Baldwin, James, 308
Barbe, Walter B., 349
Barlow, Melvin, 432
Barnard, Henry, 142, 143
Barnard College, 47
Barr, Richard H., 559
Bartlett, John, 139n
Barzun, Jacques, 4, 51–52, 59
Battle, J. A., 501
Baumeister, Alfred A., 349
Bayles, Ernest E., 410
Baynham, Dorsey, 452
Bear, Roberta Meyer, 21
Beauchamp, George A., 501
Beazley, Richard, 68n
Beck, Carlton E., 21
Beck, Frederick A. G., 177n, 382
Beck, Robert Holmes, 130n, 149
Beggs, David W., 374, 451
Behavior problems, 332–345
    curriculum and, 463–465
    dropouts, 342–345
    juvenile delinquency, 337–342
Behavior theory, 519
Bell, Daniel, 531n

Bellack, Arno A., 428–429
Belongingness, 275, 340, 345
Bendix, R., 99, 292
Benjamin, Harold R. W., 84, 352–355, 374, 411
Bennett, Lerone, Jr., 149, 282
Benny, Jack, 68
Bensman, Joseph, 276, 293
Benson, Charles H., Jr., 410
Benson, Charles S., 240, 242n, 245, 262
Bentley, Joseph C., 522
Berdie, Ralph F., 518n
Bereiter, Carl, 328n
Bernhardt, Carl L., 475
Bernier, Normand R., 21
Bernstein, Abraham, 172, 309
Best, John Hardin, 149
Bestor, Arthur, 159, 172
Bethune, Mary McLeod, 144
Bettelheim, Bruno, 23–24, 59
Beyond the Melting Pot (Glazer and Moynihan), 278
Bibens, Robert F., 476
Bible reading in school, 189
Bidna, David B., 60
Biegeleisen, Jacob I., 559
Bilinguality, 285, 288
Bill of Rights: AFT, 102, 121–122
    U.S. Constitution, 402, 469
Binet, Alfred, 326
Birmingham, John, 476
Birth rate, 362
Bjork, Robert M., 559
Black, Hillel, 501
Black Americans, 279, 281–285
    alienation of, 308–309
    bourgeois, 307
    colleges for, 47–48
    environmental conditions of, in cities, 307–308
    experiences of, and textbooks, 165
    integration of, 281, 367–368
    irrelevance of education for, 166
    leadership among, 283, 307, 471
    militancy of, 166, 221, 283, 284, 307, 367, 368, 370–371
    new expectations of teachers by, 221
    schools for, 143–144, 309–310
    separatism of, 281, 367, 368, 370–371
    and whites, relationship of, 284–285, 366–371
    and whites, studies of intelligence of, 328
    See also Negroes
Black Bourgeoisie (Frazier), 307
Black Muslims, 284
Black Panthers, 77, 308
Black power, 9, 367, 368–371
Black Power (Carmichael and Hamilton), 368
Black studies, 48, 221, 367, 422, 438
Blake, Paul, 60
Blanshard, Paul, 193
Bloom, Benjamin, 328
Blount, Nathan S., 59
Board of education, 197–200
    curriculum controlled by, 211
    expectations of teachers by, 225
    responsibility of, to community, 225
    and superintendent of schools, 200, 202
Board of Education v. Allen, 189
Bode, Boyd H., 404–406, 408, 411, 424
Bommarito, Barbara, 173, 309
Bongo, Joseph, 452
Bono, Sonny, 434
Boswash, 301, 530
Boulding, Kenneth E., 526–527, 542
Bouma, Donald H., 374
Bowen, William G., 243, 262
Bowers, C. A., 215
Bowles, Samuel, 262
Bowman, Fred Q., Jr., 523
Bowman, Garda W., 489, 502
Boy, Angelo V., 522
Braceros, 287
Braden, William, 532n, 541
Brameld, Theodore, 291, 398, 421, 434
Brazziel, William F., 328n
Brenton, Myron, 84
Brickell, Henry M., 537–538
Bridewater, William, 366n
Brighton, Stayner, 262
Brinkmeier, Oria A., 124
Broudy, Harry S., 384n, 391n, 402n, 411, 451
Brown, B. Frank, 440–441, 451
Brown, Claude, 320
Brown, H. Rap, 367
Brown, John, 282

Brown University, 47
Brown v. Board of Education of Topeka, 48, 144, 190, 367
Brownell, John A., 433
Brubacher, John S., 59
Brubaker, Dale L., 238
Bruker, Robert M., 355n, 411
Bruner, Jerome S., 426, 432
Brunner, Edmund deS., 56
Bryn Mawr College, 47
Bucchioni, Eugene, 291
Buchan, Sir John, 379
Buffie, Edward G., 451
Bundy, Clarence E., 61
Burbank, Natt B., 216
Bureaucracy in schools, 78
Burnett, Joe R., 451
Burns, Robert, 466
Burrup, Percy E., 84
Bus transportation for private school children, 189
Busaker, William E., 523
Bushnell, Don D., 541
Butts, R. Freeman, 131, 135, 136, 146, 149, 174, 193
Byerly, Carl L., 344–345

California Personality Test, 505
Callahan, Sterling, 59
Calvinism, 132
Cambodia, American troops in, 360
Campbell, Ronald F., 216
Caplow, Theodore, 101
Capp, Al, 269
Cardinal Principles of Education, 42, 394–395
Carmichael, Stokely, 367, 368–370, 374
Carns, Donald, 318n
Carson, Rachel, 363, 374
Cartwright, Dorwin, 457
Case, James, 5
Categorical aid, 236, 251–252, 257
Catholic Education Today, an Overview, 183
Cato (slave), 282
Cattell, James McKeen, 325
Caughey, John W., 282n, 291
Central office administration, 202–204
Central Purpose of American Education (Educational Policies Commission), 397
Certification, 56, 548–551
Chamberlin, Dean, 157n
Changing Education (AFT), 106
Charity schools, 130, 131
Chase, Stuart, 363
Chavez, Cesar, 288
Chemical-biological warfare, 9
Chicago: Federation of Teachers in, 108
    University of, 152, 393
Chicanos, 288–289, 307
Child benefit theory, 189
Child-centered school, 33, 153, 179, 403
Child development study, 24–25
Child guidance clinics, 342
Child study service, 513
Children of the Dream, The (Bettelheim), 23
Children of Sanchez, The (Lewis), 289
Childress, Jack R., 263
China: ancient, examination system in, 504
    and the Soviet Union, 358
Chipitts, 301, 530
Church-affiliated school, 26, 32, 131, 135, 175, 176, 178, 180–187, 189–190, 424
    See also Religion
Church-state issues, 187–191
Churchill, Winston, 329
Ciardi, John, 5
Cities: children and youth of, 304–310
    growth of, 301–302
    migration to, 307
    urban communities, 302–304
    See also Inner city *and* Urbanization
Civic education, 394
Civic responsibility, 397, 399
Civil Conservation Corps, 254
Civil Rights Laws, 9, 92, 163, 255, 283, 367
Clark, Donald H., 476
Clark, Kenneth B., 309, 320, 367
Clark, Leonard H., 59
Class in Suburbia (Dobriner), 316
Class system. *See* Social class(es)
Classes: discipline in, 64–65, 458–465
    environment in, 464
    methodology for, 390
    number of, 480–482
    self-contained, 480
    sharing responsibilities for, 487–489

size of, 482–484
Clayton, Al, 291
Clayton, S. Stafford, 193
Cleaver, Eldridge, 367, 374
Clemens, Samuel Langhorne (Mark Twain), 380
Client-centered counseling, 520, 521
Clift, Virgil A., 48n, 291, 370–371
Closed shop, 114
Cobbs, Price M., 375
Co-curricular activities, 484–485
Coeducation, 47, 394
Coffman, Lotus D., 380
Cognitive learning, 33, 419
Cohen, Arthur M., 541
Coleman, James S., 165, 215, 289n, 375
Coles, Robert, 238, 291, 297
Collective bargaining, 109–111
Collective negotiation, 113, 114
Colleges, 45–52
    for blacks, 47–48
    Catholic, 182
    class size in, 484
    counseling in, 518
    enrollment in, 46, 240, 267, 534
    faculties in, liberal arts and teacher education, 235
    future of, 50–52, 534
    homework in, 485
    influence of, on educational policies and teacher expectations, 234–235
    junior, 49, 55, 481
    land grant, 47, 253
    private school orientation to, 179
    qualifying for, by disadvantaged, 165
    requirements for entrance to, 234–235
    sexually segregated, 182
    suburban orientation to, 312, 313–314
    teachers in, 55–56, 68
    teaching load in, 481–482
    for women, 47
    See also Universities
Collier, Calhoun C., 59
Colm, Gerhard, 531
Columbia College (University), 47, 153
Combs, Arthur W., 5, 459, 460–462, 476
Comenius, John Amos, 380, 384–386, 416
Commager, Henry Steele, 174, 295

Commission on the Experimental Study of the Utilization of Staff . . . , 442
Commission on the Relation of School and College, 155
Commission on the Reorganization of Secondary Education, 42, 394
Committee on Economy of Time in Education, 41–42
Committee on College Entrance Requirements, 41
Committee of Nine . . . , 42
Committee of Ten . . . , 41
Committees, student, 467–468
Common school movement, 138–142, 143
Communication: advances in, 81, 527
    between superintendent, staff, and teacher, 204
    media of, 295–296
    of pupil progress, 511–512
    skills in, 35, 394, 395
Community(ies): black, control in, 367, 368–370
    child guidance clinics in, 342
    expectations of teachers in, 219–220
    financing of education by, 241
    inequalities of educational support by, 249–250
    influence of background of, 318
    power structure in, 195–197, 198, 234
    responsibility of board of education to, 225
    rural, urban, and suburban, 294–318
    school control exercised by, 166, 240, 241
    teacher participation in, 496–497
Community college, 49, 481, 534
Comparison, grading by, 509, 510
Compensatory education, 164–165, 255, 290
Competitive elite power structure, 196, 197
Compton, Mary, 59
Compulsory Miseducation (Goodman), 78, 421
Computers: instruction aided by, 81, 331, 468, 492, 536
    modular scheduling by, 446–447, 448
    productive power and, 531
Conant, James B., 60, 174, 238, 291, 380, 485, 517, 548n, 559
Conformity: education for, 145

need for, 345
pressure for, 271
in small towns, 298
to societal values, 420
in suburbia, 311, 315
Confrontation, 469–473
curriculum and, 437–438
Congress of Racial Equality (CORE), 284
Conservation of natural resources, 363, 365, 399–400
Constitution, U.S.: amendments relating to slavery in, 282
Bill of Rights of, 402, 469
education delegated to states by, 138, 229
and freedom of religion, 187–188, 189
Consultative council, student, 208, 209
Content of curriculum, 435–438
Content factors in intelligence, 326
Cooley, Thomas M., 147
Corbally, John E., 216, 263
Cordasco, Francesco, 291
Core program, 211, 428, 443, 444–446
structured and unstructured, 444–445
Corwin, Ronald G., 124, 239
Cottingham, Harold F., 515n
Council for Basic Education, 160
Counseling: as accepting, personal relationship, 514, 520
client-centered, 520, 521
nature of, 513–514
teacher role in, 514–519
theories of, 519–520
Counts, George S., 198n, 402–404, 408, 411, 421
Cousins, Norman, 382
Cowper, William, 479
Cox, Wally, 67
Crary, Ryland W., 432
Creativity, 34, 41, 44, 45
differences in, 333–336
encouragement of, 399
in kindergarten, 30
Cremin, Lawrence A., 131, 135, 136, 141–142, 143, 146, 149, 152–153, 159, 172, 402n
Crescimbeni, Joseph, 477
Criminality, 338; see also Juvenile delinquency

Cronbach, Lee J., 328n
Crosby, Muriel, 451
Crow, James F., 328n
Cruickshank, William M., 349
Cuban, Larry, 306–307, 320
Cubberley, Ellwood P., 145–146, 149
Curiosity: awakening of, 14
importance of, 35
Curriculum: based on demands, 437–438
based on needs, 416–419
based on structure of the disciplines, 425–427
changing content and organization of, 435–449
core, 211, 428, 443, 444–446
definitions of, 413, 414
and discipline, 463–465
as a force in school decision-making, 210–211
foundations of, 415–427, 430
future, 536
and humane values, 423–425
irrelevant, 221, 309, 422, 463, 469
new teacher's segment of, 429–430
one or several sources of, 427–429
participation of teachers in making, 206, 435–436
relation of organization and content in, 449
socially oriented, 419–423, 427
vital, need for, 341, 463
Curriculum director, 203, 224
Curti, Merle, 181n, 392n, 401n
Curtin, Thomas J., 375

Dale, Edgar, 501
Dame schools, 134, 177
Davis, Allison, 268
Davis, Mary Dabney, 26n
Day-care centers, 25–26
Death at an Early Age (Kozol), 78, 417, 496
DeBernardis, Amo, 501
DeBoer, John J., 60
Decision-making, educational: administrative influences in, 202–206, 211–212
community influences in, 195–200
influence of curriculum in, 210–211
and special interest groups, 234

teacher and student participation in, 206–210
value structure and, 35
whether to become a teacher, 544–547
Decker, Sunny, 78, 84
Deloria, Vine, Jr., 280n
Democracy: and authoritarianism, 424
and citizenship, 399
and determination of school policies, 229
and education, 169, 229–233, 242–243, 384, 389, 405–406
and freedom, 402, 405
and grouping, 332
ideal of, 12
participation in, 34
societal spokesmen for, 229–233
and student dissent, 472
values in, 39
and working for the common good, 286
Democracy and Education (Dewey), 408
Democracy in Jonesville (Warner), 270, 272, 274
Denney, Reuel, 349
Dennis, Sandy, 22, 67
Dennison, George, 78, 418, 432
Departmentalization, 480
Dependence needs, 345
Depersonalization of schools, 78
Deprivation and Compensatory Education (Rees), 310
Deputy superintendent, 203
Desegregation, 367–368
in education, 47–48, 163, 255, 283, 290
plans for avoidance of, 169, 190
Designing Education for the Future, 526
Dethy, Ray C., 239
Developing Programs for the Educationally Disadvantaged (Passow), 310
Development of Secondary Education, The (Raubinger et al.), 147
Dewey, John, 5, 139n, 152, 161, 382, 392, 402, 403, 405, 406, 407–409, 411
Dickens, Charles, 4–5
Dierenfield, Richard B., 193
Differentiated staffing and pay, 94
Director of supervision, 203

Disadvantaged, The (Fantini and Weinstein), 309
Disadvantaged children, 273–274
challenge of teaching, 78–79
concern for, 43, 257
education for, 162–168
low expectations for, 309
nursery schools for, 27
Disadvantaged Early Adolescent, The (Storen), 309
Discipline, 64–65, 458–465
curriculum and, 463–465
personality patterns and, 458–463
self, 492
Disciplines (categories of knowledge), curriculum based on, 425–427; *see also* Subject matter
Discovery: emphasis on, 40
excitement of, 35
Discrimination: against black educators, 497
against teachers, 417, 497, 498
against women as higher education teachers, 68
low self-esteem from, 289
policies of, 366–367
racial, and the voucher plan, 191
See also Segregation
Dissent. *See* Protest, youth
District superintendent, 203
Districts. *See* School districts
Diversity: education for, 36
in high school population, 267–268
of life patterns, in city, 303
in segregated neighborhood, 306–307
Dix, Lester, 172
Dobbins, Allen L., 502
Dobriner, William M., 316–317, 320
Doctor's degree, 49–50, 87, 557
Dodson, Dan, 313
Doll, Ronald C., 487n, 502
Donahue, George T., 476
Dorros, Sidney, 124
Douglas, Harl R., 174
Douglas, William O., 14
Douglass, Frederick, 282
Draper, Dale C., 60
Dreeben, Robert, 124
Dreikurs, Rudolf, 476

Dress code, 209, 472
Dropouts: student, 273, 274, 275–276, 342–345, 534
  from teaching, 498
Drugs, programs concerning, 437
Dual enrollment program, 189–190
DuBois, W. E. B., 144, 150
Dunbar, Ernest, 423n
Durante, Jimmy, 438
DuShane Emergency Fund, 104, 497
Dutch Reformed Church, colonial schools of, 135
Dykes, Archie R., 216

Ebel, Robert L., 505n
Ecology, 362, 365
Economic Opportunity Act, 26, 164, 255
Economics of Public Education, The (Benson), 240
Education: adult, 52–54, 56, 267, 482
  advanced degree in, 49
  affective and cognitive, 33, 78, 419
  American, reports on purposes of, 393–400
  of average teacher, 69
  of blacks, 47–48, 143–144, 309–310
  cardinal principles of, 42, 394–395
  challenges to, 13–14, 76–77, 144, 300–301, 420
  choosing the teaching level in, 54–56
  in colonial times, 131–137, 177
  compensatory, 164–165, 255, 290
  continuing, 96, 555–558
  decentralization of, 135, 166, 203, 240
  and democracy, 169, 229–233, 242–243, 384, 389, 405–406
  denied to slaves, 136, 143, 281
  desegregation of, 47–48, 163, 255, 283, 290, 332, 367
  for the disadvantaged, 162–168
  for diversity, 36
  dual system of, 131
  in early national period, 137–142, 178
  economic aspects of, 46, 86–98, 240–260
  economic benefits of, social and private, 242–243
  the enlightenment and, 136–137
  experimentation in, 39, 153, 166–167, 211
  failures of, 9, 78, 166, 221, 417–418
  family attitude toward, 276
  federal legislation on, 253–255, 257
  in fields of pollution and population, 366
  of the future, 534–539
  government aid to, 25–26, 190, 200, 235–236, 240–257
  history of, in America, 129–147
  home, 23, 177, 538
  for immigrants, 145–146, 181
  implications of system breaks for, 528–529
  and improvement of total environment, 419
  influences on decision-making in, 195–213
  inner-city, 179, 260, 308–310
  in-service, 163, 255, 493, 498, 557
  insufficient funds for, 19, 20
  international, 255, 360
  irrelevance of, 166, 308, 309
  and juvenile delinquency, 340–342
  for the mentally retarded, 329
  need for redefinition of, 52
  preschool, 23–26, 68, 164, 482–483
  professional status of, 116–122
  progressive, 152–162, 165, 403, 405, 416
  purposes of, 378–409, 419
  question of state vs. national control of, 138, 252, 255–257, 508
  reassessment of, 12
  reforms in, 107, 142, 145, 417
  as regarded by thinkers through the ages, 378–393
  relationship of class and ethnic backgrounds to, 289–290
  relationship of teacher salary and, 87, 91
  and religion, 131, 132, 134, 135, 180–191
  revolution in, 78–81
  segregation and discrimination in, 48, 144, 166, 170, 190, 367
  since the Civil War, 143–147
  and social problems, 352–372, 403–404

some 20th-century philosophers of, 400–409
of Spanish-speaking Americans, 288
of teachers, 49, 56, 96, 163, 469, 547, 555–558
a transition period for, 81
unequal opportunities for, 30, 249–250
U.S. Office of, 143, 240
upgrading of, 19
vocational, 147, 254, 255, 257, 300, 314, 341, 394, 399, 428
voucher plan for, 166–168, 191
Wiles' phases of, 43–45
for women, 47
See also Colleges, Parochial schools, Schools, etc.
Education for All American Youth, 158, 172
Education of Catholic Americans, The (Greeley and Rossi), 184
Education for the Disadvantaged (Miller, ed.), 309
Education of the Disadvantaged (Passow et al., eds.), 309
Education and Ecstasy (Leonard), 78
Education in the Metropolis (Miller and Smiley, eds.), 309
Education in Metropolitan Areas (Havighurst), 309
Education Professions Development Act, 255
Education of Urban Populations, The (Bernstein), 309
Educational Policies Commission, 157, 395–398
Educational Testing Service, 507
Egypt, ancient, royal schools in, 177
Ehlers, Henry, 172
Ehrlich, Paul R., 361, 375
Eight-Year Study, 155–157, 179
Einstein, Albert, 14, 382
Eisenhower, Dwight D., 382
Elam, Stanley, 124
Elazar, Daniel J., 531n
Elementary school, 32–35
 Catholic, 182, 183, 185
 church-related, 178
 class size in, 483
 core in, 444
 counseling in, 515, 516
 enrollment in, 32, 147, 178, 182, 183, 534
 of the future, 34–35, 534
 homework in, 485
 nongraded, 439
 number of classes taught in, 480
 nurturing creativity in, 335–336
 proportions of men and women teachers in, 68
 salaries in, 86, 92
 single social class or ethnic group in, 308
 spread of, 142
 teachers in, 67–76, 185
Elementary and Secondary Education Act, 26, 189, 255
Elitism, 196, 197
Elkind, David, 328n
Elkins, Stanley M., 281n, 292
Ellison, Alfred, 34, 35n
Ellison, Ralph, 308, 375
Elmira College, 47
Elmtown's Youth (Hollingshead), 274
Emancipation Proclamation, 282
Emerson, Ralph Waldo, 179, 381
Emile (Rousseau), 416
Emotion-related (affective) learning, 33, 78, 419
Emotional needs, delinquency and, 339, 340
Employment, black and white, 284
Empty Spoon, An (Decker), 78
Enabling Acts, 253
Enclaves, 304
Encounter groups, 78
Engel v. Vitale, 189
England: colleges and universities in, 45, 177
 Poor Law in, 130
English grammar school, 134
Enlightenment, the, 136–137
Enrichment, 440, 447, 449
Enrollment figures, 16–17, 178–179, 240, 267
 Catholic education, 178–179, 182–184, 267
 elementary school, 32, 147, 178, 182, 183, 534
 future, 534
 higher education, 46, 240, 267, 534

kindergarten, 29–30
nonpublic schools, 32, 43, 267
nursery school, 26
secondary school, 43, 147, 178, 182, 183
Environment: breakdown of, 303
classroom, 464
and criminality, 338
and heredity, 327
and IQ, 328
home, and education, 23
and mental retardation, 297
pollution of, 11, 362–365, 528, 529
total, improvement of, 419, 420
Epstein, Charlotte, 375
Equal Pay Act, 92
Equality of Educational Opportunity (Coleman), 289
Equalization of school support, 249–257
Erickson, Donald A., 176, 193
Erikson, Erik H., 340, 349
Essay tests, 506–507
Ethical Culture Schools, 153
Ethics: Code of (NEA), 102, 118–121
learning of, 394–395
and relations among teachers, 227
structure of, 35
Ethnic background, 277–289
and educational achievement, 289–290
middle-class, 307
of urban youth, 305, 307
Eton College, 177
Eurich, Alvin C., 451, 541
Evaluation: of achievement, 506–508
alternatives to grading in, 511–512
aptitudes and interests included in, 505–506
inescapability of, 521
in nongraded schools, 439
process of, 504–505
standards in, 508–510
See also Grading
Everson v. Board of Education, 188–189
Exceptional children, 27, 330, 336–337
Expectations of the poor and disadvantaged, 309
Expectations of teachers: administrative, 223–225
broad influences on, 233–236
of board of education, 225
community, 219–220
of fellow teachers, 227
individual, 222–223
parental, 220–222
self, 228
student, 226–227
Experience and Education (Dewey), 408
Experimentation, educational, 39, 153, 166–167, 211
Exurbs, 311, 312

Failure: by comparison grading, 509, 511
constant meeting with, 508
elimination of, in nongraded school, 441
fear of, 439
threat of, 441
Fair Employment Practices Committee, 367
Family: attitude of, toward education, 276
backgrounds, and social class interrelationships, 275–276
and criminality, 338
educational environment of, 23
suburban, 312
working class, characteristics of, 273
Fantini, Mario D., 309–310, 320
Farming. *See* Agriculture
Faust, Verne, 523
Feiffer, Jules, 310
Fields, Morey R., 541
Finch, Robert H., 260
Fisher, George D., 113
Fisher, Joseph L., 531n
Five Families (Lewis), 289
Flat grants, 250
Fleming, Robert, 487n, 502
Fletcher, Margaret I., 60
Follow-up service, guidance, 514
Ford, Henry, 296
Ford Foundation, 235
Foshay, Arthur W., 427
Foshett, John M., 84
Foster, Betty J., 559
Foster, Josephine, 29n, 31, 60
Foundation plan for equalizing school support, 250
Foundations, education supported by, 235
Foy, Rena, 21

INDEX 571

France, Anatole, 14
Franciosa, James, 67
Franklin, Benjamin, 41, 136–137, 146
Franklin, Fabian, 50n
Franklin, John Hope, 282n, 291
Franklin, Marian Pope, 216
Fraser, W. R., 193
Frazier, Alexander, 60
Frazier, E. Franklin, 307, 320
"Free" ("alternative") school, 167, 179, 180
Freedmen's Bureau, 144
Freedom(s): democracy and, 402, 405
    fear of, 213
    four, 231
    of religion, 187, 188
    and responsibility, 31
    of thought and expression, 14
French, William Marshall, 42n
Freudian psychology, 23, 519
Frey, Sherman H., 216
Friedenberg, Edgar Z., 215, 381
Frierson, Edward C., 349
Froebel, Friedrich, 30, 390–392, 416
Fromm, Erich, 213
Frost, Joe L., 35n, 60
Frost, Richard L., 196, 215
Frost, Robert, 381, 491
Fuchs, Estelle, 306, 320
Full, Harold, 172
Futurism, 525–527

Gagnon, John H., 318n
Gaines, Lloyd Lionel, 48
Galarza, Ernesto, 288n, 292
Galbraith, John Kenneth, 322
Gallagher, James J., 349
Gallegos, Herman, 288n, 292
Gans, Herbert, 268, 276, 292, 316, 317, 320
Gardner, Jim, 423
Gardner, John W., 411
Garforth, F. W., 327n
Garland, Hamlin, 298
Garrett, John S., Jr., 21
Garrison, William Lloyd, 282
Garvue, Robert J., 263
Gauerke, Warren E., 263
General factor ("g"), 326
Genius, 330
Georgiady, Nicholas P., 216

Gerwin, Donald, 263
Getschman, Keith R., 216
Ghettos: failure of schools in, 78, 370
    new teachers assigned to schools in, 498
    poverty of, 9
G.I. Bill of Rights, 253, 254
Gibbon, Edward, 384
Gibbons, Ray, 188
Gibson, John C., 375
Gifted Child Grows Up, The (Terman and Oden), 333
Giftedness, 330
Gilman, Daniel Coit, 50
Ginzberg, Eli, 320
Glaser, Robert, 502
Glasser, William, 478
Glazer, Nathan, 278, 281, 292, 349
Gleazer, Edmund J., Jr., 49, 55, 60
Glock, Charles, 375
Glock, Marvin D., 522
Gnagery, William J., 476
Goethe, Johann Wolfgang von, 9
Gold, Milton, Jr., 349
Goldberg, Miriam, 309, 477
Gompers, Samuel, 384
Good, H. G., 150
Good Morning, Miss Dove (Patton), 65
Goodbye, Mr. Chips (Hilton), 67
Goodlad, John I., 432, 434, 439, 451, 453, 502
Goodman, Paul, 78, 421, 432
Gordon, Milton M., 278, 292
Gorgias (Plato), 380
Goslin, Willard, 158
Government: aid of, to parochial schools, 190
    and day-care centers, 25–26
    early interest of, in education, 143
    and education for the disadvantaged, 163–164, 166–167
    educational expenditures by, 257–260
    legislation on education by, 253–255, 257
    manpower training program of, 164, 251–252, 254
    New England town meeting, 197–198, 298
    and nursery school education, 26

service of universities to, 50
state and local, inequalities in educational support by, 249–250
student, 207–208
and subject matter reconstruction, 33, 161
support of education by, 25–26, 200, 235–236, 240–257
and training of school personnel, 163
and vocational education, 147
and the voucher plan, 166–167
Grading: alternatives to, 511–512
by comparison or by achievement of potential, 509–510
criticism of, 510–511
social significance of, 512–513
standards for, 508–510
symbols in, 510
Graduate school, 49–50, 557
class size in, 484
teaching load in, 481
Graham, Grace, 218, 229n, 321
Graham, Hugh Davis, 375
Graham, Patricia Albjerg, 172
Grambs, Jean D., 41n, 60, 238, 375
Grammar school, 41, 132, 134, 146
Great Didactic, The (Comenius), 384
Greece, ancient, schools in, 177
Gregory, Susan, 292
Greeley, Andrew M., 184–185, 186–187, 193
Green, Robert L., 375
Greene, Mary Frances, 321
Greene, Maxine, 150, 472–473
Grier, William H., 375
Grobman, Arnold, 427
Grobman, Hulda, 226, 523
Gronlund, Norman E., 523
Gross, Beatrice, 417n, 432
Gross, Ronald, 417n, 432, 451
Gross national product (GNP), 530–531
Grossman, Ruth H., 452
Group homes, 24
Grouping: based on age, 324
of grades, 35–36, 324
homogeneous vs. heterogeneous, 330–332
of intelligence levels, 329–330
multiage, 325
for the slow learner, 329

Growing Up Absurd (Goodman), 421
Growth: conditions for, 465
economic, 9
Guidance and counseling, 513–520
for all students, 41
and juvenile delinquency, 342
nature of, 513–514
number of practitioners of, 467
teacher responsibility for, 514–519, 520
theories of, 519–520
vocational, 506
Guidance clinics, 467
Guilford, J. P., 326
Gurr, Ted Robert, 375

Haber, Harvey, 179
Hahn, Robert O., 60
Hall, Calvin S., 523
Hamilton, Charles V., 367, 368–370, 374
Hand, Harold C., 508
Handicapped children: differences in handicaps, 336–337
the mentally retarded, 297, 329
nursery school for, 27
Hansen, James C., 523
Hanslovsky, Glenda, 452
Harman, Willis, 532, 533
Harpers Ferry, 282, 283
Harrington, Michael, 296–297, 321
Harris, William Torrey, 143
Harrison, Alton, Jr., 226
Harrison, Forrest W., 249–250
Harrow, 177
Hart, Richard L., 476
Harvard College, 47, 132
Haskew, Laurence D., 9, 21
Hass, Glen, 238
Hatch Act, 253
Hauser, Philip M., 361–362, 534n
Havighurst, Robert J., 173, 268, 309
Hawkins-Brown, Charlotte, 144
Haines, Lloyd, 67
Head Start, 164, 255
Headley, Neith, 29n, 31, 60
Heald, James E., 216, 238
Health: attention to, 394
optimum, achievement of, 35
Heathers, Glen, 452
Hechinger, Fred M., 311

Heffernan, Helen, 61
Helping relationship, 518
Henderson, Algo D., 541
Henderson, George, 476
Henle, Robert J., 194
Henry, Jules, 215
Henry VI of England, 177
Hentoff, Nat, 418, 432
Herbart, Johann Friedrich, 384, 389–390
Heredity-environment debate, 327
Herndon, James, 418, 432
Herriott, Robert E., 238
Hess, Robert D., 21
High School of the Future, The (Alexander, ed.), 44, 526
High schools: academic and vocational, 42
    counseling in, 517, 520
    ethnic backgrounds of students in, 277–289
    population of, 267–268
    social class in, 268–276, 289
    teachers in, experience of, 75
    See also Junior high school, Senior high school, *and* Secondary schools
Higher education, 45–52
    black separatism and black power and, 370–371
    expenditures for, 46
    influences of, on educational policies and expectations of teachers, 234–235
    social activism in, 50–51
    teachers in, 46, 55–56
    See also Colleges, Junior college, *and* Universities
Higher Education Acts, 254, 255
Higher Horizons, 164–165
Highet, Gilbert, 84
Hilberry, Conrad, 60
Hillson, Maurie, 452
Hillway, Tyrus, 150
Hilton, James, 67
Hines, Vynce A., 59, 451
Hiroshima, 356
Hirsch, Werner Z., 542
Hispano-Americans, 285–289, 370
Hitler, Adolf, 386
Hodenfield, G. K., 559
Hodge, Robert W., 99n

Hodgkinson, Harold L., 218, 239
Hoffman, James, 374
Hoffmann, Banesh, 507, 523
Hollingshead, August B., 268, 274, 292
Holmes, Dwight Oliver Wendell, 150
Holmes, Glenn E., 61
Holmes, Oliver Wendell, 386, 425
Holt, John, 78, 416–417, 432
Holtzmann, Wayne H., 486n
Home: education at, 23, 177, 538
    group, 24
    visits in, 495
    worthy membership in, 394
Homework, 485–487
Homogeneous vs. heterogeneous grouping, 330–332
Hood, Bruce L., 410
Hook, Sidney, 476
Horrocks, John E., 345–346, 349
How Children Fail (Holt), 78
How to Teach Disadvantaged Youth (Ornstein and Vairo), 309
Howard, Alvin W., 60
Hughes, Langston, 417, 496
Hughes, Monroe James, 21
Hulburd, David, 158n, 173
Hullfish, H. Gordon, 48n, 291, 434
Human relationship and betterment, objectives of, 396, 400
Humanities, 45, 425
Hunt, Herold C., 240
Hunt, J. McV., 328n
Hunt, John Joseph, 452
Hunt, Maurice P., 424, 428
Hunter, Floyd, 196, 216
Hurley, Rodger L., 297, 321
Hurwitz, Emanuel, Jr., 239
Hutchens, Robert M., 174
Huxley, Aldous, 542
Hymes, James L., Jr., 60, 476

Identity, black, 367, 369, 371
Illinois, University of, 47n
Immigrants: Americanization of, 145–146
    from Britain and Western Europe, 277, 279
    education for, 145–146, 181
    Mexican, Puerto Rican, and Asian, 279, 285, 286–289

from Middle and Southern Europe, 277, 278
the "new," 145, 277, 278, 279
Imperatives in Education (AASA), 399–400, 410
Impersonality: of city life, 302
of standard marking system, 511
Income: of dropouts, 343
taxes on, 244, 245, 246–247, 248
teacher, salary and nonsalary sources of, 86–98
unequal distribution of, 249
variations of, in states, 250
See also Salaries
Independence, need for, 345
Independent schools, 175–180
advantages and disadvantages of teaching in, 179–180
defined, 176
history of, 177–179
progressive education in, 153
See also Nonpublic schools
Independent study, 447–449, 468
Indian Affairs, Bureau of, 280
Indiana University, 47n
Indians, American, 279, 280–281
separatism or integration of, 370
studies of intelligence of, 328
Individuality, 324, 414
in behavior problems, 337–345
and computer-aided instruction, 331
in creativity, 333–336
and curriculum, 316–318
and the dropout problem, 344–345
and expectations of teachers, 222–223
in intelligence, 325–333
methods of dealing with, 467–469
Individualized instruction, 337, 468, 512
Industrialization, 19, 300, 364
Infant and maternal mortality, black and white, 284
Information centers, 538
Information service, 513
Inlow, Gail, 502
Inner city: delinquency in, 339
master education plan for, 260
population of, 307
schools in, 179, 308–310
See also Cities

Innis, Roy, 367
"Innovative" schools, 179, 180
In-service training, 163, 255, 493, 498, 557
Inspectors (evaluators), professional, 203
Integration, racial, 367–368
and separatism, 281
Integration, subject, 33, 159–160
Integrity of individual personality, 34
Intellectual development and challenge, 34, 35
Intelligence: and acceleration or retention, 332–333
categories of, 328–332
creativity and, 334–335
differences in, 325–333
and the IQ, 326, 327–328
testing of, 325–326
Interdisciplinary studies, 162, 211; *see also* Core program
Interest, kindling of, 13
Interest inventories, 506
Interests: common, in groups, 302
of teachers, 73–74
Intergovernmental Relations, Advisory Commission on, 248–249
Intermediate school, 35
International Education Act, 255
Invisible Man, The (Ellison), 308
Iowa, University of, 47n
Irving, Washington, 64, 65
Israel: conflict of, with Arabs, 355
kibbutz method of child rearing in, 23–24

Jackson, Andrew, 139
Jackson, Philip W., 468n
Jackson, Robert H., 386
Jacobson, Philip, 193
James, Deborah, 84
James, William, 21
Jefferson, Thomas, 301
on education, 9, 138, 139, 166
on separation of church and state, 187–188
University of Virginia founded by, 139
Jencks, Christopher S., 167, 191
Jensen, Arthur, 328
Jews, educational system of, 180
Job Corps, 255

Job placement, 514
    of teachers, 553, 554
John Brown's Body, 282
Johns, Roe L., 263
Johns Hopkins University, 50
Johnson, Lyndon B., 164, 228, 355, 359
Johnson, Mauritz, Jr., 523
Johnson, Orville, 349
Johnson, Robert H., 452
Johnson, Wendell, 349
Jones, Harold R., 255–256, 263
Jorgenson, Lloyd P., 181n
Joy, Adena, 489n, 502
Junior college, 49, 481
    teachers in, 55
Junior high school, 35–41
    class size in, 483
    core in, 445–446
    functions of, 36–37, 39–41
    of the future, 39–41
    homework in, 485
    number of classes taught in, 480–481
Junior High School We Need, The (Grambs et al.), 39
Juvenile delinquency, 337–342
Juvenile Delinquency and Youth Offenses Control Act Amendment, 255

Kagan, Jerome S., 328n
Kahn, Herman, 301–302, 526, 530, 531, 532, 536, 538n, 542
Kalamazoo case, 147
Kant, Immanuel, 387
Kaplan, Abraham, 412
Katz, Martin, 517n, 519n
Kaufman, Bel, 239
Kaulfers, Walter U., 60
Keats, John, 160, 173
Keene, Melvin, 476
Keeton, Morris, 60
Keiffer, Elisabeth, 497n
Keith, Lowell, 60
Kelley, Earl, 459, 508
Keniston, Kenneth, 471, 476
Kennedy, John F., 6, 232, 284–285, 356
Kennedy, Robert F., 13, 375
Keppel, Francis, 542
Kerber, August, 173, 309
Kerner Commission Report, 375, 376

Keyserling, Leon H., 101
Kibbutz method of child rearing, 23–24
Kierkegaard, Soren, 9
Kiester, Edwin, Jr., 311n, 314–315, 321
Kilpatrick, William Heard, 400–402, 408, 411, 416
Kimbrough, Ralph D., 196, 197, 216
Kindergarten, 26, 29–31
    class size in, 483
    purposes of, 30–31
    women teachers dominant in, 68
King, Arthur R., Jr., 433
King, Martin Luther, 13, 233–234, 284
Kirtland, Ann Healy, 226–227
Klausmeier, Herbert J., 59, 61
Klein, Alexander, 476
Klein, Francis M., 432
Klopf, Gordon J., 489n, 502
Kneller, George, 263
Knezevich, Stephen J., 197n, 198–199, 201, 202n, 205–206, 216
Knowledge: categories of, 425–427
    cognitive, 33, 45, 419
    explosion of, 532
Koerner, James D., 548n, 559
Kohl, Herbert R., 78, 308n, 417–418, 433, 452
Koob, C. Albert, 185n, 187n, 193
Kozol, Jonathan, 78, 417, 433, 496
Kraft, Ivor, 542
Krug, Edward A., 134n, 150
Krutch, Joseph Wood, 425
Kuder Preference Record, 506
Kukla, David A., 471
Kunen, James Simon, 61
Kvaraceus, William C., 338, 349, 375

Labor movement: AFT and, 107, 108, 109,
    Spanish-speaking Americans in, 288
Laboratory schools, 26, 152
La Mancusa, Katherine C., 466n, 476
Land grant colleges, 47, 253
Land Ordinance Act, 137, 253
Lane, Willard R., 239
Laney, Lucy C., 144
Langdon, Grace, 502
Lange, Phil C., 502
Languages, reconstructed program for, 43
Lanham Act, 254

Larson, Richard, 84
La Vida (Lewis), 286
Latin school, 41, 132, 146, 177
Law and order in the classroom, 64–65; *see also* Discipline
Leadership: democratic, 458
    future, 532, 535
    Negro, 283, 307, 471
    by principal, 205
    in social and student activism, 180, 271, 307, 471
    specialization for, 45
    by superintendent, 201
    training for, 178, 514
Learning: cognitive and affective, 33, 78, 419
    continuous, phases of, 440–441
    by doing, 393
    home, 23, 177, 538
    individualized, 468, 512
    need for successful experience in, 344
    real, 401
    shift from teaching to, 539
    teachers as facilitators of, 535
Learning Team, A (Klopf et al.), 489
Leathers, Ronald, 69n
Leavitt, Jerome E., 61
Lecture method, 467
Lee, Everett L., 327
Lee, Gordon C., 172
Leeper, Robert R., 216, 350
Leftouts, The (Warden), 309
Leisure, use of, 35, 394, 400, 528, 532
Lenski, Gerhart, 276, 292
Leonard, George B., 78, 542
Lerner, Max, 173
Lesser, Gerald S., 476, 502
Levit, Martin, 139, 141, 150
Lewin, Kurt, 458
Lewis, Oscar, 286, 289, 292
Lewis, Samuel, 142
Libarle, Marc, 476
Library, use of, 491–492
Lieberman, Myron, 84, 107, 116–117, 124
Life expectancy, black and white, 284
Life style: changing, 76
    in city, 302, 303–304
    exurban, 312
    teacher, 220

    urban orientation of, in rural areas, 295
Lifton, Walter M., 476
Lincoln, Abraham, 229–231, 282
Lindberg, Lucile, 62
Linden, James D. and Kathryn W., 523
Lindgren, Henry Clay, 326n
Lindsey, Margaret, 548n
Lindzey, Gardner, 523
Line and staff officers, 204
Lineberry, William P., 165n
Link, Francis R., 313–314
Lippitt, Ronald, 457, 458, 477
Lipset, Seymour M., 99n, 215, 292
Lives of Children, The (Dennison), 78, 418
Living, tools for, 34–35
Living standards: of developed and underdeveloped nations, 7–8, 360
    and economic growth, 9
    rising expectations for, 97
    rural, 296
Lobbying, 77
Locke, John, 327, 387
Lombroso, Cesare, 338
Long, Nicholas J., 477
Look Homeward, Angel (Wolfe), 97
Lounsbury, John H., 37n, 62, 304n, 480n
Love: as necessary base of competence, 419
    need for, 340, 345
Low, W. A., 48n
Lower-lower class, 273–274, 276
    in city, 305, 307, 308
    life patterns of, 466
Lower-middle class, 272, 275
    suburban, 312, 316
Lower-upper class, 270–271
    in city, 304
    delinquency among, 338
Lucio, William H., 216
Lunt, Paul S., 269, 293
Lutheran educational system, 180
Lyceum, Greek, 177
Lynd, Albert, 160, 173
Lynd, Robert S., 433

McCandless, Boyd R., 349
McCarthy, Eugene, 77, 358

McCarthy, Joseph; McCarthyism, 158
McClary, George O., 523
McCloskey, Gordon, 263
McCluskey, Neil J., 181n, 194
McCollum case, 189
McCoy, Fred, 497
Macdonald, James B., 21
McGee, Reece J. M., 101
McGeoch, Dorothy M., 321
Mack, Raymond W., 375
McLendon, Jonathan C., 21
McLoone, Eugene P., 249–250
McLuhan, Marshall, 81
McLure, William P., 248
McNamara, Robert, 356–357
McNeil, John D., 216
McQuigg, R. Bruce, 61
McWilliams, Carey, 296
Madison, James, 188
Malcolm X, 284
Mann, Horace, 13, 129, 140–142, 166, 505
Manpower Development and Training Act, 164, 254
Manual on Certification Requirements . . ., 548
Marani, Jean V., 444
March, Paul E., 196, 215
Margolis, John D., 61
Marie Antoinette, 7
Marquand, John P., 268–269
Marshall, Thurgood, 283
Marx, Karl, 268
Maryland, University of, 48
Maslow, Abraham, 459
Massachusetts Bay Colony, 132–134
Massachusetts Institute of Technology, 47
Massialas, Byron G., 349
Master's degree, 49, 69, 87, 557
Masters, Nicholas A., 216
Mastery-dominance need, 346
Materialism, suburban, 315
Mathematics, reconstructed program of, 43
May, Ernest R., 282n, 292
Mayer, Frederick, 150, 386n, 387n, 389n
Mayer, Martin, 124
Mead, Margaret, 323, 477
Measurement. *See* Evaluation *and* Testing
Mechanization, 295–296; *see also* Technology

Megalopolis, 301–302, 530
Meikeljohn, Alexander, 13
Memorization, 487
Men teachers: in college, 68
    as male-role model for children, 68
    mobility of, 75
    moonlighting by, 96–97
    salaries for, 89, 92
    in secondary school, 68
Mencken, H. L., 13
Mennonites, 282
Meno (Plato), 380
Mental age score, 326
Mental health centers, 467
Mental and Physical Traits of a Thousand Gifted Children (Terman), 333
Mental tests, 325
Mentally retarded children, 329
    and environmental deprivation, 297
Merit rating and pay, 93–95
Metcalf, Lawrence E., 60, 424, 428
Mexican-Americans, 279, 285–289
    militancy of, 370
    studies of intelligence of, 328
Meyer, Adolph E., 150
Meyer, James E., 313
Michael, Donald M., 526, 542
Michaelis, John U., 452
Michigan; Kalamazoo case in, 147
    University of, and Michigan State University, 47n
Middle class: in city, 305–306
    migration of, to suburbs, 303, 304–305, 306
    prejudices of, 305, 306, 307
    protest leaders from, 471
    suburban, 220, 312, 313–316
    teachers from, 219
Middle colonies, education in, 135
Middle school, 36, 37–38
Midwest, flourishing of public education in, 142
Miel, Alice, 311n, 314–315, 321
Militancy: black, 166, 221, 283, 284, 307, 367, 368, 370–371
    Indian, 280
    of Mexican-Americans, 370
    of minority groups, 221, 368, 370–371
Military-industrial complex, 9

Miller, Carroll, 523
Miller, Delmas F., 442–443, 452
Miller, Harry L., 173, 309, 321
Miller, S. M., 292
Milliken, William G., 248
Mills, C. Wright, 276
Minar, David W., 239
Minnesota, University of, 47n
Minnesota Counseling Inventory; Minnesota Multiphasic Personality Inventory, 505
Minority groups, 280–289
   alleged favoritism to, 222
   in city, 305–308
   new expectations of teachers by, 221
   segregation and integration approaches of, 370
   in suburbs, 312
Mobility: physical, 296
   social, 306, 307
   teacher, 75–76
Modular scheduling, computerized, 446–447, 448
Monahan, William O., 239
Monopolistic power structure, 195, 196
Moon landing, 6, 81
Mooney Problem Check List, 505
Moonlighting, 54, 96–97
Moore, O. K., 536
Moore, Samuel A., II, 238
More Effective Schools, 107
Morgan, Barton, 61
Morgan, Richard E., 194
Morphet, Edgar L., 263, 362n, 526n, 542
Morrill Acts, 47, 253
Morsbach, Mabel, 292
Morse, William C., 477
Moskow, Michael, 124
Moss, Theodore C., 37, 38n, 61
Motivation: importance of, in learning, 162
   low, of blacks, 308
   in protest activities, 471
   student, 316, 468–469
   teacher, 69–72
Mount Holyoke College, 47
Moustakas, Clark, 465, 477
Moyer, Sue, 452
Moynihan, Daniel P., 278, 292
Mr. Peepers, 67

Multi-group noncompetitive power structure, 196
Multiple-choice tests, 507
Murphy, Judith, 451
Murray, Donald Gaines, 48
Muuss, Rolf E., 462

Nagle, John M., 255
Nash, Paul, 411
National assessment, 508
National Association for the Advancement of Colored People, 283, 367
National Congress of Parents and Teachers, 493
National Council for the Social Studies, 116
National Council of Teachers of English, 116
National Defense Education Act (NDEA), 43, 161, 163, 253, 254, 257
National Education Association (NEA), 102–106, 497
   Code of Ethics of, 102, 118–121
   committees, departments, etc. of, 103–104, 107, 154, 157, 395
   declining differences between AFT and, 112–113
   job-locator service of, 76
   membership in, 74, 107, 108
   organization chart of, 103
   political activity in, 77
   possibility of merger of AFT and, 113–114
   publications of, 73, 104, 106, 125, 465
   rightist criticism of, 158
   specialized organizations affiliated with, 115
   struggle between AFT and, 106–114
National Foundation for the Arts and Sciences, 255
National Institute of Mental Health, 342
National Opinion Research Center, 98, 184
National Science Foundation, 254
National Society for the Promotion of Industrial Education, 147
National Youth Administration, 254
Natural resources, conservation of, 363, 365, 399–400
Nature-nurture struggle, 327
Needs: for achievement and approval, 344, 345

adolescent, 40, 157–158, 339, 340, 341
curriculum geared to, 211, 416–419
emotional and psychological, 339, 340, 345–346
experiences adapted to, 31
high-cost, "weighting" pupils with, 250
homework related to, 486
of learners, similarity of, 345–346
mastery-dominance, 346
nursery school program and, 29
schools to meet, 153
selected, gratification of, 424
social, and education, 154
special, of culturally deprived students, 165
of suburban students, 315–316
tests made to fit, 507
varying intensity of, 346
Negroes: colleges for, 47–48
education for, after Civil War, 143–144
emergence of leaders of, 144
gains in civil rights and economic power by, 9, 367–371
improved IQ scores for, 327
racism and, 366–371
segregation of, 366–367
studies of intelligence of, 327–328
upward-mobile, 307
See also Black Americans
Neighborhood Youth Corps, 255
Neighborhoods: segregated, diversity in, 306–307
urban, 302, 304, 308
Neill, A. S., 78, 418, 433
Nelson, Gaylord, 365
Nelson, Lois N., 433
Nerbovig, Marcella H., 61
Neugarten, Bernice L., 173
Neuwien, Reginald A., 181n, 194
New Deal, 254
New England: continuation of private schools in, 142
Puritan influence in, 132–135
town meeting in, 197–198, 298
New England Primer, The, 131
New Schools Exchange, 179
New York City: Collegiate School in, 177
Higher Horizons in, 164–165
More Effective Schools in, 107

paraprofessionals in, 488
pollution in, 364
private progressive schools in, 153
Puerto Ricans in, 286
remedial work in, 488
student protest in, 472
students' rights code in, 207–210
teachers' union in, 108
New York State, educational expenditures in, 250
Newman, John Henry, 50, 61
Newman, Ruth G., 477
Newton, Huey, 367
Nichtern, Sol, 476
Nigeria-Biafra conflict, 355
Nixon, Richard M., 25, 26, 191, 228, 232, 355, 358, 359, 360, 365
Noar, Gertrude, 321, 502
Nobody Knows My Name (Baldwin), 308
Nolte, M. Chester, 125
Nonconformity, 34
Nondirective counseling, 520
Non-Graded Elementary School, The (Goodlad and Anderson), 439
Nongraded school, 40, 324–325, 438–441, 484
Nonpublic schools, 175–187
in American early history, 130, 131, 132–134, 135, 142
class size in, 483
considering whether to teach in, 179–180, 186–187
enrollment in, 32, 43, 267
number of teachers in, 16
segregation in, 190
See also Independent schools *and* Parochial schools
Northwest Ordinance, 137, 138, 253
Northwestern University, 47n
Nuclear weapons, 9, 356, 357
Nursery school, 26–29
class size in, 483
goals of, 28–29
Nursery School, The (Read), 29
Nurture-nature debate, 327
Nyquist, Ewald, 209

Objective testing, 505, 506–507
Occupational skills, specialized, 300

Occupations: information about, 35, 396–397, 420
  of Mexican-Americans, 288
  ranking of, 98–99
  studies of, 300
Oden, Melita H., 350
Of Time and the River (Wolfe), 97
O'Hara, John, 268
Ohio State University, 47n
Ohio Statehood Enabling Act, 253
Ohles, John F., 22
Ohlsen, Merle M., 505–506, 513–514, 517n, 523
Old Deluder Satan Act, 134
Oliver, Donald W., 433
Olson, James, 84
O'Neill, James M., 188, 194
O'Neill, William F., 173
On-the-job training, 45
Open admissions, 235, 534
Operation Bootstrap, 285–286
Operations factors in intelligence, 326
Oregon case, 175
Organization of curriculum, changing, 438–449
Organizations: professional, 102–116, 536
  specialized (subject), 114–116
  voluntary, and educational policy-making, 234
  teacher membership and participation in, 74, 77
Orientation: guidance in, 513
  for teachers, 557
Orlich, Donald C., 173
Ornstein, Allan C., 309, 321
Ostar, Allan W., 20
Ostrander, Raymond H., 239
Other America, The (Harrington), 296
Otto, Henry J., 333
Our Children Are Dying (Hentoff), 418
Our Miss Brooks, 67
Ovard, Glen F., 216

Paine, Thomas, 13
Palmer, George Herbert, 13
Palmer, John R., 384n, 391n, 402n, 411
Paraprofessionals, 94, 443, 487–489, 536
Parents: and children, in working-class suburbs, 317
  conferences with, 467, 495, 511–512
  of dropouts, 343
  expectations of teachers by, 220–222
  parent-teacher organizations, 493–495
  schools set up by, 26, 167
  teacher relations with, 493–497
Park, Rosemary, 174
Parker, Francis W., 152, 392–393
Parker, Hyman, 125
Parkman, Francis, 176n, 177n, 178, 180
Parochaid plan, 190
Parochial schools, 175, 176, 178, 180–187, 424
  class size in, 483
  considering teaching in, 186–187
  enrollment in, 178–179, 182–184, 267
  issues in, 184–185
  teachers in, 185–186
Parrish, Louise, 452
Passow, A. Harry, 309, 310, 321, 477
Patterson, Franklin, 433
Patton, Frances Gray, 65, 66n
Peabody, George, 47, 387
Peace Corps, 254
Penn, William, 11, 135
Pennsylvania, University of, 137
People, Yes, The (Sandburg), 438
Perception: field of, 461–462
  of relationships, and problem solving, 31
  self, 289, 299, 332
  of subject matter, by learner and adult, 408
  of teachers, by various groups, 220–222, 226–227
Perkinson, Henry J., 166n, 173
Personality: individual, integrity of, 34
  maladjusted, 333, 505
  self-actualizing, 460–462, 520
  student, 466
  of teacher, and discipline, 458–463
Personality questionnaires, 505–506
Pestalozzi, Johann, 387–389, 416
Petrequin, Gaynor, 447, 452
Pfeffer, Leo, 194
Phenix, Philip H., 426, 433
Philanthropic foundations, educational support by, 235
Phillips, John, 178

Phillips, Samuel, 178
Phillips, Wendell, 282
Phillips Andover, Phillips Exeter (academies), 178
Phoniness, 459
Piaget, Jean, 387, 412
Pickets at the Gates (Fuchs), 306
Pierce, Governor of Oregon et al. v. Society of Sisters; Pierce, . . . v. Hill Military Academy, 175n
Pierce, John, 142
Pine, Gerald J., 522
Pines, Maya, 24–25, 61
Piper, Donald L., 173
Pius XII, Pope, 11
Placement bureau, 553, 554
Planning: educational and vocational, 514
  teacher-student, 464–465, 486
Plato, 177, 380–383, 388, 424
Plessy v. Ferguson, 144
Pluralistic power structure, 196–197
Poitier, Sidney, 67
Policy-making, democratic consensus in, 229–233; *see also* Decision-making
Politics: balance-of-power, 357
  black participation in, 369
  international war and, 359–360
  school decisions and, 196
  and school support, 249
  youth participation in, 50–51, 77, 208–209, 307, 358, 360, 469–473
Pollution, 11, 362–365, 528, 529
Poor: exploitation of, 307–308
  failure of education for, 166
  low expectations for, 309
  migration of, to cities, 307
  new expectations of teachers by, 221
  and rich children, differences between, 24
  society's callousness to, 297
  and taxes, 246, 247, 248
  transportation problems of, 303–304
Poor Law (England), 130
Population: high school, 267–268
  increase in, 8, 16, 360, 361–362, 528, 529, 534
  See also Enrollment figures
Postman, Neil, 22
Potter, Robert E., 150

Poverty: in America, 471
  children of, and children of affluence, 24
  culture of, 286, 288, 289
  and mental retardation, 297
  rural, 296, 301
  war on, 26, 255, 296, 297
Poverty and Mental Retardation (Hurley), 297
Power: black, 9, 367, 368–371
  destructive, 356–359
  sense of, restored to young, 473
Power and Privilege (Lenski), 276
Power structure, community, 77, 195–197, 234
  and school board, 198
  upper-upper class and, 269
Prayer in public schools, 189
Prejudices, middle-class, 305, 306–307
Preschool education, 23–26, 164
  class size in, 482–483
  women teachers dominant in, 68
Prescott, Dan, 59
Prescott, Francis, 67
Pressure groups, 200
Pressures: community, on teacher, 496–497
  for high marks, 511
  for getting into college, 234–235
Presthus, Robert, 195–196, 216
Princeton College, 47
Principal, 205–206, 211–212
  expectations of teachers by, 223–224
  prejudices of, 306–307
  sensitivity of, to behavior problems, 467
Private schools. *See* Nonpublic schools
Problem solving, perception of relationships through, 31
Problem students, 332–345, 466–467
Process of Education, The (Bruner), 426
Product factors in intelligence, 326
Profession: characteristics of, 116–117
  education as, 116–122
Professional negotiation vs. collective bargaining, 109–111
Professional reading of teachers, 73, 106
Programmed instruction, 468, 492–493
Progressive education, 152–155, 165, 416
  evaluation of, 155–158

reactions against, 158–162, 403, 405
Progressive Education Association, 155, 158
    Eight-Year Study by, 155–157, 179
Progressive taxes, 245–249
Project approach to curriculum making, 436
Project Method, 401
Project Talent, 519
Property tax, 243, 244, 246, 247, 248
Propkin, Stan, 172
Proposals Relating to the Education of Youth . . . (Franklin), 137
Protest, youth, 10, 50–51, 271, 307, 313, 469–473
Protest in Black and White (Kukla), 471
Psychoanalysis, 519
Public Works Administration, 254
Puerto Ricans, 279, 285–289, 307
    separation or integration of, 370
Pullias, Earl V., 239
Purdue University, 47n
Puritan influence on education, 132–135, 424

Quackery in the Public Schools (Lynd), 160
Quakers, colonial education system of, 135
Question-and-answer recitation, 467
Quincy Movement, 393
Racism, 366–371
    and achieving rights, 367–371
    charges of, by blacks, 221
    nature of, 366–367
    and survival, 371
Radcliffe College, 47
Ragan, William B., 61
Ramseyer, John A., 216
Randolph, A. Phillip, 284
Raubinger, Frederick M., 147, 156n, 157n, 173
Read, Katherine H., 29, 61
Real estate tax, 246
Realms of Meaning (Phenix), 426
Reasoning effectively, 34
Recognition, need for, 346
Recreation, 538
Rector of Justin, The (Auchincloss), 67
Rees, Helen E., 310, 321
References, for teaching positions, 553
Referral to specialized agencies, 336–337
Regents examinations, 507

Reger, Roger, 349
Regressive taxes, 245–249
Reiss, Albert J., Jr., 99, 101
Released-time program, 189
Relief: expanded, 307
    as way of life, 297
Religion: and education, 131, 132, 134, 135, 180–191
    and population control, 366
Religion and Education Under the Constitution (O'Neill), 188
Remedial help, 341, 469, 488
Repas, Bob, 125
Report cards, 511, 512
Republic, The (Plato), 381, 382
Requirements for Certification . . . , 548
Research: centers of, 255
    interest in, 55
Reservations, Indian, 280
Resnik, Henry S., 173
Respect for self and others, 210, 219, 286, 461
Responsibility: administrative, 41, 225
    civic, 34, 397, 399
    freedom and, 31
    for society's evils, 471
    teacher, in counseling, 514–519, 520
Retention in grade, 332–333
Retention of teachers, 75
Reuther, Walter P., 388
Revolution: educational, 78–81
    social and political, 10, 18, 76–77, 425, 528, 529, 535
    triple, 76–81
Rice, Joseph M., 505
Richey, Robert, 22
Rickover, Hyman, 159, 160, 173, 174
Ridicule, avoidance of, 462
Riesman, David, 349
Riessman, Frank, 292, 321
Riots, 284, 308
Rise of the Meritocracy (Young), 535
Roberts, Arthur, 238
Roberts, Joan I., 310
Robinson, Donald W., 179
Rockefeller, Nelson, 358
Rogers, Carl, 459, 460, 520
Rogers, David, 217
Role(s) of teachers, 218–228

Rollins, Sidney P., 439–440, 452
Roman Catholic schools. *See* Parochial schools
Romano, Louis G., 216
Rome, ancient, schools in, 177
Room 222, 67
Roosevelt, Franklin D., 231, 367
Roosevelt, Theodore, 231, 363, 389
Rossi, Peter H., 99n, 184–185, 186–187, 193
Roszak, Theodore, 422
Rothman, Philip, 79–80
Rousculp, Charles G., 84
Rousseau, Jean Jacques, 386–387, 416
Rowe, Harold G., 173
Rowland, G. Thomas, 35n, 60
Roxbury Latin School, 177
Rudy, Willis, 59
Runes, Dagobert D., 11
Rural communities, 294, 295–298
 children and youth in, 298–301
 expectations of teachers in, 219
Rush, Benjamin, 139
Russell, Bertrand, 11, 389
Russell, William F., 389
Rustin, Bayard, 367
Rutgers College, 47
Ryan, Charles O., 362n, 526n, 542
Ryan, Keith, 451
Ryan, Orletta, 321

Saber-Tooth Curriculum, The (Benjamin), 352–355
Sachs, Benjamin M., 523
St. John, Nancy Hoyt, 238
Salaries of nonteaching personnel, 242
Salaries of teachers, 86–90, 242
 compared to those in private industry, 89
 determination of, 91–95
 differentiated pay plan, 94
 dues checkoff from, 114
 and extracurricular activities, 485
 geographical differences in, 88
 lay, in Catholic schools, 186
 merit, 93–95
 percent distribution of, 90
 single salary scale, 92–93
Sales (and gross receipts) tax, 243–244, 246, 247, 248

Salot, Lorraine, 61
Samalonis, Bernice L., 502
Samora, Julian, 288n, 292
Sandburg, Carl, 438
Sanford, Nevitt, 61
Sansan, 301, 530
Sarcasm, avoidance of, 462, 463
Sawrey, James M., 350
Saylor, J. Galen, 414n, 452, 476
Scanlon, John, 174
Schempp case, 189
Schmidt, Charles T., Jr., 125
School Children in the Urban Slum (Roberts, ed.), 310
School Construction Act, 254
School districts, 135
 power in, 196
 and school funding, 240, 250
School lunch program, 254, 257, 297
School year, extension of, 41, 95–96
Schools: academies, 41, 137, 146, 177, 178
 "alternative," 179, 180, 418
 in black community, control of, 166
 and black militancy, 370
 bureaucracy in, 78
 challenges for, 13–14, 76–77, 144, 300–301, 420
 charity, 130, 131
 child-centered, 33, 153, 179, 403
 church-sponsored, 26, 32, 131, 135, 175, 176, 178, 189–190, 424
 common, 138, 139–142, 143
 community influences on, 195–197
 dame, 134, 177
 depersonalization of, 78
 desegregation in, 47–48, 163, 255, 283, 290, 332, 367
 English grammar, 134
 expenditures for, 242, 251–252, 257–260
 experimentation in, 39, 153, 166–167, 179, 211
 failures of, 9, 78, 166, 221, 417–418
 financial support of, 235–236, 240–260
 future, 43, 44–45, 534–539
 ghetto, 78, 370
 for immigrants, 145–146, 181
 Latin grammar, 132, 146
 integration of disciplines in, 159–160

584 INDEX

irrelevance of, 166, 274
and juvenile delinquency, 340–342
laboratory, 26, 153
Latin grammar, 41, 132, 146, 177
local control of, 166, 241
for Negroes, after Civil War, 143–144
nongraded, 40, 324–325, 438–441, 484
number of teachers in, 14–16
openings for teachers in, 14–20
ownership of, 228–233, 438
problems of, 166–168
progressivism in, 152–160
public, history of, 129–147
public, rightist criticism of, 158–159
rejection by and of, 342, 343
religion and, 187–191
retention rates in, 46
rural, and urban demands, 300
secondary, development of, 142, 146–147; see also Secondary schools
segregation in, 48, 144, 166, 170, 190, 367
separate, for Negroes and whites, 144
and social class, 306
suburban, 314, 315, 318
"tickets to," 166–168
urban, 166, 179, 308–310
vocational and technical, 147, 300
"voluntary," 167, 422
See also Education, Independent schools, Parochial schools, etc.
Schools and the Urban Crisis, The (Kerber and Bommarito, eds.), 309
Schools Without Scholars (Keats), 160
Schrag, Peter, 502
Schreiber, Daniel, 345n, 350
Schroeder, Wendy, 349
Schueler, Herbert, 502
Schultz, Theodore W., 243, 263
Schwarcz, Ernest, 172
Schwebel, Milton, 350
Science program, reconstructed, 43
Science Research Associates Youth Inventory, 505
Scientific method, 393, 405, 408
Scobey, Mary M., 61
Scott, Lloyd F., 452
Scriven, E. G., 226
Seale, Bobby, 367

SEARCH (job-locator service), 76, 104
Secondary schools: Catholic, 182, 183, 185
church-related, 178
class size in, 483–484
core in, 444–446
enrollment in, 43, 147, 178, 182, 183
free, development of, 142, 146–147
homework in, 485
important issues of, in the thirties, 154–155
number and percentage of, by type, 36
principal in, 206
proportion of men and women teachers in, 68
salaries in, 86, 92
teachers in, 67–76, 185
workload in, 481
See also High school, Junior high school, *and* Senior high school
Security, feeling of, 462
Segregation, 166, 282, 366–367
de facto, 144, 170
diversity within, 306–307
in education, 47–48, 144, 166, 170, 190, 367
and low self-esteem, 289
self, 367, 368, 370–371
Selden, David, 113
Self-acceptance, 462, 520
Self-actualization, 460–462, 520
Self-centeredness, suburban, 315
Self-concept: delinquency and, 339
of dropouts, 342–343, 344
negative, 289
Self-direction, self-inspiration, 153–154
Self-discipline, 492
Self-distrust, fostering of, 4
Self-doubt of Americans, 12
Self-esteem, 308, 371
Self-examination: Catholic, 186
of teacher, 55, 544–547
Self-expectations, 219, 228
Self-identity, black, 308, 367, 369, 371
Self-interest, 196, 234
Self-perception, 299, 332
Self-realization, 82, 346, 396
Self-respect, 34, 100, 210
Self-understanding, 34, 462
Seligson, Tom, 476

Senior high school, 41–45
    class size in, 483
    of the future, 43, 44–45
    homework in, 485
    reconstructed programs in, 42–43
    teaching load in, 481
Separate but equal doctrine, 144
Service Man's Readjustment Act (G.I. Bill), 253, 254
Sesame Street, 492
Severeid, Eric, 390
Sewards, G. Wesley, 32n, 61
Sex equality in teacher salaries, 92
Sexton, Patricia, 292
Shane, Harold G., 526
Shannon, Robert L., 501
Shapiro, Eliot, 418
Sharp, D. Louise, 22
Shaver, James P., 433
Shaw, George Bernard, 390
Shermis, S. Samuel, 173
Sherwood, Elizabeth J., 366n
Shetler, Richard L., 536n
Shils, Edward B., 108n, 112–113, 125
Shores, J. Harlan, 433
Shortchanged Children of Suburbia, The (Miel and Kiester), 314
Shumsky, Abraham, 477
Shuster, George N., 181n, 182n, 183–184, 185n, 194
Siegel, Paul M., 99n
Siegelman, Ellen, 375
Silent Spring (Carson), 363
Simon, William, 318n
Simpson, Ray H., 84
Single salary scale, 92–93
Skills: basic, acquiring of, 44–45
    communication, 35, 394, 395
    social, 300
Skipping a grade, 332
Slavery: and the Constitution, 282
    prohibition of education of slaves, 136, 143, 281
Slow learners, 329, 332
Slums, 9, 303–304, 308, 338, 498
Smiley, Marjorie B., 309
Smith, B. Othanel, 433, 451
Smith, Fred M., 523
Smith, Frederick R., 61

Smith, Mortimer, 160
Smith, Robert M., 350
Smith College, 47
Smith-Hughes Act, 147, 254, 257
Smith-Lever Act, 253
Snobbery, 180
Social action, 50–51, 177, 208–209, 307, 358, 360, 469–473
Social class(es) in America, 268–276
    in cities, 304–308
    distinctions of, in independent schools, 180
    and educational achievement, 289–290
    and expectations of teachers, 220
    influence of, on school decision-making, 195
    interaction and separation of, 274–276
    and parent-teacher conferences, 495
    in the suburbs, 312–318
    of Plato, 381–382
    upper-lower and lower-lower, 272–274, 276, 305, 308
    upper-middle and lower-middle, 271–272, 275, 304
    upper-upper and lower-upper, 269–271, 275, 304
Social development, 514
Social disorganization, 303
Social problems: curriculum and, 419–423, 427
    educational inequalities, 30, 249–250
    future, 529–534
    inner city, 308–309
    and juvenile delinquency, 337–338, 339, 342
    need for more study of, 403
    population and pollution, 361–366
    progressive education and, 154
    of Puerto Rico, 285–286
    racism, 366–371
    and teaching, 371–372
    war, 355–360
Social responsibility, 34, 397, 399, 471
Social revolution, 10, 18, 76–77, 425, 528, 529, 535
Social skills, 300
Social status of teachers, 98–100
Social studies, 42, 159
Socialization of students, 420

586 INDEX

Society: alienation from, 308–309
    change in, and education, 14, 389
    future, 529–534
    ideal, of Plato, 381–382
    open or closed, 197
    role of colleges and universities in, 50–51
Society-centered school, 33
Socrates, 378–380, 412, 424
Sodola, Quentin, 523
Some Fruits of Solitude . . . (Penn), 135
South: discrimination against black educators in, 497
    education of Negroes in, after Civil War, 143–144
    lag in public education in, 136, 142
    slavery in, 136, 143
Southern Christian Leadership Conference, 284
Soviet Union: and China, 358
    engineering and scientific development in, 160
Space program, 6–7, 160
Spanish-American War, 285
Spanish-speaking Americans, 285–289
Spearman, Charles E., 326
Special interest groups, 234
Specialization: in educational field, 557–558
    and improved quality of education, 224–225
    for leadership, 45
    in occupational skills, 300
    by student, 44
    in training the mentally retarded, 329
Spencer, Herbert, 390
Sputnik, 160, 161
Srole, Leo, 174, 269n
Stamp, Dudley L., 375
Standardized tests, 507
Stanford-Binet Scale, 326
Stanley, William O., 433
States: department of education of, and curriculum, 211
    education controlled by, 138, 229, 240, 252–253
    inequalities in educational support by, 249–250
    legislatures of, and school policies, 236
    school financing shifted to, 248
    taxation by, 246, 247
    universities of, 142, 147
Status: of high school principal, 206
    occupational, 312
    and role, 218
    teacher, 98–100, 219, 220
Stefflre, Buford, 524
Stereotypes: of America, 277
    of dropouts, 342
    of gifted children, 330
    of suburbs, 318
    of teachers, 64–67, 76
Stern, William, 326
Stevie, Richard R., 523
Stinnett, T. M., 84, 108n, 109–111, 112, 125, 551, 559
Stordal, Kahmer, 523
Storen, Helen F., 309, 321
Stout, Irving W., 502
Strikes, teacher, 77, 112, 113n
Strivers, 307, 315
Strong Vocational Interest Blank, 506
Structured core, 444
Stuart, Jesse, 301, 321
Student government, 207–208
Student Non-Violent Coordinating Committee (SNCC), 284
Student personnel services, 518
Student Unrest: Threat or Promise (Greene), 472
Students: categories of, by intelligence, 328–330
    in the city, 304–310
    committees of, 467–468
    in daily attendance, expenditures for, 259–260
    educational reforms suggested by, 417
    exchange of suburban and urban, 315
    future, 535–536
    needs of, and curriculum, 211
    opposition of, to role of professor, 50
    perceptions and expectations of teachers by, 226–227
    with problems, 332–345, 466–467
    protest by, 10, 50–51, 307, 313, 469–473
    relations of, with teachers, 469–473
    rights of, 207–210, 422

role of, in university, 52
rural, 298–301
suburban, 312–318
Students for a Democratic Society (SDS), 77
Subject matter: reconstructed programs in, 42–43, 160–162, 211
  perceptions of, by learner and adult, 408
  structure of, 425–427
  teaching of, challenged, 33
Suburbs: children and youth of, 312–318
  communities of, 310–312
  expectations of teachers in, 220
  failures of schools in, 78
  flight to, 219, 303, 304–305, 306
  growth of, 310
  middle-class, 312, 313–316
  upper-class, 312–316
  working-class, 312, 316–318
Summer jobs, 96
Summerhill, 418, 433
Summerhill (Neill), 78
Superintendent of schools, 199, 200–201
  central office and staff of, 202–204, 224–225
  and curriculum policies, 211
  district, 203
  expectations of teachers by, 224
  and principal, 206
Superior students, 330
Supervisory staff, 202–204, 206
Supreme Court decisions: Allen case, 189
  Brown case, 47–48, 144, 190, 283, 367
  Engel v. Vitale, 189
  Everson v. Board of Education, 188–189
  McCollum case, 189
  Oregon case, 175
  Plessy v. Ferguson, 144
  Schempp case, 189
Swomley, John M., Jr., 190n
System breaks, 527–529, 535

Taft-Hartley Act, 109
Taitel, Martin, 362, 534n
Tale of Two Cities, A (Dickens), 4–5
Talks on Teaching (Parker), 393
Tannenbaum, Abraham J., 309, 477
Tanner, R. Thomas, 427
Tax standard, 244–245

Taxes: for education, 242–243, 244
  progressive and regressive, 245–249
  sources of, 243–245
Taylor, Calvin W., 334, 350
Taylor, Harold, 52, 61, 390, 412
Teacher aides, 443, 480, 487–489, 536
Teachers: in adult education, 56
  and behavior problems, 466–467
  in Catholic schools, 182–183, 185–186
  certification of, 548–551
  co-curricular activities of, 484–485
  college or university, requirements for, 55–56
  conferences of, with parents, 467, 495, 511–512
  continuing education of, 555–558
  coordinating, 536, 539
  creativity fostered by, 335–336
  differentiated functions of, 94
  discipline problems of, 458–465
  education of, 49, 56, 96, 163, 469, 498, 547
  expectations of, 219–228, 233–236
  as facilitators of learning, 535
  of the future, 535, 537–539
  generalizations about, 67–76
  good, 4, 5, 9, 11, 13, 72, 457
  and homework, 485–487
  as individuals, 82
  influences on, in school system, 197–213
  in inner-city schools, 309–310
  in institutions of higher learning, 46, 55–56, 68
  involved with segments of curriculum, 429–430
  junior college, 55
  length of school year and vacation periods for, 95–97
  merit rating of, 93–95
  methods of, for dealing with individual differences, 467–469
  new, worries of, 457–473
  number of, 14–16, 185
  obtaining first position as, 552–555
  participation of, in curriculum-making, 206, 207, 435–436
  participation of, in school decision-making, 206, 207

personal rights and responsibilities of, 496–497
personality of, 458, 460–462
poor, 4
problems of and helps for, 497–498
professional organizations of, 102–116
prospective, self-examination of, 55
relations of, with parents and community, 493–497
relations of, with students, 469–473
relationship of, to technology, 81
resources for use of, 490–493
roles and status of, 98–100, 218, 219–228
in rural schools, 300–301
salaries of, 86–95, 186, 485
for the seventies, 76–81
shared responsibilities of, 487–489
shortage of, 19–20, 549
and social problems, 371, 372, 404
stereotypes of, 64–67, 76
strikes by, 77, 112, 113n
supply of and demand for, 18, 19, 55, 81, 82, 549
tenure for, 94–95
tests made by, 507
varying skills of, 41
volunteer, 53–54
work of, 479–498
Teachers, Administrators and Collective Bargaining (Shils and Whittier), 112
Teaching: art of, 14
assignments in, 498
choice of level of, 54–56
competence required in, 19
defined, 13
economic aspects of, 86–98
effectiveness of, and class size, 484
experimental development in, 39
fringe benefits of, 97
and individual differences, 467–469
individualized, 337, 468, 512
leaving, 75
lower sex barriers in, 68
made by teachers, 9
motivation for, 55, 69–72
nonfinancial rewards of, 98, 100
opportunities for, 14–20
preparation for, 49, 56, 96, 163, 469, 498, 547
in public school, factors to be considered, 169–170
reasons for, 3–14, 69–72, 544–547
revolution in, 78–81
rural, rewards of, 301
subject matter, 33
team, 442–444, 480, 483
television, 484, 492
where the action is, 14, 169
Teaching machines, 18–19, 44, 492–493
Team teaching, 442–444, 480, 483
Technology, American, 7, 11, 161, 295–296, 302, 527, 531
and destructive power, 356
in education, 18–19, 41, 330–331, 468, 484, 492–493
new relationship of teacher to, 81
Soviet advances in, 160–161
Television, 81
in teaching, 484, 492
Telford, Charles W., 350
Tennessee Valley Authority (TVA), 363
Tenure, 94–95
Terkel, Studs, 322
Terman, Lewis M., 326, 332–333, 350
Testing: achievement, 506–508
and appraisal of teaching, 221
aptitude, interest, and personality, 505–506
evaluation by, 504–508
excessive use of, 507–508, 521
intelligence, 325–326
See also Evaluation
Textbooks: adaptation of, to needs of disadvantaged, 165
for children in nonpublic schools, 189
as sole "curriculum," 211
use of, 490–491
T-groups, 78
Thayer, V. T., 139, 141, 150, 194, 411
Thelen, Herbert A., 350, 457
Thinking ability, 34, 397–398
Third Plenary Council of Baltimore (Catholic), 181
Thirty Schools Study, 155–157
Thirty-Six Children (Kohl), 78, 417
This Is the Community College (Gleazer), 49, 55

INDEX 589

Thomas, George, 477
Thomas, R. Murray and Shirley M., 330n, 350
Thorndike, Edward, 505
Thorndike, Robert L., 510n
Thornton, R. James, 61
Tiedt, Sidney, 60
To Make a Difference (Cuban), 306
To Sir with Love, 67
Tocqueville, Alexis de, 150
Today's Education (NEA), 106
Todd, Vivian Edmiston, 61
Toffler, Alvin, 542
Tolerance, 11
Torrance, E. Paul, 335
Toward Balanced Growth, 530
Toynbee, Arnold, 390
Track system, 42
Trait-factor theory, 519, 520
Transformation of the School, The (Cremin), 152
Transportation; bus, for private school children, 189
    changes in, 81, 296, 528
    suburban, 311
    urban, 303–304
Trevelyan, George Macaulay, 392
Troy, Rena, 239
Truman, Harry S., 367
Trump, J. Lloyd, 442–443, 452
Tuddenham, D., 325n, 326n, 328n
Tumin, Melvin M., 292
Tunley, Roul, 350
Turner, Harold E., 560
Turner, Nat, 282
Turning Points in American Educational History (Tyack), 130
Tuskegee Institute, 47, 144
Tutoring, 177
Tuttle, Edward Mowbray, 217
Twain, Mark, 380
Tweedsmuir, Baron (John Buchan), 379
Twelve-month plan, 96
Tyack, David B., 130, 137n, 139, 140n, 142n, 150
Tyler, Leona E., 329
Tyranny of Testing, The (Hoffmann), 507

Ulben, Gerald C., 124
Understanding: international, and survival, 360
    need for, 346
    of physical and social worlds, 34
    self, 34, 462
Unemployment: black and white, 284
    of dropouts, 343
United Federation of Teachers (New York City), 108, 488
United Nations, 8, 360
United States Employment Service, 555
United States Foreign Policy (Appleton), 356
United States Office of Education, 143, 240
United States in the 1970s, 6–14
Universities, 45–52
    counseling in, 518
    European, 45, 177
    future of, 50–52, 534
    schools associated with, 26, 152
    state, 142, 147
    teachers in, 55–56, 68
    See also Colleges *and* Higher education
Unruh, Adolph, 560
Unstructured core, 444–445
Up the Down Staircase (Kaufman), 67
Upper-class suburbs, 312–316
Upper-lower (working) class, 272–273
    in city, 305, 308
    in suburbs, 312, 316–318
Upper-middle class, 271–272, 275
    delinquency among, 338
    and school dissent, 180
    in suburbs, 313, 314, 315
Upper-upper class, 269–271
    in city, 304
Upward Bound, 165
Uram, John, 125
Urban communities, 294, 296, 301–304
    children and youth of, 304–310
    delinquency in, 339
    expectations of teachers in, 219–220
    pollution in, 364
    schools in, 166, 179
    See also Cities
Urban Education Act and Task Force, 260
Urban Villagers, The (Gans), 276
Urbanization, 286, 301–302, 399, 530
Uschald, Kathie, 349

590 INDEX

Uselessness, sense of, 313

Vacations, 95–97
Vairo, Philip D., 309, 321
Values: democratic, 39, 229, 243, 405
    education oriented to, 184
    humane, development of, 423–425
    of lower-class life, 273, 274
    personal, development of, 35, 40
    professed and operative, 533
    of special interest groups, 234
    of white Anglo-Saxon Protestant America, 145–146
    of working for the common good, 286
Van Til, William, 22, 37n, 45n, 62, 223n, 268n, 304n, 428n, 465n, 480n, 526n
Vars, Gordon F., 37n, 62, 304n, 444–446, 452, 480n
Vassar, Rena L., 135n, 138n, 150, 406n
Vassar College, 47
Usdan, Michael, 239
Venable, Tom C., 411
Verner, Coolie, 53n, 56n, 62
Verville, Elinor, 477
Vidich, Arthur, 276, 293
Vietnam war, 355, 358, 359–360
Virginia, University of, 139
VISTA, 255
Vocational abilities, knowledge of, 35; *see also* Occupations
Vocational education, 147, 394, 399, 428
    in agriculture, 300
    beginnings of, 147
    federal support for, 254, 255, 257
    need for, 341
    suburban, 314
Vocational guidance, 506
Vocational placement, 514
Vocational "track," 42
Voluntary school, 167, 422
Von Stoephasius, Renata, 432
Voucher plan, 166–168, 191

Waetjen, Walter B., 350
Wagner, Helen, 452
Wall of separation, church and state, 187–188, 189
Walton, Thomas W., 21
War, 355–360
    nuclear, 528
    politics and, 359–360
    resistance to, 358
    in the seventies, 8–9, 10
    Vietnam, 355, 358, 359–360
Warden, Sandra A., 309, 322
Warner, W. Lloyd, 174, 268, 269, 270, 271, 272, 273, 274, 293
Warren, Earl, 39
Washington, Booker T., 47, 144, 282
Waskin, Yvonne, 452
Wasserman, Steve, 422–423
Watson, Goodwin, 477
Way It Spozed to Be, The (Herndon), 418
Wealth: in the city, 303, 304
    education originally a privilege of, 130
    taxing of, 246, 247, 248
    uneven distribution of, 9
Weaver, Gary R. and James H., 62
Weaver, Warren, 239
Webster, Daniel, 392
Webster, Staten W., 322, 477
Weinberg, Meyer, 376
Weingartner, Charles, 22
Weinstein, Gerald, 310, 320
Welfare-oriented state, 532
Welfare system, 25, 26
Wellesley College, 47
Wells, H. G., 4
Welter, Rush, 166n
West, Charles K., 173
West Side Story, 302
Westin, Alan F., 471
"Wetbacks," 287
Wheaton, William L. C., 362
White, Ralph, 458
White House Conference on Children, 395
Whitehead, Alfred North, 392
Whittier, C. Taylor, 108n, 112–113, 125
Wiener, Anthony J., 301–302, 526, 530, 531, 532, 536, 538n, 542
Wiles, Kimball, 43–44, 62, 238, 239
Wilhelms, Fred T., 524
Wilkins, Roy, 283, 367, 368
Willers, Jack C., 21
William and Mary, College of, 47, 138
Williams, Emmett L., 59
Williams, George, 84
Williams, Richard C., 124

Wills, Clarice Dechent, 62
Wilson, Alan, 289
Wilson, John F., 181n, 194
Wilson, Woodrow, 393
Winn, Ralph D., 401n, 411
Wisconsin, University of, 47n
Wiseman, Frederick, 63
Woellner, Robert C., 548
Wolfe, Thomas, 97
Women: average age of, in teaching, 69
    colleges for, 47
    discriminated against, as teachers in higher education, 68
    dominance of, in elementary school teaching, 68
    liberation movement of, 77
    salaries for, 89, 92
Woock, Roger R., 173
Wood, Ben D., 505
Wood, M. Aurilla, 548
Wood, Robert C., 196, 215
Woodring, Paul, 62, 174, 393
Wordsworth, William, 390, 391
Work: attitude toward, 100
    future nature and role of, 531–532
Work-experience program, 255, 341
Work stoppages, 112
Working class, 272–273, 305, 308, 312, 316–318
Works Progress Administration, 254
World situation in the 1970s, 6–12
Wrenn, C. Gilbert, 517, 519

Yale College, 47
Yamamoto, Kaoru, 84
Year 2000, The (Kahn and Wiener), 301, 526
Young, James D., 239
Young, Michael, 535
Young, Milton A., 350
Young Americans for Freedom (YAF), 77
Youth: needs of, 157–158
    rebellion by, 10, 50–51, 77, 208–209, 271, 313, 358, 360, 469–473
    sense of power restored to, 473

Zander, Alvin, 457
Zevin, Jack, 349
Zirbes, Laura, 62